Social Vulnerability to Disasters

Second Edition

Social Vulnerability to Disasters

Second Edition

Edited by
Deborah S.K. Thomas
Brenda D. Phillips
William E. Lovekamp
Alice Fothergill

CRC Press
Taylor & Francis Group
Boca Raton   London   New York

CRC Press is an imprint of the
Taylor & Francis Group, an **Informa** business

Cover photo credits: Top left: DoD photo by Mass Communication Specialist 2nd Class Michael C. Barton, U. S. Navy/ Released. Top right: FEMA photo by Liz Roll. Bottom left: FEMA photo by Michael Rieger. Bottom right FEMA photo by Vincent Clark.

CRC Press
Taylor & Francis Group
6000 Broken Sound Parkway NW, Suite 300
Boca Raton, FL 33487-2742

© 2013 by Taylor & Francis Group, LLC
CRC Press is an imprint of Taylor & Francis Group, an Informa business

No claim to original U.S. Government works

Printed on acid-free paper
Version Date: 20130521

International Standard Book Number-13: 978-1-4665-1637-3 (Hardback)

Library of Congress Cataloging-in-Publication Data

Social vulnerability to disasters / editors, Deborah S.K. Thomas, Brenda D. Phillips, William E.
Lovekamp, Alice Fothergill. -- Second Edition.
    pages cm
Includes bibliographical references and index.
ISBN 978-1-4665-1637-3 (hbk. : alk. paper)
  1. Disasters--Social aspects. 2. Risk assessment. I. Thomas, Deborah S.K. II. Phillips, Brenda.

HV553.S586 2013
363.34'2--dc23   2012039609

Visit the Taylor & Francis Web site at
http://www.taylorandfrancis.com

and the CRC Press Web site at
http://www.crcpress.com

Dedication

This volume is dedicated to

Mary Fran Myers

(1952–2004)

For many years, Mary Fran Myers served as the codirector of the Natural Hazards Research and Applications Information Center at the University of Colorado at Boulder. Many authors in this volume first met through Mary Fran, an individual dedicated to reducing vulnerability. In 1997, she received the Association of State Floodplain Managers' Goddard-White Award for her efforts, their highest award. In 2002, the Gender and Disaster Network established the Mary Fran Myers Award for her work to advance women's careers and to promote research on gender issues. In 2003, colleagues, family, and friends created the Mary Fran Myers Scholarship. Funds bring underrepresented individuals to the annual Boulder Hazards Workshop. Mary Fran is the person most responsible for weaving together the network of authors in this volume. We dedicate our work to her memory.

All proceeds from this book are donated to the Mary Fran Myers Scholarship Fund.

Contents

SECTION I   *Understanding Social Vulnerability*

SECTION II   *Socially Vulnerable Groups*

SECTION III   *Building Capacity and Community Resilience*

Preface

Since we released the first edition of this book, disasters have continued to reveal how social structure and roles produce extensive human suffering and differential impacts, bringing social vulnerability to the forefront in considering how disasters unfold. Equally important, people, even those considered vulnerable, respond in innovative and resilient ways that unveil the strength of human ingenuity and spirit. It is not a foregone conclusion that a hazard event, even a large one, will result in catastrophic loss. Like the previous volume, this second edition explicitly focuses on the social construction of disasters, acknowledging that the characteristics of an event alone do not create the tragedies that unfurl.

The primary purpose of this edition continues to be to introduce readers to the nuances of social vulnerability, how vulnerabilities compound one another, and what can be done in order to foster change, ultimately reducing vulnerabilities and building capacity. The second edition refines the original content, updates data and case studies, provides additional examples and new case studies, emphasizes the role of capacity building and resilience, and incorporates additional international examples with an explicit attempt to expand beyond the U.S-oriented first edition.

The first edition of the book was written in the wake of two catastrophes that undeniably highlighted why reducing social vulnerability is vital for risk reduction. In 2004, the world watched in horror as the Indian Ocean tsunami claimed more than an estimated 300,000 lives across 13 nations, and then in 2005 as Hurricane Katrina and the subsequent levee system failure left thousands stranded, displaced, and without homes and livelihoods across the U.S. Gulf Coast. A disproportionate percentage of the victims of both disasters were some of the most vulnerable populations, such as the elderly, the poor, children, women, people of color, and people with disabilities.

The juxtaposition of the 2010 Chile and Haiti earthquakes, as only two disaster examples in the ensuing years between the two editions, only reinforces the necessity of engaging with the social vulnerability paradigm. Sadly, many of the same themes repeated themselves from previous major disasters. The Chilean earthquake was 500 times stronger than that in Haiti, albeit more distant from population centers. Yet, 35,000 people died in Haiti for each one who died in Chile, which is only a fraction of those affected. In Haiti, the immense difference can be attributed to historical colonialism, an ineffective national government, expansive poverty, weakened infrastructure (physical and human systems), and an overall lack of building codes with enforcement. The BP Oil Spill in the U.S. Gulf reminds us that it is not just natural events that have extensive and differential impacts; small business owners struggled, fisheries were decimated, low income populations along the coast were strained, and the long-term environmental devastation will leave a lasting legacy for future generations. Even as we send this book to press, Hurricane Sandy has recently ravaged the northeastern coast of the United States as one of the most damaging natural events in U.S. history, clearly illustrating the relevance of vulnerability, sustainability, and global climate change to disaster risk reduction strategies. Early evidence from Hurricane Sandy is again highlighting how marginalized populations struggle acutely in the aftermath of a major disaster event, certainly extending to recovery processes.

The editing team for *Social Vulnerability to Disasters* gratefully acknowledges the contributions of a number of people who made this book possible. While the second edition of the book has evolved significantly, we would like to acknowledge those who contributed to the initial materials. The book is based on materials originally created for the Federal Emergency Management Agency (FEMA) Higher Education Program, which can be found at: http://training.fema.gov/EMIWeb/edu/collegecrsbooks.asp. The content of the book, however, remains the responsibility of the authors and editors and does not necessarily reflect the views of FEMA or its staff. The creators of the original material included lead course developer Dr. Elaine Enarson, who was supported by Dr. Cheryl Childers, Dr. Betty Hearn Morrow, Dr. Deborah Thomas, and Dr. Ben Wisner. Dr. Robert Bolin, Dr. Kristina Peterson, Lorna Jarrett, Dr. David McEntire, and Dr. Brenda Phillips served as consultants on the material.

The editors are extremely grateful to the chapter authors who took time from extremely busy schedules to write and update the previous volume. Authors of the original edition returned for nearly all of the chapters, with some new author additions who were willing to take on the task. Truly, the quality of the chapters reflects the immense expertise and scholarly depth of this group of authors. The book simply would not be as compelling and robust without the dedication and contributions of this impressive group. We are especially gratified to have several new, emerging scholars as authors, including several graduate students.

CRC Press editor Mark Listewnik realized the potential of bringing together a team of scholars to create a book derived from the FEMA materials in the first edition that could truly make a difference in the lives of those at risk. He continued this vision with a request for a second edition of the book. We greatly appreciate the support, guidance, and encouragement that he provided. Stephanie Morkert, Taylor & Francis production coordinator, provided answers to endless questions about formatting and organization, and Prudy Taylor Board at CRC Press, kept us on task and made sure all the elements were in place. We thank the entire publishing team for the many hours that they dedicated to this book.

As a person who worked tirelessly to integrate issues of vulnerability into emergency management, we dedicate this book to our late colleague, friend, and mentor Mary Fran Myers. Throughout her career, she worked thoughtfully and tirelessly to integrate issues of vulnerability into emergency management. Simply, her inspiration makes this book possible thought the direct and indirect association the editors and authors of this book had with her. Mary Fran's legacy lives on through dedication that all associated with this book have for improving the human condition and increasing capacity for all to reduce disaster risk.

We also dedicate this volume to all those who have suffered from natural, technological, and human-induced events, and to those who work tirelessly to reduce disaster risk. Most importantly, we hope that it will inspire, encourage and assist those who work in all aspects of emergency management to incorporate social vulnerability as a fundamental principle and goal in their work. We hope that every person who reads this book will find the chapters in this volume enlightening guides to a safer more humane world. Our work continues.

Deborah S.K. Thomas
University of Colorado Denver

Brenda D. Phillips
Oklahoma State University

William E. Lovekamp
Eastern Illinois University

Alice Fothergill
University of Vermont

About the Editors

Deborah S.K. Thomas, PhD, is an associate professor in the Department of Geography and Environmental Sciences at the University of Colorado Denver, where she also has a secondary appointment in the Department of Environmental and Occupational Health in the Colorado School of Public Health. She specializes in hazards and health geography, and has more than twenty years of experience working with geographic information systems (GIS) in disaster management and health applications, both in the United States and internationally. Her research and teaching interests focus on issues of vulnerability/resilience as they relate to both natural and human-induced hazards and health outcomes.

Brenda D. Phillips, PhD, is a professor in the Fire and Emergency Management Program and a senior researcher with the Center for the Study of Disasters and Extreme Events at Oklahoma State University. In 2010, she received the Mary Fran Myers Award from the Gender and Disaster Network, an international organization. In 2012, she received the Blanchard Award for "academic excellence in emergency management education." Dr. Phillips has been invited to teach, consult or lecture in New Zealand, Australia, Germany, India, Costa Rica, Mexico, Canada, and the People's Republic of China. She has assisted with the development of emergency management degree programs in Mexico, Canada, and New Zealand. She currently serves as graduate student coordinator for the Fire and Emergency Management Program at OSU.

William E. Lovekamp, PhD, is an associate professor in the Department of Sociology at Eastern Illinois University. He specializes in gender and disaster vulnerability, college student disaster preparedness, and social change and empowerment. Most recently, he is utilizing geographic information systems for mapping disaster risks and cultural preservation in disaster risk areas. He is a member of the U.S. Gender and Disaster Resilience Alliance, the Natural Hazard Mitigation Association, the International Gender and Disaster Network, the International Sociological Association's Research Committee on Disasters, co-organizer of the IRCD Researchers Meeting at the Annual Natural Hazards Workshop at the University of Colorado-Boulder and is an advisory council member and disaster response volunteer for the Coles and Clark Counties, IL branch office of the American Red Cross.

Alice Fothergill, PhD, is an associate professor in the Sociology Department at the University of Vermont. Her areas of interest include family and childhood studies, disaster vulnerability, gender, inequality, service learning, and qualitative methods. Her book, *Heads Above Water: Gender, Class, and Family in the Grand Forks Flood* (SUNY Press 2004), examines women's experiences in the 1997 flood in Grand Forks, North Dakota. She has conducted research on volunteerism in the aftermath of the September 11, 2001 terrorist attacks in New York City. Professor Fothergill is a member of the Social Science Research Council's (SSRC) *Research Network on Persons Displaced by Hurricane Katrina* and is currently finishing her book, *Children of Katrina* (forthcoming, University of Texas Press), with co-author Professor Lori Peek.

Contributors

Sudha Arlikatti, PhD, is an associate professor and the Emergency Administration and Planning Program coordinator in the Department of Public Administration at the University of North Texas, Denton. She has more than eight years of experience as an architect and planner prior to joining academia. She specializes in risk communication and protective action decision making; challenges of short-term sheltering and long-term housing recovery; sustainable land use planning practices, capacity building and resiliency in the United States and India. Her research and teaching interests primarily focus on disaster response and recovery management, special needs populations in disasters, and environmental planning and natural hazards mitigation in global settings.

DeeDee Bennett is pursuing her PhD in Fire and Emergency Management at Oklahoma State University. She received her BS in Electrical Engineering and MS in Public Policy at Georgia Institute of Technology. Her interests include social vulnerabilities and communications as they relate to emergency management practice and policy. Ms. Bennett has worked with the Georgia Emergency Management Agency and the Wireless Rehabilitation and Engineering Research Center on issues surrounding emergency management and people with disabilities. Ms. Bennett is currently teaching an introduction to emergency management course to undergraduates at Oklahoma State University. She is also a member of the International Association of Emergency Managers.

Lynn Blinn-Pike, PhD, is a full professor in the Department of Sociology at Indiana University-Purdue University in Indianapolis. She has previously held faculty appointments at University of Houston, University of Tennessee, University of Missouri, and Mississippi State University. She has specialized in family and adolescent studies, particularly related to resilience during stressful times. In addition, she has conducted visual sociological studies of evacuees during Hurricane Katrina, women with breast cancer, and guests at an inner city soup kitchen.

John Brett, PhD, is an associate professor in the Department of Anthropology, University of Colorado Denver. His research is focused on sustainable livelihoods and microfinance in Bolivia, dietary decision-making, and urban food systems and sustainability in the United States and Latin America. His current research is focused on food security, sustainability, and urban agriculture in collaboration with the UCD Food Systems Research Group, and he is part of a multidisciplinary team from the UCD Center for Global Health examining health, food security and development in SW Guatemala.

Nicole Dash, PhD, is the associate dean of the College of Public Affairs and Community Service and associate professor of Sociology at the University of North Texas. Her primary research interests include the sociology of disaster, vulnerability, inequality in disaster, mitigation, and bridging the gap between research and emergency management. In addition to her research work on storms such as Hurricanes Andrew and Katrina, she worked for FEMA doing post-impact GIS and currently teaches high enrollment sections of Sociology of Disaster and Collective Behavior.

Elizabeth Davis, JD, EdM, is an emergency management consultant focusing on inclusive emergency management, marginalized population planning, disaster human services, and related issues through her firms *EAD & Associates, LLC,* and the *National Emergency Management*

Resource Center (NEMRC). Both companies employ a holistic, client-focused approach to providing quality services and real-world solutions. She is also a founding board member of the relaunched charitable organization Emergency Preparedness Initiative Global. Ms. Davis is also an advisor to DHS and FEMA, sits on many research review boards, and serves on several national advisory boards

Elaine Enarson, PhD, is an "accidental" disaster sociologist whose research, writing, teaching, and consulting focus on gendered vulnerability and resilience in disasters. She has a particular interest in applied and collaborative research and in linking gender, climate, and disaster. The lead course developer of FEMA's course on social vulnerability, she initiated the on-line Gender and Disaster Sourcebook project and co-edited three gender and disaster book collections. Her monograph *Women Confronting Natural Disaster: From Vulnerability to Resilience* was released in 2012.

Maureen Fordham, is principal lecturer in Disaster Management at Northumbria University. Her PhD is from Middlesex University, working out of the Flood Hazard Research Centre and in collaboration with the Environment Agency of England and Wales. She was editor of the *International Journal of Mass Emergencies* and *Disasters* and also manages a number of disaster-related websites. She is a founding member and long time coordinator of the Gender and Disaster Network www.gdnonline.org. She is the author of a number of scientific papers. She has had various advisory roles with national and international agencies and governments. Currently, she is also the scientific coordinator of the EU funded project: embrace – Building Resilience Amongst Communities in Europe www.embrace-eu.org.

Eve Gruntfest, PhD, is professor emeritus in Geography and Environmental Studies at the University of Colorado at Colorado Springs, where she taught from 1980-2007. She is the cofounder of the WAS * IS movement (Weather and Society * Integrated Studies) and the founder of the SSWIM group (Social Science Woven into Meteorology). Her research interests have included flash floods and warnings.

Tamara Gull, DVM, PhD, is an assistant professor in the Department of Veterinary Pathobiology at Oklahoma State University's Center for Veterinary Health Sciences. She is also a lieutenant colonel in the Army Reserve Veterinary Corps with multiple deployments to Europe, Central America and the Middle East. She specializes in infectious diseases (bacteriology/mycology) and is board certified in Large Animal Internal Medicine, Veterinary Preventive Medicine and Veterinary Microbiology. Her research interests focus on infectious bacterial respiratory diseases of livestock and horses.

Rebecca Hansen, MSW, brings her experience and passion as an emergency manager and social worker together to work toward greater inclusion of diverse segments of the population in emergency management programs and practices. Working with EAD and Associates, LLC for the last ten years, Ms. Hansen has been involved in a great variety of projects that allow her to pursue this work in activities such as training, planning, exercise development, emergency response and recovery operations, writing and research. In addition, Ms. Hansen is an International Association of Emergency Managers (IAEM) member and participates on the Special Needs Caucus and is a co-founder of Emergency Preparedness Initiative Global (EPI Global). Prior to working at EAD and Associates, Ms. Hansen held positions with the American Red Cross and the NYC Office of Emergency Management planning for and responding to many emergencies in NYC including the 9/11 World Trade Center response and recovery.

Betty Hearn Morrow, PhD, is professor emerita in Sociology at Florida International University and former director of the Social and Behavioral Lab at the International Hurricane Research Center. She has more than thirty years experience studying hazard response with an emphasis on social vulnerability and community resilience. She has co-edited several related books, including *Hurricane Andrew: Ethnicity, Gender and the Sociology of Disaster, The Gendered Terrain of Disasters: Through Women's Eyes,* and *Women and Disaster.* Her current work focuses on risk communication as she continues an active research agenda applying the tools of social science to assist state and federal agencies to understand and address the needs of their constituencies related to hazard response and resiliency.

Iain Hyde, CFM, works at the Colorado Office of Emergency Management (COEM), where he has been on the Mitigation and Recovery Team since 2009. He works with communities throughout Colorado on local hazard mitigation and recovery plans, mitigation construction projects, and grants administration. In addition, he works on state level hazard mitigation and disaster recovery planning efforts, including supporting the development of the 2011 State of Colorado Natural Hazards Mitigation Plan and State of Colorado Recovery Plan. Mr. Hyde is currently enrolled at the University of Colorado at Denver School of Public Affairs, where he is pursuing a masters in Public Administration.

Maria Kett, PhD, is the assistant director of the Leonard Cheshire Disability and Inclusive Development Centre, Research Department of Epidemiology and Public Health, UCL and has many years' experience supervising and managing complex research projects in the field of disability and international development from donors such as DFID and Comic Relief. She has been employed as an expert consultant for a number of bi-multilateral organizations, including the United Nations, the World Health Organization and the UK Department for International Development. Dr. Kett has a strong focus on research in conflict and disaster-affected countries, and has undertaken policy-focused work on inclusive humanitarian responses, culminating in her role as Global Focal Point for Disability in the current revision of the Sphere Handbook on Minimum Standards in Disaster Response (2010). Dr. Kett has published widely in major peer-reviewed journals (including a special edition of *The Lancet*). She is also co-editor of the journal *Medicine, Conflict and Survival.*

Debra Jean Kreisberg, PhD, is director of the Center for Integrated Disaster Preparedness at the University of Colorado Denver, School of Emergency Medicine. Previously she was director of Emergency Preparedness and Diversity Initiatives at the Colorado Hospital Association where she worked to develop programs in the area of disaster preparedness and response with special interest around the impact for culturally diverse populations. In her work with many culturally and ethnically diverse refugee populations, Dr. Kreisberg has directly engaged with hospitals, health departments, and nonprofit organizations to develop standards of cultural competency, resources and programs that enhance access, the development of culturally appropriate assessment and intake tools, and evaluation and measurement tools in the area of healthcare access and quality of care.

Pamela Jenkins, PhD, is a research professor of sociology and faculty in the Women's Studies Program at the University of New Orleans. She is a founding and associate member of UNO's Center for Hazard Assessment, Response and Technology. Before Katrina, her research interests were diverse but focused on how communities respond to a variety of problems. Her research interests post-Katrina include documenting the response to Katrina as part of a national research team on Hurricane Katrina evacuees. She has published on first responders, faith-based communities' response to the storm, and the experiences of the elderly during and after Katrina. At a community level, she is involved in several projects that work directly with best practices for violence prevention including domestic and community violence.

Brenda McCoy, PhD, is a senior lecturer and the chair of the Department of Community and Professional Programs at the University of North Texas. Her primary research interests include social stratification and medical sociology. She has been actively involved with UNT's Next Generation Course Redesign™ Project since 2009 and is currently teaching civic engagement. Before beginning her career in higher education, Dr. McCoy worked in marketing and management for fifteen years.

Michelle Annette Meyer is a PhD candidate in sociology at Colorado State University and is a research assistant at the Center for Disaster and Risk Analysis on a NSF and NOAA funded project on hurricane risk perception along the U.S. Gulf and Atlantic Coasts. Ms. Meyer's dissertation research focuses on the role of social capital in individual and community resilience and social vulnerability in hurricane-prone communities, and she is a 2011 recipient of the National PERISHIP Dissertation Fellowship. Her research and teaching interests include disaster resilience and mitigation, climate change displacement, environmental sociology and community sustainability, quantitative and qualitative research methods, and the interplay between environmental conditions and social vulnerability.

Jenny Mincin, PhD, is regional director for the International Rescue Committee. She has worked on vulnerable population issues, disaster human services, community rebuilding/recovery and refugee resettlement as a field worker, manager and academician for almost twenty years. Dr. Mincin has responded to numerous local disasters and crises as well as federally declared disasters having worked with FEMA, Homeland Security, HHS, and international, state, and local governments. She is a former director for Human Services at Nassau County OEM and manager for City of New York 9/11 Crisis Counseling Program.

Mary Nelan, MA, is a PhD student in the Department of Sociology and Criminology at the University of Delaware and a graduate research assistant at the Disaster Research Center, the world's oldest research center focused on the social science aspects of disasters. Her research has focused on international disaster volunteers, volunteer health behaviors, social vulnerability to disasters, and evacuation and sheltering behaviors. She has volunteered in several disaster zones, including Haiti following the 2010 earthquake and Kentucky following the March 2012 tornadoes.

Mary Shannon Newell, MPA/MPH, is a research and teaching assistant at the University of Colorado Denver, where she is also pursuing a dual master's degree in Public Administration at the Colorado School of Public Affairs and Public Health at the Colorado School of Public Health. She is an honorably discharged U.S. Army veteran in which she had served as a Military Police Officer and participated in multiple combat tours in the Middle East. Her professional interests are in public health emergency preparedness and response, and improving the integration of public health and medical resources with traditional emergency management infrastructures.

Katie Oviatt, MA, is a PhD student in the Health and Behavioral Sciences Department at the University of Colorado Denver. She is also a fellow in the NSF funded IGERT program which focuses on issues involving sustainable urban infrastructure. She has a BA and an MA in anthropology, and has spent her academic career working with small-scale farmers in both Bolivia and India to understand the livelihood challenges they face. Her current research interest is focused on exploring the local food movement in the United States.

Lori Peek, PhD, is associate professor of Sociology and co-director of the Center for Disaster and Risk Analysis at Colorado State University. She also serves as associate chair for the Social Science Research Council Task Force on Hurricane Katrina and Rebuilding the Gulf Coast. Her work focuses on socially vulnerable populations—including children, women, racial, and ethnic minorities, and persons with disabilities—in disaster. She is the author of *Behind the Backlash: Muslim Americans after 9/11* (Temple University Press, 2011) and co-editor of *Displaced: Life in the Katrina Diaspora* (University of Texas Press, 2012).

Jenniffer Santos-Hernández, MA, is a PhD student in sociology at the University of Delaware, and also studied sociology at the University of Puerto Rico-Mayaguez. Her research focuses on risk communication, adaptation, and the linkages between characteristics of social vulnerability, disaster experiences, and broader social forces. Ms. Santos-Hernández has more than ten years of research experience in the United States and internationally.

Jean Scandlyn, PhD, is an assistant research professor in the Departments of Health and Behavioral Sciences and Anthropology at the University of Colorado Denver. She is a registered nurse and medical anthropologist and has more than twenty years of experience working in a variety of health care settings and doing community-based research and teaching in the United States and internationally including co-teaching a ethnographic field school in rural lowland Ecuador. Her research and teaching interests focus on social science theory and qualitative research as it relates to adolescence and early adulthood and the effects of military service on veterans, families, and communities.

Jeannette Sutton, PhD, is a senior research scientist in the Trauma Health and Hazards Center at the University of Colorado - Colorado Springs. She specializes in disaster sociology with a primary focus is on the evolving role of Information and Communication Technology, and online informal communications in disaster. Additional areas of research include the socio-behavioral aspects of disaster warning systems, outreach and service provision to vulnerable populations via online communications, and Volunteer Technical Communities in disaster.

Michael D. Thompson, PhD, has for the last decade been the Phoebe Schertz Young Professor of Religious Studies at Oklahoma State University. Prior to that he taught church history and spiritual formation for twenty-one years at the Golden Gate Baptist Theological Seminary in San Francisco, and his professional career began in 1973 as a local church minister.

Jennifer Tobin-Gurley is a research assistant at the Center for Disaster and Risk Analysis and a third year PhD student in the Department of Sociology at Colorado State University. Her work on the post-disaster resource needs of single mothers was published in the *International Journal of Mass Emergencies and Disasters*. Ms. Tobin-Gurley is also involved in a wide range of funded research projects including an examination of children's experiences following Hurricane Katrina; a gap analysis on preparedness for individuals with access and functional needs; an exploration of earthquake risk reduction activities in 11 cities in 7 different countries with high seismic risk; an analysis of disaster preparedness among childcare providers in Colorado, and; a participatory project on children's recovery after the Slave Lake fire in Canada and the Joplin tornado in the U.S.

Dr John Twigg is a principal research associate in the Department of Civil, Environmental and Geomatic Engineering and a co-director of the Centre for Urban Sustainability and Resilience, both at University College London, where he also teaches courses on disaster risk reduction, vulnerability and resilience to graduate students. His research interests include: community-based disaster risk management; socio-economic vulnerability and resilience; and disability and disasters. He has more than fifty publications on disaster risk reduction and sustainable development, including *Characteristics of a Disaster-Resilient Community* (2009) and *Disaster risk reduction: mitigation and preparedness in development and emergency programming* (2004).

Tricia Wachtendorf, PhD, is an associate professor in the Department of Sociology and Criminal Justice at the University of Delaware, and the associate director of the Disaster Research Center, the oldest center in the world focused on the social science aspects of disaster. She has worked as a community-based practitioner in harm-reduction outreach. With more than fifteen years disaster research experience, she has conducted quick response and reconnaissance field work following such disasters as the 2001 attack in New York, the 2004 Indian Ocean tsunami, the 2008 earthquake in China, and the 2011 tsunami in Japan. Her research focuses on multi-organizational coordination, improvisation, transnational disasters, and social vulnerability.

Acknowledgments

MARY FRAN MYERS SCHOLARSHIP RECIPIENTS

All royalties from the sale of this volume go to the Mary Fran Myers Scholarship, which recognizes individuals who have a "commitment to disaster research and practice and have the potential to make a lasting contribution to reducing disaster vulnerability."

Mary Fran Myers was a former floodplain manager turned scholar-practitioner and was the associate director of the Natural Hazards Research and Applications Information Center for sixteen years. She brought people together across differences, namely across academic ivory towers and disciplinary stovepipes. Myers recognized early on that reducing vulnerability and building capacity would require people to come together. One of her greatest contributions led to the emergence and development of what became the Gender and Disaster Network (GDN). Formed in 1997, the GDN (www.gdnonline.org) celebrated its fifteenth anniversary in 2012, the publication year of the second edition of this book.

Sadly, Mary Fran Myers died from cancer in 2004. Myers is remembered as an individual who reflected "leadership, guidance, grace, and laughter and established a standard of excellence admired and emulated by her colleagues. She was an innovator, a mentor, and a creative spirit who touched many lives. Her legacy has had a lasting impact on the global hazards community." (For more details, visit http://www.colorado.edu/hazards/awards/myers-scholarship.html.)

The following presents brief biographies of the scholarship recipients that illustrate their connections between research and practice, as well as their concerns for both vulnerability and resilience:

2012 WINNERS

Hsien-Ho (Ray) Chang is a currently PhD student in disaster science and management at the University of Delaware and served as a fire captain at the Taipei County Fire Department in Taiwan. Chang hopes his practical background and postgraduate studies will bridge the gap between academics and practitioners in the future.

Mike Kline manages the Vermont Department of Environmental Conservation's Rivers and Floodplain Program. Kline has developed a river corridor planning program to help more than 150 Vermont communities complete projects that improve water quality, restore river ecosystems, and mitigate floods and erosion.

Justin Moresco is a project manager at GeoHazards International, where he promotes earthquake preparedness and mitigation with an emphasis on developing countries. Moresco is working on initiatives that draw the social sciences, public health, engineering, and earth sciences to increase the impact of risk reduction efforts.

Judy Sears is pursuing a master's degree at Humboldt State University in environment and community. Her research on Community Emergency Response Teams (CERT) examined what complement of personal and community action would include most people, empower them to make neighborhood connections, and build resilience to better prepare them for slow and rapid changes.

2011 WINNERS

Keya Mitra is an associate professor in the Department of Architecture at Bengal Engineering and Science University in Shibpur, India. Mitra's research focuses on how development regulations and building rules influence the earthquake safety of the structures in urban areas.

Véronique Morin is a doctoral student in the Disaster Preparedness, Mitigation and Management (DPMM) program at the Asian Institute of Technology in Bangkok, Thailand. Morin has more than twenty years of professional experience in coastal engineering. Her research assesses the impacts of climate change and developing adaptation strategies for coastal communities in small island developing states.

2010 WINNERS

Deborah Colburn is the director of the Animal Emergency Management Program at the Colorado Veterinary Medical Foundation where she coordinates animal emergency response efforts and addresses animal issues at the Colorado State Emergency Operations Center. Colburn supported the community recovery efforts of the American Red Cross Hurricane Recovery Program in Alabama from 2006–2008.

Scott Cotton is a long-time disaster educator with firsthand response experience. He is constantly working toward better disaster preparedness, especially for agricultural and rural communities. With a research and education emphasis based on determining the most effective preparedness training and implementation, Cotton has taught disaster readiness to more than 3,000 people in 100 counties.

Peter Hanink is the director of programs at the Disaster Accountability Project (DAP), a graduate of Brooklyn Law School. During law school, Hanink worked with the Legal Aid Society's Criminal Defense Division, focusing on promoting the rights of indigent defendants. He became acquainted with DAP while serving as co-president of Brooklyn Law's Student Hurricane Network.

Terri Turner is a founding member and the outgoing chair of the Georgia Association of Floodplain Management, the Association of State Floodplain Managers No Adverse Impact Committee liaison, and chair of the Central Savannah River Area Planners Group. Turner has authored a white paper, numerous op-ed pieces, several ASFPM position letters, and a *Natural Hazards Observer* article.

2009 WINNERS

Alex Altshuler holds master's degree in community social work from the University of Haifa and in social sciences and humanitarian affairs from the University of Rome. He works as a regional project coordinator at the Israel Crisis Management Center, a nongovernmental organization assisting new immigrants faced with crisis or tragedy.

Dr. Ali Ardalan is an assistant professor of epidemiology at the Tehran University of Medical Sciences' Institute of Public Health Research and is founder of Iran's first academic Health in Emergencies and Disasters Department. His research interests focus on disaster epidemiology, community-based disaster risk management, and vulnerable groups in disasters.

Oluponmile Olonilua is a visiting assistant professor of public administration at Texas Southern University's Barbara Jordan-Mickey Leland School of Public Affairs in Houston. She became involved in disaster research after personally experiencing Tropical Storm Allison in 2001. Her research interests include hazard mitigation plan evaluation and the effect of disasters on minorities and special populations.

2008 WINNERS

Edy M. Barillas holds a master's degree in engineering geology from the Colorado School of Mines in Golden. He currently lives and works in Guatemala, but interacts with professionals and practitioners across Central America regarding disaster preparedness. As an Oxfam Project Officer, his main responsibilities focus on community organization, training and equipment monitoring for rain; early warnings; and emergency response.

Monalisa Chatterjee's "Urban Flood Loss Sharing and Redistribution Mechanisms among the Impoverished Industrial Population of Mumbai" examines informal coping methods of poor urban flood victims and studies the impact of globalization on the changing nature of coping strategies.

Charna R. Epstein directs the Crisis Prevention and Disaster Recovery Department at Heartland Alliance for Human Needs and Human Rights headquartered in Chicago. As part of her responsibilities, she helped lead the Chicagoland Katrina Relief Initiative which was responsible for the resettlement of approximately 10,000 Gulf Coast evacuees in greater Chicago.

Molly Mowery received her master's in city planning in 2008 from the Massachusetts Institute of Technology. Her research interests focus on natural hazards, sustainable development policy, and climate change adaptation. She also has worked on site planning in East Biloxi, Mississippi to address Hurricane Katrina recovery and landscape restoration efforts.

Uchenna Okoli is a native of Nigeria and is currently completing a master's in disaster management and sustainable development at Northumbria University in Newcastle upon Tyne, United Kingdom. Her work has focused on raising awareness about the importance of disaster risk reduction and integrating a culture of safety in Nigeria through advocacy and capacity building with a concentration on gender.

2007 WINNERS

Steve Samuelson works as zoning administrator, floodplain manager, residential data collector for the appraiser, and grant writer for Lyon County, Kansas. Steve advocates for how to use zoning and land use planning to prevent construction in dam breach inundation areas, even when a county has no zoning or building permits.

Saeed Ashraf Siddiqi is programme manager at the Earthquake Reconstruction and Rehabilitation Authority (ERRA) for the Government of Pakistan. With Saeed's leadership, ERRA has initiated programs for medical rehabilitation of the disabled in earthquake-affected areas, distribution of compensation to people who lost land during the earthquake, provision of legal assistance to vulnerable groups, and rehabilitation programs for widows and children.

Yu Xiao is a PhD candidate in the Department of Urban and Regional Planning at the University of Illinois at Urbana-Champaign. Her current research focuses on assessing the short- to long-run social and economic impacts of the 1993 Midwest Flood on various types of communities.

2006 WINNERS

Aurélie Brunie is a PhD candidate in city and regional planning at the University of North Carolina at Chapel Hill. Originally from France, her dissertation examines the importance of disaster management capacity building, social capital, local leadership, and middle-level institutions in the sustainability of community preparedness efforts in underdeveloped countries.

Elenka Jarolimek is an emergency management specialist at the University of Washington in Seattle. Her professional accomplishments include co-organizing Symposium 2005: Best Practices in Risk Reduction for Colleges and Universities and co-managing the University of Washington's "Report on Emergency Preparedness for Special Needs Populations."

Alessandra Jerolleman works on mitigation, community outreach, and disaster planning at the Center for Hazards Assessment, Response, and Technology at the University of New Orleans. She has worked on projects benefiting the New Orleans area flood mitigation planning for several suburban New Orleans neighborhoods, identifying and implementing outreach projects for the Disaster Resistant University project, and conducting community outreach related to the Hazard Mitigation Grant Program.

2005 WINNERS

Wei Choong, from Melbourne, Australia, has a background in international development and has worked in Bangladesh, Fiji, Lao PDR, Thailand and East Timor on development issues such as food security, poverty alleviation, and natural disaster risk management. Through research focused on reducing natural disaster risks at the community level, Choong has developed interests in disasters and development, community based disaster risk management, public awareness and education, and the exploration of indigenous coping strategies.

Ana Pamela Membreno is a civil engineer who recently finished her master of science in rural planning and development at the University of Guelph in Canada. She chose to pursue this degree after working in her native Honduras as a project manager for reconstruction projects in the wake of Hurricane Mitch. Throughout her studies, she pursued an interest in floodplain management (looking specifically at vulnerability reduction measures, institutional capacity building, and promotion of community participation) and is a certified floodplain manager.

2004 WINNER

Becky Ault lives in North Dakota. She has been Emergency Manager/9-1-1 Coordinator for Pembina County since 1995 and has led the county through ten Presidential Disaster Declarations during her tenure. Becky has been active in knowledge sharing and technology transfer with other North Dakota agencies as well as other states and federal agencies. Her other efforts include a variety of mitigation projects along the Red River, updating the county wide warning system, and assisting with the county StormReady designation from the National Oceanic and Atmospheric Administration.

Source: Natural Hazards Research and Applications Information Center, http://www.colorado.edu/hazards/awards/myers-scholarship.html. (Bios, photos of scholarship recipients, and additional details can be found here.)

1 Understanding Social Vulnerability

Maureen Fordham, William E. Lovekamp,
Deborah S. K. Thomas, and Brenda D. Phillips

CONTENTS

1.1 CHAPTER PURPOSE

This opening chapter provides an overview of why understanding social vulnerability matters for the practice and research of disaster management. The chapter content contrasts the historically dominant hazards paradigm with that of the social vulnerability paradigm and concludes with an overview of upcoming sections and chapters.

1.2 OBJECTIVES

At the conclusion of this chapter, readers should be able to:

1. Understand basic terms relevant to social vulnerability
2. Understand the dominant hazards paradigm

3. Identify the shortcomings of the dominant paradigm
4. Trace the historical development of a social vulnerability paradigm
5. Understand the general framework of a social vulnerability paradigm
6. Appreciate why considering social vulnerability is necessary in order to reduce risk
7. Recognize linkages with other major disciplinary streams, understanding how they have emerged, intertwined, and diverged from one another
8. Appreciate the relationship between vulnerability and resilience

1.3   INTRODUCTION

For many of us, images of people dying in the Indian Ocean tsunami (2004) or lying trapped in earthquake-devastated Haiti (2010) mark a point in time when we recognized the extent of human vulnerability in disaster situations. The stark images also raised deeper questions. Why were people in harm's way? Why did some subpopulations experience greater effects of the disaster? What could have been done to prevent such loss of life? How could the tragedy have been prevented from happening? What became of those affected? Were they able to return to their homes; recover psychologically; find another source of employment; reunite with their families?

The study of social vulnerability to disasters is compelling. For anyone who wondered why so many people were on the rooftops in New Orleans and why so many died, or who suffered watching complicated extrication attempts to rescue survivors buried in Haiti, many answers can be found in this volume. For researchers and professionals alike, this book is designed to make a difference in our understanding of, and efforts to reduce, conditions that threaten life safety and property, both individually and in our neighborhoods and communities. We invite you to be part of the solution.

This second edition of the text introduces updated content on various populations at risk, integrates a broader array of studies from around the world, and strengthens understanding of people's resilience to disasters. Evidence-based best practices inform the content of this book because people deserve the best science that we can offer. Indeed, understanding both vulnerability and resilience means emphasizing and explicitly applying these concepts, measuring their presence within various populations, and identifying practical solutions.

Researchers have studied and written about human vulnerability to disasters for decades. Yet, far too frequently, efforts to reduce vulnerability occur only after a major event has claimed lives and destroyed individual and community assets, including homes, businesses and savings. Measures to reduce vulnerability tend to rely on established practices, analyzing current policies and revising already-existing plans, but recent research on vulnerability has much to offer managers and practitioners in disaster-risk reduction. Consider the following examples, representing a brief glimpse of social vulnerability, noting that the topics are not entirely discrete:

Income disparity: Income disparities produce very different outcomes when an event occurs, illustrated in contrasting differential impacts between developed- and developing-country contexts or between lower- and higher-income populations within a more developed country. A major earthquake in Pakistan or Haiti will claim more lives than in the United States or Chile, causing more human suffering, and requiring more external support. Or, as another example, droughts in the United States rarely cause death, while a similar physical event in Africa can result in extensive famine, killing hundreds of thousands of people.

Class: Lower-income families and households tend to live in housing that suffers disproportionately during disasters. Such conditions are especially pronounced in lesser developed countries. Disaster managers should recognize such inequitable circumstances and endeavor to make everyone equally safe (Mileti 1999). Disparity intersects with nearly every other social factor, such as gender, race/ethnicity, and class.

Race/ethnicity: Warning messages tend to be issued in the dominant language with an expectation that people will take the recommended action immediately. Even beyond not understanding the message due to language barriers, research indicates that culture influences how people may receive and interpret warnings, further affecting how they may respond, including residents, tourists, business travelers, and family members who have not yet learned a local language (Lindell and Perry 2004).

Gender: Domestic and stranger violence increases after a disaster, yet few communities include women's advocates in their emergency operations planning (Jenkins and Phillips 2008). Further, though women tend to be the ones most likely to secure relief aid for the family, they are underrepresented and underused in recovery efforts (Enarson and Morrow 2000).

Age: Frequently, elderly populations are reluctant to secure aid after a disaster out of concern that they may lose their independence (Bolin and Klenow 1982; Fernandez et al. 2002). As a consequence, they tend to underutilize relief programs and experience delays in returning to their homes. Further, they experience higher rates of vulnerability, particularly when coupled with low income, minority status, and disability (Sharkey 2007).

Disability: People with disabilities experience considerable challenges in securing adequate transportation to evacuate threatened areas as well as to access appropriate, accessible shelters and postdisaster housing (USGAO 2006).

Health: Disasters can disrupt access to health care, particularly for the poor, the elderly, and people with disabilities. Individuals dependent on health services, such as dialysis or cancer treatment, are faced with life-threatening circumstances if these services cannot be accessed in the aftermath of an event. Disasters can also create conditions that worsen health conditions, such as debris, mold, and chemicals that cause or aggravate respiratory conditions (Lin et al. 2005; Malievskaya, Rosenberg, and Markowitz 2002). The Haitian earthquake of January 2010 resulted in near-complete collapse of an already tenuous medical care system. Coupled with contaminated water systems, a cholera outbreak toward the end of 2010 claimed an additional 3,000 lives (Farmer 2011).

Literacy: Most emergency-preparedness materials are available in written form. Few options exist to inform and prepare people with low reading levels, despite the potential for such materials to help people across literacy levels, language barriers, cognitive abilities, and age ranges (USDOJ 2008). Moreover, culture often is not taken into consideration: Communication is not just about language, but also has cultural meanings. Preparedness materials, for example, must consider the cultural context in which recommendations are made. For example, women who live in seclusion under religious codes cannot comply with evacuation orders in the absence of a male family member.

Families and households: Families provide an important unit in which people can care for each other as they rebound from disasters. Yet, many programs fail to address the diversity of families, including households of unrelated individuals. People that cohabit, renters, roommates, and couples that are lesbian, gay, bisexual, or transgendered may experience difficulty in securing aid or the comfort of people who care about them (Eads 2002; Morrow 2000). Policies and programs are often established with the assumption of a traditional nuclear family, not realizing that single-parent households (often female) may not be able stand in lines, work outside the home, or fight for access to limited resources. Such was the case in Pakistan's 2005 earthquake, when widowed women and girls feared for their safety during relief distribution (Ouellette and Ummar 2009; Sayeed 2009).

Despite these challenges, people who live within and across these population groups, or whose circumstances have not been adequately recognized, also bring valuable assets to the process of reducing risks. Consider, for example, that U.S. Presidential Executive Order 13347 advises the inclusion of people with disabilities in all phases of disaster management. More recently, the U.S. Federal Emergency Management Agency (FEMA) introduced the idea of the "Whole Community":

When the community is engaged in an authentic dialogue, it becomes empowered to identify its needs and the existing resources that may be used to address them. Collectively, we can determine the best ways to organize and strengthen community assets, capacities, and interests. This allows us, as a nation, to expand our reach and deliver services more efficiently and cost effectively to build, sustain, and improve our capability to prepare for, protect against, respond to, recover from, and mitigate all hazards. (FEMA 2011)

By integrating and incorporating a broad range of those historically vulnerable, we bring fresh views to the planning table and invite a wider partnership, which yields fresh insights, networks, and linkages that can inform every aspect of risk reduction.

In this second edition, knowledgeable authors expand on original chapters, presenting updated information on the various ways in which some populations experience higher risks than others and offering practical strategies to reduce that vulnerability. Chapter 1 compares and contrasts perspectives that have the potential to influence disaster management and how social groups experience crisis. To set the stage, this chapter begins with an introduction to the concept of social vulnerability. The emphasis then turns to presenting two major paradigms that frame our understanding of risk and influence the solutions we pursue; social vulnerability is compared and contrasted with the dominant paradigm of disasters (for an overview, see Table 1.1). The final section presents a resilience perspective, which has emerged as highly relevant to the concept and framework of social vulnerability.

1.4   DEFINING SOCIAL VULNERABILITY

The term *vulnerability* has different meanings to varying agencies and organizations, and can be conceptualized in several ways. To illustrate, some may use the term vulnerability to mean physical rather than social vulnerability. For example, the U.S. Geological Survey conducts work on coastal vulnerability to sea level rise, which mostly focuses on defining coastal inundation areas. In contrast, agencies in many nations tasked with homeland security see vulnerability as produced via the political intentions of terrorists. Some agencies (e.g., USGAO 2006) describe vulnerable populations in terms of a specific characteristic such as "transportation disadvantaged." Disaster managers at the local level apply a vulnerability approach in both of its physical and social dimensions.

In this text, while we recognize the relevance of physical risk/vulnerability, we concentrate on *social* vulnerability, which arises out of differential social relations among groups in a given society.

TABLE 1.1
The Dominant versus Vulnerability Paradigm of Disaster

Dominant Paradigm	Vulnerability Paradigm
The dominant paradigm concentrates on the physical processes of the hazard	The vulnerability paradigm addresses socioeconomic and political influences
Management style emphasizes problem solving through hierarchies and authorities	Management style emphasizes a decentralized view that involves community-based problem solving
A top-down view	A grassroots or bottom-up view
Uses technology, engineering, and science to address the hazard	Uses local knowledge, networks, imagination, and creativity to address the hazard
The goal is to reduce physical damage	The goal is to reduce social vulnerability of people
The general philosophical view is utilitarian and the conquest of nature	The general philosophical view is equitable views to reduce vulnerability and working in concert with nature
Emphasizes bounded systems	Emphasizes open systems and complexity

Source: Adapted from Blanchard (2000).

From this point forward, the term *vulnerability* will be utilized to mean social vulnerability. As Bankoff (2006) notes:

> By the 1980s, it was apparent in both the developed and the developing world that to be "at risk" was not just a question of being in the wrong place at the wrong time, and of regarding disasters as purely physical happenings requiring largely technological solutions. Disasters were more properly viewed as primarily the result of human actions; that while hazards are natural, disasters are not. Social systems generate unequal exposure to risk by making some people more prone to disaster than others and these inequalities are largely a function of the power relations (class, age, gender and ethnicity among others) operative in every society.

1.5   THE DOMINANT PARADIGM

This section reviews the dominant hazards paradigm, the most common view taken by many disaster researchers and practitioners (although not all) for many years. To do so, we examine how the dominant paradigm understands nature, chance, time, science, technology, people, and society.

1.5.1   How Does the Dominant Paradigm Understand Nature, Chance, and Time?

The dominant paradigm understands nature as the primary agent that causes the disaster to occur. While this may seem obvious, the paradigm merits fuller interpretation. As described by Tobin and Montz (1997, 8):

> The traditional view of natural hazards has ascribed all or almost all responsibility for them to the processes of the geophysical world. The view has meant that the root cause of large-scale death and destruction has been attributed to the extremes of nature rather than encompassing the human world. Frequently, disaster victims have been viewed as unfortunates who could do little but react to physical processes. The physical world, then, has been seen as an external force, separate from human forces.

The dominant paradigm explains disasters as the result of nature impinging upon human society in which there is little that can be done to change the situation. In the dominant paradigm, then, nature is the cause, the condition, and the propelling force that damages, destroys, and kills. Nature, unharnessed, is to blame. Hewitt (1983, 5) explains:

> Conceptual preambles and the development of "risk assessment" appear to have swept away the old unpalatable causality of environmental determinism... [but] [t]he sense of causality or the direction of explanation still runs from the physical environment to its social impacts.

The dominant paradigm has, for a long time, simply been accepted as the way to understand disasters. It interprets the hazards that society faces as an attack on the functioning and stability of social systems. Communities are perceived as subject to what the storm will bring to bear on their abilities to survive. The dominant paradigm has influenced powerfully both research and practice. Quarantelli (1998, 226) writes:

> The earliest workers in the area, including myself, with little conscious thought and accepting common sense views, initially accepted as a prototype model the notion that disasters were an outside attack upon social systems that "broke down" in the face of such an assault from outside.

Disasters must be managed, placed under human control, and influenced where possible, in contrast to views that integrate human activity with natural systems and honor ecological integrity.

Disasters are thus viewed as horrendous tragedies, as accidents or even as freak events. Because they are so conceived, in many locations and cultures, it is assumed that there is little one can do to prevent their occurrence and, consequently, their effects. Risk is the result of chance, of being in the wrong location at the wrong time. Society simply cannot do much about such events because they occur naturally and seemingly without prediction. We are at the mercy of nature. Steinberg (2000, xix), in his historical view on disasters, illuminates this barrier between society and nature:

> [T]hese events are understood by scientists, the media, and technocrats as primarily accidents—unexpected, unpredictable happenings that are the price of doing business on this planet. Seen as freak events cut off from people's everyday interactions with the environment, they are positioned outside the moral compass of our culture.

Disasters, as disruptive influences, are viewed as operating outside of human history and as a "break" in the "normal" flow of time. They are an "other," an "outsider" to the way in which we view our normal relations, and thus represent the untoward. In the 2008 tragedies that befell Myanmar/Burma and the People's Republic of China, both media commentators and experts in the field used the dominant paradigm to explain "donor fatigue," meaning that people had reduced their financial contributions to charitable organizations: "It might be more accurately described as disaster fatigue—the sense that these events are never-ending, uncontrollable and overwhelming. Experts say it is the one reason Americans have contributed relatively little so far" (Tolin 2008). Hewitt elaborates (1983, 10):

> The language of discourse is often a good indicator of basic assumptions. In hazards work one can see how language is used to maintain a sense of discontinuity or otherness, which severs these problems from the rest of man-environment relations and social life. That is most obvious in the recurrent use of words stressing the "un"-ness of the problem. Disasters are unmanaged phenomena. They are the unexpected, the unprecedented. They derive from natural processes or events that are highly uncertain. Unawareness and unreadiness are said to typify the condition of their human victims. Even the common use of the word [disaster] "event" can reinforce the idea of a discrete unit in time and space. In the official-sounding euphemism for disasters in North America, they are "unscheduled events."

Accepting the dominant paradigm implies that little can be done to prevent catastrophe from striking (Steinberg 2000, xix). Even the word *disaster* implies a discontinuity with normal, routine events (Hewitt 1983, 10). Time stops while we gather the injured and dead and pick up the pieces in order to move on. To recover from disaster then means to restore a sense of normal time, to bring back a routine order, and to provide social stability and functioning.

1.5.2   How Does the Dominant Paradigm Understand Science and Technology?

If we are at the mercy of nature and unexpected events, how are we to safeguard the stability and functioning of our social systems? How should we move to manage the presumably unmanageable in order to thwart the effects of such disruptions on our time? The dominant paradigm sees science and technology as the main tools available to address disasters. To manage the seeming unpredictability of earthquakes, we place seismic monitoring devices around the planet, hoping to ascertain the connection between foreshocks and main shocks. In the aftermath of the 2004 Indian Ocean tsunami, nations worked collaboratively to place wave detection systems across vast waterway expanses. Across the United States, dams and levees have been erected to ward off floodwaters and storm surges.

In short, the dominant paradigm prescribes an engineering solution to many hazards, even those that do not emanate from the natural world, including natural (hurricanes, floods, tornadoes), technological (hazardous materials accidents, oil spills, nuclear accidents), and conflict based (war and terrorism). It is clear that an emphasis on scientific or technological management is the preferred solution for the dominant paradigm. For example, after September 11, efforts focused on reinforcing buildings through integrating breakthroughs in "blast performance" research. Tremendous amounts of funding were diverted toward "hardening" targets, especially buildings, with far less funding directed toward evacuation planning, particularly for people with disabilities, seniors, and those lacking transportation. The harsh reality of Hurricane Katrina revealed the consequences of applying the dominant paradigm. Although new funding and initiatives have addressed human vulnerability to a greater extent than before the storm, far more funding and effort have targeted rebuilding the massive levee system. Environmentally oriented proposed solutions that would restore coastal integrity to stem storm surge and replenish endangered ecosystems have fared badly; in the dominant paradigm, coastal restoration, as a natural means to stem storm surge, is deemed too expensive.

Finally, turning to the practical application of science and technology offers a view consistent with, and supportive of, a capitalist economy. As Alexander (2000, 25) indicates, "Structural mitigation is preferred for obvious reasons by the construction and economic growth lobbies. Technological hardware production . . . has offered ever more complex, expensive and sophisticated solutions to the problem of hazards." Thus, because technology is seen as a near-panacea for the problems produced by disasters of all kinds, engineering and "hard science" applications receive funding far in excess of social science research. The dominant paradigm, historically, did not consider solutions that might work in concert with nature. Those who use this approach have been changing their efforts more recently to include river restoration, renaturalization projects, and dam decommissioning. However, questions linger over whether such changes truly represent a break from the dominant paradigm or simply a greener form of engineering. Rather, "the most expensive actions and the most formidable scientific literature, recommending action are concerned mainly with geophysical monitoring, forecasting and direct engineering or land-use planning in relation to natural agents" (Hewitt 1983, 5). Science and technology in this sense serve a perceived need to command and control nature. In fact, command and control is the preferred form of dealing with people too, as we discuss next.

1.5.3 How Does the Dominant Paradigm Understand People?

The dominant paradigm sees human beings as being unable to make good decisions regarding disasters. Conceptually, the term *bounded rationality* means that people lack sufficient information to make well-informed decisions regarding their risks. Although "behavior is generally rational or logical," it is "limited by perception and prior knowledge" (Tobin and Montz 1997, 5). According to the dominant paradigm, for instance, the tragedy of the cyclone in Myanmar in 2008 was attributed to such limitations. Local people lacked information or understanding regarding the impending cyclone, and thus could not or did not make evacuation decisions. The social vulnerability paradigm would extend this explanation to political, economic, and social contextual barriers beyond individual knowledge. The dominant paradigm also assumes that, even with sufficient information, people would not necessarily process the knowledge adequately and thus would choose from a bounded set of options. The dominant paradigm has also been used recently to explain why so many failed to leave New Orleans despite clear warnings to do so.

In many disaster studies, people serve as an individualized focus of inquiry. Researchers "ask how people respond to forecasts, requests to conserve water or even hazard zone legislation. They examine how people 'cope' when the volcano erupts or when a crop is destroyed" (Hewitt 1983, 7). Such research focuses squarely on the event as a disruptive extreme that causes even seasonal events, such as agricultural production, to cease. And people's responses are bounded (limited) by awareness and knowledge. Burton, Kates, and White (1978, 52) explain:

> It is rare indeed that individuals have access to full information in appraising either natural events or alternative courses of action. Even if they were to have such information, they would have trouble processing it, and in many instances they would have goals quite different than maximizing the expected utility. The bounds on rational choice in dealing with natural hazards, as with all human decisions, are numerous.

Although the intent of the research seems reasonable, it misses "the main sources of social influence over hazards" (Hewitt 1983, 7). Consequently, the conclusion has been that people must be instructed, led, and managed. Often, this is experienced as a top-down, hierarchical model designed to "command and control" events, as if the disaster itself could be herded into submission. For emergency managers who subscribe to this view, the differential responses of people to hazards and subsequent "orders" seem chaotic and nonsensical. People appear to have lost their way, to have behaved out of compliance with the clear-headed thinking of those in authority (Tierney 2005).

1.5.4   How Does the Dominant Paradigm Understand Society?

If nature is at fault, then surely the disaster is not the result of political, social, or economic systems or the misfit of interactions among these systems. Such systems, and the actors within them, are viewed as only modifying the disaster and its effects, and thus the ability of society to respond is obviously limited:

> In the dominant paradigm, then, disaster is itself attributed to nature. There is, however, an equally strong conviction that something can be done about disaster by society. But that something is viewed as strictly a matter of public policy backed up by the most advanced geophysical, geotechnical and managerial capacity. There is a strong sense, even among social scientists for whom it is a major interest, that everyday or "ordinary" human activity can do little except make the problem worse by default. In other words, the structure of the problem is seen to depend upon the ratios between given forces of nature and the "advanced" institutional and technical counterforce. (Hewitt 1983, 6)

Yet, changes within social systems, according to the dominant paradigm, can provide solutions. Consistent with the use of science, technological fixes and engineering solutions are viewed as the means by which to engage in risk reduction. Individuals cannot bear the risk because of limited means. Accordingly, measures consistent with economic interests that distribute risk will emerge. Insurance policies, for example, distribute risk when everyone buys in and shoulders the cost of an event. Burton, Kates, and White (1978, 219) describe the shared solution as "the construction of dams, irrigation systems, or seawalls, and the design of monitoring, forecasting, and warning systems with complex equipment," all of which "would be clearly beyond the scope of individual action." Socially shared risk, embedded within existing scientific and economic systems, affords a measure of security to stabilize the functioning of social systems. However, as Burton, Kates, and White (1978, 219) point out, "These favored adjustments require interlocking and interdependent social organization, and they tend to be uniform in application, inflexible and difficult to change."

1.5.5   Shortcomings of the Dominant Paradigm

A number of shortcomings of the dominant paradigm have been identified. First, the dominant paradigm does not consider all causes of disasters. Carr (1932, 221) noted that people and societies survive disasters all the time. What is important is that "as long as the levees hold, there is no disaster. It is the collapse of the cultural protection that constitutes the disaster proper." Given that Carr spoke these words 73 years before Hurricane Katrina, his words seem prophetic. The category 5 storm surge that pushed into New Orleans occurred in large part because of the decimation of natural coastal protections, coupled with engineer-driven levee solutions that were unable to withstand storms exceeding a category 3.

Second, the dominant paradigm relies heavily on understanding physical processes to the neglect of social forces. Hewitt (1983) emphasized this in his work. Too much causality has been attributed to geophysical forces. In contrast, Mileti et al. (1999) identified disasters as the result of a misfit between three systems: the physical world, the built environment, and human systems. Disasters occur because society lacks effective measures to reduce the impact; such measures reflect the values and institutions of the society. Whether or not a mitigation measure has been instigated will have much to do with economic and political will. Trailer parks, for example, are continually approved without requiring congregate sheltering facilities. Such homes routinely fail in the lowest levels of tornadic activity. Disasters consequently result from social rather than geophysical activity (Tobin and Montz 1997, 11).

Overall, critics argue that vulnerability occurs because of the ways in which social systems are constructed, choices are made, and groups are (or sometimes not) protected. In many locations, populations remain vulnerable because we have failed collectively to address the social conditions, such as inferior housing that fails to provide adequate protection. Disasters thus "bring to the surface the poverty which characterizes the lives of so many inhabitants" (Hardoy and Satterthwaite 1989, 203). The assumption (or claim) that the geophysical world is the originator of risk is called into question; critics argue instead that risk stems from "the risks, pressures, uncertainties that bear upon awareness of and preparedness for natural fluctuations [that] flow mainly from what is called 'ordinary life,' rather than from the rareness and scale of those fluctuations" (Hewitt 1983, 25).

Third, the dominant paradigm is accused of failing to consider all effects of disasters. Death, injuries, and property loss are not the only consequences:

> They can also redirect the character of social institutions, result in permanent new and costly regulations for future generations, alter ecosystems, and even disturb the stability of political regimes. Costs like these rarely, if ever, are counted as part of the disaster impacts. (Mileti 1999, 90)

Fourth, the dominant paradigm promotes an emphasis on preparedness and response rather than understanding how to reduce risk through mitigation and adaptation: a common critique levied at the U.S. Department of Homeland Security and FEMA priorities. Mileti (1999, 237) and a panel of experts in the United States recognized this disparity and wrote:

> Achieving patterns of rebuilding that generally keep people and property out of harm's way is increasingly viewed as an essential element of any disaster recovery program. Rebuilding that fails to acknowledge the location of high-hazard areas is not sustainable, nor is housing that is not built to withstand predictable physical forces. Indeed, disasters should be viewed as providing unique opportunities for change—not only to building local capability for recovery—but for long-term sustainable development as well.

To illustrate, the Northridge, California, earthquake generated $2.5 billion in direct losses, with an estimated total loss of $44 billion. Over 20,000 persons experienced displacement from their homes, and over 681,000 requested federal assistance totaling approximately $11 billion in individual and public assistance. Bolin and Stanford (1999, 104) found that all dimensions of recovery were influenced by one's location in the social system:

> From the individual's standpoint, relief accessibility is complex and takes up issues of personal knowledge of federal programs, cultural and language skills, and physical location, with the mediating effects of social class, ethnicity, and gender. It is here that language, cultural and residency barriers may hinder households in access to resources for recovery. In Fillmore, with its history of an Anglo-dominated power structure and exclusionary practices aimed at farm-workers (and lower-income Latinos in general), local political culture compounded resource access problems for Latino disaster victims.

Fifth, the dominant paradigm is charged with failing to take advantage of the full range of solutions and measures to address risk. Disasters are considered opportunities when "swift action" can be taken to "develop or implement measures" (Blaikie et al. 1994, 224), but the dominant paradigm does not deem those at risk to be possible partners in creating safer conditions. For instance:

> Women are pivotal in the intersection between household and community recovery. While their needs and experiences are in many respects gender specific, as well as deeply influenced by class and ethnicity, they also provide critical insights into neglected, yet central, problems, processes, and mechanisms of household and community recovery. We conclude that a gendered analysis is crucial to understanding and mitigating against future impacts of disasters on families and communities. (Enarson and Morrow 1997, 135)

> Churches and other bodies form the centres for citizen response to economic dislocation and crisis. Food banks, community kitchens, and pantries have sprung up all over the US and in many Latin American countries to assist and involve poor and hungry people. People's health centres and public health movements have also emerged in the slums of many of the world's mega-cities from Brooklyn and the Bronx to Rio de Janeiro, Mexico City and Manila. Such formal and informal organizations are woefully underutilized by authorities responsible for disaster mitigation. Non-governmental organizations have been quicker to recognize the potential of such groups. (Blaikie et al. 1994, 236)

Overall, the dominant paradigm provides a limited understanding of the causes of, and solutions to, disasters and fails, in particular, to recognize the true nature of vulnerability and the capacity that related populations bring to bear on their own risk as well as that of the larger society. We turn next to consideration of an alternative view, the social vulnerability paradigm.

1.6 THE SOCIAL VULNERABILITY PARADIGM

Social vulnerability to disasters is deeply rooted in historical context; current social structures, such as the lack of access to political power and the uneven distribution of income, did not just appear. Several disasters highlight this to an extent that leaves little room for disputing the relevance of social vulnerability. A comparison of Haiti and Chile earthquakes (Table 1.2) clearly reveals how social vulnerability gives rise to disaster and leads to extensive human suffering. The Chilean earthquake was 500 times stronger than that in Haiti, albeit more distant from population centers. Yet, in comparison, the death rate for those in Haiti was roughly 35,000:1, the differential arising directly out of historical colonialism, an ineffective national government, expansive poverty, and weakened infrastructure (physical and human systems).

As another example, over 8,000 people died in 1974 when Hurricane Fifi devastated northeastern Honduras. Farmers, who had been displaced from rich valley land due to the establishment of banana plantations, had cleared steep slopes to grow meager crops. Fifi's torrential rains caused the slopes to fail, leading to significant numbers of deaths and the loss of a means to feed families. Proponents of the vulnerability paradigm point out that the assumptions of the dominant paradigm fail to explain the Honduran deaths (Mileti 1999, 28):

> Although the "bounded rationality" model of human choice explicitly recognizes the existence of constraining social, political, and economic forces and cultural values, recognizing those boundaries apparently has not helped to break through them to reduce losses. It is possible, in fact, that those forces are much more powerful than previously thought.

We should not be surprised, then, that over 70% of the dead in Hurricane Katrina were over the age of 65 and that African Americans died in numbers disproportionate to whites and to their local population numbers (Sharkey 2007). Nor should we be surprised that the Indian Ocean tsunami that claimed over 300,000 lives, included an estimated 240,000 women and children (MacDonald 2005). In the Great East Japan earthquake of 2011, a relatively high number of the victims were elderly, with more than 56% aged 65 or older (Ryall and Demetriou 2012).

The characteristics of a disaster-resilient society—or the lack thereof—are undeniable in these examples. Such deaths are predictable and, with adequate preparation, the numbers are reducible. New views and practices, accordingly, have been deemed overdue and more than appropriate. Developmental

TABLE 1.2

Comparing Haiti and Chile

Characteristic	Haiti	Chile
Time and date	12 January 2012; 4:53 pm local time	27 February 2010; 3:34 am local time
Magnitude (Richter scale)	7.0	8.8
Location	25 miles west of the capital	Offshore from the west coast; twice as deep as Haiti earthquake and 70 miles from the closest city
Total population of country	9,801,664	17,067,369
Country GDP (official exchange rate)	$7.4 billion (2011 est.)	$243 billion (2011 est.)
Deaths	222,570	562
Building damage	Catastrophic, total collapses; utilities and infrastructure destroyed; hospitals destroyed; over 300,000 homes destroyed; at least 30,000 businesses destroyed	Relatively minimal and often limited to historic structures not retrofitted under the seismic code
Numbers of affected	3,700,000	2,671,556
Estimated losses	$8–$13 billion or 120% of the nation's gross domestic product	$30 billion or 18% of the nation's gross domestic product
Building codes	Limited to nonexistent; building constructed of unreinforced concrete or made from available materials in very-low-income areas	Seismic code in place since 1972, including low-income buildings; reinforced concrete often used in construction
Emergency management capabilities	Limited to nonexistent; police and fire suffer significant casualties	Fairly well developed
Emergency preparedness	Limited to nonexistent	Earthquake preparedness, including drills for children for several decades
Previous disaster experience	Limited with earthquakes; hurricane and flooding history	Significant prior events over magnitude 8.0, including a 9.5 event in 1960
Government structure	Weak; history of coups and continual transitions; national palace heavily damaged, with members of government killed	Strong and competent
Percent below poverty line	80%	20%
Social issues postimpact	Increased violence against women and girls; extensive relief camps remain open for years; water system unsafe; cholera outbreak in late 2010 claims >3,000 lives; medical infrastructure needs to be rebuilt; educational system decimated; 10 million cubic meters of debris to remove	Disproportionate recovery, with the most marginalized delayed in returning to homes; though generally considered an effective response—with many people working in and with communities—some questions of civil society arose

Sources: Block (2010); Cavallo, Powell, and Beverra (2010); Duda and Jones (n.d.); Farmer (2011); Cordero (2010); Jarroud (2012); Thurman (2010); USAID (2012).

status and poverty often lie at the heart of why people die in such predictable and disproportionate numbers. These realities cannot be easily engineered away, especially when engineering efforts benefit those more economically and politically powerful than those at highest risk (Freudenburg et al. 2009). Such counterarguments suggest that social factors like economic "growth machines" drive efforts to place levees, dams, and other seemingly protective features in place. While allowing for economic growth through access to waterways and ports, they leave people at risk when such measures fail.

At the outset, it is important to differentiate between the terms *vulnerability* and *exposure*, which clearly highlights how social processes contribute directly to the creation of risk. A whole town might be exposed to a flood risk (maybe lying within certain contours of a floodplain), but it is only some people within the flood zone that are truly vulnerable to its effects (Cardona et al. 2012). Acknowledging this difference is at the heart of where the dominant hazards and vulnerability views diverge. The dominant hazards paradigm emphasizes the underlying valorization of the triggering hazard, while the social vulnerability paradigm elevates the need to understand the socioeconomic and political root causes of disaster vulnerability. Social vulnerability results from multiple conditions and circumstances that could include health, income, disability, age, literacy, or immigration status (Wisner et al. 2004). However, it is not disability or literacy alone that produces vulnerability. Rather, it is the failure of society to recognize that a condition, such as poverty, means you cannot necessarily mitigate risk, live in a safer location, or afford to evacuate when told to do so. When disaster managers and political leaders fail to design warning systems that reach people who are deaf or to provide paratransit systems to evacuate a wheelchair user, society bears responsibility for the consequences. Social vulnerability thus results from processes of social inequality and historic patterns of social relations that manifest as deeply embedded social structural barriers resistant to change:

> Race and class are certainly factors that help explain the social vulnerability in the South, while ethnicity plays an additional role in many cities. When the middle classes (both White and Black) abandon a city, the disparities between the very rich and the very poor expand. Add to this an increasing elderly population, the homeless, transients (including tourists), and other special needs populations, and the prospects for evacuating a city during times of emergencies becomes a daunting challenge for most American cities. (Cutter 2006)

Vulnerability is "embedded in complex social relations and processes" (Hilhorst and Bankoff 2004, 5) and is situated squarely at the human-environment intersection requiring social solutions if successful risk reduction is to occur. Doing so requires us to acknowledge and address the complexity of the problem because it is not just that a hurricane has extremely high winds or an earthquake shakes the ground. Rather, the risk stems from an interface between society and its environment (Oliver-Smith 2002) that is a preexisting condition (Cutter 1996). That interface requires that we "unpack" the idea of vulnerability, not only as it affects various social groups, but also and most importantly, in how we actively and inadvertently perpetuate the social disparities that give rise to certain differential risk between individuals and groups of people.

Risk is socially produced and is not inherent to the hazard event per se. Disasters, which result from a disconnect between human systems, the built environment, and the physical world, tend to clearly reveal the social problems that make response and recovery difficult at the individual and family levels (Mileti 1999; Barton 1969). When people are exposed to an event, they may experience vulnerability resulting from social, economic, and political conditions, often beyond their control. Children who are born into poverty will experience difficulty in climbing into a higher socioeconomic level that would improve their asset base. People with disabilities experience incomes far lower than people without disabilities. Historically in the United States alone, one-third of female-headed single-parent families fall below the poverty line. Tens of thousands of elderly Americans attempt to survive solely on social security checks that fall at minimal levels. Although there are various checklists of vulnerable groups (e.g., Morrow 1999), *vulnerability is a dynamic concept* and not a label. It is not that children, people with disabilities, women, and other social groups are vulnerable as such; it is a particular amalgamation of factors in place and time that dictates that some groups will be harder hit and less able to recover successfully.

For example, when an event like Hurricane Katrina occurs before the end of the month when paychecks, social security income, and entitlement funds arrive, evacuation is virtually unafford-able for some groups. These socioeconomic realities, which represent real social problems, can be addressed through evacuation planning. Or, as done before the 2008 hurricanes that struck the Gulf Coast, entitlement checks like veterans' and social security checks can be released early to spur departures. By recognizing the nature of vulnerability, we can begin to design solutions and reduce consequences. Because power relations underlie much of the economic, social, and political segregation that marginalizes social groups and increases risk, the solution also lies in empowering those most vulnerable—in short, a political solution as well as a social solution (Hilhorst and Bankoff 2004).

Furthermore, it is important to include more "mainstream" citizen groups along with the so-called hard-to-reach groups, such as the homeless, casual workers and day laborers, and legal and illegal immigrants because these groups may be particularly exposed and have the least resources to escape from risky areas or recover after an event (Uitto 1998, 13). An example stems from events after September 11th in New York City. Hispanic day laborers, like so many of those who were at the site, were exposed to various contaminants without proper protective equipment. Mobile medical assessments uncovered related breathing issues that lingered for some time. However, due to the mobility of these workers, they could not be followed longitudinally as were the firefighters, police, and others exposed at Ground Zero (Malievskaya, Rosenberg, and Markowitz 2004; Landrigan et al. 2004).

1.6.1 Emergence of a Social Vulnerability Paradigm

Disaster management is a relatively recent profession. Most writers trace the early days of the occupation to the days of "civil defense" in the 1950s and 1960s. Disaster managers were initially viewed as "air raid wardens" who would sound an alert when an attack came from outside the United States, presumably from what used to be the United Soviet Socialist Republic (Waugh 1999; Waugh and Tierney 2007). Concern over the use of nuclear powers prompted air raid drills, the creation of bomb shelters, and fear about the possibility of an external threat. It was assumed that people would respond in panic and shock. However, a series of pivotal studies conducted by the Disaster Research Center (founded at The Ohio State University, now at the University of Delaware) demonstrated that sociobehavioral response in disaster varied from the set of assumptions under which civil defense operated. For instance, altruism and other forms of prosocial behavior were found to be typical, rather than those irrational antisocial responses, such as panic and looting. The Disaster Research Center prompted further inquiry into sociobehavioral responses to disaster—looking at organizational response, for instance—in order to arrive at a better understanding of the broader social, economic, and policy conditions that influenced disaster management.

Over time, an increasing awareness of some of the limitations of the dominant paradigm resulted in the incorporation of the concept of social vulnerability into increased research and practice. Several historically influential social or political movements began to raise questions about social vulnerability in disasters and produced new ways of thinking about various populations. In the 1930s, spatial concentrations of rural poverty were observed, which came to be known as the "Other America" (Harrington 1962). These observations laid the foundation for the development of various federally funded entitlement programs, including social security for senior citizens and even large-scale regional development projects like the Tennessee Valley Authority. These New Deal–era programs recognized that, despite their best efforts, people experienced considerable difficulty in securing housing, employment, health care, education, and more. The struggles of people at varying socioeconomic levels to secure scarce resources generated new views for the scientific study of people affected by disasters.

As an illustration of how struggles and social movements have informed the social vulnerability paradigm, the multiple social movements emerging during the 1950s and 1960s in the United States prompted deeper insights promoting the rights of various groups. The Civil Rights Movement, for example, conducted concerted efforts to retract segregation, push educational reforms, and extend voting rights for African Americans (Morris 1984). A massive women's rights campaign in the

1960s and 1970s expressed concern over political representation, economic rights, health and reproductive care, education, and more (Ferree and Hess 1985). Similarly, a Latino rights movement pursued issues ranging from agricultural labor concerns to more broadly based political representation (Gutierrez 2006). A grassroots environmental movement pushed for recognition of environmental damage (Carson 1962). Gay rights efforts attempted to secure basic human respect and laid a foundation for broader struggles in ensuing decades. In the 1980s, an environmental justice movement linked pollution and pesticides, as one example, to detrimental health effects within marginalized communities (Bullard 1990). Disability rights advocates organized and promoted inclusion and accommodation (Christiansen 1995; Barnartt and Scotch 2001). Senior advocates and senior citizens created a "gray panther" movement that leveraged growing numbers of baby boomers into a more powerful lobby group, recognizing a broad spectrum of issues including health care, elder abuse, crime, and social stereotyping (Kuhn 1978). In short, several decades of social and political organizing raised awareness of issues facing various populations and the ways in which they were historically marginalized. Organized social movements advocated for inclusion and change and, in so doing, laid a foundation to question the dominant paradigm.

Concurrent with the evolution of social and political rights movements, research on vulnerable groups began to appear in publications and as topics of discussion at professional meetings in the 1980s. Much of this work grew out of development studies and practical development initiatives in and on the Global South. For example, Andrew Maskrey's 1989 book, *Community Based Disaster Mitigation*, clearly identified sociopolitical vulnerability factors in disasters in a range of cases from Peru and put forward the (then still relatively novel) approach of managing vulnerability reduction at the community level. Disaster researchers reported evidence of race, class, age, and gender discrimination and differentiation in the effects of disasters throughout all phases of disasters (e.g., Glass et al. 1980; Bolin 1982; Perry, Hawkins, and Neal 1983; Bolin and Bolton 1986; Bolin and Klenow 1982).

It became even clearer that technological means were insufficient to prevent major damage in the United States as a result of multiple events. In 1989, Hurricane Hugo tore apart South Carolina, the same year that the Loma Prieta earthquake badly damaged the homes of Latino agricultural workers and low-income seniors. Hurricane Andrew ripped through south Florida's ethnically diverse communities in 1992 followed by the far-ranging Mississippi River floods of 1993 that affected over a dozen states. In the following year, the Northridge, California, earthquake displaced thousands of renters and low-income households. Bureaucratic procedures clearly failed when trying to reach historically vulnerable populations, as described by one Northridge survivor:

> I was not wearing my hearing aids that morning, of course, it was 4:31 in the morning. When my foot hit the floor, my bare feet felt every piece of glass that had broken. My husband was out of town, I was alone and extremely scared; my husband is profoundly deaf, no one even told him there had been an earthquake. I went to FEMA there was no interpreter. Someone later suggested I call my congress woman. Almost nine months passed before I got my FEMA check. (Phillips, personal correspondence)

FEMA, the American Red Cross, and other organizations that are among the more visible relief agencies in the United States endured criticism for not taking diversity into consideration. Simultaneously, the economic costs of disasters began to escalate rapidly, a fact that was confirmed by the U.S. insurance industry's recognition of increasing insured losses. Internationally, the 1995 earthquake in Kobe, Japan, reinforced doubts of a technological panacea. Despite the world's best engineering, many structures collapsed, the firefighting system failed, and more than 6,000 people died. Over 50% of the dead were over 60 years of age, and 1.5 times as many women died as men (Seager 2006). In 1991, flooding in Bangladesh killed five times more women than men (Seager 2006), demonstrating that social factors clearly affect life safety.

In the 1990s, the United Nations launched the International Decade for Natural Disaster Reduction (IDNDR), a decade-long effort to reduce vulnerability. While the IDNDR was successful in refocusing on preparedness and mitigation, it was criticized for the dominance of technological responses. In addition, critics argued that the IDNDR continued to attribute the cause of disasters to nature (i.e., in its use of the term *natural* to refer to disasters that many then considered to be far from natural). In contrast, a number of examples challenged this technocentric view.

In the 1990s, a major assessment of disaster research took place in the United States (Mileti 1999). This major undertaking involved over 100 scientists and experts who reviewed the extant literature and evaluated its meaning. The report recommended the adoption of a social vulnerability paradigm in distinct contrast to the dominant paradigm (Mileti 1999). Researchers recommended several ideas as a means to transform the circumstances of socially vulnerable populations. First, a participatory view that involves and includes stakeholders must be adopted, in contrast to the assumptions of a bounded rationality view where people must be led or directed. Second, social and intergenerational equity issues must be addressed to ensure that all stakeholders enjoy the right to survive. Third, economic vitality must be considered, including the full range of businesses that employ from all socioeconomic levels, including home-based work, agriculture labor, and retail and industrial employment. Fourth, quality-of-life issues, as identified by those local stakeholders, must be considered rather than imposed from outside. Fifth, environmental quality must be retained and even enhanced, including rebuilding in ways that reduce impact on marginalized populations and nonrenewable resources.

In 1994, the United Nations convened a mid-Decade conference in Yokohama, Japan, at which "a strong case was made by many representatives that more needed to be done to understand and to tap the local knowledge of ordinary people and to understand and address social vulnerability" (Wisner 2003). At the end of the IDNDR, the International Strategy for Disaster Reduction formed, with an encouraging trend toward a more social vulnerability paradigm. For example, its campaigns on safer schools and hospitals (UNISDR 2007a; Wisner 2006; UNISDR and WHO 2009) and championing of gender matters[*] both facilitate the social vulnerability paradigm. The Hyogo Framework for Action: Building the Resilience of Nations and Communities to Disasters (HFA) subsequently emerged as the key policy initiative (UNISDR 2007b), which is a 10-year plan, adopted by 168 member states of the United Nations in 2005 at the World Disaster Reduction Conference in Kobe, Hyogo. The HFA has a special emphasis on vulnerability reduction and resilience building, which are built upon five priority actions (Table 1.3). The HFA is the Millennium Development Goals of the disasters world. In 2000, 189 nations pledged to free people from extreme poverty and multiple deprivations. This pledge was consolidated in the eight Millennium Development Goals (Table 1.3).

By 2012, the regular update report on progress in achieving the MDGs reported that certain key targets had been met, including the achievement of parity in primary education between girls and boys (UN 2012). However, the 2011 Global Assessment Report on Disaster Risk Reduction (GAR) revealed that gender and public awareness are still not being adequately addressed and that girls seem to suffer most (UNISDR 2011). Importantly, the gender gap in achieving primary education widens significantly after extensive disaster events. This clearly illustrates how context is all-important when considering reported data. The HFA and the MDGs both suffer from similar limitations in focusing at national government levels and relying on self-reporting. Partly in response to that concern, the Global Network of Civil Society Organisations for Disaster Reduction produces its own reports based on some large-scale surveys (GNDR 2012). This reveals a large difference between what governments self-report to the UNISDR and what local community representatives and local government officials report. For example, over half (48 of the 82) of the national governments self-reported "substantial or comprehensive" progress on risk-governance indicators. Yet, local governments self-reported "very limited/some activity but significant scope for improvement" (GNDR 2012). Taken together, all of these reports underscore the direct relevance of *social* vul-

---

[*] UNISDR is a partner to the Gender and Disaster Network www.gdnonline.org and hosts the GDN listserv through PreventionWeb.

TABLE 1.3

United Nations Action Priorities and Development Goals

Hyogo Framework for Action Priority Actions	Millennium Development Goals
• Priority Action 1: Ensure that disaster risk reduction is a national and a local priority, with a strong institutional basis for implementation • Priority Action 2: Identify, assess, and monitor disaster risks and enhance early warning • Priority Action 3: Use knowledge, innovation and education to build a culture of safety and resilience at all levels • Priority Action 4: Reduce the underlying risk factors • Priority Action 5: Strengthen disaster preparedness for effective response at all levels	1. Eradicate extreme poverty and hunger 2. Achieve universal primary education 3. Promote gender equality and empower women 4. Reduce child mortality 5. Improve maternal health 6. Combat HIV/AIDS, malaria and other diseases 7. Ensure environmental sustainability 8. Develop a global partnership for development

Sources: Hyogo Framework (UNISDR 2007b); Millennium Development (UN 2000).

nerability within hazard and disaster management and the importance of taking a critical social vulnerability approach.

Social scientists view disasters as unique opportunities to study society, and disasters are simply amplified versions of everyday life (Nelson 2011). Traditional areas of inquiry and patterns of behavior often related to systems of *stratification*, such as race, gender, or social class mentioned previously, are examined in extreme events (Nelson 2011). Much of the current research being conducted in the social sciences examines:

1. How people are differentially vulnerable
2. How vulnerability is related to complex systems of stratification, the unique coping capacities of people within communities, and how people self-define vulnerability, etc.
3. How and why disasters are socially, culturally, and historically situated events
4. How the unequal social, economic, and political relations influence, create, worsen, or potentially reduce hazards and vulnerabilities

These aforementioned principles lie at the core of the current social vulnerability paradigm.

The current view of social vulnerability requires a discussion of stratification as one of the most important concepts for understanding the composition of any society. Stratification is defined as the layering or clustering of people into groups or strata. We stratify people and societies in many different ways, including race, ethnicity, gender, age, social class, disability, and many more. These systems of stratification shape us, our life chances and choices, and are critical organizing principles of all societies. Opportunities and rewards are explicit and implicitly available to some and withheld from others based on these groupings. Further, these groupings are often used as justification for doing so. Simply put, we do not all have the same opportunities, rewards, and barriers, which facilitates or constrains our ability to move around within these systems and improve our life chances.

These systems of stratification are intrinsically connected to opportunity, inequality, and oppression. If we consider our own experiences and backgrounds, we are all uniquely stratified in many different ways. Furthermore, some of these groupings are voluntary (achieved), while others are assigned (ascribed). Some of us are from poor families; first-generation students; graduates; wealthy; men or women; older or younger; white, black, Asian, or Hispanic; elderly; disabled; etc. We all have different opportunities and barriers based on these characteristics, and we are all unique. Unfortunately, uniqueness is often turned into unequal access to goods and resources, oppression and inequality, prejudice, and discrimination. And when we do not have the same opportunities, being successful is not as simple as "working hard and pulling ourselves up by our bootstraps." Therefore, these systems of stratification are intrinsically connected to social vulnerability in any given society. And, in disaster situations, these systems of stratification and vulnerabilities are often exposed in many ways.

Overall, the vulnerability paradigm understands that disaster-resilient communities stem from more than the physical world, and takes into consideration the full range of social institutions and populations that comprise a richly diverse human system. It is the involvement of those marginalized groups that can produce insights and views to change vulnerability, which is an emphasis of this entire text.

1.6.3 THE FRAMEWORK OF THE SOCIAL VULNERABILITY PARADIGM

The social vulnerability paradigm is not sufficient by itself to plan for disasters and must be understood as part of a larger, broader view that includes understanding geophysical hazards and technological solutions. Vulnerability assessment thus incorporates insights from the physical world but emphasizes the roles of social, economic, and political relations in the creation of hazardous situations in a specific place. Vulnerability analysis examines the social distribution of risk and why some populations bear disproportionate levels of risk to disasters. Research for a number of years has examined the notion that (Blaikie et al. 1994, 9)

> some groups in society are more prone than others to damage, loss, and suffering in the context of differing hazards. Key characteristics of these variations of impact include class, caste, ethnicity, gender, disability, age, or seniority.

Social vulnerability reflects the stratified conditions in which people compete for scarce, limited resources to mitigate against, respond to, and recover from disasters. All too often, people lack the means and opportunities to influence their risks significantly: In reality, risk is structured into the social institutions, social processes and policies, and social relationships that are difficult to influence for historically disempowered populations (Boyce 2000). People working at lower wage jobs, as well as those unable to work or those experiencing underemployment, live in housing that fails to withstand high winds, seismic activity, or flood risk. Seniors and people with disabilities lacking accessible public transportation cannot evacuate. Home-based businesses that disasters destroy undermine important incomes, especially for low-income households. Yet, government programs provide only loans to businesses, not grants. When disasters destroy domestic violence shelters, as they did in three Louisiana parishes, survivors may desperately resort to living with offenders. In short, in a society with scarce resources, there are winners and losers. As Barton argued as far back as 1969, disasters reveal deeply embedded social problems in all societies. It is in understanding those social problems that we can find places of intervention that reduce risk. International humanitarian Cuny (1983) wrote that poverty is the crucial source of risk and must be tackled to minimize human impacts; the solutions will be found in tackling issues of social justice and social change.

From the vulnerability paradigm, it is necessary to understand both the physical impact of disasters and the social conditions that underlie differential outcomes. The degree to which people receive transportation, shelter, warning, and protective action and are safe from injury, loss of life, or property damage depends on their level of income, quality of housing, type of employment, and on whether or not they are subject to discrimination and prejudice. Thus, the vulnerability paradigm seeks to understand how social, economic, and political relations influence, create, worsen, or can potentially reduce hazards in a given geographic location. The vulnerability paradigm also appreciates the importance of context, meaning that the time, place, and circumstances in which people live matters. For example, historic patterns of race relations may have resulted in segregated neighborhoods or in situations where entire towns remain situated in hazardous locations (Cutter 2006). Gendered patterns of political representation may mean that women remain excluded from policy-making positions that influence the practice of disaster management. Socioeconomic and political contexts will also differ significantly across geographic locations. Urban populations, for example, will include considerable numbers of seniors and people with disabilities that may over-stretch organizational response capacities. Rural areas, or historically impoverished states, may suffer from a lack of funding to assess and plan for those at risk. In a political context, where some hazards are deemed more important to fund than others, local repetitive hazards may fail to be addressed. Coastal areas like the states affected by Hurricane Katrina will feature diverse forms of employment, from corporate settings to fishing villages. Understanding the social distribution of risk in those settings vis-à-vis the local socioeconomic context can identify those at risk and locate community resources that would help ensure a safer environment.

Social vulnerability views can be used to inform a reinvigorated risk assessment and planning process. By assuming that social vulnerability exists, key questions can be identified to reveal areas of concern and action items. Most disaster managers, for example, rely on a four-phase life cycle of disaster management that organizes activities around preparedness, response, recovery, and mitigation.

Concern for social vulnerability in the preparedness phase, for example, might look at the types of materials developed to educate the public:

- What language are they written in?
- Do they address concerns with literacy levels? How usable are they across cultures with dramatically varying levels of literacy?
- Are they accessible to people with visual or hearing challenges? Do they take into account those who were deaf from birth versus those who lose hearing later in life? Do they consider the cultural and national differences across sign languages?
- Are they relevant for the variety of social groups present in a given community? Who is involved in creating these materials? Has the "whole community" been involved?
- Can they be understood by people of varying ages including children?

The response phase from a social vulnerability paradigm might suggest that appropriate questions would include:

- Are there sufficient numbers of paratransit vehicles to move people from nursing homes or to assist people with disabilities?
- Are first responders trained in basic words in local languages, including American Sign Language, which could help with rescue efforts and emergency medical care?
- Are shelters ready to accept a wide range of cultures, faiths, and ages with different nutritional requirements?
- Are citizens ready to respond when needed? Even in developed nations, a 72-hour waiting period may exist before help arrives. Given that neighbors will help each other, have they been trained to do so?

In recovery, social vulnerability views can be applied to identify areas of need and then to plan accordingly:

- Are sufficient numbers of local units or mobile homes available and accessible to the local population: including veterans, people with disabilities, and seniors? Are temporary shelters that are brought in resistant to future hazards? Given the likelihood that such locations will exist for some time in developing nations, how are agencies prepared to support such sites beyond their initial commitment?
- What is the local housing stock like? How old is it and who lives in it? Where is housing situated vis-à-vis local hazards and how will that housing fare in a disaster? Who is the

most vulnerable and in what kinds of hazards? Will a second disaster further undermine rebuilt structures?

- Does the recovery plan address the full range of employment and businesses that need to be supported so that people can return to work? Have historically vulnerable populations been empowered, including small businesses and woman-owned businesses? Have widows been taken into consideration for their needs?
- Has the likelihood of an increase in domestic and stranger violence been planned for?
- Have recovery planning efforts included those who were hit the hardest to empower their recovery and foster their resilience?
- Have greener initiatives been incorporated, including those that might provide a diversity of work opportunities?

Mitigation measures offer a means through which risk can be reduced, such as through strengthening a levee or building a safe room. From a social vulnerability paradigm, it would be prudent to find out:

- If high-concentration areas of those at risk have been made a priority
- Whether there are populations that require assistance in putting up mitigation measures like shutters in hurricane areas, including single parents and seniors
- If a range of options has been considered for those at risk from inexpensive fixes to those that require governmental or nongovernmental support
- Whether local hazards threaten congregate facilities, such as nursing homes, or for people with cognitive disabilities, and whether such facilities can be afforded greater protection
- Whether some mitigation measures like insurance remain unaffordable and whether local organizations might plan for the needs of those likely to suffer significant losses
- If risk reduction measures have incorporated environmentally resilient features and taken nature's predictable impacts into consideration

Social vulnerability views also emphasize the ways in which local populations bring capacities and capabilities to the disaster management process, which are largely untapped. Hurricane Katrina clearly demonstrated vulnerability through the sheer numbers of people lacking transportation and who were subsequently trapped in the flooded city of New Orleans. Few people heard stories of the tremendous efforts that were brought to aid those in need, including students and staff from the Louisiana School for the Deaf who helped with translation, the building of shelters, debris removal, and distributing donations. Experienced community organizers also pointed out that impoverished groups, though dramatically impacted by the storm, also brought coping methods to their experience by sharing what they had, including food, clothing, and homes. Families doubled and tripled up, took in strangers, and provided comfort. Children, even those separated traumatically from their families, proved resilient in forming new social bonds with peers and shelter workers.

The social vulnerability paradigm also assumes that local resources can be tapped to address the problems noted in this text. Communities include voluntary, faith-based, community, and civic organizations with track records of assisting those at risk in both nondisaster and disaster situations. Postdisaster, it is also likely that a number of emergent groups will form to address unmet needs. Organizations external to the community will also arrive in many disasters and target those who suffer disproportionately. Though disasters are not equal opportunity events, the human capacity to assist prosocially exists in abundance. Disaster managers, social service providers, health-care staff, voluntary organizations, and others concerned with socially vulnerable populations, then, must tap into these grassroots resources and fulfill their potential for change.

The social vulnerability paradigm, in concert with one that provides effective means for mitigating the physical consequences of storms, earthquakes, and terrorist attacks, can significantly reduce losses and enhance outcomes for a wider set of those at risk. The goal of this text, therefore, is to reduce human suffering by applying an empirically supported social vulnerability paradigm with practical solutions that change disaster circumstances. It is clear, though, that a selective focus on just disaster contexts remains insufficient. As Cuny (1983) understood, "Ultimately, addressing vulnerability means committing to social justice and social change."

1.7   A RESILIENCE PERSPECTIVE

Alongside work on vulnerability, there has been a growing interest in resilience (emBRACE 2012). Early work on resilience thinking, including Holling (1973), emerged out of ecological science and systems thinking, and particularly influenced resource management and climate-change literatures. It considers the response to disturbance, capacity to self-organize, and capacity to learn and adapt (Folke 2006). Ecological definitions of resilience commonly emphasize "the amount of disturbance the system can absorb without a change in its state" (Mayunga 2007, 3; Holling 1973).

From within the hazards and disasters research paradigm, Timmerman (1981) is often cited as the first to introduce the term *resilience* (Clark et al. 1998; Klein, Nicholls, and Thomalla 2003). Subsequently, Mileti (1999, 33), in his second assessment of disaster research in the United States, defined resilience as the ability of a community to "withstand an extreme natural event without suffering devastating losses, damage, diminished productivity, or quality of life and without a large amount of assistance from outside the community." While there have been many variations on these ideas (e.g., Tierney and Bruneau 2007; Peacock et al. 2008; UNISDR 2009), of particular relevance to our discussion are those that include humans more prominently in social-ecological systems and consider individual psychology and the capacity of humans to anticipate and plan for the future within a social context (Paton and Johnston 2001; Lindell and Perry 1992; Resilience Alliance 2012).

A recent review of resilience literature (Galderisi, Ferrara, and Ceudech 2010) has identified three main schools of thought. First is the *flip-side school of thought*, which sees resilience as the other face of vulnerability or the flip side of vulnerability (Galderisi, Ferrara, and Ceudech 2010). Essentially, this way of considering resilience focuses on more positive aspects of being or becoming resilient, while, arguably, vulnerability has more negative connotations of being or becoming less vulnerable (Klein, Nicholls, and Thomalla. 2003; Cannon 2008). The common perception is that a more resilient community is less vulnerable, while a less resilient community is more vulnerable. However, this does not contribute much to the debate, as it is merely a circular argument.

Next is the *inclusive school of thought*, which regards resilience as a component of vulnerability (McEntire 2001; Adger 2006). For instance, McEntire (2001) includes resilience as one of four variables of vulnerability: risk, susceptibility, resistance, and resilience. Here resilience refers to coping capacity and ability to recover quickly from a disaster and is an integral part of vulnerability.

Finally, the *separate or discrete school of thought* considers resilience and vulnerability as separate concepts (Manyena 2006; Paton 2008). Manyena (2006) presents email correspondence from various sources to support this notion. Douglas Paton (in Manyena 2006, 443) remarks:

> We can possess characteristics that can make us vulnerable and that can influence our capacity to adapt at the same time.... Until it can be demonstrated to the contrary, I think they should be viewed as discrete.

Similarly, Manyena (2006, 443) views resilience and vulnerability as two separate constructs where "the absence of vulnerability does not make one resilient." However, Miller et al. (2010) challenge those positions and take an integrationist position, stating that the separation of the concepts and the two main research communities that espouse them (the natural and the social sciences) has contributed to a failure to meet the needs of sustainable development. Yet, while Miller et al. (2010) would seek to bring the concepts together, Cannon and Muller-Mahn (2010, 622) reject the resilience concept entirely:

[D]isasters are socially constructed events: the product of the impact of a natural hazard on people whose vulnerability has been created by social, economic and political conditions. By extension, this means that resilience . . . should also be treated as being socially constructed. . . . [T]he notion of resilience—whether derived from natural (ecosystem) or technological (physics or engineering) usage—is dangerous because it is removing the inherently power-related connotation of vulnerability.

The strongly natural science-based hazards community has developed a relatively coherent social-ecological systems (SES) view (emBRACE 2012), focusing on ecosystems and natural resource management for example, but tends to discuss vulnerability (and other key terms) in an apolitical and technical and overly "scientistic" sense; they are also silent on power relations (Cannon and Muller-Mahn 2010). The latter, primarily social science-based community is represented by a more diverse vulnerability view, focusing on disaster risk reduction, livelihoods, and climate-change adaptation, for example. This community assumes a more overtly political and normative (often advocacy-based) position, but does not always give due recognition to the physical and ecological dynamics (Adger 2006, 272) or the more positive and active dynamics (Fordham et al. 2011). Overall, the common theme across all resilience is the "ability of a system to absolve, deflect, or resist potential disaster impacts and the ability to bounce back after being impacted" (Peacock 2010, 7). Building resilience is underpinned by understanding, managing, and reducing disaster risks and requires strong governance combined with bottom-up approaches with strong commitment across all sectors (NAS 2012).

It is our contention that the resilience view is not yet a fully evolved and refined view within the context of disaster management worthy of an equal weighting alongside the hazards and social vulnerability paradigms (Figure 1.1). Rather, it is useful as a corrective to, or a qualifier of, the negative implications of an overconcentration on people's vulnerability (victimhood, passivity, lack of agency, etc.). It has the potential to be used in a socially transformative way (see Pelling 2010; Fordham et al. 2011), but more often, it is reflective of a functionalist and depoliticized approach that emerges from an ecological science/systems view (Resilience Alliance 2012). The resilience concept is not inherently directional, but it has the potential to be used in either form (bouncing back to the status quo or bouncing forward to social transformation).

The ability of the resilience concept to be applied across very different disciplines and approaches makes it closer to a boundary object, facilitating communication across disciplinary boundaries, "adaptable to different viewpoints and robust enough to maintain identity across them" (Star and Griesemer 1989, 387). For example, "The boundary object sustainability has been highly successful in providing the common ground for ecologists and economists, which were formerly thought contrary, to engage together for the needs of future generations" (Brand and Jax 2007). However, Brand and Jax (2007) point to the dual nature of such boundary objects in the way they can open up

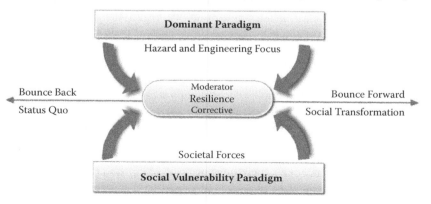

FIGURE 1.1 Model of social vulnerability and dominant paradigms in relation to resilience.

communication channels, but may ultimately hinder scientific progress because the meanings used are diluted and unclear.

To conclude, the social vulnerability paradigm is (at least currently) more apt than the resilience focus to a nuanced understanding of social differentiation and the transformative view necessary to effect the social change required to deal with the root causes (Wisner et al. 2004) of disaster risk. However, we must guard against its potential stigmatizing and labeling effects and recognize the potential of the resilience view to moderate any disempowering effects and provide an opportunity to view not just the *problem* of vulnerability reduction but also a possible *solution* in its focus on capacities and the creation of resilient, sustainable futures.

1.8 OVERVIEW OF COMING CHAPTERS

This text adopts a social vulnerability paradigm that recognizes differential impacts as well as the potential to tap into the capacities of those at risk. Throughout this text, readers will find realistic, empirical assessments of socially vulnerable populations. The emphasis is on social vulnerability coupled with sound advice on the capacities that can be fostered for further risk reduction. You will find descriptions of, and practical solutions to, the raw circumstances in which too many people find themselves before, during, and after disaster. You are invited to be a part of the transformative vision these authors promote and to join us in building a safer, more equitable society for all.

1.8.1 SECTION I: UNDERSTANDING SOCIAL VULNERABILITY

This text unfolds in several sections. In the first section, the two chapters review key theories and concepts. These chapters also globalize the concerns about social vulnerability. In Chapter 2, "Theoretical Framing of Worldviews, Values, and Structural Dimensions of Disaster," Drs. Jean Scandlyn, Deborah Thomas, and John Brett (all at the University of Colorado Denver) expand on theories and views of social vulnerability and resilience. In Chapter 3, "The Intrinsic Link of Vulnerability to Sustainable Development," Katie Oviatt (PhD graduate student) and Dr. John Brett (both at the University of Colorado Denver) situate this text in an understanding of sustainable development and its links to vulnerability, resiliency, and capacity, themes that will resonate throughout the remainder of the text. Their work helps us to grasp the Sustainable Livelihoods View, which is also incorporated into Chapter 16.

1.8.2 SECTION II: SOCIALLY VULNERABLE GROUPS

The second section of the text, consisting of Chapters 4 through 14, examines the vulnerabilities that various social groups experience along with the capacities that exist or can be developed for each. These include: race/ethnicity, class, gender, age, disability, health, literacy, family and households, violence, religion, communities, and pets/animals. Each chapter presents a demographic overview of the social group of concern followed by a summary of relevant scientific literature. Findings are organized into sections that correspond to key disaster management activities. Content first covers warning, evacuation, and response and then addresses how disasters impact those groups and how they fare during recovery periods. A concluding section discusses implications for action by addressing practical and policy considerations to reduce vulnerability as well as specific suggestions to build capacity. Each chapter offers key books, videos, and websites to provide further understanding and practical strategies.

In Chapter 4, Drs. Brenda McCoy and Nicole Dash, both from the University of North Texas, examine the influence of socioeconomic circumstances on abilities to prepare for, respond to, and recover from disaster. This chapter helps us to understand the demographic distribution of social class in the United States and how social class influences peoples' life chances. A connection is made between class and disaster vulnerability through case studies and scenarios that bring the content to life. A concluding section describes practical strategies for addressing vulnerability as experienced at lower income levels.

Dr. Dash continues her work in Chapter 5 on issues of race and ethnicity. She begins by conceptualizing race and ethnicity as socially constructed attributes that differentially influence opportunity. Dr. Dash pursues an understanding of the structural effects of race and ethnicity on U.S. society. This chapter reviews the racial and ethnic composition of the United States and specifically examines the role of race during Hurricane Katrina, suggesting ways to ameliorate existing conditions.

In Chapter 6, Jennifer Tobin-Gurley, a PhD candidate at Colorado State University, and Dr. Elaine Enarson, an independent sociologist, address gendered vulnerability. They focus on understanding how gender differentiation can influence life safety, abilities to respond, and experiences in recovery for both men and women. It is clear, though, that research finds vulnerability higher for women in most circumstances, and it is to this concern that they addresses the bulk of the chapter content.

Dr. Lori Peek, from Colorado State University, offers insights into issues of age, including children and the elderly, in Chapter 7. First, she defines children and the elderly and explains why we should distinguish between various groups of each. Disaster experiences, for example, differ between young children and adolescents, as well as those who are older or may be frail elderly. Dr. Peek then provides a demographic profile of youth and elderly populations and helps us to understand how those populations vary by age, race, class, and gender. We then learn about the experiences and risks faced by children and the elderly and what factors increase their vulnerability as well as mechanisms for reducing vulnerability.

A team of authors, including Elizabeth A. Davis (EAD and Associates, LLC), Rebecca Hansen (EAD and Associates, LLC), Dr. Maria Kett (Leonard Cheshire Disability and Inclusive Development Centre based at the University College London), Jennifer Mincin (International Rescue Committee), and Dr. John Twigg (University College London), provides insights on disability issues in Chapter 8. Their collective expertise is leveraged to understand specific conditions that contribute to increased risk for the full range of people with disabilities. This chapter also informs us about terminology and concepts used to understand and frame disability. We next move through the life cycle of disasters to understand disability issues for warning, evacuation, response, and recovery. A comprehensive set of strategies and resources are offered to promote resiliency within the disability community and for practical use by disaster managers.

Dr. Deborah Thomas returns in Chapter 9, along with Mary Shannon Newell and Dr. Debra Kreisberg (both at the University of Colorado Denver), to present issues on health and medical care. Disasters disrupt access to medical care and reveal long-standing social problems that underlie and exacerbate health concerns. Their work serves as a reminder that social institutions are not invulnerable to the effects of disaster or societal neglect.

Jenniffer Santos-Hernández, a PhD candidate at the University of Delaware, and Dr. Betty Hearn Morrow, professor emerita at Florida International University, look at language and literacy issues in Chapter 10. They begin this chapter by presenting disaster cases where language or literacy issues mattered, such as with warning messages or delivering relief. We then learn of the prevalence of language and literacy issues across the United States and its relevance for disaster management such as preparedness materials. They subsequently present and explain tools and strategies that help to translate materials into language and literacy-appropriate resources.

Dr. Tricia Wachtendorf and graduate student Mary M. Nelan (Disaster Research Center at the University of Delaware), in conjunction with Dr. Lynn Blinn-Pike (Indiana University-Purdue University, Indianapolis), examine families and households in Chapter 11. They begin by explaining current household and family composition in the United States and the implications for disaster response. Various studies then help us to understand how household and family characteristics, as well as their related resources, are tied to how well they may be able to prepare for, respond to, and recover from disasters. High-risk households and families are discussed along with strategies for reaching out to these units in an effort to reduce the effects of disasters. This important chapter updates and globalizes content, including consideration of lesbian and gay families.

Drs. Brenda Phillips (Oklahoma State University) and Pam Jenkins (University of New Orleans) work through the rarely examined topic of postdisaster violence in Chapter 12. This chapter explains how various kinds of violence differentially impact social groups in the United States. These authors explain why it is important to understand violence in disaster situations and what can be done prior to an event to build partnerships that anticipate and potentially reduce aggression, hostility, brutality, and cruelty.

Drs. Michael Thompson and Brenda Phillips, both of Oklahoma State University, then introduce readers to religious contexts in which people may experience heightened risks in Chapter 13. Their work builds on important studies conducted post 9/11 about hate crimes and integrates emerging materials on gender-based blaming that occurs in disaster contexts. Resilience is addressed through examining the functions of religious institutions and the power of personal faith as a source of resilience. Faith-based organizations and their contributions to disaster relief and recovery are also described, including the importance of continuity of operations planning for such key resource bases.

Dr. Tamara Gull, a professor in the College of Veterinary Medicine at Oklahoma State University, offers Chapter 14 (new for the second edition), concerned with pets, service animals, and livestock. Issues associated with their care before, during, and after disasters are considered, along with sound recommendations for pet owners, emergency managers, state animal response teams, and veterinarians.

1.8.3 SECTION III: BUILDING CAPACITY AND COMMUNITY RESILIENCE

The final chapters of the book fall into a section that promotes capacity building in various ways. In Chapter 15, Dr. Pam Jenkins returns and provides insights into how social capital and other community resources can be leveraged. Her work reveals the value of what the full set of community members, regardless of income or disability, can bring to the table when responding to and recovering from disaster effects.

Dr. Deborah Thomas, along with Iain Hyde, Colorado Department of Emergency Management, and Michelle Meyer, a PhD candidate at Colorado State University, reveal practical strategies for community vulnerability analysis (CVA) in Chapter 16. CVA allows emergency managers and planners (among others) to identify, analyze, monitor, and integrate social vulnerability into the full life cycle of emergency management: preparedness, response, recovery, and mitigation. Their work includes explaining how geographical information systems (GIS) can help us to map vulnerability. The chapter also emphasizes participatory mechanisms for increasing community input for vulnerability analysis as well as discussion of how to foster more sustainable communities.

Drs. William E. Lovekamp (Eastern Illinois University) and Sudha Arlikatti (University of North Texas) thoroughly cover ideas and strategies for empowerment in Chapter 17. They begin by walking us through how social change and empowerment take place. Next, we understand how community-based organizations and nongovernmental organizations can play pivotal roles in leveraging social capital found in social groups. They also help us to grasp how disasters can influence social change and specifically examine effects after September 11, Hurricane Katrina, the Indian Ocean tsunami, and the Haiti earthquake.

Finally, in Chapter 18, "New Ideas for Practitioners," DeeDee Bennett, a PhD candidate at Oklahoma State University, and Drs. Brenda Phillips (Oklahoma State University), Deborah Thomas (University of Colorado Denver), Eve Gruntfest (University of Colorado–Colorado Springs), and Jeanette Sutton (University of Colorado–Colorado Springs) present fresh ideas that promote transformative and inspiring insights. This chapter challenges us to remain current in the field in order to move forward and expand our efforts to reduce vulnerability.

1.9 SUMMARY

This chapter introduced the idea of social vulnerability to disasters, which is deemed to be a pre-existing condition deeply embedded in social, economic, and political relations between groups of people. The challenges of social vulnerability require social solutions that redress deeply embedded social problems that require concentrated effort not only from disaster managers but from the broader society as well. Such solutions require significant manifestations of political will and social effort. Because these social problems remain resistant to change, disaster managers, social service providers, elected officials, and others concerned with vulnerability and risk must design realistic strategies that impact at the individual, family, household, and community levels. This text sets out to understand how various social groups experience vulnerability and to design practical solutions that can, at least, serve as interim measures. As such, this book takes to heart the Maori proverb, "*Ha aha te mea nui? He tangata, he tangata, he tangata.*" [What is the most important thing? The people, the people, the people.]

DISCUSSION QUESTIONS

1. Why is there such a strong bias toward technology in the dominant paradigm of disasters?
2. What is the role of chance or random events in your own life? Describe a "freak occurrence" you've experienced.
3. Describe the key elements of the dominant and vulnerability paradigms.
4. What are the strong points of the dominant paradigm of disasters, in your opinion? Explain and justify your views. What critiques make sense to you?
5. Discuss the notion that a disaster is "an act of God." The dominant paradigm does not explicitly invoke divine causation or agency any more, but do you think there is still some legacy of this earlier view to be found in the dominant paradigm? Why? Why not?
6. Discuss and explain the deaths that occurred during the Indian Ocean tsunami (2004), Hurricane Katrina (2005), the Myanmar cyclone (2008), or the Chinese earthquake (2008) from both the dominant and vulnerability paradigms.
7. What are the strong points of the vulnerability paradigm of disasters, in your opinion? Explain and justify your views. What critiques make sense to you?
8. Are there social groups in your community that may experience higher vulnerability to disaster than others? Who are they, and why do you believe them to be vulnerable?
9. How might an emergency manager view warning and evacuation from the dominant and vulnerability paradigms?
10. Using the dominant and then the vulnerability views, how might an emergency manager develop a recovery effort?

ACKNOWLEDGMENTS

The first edition of this book was based upon the "Social Vulnerability Approach to Disasters" FEMA training course that developed out of the efforts of the FEMA Higher Education Project managed by Dr. B. Wayne Blanchard (http://www.training.fema.gov/EMIWeb/edu/sovul.asp). While the second edition of *Social Vulnerability to Disasters* is significantly updated and changed, the editors and authors of the second edition are indebted to Drs. Ben Wisner, Elaine Enarson, Betty Morrow, Cheryl Childers, and Deborah Thomas, who were the full team of course developers of the original FEMA course materials that provided the inspiration for our work. The interpretations and conclusions in the current edition are those of the authors and do not represent those of FEMA, the original team, or the original authors.

REFERENCES

Adger, W. N. 2006. Vulnerability. *Global Environmental Change* 16:268–81.

Alexander, David. 2000. *Confronting catastrophe*. New York: Oxford University Press.

Bankoff, G. 2006. The tale of the three pigs: Taking another look at vulnerability in light of the Indian Ocean tsunami and Hurricane Katrina. http://understandingkatrina.ssrc.org/Bankoff/.

Barnartt, Sharon, and Richard Scotch. 2001. *Disability protests*. Washington, DC: Gallaudet University Press.

Barton, Alan. 1969. *Communities in disaster*. New York: Doubleday.

Blaikie, P., Cannon, T., Davis, I. and Wisner, B. 1994. *At risk*. London: Routledge.

Blanchard, W. 2000 (July). Higher Education Project Presentation at Emergency Management Institute. Emmitsburg, MD.

Block, Melissa. 2010. Strict building code may explain lower Chile toll. http://www.npr.org/templates/story/story.php?storyId=124210386.

Bolin, Robert. 1982. *Long-term recovery from disaster*. Boulder, CO: Institute of Behavioral Science.

Bolin, Robert, and Patricia Bolton. 1986. *Race, religion, and ethnicity in disaster recovery*. Boulder: University of Colorado.

Bolin, R., and D. Klenow. 1982. Response of the elderly to disaster: An age stratified analysis. *International Journal of Aging and Human Development* 16 (4): 283–96.

Bolin, R., and L. Stanford. 1999. Constructing vulnerability in the first world: The Northridge earthquake in Southern California, 1994. In *The angry earth: Disasters in anthropological view*, ed. A. Oliver-Smith and S. Hoffman, 89–112. New York: Routledge.

Boyce, J. K. 2000. Let them eat risk? *Disasters* 24 (3): 254–61.

Brand, F. S., and K. Jax. 2007. Focusing the meaning(s) of resilience: Resilience as a descriptive concept and a boundary object. *Ecology and Society* 12 (1): 23. http://www.ecologyandsociety.org/vol12/iss1/art23/.

Bullard, Robert. 1990. *Dumping in Dixie*. Boulder, CO: Westview Press.

Burton, Ian, R. Kates, and Gilbert White. 1978. *The environment as hazard*. New York: Oxford University Press.

Cannon, T. 2008. *Reducing people's vulnerability to natural hazards: Communities and resilience*. UNU-WIDER Research Paper No. 2008/34. Bonn: United Nations University (UNU) and World Institute for Development Economics Research (UNU-WIDER).

Cannon, T., and D. Muller-Mahn. 2010. Vulnerability, resilience and development discourses in context of climate change. *Natural Hazards* 55:621–35.

Cardona, O. D., M. K. van Aalst, J. Birkmann, M. Fordham, G. McGregor, R. Perez, R. S. Pulwarty, E. L. F. Schipper, and B. T. Sinh. 2012. Determinants of risk: Exposure and vulnerability. In *Managing the risks of extreme events and disasters to advance climate change adaptation: A special report of working groups I and II of the Intergovernmental Panel on Climate Change (IPCC)*, ed. C. B. Field, V. Barros, T. F. Stocker, D. Qin, D. J. Dokken, K. L. Ebi, M. D. Mastrandrea, et al., 65–108. Cambridge, U.K.: Cambridge University Press.

Carr, L. 1932. Disasters and the sequence-pattern concept of social change. *American Journal of Sociology* 38:207–18.

Carson, Rachel. 1962. *Silent spring*. Boston: Houghton Mifflin.

Cavallo, Eduward, Andrew Powell, and Oscar Beverra. 2010. Estimating the direct economic damage of the earthquake in Haiti. Inter-American Development Bank. http://idbdocs.iadb.org/wsdocs/getdocument.aspx?docnum=35074108.

Christiansen, John. 1995. *Deaf president now!* Washington, DC: Gallaudet University Press.

Clark, G. E., S. C. Moser, S. J. Ratick, K. Dow, W. B. Meyer, S. Emani, W. Jin, J. X. Kasperson, R. E. Kasperson, and H. E. Schwarz. 1998. Assessing the vulnerability of coastal communities to extreme storms: The case of Revere, MA, USA. *Mitigation and Adaptation Strategies for Global Change* 3:59–82.

Cordero, F. 2010. Chile earthquake reveals social inequalities. Global Voices. http://globalvoicesonline.org/2010/03/10/chile-earthquake-reveals-social-inequalities/.

Cuny, Fred. 1983. *Disasters and development*. Dallas, TX: Intertech.

Cutter, S. 1996. Vulnerability to environmental hazards. *Progress in Human Geography* 20 (4): 529–39.

———. 2006. The geography of social vulnerability: Race, class and catastrophe. http://understandingkatrina.ssrc.org/Cutter.

Duda, Kenneth, and Brenda K. Jones. n.d. USGS remote sensing coordination for the 2010 Haiti earthquake. ftp://ftp.ecn.purdue.edu/jshan/000000_special_issue/09Duda/text/Duda_USGS%20Haiti%20Coordination_v10Mar2011-1808-forPDF.pdf.

Eads, M. 2002. Marginalized groups in times of crisis: Identity, needs and response. Quick Response Report #152. Boulder, CO: Natural Hazards Center.

emBRACE. 2012. Building resilience amongst communities in Europe. http://www.embrace-eu.org/documents/emBRACE-D1-1_LitReview_040412_Final.pdf.

Enarson, E. and Morrow, B. 1997. A gendered perspective: Voices of women. In *Hurricane Andrew*, ed. W. Peacock, B. H. Morrow, and H. Gladwin, 116–140. Miami, FL: International Hurricane Center.

Enarson, E., and B. Morrow. 2000. A gendered view: Voices of women. In *Hurricane Andrew*, ed. W. Peacock, B. H. Morrow, and H. Gladwin, 116–40. Miami, FL: International Hurricane Center.

Farmer, Paul. 2011. *Haiti after the earthquake*. New York: Public Books.

FEMA. 2011. Whole community. http://www.fema.gov/about/wholecommunity.shtm.

Fernandez, L., D. Byard, C. C. Lin, S. Benson, and J. A. Barbera. 2000. Frail elderly as disaster victims: Emergency management strategies. *Prehospital and Disaster Management* 17 (2): 67–74.

Ferree, Myra Marx, and Beth Hess. 1985. *Controversy and coalition: The new feminist movement*. Boston: G. K. Hall.

Folke, C. 2006. Resilience: The emergence of a perspective for social–ecological systems analyses. *Global Environmental Change* 16:253–67.

Fordham, Maureen, Suranjana Gupta, Supriya Akerkar, and Manuela Scharf. 2011. *Leading resilient development: Grassroots women's priorities, practices and innovations*. New York: UNDP and GROOTS International.

Freudenberg, William R., Robert Gramling, Shirley Laska, and Kai Erikson. 2009. *Catastrophe in the making: The engineering of Katrina and the disasters of tomorrow*. Washington, DC: Island Press.

Galderisi, A., F. F. Ferrara, and A. Ceudech. 2010. Resilience and/or vulnerability? Relationships and roles in risk mitigation strategies. Presented at 24th AESOP Annual Conference, Finland, 7–10 July 2010.

Glass, R. I., R. B. Craven, D. J. Bregman, B. J. Stroll, P. Kerndt Horowitz, and J. Winkle. 1980. Injuries from Wichita Falls tornado: Implications for prevention. *Science* 207:734–38.

GNDR (Global Network of Civil Society Organisations for Disaster Reduction). 2012. www.globalnetwork-dr.org.

Gutierrez, Rudy. A. 2006. The Chicano movement. In *Latinas in the United States*, ed. V. Ruiz and V. Sanchez Korrol, 151–55. Bloomington: Indiana University Press.

Hardoy, Jorge, and David Satterthwaite. 1989. *Squatter citizen: Life in the urban third world*. London: Earthscan.

Harrington, Michael. 1962. *The other America: Poverty in the U.S.* New York: Simon and Schuster.

Hewitt, K. 1983. The idea of calamity in a technocratic age. In *Interpretations of calamity*, ed. K. Hewitt, 3–32. Boston: Allen and Unwin.

Hilhorst, D., and G. Bankoff. 2004. Introduction: Mapping vulnerability. In *Mapping vulnerability: Disasters, development and people*, ed. G. Bankoff, G. Frerks, and D. Hilhorst, 1–9. London: Earthscan.

Holling, C. 1973. Resilience and stability of ecological systems. *Annual Review of Ecology and Systematics* 4: 1–23.

Jarroud, Marianela. 2012. Chile's earthquake reconstruction hindered by delays and profiteering. *IPS News Service*, February 29. http://www.ipsnews.net/2012/02/chilersquos-earthquake-reconstruction-hindered-by-delays-and-profiteering/.

Jenkins, P., and B. D. Phillips. 2008. Battered women, catastrophe and the context of safety. *NWSA Journal* 20 (3): 49–68.

Klein, R. J. T., R. J. Nicholls, and F. Thomalla. 2003. The resilience of coastal megacities to weather-related hazards. In *Building safer cities: The future of disaster risk*, ed. A. Kreimer, M. Arnold, and A. Carlin. Washington, DC: The World Bank Disaster Management Facility.

Kuhn, M. 1978. Insights on aging. *Journal of Home Economics* 70 (4): 18–20.

Landrigan, P., P. Lioy, G. Thurston, G. Berkowitz, L. C. Chen, S. Chillrud, S. Gavett, et al. 2004. Health and environmental consequences of the World Trade Center Disaster. *Environmental Health Perspectives* 112 (6): 731–39.

Lin, S., J. Reibman, J. A. Bowers, S. A. Hwang, A. Hoerning, M. I. Gomez, E. F. Fitzgerald, et al. 2005. Upper respiratory symptoms and other health effects among residents living near the World Trade Center site after September 11, 2001. *American Journal of Epidemiology* 162 (6): 499–507.

Lindell, M. K., and R. W. Perry. 1992. *Behavioral foundations of community emergency planning*. Washington, DC: Hemisphere Press.

———. 2004. *Communicating risk in multi-ethnic communities*. Thousand Oaks, CA: Sage.

MacDonald, M. 2005. How women were affected by the tsunami. *PloS Med.* 2 (6): e178. http://www.plosmedicine.org/article/info%3Adoi%2F10.1371%2Fjournal.pmed.0020178.

Malievskaya, E., N. Rosenberg, and S. Markowitz. 2002. Assessing the health of immigrant workers near Ground Zero. *American Journal of Industrial Medicine* 42 (6): 548–49.

Manyena, S. B. 2006. The concept of resilience revisited. *Disasters* 30 (4): 433–50.

Maskrey, A. 1989. *Community based disaster mitigation*. Oxford, UK: OXFAM Publications.

Mayunga, Joseph S. 2007. Understanding and applying the concept of community disaster resilience: A capital-based approach. Draft working paper prepared for the Summer Academy for Social Vulnerability and Resilience Building, 22–28 July, Munich, Germany. http://www.ehs.unu.edu/file/get/3761.

McEntire, D. A. 2001. Triggering agents, vulnerabilities and disaster reduction: Towards a holistic paradigm. *Disaster Prevention and Management* 10 (3): 189–96.

Mileti, Dennis. 1999. *Disasters by design: A reassessment of natural hazards in the United States*. Washington, DC: Joseph Henry Press.

Miller, F., H. Osbahr, E. Boyd, F. Thomalla, S. Bharwani, G. Ziervogel, B. Walker, et al. 2010. Resilience and vulnerability: Complementary or conflicting concepts? *Ecology and Society* 15 (3): (online). http://www.ecologyandsociety.org/vol15/iss3/art11/.

Morris, Aldon. 1984. *Origins of the Civil Rights Movement*. New York: Free Press.

Morrow, B. H. 1999. Identifying and Mapping Community Vulnerability. *Disasters* 23 (1):11–18.

Morrow, B. 2000. Stretching the bonds: The families of Andrew. In *Hurricane Andrew*, ed. W. Peacock, B. H. Morrow, and H. Gladwin, 141–70. Miami, FL: International Hurricane Center.

NAS (National Academy of Sciences) Committee on Increasing National Resilience to Hazards and Disasters. 2012. *Disaster resilience: A national imperative*. Committee on Science, Engineering, and Public Policy. Washington, DC: The National Academies Press (prepublication version—subject to further editorial revisions).

Nelson, Libby A. 2011. Sociology in the storms. *Inside Higher Ed*, August 29. http://www.insidehighered.com/news/2011/08/29/sociologists_of_disaster_see_research_in_storms.

Oliver-Smith, A. 2002. Theorizing disasters: Nature, power, and culture. In *Catastrophe and culture: The anthropology of disaster*, ed. S. Hoffman and A. Oliver-Smith, 23–47. Santa Fe, NM: School of American Research Press.

Oullette, C., and F. Ummar. 2009. Making a difference: Promoting gender equality in Pakistan's response to the earthquake. Islamabad, Pakistan: Canadian International Development Agency.

Paton, D. 2008. Community resilience: Integrating individual, community and societal perspective. In *The phoenix of natural disasters: Community resilience*, ed. K. Gow and D. Paton. New York: Nova Science.

Paton, D., and D. Johnston. 2001. Disasters and communities: Vulnerability, resilience and preparedness. *Disaster Prevention and Management* 10 (4): 270–77.

Peacock, W. G., ed. 2010. Advancing the resilience of coastal localities: Developing, implementing and sustaining the use of coastal resilience indicators: A final report. Prepared for the Coastal Services Center and The National Oceanic and Atmospheric Administration under Cooperative Agreement Award No. NA07NOS4730147. http://hrrc.arch.tamu.edu/media/cms_page_media/558/10-02R.pdf.

Peacock, W. G., Howard Kunreuther, William H. Hooke, Susan L. Cutter, Stephanie E. Chang, and Phillip R. Berke. 2008. *Toward a resiliency and vulnerability observatory network: RAVON*. Final Report, NSF Grant SES-08311115. Hazard Reduction and Recovery Center, Texas A&M University. http://archone.tamu.edu/hrrc/Publications/researchreports/RAVON.pdf.

Pelling, M. 2010. *Adaptation to climate change: From resilience to transformation*. London: Routledge.

Perry, J. B., R. Hawkins, and D. M. Neal. 1983. Giving and receiving aid. *International Journal of Mass Emergencies and Disasters* 1:171–188.

Quarantelli, E. L. 1998. Epilogue. In *What is a disaster?* ed. E. L. Quarantelli, 226–28. London: Routledge.

Resilience Alliance. 2012. http://www.resalliance.org.

Ryall, J., and Demetriou, D. 2012. Japan earthquake and tsunami: 478 bodies remain unidentified one year on. *The Telegraph*, 9 March. http://www.telegraph.co.uk/news/worldnews/asia/japan/9132634/Japan-earthquake-and-tsunami-478-bodies-remain-unidentified-one-year-on.html.

Sayeed, A. 2009. Victims of earthquake and patriarchy: The case of the 2005 Pakistan earthquake. In *Women, gender and disaster: Global issues and initiatives*, ed. E. Enarson and P. Chakrabarti, 142–52. New Delhi, India: Sage.

Seager, J. 2006. Noticing gender (or not) in disasters. *Geoforum* 37 (1): 2–3.

Sharkey, P. 2007. Survival and death in New Orleans. *Journal of Black Studies* 37 (4): 482–501.

Star, S. L., and J. R. Griesemer. 1989. Institutional ecology, translations and boundary objects: Amateurs and professionals in Berkeley's Museum of Vertebrate Zoology, 1907–39. *Social Studies of Science* 19 (3): 387–420.

Steinberg, Ted. 2000. *Acts of God: The unnatural history of natural disaster in America*. New York: Oxford University Press.

Thurman, Colleen. 2010. Chile vs. Haiti: Political economy and earthquake preparedness. The Triple Helix Online: a forum for global science in society, April 16. http://triplehelixblog.com/2010/04/chile-vs-haiti-political-economy-and-earthquake-preparedness/.

Tierney, K. 2001. Strength of a City: A Disaster Research Perspective on the World Trade Center Attack. http://www.ssrc.org/sept11/essays/tierney_text_only.htm.

Tierney, K., and M. Bruneau. 2007. Conceptualizing and measuring resilience: A key to disaster loss reduction. *TR News* 250 (May-June): 14–17. http://onlinepubs.trb.org/onlinepubs/trnews/trnews250_p14-17.pdf.

Timmerman, P. 1981. *Vulnerability. Resilience and the collapse of society: A review of models and possible climatic applications.* Environmental Monograph No. 1. University of Toronto, Institute for Environmental Studies.

Tobin, G., and B. Montz. 1997. *Natural hazards.* New York: Guilford.

Tolin, L. 2008. Americans suffering from "disaster fatigue." *Intelligencer Journal (Associated Press).*

UN (United Nations). 2000. United Nations Millennium Declaration. http://www.un.org/millennium/declaration/ares552e.pdf.

———. 2012. The Millennium Development Goals Report 2012. http://www.undp.org/content/dam/undp/library/MDG/english/The_MDG_Report_2012.pdf.

UNISDR. 2007a. Towards a culture of prevention: Disaster risk reduction begins at school: Good practices and lessons learned. 2006–2007 World Disaster Reduction Campaign. http://www.unisdr.org/2007/campaign/pdf/WDRC-2006-2007-English-fullversion.pdf.

———. 2007b. Hyogo Framework for Action 2005–2115: Building the resilience of nations and communities to disasters. UN/ISDR-07-2007-Geneva. http://www.unisdr.org/files/1037_hyogoframeworkforactionenglish.pdf.

———. 2009. *2009 UNISDR Terminology on Disaster Risk Reduction.* 2009. Geneva, Switzerland: United Nations International Strategy for Disaster Reduction, 2009. http://www.unisdr.org/files/7817_UNISDRTerminologyEnglish.pdf.

———. 2011. Global assessment report on disaster risk reduction. http://www.preventionweb.net/english/hyogo/gar/2011/en/home/index.html.

UNISDR and WHO. 2009. 2008–2009 World Disaster Reduction Campaign: Hospitals safe from disasters. http://www.unisdr.org/2009/campaign/pdf/wdrc-2008-2009-information-kit.pdf.

USAID. 2012. Earthquake. http://haiti.usaid.gov/issues/earthquake.php.

USDOJ (U.S. Department of Justice). 2008. Executive Order 13166: Improving access to services for persons with limited English proficiency. http://www.usdoj.gov/crt/cor/Pubs/eolep.htm.

USGAO (U.S. Government Accountability Office). 2006. Disaster preparedness: Preliminary observations on the evacuation of hospitals and nursing homes due to hurricanes. GAO-06-790T.

Uitto, J. I. 1998. The geography of disaster vulnerability in megacities: a theoretical framework. *Applied Geography,* 18 (I): 7–16.

Waugh, William. 1999. *Living with hazards, dealing with disasters.* Armonk, NY: M. E. Sharpe.

Waugh, William, and Kathleen Tierney. 2007. *Emergency management: Principles and practice for local government.* 2nd ed. Washington, DC: ICMA Press.

Wisner, B. 1993. Disaster vulnerability: Scale, power, and daily life. *GeoJournal* 30 (2): 127–40.

———. 2003. Disaster risk reduction in megacities. In *Building safer cities*, ed. A. Kreimer, M. Arnold, and A. Carlin, 181–96. Washington, DC: The World Bank.

———. 2006. Let our children teach us! A review of the role of education and knowledge in disaster risk reduction. Prepared on behalf of the ISDR system Thematic Cluster/Platform on Knowledge and Education. http://www.unisdr.org/2005/task-force/working%20groups/knowledge-education/docs/Let-our-Children-Teach-Us.pdf.

Wisner, B., P. Blaikie, T. Cannon, and I. Davis. 2004. *At Risk.* London: Routledge.

RESOURCES

- A series of papers, including many from the vulnerability view, can be found at the Social Science Research Council website, "Understanding Katrina," at http://understandingkatrina.ssrc.org/.

- An additional set of papers on a broader array of disasters can be found at the Radix website, http://www.radixonline.org/resources_papers.htm.

- For a community-based examination of the vulnerability view, visit the Greater New Orleans Community Data Center at http://www.gnocdc.org.

Section I

Understanding Social Vulnerability

2 Theoretical Framing of Worldviews, Values, and Structural Dimensions of Disasters

Jean Scandlyn, Deborah S. K. Thomas, and John Brett

CONTENTS

2.1 CHAPTER PURPOSE

This chapter explores the fundamental and significant ways that our worldviews—our representations and assumptions about the world—frame our understanding of, and response to, hazards and disasters. We begin by defining theory: the formal, explicit, and systematic worldviews that provide the foundation for the scientific analysis of hazards and disasters. This is followed by a discussion of the shift in theory from framing hazards and disasters as primarily natural and unexpected events to framing them as expected outcomes of complex human-environment interactions. This theoretical shift has led to a focus on social vulnerability: why some individuals, groups, communities, and nations differentially experience the effects of hazard events. Most recently, scholars and policy makers are also placing more emphasis on community resilience in conjunction with social vulnerability, adding to theoretical complexity. We then discuss how critical and conflict

33

theories contribute to a comprehensive understanding and analysis of vulnerability at multiple levels of analysis. Because these theories focus primarily on social structure, the structure and agency perspective is introduced to examine how vulnerable individuals and communities view and respond to hazards and disasters within a given social structure. Finally, systems theory, specifically political ecology theory, provides a practical analytic framework to understand and evaluate social vulnerability and reduce vulnerability by linking it to sustainable development and social justice.

2.2   OBJECTIVES

At the conclusion of this chapter, readers should be able to:

1. Understand what theory is and how it contributes to framing social vulnerability in a way that illuminates the critical elements of this complex issue
2. Define critical and conflict theories and explain how they contribute to understanding vulnerability in a more comprehensive fashion
3. Appreciate how structure and agency interplay in the creation of vulnerability and resilience
4. Explain how theory leads to an explanation of worldviews and values that in turn influences how disasters are viewed by disaster planners and by individuals and communities who are vulnerable to hazards and disasters
5. Appreciate how the theoretical framing of structure and agency illuminate how worldviews and values affect our approaches to tackling disaster reduction and increasing resilience
6. Discuss how systems theory guides a mechanism for understanding and evaluating vulnerability, also linking to sustainable development

2.3   INTRODUCTION

On February 19, 2002, a severe rainstorm "pummeled" La Paz, the capital of Bolivia, "killing 60, injuring 100 and leaving over 500 homeless. Hailstorms, heavy rains and flash floods tore through the region, destroying homes, washing away bridges and ripping up road surfaces and brick walls." The mayor of La Paz, Juan del Granado, estimated damages at $60 million (Steen 2002). Bolivia's president, Jorge Quiroga, declared a state of emergency, and volunteers joined the city's emergency staff and the Bolivian Red Cross to provide relief to the injured and homeless, stabilize buildings, and search for missing persons. (Enever 2002)

Why include a chapter on theory in a book about vulnerability to natural disasters? What role can theory possibly play in understanding or responding to a disaster, such as the flood that occurred in La Paz in 2002? In this account of a flood disaster, which is presented as a simple recounting of a current event, theory plays a critical, though unstated, role. It identifies the agents or actors in the story, explains the results of their actions, provides direction for appropriate response, and predicts what will happen if appropriate responses are (or are not) made. Theories help us to understand the world around us, but they can also limit what we see and how we perceive it. Consequently, if we want to minimize the human, environmental, and social losses from hazards and disasters, it is critical that we be aware of, and deliberate in, our use of theory.

Worldviews are shared assumptions and values about human character and our relationship with the natural environment that we learn first informally from family, friends, and other caregivers who undertake our early socialization and, later, through school and other formal institutions. Like formalized scientific theories, worldviews also provide us with explanations of how the world works and what motivates and directs human behavior. As much or more than the scientific theories espoused by disaster managers and planners, our various worldviews and values—shaped by history, the physical environment, and social institutions—affect our perceptions of hazards and disasters, influencing preparedness, mitigation, response, and recovery efforts.

This chapter defines theory and the role it plays in framing social vulnerability to identify and illuminate the various dimensions of this complex issue. We then discuss the emerging focus on social vulnerability and resilience within the context of two major theories—conflict and systems theory—that have been used to understand hazards and disasters from this perspective. Critical and conflict theories explain how differential access to resources and power, embedded in social institutions or social structure, and the actions or agency of individuals and groups interact to create vulnerability (see Box 2.1). In addition, these theories explain why some groups are more vulnerable

---

BOX 2.1   CASE STUDY: POLITICS AND PUBLIC IMAGE IN DISASTER RELIEF

Cyclone Nargis, which passed over the Irrawaddy Delta region of Myanmar (Burma) on May 2, 2008, illustrates how disasters can highlight internal and external political conflicts. It also demonstrates the importance of considering individual and collective agency in providing resilience to hazards and disasters.

The cyclone, a category 4 storm, affected over 10,000 square kilometers and 2.4 million people (Figure 2.1). The UN estimates deaths at 63,000–101,000, with 220,000 persons missing (http://www.nytimes.com/2008/06/17/world/asia/17iht-myanmar.3.13783386.html?pagewanted=all). Myanmar is one of the poorest countries in Southeast Asia. Although it has reduced child mortality since 1990, it ranks 40th among nations for under-5 child mortality; life expectancy is 59 years for men and 61 for women; and 32% of children under 5 are moderately or severely underweight (UNICEF 2008). Malnutrition and food security are major concerns for the entire population. Consequently, Myanmar's population is vulnerable to a host of potential problems in the face of an event like Cyclone Nargis: measles outbreaks among children who have not been adequately vaccinated, diarrhea and other waterborne diseases from damaged sewage and potable water systems, and outbreaks of malaria and dengue fever from increased exposure to mosquitoes as homes are damaged and people must spend more time outdoors. As a press release from the Johns Hopkins Bloomberg School of Public Health observes, "Disease outbreaks have not occurred following the majority of tropical cyclones in the past several decades, primarily because of timely humanitarian response" (Beyrer, Doocy, and Robinson 2008, 3).

At the time of the cyclone, Myanmar had been under military rule since 1962, and Senior General Than Shwe had controlled the country since 1992. In the fall of 2007, Buddhist monks led a series of protests against the military government's decision to double the price of fuel; the government responded with a violent suppression of monasteries that evoked strong international censure and increased control over the media and isolation from the international community (http://news.bbc.co.uk/2/hi/asia-pacific/7016608.stm). Government statistics on the scale of deaths and destruction from Cyclone Nargis reflected the government's desire to control foreign perceptions of the emergency. In contrast to UN statistics that estimated 3.2 million citizens affected, 220,000 missing and 63,000 to 101,000 dead, official sources in Myanmar listed the death toll at 29,000, with 42,000 persons missing and 1.5 million persons displaced (Beyrer, Doocy, and Robinson 2008). Several days passed before General Shwe agreed to allow foreign aid agencies to provide relief, and he initially restricted relief to supplies and food, but not personnel. Journalist Gavin Hewett reported from Myanmar that senior military officers worried that "foreigners will undermine their power. The military regime hopes, bizarrely, that this crisis might even enhance their prestige. Much of the aid is transferred to army trucks. They want the people to see Burmese soldiers saving the people" (http://news.bbc.co.uk/2/hi/asia-pacific/7416952.stm).

International aid workers feared that the delay in providing aid, both supplies and skilled personnel, would lead to widespread deaths from infectious diseases and starvation and were publicly critical of the government's response.

Despite these fears, an article in the *International Herald Tribune* six weeks after the storm reported that survivors were recovering slowly. "'The Burmese people are used to getting nothing. They just did the best they could,' said Shari Villarosa, the highest-ranking U.S. diplomat in Myanmar, formerly known as Burma. 'I'm not getting the sense that there have been a lot of deaths as a result of the delay'" (http://www.nytimes.com/2008/06/17/world/asia/17iht-myanmar .3.13783386.html?pagewanted=all). In the face of widespread poverty and a government slow to respond, the people of Myanmar demonstrated resilience, providing food and shelter to survivors and some actively protesting for allowing more foreign aid workers to enter the country. Yet, how much additional mortality, illness, and economic loss occurred because of a tightly controlled and slow response? In a recent shift toward a more open and democratic government, Aung San Suu Kyi, who opposed the military government for decades, was elected as a member of Parliament and sworn in on May 2, 2012. How these national political changes will affect Myanmar's planning for and response to disasters remains to be seen.

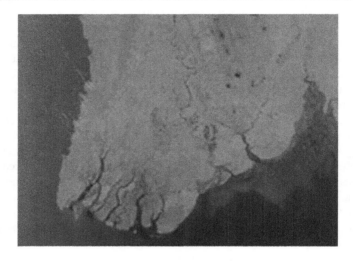

FIGURE 2.1   The top image is the Burma coastline on April 15, 2008, prior to Tropical Cyclone Nargis, and the bottom image is the same coastline on May 5, 2008, showing the extensive flooding the cyclone caused. (*Source*: NASA/MODIS Rapid Response Team, http://www.nasa.gov/topics/earth/features/nargis_floods.html.)

to hazards and disasters than others and also contribute to understanding the worldviews and values that direct how disasters and hazards are viewed in various communities. Critical and conflict theories also provide important cautions in understanding resilience so that attention and resources are not deflected from disaster planning. Systems theory is valuable in analyzing the interaction of critical variables—e.g., the physical environment, human societies and institutions, and animal and plant species—at different levels of analysis, from the individual to the global system. Because systems theory makes it possible to view these phenomena as interdependent components of an encompassing world system, it permits the integration and application of theory and knowledge from many disciplines, including geography, geology, anthropology, sociology, engineering, biology, and political science, among numerous others.

2.4   WHAT IS THEORY?

"At a basic level, though, theory is just a version of some aspect of reality" (Perry 2003, 2). In science, theory is elaborated, can be explicitly stated, and is frequently associated with an individual who first set it out in a formal manner, for example, Darwin's theory of natural selection or Einstein's theory of relativity. Scientific theories are rarely the product of one person's thought or work; they emerge from a body of observation and experiment and scholarly exchange that has accumulated over time. For example, contemporary geologists use plate tectonic theory to understand earthquakes, volcanoes, and other changes in the earth's surface. Plate tectonics theory defines the relevant agents of geologic events: magma, oceanic crust, ocean ridges and trenches, and tectonic plates. It defines the processes that drive the movement of plates: Radioactive decay at the earth's core creates convection currents in the molten magma beneath the earth's surface that move the plates in different directions. And, it explains and predicts what results from the interaction of tectonic plates: earthquakes, volcanoes, and mountain ranges. Understanding the characteristics and movements of tectonic plates and their boundaries allows geologists to explain past events such as the formation of the Himalayas in Asia and the Great Rift Valley in Africa and to predict, at least to some extent, where earthquakes and volcanic eruptions are likely to occur in the future. This theory, which was formulated in the 1960s and 1970s, transformed geology by bringing together findings from studies of fossils, the earth's magnetism, and the distribution of earthquakes and volcanoes explain them with one set of unified concepts and principles. Plate tectonics is an excellent example of scientific theory.

Plate tectonics theory and others like it form the foundation of scientific inquiry. Because they define the relevant agents, conditions, and relationships of a given aspect of reality, they determine the questions that we ask, how we ask them, and how we interpret the answers we obtain. Consider the case of earthquakes. Because plate tectonics is so powerful in explaining geologic events, investigations into the causes and processes of natural disasters are framed by that theory. After the tsunami in Southeast Asia in 2005, scientists focused their attention on how the earthquake generated the tsunami, the pattern of where it struck land, and how to augment and improve warning systems to prevent loss of life from tsunamis in the future. In other words, many scientists assumed that the cause of the disaster was a natural event and that plate tectonics could explain its occurrence. Many did not directly consider as readily the patterns of human settlement and land use that placed people, animals, and property in the wave's path as equally significant causes.

Not all theories are as well developed or explicitly stated as plate tectonics. We use theory every day, in the more informal sense of worldview, to understand and respond to common events in our daily lives. For example, there are theories about who and what are safe (friends and family, pets, home) and who and what are potentially or actually dangerous (strangers and enemies, wild animals, tornadoes). Although not usually labeled "theory," these worldviews or common sense theories, like formal theories, are nonetheless versions of reality that contain the same elements—assumptions, concepts, and propositions—as scientific theory. Like scientific theories, worldviews offer shared explanations and predictions about the world around us. For the most part, our experience supports these theories (or we ignore it when it does not), which we learn as part of our cultural and historical heritage. Worldviews remain largely unstated and unconscious as part of the world in which we live, much like the air we breathe. Unlike formal theory, worldviews are not subjected to rigorous and systematic testing, and their assumptions, concepts, and propositions may contain contradictions and logical inconsistencies not present, at least not intentionally, in scientific theories. But occasionally events contradict our theories in ways that we cannot ignore or easily dismiss. For example, an enemy performs an act of kindness, a stranger says "hello," or a family member betrays or hurts us. This may cause us to revise our theories or to reject the evidence as an outlier to the general theory, the "exception that proves the rule."

2.5 HAZARDS AND DISASTERS: THE DOMINANT PARADIGM

Returning to the case of the flood in La Paz, in the immediate aftermath of an event like this, we rely on the commonly shared theory that disasters are "natural events," the result of "extremes of nature." Media accounts of the flood in La Paz depict the rainstorm as the active agent of the disaster: It "pummels" the city, kills 60 people, and destroys property. It is an unusual event that disrupts the normal order. Reporting on the flood in La Paz, Steen (2002) noted that "[t]he Bolivian National Meteorological Service said that the city has not had such an intense rain in the 50 years it has kept records." In this account, humans are passive victims swept away by the rushing torrents of water despite their efforts to cling to tree branches and other fixed objects. Responses to the disaster are technological, dictated by accommodating natural forces: removing people from the rushing water, repairing buildings, and restoring damaged systems. Prevention of future disasters requires shoring up structures to withstand the pressure of the water, or, as noted in a United Nations report issued after the flood in La Paz, creating a system to warn people when water levels rise rapidly and dangerously (UN/ISDR 2007).

The way the story of the 2002 flood in La Paz is told illustrates what Hewitt (1983) calls the dominant or scientific view of hazards (see Chapter 1). Scholars who approach the study of hazards and disasters from the perspective of social vulnerability criticize the dominant paradigm as being based in common sense theories or worldview. The following quotation by Quarantelli (1998) illustrates the unconsciously accepted character of this theory:

> The earliest workers in the area, including myself, *with little conscious thought* and accepting *common sense views*, initially accepted as a prototype model the notion that disasters were an outside attack upon social systems that "broke down" in the face of such an assault from outside [emphasis added].

Tobin and Montz (1997, 8) criticize the dominant paradigm for failing to incorporate human action as a root cause of hazards and disasters:

> The traditional view of natural hazards has ascribed all or almost all responsibility for them to the processes of the geophysical world. The approach has meant that the root cause of large-scale death and destruction has been *attributed to the extremes of nature rather than encompassing the human world*. Frequently, disaster victims have been viewed as unfortunates who could do little but react to physical processes. The physical world, then, has been seen as an external force, separate from human forces [emphasis added].

Although scientific theory is supposed to be a model of universal and timeless laws and processes and therefore objective and impartial, in reality theory arises within specific historical and cultural contexts. McEnaney (2000) argues that the dominant approach to disasters formed during the Cold War, a time when the United States focused on having a strong civil defense system to protect against attack from external enemies. This civil defense model, argues McEnaney, was applied to disasters and hazards, which were conceived of as attacks by natural forces. Watts (1983, 233) traces the dominant approach to hazards and disasters to the positivist science of the Enlightenment, in which nature can be studied and observed empirically and objectively, but human behavior and society are vague and metaphysical phenomena and therefore fall outside the domain of science. Thus logically, a scientific and technological approach to disasters must examine their natural rather than their human causes.

Scientific theories, especially those that involve human beings and social phenomena, are also shaped by the social position and power of those who propound them (see discussion of Gramsci's concept of hegemony and Foucault's ideas of knowledge and power in Section 2.8.1). To view natural disasters as isolated events or accidents of nature keeps us from recognizing both the regularity with which they occur and the human decisions and actions that place some, but not all, people in the way of natural forces or create changes in the environment that place them at risk. For example, the United Nations environment report on the flood in La Paz notes that floods and mudslides are common in La Paz, which "lies along a narrow valley crossed by more than two hundred rivers, including subterranean rivers, and suffers from unstable geological conditions." The large numbers of migrants who have moved to the capital city from impoverished rural areas have built housing on the steep hillsides on unstable soil or on the floodplains, "making them particularly vulnerable to floods and mudslides during the rainy season (December to March)" (UN/ISDR 2007). This report challenges the dominant paradigm in several ways and raises many important questions. First, floods and mudslides are not uncommon in La Paz; the area is geologically unstable with major water drainage issues. Second, people as much as nature are at the nexus of risk and vulnerability. (See Photos 2.1, 2.2, and 2.3.)

This description raises a series of important questions about the social causes of the "natural" hazard of floods in La Paz. Why is Bolivia's capital built in a geologically unstable area? Who in La Paz is most at risk from floods and mudslides? Who or what "forces" or requires that people live in floodplains and on high, unstable slopes?

2.6 CHALLENGING THE DOMINANT PARADIGM: SOCIAL VULNERABILITY

In the United States during the 1960s and 1970s, the Civil Rights Movement, the War on Poverty, and the emerging environmental movement provided conditions that stimulated emergency managers,

PHOTO 2.1   La Paz, Bolivia, showing development and building practices with flood and landslide risk. (*Source*: Photo by Jean Scandlyn. With permission.)

PHOTO 2.2 La Paz, Bolivia, showing pockets of development on hillsides and buildings at the base of steep slopes also in flood and landslide risk zones. (*Source*: Photo by Jean Scandlyn. With permission.)

PHOTO 2.3 Street vendors along a shopping street in La Paz, Bolivia. (*Source*: Photo by Jean Scandlyn. With permission.)

social scientists, and those affected by disasters and hazards to question the assumptions of the dominant paradigm (see Chapter 1). Additionally, fieldwork in disaster research beginning in the 1970s revealed complex social structural factors contributing to disasters. Globally, contextual conditions also challenged the dominant paradigm of hazards, with numerous examples demanding a more comprehensive and systematic view of how disasters emerge out of human systems.

Agricultural development in northeastern Honduras provides an illustrative case. During the early to mid-twentieth century, many subsistence farmers in this region sold their land in valley bottoms to companies that developed the land for large-scale commercial banana plantations. The displaced farmers subsequently moved higher up to less expensive and more agriculturally marginal land above the valleys. In clearing these plots for their subsistence farming, they destabilized the soil on these steep hillsides. In 1974, when Hurricane Fifi struck Honduras, heavy rains produced major landslides and collapsed an irrigation dam. Eight thousand people died, and the banana crop was largely destroyed (Pielke et al. 2003). Was this only a "natural" disaster?

In the 1980s and 1990s, technological approaches to disaster and hazard mitigation failed to prevent widespread destruction from events such as the Northridge earthquake in 1994, Hurricane Andrew in 1992, and floods in Mississippi in 1993. Despite the Japanese using the world's most advanced structural engineering in its new construction, 6,000 people died and many older buildings collapsed in the 1995 earthquake in Kobe, Japan (Geosources 2002). At the same time, a rising number of events resulting in differential impacts on various subpopulations forced disaster planners to recognize that race and ethnicity, class, economic status, age, disability, and gender all directly give rise to increased risk in the face of disaster.

During the same period, social scientists accumulated evidence that people were usually very knowledgeable about recurrent risks and hazards in their local environment and had often developed means to mitigate their risk. An important feature of the human species is its ability to adapt to a wide variety of physical and social environments. Successful adaptation requires balancing competing needs, e.g., balancing the need to be close to sources of water and food with the need to minimize risk from floods (Oliver-Smith 1999). For example, rice farmers in Bangladesh deliberately live in concentrated settlements in the floodplain of the Ganges River, where they depend upon predictable annual floods to replenish soil and nutrients for rice crops and nutrients that support fish harvests. Moving away from flooded land; obtaining assistance from extended kin during and after floods; selling land, livestock, and belongings to recover from losses; and spending savings are all regular, accepted ways that Bangladeshis mitigate risks from floods (Zaman 1999).

Yet social changes, especially those that increase poverty or undermine local power, may make it difficult for people to act on their knowledge of hazards and disasters and usual patterns of response. After a particularly severe flood in Bangladesh in 1998, the initial proposals of aid agencies such as the United Nations Development Program (UNDP) and South Asian Association for Regional Cooperation (SAARC) to permanently reduce risks from floods included "expensive structural engineering 'megaplans' that called for construction of massive embankments on major rivers throughout the country and the dredging of rivers to obtain lower water levels" (Zaman 1999, 203). Following evaluation of the plans, these technological solutions were replaced with programs to improve long-term economic development and welfare to enhance residents' ability to recover from flood damage and losses.

Even in countries where poverty is less of an issue, differences in the authority of local knowledge based in historical experience and technical and professional authority based in science can also interfere with preparedness and mitigation efforts. Japan's recent tsunami provides a forceful example. In the seaside community of Aneyoshi, residents placed a stone tablet on a hillside to mark the place where a tsunami struck in 1896. Following this warning, Aneyoshi residents no longer build houses close to the water, and there were no fatalities when a major tsunami struck in March 2011. In contrast, in the Taro district of Miyako, after a tsunami struck the area in 1930, the community built a 30-foot-high levee. Many residents built houses behind the wall, lured by a false sense of security. Although the levee did not collapse under the tsunami and slowed its impact, more than

200 people in the district died when they failed to evacuate, thinking that the wall would protect them (Macleod 2011). As one newspaper account reported:

> "I want everyone to tell their children, they must be better prepared," said Waita, 55, who moved his own house to higher ground 20 years ago after his parents warned of the area's frequent tsunamis. "If you feel an earthquake, don't wait for any announcement, just run to higher ground. I'm no scientist, but building a wall will always have limits," he said.

These intellectual developments stimulated the search for new perspectives and theories about hazards and disasters that would take social factors, local knowledge, and inequity in exposure to risk into account. Vulnerability or social vulnerability was the concept that emerged to redirect research and analysis. The United Nations International Strategy for Disaster Reduction defines vulnerability as "[t]he conditions determined by physical, social, economic and environmental factors or processes, which increase the susceptibility of a community to the impact of hazards." Wisner, Blaikie, and Cannon (2004, 11) expand the definition to include the "capacity to anticipate, cope with, resist and recover." There are many definitions of this term, but they all include considerations of individual and collective susceptibility to natural events and the capacity to respond to those events, often linked to the concept of resilience. Drawing from a number of sources, Birkmann (2006, 15) provides the following definition of resilience: "Generally, a common ground can be seen in the understanding that resilience describes the capability of a system to maintain its basic functions and structures in a time of shocks and perturbations." Resilience is closely related to the concept of adaptation, mentioned previously and discussed in relation to systems theory later in this chapter. While many definitions exist of resilience and the specifics debated, it can generally be thought of as the ability to adjust material and nonmaterial culture (norms, ideals, and values) to varying environments, both physical and social, and to changes in those environments over time, with vulnerability very much a part of the equation.

Those working within the framework of vulnerability further recognize that vulnerability occurs on many levels of interaction, i.e., individual, community, regional, national, and global, and that vulnerability is determined by a host of physical *and* social factors, such as gender, race, ethnicity, age, and social class. As Hewitt (1983) notes, one of the most important developments of the social vulnerability paradigm is that it views disasters not as exceptional events, but as the product of normal or usual processes. Consequently, a theory that can describe, explain, and predict social vulnerability to disasters must take into account social as well as environmental determinants, analyze causality at multiple scales or levels, and view disasters as resulting from normal or usual and not exceptional events and processes. (See Chapter 3 for a discussion of the sustainable livelihoods approach that seeks to accomplish this.)

Finally, the concept of social vulnerability raises questions of social justice. With few exceptions, the poor and marginalized are most vulnerable to disasters, whether they live in rich or poor nations, and are less able to act upon their knowledge and awareness of risks and hazards stemming from power arrangements and resource distribution. A notable example is coastal real estate development. Although both types of property owners are exposed to risk from hurricanes, the meaning and implications of risk for a wealthy individual who builds a second home on beachfront property, which is likely insured, are quite different from those of the individual of more modest means from a commercial fishing village whose family has lived and worked there for several generations.

This discussion underscores not only the importance of theory in understanding and responding to disasters and hazards, but the need to make the theories we use explicit if we are to:

- Understand the differential effects of hazards and disasters on individuals, communities, regions, and nations
- Understand how human actions, knowledge, and beliefs affect vulnerability and resilience to hazards and disasters

- Decrease inequities in risk and exposure within and across populations and increase capacity and resilience in all kinds of communities (social justice)
- Develop more flexible, locally adaptable interventions and approaches

2.7 CONFLICT AND CRITICAL THEORY

Why are some people more vulnerable to hazards and disasters than others? In the case of the 2002 street floods in La Paz, street vendors, the majority of whom were poor women, bore the highest risk and exposure. Although that particular flood was a relatively rare event, those women who survived the flood returned to sell their goods in the same locations. How do we understand this response and the processes that created it? Social scientists have applied two major theoretical perspectives to understanding social vulnerability: political economy and systems theory and their combination in political ecology.

Strictly speaking, political economy is a not a theory, but a perspective from which several distinct social theories have developed. During the European Enlightenment, social philosophers began to investigate the origin, nature, and relationships between nation-states and their colonial holdings. Swiss philosopher Jean-Jacques Rousseau was the first to use the phrase "political economy" in *A Discourse on Political Economy* published in 1755. Rousseau defined the general or "political economy" as an extension of the "particular economy," that is, "the wise and legitimate government of the house for the common good of the whole family" to "that great family, the State" (Rousseau 1973, 128). Just as in a household, the state had an *economy*, the production and exchange of goods and services, and *politics*, the just (ideally) use of power and legitimate authority to allocate goods and benefits, set policy, protect rights, and resolve disputes. A key aspect of this perspective is the link between politics and economics. Although often separated into distinct areas of study in subsequent eras, i.e., political science and economics, Enlightenment-era theorists saw them as inextricably linked. Political power and processes supported the national economy through the creation and protection of institutions such as private property and taxation. The economy, through tax revenues, enabled the state to establish its authority internally and expand it externally through wars of conquest and colonization, setting domestic and foreign policies favorable to economic development and supporting them by force when necessary.

At the same time that the political economy perspective emerged, the critical tradition that developed in Europe in the seventeenth century to analyze texts such as the Bible was expanded and applied to a critical assessment of, and need for, reform of government, law, and other social institutions to improve the human condition (Therborn 1996). The convergence of political economy and the critical tradition yielded conflict theory, expressed most fundamentally in Karl Marx's critique of political economy in *Capital* (1867/1990). Conflict theory rests on the assumption that conflict and contradiction are inherent in human social life and that this conflict produces historical changes, sometimes violent and revolutionary, that generate progress in social organization and life. For example, in the capitalist political economy or mode of production, conflict and contradiction are inherent in control over the means of production: those physical resources, e.g., raw materials, electricity, or machinery, necessary for the production of goods and services by a given class of people. Those who control or own the means of production, the capitalist class, are in conflict with those who do not, the laboring or working class, who must sell their labor to sustain themselves and their families. Whereas Marx acknowledged that capitalism is a powerful engine of production and technological innovation that could benefit the state and that would ultimately become the dominant form of political economy globally, he also argued that class conflict inevitably creates inequality, exploitation, and oppression both within and among nations. Once workers recognized their exploitation by the capitalist class, this internal contradiction would generate social revolution and the formation of a new, more equitable mode of production.

Within capitalist societies, inequality becomes institutionalized through various forms of capital: human, social, cultural, institutional, financial, and political. For example, human capital is the attainment of valued skills and knowledge by individuals through training and education. In the United States, lawyers, doctors, and engineers have high human capital; they speak English and perhaps other languages, are literate, and have mastery and expertise of a professional body of knowledge and related skills that are highly valued in the society and the labor market. A CEO of a large corporation, if she or he owns stock in the company, may have a great deal of financial capital as well as institutional capital, the power that comes from holding an official position of leadership in an established financial entity supported by the laws of the state. These forms of capital can be translated into power to affect the social and physical environment, power that is often subtly exercised to maintain prestige and wealth. But not everyone has an equal chance of obtaining various forms of capital, nor do all forms of capital provide the same kinds of resources for responding to hazards and disasters. Opportunity is highly structured, even in a nation like the United States that values equality, freedom, and self-determination.

Globally, the division between capitalists and laborers was re-created among nations and regions of the world through colonialism. European nations extracted raw materials from their colonies using slave labor from Africa or the forced labor of indigenous people in South America and Asia, but retained a monopoly on manufacturing and processing of those raw materials in Europe. Investment in all kinds of infrastructure, from courts of law to schools to roads and railways, was concentrated in Europe, with only those resources necessary to meet the needs of extracting raw materials invested in the colonies. As Rodney (1982, 25) noted with regard to Africa over 30 years ago, "African economies are integrated in the very structure of the developed capitalist economies, and they are integrated in a manner that is unfavorable to Africa and insures that Africa is dependent on the big capitalist countries." Many postcolonial nations still lack the infrastructure and wealth to prepare for and mitigate the effects of disasters and suffer higher losses of life when disasters occur (Dilley et al. 2005; Wisner, Blaikie, and Cannon 2004). A prime example is Haiti. Although Haiti secured its independence from France in 1803, prior to the earthquake of January 12, 2011, it ranked 145th of 169 countries in the UN Human Development Index, contributing to the extent of the death and destruction (Disaster Emergency Committee, n.d.).

2.8 STRUCTURE AND AGENCY

In conflict theory, inequality is viewed as an inherent feature of the social *structure*. Elements of social structure include the institutions that form the context of our daily lives: schools, religions, courts of law, financial markets, professions, government agencies, the police and military, businesses and corporations and their regulation, hospitals and clinics, and marriage and the family. This structure largely determines the conditions within which individuals live their lives and the resources available to them. Schools in poor neighborhoods receive less funding, have larger average class sizes, have higher rates of absenteeism and change in their student populations, and have a harder time recruiting and retaining high quality teachers than those in affluent suburbs. Thus, children growing up in poor neighborhoods and attending these schools are at an educational disadvantage from the day they enter kindergarten (Kozol 1991). The result of the institutionalization of inequality results in *structural* violence. As Farmer (2005, 307) notes, "Structural violence is violence exerted systematically—that is, indirectly—by everyone who belongs to a certain social order." For example, the systematic neglect of levees that protected poor neighborhoods of New Orleans left African Americans disproportionately vulnerable to loss of life and property from Hurricane Katrina. Their vulnerability was compounded by their reliance on public transportation to leave the city and their mistrust of public institutions' willingness to help them or to provide accurate information about evacuation based on long-standing racism (Elder et al. 2007).

Some social observers view globalization as a process that can reduce inequality within and among nations and regions by increasing "transnational flows of capital/goods, information/ideas, and people" (Kalb 2000, cited in Lewellen 2002, 8). As more of the world's people participate in the production and exchange of goods and services, ideas and values, standards of living, life expectancy, and quality of life will improve everywhere. In contrast, Rapley (2004, 6) argues that the economic policies of neoliberalism underlying globalization "have had the effect of raising aggregate income but skewing its distribution." In other words, average incomes have risen, but the gap between rich and poor has widened. In the 1960s and 1970s, large multinational banks actively marketed loans to governments in Africa and Latin America for economic development—loans that those governments readily secured. When they could not keep up with repayment, the International Monetary Fund (IMF) and World Bank mandated restructuring of the loans and demanded "austerity measures" to ensure their adherence to the terms of restructuring. Many of these measures required that governments of debtor nations make massive cuts in spending on health care, infrastructure, education, agricultural development, and other social programs that increased the vulnerability of their citizens to a variety of hazards and disasters and eroded the state's ability to provide assistance in times of need (Gill 2000; von Braun, Teklue, and Webb 1998). Whereas there is greater economic integration globally at the macro level of nations and regions, at the local level of families and communities, inequalities in the ability to participate in global processes persist (Lewellen 2002). Although cell phones have increased access to global communication for many people in poorer countries, computers and the Internet remain beyond the reach of the majority of the world's population (Chinn and Fairlie 2007).

2.8.1 Understanding Vulnerability

How does conflict theory help us to understand social vulnerability to disasters? Various forms and amounts of capital affect where people live, work, travel, how many children they have, the resources in their social networks, and thus both their exposure to risk and their ability to respond to a hazard or disaster. Although wealthy individuals who own waterfront or coastal property (high financial capital) are at high risk from floods and storms, they usually have the means to leave the area when conditions threaten and can purchase insurance to protect them against some if not all of the damage to their property. In addition, they usually have the social connections (social capital) and skills (human capital) to ensure that their insurance claims are processed quickly and successfully and that their livelihoods are less likely to be fully at risk (Wisner, Blaikie, and Cannon 2004). The purchase of insurance is evidence that those individuals who purchase it understand that their property is at risk. Those who are poor (low financial capital) may be just as aware of the risks they face from storms and floods, but they usually have fewer choices of where they can live or over the quality of their housing, and may not be able to afford insurance or feel that more personal forms of insurance, such as sharing resources among family members, are more reliable. The family whose livelihood depends on commercial or subsistence fishing needs to live on the coast, where both their homes and their business are at risk from storms, flooding, and other hazards. Furthermore, residents in a fishing village in Southeast Asia are more vulnerable to loss of life and property than those living in coastal villages in Australia or Europe. Although the concepts and principles of conflict theory are relatively simple, their application suggests the complex interplay of social, economic, and historical factors that contribute to differences in risk and vulnerability to disasters and hazards for different populations within countries and for different countries and regions globally.

So far we have considered the *material* aspects of social structure and power as discussed by conflict theorists. Material aspects include, among others, control over natural resources; the accumulation of wealth; investment in roads, buildings, and manufacturing capacity; the creation of universities and research facilities; and the development of technology and science. Other theorists working within this paradigm have focused on how *nonmaterial* elements of social structure—symbols, beliefs, values, and knowledge itself—play a critical role in maintaining and reproducing inequality and exercising power. One of the key questions that conflict theorists must answer is how one class of people can not only be exploited and dominated by a much smaller class of people without the constant use or threat of force and violence, and may even actively embrace and uphold the structures of power that dominate them. Most contemporary capitalist societies do not rely primarily on organized religion to support the power of the state, and many actively espouse values such as freedom, individual rights and civil liberties, and popular participation in democratic government. Gramsci (1971) discussed aspects of the role of ideology in social structure through his development of the concept of hegemony. Hegemony, Gramsci argues, is the exercise of power indirectly by the use of ideas, ideology, and a view of life that supports the social structure and those in power. This process is complex and contradictory, with various groups vying to dominate popular thought and media. Nonetheless, an overarching set of values becomes those that the majority of a society's members internalize and thus becomes a major component in their worldview.

The dominant paradigm of disasters may be viewed as having hegemonic aspects or qualities. By viewing disasters as events caused by natural forces and processes outside human history and beyond human control, governments and other powerful organizations can deflect criticism for inadequate enforcement of building codes, lack of investment in warning systems and disaster planning, and for allowing some communities to suffer higher costs than others when disasters occur. Because this paradigm also infuses media accounts of disasters and hazards and appears in disaster management literature and courses, it is accepted as "common sense" and is therefore sometimes difficult to recognize or effectively challenge. Thus, the focus in the accounts of the flood in La Paz focus on its rarity and unusual strength rather than on the social and economic structure that compels many people to live on unstable hillsides and sit daily in the streets trying to sell something to provide income to feed and clothe their families.

Foucault (1980, 133) examined the ways in which we internalize the dominant views of the powerful in social institutions through scientific discourse and knowledge. Under capitalism, Foucault argues, science supplants religion as the primary means of determining truth in most societies. "Truth is linked in a circular relation with systems of power which produce and sustain it, and to effects of power which it induces and which extend it. A 'régime of truth.'" Consequently, those who control the production of scientific knowledge and its applications through technology also control our conversations or discourse and thus can affect how we view, study, and respond to phenomena such as disasters and hazards. Jason Corburn (2005) describes how discourse affected planning for development in western North Dakota. "Community voices were marginalized despite public efforts to involve residents. Even when local residents managed to gain an audience, they had little impact on development decisions in part because planners and residents did not speak the same language and understand each other's politics" (Tauxe [1995] quoted in Corburn [2005, 147]).

Charts, tables, and lengthy written documents often carry more weight in such public conversations than do the evidence of what Corburn calls "street science" or what anthropologists call "local knowledge," which may be presented in the form of stories or oral history that appears anecdotal even if it condenses years of accumulated empirical observation and experience (Corburn 2005), much like the tablets erected on Japanese hillsides to mark the impact of a tsunami. Control of discourse reinforces inequalities among and within nations in understanding and responding to disasters and hazards. Because the dominant paradigm of disasters sees them as products of nature, natural and earth sciences have, until recently, received the majority of funding for research, and the focus of mitigation has been on technology instead of social issues.

According to Foucault, an important aspect of the power of truth through science is how it internalizes social control within the individual members of a society. Biology and psychology, applied through organized medicine and psychiatry and communicated through schools and mass media, define what is considered normal behavior or a normal body. We internalize these standards of normality and discipline our behavior to achieve them. Bourdieu (1998) called this embodiment of social standards and scientific knowledge *habitus*. Habitus is internalized social structure: An individual's habitus consists of the largely unconscious patterns of thinking, feeling, and acting that she or he exhibits in daily life. According to Bourdieu, habitus not only incorporates mainstream or dominant standards of behavior and physical qualities and values, but those that are particular to an individual's location in the social structure, i.e., his or her class status. Because local knowledge is so frequently dismissed as unscientific or anecdotal, community members, particularly those with little formal education, may dismiss the authority of their own knowledge and experience, at least in discussions with those identified as experts. At the same time, when internalized, shared worldviews or habitus include a sense of futility or powerlessness in the face of social injustice, it can represent a barrier to effective social and political action to mitigate hazards and disasters.

Just as those working within the dominant paradigm of hazards can focus too much attention on natural causes of disasters, so conflict theorists can focus too much on the constraints and dominance of social structure and fail to recognize the role of individual and human action to generate change that can affect social life and the physical environment. For Foucault and Bourdieu, structure, external and internalized, does not completely determine individual and collective behavior and action. Individual and collective action or agency also affects social structure. Foucault acknowledged that alternative sources of knowledge and understanding and models for action exist outside mainstream images and institutions (Moore and Sanders 2006, 13), for example, in the coded opposition to power of the Brer Rabbit stories of rural blacks in the United States (Kushnick 1998) or in local forms of resistance such as seasonal workers in Malaysia delaying the harvest of crops of landowners who have overly exploited or mistreated them (Scott 1985). For Bourdieu, habitus is not only the product of what we receive and are taught, but also of our everyday actions and social encounters or practice, and thus is subject to innovation and change.

2.9 SYSTEMS THEORY AND SOCIAL VULNERABILITY

General systems theory is another major theory, also frequently implicit, that underlies social vulnerability approaches to understanding hazards and disasters. As we will discuss later in the chapter, it is often combined with political economy in *political* ecology and with culture in *cultural* ecology. Historically, the scientific approach that developed during the Enlightenment in Western Europe was based on the assumption that a phenomenon (whole) consisted only as a sum of its smallest identifiable parts. To understand a phenomenon, for example, the human body, it is necessary to determine its smallest parts, i.e., the cell, and understand their characteristics and behavior. Once these are understood, individual organs and whole bodies could be understood as well. This breaking down of a phenomenon into its constituent parts, or reductionism, is evident in different scientific disciplines: biologists break down living organisms into their smallest units, cells; chemists break down matter into atoms and molecules; and physicists break atoms further into subatomic particles and waves. By the early twentieth century, the various scientific disciplines worked largely independently of each other, each examining the parts of the world that formed the object of their study.

In the 1930s, biologist Ludwig von Bertalanffy (1950) reacted against scientific fragmentation and reductionism, arguing that a more holistic approach was needed. Writing in 1956, Boulding described the consequences of reductionism: "[T]he more science breaks into sub-groups, and the less communication is possible among the disciplines, however, the greater chance there is that the total growth of knowledge is being slowed down by the loss of relevant communications" (1956, 198). In the case of hazardous events, a reductionist approach may fail to consider key factors or processes that can mitigate the risks of damage, injuries, and deaths. In the case of Hurricane Katrina, for example, understanding the dynamics of levees, hurricanes, and flooding might have prevented much of the physical destruction in New Orleans' Ninth Ward. But by itself this knowledge is insufficient. Instead, to comprehensively reduce risk, the entire system must be understood at the individual and community levels and must take into account not only physical forces and conditions, but economic, political, historical, and social factors. In the aftermath of Hurricane Katrina, many of the deaths occurred because many poor residents, many of whom had limited physical mobility, relied on a public transportation system that could not adequately evacuate large numbers of people in an emergency (Wolfshon 2006). Thus knowledge of the Delta region's physical and meteorological characteristics and the city's social geography are both essential for mitigating risk from hurricanes.

General systems theory provides a way to increase communication among scientific disciplines through the concept of the system. Though the origin of the fundamental idea behind systems theory can be traced to scientists and philosophers such as Aristotle, Descartes, and Galileo, its contemporary incorporation into general systems theory is generally credited to Ludwig von Bertalanffy (1972).

2.9.1 What Is a System?

Although the definition of *system* might seem obvious, it is important to examine its elements. By definition, a system is composed of at least two interrelated parts or elements (Kast and Rosenzweig 1972). A more applicable definition is "a collection of interacting or independent entities that produces a unified functional whole, whose properties or behaviors cannot be predicted from a separate understanding of each individual level component" (Dale et al. 2004). Systems theory is based on the assumption from the Greek concept of holism that "the whole is something different from the sum of its parts" (Koffka 1935, 176). In other words, wholes are not merely a collection of different parts, but are organized, distinct phenomena that have characteristics, qualities, and behavior unique to them and different from the qualities of their component parts. This principle, known as *emergentism* (the character of the whole *emerges* from its parts), is fundamental to systems theory and distinguishes it from reductive approaches. What makes the whole unique is how the parts are linked to one another through organizing functions, the tasks or jobs that various parts of the system perform. Whereas some parts may perform more than one job, and many systems have redundant parts, the whole is dependent upon its parts working together in unity. Changes in one part of a system generate responses and changes in other parts of the system. As Koffka (1935) notes, it is the relationship between the parts and the whole that is meaningful and important.

An important feature of systems is whether they are open or closed. Closed systems have impermeable boundaries and so do not exchange energy or materials with their surrounding environment but must regulate themselves internally. Open systems, on the other hand, have permeable boundaries and freely exchange energy and materials with other systems in their environment. These are relative qualities: Most systems are more or less open or closed. Culture, for example, is a relatively open system that exchanges materials and energy through human interactions with the physical environment, plants, animals, and other societies. In turn, those systems are also altered by the exchange.

2.9.2 Ecological Systems

An ecosystem is greater than the sum of its parts.

—Eugene P. Odum (1913–2002)

In the 1970s, scientists applied general systems theory to the emerging science of ecology. Odum presented the idea of the "new ecology" in 1964 in an article by that title in which he links ecology—the study of the interaction between organisms and their environment—with general systems theory. Because it identifies similarities among phenomena of different disciplines, general systems theory provided a common ground to link physical geography with biology and human geography, particularly the interaction between human individuals and communities and their environment, both living and nonliving. Moreover, the new ecology recognized that explaining structure and function at only one level of analysis could not explain the whole picture. For example, understanding the effect of building a dam on the price and availability of electricity will not explain its effects on human communities displaced by the dam or the increased burden of parasitic, waterborne diseases in people who live above the dam. In addition, the new ecology acknowledged that descriptive research is insufficient to link different layers of scientific research. For example, studying the nature of plant growth and nutrient cycling will not produce larger crop yields. However, if the functions of these two phenomena are studied together, common denominators can be determined, leading to an understanding of their interactions. Odum (1964) describes the ecosystem concept as a basic unit of structure and function that must be dealt with: "The new ecology is thus a *systems ecology*" [emphasis added].

The power of systems theory lies in its ability to examine complex interrelationships at multiple levels and thus analyze vulnerability to disasters and hazards as well as identifying ways to mitigate them. In the case of the flood disaster in La Paz, for example, multiple systems were affected by the rushing water: transportation systems in the city; sewer systems that contain waste and keep it from contaminating drinking water; communication systems where utility and phone lines are damaged; power systems that supply electricity to homes and businesses, but also to police, fire, and rescue departments; and health care systems that must cope with multiple victims during the flood and patients who present with waterborne diseases from contaminated drinking water after the waters subside. Additionally, the political-economic system means that many poor Bolivians, particularly women, must sit on city streets to sell their goods and remain with those goods even as flood-waters rush down the streets. The failure of the government to build and maintain roads and drainage ditches, and to enforce building codes, coupled with migration of the rural poor to the city's unstable hillsides, all increase the vulnerability of the poor to flood disasters. With few options and resources, and low value placed on public safety by the state, La Paz's poor street vendors have little choice but to adopt the worldview that a flood disaster is "God's will" and to return to the streets.

The emergence of ecological systems perspective was a significant scientific and theoretical development that arose from increasing awareness of (a) environmental pollution and its effect on health, (b) increasing human population and the demand on natural resources, and (c) the extinction of plants and animals resulting from human actions (Holling and Chambers 1973). Within this context, ecological systems theory represents a shift in scientific and popular (in those areas of the world where Western science is dominant) conceptions of the relationship between humans and nature.

2.9.3 CRITIQUE OF ECOLOGICAL SYSTEMS: POLITICAL ECOLOGY

Although ecological systems theory provides an excellent framework for describing the "whats" and "hows" of these relationships and the social vulnerabilities that exist within these systems, they tend to focus on equilibrium and balance instead of conflict and change. Within the ecological systems view, it is hard to see disasters as anything other than extreme natural events or disturbances to the system, with resilience as a system's ability to recover from external forces (Wilcox and Horwitz 2005). Political ecology, which combines ecological systems theory with political-economic perspectives, most notably those of conflict theorists such as Wolf (1982), Frank (1969), and Wallerstein (1974), became an important framework for examining the role of power, inequalities, and inequities in the distribution of resources and of global capitalism on ecological changes at local, regional, and global levels of analysis (Walker 2005). "Whereas cultural ecology and systems theory emphasized adaptation and homeostasis, political ecology emphasized the role of political economy as a force of maladaptation and instability (Walker 2005, 74).

The creation of large dams to harness hydroelectric power in many developing countries in the 1960s and 1970s is a case in point. The dams did generate power, but in creating large freshwater lakes they also greatly increased the habitat for freshwater snails and altered patterns of human agriculture, fishing, and transportation to increase settlement near the lakes and human contact with the water. Thus, the stage was set for the rapid spread of schistosomiasis, a debilitating, chronic parasitic infection, throughout the world's tropical regions (Desowitz 1976; Steinman et al. 2006). In India, despite decades-long protests from people threatened with displacement from dam projects, the government has built 4,300 large dams that "have submerged about 37,500 square kilometers—an area almost the size of Switzerland—and displaced tens of millions of people" (International Rivers 2008). Underlying the decisions to build these dams and the responses to their construction and the changes they brought were competing worldviews and values.

2.10   WHAT ARE WORLDVIEWS?

Whereas disaster planners draw from explicitly stated formal theories as a basis for their assessments and planning, all of us—professionals and lay people—rely on our worldviews to make sense of events in our lives, including disasters and their consequences. Like formal theories, worldviews also describe, explain, and predict features of our natural and social environments. Worldview, from the German *weltanschauung*, refers to ways of thinking about the world and its events that are more or less shared by a group of people. Worldviews provide answers to questions about the meaning of life and death and what the appropriate human response to those events should be. Implied in the concept of worldview is a direct relationship between the way an individual or group views the world and their behavior. Worldviews are learned through social interactions with parents, friends, and others in one's community from early childhood. They may be expressed through religion or philosophy, or they may be implicit in the structure, norms, and values of institutions such as public schools or medical clinics. Worldviews are largely unconscious and may guide our actions without our awareness. The concept of worldview is conceptually problematic in that worldviews are only "more or less" shared among members of a society or social group; like habitus, worldviews vary by an individual's or a community's position within the social structure and by their unique experiences. The world may look very different if you are a small landholder working to produce food for your family than if you are a commercial fisherman who supplies fish for sushi on the global market or an investment banker on Wall Street. For this reason, many contemporary anthropologists prefer *ideology* or *habitus* to *worldview*.

Worldviews respond to questions about human relationship with nature, and thus to understand vulnerability and response to hazards and disasters, it is critical to take worldviews into account. Broadly speaking, there are three ways of understanding the society-nature relation:

* People under nature (nature's theory): humans are at nature's mercy
* People with nature: humans live their collective lives in harmony with nature
* People over nature (human's theory): humans dominate nature through manipulation of the natural world

Under the first worldview, an earthquake or tornado might be seen as an "act of nature" or as an "act of God" if God is accepted as the creator of nature. The response might be to accept it as an unavoidable though unfortunate event and to rebuild damaged structures. Under the second worldview, the same event might be viewed as something to which human society must adapt and for which it must plan by understanding weather patterns, locating cities on stable ground and away from common tornado pathways, and using knowledge and cooperation to provide safe places of refuge. Under the third worldview, damage to structures or lives lost result from human failure to master nature, and the response is to design and build structures that can better withstand the forces of earthquakes or learn to predict and warn against tornadoes.

The relationship between a society's political, economic, and social structures and its view of the relationship between humans and nature has been a subject of debate among anthropologists. Some, like Harris (1979), argue that a society's material, economic bases, i.e., how its members obtain their needs from nature or mode of production, determines their worldview. Thus, a society based on hunting and gathering in which success depends on an intimate knowledge of the local environment and its plants and animals will tend to have a worldview of people with nature. A society based on industrial technology, where most people live far removed from nature, will tend to have a worldview of people over nature. And a society or community that has few resources and whose members have little control over where they live and how they make a living are likely to adopt the worldview of people under nature. Most social scientists would agree that the relationship between environment, mode of production, and view of nature is complex and can work in both directions: Our view of nature can change.

2.11 WORLDVIEWS AND VALUES

Values are guidelines for actions and decisions that are generally consistent with and derived from worldviews. For example, in the general worldview of human over nature, human life is valued over that of other species. The human need or desire to increase crop yields through the application of pesticides is justified through this value, even though it may never be stated unless someone challenges that decision and its underlying value. Values address questions of morality, of right and wrong action, and what is good and desirable. Like worldviews, they may be explicitly stated or unconscious and implicit in the form of "gut feelings" that a given action or decision is the "right" or "wrong" thing to do.

Values express equity or fairness, justice, and the relationship of the individual to society. What do I owe a stranger simply because that person is a human being in need? How much should my individual opinion or need or desire count in society? What is "consent," and how should it be expressed? Philosophers distinguish between intrinsic values, those things that are good, desirable, or important in and of themselves without relation to any other thing, and extrinsic values, those things that are valuable because they are a means to obtaining, enjoying, or protecting something that is intrinsically good (Flew 1979, 365). Intrinsic and extrinsic values are considered when we invoke the sacredness of the Earth as part of creation (Hayden 1995; Khalid 1992) or assign monetary value to a unique geological feature or to preserving remote areas so that humans can experience wilderness (Foster 1997). Values also guide discussions of which risks can be mitigated and for whom, and which risks are acceptable and at what level. For example, are the risks from landslides and earthquakes viewed as impossible to manage, whereas nuclear power accidents or terrorist attacks must be prevented at any cost?

Values exist and affect decisions and behaviors at various levels and through various systems, and they often come into conflict with one another. For instance, disaster managers and economic planners in a city may believe that they should provide protection from disasters equally across the entire population; thus, equality is valued. They probably also want to achieve this by using scarce or limited resources wisely; thus, efficiency is valued. If there is a small population of the city that is very hard to protect, it may not be efficient to spend 90% of the resources to protect only 10% of the population. The issue becomes more problematic if that small group is also an ethnic, racial, or occupational minority group. Many planners and officials believe that historically marginalized or deprived groups should receive assistance in greater proportion than their strictly equal share—the value of equity.

Returning to the example of dams in India, the worldview embraced by the Indian government is one of humans over nature, expressed in its willingness to use technical solutions—dams—to solve human needs for energy. The government also values economic development more than the possible harm or disruption caused to the millions of people displaced by the dams. The worldview embraced by the protestors, in contrast, is one of nature with humans, expressed in the desire for economic development that values environmentally sustainable solutions to the need for power and that values local community needs over national needs or special interests.

2.12 COMMUNITY-BASED APPROACHES AND SOCIAL AND ENVIRONMENTAL JUSTICE

Conflict theory forces us to acknowledge social inequity as a source of vulnerability to disasters and to redefine hazards to include not only extreme events such as earthquakes and volcanic eruptions, but conditions that millions of people live with daily: contaminated water, lack of sanitary facilities, unsafe roads, and inadequate food and nutrition. These theories also direct us to consider different approaches to mitigating hazards and disasters that incorporate social justice and participatory approaches to research and planning.

Freire (1970) examined how individuals and groups could challenge structures of power and inequality through literacy and *conscientização* or critical consciousness. Freire observed that becoming literate, i.e., learning to read and write especially as taught in schools, is a process whereby society inculcates dominant values and views. It is thus dehumanizing and oppressive for poor and marginalized members of society. Learning to read and write can, however, be a process of humanization and liberation if it is taught in a way that demonstrates the power embedded in language and if teachers work in equal partnership with the persons learning to read to control that power themselves (Freire 1970).

Analogously, research on hazards and disasters can be a process that empowers residents of communities at high risk. Participatory Rural Appraisal or Assessment (PRA) and Community Based Participatory Research (CBPR) (Israel 2005) rest on principles that emphasize the knowledge and strengths of local communities and their members and strive to equalize the power between researchers or technical experts and those they are studying. It is no easy task for professionals whose technical or academic knowledge confer power and authority not to dominate the process. "They must take time, show respect, be open and self-critical, and learn not to interrupt. They need to have confidence that local people, whether they are literate or not, women or men, rich or poor, are capable of carrying out their own analysis" (IDS 1996, 2).

The sustainable livelihoods approach (SLA) (described in Chapter 3) uses PRA and community-based strategies to assess a community's vulnerability and resilience to hazards and disasters.

These are lofty ideals, and PRA and CBPR projects often fall short of truly equal partnership and collaboration. Nonetheless, these models offer an approach that values local knowledge of the physical and social environment and has the potential to recognize and incorporate indigenous ways of living with hazards and disasters that may prove more sustainable than purely technological approaches (Zaman 1999). Although this knowledge and participation could be extracted and used for top-down programs and interventions imposed by government or civic agencies and institutions outside the community, these approaches are guided by the view that community members must be equal partners in all aspects of research, program design, implementation, and evaluation and that this process should be used to empower local communities. Consequently, PRA and CBPR have been used to directly respond to issues of social and environmental justice (Shepard et al. 2002) such as pesticide exposure among farm workers (Arcury, Quandt, and Dearry 2001). "Fundamentally, *street science* is about the pursuit of environmental-health justice. Mobilizing local knowledge helps disadvantaged communities organize and educate themselves, as well as increases control over the decisions that impact their lives" (Corburn 2005, 216) [emphasis in the original]. Thus, these frameworks support the position that communities have the right to know about local hazards and a right to protection from disasters.

Discussion of human rights and social justice returns us to the power of conflict and critical theory to analyze inequities in social vulnerability. Conflict and critical theory propose that a society's dominant or hegemonic worldview and underlying values, and its institutions and policies regarding those factors that govern human and environmental interactions, are mutually reinforcing. In other words, if a society's economic system of production is based on exploiting natural resources and human labor and exchanging its products in a free market, its social structure will incorporate unequal access to and control over productive resources. Its worldview will be one of humans over nature; its core values will support efficiency over equity; and the view that hazards and disasters are uncontrollable natural events will predominate. These structures and values will generate policies that result in differential social vulnerability to hazards and disasters based on a variety of factors including race, gender, age, ethnicity, and social class.

But to focus solely on structure and hegemony denies the power of individual and collective agents to change their interaction with the environment and the values and worldview that guide those interactions. Through concerted action in a variety of scientific disciplines, in social policy, and in hazard and disaster management, the dominant paradigm of hazards and disasters is slowly being transformed. The application of conflict and critical theory forces attention on the role of social structure, worldview, and values on social vulnerability. The concept of sustainability forces us to consider the real costs of the inequalities and inequities that result from a worldview of humans over nature and points to the value of local knowledge in creating sustainable interactions with the environment. As Oliver-Smith (1996, 2) notes, "In effect, if a society cannot withstand without major damage and destruction a predictable feature of its environment, that society has not developed in a sustainable way." Finally, attention to agency through participatory research and planning offers the promise of empowering those who are disproportionately at risk to demand equity in mitigation and planning.

Things are changing in Bolivia as national and local governments and communities work to improve disaster planning. In February 2011, following several weeks of heavy rains, a dozen neighborhoods in La Paz were placed on "red alert" (Los Tiempos 2011). As the land began to crack and slide, neighbors and soldiers in the Bolivian army helped evacuate the neighborhood of Callapa. Over 800 buildings and homes were destroyed, and approximately 5,000 people were affected by what city government spokesperson Edwin Herrera called "the worst that La Paz has ever seen" (AP 2011). But what was different about this landslide was that residents quickly evacuated and were prohibited from returning to the unstable area. Consequently, there were a few injuries, but no deaths.

2.13   SUMMARY

Theory is critical to our scientific approach to hazards and disasters. To view hazards and disasters as extraordinary natural events or as basic features of human environmental systems is more than a matter of semantics: It represents critical choices in how we study the disasters that affect our environment and millions of lives every day, and how we adapt to reduce risk in practice. Disasters, such as Hurricane Katrina and the floods and landslides in La Paz, demonstrate that risk and vulnerability are not distributed equally within a society. Critical and conflict theory explain these inequalities and inequities as the product of social structure, worldviews, and values. Combined with systems theory, the political ecology framework provides a powerful mechanism to analyze the complex interplay of variables that result in disasters. Adding the concept of human agency and using participatory approaches to research guided by a theoretical lens creates disaster planning that decreases social vulnerability and promotes sustainable human-environment interactions.

DISCUSSION QUESTIONS

1. Using a conflict and critical theory approach, how do the zoning policies and building codes in your local community affect social vulnerability to hazards and disasters?
2. What individuals or organizations can you identify at the local, national, and international levels that have succeeded in changing worldviews and values that directly affect disaster planning and mitigation? How have they achieved these changes?
3. How do you see institutions responsible for disaster planning and mitigation responding to the use of participatory approaches to research and planning in your community? Should community members and organizations be full and equal partners? Why or why not? How do you determine who should be included and which voices should be heard?
4. Analyze media reports for a disaster or hazard. What values and worldview guide how the event is reported? What is the view of hazards and disasters they present? How might you go about informing journalists and media representatives about alternative ways of viewing these events?
5. How does the concept of sustainability challenge the view of hazards and disasters as natural events? What does it tell us about the costs of social vulnerability? What worldview of the relationship of humans to nature does it support?
6. Is protection from hazards and disasters a human right?

REFERENCES

AP (Associated Press). 2011. La Paz landslide wrecks 400 homes. *The Guardian*, February 27. http://www.guardian.co.uk/world/2011/feb/27/la-paz-landslide-wrecks-homes.

Arcury, T. A., S. A. Quandt, and A. Dearry. 2001. Farmworker pesticide exposure and community-based participatory research: Rationale and practical applications. *Environmental Health Perspectives* 109 (3): 429–34.

Beyrer, C., S. Doocy, and C. Robinson. 2008. Cyclone Nargis: 3.2 million Burmese affected, limited humanitarian assistance poses health threat as conditions worsen. Johns Hopkins Bloomberg School of Public Health Press Release, May 13.

Birkmann, J. 2006. Measuring vulnerability to promote disaster-resilient societies: Conceptual frameworks and definitions. In *Measuring vulnerability to natural hazards: Towards disaster resilient societies,* ed. Jörn Birkmann, 9–54. Tokyo: United Nations University Press.

Boulding, K. E. 1956. General systems theory—The skeleton of science. *Management Science* 2 (3): 197–208.

Bourdieu, P. 1998. *Practical reason: On the theory of action.* Stanford, CA: Stanford University Press.

Chinn, M. D., and R. W. Fairlie. 2007. Determinants of the global digital divide: A cross-country analysis of computer and Internet penetration. *Oxford Economic Papers* 59 (1): 16–44.

Corburn, J. 2005. *Street science: Community knowledge and environmental health justice.* Cambridge, MA: MIT Press.

Dale, V., S. Bartell, R. Brothers, and J. Sorensen. 2004. Systems approach to environmental security. *EcoHealth* 1:119–23.

Desowitz, R. S. 1976. *New Guinea tapeworms and Jewish grandmothers.* New York: W. W. Norton.

Dilley, M., R. S. Chen, U. Deichmann, A. L. Lerner-Lam, and M. Arnold. 2005. Natural disaster hotspots: A global risk analysis, synthesis report. New York: International Bank for Reconstruction and Development, The World Bank, and Columbia University. http://sedac.ciesin.columbia.edu/hazards/hotspots/synthesisreport.pdf.

Disaster Emergency Committee. n.d. Haiti earthquake facts and figures. http://www.dec.org.uk/haiti-earthquake-facts-and-figures.

Elder, K., S. Xrasagar, N. Miller, S. A. Bowen, S. Glover, and C. Piper. 2007. African Americans' decisions not to evacuate New Orleans before Hurricane Katrina: A qualitative study. *AJPH* 97 (Suppl. 1): S124–29.

Enever, A. 2002. Fifty dead in shock Bolivian flood. *BBC News.* http://news.bbc.co.uk/2/hi/americas/1833002.stm.

Farmer, P. 2005. *Pathologies of power: Health, human rights, and the new war on the poor.* Berkeley, CA: University of California Press.

Flew, A., ed. 1979. *A dictionary of philosophy.* New York: St. Martin's.

Foster, H. D. 1997. *The Ozymandias principles: Thirty-one strategies for surviving change.* Victoria, BC: Southdowne Press.

Foucault, M. 1980. *Power/knowledge: Selected interviews and other writings, 1972–1977.* Ed. C. Gordon. New York: Pantheon Books.

Frank, A. G. 1969. *Capitalism and underdevelopment in Latin America: Historical studies of Chile and Brazil.* New York: Monthly Review Press.

Freire, P. 1970. *Pedagogy of the oppressed.* Trans. M. B. Ramos. New York: Seabury Press.

Geosources. 2002. Kobe earthquake. http://www.georesources.co.uk/kobehigh.htm.

Gill, L. 2000. *Teetering on the rim: Global restructuring, daily life, and the armed retreat of the Bolivian state.* New York: Columbia University.

Gramsci, A. 1971. *Selections from the prison notebooks.* Trans. and ed. Q. Hoare and G. N. Smith. New York: International Publishers.

Harris, M. 1979. *Cultural materialism: The struggle for a science of culture.* New York: Random House.

Hayden, D. 1995. *The power of place: Urban landscapes as public history.* Cambridge, MA: MIT Press.

Hewitt, K. 1983. The idea of calamity in a technocratic age. In *Interpretations of calamity,* ed. K. Hewitt, 3–32. Boston: Allen and Unwin.

Holling, C. S., and A. D. Chambers. 1973. Resource science: The nurture of an infant. *BioScience* 23 (1): 13–20.

IDS (Institute of Development Studies). 1996. The power of participation: PRA and policy. IDS Policy Briefing, Issue 7. Brighton, UK: Institute of Development Studies. http://www.ids.ac.uk/files/dmfile/P87.pdf.

International Rivers. 2008. India. http://www.internationalrivers.org/campaigns/india.

Israel, B. A. 2005. Community-based participatory research: Lessons learned from the Centers for Children's Environmental Health and Disease Prevention research. *Environmental Health Perspectives* 113 (10): 1463–71.

Kalb, D. 2000. Localizing flows: Power, paths, institutions, and networks. In *The ends of globalization: Bringing society back*, ed. D. van der Land, M. Staring, R. van Steenbergen, B. Wilterdink, and N. Kalb. Lanham, MD: Rowman and Littlefield. Quoted in T. C. Lewellen. *The anthropology of globalization: Cultural anthropology enters the 21st century* (Westport, CT: Bergin and Garvey, 2002), 8.

Kast, F. E., and J. E. Rosenzweig. 1972. General systems theory: Applications for organization and management. *The Academy of Management Journal* 15 (4): 447–65.

Khalid, F. M., ed., with J. O'Brien. 1992. *Islam and ecology*. New York: Cassell.

Koffka, Kurt. 1935. *Principles of Gestalt psychology*. New York: Harcourt, Brace and World.

Kozol, J. 1991. *Savage inequalities: Children in America's schools*. New York: Crown Publishers.

Kushnick, L. 1998. Review of the Norton anthology of African American literature, the Norton companion to African American literature, and the Oxford book of the American South. *Race and Class* 39 (3): 105–8.

Lewellen, T. C. 2002. *The anthropology of globalization: Cultural anthropology enters the 21st century*. Westport, CT: Bergin and Garvey.

Los Tiempos. 2011. En La Paz siguen los derrumbes. Los Tiempos.com, February 3. http://www.lostiempos. com/diario/actualidad/nacional/20110301/en-la-paz-siguen-los-derrumbes_115142_228243.html.

Macleod, Calum. 2011. Japanese towns reconsider sea walls after deadly tsunami. USA Today, August 13. http://www.usatoday.com/news/world/2011-08-11-japanese-town-undeterred-by-record-wave_n.htm.

Marx, K. 1867/1990. *Capital: A critique of political economy*. Trans. B. Fowkes. New York: Penguin Books.

McEnaney, L. 2000. *Civil defense begins at home: Militarization meets everyday life in the fifties*. Princeton, NJ: Princeton University Press.

Moore, H. L., and T. Sanders. 2006. Anthropology and epistemology. In *Anthropology in theory: Issues in epistemology*, ed. H. L. Moore and T. Sanders, 1–21. Malden, MA: Blackwell Publishing.

Odum, E. P. 1964. The new ecology. *BioScience* 14 (7): 14–16.

Oliver-Smith, A. 1996. Anthropological research on hazards and disasters. *Annual Review of Anthropology* 25:303–28.

———. 1999. What is a disaster? Anthropological perspectives on a persistent question. In *The angry Earth: Disaster in anthropological perspective*, ed. A. Oliver-Smith and S. M. Hoffman, 18–34. New York: Routledge.

Perry, R. J. 2003. *Five key concepts in anthropological thinking*. Upper Saddle River, NJ: Prentice Hall.

Pielke, R. A. Jr., J. Rubiera, C. Landsea, M. L. Fernández, and R. Klein. 2003. Hurricane vulnerability in Latin America and the Caribbean: Normalized damage and loss potentials. *Natural Hazards Review* 4 (3): 101–14.

Quarantelli, E., ed. 1998. *What is a disaster?* New York: Routledge.

Rapley, J. 2004. *Globalization and inequality: Neoliberalism's downward spiral*. Boulder, CO: Lynne Reiner.

Rodney, W. 1982. *How Europe underdeveloped Africa*. Washington, DC: Howard University Press.

Rousseau, J. 1973. A discourse on political economy. In *The social contract and the discourses*, trans. G. D. H. Cole, 128–68. London: David Campbell Publishers.

Scott, J. C. 1985. *Weapons of the weak: Everyday forms of peasant resistance*. New Haven, CT: Yale University Press.

Shepard, P. M., M. E. Northridge, S. Prakesh, and G. Stover. 2002. Preface: Advancing environmental justice through community-based participatory research. *Environmental Health Perspectives* 110 (2): 139–40.

Steen, R. 2002. Bolivian floods kill 60, over 500 homeless. Red Cross. http://www96.reliefweb.int/report/ bolivia/death-toll-rises-70-bolivian-floods.

Steinman, Jennifer Keiser, Robert Bos, Marcel Tanner, and Jürg Utzinger. 2006. Schistosomiasis and water resources development: Systematic review, meta-analysis, and estimates of people at risk. *Lancet Infectious Diseases* 6 (7): 411–25.

Tauxe, C. S. 1995. Marginalizing public participation in local planning: An ethnographic account. *Journal American Planning Association* 61 (4): 471–81. Quoted in J. Corburn. *Street science: Community knowledge and environmental health justice* (Cambridge, MA: MIT Press, 2005), 147–48.

Therborn, G. 1996. Dialectics of modernity: On critical theory and the legacy of 20th century Marxism. In *A companion to social theory*, ed. B. S. Turner. Oxford: Blackwell.

Tobin, G. A., and B. E. Montz. 1997. *Natural hazards: Explanation and integration*. New York: Guilford Press.

UNICEF. 2008. At a glance: Myanmar. http://www.unicef.org/infobycountry/myanmar_statistics.html#51.

UN/ISDR. 2007. Bolivia: Flood early warning system projected for La Paz. http://www.eird.org/newsroom/ bolivia.pdf.

von Bertalanffy, L. 1950. An outline of general systems theory. *British Journal for the Philosophy of Science* 1 (2): 134–65.

———. 1972. The history and status of general systems theory. *Academy of Management Journal* 15 (4): 407–26.

von Braun, J., T. Teklue, and P. Webb. 1998. *Famine in Africa: Causes, responses and prevention.* Baltimore: Johns Hopkins University Press.

Walker, P. A. 2005. Political ecology: Where is the ecology? *Progress in Human Geography* 29 (1): 73–82.

Wallerstein, I. 1974. *The modern world-system: Capitalist agriculture and the origins of the European world economy in the sixteenth century.* New York: Academic Press.

Watts, M. 1983. On the poverty of theory: Natural hazards research in context. In *Interpretations of calamity*, ed. K. Hewitt, 231–62. Boston: Allen and Unwin.

Wilcox, B. A., and P. Horwitz. 2005. The tsunami: Rethinking disasters. *EcoHealth* 2:89–90.

Wisner, B., P. Blaikie, and T. Cannon. 2004. *At risk: Natural hazards, people's vulnerability and disasters.* 2nd ed. London: Routledge.

Wolf, E. 1982. *Europe and the people without history.* Berkeley, CA: University of California Press.

Wolfshon, Brian. 2006. Evacuation planning and engineering for Hurricane Katrina. *The Bridge* 36 (1): 27–34.

Zaman, M. Q. 1999. Vulnerability, disaster, and survival in Bangladesh: Three case studies. In *The angry Earth: Disaster in anthropological perspective,* ed. A. Oliver-Smith and S. M. Hoffman, 192–212. New York: Routledge.

RESOURCES

- *National Institute of Environmental Health Science, Environmental Science, and Community-Based Participatory Research.* http://www.ncbi.nlm.nih.gov/pmc/articles/PMC1241159/.
- *Office of the United Nations High Commissioner for Human Rights.* "Issues in Focus: Natural Disasters and Internal Displacement. http://www.ohchr.org/EN/Issues/IDPersons/Pages/Infocus.aspx.
- *Wageningin UR.* "Participatory Planning Monitoring and Evaluation" (PPM&E). http://portals.wi.wur.nl/ppme/.

3 The Intrinsic Link of Vulnerability to Sustainable Development

John Brett and Kate Oviatt

CONTENTS

3.1 CHAPTER PURPOSE

This chapter explores a variety of perspectives around the argument that sustainable development (SD) can reduce vulnerability and enhance community resilience to hazard events. We first review the relationship between development, especially focusing on various aspects of poverty reduction, vulnerability, and resilience, followed by a discussion of the core principles of sustainable development and its promises. The concepts of sustainable development are often abstract so we introduce the sustainable livelihoods approach (SLA) which creates an explicit model and process of development, allowing planners and practitioners to identify and develop specific approaches for addressing vulnerabilities and enhancing resilience. This is followed by a discussion of sustainability and vulnerability and of sustainability and resiliency. We develop two case examples drawn from the authors' research in rural tropical regions of northwestern Guatemala and northern Ecuador.

3.2   OBJECTIVES

At the conclusion of this chapter, readers should be able to:

1. Understand the need for addressing "root causes" for disaster loss reduction
2. Explain the basic elements of sustainable development and why it makes sense to integrate disaster planning/emergency management with this framework
3. Elaborate on the explicit links among vulnerability and resilience and sustainable development, understanding how taking a sustainable development approach can increase resiliency and capacity
4. Gain an appreciation for the sustainable livelihoods approach (SLA) and how it addresses root causes of vulnerability and contributes to resiliency

3.3   INTRODUCTION

According to Didier Cherpitel, secretary general of the International Federation of Red Cross and Red Crescent Societies (IFRC), "Disasters are first and foremost a major threat to development, and specifically to the development of the poorest and most marginalized people in the world. *Disasters seek out the poor and ensure they stay poor*" [emphasis added] (Twigg 2004, 9). This is an important sentiment; however, following from the arguments on root causes and alternative perspectives on vulnerability presented in Chapter 2, it neglects an extremely important distinction: Disasters do not "seek out" the poor; rather, social and political-economic processes ultimately create the conditions that preferentially expose the poor to hazards and minimize capabilities for responding to, and recovering from, hazard events.

The cause lies only partly in the event; it is the social and political-economic conditions that often have deep historical roots, increasing the risk of a disaster and almost always impacting subsets of the population disproportionately when a hazard event occurs. Because the root causes of vulnerability arise primarily through inequality, power structures, worldviews, and belief systems, changing them in meaningful ways is extremely challenging. A bridge is relatively easy to repair in the aftermath of an earthquake or can be strengthened prior to an event, but addressing poverty, gender inequality, racism, and other social and political-economic factors is significantly more complicated. Twigg (2004, 2) argues that disaster planning has too often been considered part of a humanitarian aid orientation, rather than being part of overall (sustainable) development efforts. Humanitarian aid, though necessary, provides only immediate and temporary assistance after an event but does not address the root causes that contributed to the disaster in the first place. This lack of integration between development and disaster planning can, and has, perpetuated an increase in disaster vulnerability. A single disaster is capable of destroying years of development work; likewise, development projects that fail to consider disaster risk can increase both the effects and the likelihood of a disaster (UW-DMC 1997).

Unfortunately, because the political-economic and social contributors are more complex, the result can be inaction. Some might even argue that issues of vulnerability do not belong in the emergency management realm; nothing could be further from the truth if the goal is actually disaster loss reduction. By directly incorporating disaster and emergency management into sustainable development and planning programs in the United States and internationally, we can potentially reduce vulnerability and enhance resilience. Sustainable development (SD), with its attention to environmental, economic, and social issues, is a significant theme within discussions on disaster vulnerability reduction. There is an increasing recognition that "the social and the economic are closely linked with the environmental sphere" (Birkmann 2006, 44). These elements are intrinsically connected to reducing disaster vulnerability, and yet Birkmann argues that rarely are these frameworks used in conjunction with one another in practice, although a few examples exist. (See Twigg [2004, 5] and Cannon, Twigg, and Rowell [2003] for case examples.)

In this chapter, we explore how sustainable development approaches can potentially decrease vulnerability to disasters, explicitly focusing on the sustainable livelihoods approach (SLA) as a model to operationalize sustainability and vulnerability reduction. This chapter explores the direct associations between SD, vulnerability and resilience, both conceptually and through a focused review of the literature. To illustrate some of these elements and processes, we present contrasting case examples of the lowland Ecuador community of Mondaña, which is actively developing and implementing sustainable practices, with the Trifinio region of northwestern Guatemala, which has been involved in a modicum of disaster preparedness but no systematic development programming. We begin with a short review of the concept and principles of SD followed by a discussion on how sustainable development, as conceptualized and practiced through SLA, can provide a model for considering both sustainable development and vulnerability reduction in the same planning processes. The relationship between participatory, community-based vulnerability assessment and SLA is presented in more detail in Chapter 16.

3.4 DEVELOPMENT AND VULNERABILITY

Around the world, a growing share of the devastation triggered by "natural" disasters stems from ecologically destructive practices and from putting ourselves in harm's way. Many ecosystems have been frayed to the point where they are no longer resilient and able to withstand natural disturbances, setting the stage for "unnatural disasters"—those made more frequent or more severe due to human actions. By degrading forests, engineering rivers, filling in wetlands, and destabilizing the climate, we are unraveling the strands of a complex ecological safety net. (Abramovitz, cited in UNISDR 2004, 27)

The relationship between disaster vulnerability and development is a complicated one. Disasters have often been considered deviations or interruptions from "normal" human activity or development (UNDP 2004). Within moments, a hazardous event can undo years of development gains. However, it is increasingly recognized that the relationship between disasters and development is not one-way. Poorly planned, narrowly defined, and inadequately executed development practices themselves can increase the likelihood and the effects of a disaster, directly influencing and shaping disaster risk (UW-DMC 1997; UNDP 2004). It is often the consequences of development that result in environmental degradation, rapid population growth, and urbanization that create the disaster, rather than the actual hazardous event (UW-DMC 1997). The Brundtland Commission recognized this relationship, commenting eloquently on the 1980s droughts in Africa:

The recent crises in Africa best and most tragically illustrate the ways in which economics and ecology can interact destructively and trip into disaster. Triggered by drought, its real causes lie deeper. They are to be found in part in national policies that gave too little attention, too late, to the needs of smallholder agriculture and to the threats posed by rapidly rising populations. Their roots extend also to a global economic system that takes more out of a poor continent than it puts in. Debts that they cannot pay force African nations relying on commodity sales to overuse their fragile soils, thus turning good land to desert. (Brundtland Commission 1987)

To reduce disaster vulnerability, both the impacts of natural hazards on development efforts and the impacts of development on natural hazards risk must be considered. Both loss of infrastructure, such as roads, bridges, communication lines, energy sources, etc., and loss of people, through death, disablement, and migration, can have devastating effects on local, regional, and national economic and social development (UNDP 2004). Such losses usually have a much greater net effect in less-developed countries with less robust economies. For example, in 2001, both the United States and El Salvador experienced roughly US$2 billion in losses due to damage from earthquakes. Whereas the United States could accommodate such expenses without difficulty, such a loss accounted for 15% of El Salvador's annual gross domestic product (UNDP 2004). The effects of a single hazard event can have lasting repercussions on an area by undoing years of development gains, setting back both social and economic development.

Although less obvious than a disaster's impacts on development, the impact that development can have on disaster vulnerability can be, in some respects, more important. There are many ways in which development can increase disaster vulnerability, most notably by failing to incorporate hazards planning into development strategies. In areas that are prone to certain hazards, the impacts can be mitigated if the relationships between hazards, vulnerability, and development are considered throughout the planning process. Development that fails to consider the hazard risk of an area can directly increase the population's vulnerability. The 1992 earthquake in Cairo, Egypt, exemplifies this. The earthquake, which measured 5.2 on the Richter scale, an event that would be considered small to moderate in the United States or Western Europe, caused massive damage with over 500 deaths and 4,000 injuries. Failure to account for earthquake risk in construction of older as well as newer buildings resulted in tremendous loss of life and property damage from a relatively minor earthquake. Over 2,500 houses were completely destroyed, 1,087 schools had to be closed, and 5,780 more required extensive repairs (UW-DMC 1997, 34). Similarly, the 2008 Sichuan, China, earthquake graphically illustrated the importance of consistent planning and policy implementation. Although official policy required building to earthquake standards, the codes were not enforced for many buildings, including schools. As a consequence, these poorly designed and built buildings collapsed in much greater numbers than those properly designed and built, disproportionately contributing to the very high death toll. Had the existing earthquake building requirements been implemented during the construction of these houses and schools, the loss of life and damage would undoubtedly have been lower.

Development increases disaster vulnerability through unintended consequences that weaken the social, ecological, or economic factors that allow systems to absorb and rebound from hazard events (resilience). Population growth, migration, the introduction of new production/consumption patterns, the implementation of new technologies, etc., can alter existing social and environmental relationships, which in turn can lead to a change in vulnerability. Such changes can result in severe environmental degradation due to increased pressure on environmental resources, the creation of more waste and pollutants, and the use of marginal lands (UW-DMC 1997). "Environmental degradation increases the intensity of natural hazards and is often the factor that transforms the hazard into a disaster" (UNISDR 2004, 27). An explicit example of these interactions can be seen on many Caribbean islands, where bananas and other crops for export are planted on fertile valley bottomlands, a practice that forces subsistence farmers up onto steep slopes. Widespread forest clearing and short fallow cycles expose broad areas to erosion. When heavier than usual rains occur, extensive erosion and landslides are the inevitable result, leading to downslope pollution, loss of life, and property damage (UNISDR 2003). Current economic models encourage consumption and production practices that often ignore environmental constraints, leading to an increase in vulnerability (see Section 3.5.2 for further details).

The 1984–1985 famine in Sudan is a clear example of how the unintended consequences of development increase vulnerability. Before the 1970s, Sudanese farmers largely practiced subsistence farming and employed techniques such as crop rotation, migratory grazing, and leaving land fallow to protect and maintain soil fertility. Beginning in the 1970s, industrial agricultural techniques were introduced to boost the nation's agricultural export economy. Industrial agriculture requires more land per farm than traditional agriculture and is focused on producing cash export crops rather than food for local consumption. The expansion of industrial agriculture, coupled with increasing population pressures, reduced the land available for subsistence farming and displaced many people from their land. The cumulative effect of this was an overall increase in vulnerability: Social networks were destroyed; traditional farming techniques and coping mechanisms were abandoned; and those who still had land farmed it more intensively to produce enough food to survive, leading to an increase in deforestation and soil degradation. With the emphasis on cash crops, people became more vulnerable to fluctuations in market prices and job availability. Drought is a common hazard in Sudan, but the introduction of industrial agriculture reduced the effectiveness of traditional coping mechanisms and resulted in an increase of vulnerability. When the drought began in the early 1980s, traditional methods of coping proved ineffective and nearly 25,000 people were gravely affected (UW-DMC 1997, 35).

3.5   THE SUSTAINABLE DEVELOPMENT FRAMEWORK

In 1987, the United Nation's Commission on Environment and Development met to discuss issues of poverty, population growth, and environmental degradation. The commission, commonly known as the Brundtland Commission (named after the chairwoman, Gro Harlem Brundtland), recognized the importance of integrating economic development with environmental issues. The commission codified a long-standing critique that traditional approaches to development had left an "increasing number of people poor and vulnerable, while at the same time degrading the environment" (Brundtland Commission 1987). (See the Sustainable Development Timeline for the antecedent events and discussions leading up to the commission [Earth Summit 2012].)

The Brundtland Commission emphasized the concept of sustainable development as a way to bridge the gap between economic development and the environment. The commission recognized that development and the environment are tightly linked: Development orientations and practices that erode environmental resources will ultimately undermine and inhibit economic development (Brundtland Commission 1987). The commission defined sustainable development as "development that can meet the needs of the present without compromising the ability of future generations to meet their own needs" (Brundtland Commission 1987). The sustainable development orientation seeks to improve people's quality of life in an equitable way without undermining the environmental resource base. It considers longer-term ramifications of development and practices in such a way that the natural resource base is preserved for future generations. In various ways, practitioners consider environmental, economic, and social factors (Kates, Parris, and Leiserowitz 2005; Kates et al. 2001); see Figure 3.1. The challenge of sustainable development is to understand how these three components, the "sustainability triad," interact and affect one another through development and to consider each in development planning.

3.5.1   ENVIRONMENT

It was felt that the sky was so vast and clear that nothing could ever change its colour, our rivers so big and their water so plentiful that no amount of human activity could ever change their quality, and there were trees and natural forests so plentiful that we will never finish them.... Today we should know better.

—Hon. Victoria Chitepo

Minister of natural resources and tourism, government of Zimbabwe,
on the Industrial Revolution (Brundtland Commission 1987)

The primary foundation for sustainable development is the recognition that human social and economic activities are tightly linked to the environment. Maintaining the "resilience and robustness of biological and physical systems" is a central component of sustainable development (Rogers, Jalal, and Boyd 2008, 23). Current economic practices favor wasteful consumption and production patterns, resulting in loss of environmental diversity and economic production potential. Environmental degradation is occurring on an unprecedented global scale: Deforestation, nonrenewable resource consumption, environmental contamination, and global climate change are just a few of the environmental issues facing us today (Horrigan, Lawrence, and Walker 2002; Raskin et al. 1998; NRDC 2005). While ultimate outcomes are unknowable, a range of dramatic impacts on

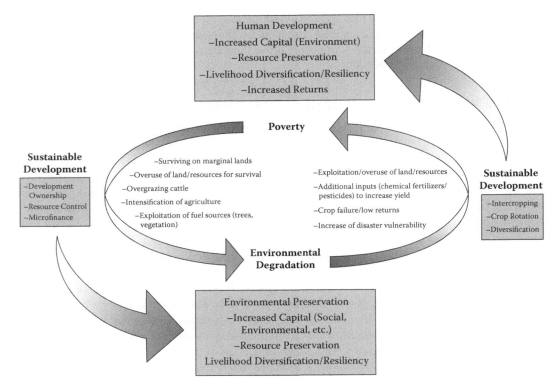

FIGURE 3.1 Relationship of development and sustainable development. (*Source*: John Brett and Kate Oviatt. With permission.)

human populations and global ecosystems is likely if the intimate relationships of environmental, economic, and social well-being are not adequately addressed.

Lasting and stable social and economic development requires reframing the use of environmental resources and services in terms of long-term use versus immediate consumption. Environmental sustainability means that resources are not depleted beyond their ability to regenerate (Brundtland Commission 1987). Diverse biological systems, clean air and water, and productive soil are all limited resources upon which human well-being depends. Environmental, or ecosystem, services are an expanding economic consideration regarding environmental sustainability where natural processes that, in many cases, literally make life possible are attributed an explicit monetary value, examples of which include the production of soil (upon which all agriculture depends), the hydrologic cycle that provides regular supplies of fresh water, and the dilution and breakdown of many toxic substances. In other words, the actual cost of economic and social processes is calculated, seeking to incorporate hidden and intangible costs into economic equations. Efforts to place a value on these ecosystem services have demonstrated that if we had to pay for them, the costs would be astronomical, lending weight to the argument that it is better to preserve the function of these ecosystem services than to have to replace them (Costanza et al. 1997; Keohane and Olmstead 2007). Since Costanza's pioneering work, explorations of the real costs of environmental damage to human health, equity, quality of life, and risk have been developed. (See the excellent collection of approaches in Ingram, DeClerck and Rumbaitis del Rio 2012.)

3.5.2 ECONOMIC FACTORS

The Brundtland definition stresses meeting the needs of the present as an essential element of sustainable development. This involves improving living standards for people throughout the world.

Despite significant improvements in global food production, education, and overall health, populations worldwide still suffer from crushing poverty. Roughly 20% of the world's population (1.3 billion people) lives in extreme poverty, defined by the World Bank as living on US$1.25 or less per day. People experiencing this extreme degree of poverty are chronically malnourished, lack safe drinking water and sanitation, cannot afford education for their children, and lack access to basic health care (Sachs 2005a). An additional 3 billion people, roughly half of the world's population, live in "moderate" poverty, defined as living off a mere US$2 or less per day (Rogers, Jalal, and Boyd 2008).

Under these conditions, basic needs are barely met, and individuals, families, and communities are highly vulnerable. They often live on the most marginal lands, have the most limited access to basic services, and have incomes that are uneven, uncertain, and easily disrupted (Collins et al. 2009). Addressing the income gap is a central social justice component in the sustainable development argument. Additionally, poverty has important implications for environmental resource use. Many people throughout the world live in ecologically fragile environments. Faced with limited economic opportunities, overexploitation of environmental resources is often necessary for basic survival (Rogers, Jalal, and Boyd 2008). Such exploitation of already degraded and at-risk environments keeps populations impoverished through consumption of vital resources needed for basic survival. Poverty and environmental degradation create a complex cycle, making both poverty alleviation and environmental protection difficult. Thus, improving living standards is requisite for successful sustainable development, which can only occur by addressing the availability of essential needs such as food, water, sanitation, health care, and education (World Bank Development Web 2001).

Although it is the cornerstone to SD, the full integration of environmental and economic considerations is extremely challenging. Many argue that economic interests are inherently at odds with environmental interests. Current economic development models are based on assumptions of continuous growth and ever-increasing consumption, largely ignoring environmental limitations (Osorio, Lobato, and del Castillo 2005).

Given that the current economic approaches are not sustainable, how are economic issues to be incorporated into sustainable development? Here it is important to distinguish between economic growth and economic development. Daly (1993, 268) notes: "When something grows it gets bigger. When something develops it transforms into something different. The earth ecosystem develops (evolves), but does not grow.... [T]he economy must eventually stop growing, but can continue to develop." Continual economic growth is an impossibility considering inherent environmental limitations. However, the economy can continue to develop, to change. One of the challenges of sustainable development is to foster this development and change by designing and implementing innovative economic practices that are consistent with environmental and social goals. For example, the concept of "natural capitalism" argues that four interlocking business principles can create financially profitable and ecologically sustainable business:

1. Dramatically increase the productivity of natural resources
2. Shift to biologically inspired production models
3. Move to solutions-based business models
4. Reinvest in natural capital

The authors argue that adopting "some very simple changes to the way we run our businesses can yield startling benefits for today's shareholders and for future generations" (Lovins, Lovins, and Hawken 1999, 146). (See also Hawken, Lovins, and Lovins [1999] for an extended treatment of the concept.)

Sustainable economic practices consider both social and environmental issues. They enhance the welfare of individuals while simultaneously considering environmental resource limitations. Ideally, sustainable economic practices incorporate the regenerative capacity of natural resources and do not use more resources or create more waste than can be renewed or assimilated by the environment (Rogers, Jalal, and Boyd 2008). Pollution can be reduced by producing and selling goods locally. Goods can be produced that are durable, repairable, recyclable, or biodegradable, thus reducing unnecessary waste. Through improvements in technology, efficiency, and resource management, economic practices can be made more sustainable. In addition to environmental concerns, sustainable economic practices consider social ramifications and strive to improve human well-being.

Making business decisions and changes that bring an enterprise in line with available environmental resources must make good "business sense" if it is to succeed in a highly competitive international business climate. While "greening" a business or manufacturing process may be the "right thing to do," few enterprises can justify major capital outlays without concomitant increases in efficiency and capacity. As research and practice advance, the potential for minimizing environmental impacts in the built environment expands dramatically, particularly if incorporating actual (hidden and intangible) costs over time into cost/benefit analyses.

3.5.3 SOCIAL FACTORS

While economic and environmental factors are obvious concerns in any consideration of sustainable development, social conditions are no less important. A population that is inadequately nourished, that does not have access to basic health care and clean water, or that lacks educational resources is constrained in its ability to develop viable livelihoods that would reduce vulnerability to environmental shocks and increase its resilience when confronted with a hazard event. Beyond merely meeting the basic needs of people, many practitioners of sustainable development place significant emphasis on issues of equity, participation, empowerment, and cultural preservation (Kates, Parris, and Leiserowitz 2005). Quality of life requires that more than just basic survival needs be met; people deserve to preserve their cultural identity and be part of the process of their development (Brundtland Commission 1987).

One of the primary social concerns of sustainable development is equity. Equity is considered in terms of both intra- and intergenerational equity. *Intra*generational equity, as indicated by the Brundtland's definition, is "meeting the needs of the present" (Brundtland Commission 1987). As discussed in Section 3.5.2 on economic factors, there exists an enormous gap between the rich and the poor of this world; the basic needs of many people are simply not being met, while others have exorbitant wealth. The global disparities in access to basic services are profound; nearly 1 billion people lack access to clean drinking water; a child in a developing country is over 13 times more likely to die before the age of five than a child in a developed country; malnutrition is rising globally, and now affects nearly 1 billion people (FAO 2008). Addressing such disparities is imperative, as "everyone has the right to a standard of living adequate for health and well-being," including food, clothing, housing, and medical care, according to the United Nations Universal Declaration of Human Rights (UN 2012). Furthermore, as previously discussed, poverty and environmental degradation are often related. Thus, addressing poverty is a requisite part of sustainable development.

Similarly, *inter*generational equity requires that the development of the current generation be practiced in a way that does not compromise "the ability of future generations to meet their own needs" (Brundtland Commission 1987). This concept is founded on the belief that current populations have an obligation to maintain the well-being of the environment for future generations. Our actions today should not negatively influence the welfare of future generations. Thus, preserving environmental resources is of chief importance for intergenerational equity. "[E]nvironmental quality is not something that can be swapped for other goods without a loss of welfare" (Beder 2000). Meeting the needs of both the present generations and those to come is fundamental to sustainable development.

Gender and gender equity have long been recognized as central components in any consideration of sustainable development, beginning with explicit statements in the Brundtland report and reinforced in each of the subsequent efforts. The importance of gender and gender relations lies in the fact that men and women have different relationships to livelihoods, the environment, and the economy. Women in most societies have primary responsibility for the household and are generally the most direct link between the household and the broader environment, whether in rural or urban areas; limits on access to water, education, health care, and food often fall heaviest on women and children. A failure to examine and understand these relationships necessarily means a failure to involve the majority of the population in development efforts (women and children). While a major focus on women and sustainable development has been central to discussions of sustainable development for decades and much has been accomplished, much more remains (Dankelman 2004).

3.5.4 Post-Brundtland

Since the Brundtland Commission in 1987, sustainable development has emerged as a widely held paradigm shift and is a major concern of nongovernmental organizations (NGOs), development organizations, governments, and communities throughout the world. In the years since the Brundtland Commission, the core concepts of sustainable development have remained relatively unchanged, but significant effort has been devoted to identifying specific meanings and mechanisms for implementation at local, regional, and global levels.

In 1992, people from 178 countries gathered in Rio de Janeiro, Brazil, for the United Nations Conference on Environment and Development (UNCED). Also known as the Earth Summit, this conference was hailed as the largest international conference ever held (Reid 1995). The focus of the Earth Summit was to develop agreements and plans on addressing issues such as climate change and conservation of biodiversity. One of the central documents to emerge from the Rio conference was Agenda 21 (UN 2005a). Basically a plan of action for sustainable development, Agenda 21 develops four primary points: social and economic development, conservation and management of resources for development, strengthening the roles of major groups involved in sustainable development, and the means of implementation (Reid 1995). It discusses specific actions for implementing the sustainable use of natural resources and provides concrete measures for confronting poverty, population growth, and destructive environmental practices (Sitarz 1993) and so has become one of the leading documents regarding sustainable development.

Ten years after the Earth Summit in Rio, world leaders and NGOs met again for the World Summit on Sustainable Development in Johannesburg, South Africa, to discuss both the successes and failures since Rio, and to refine and redefine plans of action. During this conference, commonly called the Johannesburg Summit, a new document called the Plan of Implementation was written that provided specific commitments regarding issues such as water, sanitation, energy, health, agriculture, and biodiversity (Middleton and O'Keefe 2003; UN 2005b). Although frustration surrounded the lack of progress since Rio, the Johannesburg Summit reaffirmed the principles of the original Earth Summit and supported the further implementation of Agenda 21 (UN 2002).

In 2000, world leaders met at the United Nations Millennium Summit and defined the Millennium Development Goals (MDGs). The underlying rationale of the MDGs was to provide an agreed-upon blueprint on how to proceed in addressing the needs of the world's poorest populations (UN 2010). This broad consensus was made concrete through the UN Millennium Project, published in 2005 (Sachs 2005b), which took the broad framework and broke it into operational goals and recommendations around which specific plans and targets could be built. The first seven goals aim at a monumental decrease in poverty, disease, and environmental degradation, all of which contribute to disaster vulnerability, while simultaneously calling for significant improvements in education and gender equality by the year 2015. The eighth goal is significant in that it requires a partnership between developed and developing nations and demands commitment from developed nations to assist developing countries in their struggles (Sachs 2005a). Through goal 7 (ensure environmental sustainability), target 9 of the UN Millennium Project, sustainable development, is linked directly with the other goals and targets by "[i]ntegrat[ing] the principles of sustainable development into country policies and programs and revers[ing] the loss of environmental resources" (Sachs 2005b). While the emphasis of the MDGs is on meeting the basic needs of the world's poorest and not solely on sustainable development, addressing such needs is essential in any sustainable development effort: A healthy and educated population will be more productive and more able to invest in environmental considerations.

In 2012, during the 20th anniversary of the Earth Summit, the world revisited the lofty goals of 1992 at what was called Rio+20, or the Earth Summit 2012. The objectives of the summit were

> to secure renewed political commitment to sustainable development; to assess progress towards internationally agreed goals on sustainable development and to address new and emerging challenges. The Summit . . . also focus[ed] on two specific themes: a green economy in the context of poverty eradication and sustainable development, and an institutional framework for sustainable development. (Earth Summit 2012)

A brief history of important events in and around sustainable development can be found in the Sustainable Development Timeline (IISD 2012), and primary events and accomplishments over time can be found at the UN Rio+20 website (UNCSD 2012).

3.5.5   The Promise, Shortcomings, and Limitations of Sustainable Development

The integration of the social, economic, and environmental factors is what differentiates sustainable development from previous development approaches. Common development practices have focused primarily on economic development, assuming that social and environmental problems would be addressed when a certain level of economic development has been reached. Furthermore, as identified by the Brundtland Commission and subsequent research and practice, the processes of economic development often have negative social and environmental effects. In contrast, sustainable development seeks to maximize economic gains in relation to social and environmental concerns. Sustainable approaches seek to synthesize the three areas and find solutions that are environmentally, economically, and socially viable.

Although it is the most cited and widely known definition of sustainable development, the Brundtland Commission definition has shortcomings. A primary criticism of this definition is its ambiguity, only partially addressed in subsequent efforts. How does sustainable development actually integrate development and the environment? Critics claim that such vagueness enables current consumption-oriented development, which is inherently at odds with environmental protection, to continue under the guise of sustainability (Jabareen 2008; Osorio, Lobato, and del Castillo 2005). Furthermore, the vague use of the word *needs* is problematic. What are needs? Are needs merely basic food, water, and shelter, the things indispensable for survival? What about education, health care, cultural identity, security, and quality of life? Are these needs or wants? Moreover, who gets to define needs? Another criticism of sustainable development is that it is a Western approach, and that it is Westerners who define and guide the process (Osorio, Lobato, and del Castillo 2005). These issues have been partly addressed through the Millennium Development Goals process because it sets explicit goals and targets and defined processes on how to achieve them.

3.6   SUSTAINABLE LIVELIHOODS APPROACH

The sustainable livelihoods approach (SLA) and related variations offer comprehensive and practical frameworks that integrate sustainability with development at the local level and address some of the limitations inherent in global definitions and approaches advocated by the Brundtland Commission and the Rio and Johannesburg summits (DFID 1999; Ashley and Carney 2002; Frankenberger et al. 2002; Witteveen and Ruedin 2008). Its primary goal is poverty reduction, which is tackled through regional, people-centered, and participatory means. A livelihood is defined as "the capabilities, assets (both material and social), and activities required for a means of living," and is considered sustainable when "it can cope with and recover from stresses and shocks and maintain or enhance its capabilities and assets both now and in the future without undermining the natural resource base" (DFID 1999). More concrete and process-oriented than the generally abstract definitions of sustainable development, the SLA explicitly accepts the triad of social, economic, and environment

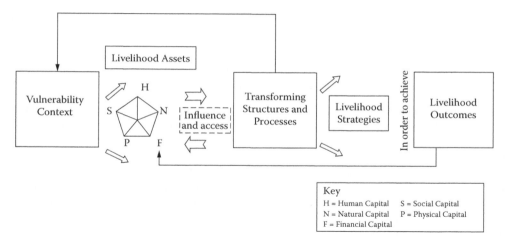

FIGURE 3.2   Sustainable livelihoods. (*Source*: DFID [1999]. With permission.)

factors, but it places people and their livelihoods as the essential outcomes of development processes. It recognizes that the need for a secure and sustainable livelihood is a central priority for most individuals and anchors development projects in the day-to-day reality of local populations and their environmental context (Carney 2002).

The "translation" of the sustainability triad developed through the Brundtland Commission Report in the sustainable livelihoods approach is achieved through an exploration of five primary assets to which people have access (Figure 3.2). Through the planning process, these assets are evaluated and developed to reduce vulnerability and increase livelihood security. These assets are defined as different kinds of "capital": human, social, physical, financial, and natural (DFID 1999). Similar to the triad concept of sustainable development, these capitals represent the environmental, economic, and social factors that affect people's livelihood security.

3.6.1   SUSTAINABLE LIVELIHOODS APPROACH ASSETS DEFINED

Much less ambiguous than the definition of sustainable development, the SLA clearly identifies its main objective as poverty reduction. As SLA is necessarily local, or at most regional, it is important to acknowledge that it does not replace broader-scale planning efforts that are likely more quantitative and macro level (e.g., Estrategia 2009). Furthermore, by placing people at the center of development, the sustainable livelihoods approach focuses on understanding what most directly impacts local populations. When the needs, perspectives, and strengths of local communities are understood and given priority, poverty-reduction initiatives become more compatible with local strategies and will be more effective (DFID 1999). Participatory approaches identify local priorities and strategies, putting control of development into the hands of the people, rather than outsiders. The types of capital are defined as:

- *Human capital*: The skills, knowledge, ability to labor, and good health that enable people to achieve their livelihood objectives
- *Social capital*: The social networks, group membership, and relationships upon which people can draw
- *Physical capital*: The basic infrastructure needed to support a viable livelihood, including affordable transportation, adequate shelter, clean water supply, and adequate sanitation
- *Financial capital*: The financial resources people can access, including cash, livestock, income, pensions, and remittances

- *Natural capital*: The natural resource base from which people derive their livelihoods, and which provides basic environmental services such as water and air purification, erosion protection, and hazard defense (DFID 1999)

3.6.2 SUSTAINABLE LIVELIHOODS AND VULNERABILITY

SLA integrated with the vulnerability paradigm provides a comprehensive process for reducing vulnerability and ultimately decreasing loss. Where the "vulnerability approach" drives the orientation of this volume, we are talking in this chapter about what could be called a "resiliency approach" (Folke et al. 2002; Folke 2006; Rose 2011). The vulnerability approach acknowledges that political-economic, historic, and social factors make certain individuals, populations, or segments of populations more vulnerable to hazard events; these subpopulations then disproportionately suffer the consequences of disasters. In current thinking, taking all groups of people into account is necessary for disaster loss reduction. Thus, considering vulnerability and hazard risk in the context of sustainable livelihoods development projects offers a greater opportunity to tackle the difficult challenges of broader social, political-economic, and historical forces. A failure to acknowledge these factors at the local level during a planning effort potentially misses important opportunities for change, decreases the impact of specific interventions, or puts entire projects at risk. Additionally, there may be opportunities to reduce vulnerability and enhance resiliency at the macro level if attention is paid to the possibility during the planning process.

Instead of just acknowledging "root causes," a SLA along with community vulnerability assessment (CVA) can truly attend to root causes by enhancing livelihoods, reducing vulnerability, and increasing resiliency. "Of particular importance is the idea of a 'chain of causation' that goes from 'root causes' through 'dynamic pressures' in the production of 'unsafe conditions'" (Blaikie et al. 1994; Wisner, Blaikie, and Cannon 2004). This "chain of causation" analysis is similar to the modeling proposed in sustainable livelihood approaches, and so could be easily adapted to consider livelihoods as a component of this chain of causation analysis. (For more on a similar approach, see Kohler, Jülich, and Bloemertz [2004].) Instead of simply asking, "What can be done?" in the context of reducing vulnerability to a particular hazard or set of hazards, through the SLA we can directly ask, "What can be done?" in the context of sustainable development efforts to address the kinds of factors that put populations, or segments of populations, at greater risk in the first place. If embedded within comprehensive planning and the systems theory modeling (see Chapter 2) that underlies both emerging disaster planning approaches and the sustainable livelihoods approach (Norberg and Cumming 2008; Waltner-Toews, Kay, and Lister 2008), it could be possible to address both issues at once, realizing benefits for livelihoods as well as vulnerability reduction. Increasing livelihood options should lead to reduced vulnerability and enhanced resiliency because populations with a broader base of opportunities are generally less exposed to hazard events and have more resources upon which to draw following a hazard event. On the other hand, working to reduce vulnerability should enhance livelihood opportunities because such measures should create a framework or context of lowered risk in which a greater diversity of livelihood options can be developed.

The central connection between SLA and CVA is the factors that make households, segments of populations, or regions vulnerable to income shocks (threats to livelihoods), which are strikingly similar to those that place them at greater risk to natural hazard events. It is the constellation of natural, socioeconomic, and political forces that limits livelihoods, thus decreasing resilience while increasing vulnerability. (See Chapter 16, Section 16.5.3, for a further discussion of SLA and vulnerability assessment.)

3.7 SUSTAINABILITY AND RESILIENCY

Recognizing that it is often inappropriate, inadequate, or misguided development activities that increase vulnerability to disasters, much can be gained by incorporating risk and disaster

FIGURE 3.3 Relationship of vulnerability, resilience, and sustainability. (*Source*: Kate Oviatt and John Brett. With permission.)

considerations into comprehensive development planning. The relationships between development and hazards can help identify possible interactions among development plans and existing risks and vulnerabilities. Sustainable development is increasingly recognized as an important perspective in disaster research and planning (Birkman 2006; UNISDR 2004; Mileti 1999; Schneider 2002). As opposed to traditional development, the more holistic framework of sustainable development considers the relationship between environmental, economic, and social issues. By understanding these relationships and by identifying the best use of available connections, sustainability can contribute to a reduction of disaster vulnerability (UNISDR 2004).

This section utilizes one model of resiliency and vulnerability where they are considered as opposite poles of a spectrum with an inverse relationship (Folke et al. 2002). Sustainable development acts as the "slider" or the motive force that moves a population from more vulnerable to more resilient (Figure 3.3). As in the SLA, sustainable development and vulnerability reduction do not have particular end points; rather, they are processes over time that enhance resiliency and reduce vulnerability. While this is conceptually obvious, in practice it is, of course, much more complex.

Environmental degradation can significantly influence disaster vulnerability because a severely altered environment is generally much less able to absorb the impact of a hazard event and is therefore more susceptible to disasters. The short-term, one-way use of natural resources characteristic of much market-oriented development frequently exacerbates risk and heightens vulnerabilities. A central tenet of sustainable development holds that development initiatives must operate within environmental limits. This ensures that resources are not used beyond their capacity to regenerate, thus providing longer-term economic benefits, and maintaining hazard protections and buffering capacities that come from an intact natural environment. Sustainable use of natural resources "will increase the resilience of communities to disasters by reversing current trends of environmental degradation" (UNISDR 2003, 9).

In much of the developing world, careful consideration of land-use strategies is especially important in sustainable development to help lower disaster vulnerability. For example, the growing demand for food, timber, and other resources has placed increased pressure on the Earth's ecosystems; land that has been overworked, through intensive agriculture, deforestation, and other forms of resource exploitation is more prone to erosion, desertification, and landslides (FAO 2012; Raskin et al. 1998). The central consideration in sustainable development is maximization of social and economic output while minimizing negative environmental consequences that increase vulnerability over the long term. This holistic approach requires a change in focus for planning. There can be, for example, little argument that agricultural intensification is inevitable given population increases and rising incomes internationally (wealthier people consume more food resources than poorer ones).

Conventional agricultural intensification considers available markets, necessary agricultural inputs, highest producing varieties, land ownership that inhibits intensification, and related factors with the aim of maximum return relative to inputs. The focus is nearly always on near-term benefits of increased production and income, generally at the expense of environmental well-being. The wider perspective of sustainable development considers all of these same factors but in the context of social and environmental outcomes with the aim of long-term benefits across the economic, social, and environmental spectrum. SD does not preclude using particular agricultural methods of intensification (e.g., improved seed varieties, fertilizers, tractors, etc.); rather, what it does is weigh those against the desired longer-term outcomes. In terms of lowering disaster vulnerability, because sustainable development places increased value on long-term environmental outcomes, agricultural practices would more likely focus on maintaining a healthy agro-ecological system, making it more resilient in the face of natural hazards.

While the consequences of ecological practices are perhaps the easiest to see, social and economic aspects of development play an equally important role in increasing resiliency. Economic practices that encourage environmental and social welfare can potentially increase disaster resiliency by creating more diverse opportunities for populations in disaster-prone regions. For example, the practice of mixed cropping not only has environmental benefits, but it can also enhance household income security in at least two ways: First, it decreases household agricultural expenses by reducing the need for expensive chemical pesticides and fertilizers, enabling farmers to grow more of their own food as part of an integrated, mixed-use agro-ecological system. Second, growing multiple crops helps protect against major losses due to fluctuations in international market prices (Horrigan, Lawrence, and Walker 2002; Twigg 2004). If the market value of one crop (e.g., coffee, cacao) decreases, farmers who practice monocropping will experience more severe economic losses than those who rely on a mixture of crops. Increased household livelihood security can make a family more resilient in the face of a disaster.

Similarly, fair-trade practices can also enhance resiliency through income augmentation by offering prices that more accurately reflect the underlying labor inputs. Offering prices above minimum market rates seeks to provide opportunities not otherwise available (UNDP 2004; Ruben 2008). Despite market fluctuations in the value of agricultural products, primary producers receive a superior price. Access to increased and more stable income can help increase disaster resiliency. Fair-trade efforts also often try to identify value-added processes that can further increase local income (e.g., selling processed cacao paste versus the raw beans). Beyond economic benefits, fair trade promotes "collaborative decision-making and the setting aside of resources [for] enhancing social development or ecological protection" (UNDP 2004, 68). Such broad-based empowerment can increase the ability to withstand and respond to disasters.

Education is also a key element in sustainable development and is especially important for enhancing resiliency. An educated population has a wider range of income-generating options and a wider exposure to the world outside their home community. They are often better able to understand the risks and vulnerabilities they face and identify options for addressing them. Engagement through community participation has become a focus for sustainable development, and this is increasingly being recognized as an important element for vulnerability reduction (Twigg 2004).

Implicit in these discussions is the third, arguably most complex piece of sustainable development: the social. When addressing the social third of the sustainability triad, difficult issues must be addressed: social justice, inequity, and inequality. While there are a variety of perspectives, none has been more influential than the work of Sen (1999), who writes broadly of "freedoms" and "capabilities," meaning that development cannot be just about infrastructure and material wealth. Rather, he argues that "development," if it is to be socially just and inclusive (versus simply raising the GDP), must enhance the population's freedoms and capabilities. His arguments are too complex to take up here, but his writings underlie much of the Millennium Development Project and have been highly influential in the crafting of the United Nations Development Program annual reports and the Human Development Index (UNDP 2011b). (For a thorough review of Sen's arguments in development broadly and sustainable development in particular, see the UNDP Human Development Reports for 2010 and 2011 [UNDP 2010, 2011a].)

Planning for both development and disasters has traditionally been a top-down approach, generally lacking locally relevant information about the context as residents understand it. Community-based planning efforts are increasingly being utilized as a way to gain a thorough and more accurate understanding of the situation at the local level. Local talent, knowledge, abilities, and resources are used, and communities become empowered participants rather than passive recipients of development (UW-DMC 1997). A more educated and empowered population may become less vulnerable and will likely be able to cope with a disaster more effectively. Thus, education, engagement, and empowerment become important elements for sustainable development and increased disaster resiliency.

3.8 SUSTAINABILITY AND EMERGENCY MANAGEMENT: A U.S. PERSPECTIVE

While bringing together the different pieces of sustainability can be challenging, it is an important part of addressing vulnerability and increasing resiliency. Traditional disaster management in the United States has taken a very narrow approach to addressing the threat of hazards, focusing on hazard preparedness/response and technological fixes (Mileti and Gailus 2005; Britton 2001; Schneider 2002). Such an approach is inadequate for addressing the root causes of disaster vulnerability: social and political-economic systems that create conditions of environmental degradation and social marginalization. Effective disaster risk reduction requires addressing these root causes so that environmental and social well-being are strengthened and are capable of mitigating the effects of hazardous events. It also requires that issues of disaster management be integrated into related fields, such as community planning, development, and land-use management so that it is part of planning and development programs rather than a separate, independent field (Schneider 2002). The integration of sustainability and disaster management into the processes of development will more effectively address issues of vulnerability and resiliency than would traditional approaches alone.

How can issues of sustainability and disaster management be translated from a conceptual level into an effective on-the-ground implementation strategy? While the basic importance and tenets of sustainability are the same in both the United States and abroad, the process of implementation may vary in these different contexts. Internationally, especially in developing nations, the SLA framework presented in Section 3.6 works well as a model for integrating sustainability and disaster management into the process of development. However, because SLA is designed *for development* and is explicitly aimed at poverty reduction, it may not be entirely appropriate in the U.S. context. While issues of poverty and economic development remain salient in the United States, the country's issues and processes differ significantly from those in developing nations. In the United States, community planning, rather than development, is the primary area within which communities can facilitate change toward sustainability and disaster mitigation (Britton 2001; Schneider 2002).

Community planning is a key area for initiating change in the local context. In terms of sustainable development, many cities throughout the United States are working to integrate the environmental, social, and economic principles into their city plans. Two cities leading the way are Portland, Oregon, and New York; both have made significant efforts to establish sustainability as an essential part of the planning process, going so far as creating departments dedicated to sustainability (Saha and Paterson 2008). Portland's efforts focus on reducing climate emissions, reducing waste, encouraging local food production/consumption, green energy, and green building (City of Portland 2012). New York's approach is more inclusive, with 17 different areas of interest, including everything from climate change and clean energy to parks and housing opportunities (City of New York 2012). New York has also developed a set of sustainability indicators, allowing the city to track its progress toward its goals. Indicators include the per capita water consumption, the average vehicle miles traveled per resident, the availability of affordable housing, and residents' access to parks and public space. Both cities use the three principles of sustainability (environmental, social, and economic) to inform what they include in the planning process and how they define and measure success. While the efforts of Portland and New York do not explicitly focus on disaster mitigation, their work to increase the general well-being of both their city's environment and their residents helps to decrease the cities' overall vulnerability.

To address this issue of the lack of integration of disaster management with community planning and sustainability, Mileti (1999), in his monumental work on hazards in the United States, identifies a number of objectives that communities can use to guide local planning efforts (Table 3.1). These objectives provide community planners with factors to consider in disaster management planning

TABLE 3.1

Objectives for Local Sustainability

Maintain and Enhance Environmental Quality

Human activities to mitigate hazards should not reduce the carrying capacity of ecosystems, in recognition that to do so will increase long-term losses from hazards.

Hazard mitigation activities should link efforts to control and ultimately reverse environmental degradation by coupling hazard reduction to natural resource management and environmental preservation.

Maintain and Enhance People's Quality of Life

A population's quality of life includes, among other factors, access to income, education, health care, housing, and employment, as well as protection from disaster.

Local communities must consciously define the quality of life they want and select only those mitigation strategies that do not detract from any aspect of that vision of sustainability.

Foster Local Resiliency and Responsibility

Resiliency to disasters means taking mitigation actions such that a locale can withstand an extreme natural event with a tolerable level of losses.

Recognize that Vibrant Local Economies Are Essential

Take mitigation actions that foster a strong local economy rather than detract from one.

A diversified local economy, not overly dependent on a single productive force, would be more sustainable over the long term and less easily disrupted by disasters.

Ensure Inter- and Intragenerational Equity

Select mitigation activities that reduce hazards across all ethnic, racial, and income groups—and between genders— equally to avoid shifting the costs of today's advances onto later generations or less powerful groups.

Adopt Local Consensus Building

Demonstrate sustainability by selecting mitigation strategies that evolve from full participation among all public and private stakeholders.

The participatory process itself may be as important as the outcome.

Source: Adapted from Mileti and Gailus (2005).

---

in light of the environmental, economic, and social principles of sustainable development. These objectives reflect many of the same concerns as the SLA but adapt them to the context of planning in the United States.

Mileti (1999) and others (Schneider 2002; Britton 2001; Burby 1998) argue that these objectives should be part of a community's planning process to ensure sustainability within the community and to integrate disaster management into all phases of planning. Furthermore, the emphasis these objectives place on local participation and engagement is key for successful disaster management; studies have shown that both pre- and postdisaster mitigation efforts have been more successful when community groups/nonprofits and regional organizations are involved (Smith 2011; Welsh and Esnard 2009; Dyer 1999). These objectives are helpful in that they provide communities with a more tangible understanding of what the integration of sustainability and disaster management actually looks like in terms of community planning.

3.9 SUSTAINABLE DEVELOPMENT AND VULNERABILITY: THE CASE OF MONDAÑA, ECUADOR, AND TRIFINIO, GUATEMALA

Many of the abstract concepts discussed previously can be illustrated through contrasting case examples using findings from research conducted by this chapter's authors between 2006 and

2010 in a lowland tropical region of northern Ecuador around the rural town of Mondaña on the Napo River, roughly 70 km south of the Colombian border, and in northwestern Guatemala, where research began in 2011 and is ongoing. The Ecuador research focused on sustainable development and health, conducted in the context of a multiyear field school through the Departments of Anthropology and Health and Behavioral Sciences, University of Colorado Denver (UCD), while the Guatemala research is part of a long-term development project in part sponsored by the Center for Global Health at UCD.

3.9.1 Trifinio, Guatemala

The Trifinio region in northwest Guatemala, where lowland tropical rainforest was once dominant, is now banana, oil palm, and sugar cane plantations from horizon to horizon. Nearly everyone in the region in-migrated from elsewhere and is in some way connected to plantation agriculture, the majority as poorly educated, low-wage laborers on the plantations and small business owners in town. Most live in small towns or hamlets tucked in among plantations, but not on plantation land, connected by poorly built and maintained roads with few services (e.g., health clinics, police protection). Only one of the towns has a functioning central water supply with water drawn from a deep, sealed well (and therefore largely potable), with the vast majority relying on open, shallow, hand-dug wells in individual house yards. None of the towns has sewage disposal beyond household latrines. The inevitable result is contamination of the water supply when the frequent floods cause latrines to overflow into shallow wells. This in turn results in high rates of serious gastrointestinal illness, especially in young children, which, along with other causes, results in an extraordinarily high death rate for those under five years old. As a lowland, flat tropical area with relatively impervious soils that receives very high rainfall, flooding is common, washing out roads, flooding most homes to a depth of 2-4 feet, contaminating the water supply, destroying small-holder agriculture, and disrupting daily activities. While a number of NGOs have established concrete refuges on higher ground (that are supposed to be stocked with basic survival supplies), there has been no comprehensive development or disaster planning. The population is basically on its own; disaster planning assessed as part of a livelihoods approach to development in the region could realize major benefits.

3.9.2 Mondaña, Ecuador

Mondaña, like much of tropical America, is characterized by poverty and relative lack of opportunity. The Napo River basin is one of the primary oil-producing regions in Ecuador, providing limited opportunities to local populations for unskilled labor jobs. The majority of the population relies on agriculture, working as laborers on large farms or producing subsistence crops as well as cacao and coffee for sale in international markets. Prices and production for coffee and cacao fluctuate annually, sometimes dramatically resulting in uneven income and uncertainty.

Tropical soils typically have low levels of nutrients and so tend to be relatively unproductive over the long term or require intensive and expensive agricultural inputs (fertilizer, pesticides) to maintain the production cycle. Most people in the area live on 5-hectare plots granted to them by the government beginning in the 1970s. Five hectares was deemed adequate for subsistence and cash-crop production, with an initial emphasis on coffee. Coffee prices were initially maintained at relatively high levels through international price agreements, which ended in the early 1990s, drastically reducing cash income and imperiling already fragile livelihoods. As prices fell, people planted more and more coffee in an effort to maintain income, often resulting in less land available for subsistence crops. In consequence, people had to buy more produce and staples from markets, further reducing available cash. People also often turned to wildcat logging, cutting and selling high-value trees from the forest, receiving $10 for logs with a value of thousands of dollars on the international markets. This damages forest resources, as much of this illegal harvesting is from public lands and is not done with any attention to sustainable harvest.

3.9.2.1 Education and Practice at Colegio Técnico Yachana

One of the central components in sustainable development in the Mondaña region is an innovative educational program being developed by the Yachana Foundation. The Colegio Técnico Yachana (CTY) is a private not-for-profit secondary school dedicated to creating sustainable livelihoods through innovative, quality education that seeks to provide students with a range of skills usable in the regional economy. As a technical school, the curriculum is a mix of academic and practice-based education broadly focused on sustainable agriculture, micro-enterprise, and ecotourism. The goal is to provide students with knowledge and a range of practical and leadership skills that will facilitate their becoming the center of an emerging sustainable economy in the region.

An important aspect of the overall training program at the CTY is the diffusion of what students learn in school throughout the region. The school is residential, meaning students come from a wide area. One of their requirements when they are visiting their home communities is to create demonstration agricultural projects to diffuse knowledge across the region.

3.9.2.2 Sustainable Agriculture

A major effort on the part of CTY faculty and students is the development and testing of a sustainable agriculture system for the region. The sustainable agriculture effort has three major goals:

1. Produce food for students and teachers at the CTY
2. Produce food products for sale in the local markets and to the nearby Yachana Lodge
3. Serve as a testing and demonstration project on what is possible in the region

Collectively, these goals are designed to enhance agricultural and livelihood sustainability, thereby reducing vulnerability to economic shocks and environmental hazards. Practices put into place and the resulting findings include using a mixed cropping approach (Photo 3.1), which takes advantage of different plant habits, allowing more production in the same area for roughly the same amount of work. Because different crops mature at different times, it is possible, for example, to plant corn (maize), manioc (cassava), and bananas/plantains, which begin yielding at about 4 months (corn), continuing with manioc at about 9 months (continuing for up to 6 months), followed by plantain, which matures in 18 months and continues for several years.

Using a system of crop rotation allows repeated harvests from the same land before requiring a fallow (rest) period. Most tropical soils require a fallow period every few years, which allows them to recover soil nutrients lost to crop growth, but if crops are carefully rotated through fields, soil fertility can be maintained for longer periods. Crops that use large quantities of nitrogen can be rotated with crops that use more potassium and crops that replace soil nitrogen (legumes). Tropical soils do not contain many nutrients and generally have a very poor structure. In order to maintain fertility and improve structure for gardening and agriculture, organic matter through composting can be highly beneficial (Photo 3.2). The CTY has created a composting operation that uses all of the organic material produced by the kitchens at the lodge and at the school. This compost is added to raised beds created for intensive vegetable production. Intensive production of vegetables through raised beds can yield large quantities of fresh produce, reducing the amount of imported fresh vegetables local populations need to buy and with the potential of producing surpluses for sale. As of 2010, the agricultural system was producing all of the plantains and manioc needed for the school and lodge, with some left over to sell into the local market, about half the chickens and eggs, all of the fish (tilapia), and with the potential to produce most of their fresh vegetables.

A very important aspect of reducing vulnerability to natural hazards is planting according to the landscape. Local knowledge of soils, flood conditions, and wet and dry seasons are well established and can be used to reduce vulnerability. A 10-meter buffer of trees near the river slows annual flood waters, reducing bank erosion while allowing the accumulation of high-quality soil over fields next to the river. Planting of certain tree crops like cacao that are tolerant of the annual flooding near the

PHOTO 3.1 Sustainable practices: mixed planting of plantains, cassava, and maize in Mondaña, Ecuador. (Photo by John Brett. With permission.)

PHOTO 3.2 Sustainable practices: composting in Mondaña, Ecuador. (Photo by John Brett. With permission.)

river allows for production in an area otherwise at risk from flooding hazard. While flooding can be damaging to crops and farmsteads near the river, it also brings important nutrients to area soils. The intercropping of annual crops (e.g., pineapple, maize) between flood-tolerant tree crops in riverside fields during the drier parts of the year takes advantage of annual soil renewal and increases production on specific plots of land.

Tree crops (cacao, coffee) are planted to mimic the multiple layers of tropical forest structure, with an understory of shade-tolerant commercial crops (e.g., ginger), with the coffee or cacao as the middle layer and an overstory to provide shade (the highest quality coffee and cacao are shade grown), restore soil nutrients, and provide fruit. If the overstory trees are leguminous, they add nitrogen to the soil, reducing the need for fertilizer. The use of a variety of plants in the same area reduces insect damage and disease incidence because plant diversity creates a less ideal environment for insect and disease pests. This in turn reduces the need for pesticides, thus reducing costs and potential environmental damages.

Much feed for farm animals is produced locally, reducing the need to spend scarce cash on imported feed. Chickens (for eggs and meat), pigs, and tilapia (a tropical fish well adapted to farm production) can be incorporated into a comprehensive production system. A variety of crops are easily grown that can provide much of the feed for local animals, and animal waste in turn can be incorporated into the composting program.

3.9.2.3 Fair-Trade Cacao Projects

Cacao, the primary raw ingredient for chocolate, is native to tropical South America and so is well adapted to and grows well in these conditions. Among the problems in growing primary agricultural products is that they are subject to tremendous price fluctuations according to world markets. Even under the best of circumstances, the prices paid are generally very low, dramatically limiting income relative to labor input. One of the major international efforts directed toward social and economic sustainability is the fair-trade movement, where producers are paid a higher-than-market price for their agricultural products; consumers accept the additional cost in support of farmers earning a higher wage. Combining fair trade with organic production allows growers to produce a higher quality product and, in many cases, to create value-added products (locally packaged coffee, processed chocolate, etc.) that command higher prices and are less susceptible to price fluctuations on international markets. Beginning in the late 1990s, the U.S.–Ecuadorian nongovernmental organization FUNEDESIN (now the Yachana Foundation) began organizing cacao growers into cooperatives, offering technical assistance to improve quality and yield (improved varieties and production processes). As quality increased and many farms became organic, FUNEDESIN was able to begin a fair-trade program, thus reinforcing the value of producing a superior crop. While their price also fluctuates, it is generally about 15% above international prices, reflecting the higher quality product. It is important to note that these are not subsidies in any sense, but higher prices paid for higher quality products that acknowledge the work and care required to produce quality products.

This package of educational and agricultural activities is beginning to create a more stable, ecologically sound economy in the region, thus reducing vulnerability and enhancing resilience. By developing systems of sustainable agriculture through an innovative education program that takes advantage of tropical conditions while working to accommodate to the limitations inherent in the region: crops will be at less risk from natural events (especially heavy rains and flooding); agriculture outputs will increase in yield and quality; and incomes will rise. Creating a cadre of well-educated young people with job skills applicable to the local economy creates opportunities that reduce the need for young people to migrate to urban areas in search of work. Having a motivated, skilled workforce with training as micro-entrepreneurs, and in ecotourism and sustainable agriculture, has the potential to develop the local economy in ways that single-focus interventions cannot. Similarly, the requirement that students apply what they learn in school in their home communities diffuses the core knowledge throughout the region, thus increasing the impact to a much larger area than the immediate surrounding community.

3.10 SUMMARY

After more than 25 years since the Brundtland Commission published its report, nearly half of humanity lives in significant poverty (<US$2 per day); the global population is at 7 billion and growing; and environmental emergencies range from tropical forest destruction and air pollution to worldwide climate change (Rogers, Jalal, and Boyd 2008; UNFPA 2011). In this context, disasters appear ever more devastating, with damage and death largely attributable to factors related to social vulnerability and lack of resiliency, rather than an increase in hazard events. In the face of these seemingly insurmountable challenges, the necessity for merging sustainable practices with vulnerability reduction efforts is arguably more important than ever.

DISCUSSION QUESTIONS

1. What is the sustainability triad and why is it so difficult to achieve?
2. Choosing specific cases for analysis, discuss how sustainable development interrelates with vulnerability.
3. What is the sustainable livelihoods approach? How does it interact with the vulnerability paradigm?
4. How might attending to root causes reduce vulnerability to disasters?

REFERENCES

Ashley, C., and D. Carney. 1999. Sustainable livelihoods: Lessons from early experience. UK Department for International Development, London.

Beder, S. 2000. Costing the earth: Equity, sustainable development and environmental economics. *New Zealand Journal of Environmental Law* 4:227–43.

Birkmann, J., ed. 2006. *Measuring vulnerability to natural hazards: Toward disaster resilient societies.* New York: United Nationals University Press.

Blaikie, P., T. Cannon, I. Davis, and B. Wisner. 1994. *At risk: Natural hazards, people's vulnerability and disasters.* London: Routledge.

Britton, N. 2001. A new emergency management for the new millennium? *Australian Journal of Emergency Management* 16 (4): 44–54.

Brundtland Commission (World Commission on Environment and Development). 1987. *Our common future.* New York: Oxford University Press.

Burby, R. 1998. *Cooperating with nature: Confronting natural hazards with land use planning for sustainable communities.* Washington, DC: Joseph Henry Press.

Cannon, T., J. Twigg, and J. Rowell. 2003. Social vulnerability, sustainable livelihoods and disasters. Report to DFID (Department for International Development), London. http://www.eldis.org/assets/Docs/21628.html.

Carney, D. 2002. Sustainable livelihood approaches: Progress and possibilities for change. UK Department for International Development, London.

Chambers, R., and G. Conway. 1992. *Sustainable rural livelihoods: Practical concepts for the 21st century.* Brighton, UK: Institute of Development Studies.

City of New York. 2012. Plan NYC. http://www.nyc.gov/html/planyc2030/html/home/home.shtml.

City of Portland. 2012. Bureau of Planning and Sustainability. http://www.portlandonline.com/bps/index.cfm?c=28534.

Collins, D., J. Morduch, S. Rutherford, and O. Ruthven. 2009. *Portfolios of the poor: How the world's poor live on $2 a day.* Princeton, NJ: Princeton University Press.

Costanza, R., R. d'Arge, R. de Groot, S. Farber, M. Grasso, B. Hannon, K. Limburg, et al. 1997. The value of the world's ecosystem services and natural capital. *Nature* 387 (15): 253–60.

Daly, H. E. 1993. Sustainable growth: An impossibility theorem. In *Valuing the Earth: Economics, ecology, ethics,* ed. H. E. Daly and K. N. Townsend, 267–73. Cambridge, MA: MIT Press.

Dankelman, I. 2004. *Women and the environment.* United Nations Environment Program, Policy Series.

DFID (Department for International Development). 1999. Sustainable livelihoods guidance sheets. Department for International Development, London.

Dyer, C. 1999. The Phoenix Effect in post-disaster recovery: An analysis of the Economic Development Administration's culture of response after Hurricane Andrew. In *The angry Earth: Disaster in anthropological perspective*, ed. A. Oliver-Smith and S. Hoffman. New York: Routledge.

Earth Summit. 2012. Sustainable development timeline. http://earthsummit2012.org/about-us/sd-timeline.

Estrategia (Estrategia Andina para la Prevención y Atención de Desastres). 2009. Decisión número 713 del Consejo Andino de Ministros de Relaciones Exteriores. http://www.caprade.org/doc_estrat/eapad_esping.pdf.

FAO (Food and Agriculture Organization). 2008. Hunger on the rise. http://www.fao.org/newsroom/en/news/2008/1000923/index.html.

———. 2012. Land resources. http://www.fao.org/nr/land/degradation/en/.

Folke, C. 2006. Resilience: The emergence of a perspective for social-ecological systems analyses. *Global Environmental Change* 16 (3): 253–67.

Folke, C., S. Carpenter, T. Elmqvist, L. Gunderson, C. S. Holling, B. Walker, J. Bengtsson, et al. 2002. Resilience and sustainable development: Building adaptive capacity in a world of transformations. Paper prepared for the process of the World Summit on sustainable development on behalf of the Environmental Advisory Council to the Swedish Government. http://www.resalliance.org/files/1144440669_resilience_and_sustainable_development.pdf.

Frankenberger, T., K. Luther, J. Becht, and M. K. McCaston. 2002. *Household livelihood security assessments: A toolkit for practitioners.* Atlanta: CARE USA.

Hawken, P., A. B. Lovins, and L. H. Lovins. 1999. *Natural capitalism: Creating the next industrial revolution.* Boston: Little-Brown.

Horrigan, L., R. S. Lawrence, and P. Walker. 2002. How sustainable agriculture can address the environmental and human health harms of industrial agriculture. *Environmental Health Perspectives* 110 (5): 445–56.

IISD (International Institute for Sustainable Development). 2012. Sustainable development timeline 2012. http://www.iisd.org/pdf/2012/sd_timeline_2012.pdf.

Ingram, J. C., F. DeClerck, and C. Rumbaitis del Rio, eds. 2012. *Integrating ecology and poverty reduction: Ecological dimensions.* New York: Springer.

Jabareen, Y. 2008. A new conceptual framework for sustainable development. *Environment, Development, and Sustainability* 10:179–92.

Kates, R. W., W. C. Clark, R. Corell, J. M. Hall, C. C. Jaeger, I. Lowe, J. J. McCarthy, et al. 2001. Environment and development: Sustainability science. *Science* 292 (5517): 641–42.

Kates, R., T. M. Parris, and A. A. Leiserowitz. 2005. What is sustainable development? Goals, indicators, values, and practice. *Environment* 47 (3): 8–21.

Keohane, N., and S. Olmstead. 2007. *Markets and the environment.* Washington, DC: Island Press.

Kohler, A., S. Jülich, and L. Bloemertz. 2004. Guidelines: Risk analysis—A basis for disaster risk management. Deutsche Gesellschaft für Technische Zusammenarbeit (GTZ). http://www.preventionweb.net/english/professional/publications/v.php?id=1085.

Lovins, A. B., L. H. Lovins, and P. Hawken. 1999. A road map for natural capitalism. *Harvard Business Review* 77 (3): 145–58.

Middleton, N., and P. O'Keefe. 2003. *Rio plus ten: Politics, poverty and the environment.* Ann Arbor: University of Michigan Press.

Mileti, D. 1999. *Disasters by design: A reassessment of natural hazards in the United States.* Washington, DC: Joseph Henry Press.

Mileti, D., and J. Gailus. 2005. Sustainable development and hazards mitigation in the United States: Disasters by design revisited. *Mitigation and Adaptation Strategies for Global Change* 10:491–504.

Norberg, J., and G. S. Cumming, eds. 2008. *Complexity theory for a sustainable future.* New York: Columbia University Press.

NRDC (Natural Resources Defense Council). 2005. Global warming basics. http://www.nrdc.org/globalWarming/f101.asp.

Osorio, L. A. R., M. O. Lobato, and X. Á. del Castillo. 2005. Debates on sustainable development: Towards a holistic view of reality. *Environment, Development and Sustainability* 7 (4): 501–18.

Raskin, P., G. Gallopin, P. Gutman, A. Hammond, and R. Swart. 1998. Bending the curve: Toward global sustainability. Report to Global Scenario Group. Stockholm Environment Institute, PoleStar Series Report no. 8.

Reid, D. 1995. *Sustainable development: An introductory guide.* London: Earthscan.

Rogers, P. P., K. F. Jalal, and J. A. Boyd. 2008. *An introduction to sustainable development.* London: Earthscan.

Rose, A. 2011. Resilience and sustainability in the face of disasters. *Environmental Innovation and Societal Transition* 1 (1): 96–100.

Ruben, R. 2008. The development impact of fair trade: From discourse to date. In *The impact of fair trade*, ed. Ruerd Ruben. Wageningen, Netherlands: Wageningen Academic.

Sachs, J. 2005a. *The end of poverty: Economic possibilities for our time.* New York: Penguin Press.

———. 2005b. Investing in development: A practical plan to achieve the Millennium Development Goals. http://www.unmillenniumproject.org/reports/fullreport.htm.

Saha, D., and R. Paterson. 2008. Local government efforts to promote the "three Es" of sustainable development: Survey in medium to large cities in the United States. *Journal of Planning Education and Research* 28:21–37.

Schneider, R. 2002. Hazard mitigation and sustainable community development. *Disaster Prevention and Management* 11 (2): 141–47.

Sen, A. 1999. *Development as freedom.* Oxford, UK: Oxford University Press.

Sitarz, D. 1993. *Agenda 21: The earth summit strategy to save our planet.* Boulder, CO: Earthpress.

Smith, G. 2011. *Planning for post-disaster recovery: A review of the United States disaster assistance framework.* Fairfax, VA: Public Entity Risk Institute.

Twigg, J. 2004. *Disaster risk reduction: Mitigation and preparedness in development and emergency planning.* London: Overseas Development Institute.

UN (United Nations). 2002. *Report of the world summit on sustainable development.* New York: United Nations.

———. 2005a. Agenda 21. http://www.un.org/esa/sustdev/documents/agenda21/index.htm.

———. 2005b. Johannesburg Plan of Implementation. http://www.un.org/esa/sustdev/documents/WSSD_POI_PD/English/POIToc.htm.

———. 2010. What's going on? Millennium Development Goals. http://www.un.org/millenniumgoals/index.shtml.

———. 2012. Universal Declaration of Human Rights. http://www.un.org/Overview/rights.html.

UNCSD (United Nations Conference on Sustainable Development). 2012. The history of sustainable development in the United Nations. http://www.uncsd2012.org/rio20/history.html.

UNDP (United Nations Development Programme). 2004. *Reducing disaster risk: A challenge for development.* United Nations Development Programme, Bureau for Crisis Prevention and Recovery.

———. 2010. Human Development Report 2010: The real wealth of nations: Pathways to human development. http://hdr.undp.org/en/reports/global/hdr2010/.

———. 2011a. Human Development Report 2011: Sustainability and development: A better future for all. http://hdr.undp.org/en/reports/global/hdr2011/.

———. 2011b. Human development index (HDI). http://hdr.undp.org/en/statistics/hdi/.

UNFPA (United Nations Population Fund). 2011. Linking population, poverty and development. http://www.unfpa.org/pds/trends.htm.

UNISDR (United Nations International Strategy for Disaster Reduction). 2003. *Disaster reduction and sustainable development: Understanding the links between vulnerability and risks to disasters related to development and environment.* Geneva, Switzerland: UNISDR.

———. 2004. *Living with risk: A global review of disaster reduction initiatives.* Geneva, Switzerland: UNISDR.

UW-DMC (University of Wisconsin–Disaster Management Center). 1997. *Disasters and development, study guide and course text.* Madison: University of Wisconsin, Disaster Management Center.

Waltner-Toews, D., J. J. Kay, and N.-M. Lister, eds. 2008. *The ecosystem approach: Complexity, uncertainty, and managing for sustainability.* New York: Columbia University Press.

Welsh, M., and A. Esnard. 2009. Closing gaps in local housing recovery planning for disadvantaged displaced households. *Cityscape: A Journal of Policy Development and Research* 11 (3): 195–212.

Wisner, B., P. Blaikie, and T. Cannon. 2004. *At risk: Natural hazards, people's vulnerability and disasters.* 2nd ed. London: Routledge.

Witteveen, A., and L. Ruedin. 2008. Putting a livelihood perspective into practice: Systematic approach to rural development—A guide for analysis, appraisal and planning in rural areas. Berne: Swiss Agency for Development and Cooperation (SDC). www.poverty-wellbeing.net.

World Bank Development Web. 2001. What is sustainable development? http://worldbank.org/depweb/english/sd.html.

RESOURCES

- Chiwaka, E., and R. Yates. "Participatory Vulnerability Analysis: A Step-by-Step Guide for Field Staff." 2005. http://www.who.int/management/programme/ep/en/index1.html.
- *Eldis.org.* Livelihoods Connect: Gateway to Resources on Sustainable Livelihoods Approach. http://www.eldis.org/go/topics/dossiers/livelihoods-connect. This is a very rich site. While the roots of the sustainable livelihoods approach go back to the early 1990s

(Chambers and Conway 1992), DFID and other organizations (CARE, OXFAM, UNDP) took the central concepts and tried, tested, and revised the approach over a number of years. Much of that information is at this very in-depth site.

- *International Federation of Red Cross and Red Crescent Societies* (IFRC). "What Is VCA? An Introduction to Vulnerability and Capacity Assessment." Geneva, Switzerland: IFRC. 2006. http://www.ifrc.org/Docs/pubs/disasters/resources/preparing-disasters/vca/whats-vca-en.pdf.
- ————. "How To Do a VCA: A Practical Step-by-Step Guide for Red Cross Red Crescent Staff and Volunteers." 2007. http://www.preventionweb.net/english/professional/trainings-events/edu-materials/v.php?id=8277.
- *Poverty-Wellbeing.net*. The platform on livelihoods, equity, and empowerment is a feature of the Swiss Development Agency (SDC) and has a host of up-to-date information on livelihoods thinking and approaches. http://www.poverty-wellbeing.net/.
- Rodríguez, H., and J. Barnshaw. "The Social Construction of Disasters: From Heat Waves to Worst-Case Scenarios." *Contemporary Sociology* 35, no. 3 (2006): 218–23.
- Rodríguez, H., and D. Marks. "Disasters, Vulnerability, and Governmental Response: Where (How) Have We Gone So Wrong?" *Corporate Finance Review* 10, no. 6 (2006): 5–14.
- Rodríguez, H., and C. N. Russell. "Understanding Disasters: Vulnerability, Sustainable Development, and Resiliency." In *Public Sociologies Reader*, edited by J. R. Blau and K. E. I. Smith. Lanham, MD: Rowman and Littlefield, 2006.

Section II

Socially Vulnerable Groups

4 Class

Brenda McCoy and Nicole Dash

CONTENTS

4.1 CHAPTER PURPOSE

One of the key features of social life in the United States is the stratification of the population into different social classes. Social class includes both material resources like money and non-material resources such as education or power. This chapter first discusses the complex nature of social class in the United States and around the world and then illustrates how it impacts disaster vulnerability.

4.2 OBJECTIVES

As a result of reading this chapter, the reader should be able to:

1. Define "social class" and describe its component attributes
2. Explain the difference between social class and social castes
3. Describe the stratification of social classes in the United States and around the world
4. Explain how "social class" and "social castes" structure people's life chances and opportunities
5. Articulate the connections between social class, social caste, and disaster vulnerability
6. Apply your knowledge of lower class or caste status and vulnerability to both disaster case studies and disaster scenarios
7. Describe ways in which emergency personnel can help to address vulnerability issues associated with lower class status

4.3 INTRODUCTION

The ability to prepare for and respond to a disaster or hazardous event and to reduce its impact on our lives largely depends on available resources. Common wisdom (and lots of research) suggests that people who have more money, education, or power are better prepared, respond more quickly, and recover faster than those who have less. But personal resources are only one part of the equation. Where you are when disaster strikes is just as important. Wealthier and more powerful communities, states, and nations are better equipped to prepare for and deal with hazardous events. They have more extensive and sophisticated infrastructure such as roads, health-care facilities, communication networks, and emergency response equipment. They also can draw on a variety of highly trained emergency personnel—fire, police, medical, and military. This chapter describes different types of resources and how they are distributed in the United States and in other parts of the world. It also specifically examines how inadequate resources may result in increased vulnerability of individuals and communities in the face of disaster and the ways emergency management operations can reduce the harm to these segments of the population.

4.4 DEFINITIONS AND CONCEPTS

All societies in the world rank their members into social strata or categories based on some set of criteria such as money, education, employment, prestige, or power. In some societies, stratification may take the form of social classes, while in others it manifests as a caste system. In either case, social stratification is illustrative of the inequality that exists among individuals in a particular society. Stratification also exists at a broader level as a result of the unequal distribution of resources among nations, states, cities, and regions.

In addition to reflecting different levels of resource distribution, stratification includes belief systems used to justify why some people have more (or less) than others. A value is also implicitly assigned to the people, depending on their particular class or caste. Those in higher castes or social classes are considered more important or valuable to society than those in lower groups.

Class systems are a form of social stratification based on a combination of birth and individual achievement. People within a specific social class tend to have similar amounts of money, education, and opportunities for advancement. Class systems are more fluid than caste systems and are typically associated with the belief that with enough work, demonstrated skill (and perhaps a little luck), individuals can attain a higher class position. In the United States, this belief system is referred to as the "American dream," but similar belief systems exist in other highly developed countries. It is important to understand, however, that the belief systems associated with class or caste systems may or may not reflect reality.

With caste systems, there is little or no possibility of social mobility. Social standing in a particular caste or category is inherited or ascribed at birth and is not connected with individual effort or achievement. Two characteristics are common to most caste systems. The first is endogamy—a requirement that people are only allowed to marry others in the same caste or social category. They may not marry "up" or "down." The second characteristic of most caste systems is occupational specialization. Families in each caste are permitted to pursue only certain types of employment that, in turn, determines the type of education or training necessary to prepare for that work. Caste systems are more typical in less developed countries and in agrarian societies. The caste system in India is perhaps the best known; however, various forms of caste systems also exist in Nepal, Pakistan, Bangladesh, and in some countries in Africa and other parts of the world.

Our social class position, or our membership in a particular caste, affects our lifestyle, the opportunities available to us, and the neighborhoods we live in. (For an illustration of these effects, see Box 4.1.) It affects the schools we attend, the type and amount of education we receive, our choice of occupation, and our income potential. Max Weber (1922) was perhaps the first to describe the interplay between a person's financial resources and lifestyle. For Weber, lifestyle is a product of a person's life chances and life conduct. Lifestyle is the visible expression of a person's social standing and refers to a person's patterns of expenditure, consumption, and tastes. Examples of lifestyle include the types of leisure activities we engage in, the social networks we are a part of, our diet and cuisine, the type of house and neighborhood we live in, and the type of car we drive.

BOX 4.1   STRATIFIED MONOPOLY

Often it is hard for us to put ourselves in the position of others. In other words, in the context of social class, those of us who are middle or upper class find it difficult to imagine what it is like to be lower or working class, and those of us who grew up lower or working class find it hard to imagine what it is like to be middle or upper class. Huge stereotypes about the poor, in particular, exist in American society. Some of these stereotypes include "poor people choose to be poor and if they only worked harder they would be able to earn more money." These stereotypes are based on the idea that everyone has the same opportunity to pull himself up by his bootstraps, and those who do not make it simply are not working hard enough. The reality, however, is very different. As the beginning of this chapter emphasized, class mobility is very challenging. If you are not born into a certain level of wealth, the playing field is unequal from the beginning. Your life chances are affected, and part of those chances is opportunity.

The game Monopoly can be used to illustrate the effects of a class-based stratification system. Using a regular Monopoly board, we can slightly change the rules to illustrate the challenges to class mobility. To play, you and five others should set up the game as instructed in the game directions. However, do not hand out any starting money. Once the game is ready, each person playing should count off from one to six. Once each player has a starting number, distribute money based on the following: player 1, $900; player 2, $3,750; player 3, $0; player 4, $1,500; player 5, $200; and player 6, $450. Play the game for an hour just as the directions describe except for one deviation: The rules indicate that a person who has no money is bankrupt, and no longer plays the game. In this version, instead of being bankrupt, players who lose all their money (or start with none) may borrow from other players willing to make loans. Players should keep track of how much money is owed to them or they owe others. As you will see when playing the game, those who started with little money find it challenging to increase their wealth. They may have some limited cash in their hands, but they are less likely to own property, homes, and hotels. What you will find, however, is that it is not impossible for players to improve their position, but it is difficult. Seeing how difficult this is, imagine how challenging it would be if you changed a few parameters. What if someone had no source of income, so that every time they passed "Go," they received nothing? What if you designated some people as female, and those who were female received less money each time they passed "Go"? As you can imagine, modeling different life experiences in the game would lead to different results. But what becomes clear during this exercise is that when the playing field from the beginning is not equal, those with fewer resources struggle more. Before you put the game away, make sure you record the following information for each player so we can use it later: cash on hand, how much money is owed to you, how much money you owe others, value of properties you own, and value of houses and hotels.

Without access to resources, individuals, families, and even poor communities face challenges when trying to mitigate against and prepare for hazardous events. Poor health and education levels also play a critical role in hazard outcomes by rendering some more vulnerable than others. The key to this vulnerability is the structural impediment resulting from limited access to material and nonmaterial resources. Likewise, poor communities have similar issues with increased vulnerability, as they also, as a community, have less ability to garner resources needed for disaster.

A person's lifestyle is directly connected to their life chance—the probability that they will be able to get what they want or need in life. It is largely, but not exclusively, rooted in a person's financial strength. Life chance is most challenging for those with low social standing and is greatest for those in the upper classes or castes (Mantsios 2001). Life conduct involves personal choice and self-direction. Just because a person can afford a particular home or car does not necessarily mean they will choose to do so. Similarly, some people will choose to expend financial resources on things they cannot afford in order to maintain the appearance of a certain lifestyle.

Our social standing affects more than our lifestyle. It also has a direct impact on our interactions with others. While people have contact with others outside their own class or caste, their primary interactions are with those of the same class or caste. They live in comparable neighborhoods, shop in similar stores, eat in the same kinds of restaurants, and share similar values and belief systems. For social scientists, stratification into social classes or castes is a macro issue because it is widely focused on the organizational structure of society. However, social scientists also focus more narrowly on the social interactions of individuals—a micro issue—because these interactions create and shape people's perceptions of reality. This sense of reality frames how people interpret events, including what is normal. How people perceive events is an extremely important consideration for emergency planners. People from various social strata often interpret hazardous events in different ways. What one group considers an emergency may be considered "normal" by another.

4.5   DEMOGRAPHIC OVERVIEW

Considering the complex nature of stratification, it is not surprising that most Americans do not understand its meaning or its nature. The following sections describe the different components that define or are reflective of levels of stratification or social standing such as income, wealth, and education, and the demographic distribution of these components in the United States and around the world.

4.5.1   INCOME

Income is a major indicator of a person's social standing and is strongly connected with membership in a particular social class or caste. Income typically consists of receipts in the form of salary, wages, or pension payments. It also includes earnings, if any, from investments or from other nonlabor sources such as child support, disability, and unemployment insurance. Most researchers examine household income in the United States rather than individual income because most people live

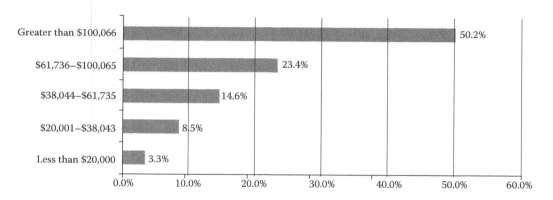

FIGURE 4.1 Percent of U.S. households by income group, 2010. (*Source*: U.S. Census.)

with other earners and share their financial burdens as well as benefits. In most cases, households consist of people related by marriage. However, many nonrelated people share the same residence and the expenses associated with running that household. While they may or may not share their income, they are assumed to share similar economic circumstances. Nonfamily households are not uncommon—especially in modern, industrialized nations. For example, nonfamily households accounted for 32.9% of all U.S. households in 2010 (DeNavas-Walt, Proctor, and Smith 2011).

Median income is more commonly reported than average income because of the magnitude of the difference between the lowest incomes (zero) and the very highest. In addition, because the highest earners often account for a disproportionately large share of the aggregate earnings, use of average income would produce a distorted picture. In 2010, median household income in the United States was $49,445. Median household income has declined 6.4% since 2007, the year before the most recent recession (DeNavas-Walt, Proctor, and Smith 2011). Thus, members of the middle-ranked households in the United States would have had approximately $4,100 per month in income before payment of taxes, leaving some amount less than that to pay for housing, groceries, clothing, transportation, other necessities, and any leisure activities or nonessential items.

In the United States, there is considerable income inequality—the difference between those who make a lot of money and those who do not. In order to study income distribution, researchers first sort all American households from the highest gross earnings to the lowest. The sorted households are then divided into five equal groups, which are referred to as quintiles. In other words, each quintile accounts for 20% of the American population. A fairly small portion of the U.S. population claims the bulk of the total personal income earned in the United States. In 2010, households in the top quintile earned half (50.2%) of all personal income in America, while the top 5% made 21.3%. Households in the top quintile had earnings greater than $100,066 annually, but the average income among households in this stratum was $169,333 per year (see Figure 4.1). Those in the second highest quintile accounted for 23.4% of the country's aggregate income, with receipts starting at $61,736 per year. The average household income in this stratum was $79,040. The top 40% of households in the United States accounted for nearly 75% of all dollars earned by all households in the country. In contrast, households in the lowest quintile garnered only 3.3% of all income and earned less than $20,000 per year. Average income for households in the lowest stratum was $11,034 (DeNavas-Walt, Proctor, and Smith 2011).

There is even more income inequality between nations. Americans—even those with the least income—tend to earn more and be much better off than most people in the world. According to Branko Milanovic, an economist with the World Bank, nearly half of the richest of people in the world (top 1%) live in the United States (Milanovic 2011). Membership in this elite group requires that an individual earn at least $34,000 per year after taxes. A household consisting of a married couple would need an after-tax income of at least $68,000. In contrast, material circumstances for those in the global middle class are very, very poor by American standards. Global median income is only $1,225 a year, or about $102 per month—a number that is already adjusted to account for variations in the cost of living and purchasing power that exists between poorer and wealthier nations (Milanovic 2011).

The World Bank stratifies countries into four basic categories (low, lower-middle, upper-middle, and high income) based on their gross national income (GNI) per capita. GNI per capita is not a measure of individual income. It is calculated by dividing the gross national income of a particular country by its midyear population. GNI per capita is often adjusted for purchasing power parity (PPP), which makes it possible to compare income between countries. In countries with low-income economies, most people are desperately poor. Examples of countries in this category are Afghanistan, Bangladesh, Cambodia, Haiti, Nepal, Niger, Somalia, and Uganda. The GNI per capita for the 35 countries in this category is $1,005 or less. Lower-middle economies have a GNI per capita of $1,006–$3,975. The 56 countries in this group include Egypt, Honduras, Indonesia, India, Iraq, Sudan, Ukraine, and Vietnam. The upper-middle-income category also includes 56 countries, many of which are located in South and Central America. Among other countries in this category are China, Thailand, and Turkey. The GNI per capita for upper-middle-income countries ranges from $3,976 to $12,275. Countries with high-income economies—those with GNI per capita of $12,276 or more—include the United States and 69 other nations in the industrialized Western world such as Australia, Canada, France, Germany, Japan, Norway, Sweden, Switzerland, and the United Kingdom (World Bank 2012a). In 2010, the GNI per capita for the United States was $47,340 compared with $400 in Afghanistan, $1,270 in India, and $8,930 in Mexico. Income inequality, both within a country and between nations, is an important indicator of which populations are most vulnerable to hazardous events or disasters.

4.5.2 Low Income and Poverty

According to the U.S. federal government, an American household with four members who together earned less than $22,050 per year or an individual who earned less than $10,830 annually was classified officially as poor (HHS 2010). Approximately 46.2 million Americans, or 15.1% of the U.S. population, fell into that category in 2010. Approximately 20.5 million Americans (6.7%) had incomes that were less than one-half of the official poverty level (DeNavas-Walt, Proctor, and Smith 2011).

Many Americans believe that the poor are people who are simply unwilling to work, or who do not work hard enough. And that may be true for some individuals. However, the majority of poor people in the United States work very hard—sometimes at more than one job. The problem is that they do not make enough money at their jobs to pay for essential goods and services.

An American who earned minimum wage in 2010 and worked full-time made $7.25 per hour. Working 50 weeks per year, a minimum wage worker earns $290 per week, approximately $1,160 per month, and $14,500 per year before taxes. In 2010, an estimated 4.4 million workers earned the minimum wage or less (DOL 2011). According to the U.S. poverty standard, however, a minimum wage worker is not considered officially poor by the federal government if he or she is single and living alone. After taxes, this single woman or man would have had approximately $32 per day to pay for housing, food, and other essentials. If this individual were a single mother supporting a child, she would barely have qualified as poor since her yearly wages were just less than the $14,570 poverty threshold defined for a household with two people (HHS 2010).

The concentration of poor people varies across the United States. In 2010, many cities in the United States had poverty rates that far exceeded the national average of 15.1% and others were less. For example, the poverty rate in the nation's capital and surrounding metro area was 8.4% in contrast to 37.6% in Detroit, Michigan. Some of the cities with high poverty rates are considered by emergency planners to be at higher risk for some type of hazardous event (Table 4.1). Preparing

TABLE 4.1

Poverty Rates 2006–2010 for 10 Major U.S. Cities with Hazard Risks

City	Poverty Rate (%)	Type of Event	City	Poverty Rate (%)	Type of Event
Brownsville, TX	35.8	hurricane	Memphis, TN	25.4	earthquake
Dallas, TX	22.3	tornado	Miami, FL	27.3	hurricane
Fayetteville, AR	22.4	tornado	North Charleston, SC	22.9	hurricane
Fresno, CA	24.9	earthquake	Oklahoma City, OK	16.6	tornado
Los Angeles, CA	19.5	earthquake	Mobile, AL	21.5	hurricane

Source: U.S. Census Bureau, State and County Quick Facts, 2012.

for, mitigating against, and responding to disasters or hazardous events in cities or areas with large, vulnerable populations is a serious and ongoing challenge for emergency planners.

While poverty is a problem in America, those defined as poor in the United States are very well off by global standards. One expert estimates that the poorest Americans—the bottom 5%—earn more than two-thirds of the rest of the world (Milanovic 2011). Most of the poor in the United States and other developed countries experience relative poverty, a lack of resources compared to others in the same country. In contrast, persons who lack sufficient means for survival suffer from absolute poverty.

Experts at The World Bank estimate that, in 2008 (latest available figures), 1.29 billion people or 22% of the world's population, lived in absolute poverty (Olinto and Saavedra 2012). Put another way, the number of extremely destitute citizens of the world is four times greater than the current population of the United States. These abjectly poor people subsist on $1.25 per day or less—a figure that is already adjusted for purchasing power parity (PPP). Approximately 2.5 billion people globally live on less than $2 per day. People experiencing poverty at this level already live a disastrous existence. They lack adequate access to clean water, food, housing, clothing, health care, and sanitation facilities. They also have little or no education, low skills, and limited work opportunities.

The largest numbers of extremely poor people are found in the countries comprising South Asia: Afghanistan, Bangladesh, Bhutan, India, Maldives, Nepal, Pakistan, and Sri Lanka. This area—especially the Indian peninsula—also has a higher risk for hazardous events, including tsunamis, earthquakes, cyclones, and flooding associated with the monsoon season.

The deepest and most extreme poverty in the world is found in sub-Saharan Africa. Existence for most people in this part of the world is a day-to-day struggle. In 2008, nearly half of the population lived on $1.25 (PPP) per day or less. The poverty rates in some of these countries are staggering. For example, approximately 88% of the people in the Democratic Republic of the Congo live on $1.25 (PPP) per day or less. In Nigeria, 85% of the population subsists on less than $2.00 (PPP) per day or less (World Bank 2012b). Everyday life is tenuous for the people of sub-Saharan Africa and they are especially vulnerable to emergency events such as droughts, famines, communicable disease, cyclones, and even civil war.

4.5.3 WEALTH

The presence or absence of wealth is a major factor in a person's life chances. Wealth is a pool of stored financial value that is available when needed and thus is a good reflection of material comfort and security. Those with greater wealth belong to the upper classes or castes, and those with little or none belong to the middle or lower classes. Wealth consists of the total net value of a person's cash assets and savings, housing and other real estate, investments, the surrender value of life insurance, and pension plans. In short, wealth consists of any financial resources that a person has left over after all his or her debts have been paid. Wealth is more difficult for researchers to compute and analyze than income because it involves components that change in value like housing and stocks. As a result, the latest wealth figures lag behind income by 2–3 years.

The computation of wealth does not include income. People who have earnings from jobs and/or investments that exceed their requirements for everyday living may choose to build their personal wealth by saving or investing a portion of their income. However, simply having a sizeable income is no guarantee that a person will accumulate wealth. Moreover, income streams may be interrupted through the loss of a job or by making a poor investment decision.

The connection between wealth and social standing has long been recognized. Karl Marx (1845/1978) first distinguished between capitalists—the holders of sufficient wealth to own the means of production—and workers, who had only their labor to sell. Since Marx, numerous social theorists have refined the notion of social standing to include other dimensions, but all have maintained that wealth is a crucial component. Many Americans believe that the United States is fundamentally a classless society or that the United States is a nation largely composed of a middle class (Mantsios 2001).

Contrary to what many Americans believe, however, wealth is far from being evenly distributed in the United States and most of it is not controlled by a large middle class. In fact, the distribution of wealth in the United States is far more lopsided than income. In 2007, over a third (34.6%) of the wealth in the United States was concentrated in the hands of the most affluent Americans—the top 1% (Wolff 2010). The wealthiest 20% held 85.1% of the total personal wealth. Viewed from another perspective, the richest 1% of Americans had more wealth at their disposal (34.6%) than the bottom 90% (27.1%).

Actual dollar figures provide greater insight into the financial reserves that may or may not be available to many Americans. In 2007, 18.6% of the population possessed no wealth at all or their debts exceeded the total value of their assets. Just over one out of four Americans (26.6%) possessed less than $5,000 in wealth, and 30% had less than $10,000 (Wolff 2010).

In the United States in 2007, median wealth was $102,500. In other words, half of the population had more than $102,500 in financial resources or wealth and half had less. For many Americans, equity in their homes constitutes a considerable portion of their wealth. Home equity, while valuable, is illiquid. It takes longer to convert it to cash than other types of investments. Homeowners must either wait until their home is sold to gain access to their net equity, or go through the process of securing a home-equity loan. Because of this, Edward Wolff (2010) argues that a computation of wealth that excludes net equity in an owner-occupied house more accurately reflects financial resources that are immediately available for expenditure. By his estimation, median non-home wealth in the United States in 2007 was only $23,500.

The distribution of wealth across the globe is considerably more uneven than its distribution in the United States. More than half of global household wealth is owned by the richest 2% of the adults in the world (UNU-WIDER 2006). The top 10% hold 85% of global household wealth. In contrast, half of the adult world population controls only 1% of global household wealth. Membership in the top 10% bracket of global household wealth required net assets of $61,000 or more (UNU-WIDER 2006).

This lopsided distribution of wealth has important implications. One of the most important is that those who are wealthy have considerable power—political and otherwise. They populate the ranks of the decision makers and shape public policy—including policies affecting preparation for and responses to emergencies. In contrast, most people in the world have no personal financial reserves that they can rely on in the event of an emergency. They simply live from paycheck to paycheck and hope that nothing happens to disrupt their regular source of income. Unfortunately, many disasters or catastrophes destroy businesses and the jobs associated with those businesses.

4.5.4 EDUCATION

Like wealth and income, education plays an important role in people's life chances and is a critical component for the social and economic development of a country. It has a direct impact on employment, health, personal empowerment, and participation in the political process. Education is connected with social standing because it because it is a fairly consistent predictor of a person's earnings capability. People who have completed more formal education tend to earn more than those who have not.

In 2009, 85.3% of American adults ages 25 and older had at least a high school diploma or more education. Nearly 30% of U.S. adults had earned a bachelor's degree or higher (Ryan and Siebens 2012). Median earnings for individuals with only a high school diploma were $26,776 per year compared with $47,510 for those who earned a bachelor's degree. Those with advanced degrees had median earnings of $62,313.

Educational attainment is affected by structural factors such as the tendency of people to live in close proximity to others with similar economic resources. Because public schools are frequently financed with taxes based on property values, schools located in poorer areas often do not have the same resources as those located in more expensive neighborhoods. This pattern is also evident among states. For example, 91.5% of the population in Minnesota completed a high school education in contrast to 79.9% in Texas. The poverty rates for these two states are 10.6% and 16.8%, respectively. Moreover, children who live in poorer neighborhoods are often exposed to environmental hazards or have health issues that impede academic performance. For these reasons and others, many scholars believe that children from working-class families are prevented from attaining levels of education that would improve their class position (Blau and Duncan 1967; Conley 1999).

Many Americans believe with good reason that getting a good education is a key to success. However, they often overlook the role that financial resources play in getting a good education. Numerous studies show that getting a good education is as much about opportunity and mentorship as it is about basic intelligence. Thus, for example, parents with money are able to pay to enhance their children's educational experiences and shape their children's educational choices. The children of parents with financial resources have the opportunity to study more and work less, and they do not tend to be shackled with repaying student loans after graduation.

The extreme lack of economic resources in other parts of the world—especially in developing countries—has a direct impact on educational attainment. At least four years of education is required for basic literacy. UNESCO (2010) defines education poverty as fewer than four years of education. Those with fewer than two years of education live in extreme education poverty.

Education poverty is prevalent in 22 developing countries, with 30% or more of adults aged 17 to 22 having less than four years of education. In sub-Saharan Africa, 50% of adults ages 17 to 22 experience education poverty. However, one in five adults in 26 developing countries has fewer than two years of education. Altogether, there are an estimated 759 million illiterate people in the world—both adults and youth—two-thirds of whom are women (UNESCO 2010).

Education possesses intrinsic qualities that transcend its economic value. People who have low levels of education may have lower self-esteem. They may have difficulty reading and with verbal communication, which makes it harder for them to access other resources or social assistance. It also complicates their ability to recognize health risks and follow the instructions of health-care providers. Lower levels of education serve to narrow the lens through which people see their world. It constrains where and how people get information—an issue of vital importance to emergency planners.

4.5.5 OCCUPATION AND PRESTIGE

A person's occupation—an indicator of both social class and caste—is the primary source of income for most people and is closely related to a person's level of education. People in the uppermost strata in a society may not work or derive most of their income from employment. However, those in lower classes often work more than one job to make ends meet. A person's occupation is also an important source of prestige.

Even though the U.S. Bureau of Labor Statistics classifies workers into 820 different occupations, jobs are often grouped into two broad categories: white collar and blue collar. Jobs believed to require greater skill and training and that are typically held by people with college or professional degrees are referred to as *white collar*. These occupations are associated with higher levels of prestige, higher pay, and are usually conducted indoors or in more pleasant surroundings. Blue-collar jobs, in contrast, are believed to require less mental skill, tend to be more physically labor intensive, and pay less money. Some of these jobs are also more dangerous.

In 2011, the highest-paying occupation groups in the United States included management, legal, computing, and engineering. However, low-paying jobs comprised most of the 10 largest occupations groups. These groups accounted for 20% of the employment in the United States and included positions such as office clerks, retail sales, food preparation, waiters and waitresses, janitors, and freight workers (DOL 2012).

In an effort to study the problems and challenges facing low-wage workers, Barbara Ehrenreich took jobs in different parts of the country as a waitress, hotel maid, house cleaner, nursing-home aide, and Wal-Mart salesperson. Her experiences are recorded in her best-selling classic, *Nickel and Dimed*, first published in 2001. Ehrenreich, who holds a PhD, reported that her first discovery was that "no job, no matter how lowly, is truly 'unskilled.' Every one of the jobs…required concentration, and most demanded that [she] master new terms, new tools, and new skills" (2001, 193). She also noted that the often physically demanding nature of these jobs—some even damaging—rarely provided health insurance benefits. Ehrenreich made other important observations about minimum- and low-wage work. Compared to white-collar workers, low-wage blue-collar workers tend to have very little control over their schedule or how they work. They are more closely monitored than white-collar workers and must be more careful about taking breaks and making or receiving personal phone calls. Low-wage workers often find it much more difficult to take time off from work for personal appointments such as meeting with a child's teacher or going to the doctor. While many white-collar workers work longer than 40-hour weeks, they are often able to afford help at home in the form of a housekeeper or lawn service. White-collar workers also have more flexibility in determining when they will work longer hours.

The low wages and/or lack of control associated with some jobs are more pronounced in developing countries and sometimes take the form of contemporary slavery. Forced labor includes bonded labor, human trafficking, forced marriage, and child labor. Anti-Slavery International (2012) has identified four characteristics of contemporary slavery. The first is that enslaved people are forced to work through mental or physical threat and abuse. They are also owned or controlled by their employer. Another characteristic is that people who are enslaved are dehumanized and treated as commodities. Finally, their freedom of movement is restricted. The International Labour Organization (2012) has estimated that 20.9 million people are currently victims of some form of forced labor.

These issues are especially pertinent for emergency planners. Many people have jobs that they have little or no freedom to leave—even in the face of a pending disaster or hazardous event—because they believe that, if they elect to do so, their job and livelihood are at risk. Moreover, people working long hours or two jobs may have little time to consider or prepare for a potential disaster.

4.6 RELEVANCE

As we have seen, our placement in the social strata plays an important role in our life chances. In the following section, we will discuss some of the ways in which social class or caste impacts our lives. What should be clear is that those in the top of the social hierarchy have an easier time in life than those at the bottom.

4.6.1 Health

Research has consistently shown that our place in the social hierarchy impacts our health in a variety of different ways. Those with less money are more likely to have health-related issues. The number one health risk in the world is hunger. It is responsible for the deaths of more people than AIDS, tuberculosis, and malaria combined (UN World Food Programme 2012). An estimated one in seven people (925 million) in the world are undernourished (FAO 2010). In the United States, the problem of hunger exists but is much less severe. In 2010, nearly 15% of households at some point during the year lacked sufficient financial resources to buy food for all of its members (USDA 2011).

People who lack sufficient resources to take care of their health do not seek preventive services or pre- or postnatal care, and they are far less likely to get treatment when they are ill. As a result, minor conditions can quickly develop into acute or life-threatening conditions. This issue is further complicated by the fact that poor families are more likely than nonpoor families to live in less sanitary and more hazardous or toxic environments (Syme and Berkman 1997).

Lack of personal resources for health care, however, is only one part of the equation. The other part is the availability of health-care personnel, treatment facilities, drugs, and vaccines. Poorer countries (and some regions in wealthier countries) do not have enough doctors, hospitals, clinics, pharmacies, or medical equipment. Total annual per capita expenditure on health from all sources ranged from $11 in Eritrea in Africa to $8,262 in Luxembourg in Europe. The World Health Organization (WHO) has indicated that a minimum of $44 per capita, on average, was required for a country to scale up to provide essential health services to its citizens (WHO 2012). Most of these services would be directed at dealing with communicable disease as well as maternal and child health. Much more is required to address other health issues. Expenditure varies significantly across global regions from an average of $48 in the WHO Southeast Asia region to $3,187 in WHO Region of the Americas. In 2009, 29 countries were unable to reach the $44 minimum requirement.

Per capita spending on health in the United States in 2009 was $7,960 (WHO 2012). In spite of this expenditure, many Americans lack access to basic health care. In 2010, approximately 16.3% (49.9 million people) of Americans had no health insurance (DeNavas-Walt, Proctor, and Smith 2011). Those in the lower classes are most vulnerable—especially the lower working classes. The federal government provides some health coverage to the very poorest Americans.

The genesis of the health problems of those lower in the social hierarchy, however, is less important than the consequences of them. As we will investigate later, the ability of the most vulnerable people in a society to prepare for, respond to, and recover from disaster is compromised. Individuals with more wealth are more likely to have better health overall through better access to resources. Wealthier regions or countries are also better prepared to respond to the needs of their citizens irrespective of personal resources.

4.6.2 Housing

One of the most significant consequences of social class is its impact on housing. For those with wealth or in a higher social class, access to almost any type of housing that they desire is possible. With enough money, they can buy or build homes in the best neighborhoods with the strictest safety standards. For those with little financial resources, their housing options are much more limited (Donner and Rodriguez 2008). The poor are less likely to own their own homes and have fewer options with rental properties.

Those in the lower social classes tend to spend a greater proportion of their income on housing. In 2009, 19.4 million Americans paid more than half of their incomes on housing (State of the Nation's Housing 2011). Even middle-income households devoted a significant share of income to housing. Households with annual earnings between $45,000 to $60,000 spent an average of 30% of their income for housing. As a result, those with more income are more likely (but not guaranteed) to have more discretionary income available for other necessities and emergencies. Daskal (1998, 2) argues that the typical poor—those who received no subsidy for housing, spent about 77% of their household income on housing in 1995.

More significant is that available affordable housing for low-income renters becomes more challenging to find. In its annual report on "worst-case housing needs," the U.S. Department of Housing and Urban Development (HUD 2005, 4) reported that

> there continues to be a shortage of affordable housing that is available to very-low-income and, more significantly, extremely-low-income renters. In 2003, there were 78 rental units affordable to extremely-low-income renters for every 100 such households, but only 44 were available for these households (the remainder being occupied by higher-income households).

This lack of affordable housing is a major reason why the poor often end up homeless. In addition, there is significant concern that this housing may be substandard and greatly at risk during hazards such as earthquakes, tornadoes, and hurricanes. In 1998, Daskal (1998, 22) found that approximately 14% of poor renters lived in housing with moderate or severe physical problems, while about 40% of poor homeowners lived in poor-quality housing in 1995. As we will see later when we discuss vulnerability across the disaster life cycle, quality of housing plays a significant role in hazard vulnerability. The need to find affordable housing restricts housing options. When such a significant percentage of one's income is going to housing, even when safety is a goal, price dominates housing decisions. As a result, many financially marginal families and individuals live in housing that is more likely to suffer serious damage or total destruction in a hazardous event.

4.6.3 EDUCATION

In addition to the challenge of finding housing, social class also impacts access to and quality of education. Children from poor families are more likely than children from nonpoor families to attend schools with inadequate funding (Kozol 1991). Significant consequences result from poorly funded schools, which are more likely to have fewer teachers, larger class sizes, inadequate instructional materials such as books and computers, and often dangerous building structures. These same children are less likely to finish high school than nonpoor families (Shanahan, Miech, and Elder 1998), and poor and working-class children are more likely to be tracked into general or vocational programs in schools, while children from higher classes are more likely to be tracked into college-preparatory programs (Oakes 1985). As a result, class becomes a vicious cycle where kids born into low-income or working-class families find it difficult to improve their class position. Their opportunities, regardless of intelligence and ability, are limited because of structural impediments to success. With less education, they are more likely to have low-paying jobs with limited, if any, benefits. Thus, the system itself creates replicating channels of vulnerability by limiting opportunities to move to higher social classes, where access to resources such as money and power reduces vulnerability across the disaster life cycle (Box 4.1).

4.6.4 SOCIAL CAPITAL

Another important way that our social standing is important involves our connections with other people. Many social scientists refer to the interpersonal networks of family members, friends, coworkers, neighbors, and other voluntary associations as social capital. The term *social capital* implies that our social networks have economic value in addition to the emotional support, advice, companionship, and other forms of assistance we typically associate with interpersonal relationships. In fact, most people have either received material support in the form of a gift, loan, or other goods such as food from others in their network, or have rendered this type of aid to others.

Moreover, assistance either to or from others may also take the form of some service that would otherwise need to be purchased, such as home repair or child care.

Another way that social capital is translated into economic value involves the types of relationships that people have in their networks. For example, those individuals who have powerful contacts in the work world are often able to use those connections to find a job or to get a better job either for themselves or for someone else in their network. Similarly, people may have contacts who have political power and who are able to influence the types and amounts of governmental or other resources that are made available to a business, neighborhood, community, or city. Employment status and age also affect the size of an individual's social network. People who are younger and those who are employed tend to have larger personal networks to draw support from than the unemployed or elderly. People rely on and utilize their social networks irrespective of size; however, the important point is that those from lower classes tend to have fewer resources of all types to share with other members in their networks.

People's social capital is a vital consideration for emergency planners. It affects how people get information about potential hazardous situations and how that information is perceived, since we often consult with those closest to us about important matters. Level of social capital is also reflective of the "people resources" available to an individual to prepare for, respond to, or attempt to recover from a disaster or hazardous event. Social capital and the other components of social standing—wealth, income, education, and occupation—are inextricably linked. People with fewer of these resources are far and away more vulnerable to disasters and other hazardous events than those who possess more. In fact, in a study of Kobe, Japan, and Gujarat, India, Nakagawa and Shaw (2004) found that communities with higher social capital experienced the fastest recovery. More detail on this topic can be found in the next section of this chapter.

4.7 VULNERABILITY ACROSS THE DISASTER LIFE CYCLE

How does social class impact disaster vulnerability? In this section, we will examine this question by looking at how limited access to both material and nonmaterial resources affects vulnerability across the disaster life cycle. Researchers are in general agreement that the poor lose relatively more in disasters (Beatley 1989; Dash, Peacock, and Morrow 1997; Fothergill and Peek 2004; Wisner et al. 2004; Elliott and Pais 2006). The most devastating disasters in the twentieth century are believed to have had the greatest impact on relatively poor populations (Beatley 1989). This is not to say that absolute dollar loss has been highest among the poor, but rather that the poor proportionately lose more during disasters, and likewise have a more challenging time recovering.

In other words, the vulnerability of the poor is greater, as they have less ability to withstand their losses. During Hurricane Andrew in 1992, for example, one family living on Miami Beach had $60,000 worth of damage to their home, while a family in Florida City lost $40,000. On the surface, we might conclude that the home in Miami Beach had the greater loss, but in reality the impact of that loss was much less. The Miami Beach home was valued at over $1 million, whereas the Florida City home was valued at only $55,000. The family in Miami Beach simply lost things like awnings or had damage to their pool, while the Florida City family lost almost their entire home. The Florida City family was displaced after the storm for over a year, while the family in Miami Beach was able to continue living in their home. So, as you can see, looking at just the absolute dollar amount of loss does not reflect the true reality of who is bearing the brunt of the cost of disaster. Nor does it reflect the challenges the poor face in all phases of disaster. And these types of differences are even more significant when we look at developing nations, where absolute poverty is widespread.

4.7.1 WARNING/EVACUATION/RESPONSE

Warning, evacuation, and response all belong to what is considered the preparedness phase of the disaster cycle. For some types of hazards such as earthquakes, there is little or no warning phase, and as a result, there are often few options for evacuation. Other hazards such as hurricanes often have lengthy warning phases that offer opportunities for pre-impact protective action such as evacuation. While on the surface this seems like an easy concept to understand, the reality is that warning and evacuation are complex social processes that require individuals to understand and process the information they receive. Social class impacts this process in multiple ways.

Social class may impact how people understand the information they receive, whom they receive information from, and the options people have once they understand the dangers. During warnings, social class plays a role in perceptions of danger (Fothergill and Peek 2004). Think of social class as a type of lens in which information is filtered. One's experiences at the bottom of the class hierarchy or at the top will impact how that information is filtered. One of the lenses that impacts whether people recognize danger is education. Education impacts vulnerability in that those who have more exposure to education about hazards are better able to recognize danger and consequently prepare for the hazards. School systems in wealthier neighborhoods are more likely to provide opportunities for education about area hazards. For example, in some parts of North Texas, school children regularly attend programs that introduce them to how tornadoes are formed and what types of things they can do when tornado warnings are issued. These children then take this information home to parents, and ultimately the household knows, generally, what to do in case a tornado is in the area. These programs are more likely to exist in middle-class and wealthy communities, where the school district has financial resources for things like transportation to off-campus programs. In addition, with the emphasis of the federal government's No Child Left Behind educational program, where school funding is tied to student performance on standardized tests, even less school time is available to explore hazards, as it takes away time from teachers preparing students for state-mandated testing. As a result, students from particularly poor school districts are even less likely to learn about earthquakes, floods, tornadoes, hurricanes, and wildfires. With less knowledge, they are less likely to perceive danger.

What is interesting is that the empirical evidence on the impact of social class is somewhat mixed, with some research finding that those with lower socioeconomic status (SES) are more likely to perceive risks, while others have found little or no support for this finding (White 1974; Flynn, Slovic, and Mertz 1994; Armas 2006; Gaillard 2008). Some empirical research has found a connection between the type of employment someone has and that person's risk perception, with those with riskier jobs being less likely to perceive dangers, since they have to cope with dangers every day (Moreau 1987). And as we discussed previously, people with lower SES are more likely to work in riskier jobs. Inaccurate risk perception puts people in greater danger, since most people will not act on warnings, for example, without recognizing that they are in danger. As a result, those who do not perceive the danger are less likely to take preparedness measures such as gathering supplies, putting up hurricane shutters, or evacuating at-risk areas. Likewise, those who live more dangerous lives, such as the homeless, are often more likely to underestimate their risk, since their everyday existence constantly requires them to negotiate dangerous situations, and as a result, they may not take warnings seriously (Mileti, Drabek, and Hass 1975). Hazard vulnerability, then, is greater, since they are less likely to recognize the extraordinary dangers the hazard may pose to them or their families. However, even when those with lower socioeconomic status do recognize their risk, their options for protective action are limited. (For an illustration of these effects, see Box 4.2.)

BOX 4.2   STRATIFIED MONOPOLY AND DISASTER

Box 4.1 described a game of stratified Monopoly where the playing field was not even for everyone in the game. After the game, you recorded how much money and assets you gained while playing. Take all of those assets and add them up. This is your current level of wealth. If you ended up with a negative amount, this means that you are overwhelmed with debt. Using the information you know about disaster and vulnerability, the rules outlined below, and the assets and debt you earned while playing stratified Monopoly, prepare for the following disaster. You must consider each individual and their attributes, and consider all individuals as a community (those playing the game with you). Discuss and outline what each individual would do and what limitations you would have. Here are some of the things you can consider: What would you need to be prepared? Would you have what you need to prepare? Would you need to evacuate? Would you be able to evacuate? Where are your children? What would you do first in this scenario? If you survived, do you believe your home would still be standing? Would you be able to live at your home? If not, where would you go? How long would it take for you to recover? What would your community look like? Would the community be the same or different 2 years post event?

Rules (the amounts here are general guidelines, as the amount of money you will acquire will vary based upon how long you play the game):

- The disaster happens three days before the end of the month.
- If you earned less than $450, you do not own a car.
- If you earned less than $1000, you do not own a house; you rent. Any property you own is where you would like to build a house, but you have not been able to get enough money together yet to build on it.
- If you earned less than $1600, you have no money in the bank at the end of the month. All cash goes to your daily living expenses.
- If you earned more than $650 but less than $1600, you have done no mitigation (no shutters for hurricanes, no tying down of roof, no earthquake or flood protection).
- If you have less than $250 of total assets, you are homeless.
- Ultimately, at least one person playing the game will be homeless, one or two will not have cars, and about half will be renters.

Disaster scenario: You live in a city in the Midwest, population about 100,000. The downtown area is thriving with commercial and residential activity. Many people who live in the downtown area do not have cars because everything they need is there. There is some public transportation around the city, but nothing that leaves the city. There are two major highways running through the city, with many minor arteries that feed into the major highways. Few people consider the area to be at risk despite the fact that a major fault line runs through the area. Very few tremors have been experienced, and while there is some public education on the risk, it is usually focused on yearly announcements on grocery bags at one of the major food stores in the city. Earthquake drills are not routine in the school system. New, more expensive homes have some earthquake mitigation built in to the structures, such as pipes and hot-water heaters being secured, but older, inexpensive homes were built before mitigation measures were thought to be important. Out of the blue, the U.S. Geological Survey (USGS) issues a prediction for a major earthquake (7.0 or greater) to strike the city within the month. The suggestion from the USGS is that people begin preparations immediately by securing their homes, developing a disaster kit, and having an evacuation plan in place should there be significant damage in the area when the earthquake happens. Within a week, the city begins to feel some minor earthquake shocks. As the shocks get stronger, buildings begin to show significant signs of structural damage. Some housing in the poorer area of town begins to crumble. Not knowing what to do at this point, the mayor calls for an immediate citywide evacuation. Are you prepared? How do you get out of the city? Where will you go? After the earthquake strikes, what do you think you will find when you come back to your home? What happens then? You and your community (those playing the game with you) should work together to develop these answers. Develop a response-and-recovery plan for you and your community.

In an analysis of the Kobe, Japan, earthquake, Wisner (1998) found that sophisticated models of earthquake prediction used in Japan did not include variables for known at-risk groups such as the elderly and poor. Even when planners realized that the models failed to include important demographic variables, new models that were developed still failed to include any measure of homelessness. While the homeless population in the area was small, Wisner (1998, 29) emphasized that this population included significant vulnerable characteristics. The homeless population was older, more isolated, less wealthy, and less healthy. These consequences of being poor play an important role in earthquake planning, both for the individual and the community, yet this vulnerable population was not included in earthquake planning.

Such oversight often happens in the United States as well. Consider the advice that is often given by response agencies such as the Federal Emergency Management Agency (FEMA) and the American Red Cross. Both agencies believe that households are responsible for having survival supplies (water, food, radio, flashlight, etc.) to last a family for at least three days. In other words, all of us should have these supplies on hand all the time in our "disaster" kit so that we are prepared for any type of event, whether it has a warning phase or not. While this is sound advice for the majority of Americans, it poses somewhat of a problem for those who are the most financially marginal. Think back to our previous discussion of housing: The most extreme poor may spend up to 77% of their income on housing, leaving a relatively small amount left for transportation and food. Many of the extreme poor, in fact, do not have enough money in a month to cover all their expenses and often, as the health data indicate, the poor do not have enough money to eat. If this is the reality for some, expecting the use of limited resources to stockpile water and food for an event that may or may not happen when—right at that moment—they or their children are hungry is unrealistic. Often the assumption is that people simply refuse to prepare themselves for hazardous events, but the reality is that many simply cannot. Their inability to have the resources needed to have supplies on hand renders them more vulnerable. The wealthy, in comparison, have the resources to invest in food and water that they may never need; the poor do not have this luxury, even if they clearly recognize the need. Similarly, lack of resources negatively impacts the poor's ability to take other protective measures such as evacuation.

Significant research has focused on understanding evacuation and evacuation decision making. In their summary of evacuation research, Sorensen and Vogt Sorensen (2006, 191) summarize some of the key factors that have been examined in evacuation research in the United States. They conclude that overall higher socioeconomic status yields higher evacuation rates and that the empirical support for this finding is high. Those with more resources have more options for evacuation. They are more likely to have transportation and the financial resources needed to protect themselves and their families. For example, people on the upper end of the social-class hierarchy are more likely to have wider social networks. As a result, middle- and upper-class families are more likely to have people outside of the evacuation zone with which to stay, and if not, they are more likely to have the financial means to stay at a hotel. Those who are poorer, on the other hand, are less likely to have the same options. As a result, those who are poorer are more likely to evacuate to public shelters or remain in their homes (Gladwin and Peacock 1997).

In a study of Hurricane Katrina evacuees in Houston, researchers found that evacuees in Houston shelters were disproportionately poor, with low rates of home ownership, health insurance coverage, and education. While only 10% of the residents of New Orleans earned less than $10,000 in 2004, about one-third of the evacuees in Houston reported earnings in this range (Brodie et al. 2006, 1403). Even the ability to go to public shelters may be problematic, as the poor are less likely to have cars, and thus must rely on public transportation during evacuation (Berube et al. 2006). These types of experiences may help explain why, during Hurricane Katrina, those with more financial resources evacuated earlier than those who were poorer (Elliott and Pais 2006). The homeless have even fewer options, as shelters often require identification for entrance, which the homeless often cannot provide. In addition, shelter locations are often reported through radio or television media, which are not readily available to the homeless.

In addition, renters and poor homeowners are less likely to have hazard insurance (Fothergill and Peek 2004). Poor homeowners often have no or inadequate insurance covering both their home's structure and personal property; renters often have no coverage at all for the contents of their apartments. Although renters' insurance is considered affordable by many, it is often out of reach for those who are even minimally financially marginal, since renter's insurance often requires adequate credit. For those who are poor or who have struggled out of poverty, their credit history is often spotty, if not worse. Without an adequate credit score, insurance underwriters often assume the individual is a risk and will deny coverage. Thus, the poor, who cannot afford to lose and replace their belongings, are often the most exposed to losses. Similarly, homeowners face the same dangers when they are underinsured, as will be discussed later in this chapter.

4.7.2 IMPACTS

As discussed previously, it is often the poor who bear the greatest costs during a disaster. While these costs may not be higher in absolute dollars, they are much higher in proportional losses. One of the reasons that the poor have a greater vulnerability to disaster impacts is their limited housing opportunities. People in the lower part of the social-class hierarchy are more likely than people in the higher part of the social-class hierarchy to live in substandard housing, which includes, but is not limited, to the following:

Housing in bad repair
Housing located in hazardous areas, but not built to building codes
Manufactured housing (mobile homes)
Older housing that has not been retrofitted to meet newer building codes
Rental housing and poorly constructed housing

Homes that are built more poorly are more likely to be damaged during disasters. Since the poor are more likely to live in this type of housing, they are more susceptible to losses. In addition, as discussed previously, in countries such as the United States, Canada, Australia, and the United Kingdom, the poor are more likely to be renters, and as renters they have little, if any, control over the structural soundness of their homes. They have few options for mitigation even when they themselves are willing to invest in the cost. For example, in areas with high hurricane risks, renters are often not allowed to put up their own window protection for threatening storms, since to do so would require them to drill into the building itself, which they do not own. As a result, in areas with a large number of renters, you often see most windows of multiunit structures with taped Xs on them. The tape is believed to help during high-wind events, but the reality is that the tape offers no additional protection at all.

If the poor, then, are living in more dangerous housing to start with, it is no wonder that research has found that they are more likely to have significant disaster losses (Dash, Peacock, and Morrow 1997; Perry and Mushkatel 1986; Cochrane 1975). In earthquakes, unreinforced masonry buildings are at the greatest risk, and they are most likely to be inhabited by the poor (Fothergill and Peek 2004), and in wind events such as tornadoes and hurricanes, manufactured housing units (mobile homes) are at the greatest risk. While new manufactured housing today is built for the specific wind zone in which it will be placed, prior to 1994, wind standards were not considered in the manufacture of the units. Prior to 1976, no structural standards were in place at all. In 1976, the U.S. Housing and Urban Development Agency began to oversee the building of manufactured housing and, at that time, imposed minimum guidelines for structural soundness. However, most of the guidelines were to mitigate fire risk and not wind dangers (Dash 2005). And while it is hard to believe, older mobile homes do not leave the housing stock; instead, it appears that these units simply get sold to those who are even more financially marginal. In other words, some of the most financially vulnerable populations live in the most physically vulnerable housing.

While data for the entire United States is a challenge to gather, Florida can be used as a case study. As of 2005, the state of Florida's building stock included over 300,000 pre-1976 mobile homes and in excess of 643,000 manufactured housing units built between then and the middle of 1994 (Dash 2005). In a small study of residents who live in the oldest, most vulnerable mobile homes in Florida (sample size about 500), Dash (2005) found that about 20% of those living in pre-1976 mobile homes have annual incomes of $10,000 or less, with another 32% reporting household incomes between $10,000 and $20,000. During Hurricane Andrew, out of 6,600 mobile homes in south Florida before the storm, only nine remained afterward (Morrow 1997). Clearly, the poor are more vulnerable due to the type of housing they inhabit. As a result, the poor are more vulnerable to injuries and fatalities. In the 1992 Chicago heat wave, for example, the poor were more likely than the wealthy to perish from the extreme heat (Klinenberg 2002). Their health beforehand was more tenuous; thus putting them more at risk to feel the effects of the heat along with their physical locations (in urban areas where the heat concentrates, for example) were more dangerous as well.

Vulnerability, then, emerges for the poor due to the limited choices they have in housing location. Vulnerable land is increasingly used as locations to build affordable housing for lower-income families (Tierney 1989). Consequently, people in the lower half of the social-class hierarchy are more likely than those in higher social classes to live on vulnerable land. This dangerous combination of socially vulnerable people on physically vulnerable land is seen when analyzing damage from Hurricane Andrew and the 2008 Wenchuan earthquake in China. During Hurricane Andrew, nearly all of the state and federal public housing in the hardest hit area of south Florida was severely damaged (Yelvington 1997), leaving many either living in damaged units without power for months or in tent cities set up by the U.S. Army. Despite the danger of mobile homes in hurricane-prone areas, FEMA's alternative solution was to move the poor into small mobile homes. While this may have been a feasible short-term solution, many, due to their poverty status or family size, ended up living in these units for years. As a result, the poor who lost everything remained at increased risk through the very policies that were being used to help them recover from the storm.

Some argue that the poverty regions of China are the same regions that are at risk for natural disasters (Sun et al. 2010), and the Wenchuan earthquake is a prime example of this danger. The earthquake struck rural counties and districts that were particularly poor, destroying over 7.7 million houses, damaging another 24 million, killing over 69,000 people, leaving more than 17,000 missing and injuring close to 375,000 (Dunford and Li 2011). Of the counties and districts that suffered the most losses, "15 were designated state-level and 28 provincial key counties of poverty alleviation and development" (Sun et al. 2010).

While much of the previous discussion has focused on individuals and families, it is important to note that poor communities also bear a significant burden in disaster. As discussed previously, the poor are more likely to have social networks with fewer resources and to live geographically close in poor communities. Poor communities in larger urban ecological networks are more likely to be ignored and underserved even during periods without disaster, thus creating what some have called a "cycle of poverty" (Logan and Molotch 1987, 197), where those who grow up poor do not have the opportunity for upward mobility. Poorer communities are more likely to have less-organized local governments that, even when trying their best, do not have resources to protect their community. As a result, in addition to the damage that households in poor communities experience, the communities themselves often suffer significant damage. One of the poorest communities in the impact area of Hurricane Andrew, Florida City, not only had significant damage to its housing stock (see Box 4.3 for a case study), but all the city structures were also completely damaged. The city hall, for example, was a complete loss, and during the storm, city workers who stayed in the building to meet community needs during the storm literally tied themselves to support columns during the storm in order to survive. The ultimate consequence, however, is that those who most need community support and assistance (the poor) are unable to receive it when the community itself loses all of its structures.

How poverty affects disaster impact is clear when examining the 2010 Haitian earthquake. To understand the impact of the earthquake, it is first important to examine Haiti before the earthquake.

BOX 4.3   CASE STUDY: FLORIDA CITY AND HURRICANE ANDREW

Hurricane Andrew made landfall August 24, 1992, in the southernmost portion of Florida after a quick strengthening as it spun in the Atlantic basin. The storm came ashore as a category 5 hurricane with sustained winds over 145 mph and gusts over 175 mph. The winds were so severe that they blew the measuring instruments off the roof of the National Hurricane Center's building on the campus of the University of Miami. Andrew's storm track was significant for two critical reasons. First, it went south of downtown Miami, where population was denser and losses were expected to be even greater than they were. And second, the eye of the hurricane tracked near Florida City—one of the poorest incorporated cities in south Florida, if not the country. According to the 1990 U.S. Census, Florida City had a population of about 5,800, with a median household income of $15,917 as compared to a U.S. median of $30,056. In Florida City, 37% of the population in 1990 fell below the poverty line compared to 13.5% in the United States as a whole. In addition, 55% of housing units were renter occupied. Clearly, Florida City was a poor community, and in the larger context of the area as a whole, it wielded very little political power as both citizens and as an incorporated community. It had a weak government that was somewhat unorganized before the storm, and even more so afterward, and as a community it had very little power in the larger county government. Using property tax data from the county, analysis showed that Florida City single-family homes lost 81% of their value as a result of the hurricane. While the dollar amount lost may not have been as significant as it was in other areas, nowhere was the proportional loss greater.

In fact, its neighboring incorporated city, Homestead, lost only 47% of its single-family housing value. But overall, Homestead was not as economically marginal as Florida City. Its median household income was higher, although lower than the United States as a whole, and its poverty rate was similarly lower. Home values, however, were over $10,000 higher, and more important, as a community Homestead wielded more power in the larger context of the county. Homestead also had a strong city government that was more organized and able to garner resources for the community. Nowhere can the effects of this be seen more clearly than in an analysis of long-term single-family housing recovery. Florida City's single-family property values did not reach their pre-impact level until about 7 to 8 years after the hurricane, whereas Homestead reached pre-Andrew levels within two assessments of Hurricane Andrew, or about two years.

More significant is looking at the long-term patterns in both of these communities. The 2000 U.S. Census occurred about 7 to 8 years after Hurricane Andrew, and illustrates how disaster can exacerbate inequality. In 2000, Florida City's median household income actually fell to $14,923 while Homestead's increased to $26,775, and the United States as a whole increased to $41,994. Poverty rates in Florida City increased in 2000 to 43.3% while the United States as a whole fell to 12.4%. In 2010, almost 20 years after Hurricane Andrew, Florida City's median income increased significantly to $25,132, but still lagged significantly behind Homestead at $37,901 and the State of Florida at $47,661. And 40% of the population still remained under the poverty line. While it is hard to attribute all these negative changes to Hurricane Andrew, it is clear that the hurricane played some role. Decisions made by community leaders and the relocation of agriculture out of the area as a result of the storm all played a role in making a poor community even poorer in the wake of a major disaster (Dash and Peacock 2003).

Haiti's long history of poverty was evidenced by at least 10,000 nongovernmental organizations that were in the country before the earthquake trying to address issues related to the lack of basic needs such as clean water, adequate shelter, and acceptable levels of nutrition (Kidder 2010). According to the World Bank, 77% of Haiti's citizens are considered to be in poverty, with only 51% having access to "improved water sources." It is the poorest country in the Western Hemisphere and one of the poorest in the world, with a GDP per capita of $671. The literacy rate is a little under 53%, and the country experiences unemployment rates over 40% (CIA 2012). In 2010, more than half of the population lived on less than $1 per day, with 80% surviving on less than $2 per day (World Bank 2012). It is within this social context that Haiti experienced a 7.0-magnitude earthquake on January 12, 2010.

The epicenter of the earthquake was only 16 miles from the capital city of Port-au-Prince, which is a population center of the country. Significant damage to buildings occurred, including the presidential palace, all but two government ministries, and the United Nations Headquarters (IFRC 2010). According the International Federation of the Red Cross (2010), the earthquake impacted 3 million people, killing over 222,000 and injuring another 300,000. In addition, over 188,000 homes were destroyed or damaged, leaving over 1.5 million people displaced (Goldberg 2010).

While some would argue that earthquakes of such high magnitudes will always have significant impact, a little over a month after the earthquake in Haiti, Chile experienced an even stronger earthquake. On February 22, 2010, an 8.8-magnitude earthquake also impacted about 1.5 million people in the area of Concepcion, yet official reports of casualties indicate that only 500 people died (Mandariaga et al. 2010). Why such a contrast? One might think that the answer is that the people of Chile are not as poor, and while that is true, the impact of class in this case is much more complicated. Unlike Haiti, Chile has a relatively low poverty rate at around 15.1% (as of 2009), and it is classified as an upper-middle-class country (World Bank 2012d), unlike Haiti, which is categorized as low income. Additionally, Chile's literacy rates are over 95%, with a 22% unemployment rate (CIA 2012). What is most important, however, is that Chile's wealth as a country allows it to implement building codes that require modern earthquake-resistant building designs. While there was major damage in many buildings, very few collapsed (Madariaga et al. 2010), unlike in Haiti, where pictures of the devastation show that the majority of buildings collapsed in the earthquake's aftermath.

So while we often think of class, poverty, and wealth as individual characteristics with effects on people and families, the stark contrast between the 2010 earthquakes in Haiti and Chile shows that the impact may also be on a much larger scale. The ability to implement building codes, require inspection, and instill confidence in the safety of buildings is a product of the social structures in which these activities happen. Likewise, the ability to recover after disasters is also a function of these same structures. In fact, it is during recovery from disaster that the most significant vulnerabilities of the poor often surface.

4.7.3   Short- and Long-Term Recovery

Clearly, we have seen that the poor are more vulnerable to hazards in both the preparedness/warning stage of a disaster and during impact. The reasons for this increased vulnerability lie not in any flaw of the individual or family, but rather in the systems of social stratification that put them at greater risk. However, as challenging as it is for the poor in the first two phases of disaster, their most significant challenges appear during the recovery phase of disaster (Bolin 1986; Bolin and Bolton 1986; Bolin and Stanford 1991; Phillips 1993; Hooks and Miller 2006; Dunford and Li 2011).

In part, recovery is challenging because of the significant impacts experienced by those who are poor, but more than the impacts, their vulnerability arises from social structures that make it more difficult for them to garner the necessary resources for recovery. The foremost short-term recovery need for the poor is often housing. While permanent housing is the most important long-term recovery goal, temporary housing or sheltering is the most significant short-term issue. Without financial resources, the options for the poor are often limited, and recovery as a whole is significantly influenced by housing recovery (Peacock, Dash, and Zhang 2006). Renting hotel rooms requires access to credit cards with available credit as well as transportation to the site. We often forget that the poor are not likely to have credit cards or access to significant amounts of cash. Research has found that those with higher incomes were more likely to stay at hotels and motels, while those with lower incomes stayed with family (Morrow 1997). In addition, the length of time for those who stay with family is higher for the poor than others. Morrow (1997) found that the poor were three times more likely to still be staying with family three months after Hurricane Andrew than higher-income groups.

In some situations, few options for the poor exist, and the federal government may step in to shelter poor families. After Hurricane Andrew, the U.S. Army built tent cities to house the poor. While this was considered temporary sheltering that would last for only days to a couple of weeks, it lasted for over two months and was an important step in being able to keep families together in the area (Yelvington 1997). Without the development of the tent cities, recovery for the poor may have been even more impeded, with a high likelihood of displacement out of the south Florida area, similar to that of the poor after Hurricane Katrina. Recovery after Katrina was complicated by the displacement of residents throughout the United States. This displacement began when the poor were sheltered significant distances outside of the city with little opportunity to easily return.

In addition, social networks during recovery are extremely important for the poor. We have emphasized that the wealthy have more elaborate social networks—networks that are geographically wider and politically more powerful. For the wealthy, these social networks help during all phases of a disaster. Recovery of the social networks, however, is of particular importance for the poor. Poor families use their networks for child care, food, transportation, and support. Displacement destroys these networks and makes recovery much more challenging for the poor. For those who were displaced from New Orleans during Hurricane Katrina, for example, returning to New Orleans was difficult without the support and assistance of their former social networks. Likewise, being displaced is problematic, as the networks that people had relied on at home do not exist in their new towns or cities. As a result of these complicated social processes, measuring recovery is challenging, as some people continue to struggle to return to their homes and a city that they believe is not getting enough resources for long-term recovery. (For more information on the issues related to displacement, see L. Weber and Peek [2012].)

Indeed, it is during the long-term recovery phase that a community's ability to wield power in larger sociopolitical structures makes a significant difference in long-term recovery. As Peacock and Ragsdale (1997) point out, the recovery process requires different political structures within a community network to compete for limited recovery resources. Those "systems" that can best compete will get the most resources. For the poor, in particular, recovery is a combination of what little resources they can garner on their own but, more importantly, the resources a community receives to aid them during the process, such as grants. Communities that are well developed, wealthy, and with strong leadership are the communities most likely to succeed during the very competitive recovery period (Klinteberg 1979; Rubin 1985). Long-term recovery, then, is impacted by resources on both a personal level and a community level.

The case of Florida City (Box 4.3) emphasizes that community structures play a vital role in recovery processes; however, there is no doubt that adequacy of other types of resources also play a major role in recovery. Families in the lower half of the social-class hierarchy have fewer internal and external resources for recovery than families in the higher social classes. As mentioned previously when discussing preparedness, the poor are more likely than others to have substandard insurance. When they do have insurance, it is often with smaller insurance agencies that are less likely to make adequate settlements (Peacock and Girard 1997). Without insurance, individuals and families must rely on their own personal resources to recovery; however, the poor are less likely to have these resources available. To complicate matters, most disaster assistance is readily available for homeowners, with renters less likely to receive aid.

As a result of their limited ability to access resources, poor families recover at a slower rate than do nonpoor families. For families of all social classes, the more quickly they can return to permanent housing, the more quickly they recover. However, returning to permanent housing is particularly challenging for the poor. In a summary of housing recovery following disaster, Peacock, Dash, and Zhang (2006) highlighted that housing recovery in the United States is a market-driven process and, as such, predisaster inequalities tend to be replicated during postdisaster recovery. Unless recovery plans give attention to the additional needs of the poor, a market-based solution, by nature, benefits those who have the power and wealth to access the resources necessary to rebuild and repair. Those with adequate resources are more quickly able to find contractors, acquire building materials, and navigate the complicated system of city/county permitting and rules. Those with fewer resources may attempt to do repairs themselves or find a less expensive contractor who may not have the same skills as those selected by those with more wealth. Thus, even with some resources, those who are poorer may find the rebuilding process lengthier.

The need for long-term temporary housing, then, becomes more critical for poor homeowners, but finding permanent postdisaster housing for renters is even more of a challenge. Many of the same challenges they have finding housing in a predisaster context continue postdisaster. Of particular concern is that the stock of affordable permanent housing is often limited after disasters. For example, the cost of rental housing often increases significantly after a disaster as landlords attempt to benefit from the limited nondamaged housing stock. Under the best of conditions, there is no surplus of housing for low-income families, and this is exacerbated in a postdisaster environment (Bolin and Stanford 1991), as the limited rental housing pool is reduced even further by landlords who choose not to rebuild or repair (Childers et al. 1998).

In addition, poor families receive less aid than nonpoor families (Bolin and Stanford 1991; Phillips 1993; Dash, Peacock, and Morrow 1997), which makes recovery even more challenging, considering that their own internal resources will be significantly limited. The reason for this inequality is twofold. One reason for this disparity is that low-interest loans are an important factor in family recovery after disaster, and the poor are less likely to be able to qualify for such loans (Bolin and Bolton 1986; Bolin 1986; Tierney 1989). For homeowners with no or limited insurance, the primary government form of aid is Small Business Administration (SBA) loans (Peacock, Dash, and Zhang 2006). Since this is not a grant program, but rather a loan program, the application process is more complicated and requires a level of approval not usually necessary for grant-based programs. Applications for SBA loans are initially subjected to an income-level test, and if applicants pass this test, they are then subjected to an analysis of "ability to repay loan." As a result, loan approvals are more likely for moderate- to higher-income families who appear to be less of a risk.

Other FEMA programs tend to focus only on short-term emergency repairs so that no further damage occurs. As a result, when poor families fail to qualify for SBA loans, they often cannot repair their homes. In the end, they end up with very few options. They can try to sell their damaged home without repairs; however, if the amount they receive is lower than the amount they owe on their mortgage, they must continue to pay the difference. More often, what happens is that families abandon their homes unrepaired, and those with mortgages are foreclosed upon. In addition, the state or local government may come in and secure homes that are not repaired. Once this is done, homeowners are often given a period of time in which to repair the home. If it is not repaired, the state may take ownership. This was a significant issue after Hurricane Andrew for the poorest and hardest-hit families, and it continues to be an issue in the poorest areas of New Orleans after Hurricane Katrina (Chamlee-Wright and Rothschild 2006).

Perhaps understanding the issues would be easier if we could simply argue that the poor are denied aid, such as loans, more than those who are wealthier. If all we had to consider were the complexities of postdisaster loans, then perhaps the solution to the problem would be more readily evident. The problem, however, is that the issue of aid is complicated by the fact that the poor simply apply for aid at lower rates than those who are wealthier (Dash, Peacock, and Morrow 1997). This may happen for several reasons. The poor are less likely to have documentation of residence, which is required for aid. Without such documentation, they cannot apply for aid. The poor are also more likely to live "doubled up" in a house. In other words, more than one family may live in the same house. In these cases, only one head of household may apply for aid, and as a result, an entire family may get no assistance. Although this is problematic in many disasters, FEMA rules have not changed. And as already noted, most federal aid goes to homeowners over renters (Bolin and Stanford 1991), and since the poor are more likely to be renters, they are often left relying on charitable organizations for recovery assistance. Clearly, without aid, the recovery process is stymied.

For developing countries, international aid postdisaster plays a significant role in the recovery process, yet research findings indicate that humanitarian aid "failed to meet the needs of developing countries in reducing their exposure to disaster risks and ensuring sufficient funds to governments and individuals for financing the recovery process" (Linnerooth-Bayer, Mechler, and Pflug 2005). In a 2005 *Science* article, Linnerooth-Bayer, Mechler, and Pflug (2005, 1045) argue that low-income countries experience more fatalities and larger economic losses than both middle- and high-income nations, and yet, simultaneously, only about 1% of households in low-income nations have catastrophe insurance as compared to 30% in high-income countries. The authors argue that the focus on giving postdisaster aid leaves little incentive to countries to prevent losses, but the aid that they expect and rely on covers under 10% of what they need to recover.

Morris and Wodon (2003) investigated the distribution of aid on a more micro level after Hurricane Mitch. In their study, they looked at whether the significant amount of international aid was distributed to those with the greatest need. Using data collected in the poorest areas of Honduras, Morris and Wodon found that when you control for damage to dwellings, the odds of receiving aid were negatively correlated with wealth and positively correlated with asset loss. They concluded that aid is distributed based on asset loss rather than on wealth. We can conclude, then, that those with the greatest need for relief postdisaster—such basic needs as food, clothing, and medicine—may not be the ones actually receiving the aid, because organizations distributing the relief are simply looking at asset losses related to the disaster rather than the capacity of a household to live in the postdisaster environment.

Social class, then, plays a significant role in generating vulnerability for those on the bottom of the social-class hierarchy in each phase of the disaster cycle. Whether it is having limited resources for preparedness or more structurally dangerous housing or little political power during the recovery period, the poor disproportionately feel the effects of disaster. As individuals, they have little ability to garner the financial means necessary to withstand hazards and, ultimately, even less to recover from them. Yet, even knowing this, as a society we have yet to fully address the needs of this population. In many ways, this should not be surprising, since, as a society, we tend to want the poor to be and stay invisible. We close our eyes to the homeless every day and fail to recognize the everyday threats the truly poor and disadvantaged face in trying to meet their material needs in a nondisaster context. Yet, when disasters strike, political leaders, in particular, continue to consider them "acts of God" or equal-opportunity events, and they fail to recognize that planning for the poor before a disaster happens ultimately saves money in the long run. With disaster after disaster, we see these differential impacts and effects, yet as much as we talk about "lessons learned," these lessons rarely seem to be implemented (see Box 4.2).

4.8   IMPLICATIONS FOR ACTION

While much of what we have discussed in this chapter results from structural features of society, there are some ways that emergency personnel can address the needs of those in the lower social classes. Focusing planning on the issues outlined in this chapter is the first step in minimizing the vulnerability that the poor experience during hazardous events. Through programs focused on this population, planners may be able to develop a capacity for resilience in the lower classes. The key when thinking about resilience for this group is to understand that this capacity will not develop without assistance. The vulnerability that exists for this group, whether in terms of health, education, housing, or disaster, in part reflects a laissez faire attitude toward the poor. As long as people believe that the poor deserve to be poor or that everyone has equal opportunity, we as a society will continue to fail the groups that need our help the most. Changing attitudes, then, is the first thing that must be done to begin to address the specific needs and issues of the poor. While attitudes in general need altering, specific programs of education for emergency managers are needed to bring poverty to the forefront as a planning issue.

4.8.1   Recognize that Disasters Worsen Social Inequalities

We must first recognize that disasters can exacerbate already-existing inequalities within the community. While disasters in general bring communities together, this altruistic state (where stratification and inequality issues disappear) is very short-lived. As we saw with the case study of Florida City, disasters often make the divide between the haves and have-nots even greater. To address this, programs that address the needs of the poor need to be in place before disaster strikes. Programs that recognize that those who are poor may not be able to have a disaster kit on hand will begin to address some of these needs. In addition, considering that poorer families will have a harder time evacuating and finding shelter, emergency managers need to go into their communities and learn what the needs are from those who live in the community. Programs that have local community-based town hall meetings to discuss disaster preparedness and evacuation may be one way to address needs. These programs must be held where the poor live and work if they are to participate. Programs that require travel to attend will not help those who do not have the means to get to the locations.

Furthermore, communities must recognize the power that they have and how much citizens rely on them. A study of African Americans after Hurricane Katrina found that many did not evacuate or delayed evacuation because the mayor's messages were inconsistent. As one respondent who did not evacuate stated, "The mayor did not say it was a mandatory evacuation at first. One or two days before the hurricane hit, he said it was mandatory. It was too late then" (Elder et al. 2007). Until the mandatory evacuation was called, they did not think the danger was significant, and once he did call it, they felt it was too late to leave. Those with more wealth and income were able to leave earlier, as they had less to risk and more resources with which to go. The working poor could not leave until they were allowed to leave and not report back to work. As expensive as evacuation is for a community, leaders must learn to make the hard decisions earlier in order to allow all residents to have an equal opportunity to get out.

Internationally, poverty rates may increase postdisaster, as the poor have more challenges in meeting their daily needs. Likewise, disasters may also significantly impact their short-term and long-term livelihood (Sanderson 2000; Carter et al. 2007). In fact, some argue that the urban poor in the cities and towns of Africa, Asia, and Latin America are the most at risk not only for future disasters, but also because of their increasing poverty after these events due to their vulnerability socially and geographically. Much of this may be due to the impromptu nature of development of urban housing for the poor, who settle where they can without thought to the risks or dangers of losing what little they may possess (Sanderson 2000). Leaders must stop blaming those who settle so haphazardly and, instead, intervene before disaster in order to help move the poorest to safer, more sustainable locations.

4.8.2   Develop Mitigation Programs that Target the Poor

Another significant way we can address the needs of the poor is to not only implement, but also encourage participation in mitigation programs targeting lower social classes. In the United States, some fundamental shifts in mitigation methodology may be required to do this. Most mitigation projects are funded based upon the completion of a cost–benefit analysis. This analysis estimates the cost of a mitigation project and, then, the benefits that can be expected once the project is completed. The inherent problem with this type of analysis for the poor is that it is often very hard to get a cost–benefit ratio that meets the required threshold. This inability to meet the threshold is a direct result of using only specific costs (such as the cost of retrofit material) and specific benefits (i.e., the amount of damage that is avoided). However, as we know, avoiding damage also has other significant benefits that cannot always be quantified, particularly for the poor. Thus, there is a need to develop new methods that consider the nonmonetary benefits of mitigation or methods that can provide a credible basis for monetizing such benefits.

Programs for mitigating the damage to private structures have been attempted (such as Florida's Residential Construction Mitigation Program in the early 1990s); however, the biggest criticism of these programs is that they often mitigate damage to the homes of the rich, as their cost–benefit ratios are highest. Those on the upper end of the social-class hierarchy are also the ones most capable of investing in mitigation without government assistance. Consequently, grant programs that qualify households based on factors other than cost–benefit ratios are needed to address the structural vulnerabilities of the housing of the poor. Considering that those on the lower end of the hierarchy tend to bear the highest burden during disaster, investment in mitigation must be based on something other than the traditional costs and benefits (Heinz Center 1999).

In order to target appropriate structures, mapping of housing located on vulnerable land and socioeconomic demographics is necessary. By combining social and geographical data, emergency managers can assess locations that are the most physically and socially vulnerable, and then target mitigation projects in those areas. To be successful, emergency managers must work with community leaders who are trusted by the citizens most in need. Without these partnerships, the poor will be skeptical of the intentions of the program. The likelihood of success grows by working with community leaders (not necessarily politicians) who can explain the program and recruit participants.

Linnerooth-Bayer, Mechler, and Pflug (2005) emphasize that international aid focuses on postdisaster response and not pre-impact mitigation. With low-income countries bearing disproportionate loss of life and economic losses, the international aid community should be urged to invest more in pre-impact mitigation programs that engage community members in developing programs and relationships that will minimize the impact of disasters. While some of these programs will directly address hazards themselves, others need to focus on issues such as risk transfer (Linnerooth-Bayer, Mechler, and Pflug 2005) and the development of social capital (Nakagawa and Shaw 2004).

4.8.3 INCLUDE COMMUNITY MEMBERS IN DISASTER PLANNING

Including members of lower social classes in disaster planning and development meetings is key to developing programs that pay particular attention to the needs of community members. By engaging community members, particularly those in the lower half of the social-class hierarchy, in developing education programs on disaster mitigation and preparedness, the particular needs of the poor will be integrated. Again, think of the issue of disaster kits. As we have discussed previously, the poor may recognize the need for a disaster kit, but they simply do not have the resources necessary to have the supplies on hand. Educational programs that focus on disaster kits alienate those who cannot have the items available. This is not to suggest that disaster kits and supplies should not be consistently mentioned in disaster education; however, limitations of the poor must be recognized and alternatives recommended. If your target audience feels left out from the beginning, they will not listen or participate in the effective plans that might come later.

Members of planning committees representing the poor can offer insight into what types of things will be successful in poorer communities. As long as we continue to impose "one size fits all" emergency plans on all parts of a community, we fail to address the special needs of those who bear the greatest burden in disaster.

4.8.4 RECOGNIZE THE UNIQUE NEEDS OF THE POOR

Recognizing that lower social classes have unique needs that are not often met by federal, state, and local disaster aid policies, emergency managers need to be proactive by identifying specific sources of disaster relief before any type of event occurs. Planning for recovery is vital for success for everyone during recovery. If you know before a disaster occurs that the poor will have less opportunity for traditional aid in the United States, then knowing what alternative sources are available will be key to their recovery. If you wait until after a disaster occurs to compile a list of resources, then those who most need the information and help will already be negatively impacted during the recovery phase. The key is for emergency managers and nonprofit organizations to plan ahead for the challenges that the poor will face. These challenges include struggles to find new, safe, affordable housing, and emergency managers must plan ahead for this challenge.

Quick damage assessments regarding the available stockpile of affordable housing in a community after disaster allow for a more rapid needs assessment for those who have lost their homes. Understanding the extent of the problem will help to address it. Since affordable housing options are critical for the poor to begin the long-term recovery process, there is a clear need for programs that help motivate owners of these properties to rebuild quickly. Incentives should be used to restore and repair these units, with guarantees from the owners that rents will remain affordable. Similarly, just as most communities have laws that prevent price gouging for pre- and postdisaster supplies (such as water, ice, and wood), there is a clear need to develop programs that offer property owners incentives to keep rents reasonable in disaster-impacted areas. Issues related to housing are among the most challenging to address, since housing recovery is allowed to be market driven. However, without intervention, the poor will continue to struggle—and suffer greater consequences than others—in the aftermath of disaster.

4.9 SUMMARY

The problems highlighted in this chapter focus on ways the poor, in particular, are more vulnerable to disaster due to their inability to garner resources. These resources may be obvious, such as international disaster aid, money, or housing, or much more subtle, such as education, political will, and power. Without all of these things, the poor bear the greatest burden during disaster. While their absolute losses may not be as high as those in the upper classes, their proportional losses are often greater. In addition, they are less likely to have the necessary resources to recover from these losses. Those who find themselves at the lower end of the class structure often find themselves struggling more in the wake of disaster. Stated simply, disaster exacerbates inequality, and the gap between those considered the "haves" and those considered the "have nots" increases. The inherent problem, however, is that to reduce the effects of disaster on this population requires structural changes to society that address class/caste issues. In other words, to best reduce the vulnerability of the poor, we must eliminate poverty. Clearly, this is easier said than done. Ultimately, while emergency responders, governments, and nonprofits can develop programs as discussed here to minimize the impact of class on disaster impact and recovery, the reality is that, within our current social structure, the basic need is for more programs that address global poverty in and of itself. Until society as a whole recognizes this, disasters will continue to significantly impact the poor. The job of emergency personnel is to recognize this and minimize the effects as much as possible.

DISCUSSION QUESTIONS

1. Define social class and explain its attributes.
2. Discuss the demographic distribution of social class and its attributes globally.
3. Explain the connection between social class and caste and life chances and life styles.
4. Discuss the distribution of poverty globally and its impact on vulnerability.
5. What are some of the ways in which social class affects vulnerability to disaster across the disaster life cycle?
6. How are social class and international aid after disasters connected?
7. Develop strategies for your local community to meet the unique needs of those on the lower end of the social-class hierarchy. What types of programs would be the most useful?

ACKNOWLEDGMENTS

This chapter is modeled on Session 7 of the FEMA Higher Education Course titled, "A Social Vulnerability Approach to Disaster," originally designed by Cheryl Childers. The authors thank Dr. Childers for the work she did that made this chapter possible.

REFERENCES

Anti-Slavery International. 2012. What is modern slavery? http://www.antislavery.org/english/slavery_today/what_is_modern_slavery.aspx.

Armas, I. 2006. Earthquake risk perception in Bucharest, Romania. *Risk Analysis* 26 (5): 1223–34.

Beatley, T. 1989. Toward a moral philosophy of natural disaster mitigation. *International Journal of Mass Emergencies and Disasters* 7 (1): 5–32.

Berube, A., E. Deakin and S. Raphael. 2006. "Socioeconomic Differences in Household Automobile Ownership Rates" Implications for Evacuation Policy." http://gsppi.berkeley.edu/faculty/sraphael/berubedeakenraphael.pdf (retrieved December 12, 2012)

Blau, P., and O. Duncan. 1967. *The American occupational structure*. New York: Free Press.

Bolin, R. C. 1986. Disaster impact and recovery: A comparison of black and white victims. *International Journal for Mass Emergencies and Disasters* 4 (1): 35–50.

Bolin, R. C., and P. Bolton. 1986. *Race, religion and ethnicity in disaster recovery*. Boulder: University of Colorado Press.

Bolin, R., and L. Stanford. 1991. Shelter, housing and recovery: A comparison of U.S. disasters. *Disasters* 15 (1): 24–34.

Brodie, M., E. Weltzien, D. Altman, R. J. Blendon, and J. M. Benson. 2006. Experiences of Hurricane Katrina evacuees in Houston shelters: Implications for future planning. *American Journal of Public Health* 96 (5): 1402–8.

Carter, M. R, P. Little, T. Mogues and W. Negatu. 2007. "Poverty Traps and Natural Disasters in Ethiopia and Honduras." *World Development* 35 (5): 835–856.

Chamlee-Wright, E., and D. Rothschild. 2006. Government dines on Katrina leftovers. *Wall Street Journal*, June 15. http://americandreamcoalition.org/landuse/WSJ_Jul06.pdf.

Childers, C., B. Phillips, A. Herring, and C. Garcia. 1998. Defining and applying sustainability after disaster: The experience of Arkadelphia, Arkansas (USA). Paper presented at the Sustainability, Globalisation and Hazards: Enhancing Community Resilience Conference, London.

CIA (Central Intelligence Agency). 2012. The world factbook—Chile. https://www.cia.gov/library/publications/the-world-factbook/geos/ci.html.

Cochrane, H. C. 1975. *Natural disasters and their distributive effects*. Boulder: University of Colorado Press.

Conley, D. 1999. *Being black, living in the red*. Berkeley: University of California Press.

Dash, N. 2005. Mobile home replacement program in Florida: What we know today and where we should go in the future. Final report Year 5 submitted to the International Hurricane Research Center, Florida International University. http://www.ihrc.fiu.edu/lwer/docs/Year5_Tab03_MHReplacement.pdf.

Dash, N., and W. G. Peacock. 2003. Long-term recovery from Hurricane Andrew: A comparison of two ethnically diverse communities. Presentation at the 2003 Southwest Sociological Conference Meetings, San Antonio, TX, April 16–19.

Dash, N., W. G. Peacock, and B. H. Morrow. 1997. And the poor get poorer. In *Hurricane Andrew: Ethnicity, gender, and the sociology of disasters*, ed. W. G. Peacock, B. H. Morrow, and H. Gladwin, 206–25. New York: Routledge.

Daskal, J. 1998. In search of shelter: The growing shortage of affordable rental housing. Center on Budget and Policy Priorities. http://www.cbpp.org/615hous.pdf.

DeNavas-Walt, C., B. D. Proctor, and J. Smith. 2011. Income, poverty and health insurance coverage in the U.S.: 2010. U.S. Census Bureau, Current Population Reports, P60-239. Washington, DC: U.S. Government Printing Office. http://www.census.gov/prod/2011pubs/p60-239.pdf.

DOL (U.S. Department of Labor, Bureau of Labor Statistics). 2011. Characteristics of minimum wage workers: 2010. http://data.bls.gov/cgi-bin/print.pl/cps/minwage2010.htm.

DOL (U.S. Department of Labor, Bureau of Labor Statistics). 2012. Occupational employment and wages, May 2011. http://www.bls.gov/news.release/pdf/ocwage.pdf.

Donner, W. and Rodriguez, H. 2008. Population composition, migration and inequality: The influence of demographic changes on disaster risk and vulnerability. *Social Forces* 87 (2): 1089–1114.

Dunford, M., and L. Li. 2011. Earthquake reconstruction in Wenchuan: Assessing the state overall plan and addressing the "forgotten phase." *Applied Geography* 31:998–1009.

Ehrenreich, B. 2001. *Nickel and dimed.* New York: Henry Holt and Co.

Elder, K., S. Xirasagar, N. Miller, S. A. Bowen, S. Glover, and C. Piper. 2007. African Americans' decisions not to evacuate New Orleans before Hurricane Katrina: A qualitative study. *American Journal of Public Health* 97 (S1): S124–29.

Elliott, J. R., and J. Pais. 2006. Race, class, and Hurricane Katrina: Social differences in human responses to disaster. *Social Science Research* 35 (2): 295–321.

FAO (Food and Agriculture Organization of the United Nations). 2010. Global hunger declining, but still unacceptably high. Economic and Social Development Department. http://www.fao.org/docrep/012/al390e/al390e00.pdf.

Flynn, J., P. Slovic, and C. K. Mertz. 1994. Gender, race, and perception of environmental health risks. *Risk Analysis* 14 (6): 1101–8.

Fothergill, A., and L. A. Peek. 2004. Poverty and disasters in the U.S.: A review of the recent sociological findings. *Natural Hazards* 32 (1): 89–110.

Gaillard, J. C. 2008 Alternative paradigms of volcanic risk perception: The case of Mt. Pinatubo in the Philippines. *Journal of Volcanology and Geothermal Research* 172 (3–4): 315–28.

Gladwin, H., and W. G. Peacock. 1997. Warning and evacuation: A night for hard houses. In *Hurricane Andrew: Ethnicity, gender, and the sociology of disasters*, ed. W. G. Peacock, B. H. Morrow, and H. Gladwin, 52–74. New York: Routledge.

Goldberg, M. L. 2010. Haiti at six months after earthquake. UN Dispatch, July 12. http://www.undispatch.com/haiti-at-six-months-after-earthquake.

Heinz Center (H. John Heinz III Center for Science, Economics, and the Environment). 1999. *The hidden costs of coastal hazards: Implications for risk assessment and mitigation.* Washington, DC: Island Press.

HHS (U.S. Department of Health and Human Services). 2010. The 2010 HHS poverty guidelines. http://aspe.hhs.gov/poverty/10poverty.shtml.

Hooks, J. P., and T. B. Miller. 2006. The continuing storm: How disaster recovery excludes those most in need. California Western Law Review, essays from the 2006 Western Law Professors Conference, Pale Promises: Confronting the Rights Deficit. http://cwsl.edu/content/journals/Hooks-Miller%20camera%20ready%20final.pdf.

HUD (U.S. Department of Housing and Urban Development). 2005. Affordable housing needs: A report to Congress on the significant need for housing. http://www.huduser.org/publications/affhsg/affhsgneed.html.

IFRC (International Federation of the Red Cross and Red Crescent Societies). 2010. Annual Report 2010. http://www.ifrcmedia.org/assets/pages/annual-report/resources/IFRC-Annual-report-2010-English.pdf.

International Labour Organization. 2012. Summary of the ILO 2012 Global Estimate of Forced Labour. http://www.ilo.org/sapfl/Informationresources/ILOPublications/WCMS_181953/lang--en/index.htm.

Kidder, T. 2010. Recovering from disaster: Partners in health and the Haitian earthquake. *New England Journal of Medicine* 362 (9): 769–72.

Klinenberg, E. 2002. *Heat wave: A social autopsy of disaster in Chicago.* Chicago: University of Chicago Press.

Klinteberg, R. 1979. Management of disaster victims and rehabilitation of uprooted communities. *Disasters* 3 (1): 67–70.

Kozol, J. 1991. *Savage inequalities.* New York: Crown.

Linnerooth-Bayer, J., R. Mechler, and G. Pflug. 2005. Refocusing disaster aid. *Science* 309 (5737): 1044–46.

Logan, J., and H. L. Molotch. 1987. *Urban fortunes: The political economy of place.* Berkeley: University of California Press.

Madariaga, R., M. Metois, C. Vigny, and J. Campos. 2010. Central Chile finally breaks. *Science* 328 (5975): 181–82.

Mantsios, G. 2001. Class in America: Myths and realities. In *Race, class, and gender in the U.S.* 5th ed., ed. P. S. Rothenberg, 168–82. New York: Worth.

Marx, K. 1845/1978. The German ideology. In *Marx–Engels reader.* 2nd ed., ed. R. Tucker, 146–200. New York: W. W. Norton.

Milanovic, B. 2011. *The haves and the have-nots: A brief and idiosyncratic history of global inequality.* New York: Basic Books.

Mileti, D., T. E. Drabek, and J. Eugene Hass. 1975. Human systems in extreme environments: A sociological perspective. Program on Environment and Behavior monograph no. 21. Boulder: University of Colorado, Institute of Behavioral Science, Natural Hazards Research and Applications Information Center.

Moreau, A. 1987. Is your risk assessment credible? *Emergency Preparedness Digest* 14 (1): 9–13.

Morris, S. S., and Q. Wodon. 2003. The Allocation of natural disaster relief funds: Hurricane Mitch in Honduras. *World Development* 31 (7): 1279–89.

Morrow, B. H. 1997. Disaster in the first person. In *Hurricane Andrew: Ethnicity, gender, and the sociology of disasters*, ed. W. G. Peacock, B. H. Morrow, and H. Gladwin, 1–19. New York: Routledge.

Nakagawa, Y., and R. Shaw. 2004. Social capital: A missing link in disaster recovery. *International Journal of Mass Emergencies and Disaster* 22 (1): 5–34.

Oakes, J. 1985. The reproduction of inequality: The content of secondary school tracking. *Urban Review* 14 (2): 107–20.

Olinto, P., and J. Saavedra. 2012. An overview of global income inequality trends. In *Inequality in focus* 1 (1). http://siteresources.worldbank.org/EXTPOVERTY/Resources/Inequality_in_Focus_April2012.pdf#page=1&view=FitH,400.

Peacock, W. G., N. Dash, and Y. Zhang. 2006. Sheltering and housing recovery following disaster. In *Handbook of disaster research*, ed. H. Rodriguez, E. L. Quarantelli, and R. Dynes, 258–74. New York: Springer.

Peacock, W. G., and C. Girard. 1997. Ethnic and racial inequalities in hurricane damage and insurance settlements. In *Hurricane Andrew: Ethnicity, gender, and the sociology of disasters*, ed. W. G. Peacock, B. H. Morrow, and H. Gladwin, 171–90. New York: Routledge.

Peacock, W. G., and A. K. Ragsdale. 1997. Social systems, ecological networks and disasters: Toward a socio-political ecology of disasters. In *Hurricane Andrew: Ethnicity, gender, and the sociology of disasters*, ed. W. G. Peacock, B. H. Morrow, and H. Gladwin, 20–35. New York: Routledge.

Perry, R. W., and A. H. Mushkatel. 1986. *Minority citizens in disaster*. Athens: University of Georgia Press.

Phillips, B. 1993. Cultural diversity within disasters: Sheltering, housing and long-term recovery. *International Journal of Mass Emergencies and Disaster* 11 (1): 99–110.

Rubin, C. B. 1985. The community recovery process in the U.S. after a major disaster. *International Journal of Mass Emergencies and Disasters* 3 (2): 9–28.

Ryan, C., and J. Siebens. 2012. Educational attainment in the United States: 2009. U.S. Census Bureau, Current Population Reports, P20-566. Washington, DC: U.S. Government Printing Office.

Sanderson, D. 2000. Cities, disasters and livelihoods. *Environment and Urbanization* 12 (2): 93–102.

Shanahan, M. J., R. A. Miech, and G. H. Elder Jr. 1998. Changing pathways to attainment in men's lives: Historical patterns of school, work, and social class. *Social Forces* 77 (1): 231–56.

Sorenson, J., and B. Vogt Sorenson. 2006. Community processes: Warning and evacuation. In *Handbook of disaster research*, ed. H. Rodriguez, E. L. Quarantelli, and R. Dynes, 183–99. New York: Springer.

Sun, M., B. Chen, J. Ren, and T. Chang. 2008. Natural disaster's impact evaluation of rural households' vulnerability: The case of Wenchuan earthquake. *Agriculture and Agricultural Science Procedia* 1:52–61.

Syme, S. L., and L. F. Berkman. 1997. Social class, susceptibility, and sickness. In *Sociology of health and illness*. 5th ed., ed. P. Conrad, 29–35. New York: St. Martin's Press.

Tierney, K. 1989. Improving theory and research on hazard mitigation: Political economy and organizational perspectives. *International Journal of Mass Emergencies and Disasters* 7 (3): 367–96.

UNESCO. 2010. EFA global monitoring report 2010. Reaching the marginalized. http://www.unesco.org/new/en/education/themes/leading-the-international-agenda/efareport/reports/2010-marginalization/.

UNU-WIDER (United Nations University World–World Institute for Development Economics Research) 2006. The world distribution of household wealth. http://www.wider.unu.edu/events/past-events/2006-events/en_GB/05-12-2006/.

UN World Food Programme. 2012. Hunger. http://www.wfp.org/hunger/stats.

USDA (U.S. Department of Agriculture). 2011. Food Security in the U.S. http://www.ers.usda.gov/briefing/foodsecurity/.

Weber, L., and L. Peek, ed. 2012. *Displaced: Life in the Katrina diaspora*. Austin: University of Texas Press.

Weber, M. 1922. *Economy and society*. Tubingen, Germany: Mohr.

White, G. F. 1974. *Natural hazards: Local, national, global*. New York: Oxford University Press.

WHO. 2012. World Health Statistics 2012. http://www.who.int/gho/publications/worldhealthstatistics/ENWHS2012Full.pdf.

Wisner, B. 1998. Marginality and vulnerability: Why the homeless of Tokyo don't "count" in disaster preparations. *Applied Geography* 18 (1): 25–33.

Wisner, B., P. Blaikie, T. Cannon, and I. Davis. 2004. *At risk: Natural hazards, people's vulnerability and disasters*. London: Routledge.

Wolff, E. N. 2010. Recent trends in household wealth in the United States: Rising debt and the middle-class squeeze—An update to 2007. Working paper no. 589. New York: Levy Economics Institute of Bard College.

World Bank. 2012a. How we classify countries. http://data.worldbank.org/about/country-classifications.

World Bank. 2012b. Regional dashboard—Sub-Saharan Africa. http://povertydata.worldbank.org/poverty/region/SSA.

World Bank. 2012c. Haiti overview. http://www.worldbank.org/en/country/haiti/overview.

World Bank. 2012d. Chile. http://data.worldbank.org/country/chile.

Yelvington, K. 1997. Coping in a temporary way: The tent cities. In *Hurricane Andrew: Ethnicity, gender, and the sociology of disasters*, ed. W. G. Peacock, B. H. Morrow, and H. Gladwin, 92–115. New York: Routledge.

RESOURCES

BOOKS, ARTICLES, AND CHAPTERS

Anderson, M. B. "Vulnerability to Disaster and Sustainable Development: A General Framework for Assessing Vulnerability." In *Disaster Prevention for Sustainable Development: Economic and Policy Issues*, edited by M. Munasinghe and C. Clarke, 41–50. Washington, DC: The World Bank, 1995.

Barr, D. *Health Disparities in the U.S.: Social Class, Race, Ethnicity, and Health*. Baltimore: Johns Hopkins University Press, 2008.

Keister, L. A., and S. Moller. "Wealth inequality in the U.S." *Annual Review of Sociology* 26 (2000): 63–81.

Morrow-Jones, H. A., and C. R. Morrow-Jones. "Mobility Due to Natural Disaster: Theoretical Considerations and Preliminary Analysis." *Disasters* 15, no. 2 (1991): 126–32.

Phillips, B. D. "Sheltering and housing of low-income and minority groups in Santa Cruz County after the Loma Prieta earthquake." In *The Loma Prieta, California, Earthquake of October 17, 1989—Recovery, Mitigation, and Reconstruction*. Professional paper 1533-D, U.S. Geological Survey (1998): 17–18.

Westgate, K. "Land-Use Planning, Vulnerability and the Low-Income Dwelling." *Disasters* 3, no. 3 (1979): 244–48.

FILMS

Down, but Not Out; Dos Americas: The Reconstruction of New Orleans. 2008. Upheaval Productions (33 min).

The End of Poverty. 2010. Cinema Libre Studio (104 min).

People Like Us: Social Class in America. 2001. CNAM Film Library (124 min).

WEBSITES

Shah, A. *Global Issues: Social, Political, Economic and Environmental Issues That Affect Us All*. "Causes of Poverty." http://www.globalissues.org/issue/2/causes-of-poverty.

UC Atlas of Global Inequality. http://ucatlas.ucsc.edu/.

Wikipedia. "Social Class in the United States." http://en.wikipedia.org/wiki/Social_class_in_the_United_States.

———. "Wealth Inequality in the United States." http://en.wikipedia.org/wiki/Wealth_inequality_in_the_United_States.

5 Race and Ethnicity

Nicole Dash

CONTENTS

5.1 CHAPTER PURPOSE

This chapter focuses on two key features of social vulnerability to disaster: race and ethnicity. The chapter explains the nature of race and ethnicity and the ways in which they impact vulnerability to disaster.

5.2 OBJECTIVES

As a result of reading this chapter, the reader should be able to:

1. Conceptualize race and ethnicity as socially constructed attributes
2. Understand the racial and ethnic makeup of the United States
3. Explain why race and ethnicity are not the same across cultures
4. Examine the structural effects of race and ethnicity on society
5. Describe ways in which race and ethnicity result in hazards vulnerability across the disaster life cycle
6. Understand the role that race played in Hurricane Katrina and other disasters globally
7. Suggest ways to address the vulnerability of racial and ethnic minorities with emergency and mitigation measures

5.3   INTRODUCTION

When Hurricane Katrina struck the United States in 2005, the intersection of race and ethnicity and disasters became headline news; similar discussions occurred after the 2010 earthquake in Haiti which devastated parts of the primarily Afro-Caribbean nation. While disaster researchers long knew that race and ethnicity were issues in the experience of and recovery from disasters (Bolin and Bolton 1986; Phillips 1993; Dash, Peacock, and Morrow 1997; Fothergill, Maestas, and Darlington 1999; Wisner et al. 2004), the relationship became much more evident particularly after these events. This chapter attempts to illustrate how social structures of race and ethnicity generate increased vulnerability for minorities in disasters in locations where social life is particularly structured around these differences. While it is not uniformly practiced, many countries around the world use race and/or ethnicity as a way to group citizens (Morning 2008). This chapter focuses on four broad issues:

1. What are race and ethnicity and how are these structured?
2. How do race and ethnicity create vulnerability?
3. What are the consequences of this vulnerability in the experience of disaster?
4. What types of actions can be taken to address the increased vulnerability and develop more resiliency of racial and ethnic minorities?

5.4   DEFINITIONS AND CONCEPTUALIZATION

Race and ethnicity are often taken for granted—not the race or ethnicity of an individual per se, but what it means when we use the terms. Most people, when thinking about the ideas of race and ethnicity, simply draw upon common usage within their own culture to understand the concepts. The reality is that most people's conceptions of race and ethnicity are based on incorrect assumptions and stereotypes. And while both have similar consequences in disaster, the two ideas are not the same or interchangeable. Ethnicity is based on a shared culture such as language, religion, or common norms and practices, rather than specific physical traits. On the other hand, people often assume that race pertains to genetically based biological differences that manifest themselves as different physical characteristics. While members of different races have different physical attributes such as different skin tone or eye shape, people of different races are not inherently genetically different in the sense of creating biological subspecies (Sykes 2001). In other words, people with lighter skin tones are biologically categorized the same as those with darker skin tones. In fact, unlike other animal species that have a variety of subspecies, there is only one type of human.

If race is not necessarily genetically based, then what is it? Race is primarily a social construction. In other words, it is an arbitrary way to organize people based upon easily distinguishable physical features. The categories, however, are not part of some natural biological order, but rather are created and imposed by members of a given society. In fact, in a cross-national study of 141 countries, only three countries used race as a primary term in their 2000 census (Morning 2008). Race as an idea and concept and the racial categories that go along with it are culturally defined. Not every culture uses physical characteristics as a way of organizing and defining their populations.

In the United States, for example, three racial categories are commonly used: white, black and Asian. However, according to the U.S. Census, the agency that counts the population in the United States, there are five races: white, black, American Indian or Alaska Native, Asian, and Native Hawaiian or Pacific Islander. In fact, the U.S. Census even has an option for "other race," once again illustrating the arbitrary nature of the categories. Starting with the 2000 census, individuals were given the option to choose membership in multiple racial categories. In addition, the categories used in the United States illustrate how specific racial grouping is to specific cultures. The categories used in the United States, for example, would not help delineate populations in other parts of the world.

In Australia, race is not used as part of their census. Instead, Australians are asked if they are aboriginals or Torres Strait Islanders. Brazil does use the term *race* in their census, but their categories are similar to those of the United States. In Brazil, the racial categories are: white, black, yellow, brown, or native/aboriginal (Morning 2008).The census in Mexico, on the other hand, only focuses on categorizing indigenous populations. As you can see, race, then, is not a universal concept across the globe. But while different ways of classifying exist, what is clear is that many if not all countries do classify their population based on race or ethnicity. While in many countries the differences between race and ethnicity are unimportant, in others, like the United States, the two are distinct.

As discussed earlier, race and ethnicity are often confused as the same. Looking at the ethnic category of Hispanic in the United States helps to illustrate the difference. When thinking of Hispanics, people commonly consider Hispanics a different racial group, but in actuality, being Hispanic is considered an ethnicity. People from Spanish-speaking cultures can be any race, although most in the United States have Latin American roots and are likely to be considered "people of color" even though they are not designated as being in a racial category by the U.S. Census. When completing the census, individuals are asked first to designate their race, and then, second, to designate whether they are Hispanic. And similar to race, ethnic issues in the United States are very different from those in other parts of the world. How ethnicity is defined is different in different geographical areas. In the United States, for example, the focus is on groups such as Hispanics, Italian Americans, and Irish Americans, where people within the groups have a shared identity based on either genealogical country of origin, language, or religion. Ethnic categories in other parts of the world are different and may be based on dialect, religious beliefs, or other cultural features. Just like racial categories, they are socially constructed and culturally defined.

In Romania, for example, people are asked about their nationality, and the categories included are brief: Romanian, Hungarian, Gypsy/Roma, German, and other (Morning 2008, 250). Guatemala, Paraguay, and Argentina, on the other hand, include between 19 and 22 different categories for selection (Morning 2008). Censuses in other regions not only give categories for selection, but also request the delineation of any selection of the "other" category. In Estonia and Singapore, for example, ethnic and/or nationality categories are given as options, and then there is an additional open-ended selection that respondents are asked to complete. In other parts of the world, such as China and Senegal, ethnicity is so broad that no categories are given. Instead, they are asked to simply write in their ethnic identity (Morning 2008). As you can see, developing a global picture of ethnicity is just as complicated as developing one for race. Both concepts are very place based and culturally rooted. So while some categories may overlap from country to country, there are more differences than similarities in the categories of enumeration. What is common across the globe is that many countries officially categorize their population using categories that we would say are racially or, more often, ethnically based.

What is important to realize is that while in theory race and ethnicity are different, in practice these groups are often merged together. For example, in social science research focused on the United States, when looking at differences among groups, the most common groups considered are white, black, and Hispanic. The key is that regardless of whether considering race or ethnicity, different traits of an individual tend to create trait generalizations, such as intelligence or work ethic, where individuals are assumed to have specific characteristics based upon their race or ethnicity. So, if the categories are arbitrary and socially constructed, why do race and ethnicity receive so much attention?

One of the reasons race, in particular, is a significant feature in some societies is that physical attributes serve as visual markers designating one person different from another. Those characteristics that we consider ethnic traits are often visual through dress, language, or other obvious practices. With visual markers, we can more easily create the notion of the "other." In other words, differences allow us to separate "us" from "them." This notion is significant for how society is structured. What ultimately happens is the creation of majority and minority populations, where the majority has power and the minority does not. Once these power dynamics are integrated into society, then physical difference gives us a convenient system to segregate, isolate, and discriminate. Those in the majority separate themselves from the minority, and as a consequence, structures of inequality are formed that have significant consequences and benefits for minority and majority populations. Because some are benefiting from the system, changing the system is difficult. And while race and ethnicity can be markers for group membership that offers pride and identity, for the most part in society today they serve mainly as a basis for prejudice and discrimination. Thus, it is not race or ethnicity that inherently creates increased disaster vulnerability for groups of people, but rather, it is how race and ethnicity are interpreted by a given society, and the structures surrounding race and ethnicity that relate to vulnerability and resiliency, as we will discuss later in the chapter.

5.5   DEMOGRAPHIC OVERVIEW: RACE AND ETHNICITY IN THE UNITED STATES AND THE WORLD

Understanding how race and ethnicity vary globally is challenging and perhaps impossible. There are no universal categories, so discussions become very complicated. In this section, we discuss the racial and ethnic composition of the United States first, followed by an overview of some Canadian statistics and a brief look at some selected countries across the globe.

The U.S. Census is the agency responsible for collecting race and ethnicity data in the United States. The categories used to collect race and ethnicity data in the 2010 census were determined by the Office of Management and Budget (OMB) in October of 1997 (Humes, Jones, and Ramirez 2011). Starting with the 2000 census, respondents were able to designate more than one racial category. In other words, they could choose both white and black (or any other combination) to reflect a multiracial family of origin. Racial categories according to the U.S. Census have very specific definitions. The following are brief definitions of the five racial categories according to the U.S. Census (Grieco and Cassidy 2001, 3):

- "White"—people having origins in any of the original peoples of Europe, the Middle East, or North Africa
- "Black or African American"—people having origins in any of the black racial groups of Africa
- "American Indian and Alaska Native"—people having origins in any of the original peoples of North and South America (including Central America) and who maintain tribal affiliation or community attachment
- "Asian"—people having origins in any of the original peoples of the Far East, Southeast Asia, or the Indian subcontinent
- "Native Hawaiian or other Pacific Islander"—people having origins in any of the original peoples of Hawaii, Guam, Samoa, or other Pacific Islands
- "Other Race"—included for respondents who were unable to identify with the five OMB race categories

The majority of the population in the United States is white. Table 5.1 shows the racial composition of the United States in 2010. A little less than three-fourths of the population is white. Of the remaining population, a little less than half are black. Two significant features of the data are that they do not include a separate category for Hispanics, so Hispanics are included in each of the categories, and those who selected more than one race are included as a separate category. In addition, Table 5.1 shows a significant number of people who consider themselves some "other race." One of the reasons this number is so high is the confusion by the general public of race and ethnicity. Many Hispanics do not consider themselves white or black; rather, they see themselves as a different racial category. Therefore, many Hispanics either chose "other" as their racial category or they wrote in that they are Hispanic, which is included in the "other" category.

TABLE 5.1
Racial Composition of the U.S. Population, 2010

Race	Number	Percent
White	229,397,472	74.2
Black or African American	38,874,625	12.6
American Indian or Alaska Native	2,553,566	0.8
Asian	14,712,302	4.8
Native Hawaiian or Pacific Islander	507,916	0.2
Other race	14,889,440	4.8
Two or more races	8,398,368	2.7
Total	309,349,689	

Source: U.S. Census Bureau, American Community Survey 2010.

As the categories of race are arbitrary, we can also look at the composition of the United States in an attempt to capture a clearer majority–minority picture. To do this, we can re-create the data to include a category for Hispanic. Each of the other categories in Table 5.2, then, does not include those who consider themselves Hispanic. Whites and blacks, for example, are now non-Hispanic whites and non-Hispanic blacks. Table 5.2 illustrates the population percentages with the new category configuration. One of the most significant changes is in the number and percent in the "other race" category. When including Hispanic as its own category, the "other race" category becomes rather insignificant. This change highlights the confusion between race and ethnicity. Although the difference between race and ethnicity may be important to the U.S. government, the difference is not widely understood by its citizens. For its citizens, difference in general seems to be the more important feature of how people categorize themselves. For the population, what makes someone a minority (race or ethnicity) appears less important than the acknowledgment of the difference. Hispanics clearly recognize themselves as different from whites in the United States, and as a result, are less likely to report themselves as white.

To see how this compares in other countries, we are going to examine the Canadian Census. Table 5.3 re-creates data from the 2006 Canadian Census. What is the most notable is the language used to categorize their population. As you see, their data is framed in relation to the idea of "visible minority." A visible minority in this case is defined as "persons, other than Aboriginal peoples, who are non-Caucasian in race or non-white in colour" (Statistics Canada 2006). Clearly, the majority of

TABLE 5.2
Racial and Hispanic Composition of the U.S. Population, 2010

Race	Number	Percent
White	196,929,412	63.7
Black or African American	37,897,524	12.3
Hispanic	50,740,089	16.4
American Indian or Alaska Native	2,074,523	0.70
Asian	14,566,264	4.7
Native Hawaiian or Pacific Islander	474,799	0.2
Other race	558,211	0.2
Two or more races	6,108,867	2.0
Total	309,349,689	

Source: U.S. Census Bureau, American Community Survey 2010.

TABLE 5.3

Visible Minority Groups, Canada, 2006

Visible Minority Group	Number	Percent
Chinese	1,216,565	3.89
South Asian	1,262,865	4.04
Black	783,795	2.51
Filipino	410,700	1.31
Latin American	304,245	0.97
Southeast Asian	239,935	0.77
Arab	265,550	0.85
West Asian	156,695	0.50
Korean	141,890	0.45
Japanese	81,300	0.26
Visible Minority, other	71,420	0.23
Multiple Visible Minority	133,120	0.43
Not a Visible Minority	26,172,940	83.78
Total	31,241,030	

Source: Statistics Canada, 2006.

Canadians are considered to be not a visible minority (includes Aboriginal people). What is equally interesting is the remainder of the categories that are delineated. While comparable to the U.S. Census in some ways, with categories for black and Latin American, Canada enumerates for a variety of differences in their Asian populations. From this, we can predict that in Canada differences between those categorized as West Asian (Iranian or Afghani) and those as Southeast Asian (Vietnamese, Cambodian or Malaysian) manifest themselves differently than they do in other locations.

Whether difference is manifested by race, ethnicity, or a combination of both, the consequences remain the same. Table 5.4 lists a sampling of countries from around the world with some examples of the racial/ethnic enumeration of their population. As you can see, while there are some similarities among some of the countries, many are very different. Israel, for example, focuses on whether a person is Jewish or not. Interestingly, Israel does not focus on religion as a whole, but being Jewish is

TABLE 5.4

Selected List of Countries and Ethnic Data

Country	Ethnic Groups
Australia	white 92%, Asian 7%, aboriginal and other 1%
Bahamas	black 85%, white 12%, Asian and Hispanic 3%
Belize	mestizo 48.7%, Creole 24.9%, Maya 10.6%, Garifuna 6.1%, other 9.7% (2000 census)
Brazil	white 53.7%, mulatto (mixed white and black) 38.5%, black 6.2%, other (includes Japanese, Arab, Amerindian) 0.9%, unspecified 0.7% (2000 census)
Estonia	Estonian 68.7%, Russian 25.6%, Ukrainian 2.1%, Belarusian 1.2%, Finn 0.8%, other 1.6% (2008 census)
Indonesia	Javanese 40.6%, Sudanese 15%, Madurese 3.3%, Minangkabau 2.7%, Betawi 2.4%, Bugis 2.4%, Banten 2%, Banjar 1.7%, other or unspecified 29.9% (2000 census)
Israel	Jewish 76.4% (of which Israel-born 67.1%, Europe/America-born 22.6%, Africa-born 5.9%, Asia-born 4.2%), non-Jewish 23.6% (mostly Arab) (2004)
New Zealand	European 56.8%, Asian 8%, Maori 7.4%, Pacific islander 4.6%, mixed 9.7%, other 13.5% (2006 census)
Turkey	Turkish 70%–75%, Kurdish 18%, other minorities 7%–12% (2008 est.)

Source: CIA World Factbook.

seen as an ethnic identity as compared to all others who are not Jewish. As you can see in Table 5.4, the majority of those who are considered not Jewish are Arab, not specifically another religious identity. While the examples in Table 5.4 are not exhaustive and the ethnic data is collapsed into manageable categories, what it illustrates is the constructed nature of the categories themselves. As Americans, Canadians, or Brazilians, how we see race and ethnicity is shaped by our specific cultural reality. But while the groups may change, the overall impact remains the same: One group is set as the majority, while the remainder is set as the other. Because of the "othering" that occurs to those who are not part of the majority, the following discussion of the consequences of being "minority" applies to both racial and ethnic groups.

5.6 RELEVANCE

Society is structured, to some degree, based on status or the position someone holds in society. These positions come with social roles and expectations. In other words, when we know someone is a daughter, student, doctor, or minority woman, we use our knowledge and experience of society to define what and how we expect a person to act. Everyone has a variety of achieved and ascribed statuses. Achieved status is earned through activities and includes student, doctor, lawyer, or president. Others are inherited or ascribed to us at birth. These include gender and race. But while each individual has a variety of these statuses, they are not all equal in the eyes of the individual or society. As individuals, we tend to value our achieved statuses, while society tends to focus on ascribed status. A female doctor, for example, tends to be seen as a woman first in society and as a doctor second. Gender, then, is a master status—what people see and judge first. Race is also a master status; it is what people notice first, and thus how they judge the individual. Ethnicity may also be a master status in some cultures, as the way we look, dress, or act may give a clear indication of our ethnicity. While some would like to argue that society is color-blind, people tend to be very aware of skin color and obvious ethnic differences. Along with this comes a strong tendency for minority status to take precedence over other statuses. An individual, then, is seen first by race and ethnicity and second by achieved statuses, and thus interactions are dominated by the assumptions or stereotypes people have of the members of these groups.

Stereotypes are a set of oversimplified generalizations about a group based upon either observed or perceived qualities of the group members. Stereotypes may be positive or negative, but negative stereotypes have the greatest consequence for life experiences, particularly for minorities. Negative stereotypes are hard to eliminate from society because the stereotype itself, while often false, reinforces the ideas contained within it. Consider the following examples where stereotypes create a vicious cycle:

- An American teacher does not expect as much from black students, and as a result black students do not perform as well.
- A Canadian boss does not expect Latin American employees to think for themselves, and as a result Hispanics are less likely to take on leadership roles at work that require decision making.
- An Israeli human resources manager believes Palestinians are farmers with little computer knowledge, and thus does not consider any for employment in his high-tech company.
- A disaster worker does not think minority victims' losses are great enough to qualify for assistance, and the worker makes this opinion known to people. As a result, minority victims will file fewer applications for aid than might be expected because they believe their losses are not large enough.

Because individuals are treated based upon a stereotypical expectation, they often reinforce the stereotypes themselves. Life chances, then, are altered because what people assume about a group of people is applied to every individual of that group as well. The stereotypes perpetuate themselves because of the limited opportunities, and the cycle begins anew. But it is a fallacy to think that all assumptions about race and ethnicity are negative. For those in the majority, the assumptions are often positive, which offer everyone in the group added opportunity. These positive opportunities or experiences are often called privilege. Privilege is the opportunity one has simply because of membership into a specific majority group such as whites, males, or in the case of Israel, being Jewish. The tendency is to think that prejudice always puts someone at a disadvantage, but the other side of it is that it also creates advantages. Privilege is not easy to see because it is taken for granted. Some examples of white privilege in the United States, for example, include not being regularly viewed with suspicion, not being asked to speak for your entire race, and dealing with people in authority who look similar to you. As a result, opportunities and experiences are completely different for those in the majority when compared to those in the minority. This institutional racism, racism that is embedded in social structure and social systems, is reflected in different ways throughout the world. In many locations, it manifests itself into residential segregation, ghettoization, and political marginalization. Segregation and ghettoization restrict where minorities live, and political marginalization limits the voice minorities have in policy making. As a result, minorities are more vulnerable in every phase of the disaster cycle. However, before a discussion of the specific phases of disaster, a general discussion of how race and ethnicity impacts vulnerability is needed.

Wisner and others (2004, 7) argue that vulnerability emerges from "social, economic and political processes that influence how hazards affect people in varying ways and with differing intensities." In their model of understanding disasters, they focus on societal features that generate more vulnerability for minority members of the population. These structural forces shape the experience of disasters. Segregation, ghettoization, and political marginalization restrict access to resources in a variety of ways. And while this chapter focuses on the relationship of race and ethnicity to disaster, it should be noted that disentangling race and ethnicity from issues of social class and gender is challenging. Social systems, whether race or gender, for example, are interrelated, and as a result vulnerability is not uniform for everyone. While vulnerability has specific outcomes within the disaster cycle, we first need to understand the connections between race and vulnerability more broadly. However, much of what comes into play when considering how race and ethnicity impact vulnerability centers on limits of opportunity as a result of issues like segregation. Ultimately, issues of race and ethnicity are often environmental justice issues. Environmental justice focuses on the equitable distribution of environmental risks and dangers across racial and ethnic groups, as well as social classes.

Environmental decision making and policies often mirror the power arrangements of the dominant society and its institutions. Environmental racism disadvantages minorities while providing advantages or privileges for those in the majority. The question of who pays and who benefits from environmental and industrial policies is central to this analysis of environmental racism and other systems of domination and exploitation. Racism influences the likelihood of exposure to environmental and health risks as well as accessibility to health care. Some examples:

- "International Environmental Justice: Building the Natural Assets of the World's Poor" (Harper and Rajan 2004) highlights that poor, often racially or ethnically marginalized communities face a disproportionately heavy burden from degradation of the environment. Citing examples from the literature, they highlight the uneven impact of environmental policy on the Roma (Gypsies) in Eastern Europe, ethnic minorities in Southeast Asia, and the Ogoni minority in Nigeria. The impact on minorities is a direct result of the political disenfranchisement of minorities.
- *Toxic Waste and Race in the United States* (Lee 1987) was the first national study to correlate waste facility sites and demographic characteristics. Race was found to be the most potent variable in predicting where these facilities were located—more powerful than poverty, land values, and home ownership.
- Alston and Brown (1993) examine how ethnic and racial minorities across the globe bear the brunt of nuclear testing. Some examples include ethnic minorities in central Asia,

Aborigines in Australia, minorities in Algeria, and indigenous people in the South Pacific; all experienced significant health problems related to radiation testing.

- *Dumping in Dixie: Race, Class, and Environmental Quality* (Bullard 2000) chronicled the convergence of two social movements—social justice and environmental movements—into the environmental justice movement. This book highlighted blacks' environmental activism in the South, the same region that gave birth to the modern Civil Rights Movement. What started out as local and often isolated community-based struggles against toxics and facility siting blossomed into a multi-issue, multiethnic, and multiregional movement (Environmental Justice Resource Center, www.ejrc.cau.edu).
- Stretesky and Hogan (1998) found that census tracts with higher percentages of minorities, specifically blacks and Hispanics, are more likely to be located in census tracts with a Superfund site (a property with significant chemical contamination that the U.S. Environmental Protection Agency has designated for cleanup).

While these examples focus on toxic contamination, the same issues hold true across other types of hazardous locations. While the land is problematic in and of itself, the broader issue is the social systems that contribute to minorities living in these locations. Vulnerability, then, is not simply due to being minority, but rather it is due to social conditions that marginalize minorities to dangerous locations. Some would question why minorities choose to live in these risky locations, but such questions fail to recognize the structural forces that limit agency. Societal conditions also impact vulnerability by limiting not only land choices, but housing choices as well.

As a consequence of segregation and racism, ethnic and racial minorities have limited housing options. Research has found that racial and ethnic minorities tend to live in more marginal or low-quality housing (Logan and Molotch 1987; South and Crowder 1997). Vulnerability is generated through a greater likelihood that the homes are poorly maintained and built with older building codes and poorer construction materials (Bolin 1994; Bolin and Stanford 1998; Peacock and Girard 1997). In the United States, this is particularly problematic for renters, who have little control over structural maintenance and mitigation. With about 54% of all blacks living in rental housing (compared to 34% of whites) in 2000 (McKinnon and Bennett 2005), the instability of poor black communities dominated by rental housing and unsupported infrastructure significantly contributes to increased vulnerability. In addition, Klinenberg (2002, 91), in his study of the 1995 Chicago heat wave, found that increased vulnerability to extreme heat was not simply a function of poverty. In comparing two poor communities, one predominantly white and the other predominantly black, he found that "the dangerous ecology of abandoned buildings, open spaces, commercial depletion, violent crime, degraded infrastructure, low population density, and family dispersion creates an atmosphere of increased vulnerability." His findings underscore the role that race plays in creating structural conditions that generate vulnerability.

Race and ethnicity, then, are social constructions with arbitrary categories based on specific time and place. The importance of race and ethnicity is not that they exist as differential categories, but rather that the significance of race is the consequences of racial structures. Race and ethnicity are not inherently problematic in their existence; what is problematic is their use as a mechanism for discrimination and political marginalization. Racism, and thus discrimination, is the inherent problem, as it creates structural conditions that impact the ability of minority groups to garner the necessary resources (money and power, for example) to prepare for and respond to hazardous events. If structural conditions were different, race and ethnicity would not, in and of itself, create vulnerability. This distinction is important. Vulnerability, while often applied on a micro or individual level, is actually about the macro or structural level. What puts people at greater risk is the structural elements of society that place minorities in positions of greater vulnerability through features such as segregation that limit free selection of housing options. Institutional racism built into the structural systems of different countries, cultures, and accompanying stereotypes and expectations from individuals creates an environment where the experiences of racial and ethnic minorities in disaster are significantly different from those of the majority. These differences hold true across the disaster life cycle (for related content, see Box 5.1).

As stated previously, minority populations are more likely to live on marginal lands. According to the Brookings Institute (2005, 16), almost three-fourths of minority residents and a little over

---

BOX 5.1   HURRICANE KATRINA CASE STUDY

Hurricane Katrina made landfall as a Category 3 hurricane on the Gulf Coast of the United States on Monday, August 29, 2005, with the eye of the storm coming ashore between New Orleans, Louisiana, and Biloxi, Mississippi. While the storm impacted a variety of communities along the Gulf Coast, the storm's impact in New Orleans illustrates the consequences of the increased vulnerability of a predominantly black community in the United States. It is believed that the storm surge in the New Orleans area was between 15 and 19 feet in the eastern area and 10 to 14 feet in the western portion of the city (Knabb, Rhome, and Brown 2005). New Orleans, built below sea level, was inundated with water as the surge breached the levee system and flooded the city.

In the end, over 1,450 people lost their lives in Louisiana, the majority in the New Orleans area. While no one knows exact numbers, tens of thousands of people in New Orleans remained in the city as the storm made landfall. Estimates suggest that 30,000 to 40,000 made their way to the Superdome and convention center in New Orleans either shortly before the storm made landfall or in its aftermath. While there are no good statistics on the racial composition of the evacuees in the Superdome and convention center, media images, personal accounts, and research interviews suggest that the majority were black. Of these, many were rescued by helicopter as the water continued to rise and stranded people on their roofs or in their attics with few options.

The city of New Orleans, well known for its French Quarter and jazz music, is also known for its poverty. According to U.S. Census data at the time of Hurricane Katrina, 22.9% of all individuals in the city lived below the poverty level as compared to 12.4% of the United States as a whole. However, to argue that poverty was the cause of the disaster is to ignore another significant feature of the area—the racial stratification. New Orleans is a city that is majority minority, with a little over 67% of its population being black. However, while the city always had a large population of blacks, by 2000 the city had become extremely segregated, with most blacks living in neighborhoods that were more than 75% black (Brookings Institute 2005, 6). With these clear geographic divisions along racial lines came concentrated levels of poverty as well:

- The great majority (84%) of the poor population was black.
- Median income for blacks was half that of whites.
- Poverty rate for blacks was three times higher than white poverty rate.
- Poor blacks were five times as likely to live in areas of extreme poverty.
- College attainment was four times lower for blacks than for whites.
- Only 41% of black households owned their own homes as compared to 56% of whites. (Brookings Institute 2005, 7–8)

This case study of Hurricane Katrina and New Orleans illustrates how the effects of disasters are not natural, despite our tendency to think of them that way. Instead, disasters result from the interaction of a hazard with social systems that often render some more vulnerable than others. The impact of Hurricane Katrina on New Orleans resulted from a history of racial segregation, discrimination, and economic inequalities that increased the vulnerability of blacks, particularly poor blacks, in New Orleans.

half of renters in New Orleans during Hurricane Katrina lived in the flood plain. The areas of the city with the lowest number of minority residents did not flood, while those areas with the highest number of minority residents did flood. Those in the majority have the power to live on lands that are at lesser physical risk. Racial minorities have fewer options for housing, and as a result live on lands that are least desirable, such as lands in or closer to the flood zone. Beyond having a greater flooding risk, minorities were less likely to have evacuated during the storm. While some question why people would choose not to evacuate, the reality for many is that they did not have the resources to evacuate.

First, it is estimated that over 100,000 people in the New Orleans area did not have access to a car before the storm hit, and that a little over half of poor blacks had no access as compared to 17% of poor whites (Center for Social Inclusion n.d.). Without transportation, leaving the area was difficult, if not impossible. As a result, many blacks in the area wound up in the refuge of last resort, the Superdome. As more and more people found their way to one of the only known locations of safety, conditions at the Superdome continued to deteriorate both as a consequence of the damage it received during the storm and overcapacity of the shelter. Some estimates suggest that 30,000 people evacuated to the Superdome—the majority being black.

Second, even those who evacuated the storm often had no home to return to, and as a result, tens of thousands of residents were bussed and flown all over the country in the days and weeks after the storm. Large numbers of people went to the Houston, San Antonio, and Dallas areas in Texas, while still others were flown to areas as far as Denver, Colorado, and Atlanta, Georgia. In the process of relocating, families were often split up—with one member on a bus to Dallas while another was on a plane to Atlanta, for example. Parents were separated from their children, and little record keeping made it a challenge to reunite families. In the longer term, while wealthier, whiter areas of New Orleans recovered quickly, such as the French Quarter, not surprisingly, predominantly poor black neighborhoods continue to struggle. With significant rental property destroyed, rents in the area skyrocketed, leaving many unable to afford to return to the city. In addition, FEMA (Federal Emergency Management Agency) gave little assistance to help people return.

Hurricane Katrina was not an equal-opportunity event. The example of Hurricane Katrina and the metropolitan New Orleans area emphasizes how segregation and institutionalized racism generate differing vulnerabilities for racial and ethnic minorities. While blacks are still a majority, 2010 population estimates suggest that fewer blacks live in New Orleans. The 2010 U.S. Census shows that the black population is now at about 62%. However, poverty estimates remain about the same. These changing demographics, in part, result from displaced residents not being able or not wanting to return to the city. In addition, there is a sense that some parts of the area are being gentrified as developers purchase destroyed low-income properties and redevelop them into more high-rent districts with vastly different social landscapes. Similarly, HUD (U.S. Department of Housing and Urban Development) is destroying many of the public housing projects in the city, making it even harder for many to return home. Driving through the city today tells the story of two different Americas, one in which those with power and money (the "haves") experience less storm impact and recover faster than those without power and money (the "have nots"), who continue to struggle. In New Orleans, the "have nots" are racial and ethnic minorities, and thus it is this group that faces an unknown future

The problems and issues seen in Hurricane Katrina in the United States can also arise anywhere in the world, at any time. During the 2008 Great Wenchuan Earthquake, for example, the epicenter was in one of China's four minority counties; Wenchuan County was populated by 27% of the Quingzu minority (Zifa 2008). The Quingzu people tend to live in the most seismically vulnerable structures built from stone masonry or rammed earth. As a result, the Quingzu homes were more vulnerable to the intense shaking and more likely to experience collapse or significant damage (Zifa 2008). The complete stories of Hurricane Katrina and the city of New Orleans and of the Quingzu people in China have yet to be told, as the regions continue to struggle to recover and rebuild, but the glaring vulnerability of minority communities cannot be denied.

5.7 VULNERABILITY ACROSS THE DISASTER LIFE CYCLE

The effects of vulnerability are not similar across the different stages of the disaster life cycle. While vulnerability is rooted in the same structural systems discussed previously, the actual outcome of that vulnerability will vary based upon the actual processes that occur at changing points of time during the buildup toward, the outcome of, and the recovery from disaster. During the warning, evacuation, and response stages, race and ethnicity play a role in how individuals process and respond to information given to them. Race and ethnicity also play a role in the options available when the risk is recognized. While many of the effects may appear to be due to economics, it is challenging to disentangle the two issues. However, minorities receive, interpret, and process warning information differently for a variety of reasons. In addition, minorities are more likely to be more impacted by disaster events both in terms of casualties and damage. The same social systems that generate vulnerability also impact short-term and long-term recovery by limiting access to recovery aid, emergency sheltering, and long-term housing options.

5.7.1 WARNING/EVACUATION/RESPONSE

Warnings for disaster are social processes. This idea is sometimes not easy to understand. Most people think that a warning is issued and people simply act in response to it. But in reality, warning is a process in which the receiver of the warning goes through a series of steps, or processes, before a decision is made. Warnings have multiple actors (such as the giver of the warning and the receiver) involved and numerous feedback cycles where one thing is decided and then feeds back into the larger picture. The complexity of these intertwined processes reflects many social factors. Race and ethnicity are two factors that influence not only how warning is processed, but also what types of protective measures are taken.

How does increased vulnerability resulting from race and ethnicity impact the warning process? One of the ways to impact that process centers on the channels of communication to disseminate the warning. The same social structures that isolate minority populations in segregated communities also impact the warning messages they receive. For example, minorities are more likely to rely on family and social networks for disaster information (Perry and Mushkatel 1986; Perry and Lindell 1991; Peguero 2006; Benavides and Arlikatti 2010), rather than official sources such as local emergency managers. These same friends and family are likely to be living in the same geographic area, and as a result are just as likely as the respondent to not have accurate information. If everyone in the social network is relying on each other for information and no one has accurate information, then many people within an at-risk area may make decisions based on false information. However, even when information is received from official sources, there is no guarantee that those are trusted sources. Racial and ethnic minorities may not automatically see police, news media, or emergency management personnel, for example, as trusted sources, as experiences with them prior to the hazard event may influence perceptions (Donner and Rodriguez 2008). Thus, individuals interpret warnings differently based upon who they are, whom they are with, who and what they see or do not see, and what they hear (Mileti, Drabek, and Haas 1975, 43). As a result, even "fire" yelled in a large university classroom will be heard, understood, interpreted, and reacted to differently by individuals who hear it.

Warnings for any kind of hazard are filtered through experience, and this experience influences the interpretation of the messages. Being a minority does not inherently mean people interpret things differently; rather, it is the social experiences of being a minority that influence that interpretation. Ultimately, warnings are part of a process that leads to risk perception where an individual actually recognizes danger. If people do not recognize the danger of a hazardous event, they usually fail to take protective measures for the hazard.

In a study of three ethnic groups after the December 26, 2004, tsunami in Indonesia, Gaillard and others (2008) found significant differences in how ethnic groups realized the tsunami danger.

The Acehnese, Simeulue, and Minangkabau people all reacted very differently and experienced significantly varied outcomes. While all were in very similar geographic proximity to the critical danger, each group reacted to the earthquake, as it related to a possible tsunami, differently. When the earthquake was felt, 25% of the Simeulue respondents reported immediately fleeing to the mountains, while none of the other ethnic group respondents reported similar actions. Similarly, upon experiencing the earthquake, a little less than 20% of both the Acehnese and Minangkabau reported that their immediate response was praying, while none of the Simeulue reported praying. The study surmises that the different responses—and thus varying risk perception regarding the tsunami—were due to different cultural knowledge about the environment.

Recognizing risk before a disaster is critical for people to take precaution. And while perceiving danger is often a necessary condition for taking protective measures, it is not a sufficient condition, as other social factors may influence the ability to protect oneself regardless of the amount of danger one perceives. One argument for why racial and ethnic minorities may not recognize their risk to the same extent as others is that the hazard or disaster agent seems no more dangerous than their everyday social conditions. Ghettoized neighborhoods to which racial and ethnic minorities are often socially confined may be extremely dangerous, with high crime rates. Klinenberg (2002) focuses on some of these everyday dangers in his study of the 1995 Chicago heat wave. In areas that were considered particularly dangerous, such as Cabrini Green (at the time one of the most dangerous public housing developments in the country), people were afraid to open their windows to mitigate the heat. One of the things that can be concluded is that individuals who find themselves in everyday dangerous situations may be less likely to perceive the true risk of a hazard. Similarly, religious affiliation may also play a role in how people prepare for disaster. During Hurricane Andrew, for example, Lubavitch Jews who live in Miami Beach refused to evacuate because their rabbi in Israel told them they would be safe. A study of Muslims living in Tampa, Florida, found that most do not consider public shelters as an evacuation option due to their lack of perceived safety and prayer rooms (Mando et al. 2011). Consequently, ethnic and racial minorities may also respond differently to dangers. These differing responses may be a result of limited risk recognition or may be a consequence of structural impediments that restrict options.

Some of these restricted options are due to cultural factors, while others are due to economic factors. The role of class or economic factors was discussed in Chapter 4, and these cannot simply be dismissed when discussing racial and ethnic minorities due to how inexplicitly race and class structures are often tied together. While this is true, this section will attempt to focus on some of the unique characteristics of race and ethnicity. Think back to what you read earlier about Hurricane Katrina (see Box 5.1); the problems that arose were not singularly a result of class issues. Rather, the significant issue was how race and class intersected to create more danger for some individuals. In addition, those who were both black and poor were more likely to live in dangerous locations. This type of development pattern holds true across hazards. As a result, minorities are often in areas that need to be evacuated. Research on how race and ethnicity impact evacuation is somewhat mixed in its results, with some studies finding that it is a significant predictor of evacuation and others finding that it is not (Drabek and Boggs 1968; Perry and Mushkatel 1986; Gladwin and Peacock 1997; Elliott and Pais 2006; Elder et al. 2007).

Gladwin and Peacock (1997), in particular, found that black households that resided in an evacuation zone during Hurricane Andrew were less likely to evacuate. Compared to whites, they were two-thirds less likely to evacuate. In coming to this conclusion, however, Gladwin and Peacock failed to examine the role of risk perception in evacuation behavior. Thus, the question remains as to whether those who did not evacuate did so due to decreased risk perception or simply because they chose not to act upon the danger they recognized. One of the things we do know that impacts evacuation compliance is whether those asked to evacuate have an evacuation destination. While evacuation shelters are opened for most hazards and disasters, public shelters are considered a last resort by most evacuees. The majority of those who leave before a storm go to the homes of family and friends. However, minority evacuees are more likely to use public shelters than those who are part of the majority (Yelvington 1997; Lindell, Kang, and Prater 2011). This increased use of shelters may result from a variety of different vulnerabilities.

First, family members are more likely to also live in evacuation zones. Second, as racial and ethnic minorities continue to process warning information and determine their risk, it is possible that they simply wait too long to go to any other type of safe location. Third, in areas where race and ethnicity intersect with poverty, transportation may be a significant issue. Many communities will provide public transportation to people trying to evacuate to a public shelter. However, no transportation assistance is afforded to those who try to evacuate to nonpublic shelters. Fourth, evacuation may be costly, thus restricting minority evacuees from traveling longer distances for shelter. In addition, once the initial hazard passes, minorities may react differently to continuing dangers. For example, after earthquakes, ethnic minorities are believed to be less willing to reenter their homes regardless of the level of damage that the structure sustained. Fears such as these result from a shared ethnic culture in which past experiences may be remembered. Mexicans in California, for example, may remember stories they were told of previous earthquakes in Mexico during which aftershocks caused further damage or injury (Rubin and Palm 1987).

Therefore, the key to understanding how race and ethnicity generate vulnerability during the warning/evacuation/response phase of a disaster lies in recognizing how experiences as a minority impact the social lenses that one uses to interpret warnings and perceive risk. Then, in conjunction with how warnings are interpreted, evacuation is impacted by limited access to evacuation options in part due to the intersection of race, ethnicity, and class. This connection between race, ethnicity, and class also plays a key role in the impact stage of disaster.

5.7.2   IMPACTS

In disasters, it is often minorities and the poor who bear the brunt of the disaster impact. They bear this cost not in absolute dollars, but rather in their proportional losses. In other words, minorities are more likely to lose more of their homes and belongings, even when the dollar amount of that loss is less. To illustrate, imagine a home whose structure is valued at $150,000 being in an earthquake zone and sustaining $50,000 worth of damage. While this is a significant amount of damage, the home itself may be inhabitable and relatively easy to repair. Now consider a home worth $60,000 that sustains $50,000 worth of damage. This home is not inhabitable, nor is it easy to repair. It is possible that all that remains is the foundation and some plumbing. Both homes sustained the same dollar amount of damage; however, the consequences of that damage are completely different. One received damage equivalent to 83% of its value (the second example), while the other lost the equivalent of 33% of its value. As a result, not only are the impacts of the earthquake different in terms of loss, but also, as we will see later, they also affect the recovery process. The question that needs to be answered is why minorities are more likely to have greater proportional losses. The answer to this question is not an easy one, since, similar to the issues that impact the warning phase of a disaster, impact is influenced by both class and race or ethnicity. In addition, impacts are influenced by societal features such as racism and segregation.

As discussed earlier, one of the consequences of the institutional racism that exists in many parts of the world is residential housing segregation, and this segregation significantly affects how disasters impact racial and ethnic minorities. Minority populations live in less desirable locations, and as a result they are often concentrated geographically. Disasters occur in geographic space. Whether earthquakes, tornadoes, hurricanes, fires, or nuclear power plant accidents, the extent of the impact area may be narrow or wide, but more important than the extent of the damage is the population that lives in those areas. Because space is, for the most part in the United States and other locations across the globe, racially and ethnically segregated, disasters may impact a concentrated population. For an illustration, Figure 5.1 depicts a census tract map for Tarrant County, Texas, illustrating the locations of census tracts where the population is over 40% nonwhite. Minority populations are, for the most part, concentrated in contiguous areas in a band along the south and southeastern part of the county.

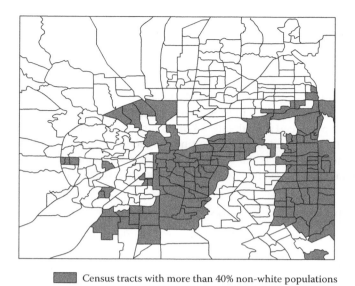

Census tracts with more than 40% non-white populations

FIGURE 5.1 Segregation in Tarrant County, TX. (*Source*: 2010 U.S. Census.)

Since we know that minority populations are more likely to live in more vulnerable locations, we can see why impacts may be higher for minorities depending on where a disaster event occurs.

Even when disasters hit areas with equal amounts of minority populations, minorities still experience more proportional losses, as discussed previously. When Hurricane Andrew struck south Florida during the early morning hours of August 24, 1992, the strongest category 5 winds crossed over the cities of Homestead and Florida City. Yet, even though these areas suffered similar hurricane-force winds, damage was more significant in Florida City. According to the 1990 census, Florida City's population was 61% black, while Homestead's population was only 23% black. In addition, Florida City's population was considerably poorer, with a median income about $5,000 lower than that of Homestead. So in this context, with storm experience being very similar, Florida City's single-family homes lost 81% of their value as a result of Hurricane Andrew, while Homestead's lost only 47%. While both were significant, Florida City clearly experienced a greater impact. Again, the dual impact of class and race placed this community more at risk.

In addition to increased risk to physical structures, some research has also found that mortality rates often are higher among minorities (Moore 1958; Bolin and Bolton 1986; Liang et al. 2001). In his study of the Chicago heat wave, Klinenberg (2002) found that blacks had the highest proportional death rate compared to any other ethnic or racial group, while Hispanics had a relatively low mortality rate. He argues, in part, that the increased vulnerability of blacks stemmed from the locations where they lived in the Chicago area. For example, blacks were more likely to be living in locations with high crime rates and isolated streets. As a result, the level of fear in these areas was higher, and people's willingness to open windows was lower, putting them at greater risk for high temperatures in their homes. Minorities living in public housing were at particular risk because most of the units were without air conditioning. In addition, older black men were more likely to be socially isolated—the leading cause of death during the heat wave according to Klinenberg. Analysis of deaths after Hurricane Katrina found that the majority of those who died as a result of Hurricane Katrina were black, and that blacks had a 1.7 to 4 times higher mortality rate than whites (Brunkard, Namulanda, and Ratard 2008). This is not surprising, considering the racial composition of New Orleans, but it does illustrate the consequences of living in riskier areas.

During the 2004 tsunami in Sri Lanka, ethnic differences were also evident in both mortality rates and damage (de Silva 2009). In the coastal areas of Ampara, Muslim minorities experienced

high rates of mortality, morbidity, and damage in part due to their minority status and lack of political power in the region, and they were also less likely to access assistance than those in other areas
(de Silva 2009). The Muslim population's increased vulnerability was due to: their living on the
coast; working in the fishing industry; and high-density housing (de Silva 2009). Other locations
have seen similar relationships between ethnicity and mortality.

In a reanalysis of historical pandemic data, Wilson and others (2012) also found a connection
between ethnicity and mortality rates in New Zealand. Their findings indicate that the Maori minority in New Zealand experienced a death rate 7.3 times higher than Europeans in the 1918 pandemic,
6.2 times higher in the 1957 pandemic, and 2.6 times higher in the 2009 pandemic. One explanation
for this increased mortality risk is that the Maori tend to live remotely, with less access to public
health information, including vaccines, and to stable and safe housing conditions.

5.7.3 SHORT- AND LONG-TERM RECOVERY

Trying to demonstrate the effects of vulnerability in these three distinct phases of disaster is challenging, as the phases themselves are interconnected. Early research found that minority communities struggle more during recovery (Bolin 1986; Bolin and Bolton 1986; Bolin and Stanford 1998;
Phillips 1993). While these studies have highlighted the challenges minorities face in the aftermath
of disaster, they are less clear on how discriminatory structures impact the recovery process. As we
have discussed, one of the reasons race and ethnicity play a significant role in disaster is their connection to social class or economics in the United States. In other locations, the key issues that arise
during the disaster cycle may be due to historical ethnic conflicts. This also remains true when discussing recovery from disaster. The ability to garner resources in the wake of disaster is one of the
keys to recovery, and racial and ethnic minorities often have limited access to necessary resources.
And while this clearly does include financial resources, in the recovery stage the issues are broader
and also include the ability to leverage political power for the benefit of the community. Minority
communities often have little political power in the larger political context, and as a result, after
disaster, they are often least likely to get assistance. Likewise, in Western cultures, homes in minority areas are often less likely to have adequate insurance coverage. Since there is a direct correla-
tion between insurance coverage and recovery, the lack of insurance resources negatively impacts
minority homeowners' ability to recover. Recovery then is a complicated process that involves both
the individual's ability to garner resources and the community's ability to compete for required
resources. (See Peacock and Ragsdale [1997] for more information on community competition.)
Without adequate resources, recovery is slowed.

Looking at resources on the individual or household level first, research finds that minorities
often have inadequate insurance coverage (Bolin and Bolton 1986; Peacock and Girard 1997). Since
recovery, for the most part, is market driven, insurance plays a key role in the recovery process.
Without adequate coverage, recovery is slowed. Peacock and Girard (1997) analyzed the connection between race and ethnicity and insurance coverage in the wake of Hurricane Andrew. While
most households had some insurance coverage, blacks and non-Cuban Hispanics had the greatest
likelihood of not having coverage. Likewise, non-Cuban Hispanics and blacks were more likely
than non-Hispanic whites and Cubans to report that their insurance companies were not adequately
covering their losses. To try to understand the significant difference between these racial and ethnic
groups, Gladwin and Peacock (1997) analyzed insurance coverage in the hardest hit area. They
found that those without sufficient coverage were more likely to not be insured with one of the three
major insurance companies (State Farm, Allstate, or Prudential). Ultimately, they found that of the
homeowners who were not insured by one of the major carriers, black homeowners were four times
more likely than whites to report insufficient coverage, whereas no racial differences emerged for
the group who were insured by one of the major insurance agencies (Peacock and Girard 1997, 183).
In their attempt to understand this pattern, they found that black households were half as likely as
white households to be insured by one of the big three companies. Their ultimate conclusion is that

"residential segregation deters blacks, but not Hispanics, from obtaining a policy from a top insurance company" (Peacock and Girard 1997, 187). Thus, if insurance is the cornerstone of disaster recovery in the United States, and blacks, in particular, are less likely to have adequate coverage due to structural impediments against attaining insurance from a top insurance company, then it is clear that recovery will be significantly impacted.

Minority communities are also less likely to have the political power to garner necessary resources within larger social systems. Recovery is often seen as a competitive process, where different segments of a larger community fight for limited resources (Peacock and Ragsdale 1997). Areas with significant ethnic conflict prior to the disaster in particular struggle in the aftermath of disaster. Segments of the population that can wield more power are more likely to garner the resources they need in the aftermath of disaster. Local governments that are strong and well organized with strong leaders and a readiness to act are more likely to quickly and adequately recover (Rubin 1985; Dash, Peacock, and Morrow 1997). Minority communities often have little power in larger political systems, and often they struggle both organizationally and financially. As a result, recovery is delayed due to the inability to fight for limited resources. In addition, these weaker local governments may be more susceptible to power elites who push and pressure them into making decisions that may not be in the best interest of their communities. Minority communities, both the property within the community and the inhabitants, are often forgotten by those with power, and what often results is a cycle in which the community members themselves are blamed for the poor community conditions that resulted from not getting adequate resources in the first place (Logan and Molotch 1987). As a result, the distribution of aid to minority neighborhoods is often inadequate, resulting in both short-term and long-term recovery struggles. In the United States, examples of this effect can be seen in recovery efforts from both Hurricanes Andrew and Katrina. Internationally, recovery issues may be complicated by additional factors.

Some have argued that the significant amount of humanitarian aid that enters a region after a disaster may lead to "conflict, tension and even the widening of the distance between various ethnic groups" (de Silva 2009, 253). In Sri Lanka, ethnic conflict significantly influenced the recovery process after the 2004 tsunami. At the time of the tsunami, there was significant international work being done to barter a cease-fire in the area between multiple warring groups. Uyangoda (2005, 344) argues that "events after the tsunami indicated that even the responses to such a massive human disaster had been fundamentally intertwined with some core issues of the ethnic conflict." Muslim minorities in the region affected by the tsunami were less likely to receive land to rebuild housing, in part because of the ethnic conflict. Those with political power deemed land too close to the sea unsafe for housing and, therefore, Muslim minorities lost the ability to rebuild in their traditional locations (de Silva 2009).

In settings such as these, the complex natures of ethnic relationships play an important role in the recovery process and environment. In the case of Sri Lanka, civil society leaders wanted the peace process and recovery process to be tied together, but in the end, those were delinked in an attempt to help the various groups meet their recovery needs. And even with these changes, the recovery process continued to be affected by ethnicity. These types of ethnic issues may not always create an environment where one group recovers faster than another, but such ethnic conflicts do influence the entire recovery process and environment.

5.8 IMPLICATIONS FOR ACTION

Race and ethnicity generate vulnerability not simply through cultural differences, although those play a role. Beyond cultural differences, racism embedded in the structural foundations of communities limits opportunity and mobility, and this plays the larger role in vulnerability to disaster. The problem with this connection is not that we recognize its existence, but rather that we are limited in many ways in our response to it. As argued in Chapter 4, the best way to mitigate the vulnerability of the poor to disaster is to eliminate poverty in the first place. And while this is a simple answer to a complex problem, it is not a solution that can be implemented without major changes and alterations to culture and society. Similarly, the best option to reverse the vulnerability to disaster for racial and ethnic minorities is to eliminate racism and its accompanying ethnic and racial stereotypes. The problem with such a needed solution is that it, too, requires significant societal change. This is not to say that it cannot or will not happen, but it is not a practical response that can immediately alter the disaster experiences of minority groups. This is particularly the case in countries where long-standing ethnic tensions exist. The following section outlines a variety of actions that can be applied to address the increased vulnerability of racial and ethnic minorities.

5.8.1   Understanding Stratification

While the profession of emergency management continues to advance, particularly in Western societies, more work needs to be done to educate emergency, political, and humanitarian aid leaders of the impact of race and ethnicity on the disaster experience. Books like this one represent a good first step in understanding the structural inequalities that exist. As this chapter shows, it is not always easy for those in the majority to recognize the experiences of those in the minority. From the outside, it is not always easy to see how stratified social systems like those in the United States result in overt and institutionalized discrimination. And even more complicated is that the notions of race and ethnicity vary globally, and little systematic research outside of the United States has been conducted to understand the issue in this larger context.

To develop a better understanding of the issues, students of emergency management should consider taking classes that focus on race, ethnicity, and culture that use both domestic and international examples for illustration. There is much to be learned from one's own culture as well as other cultures. Classes that focus on these issues are available in both anthropology and sociology departments at most colleges and universities. These classes can be taken as electives while completing emergency management programs, or emergency managers already in the field can take classes as nondegree-seeking students at local colleges and universities. To understand the effects that disasters have on communities and their citizens, it is vital to first understand the structure of society itself. Understanding how race and ethnicity impact individuals and communities in nondisaster times will help decision makers to better meet the needs of minority populations during disasters. Along with this general knowledge, reducing vulnerability also entails emergency personnel knowing their own communities.

5.8.2   Know Your Community

To best meet the needs of survivors of disasters, responders at all levels, then, need to first know their communities. One of the ways to do this is to make sure that social vulnerability is included in community vulnerability maps. While it is important to know the locations of nuclear power plants, hospitals, and schools, it is just as important to know where racial and ethnic minorities live, and what risks exist in those particular locations. Thinking about the example of the 2004 tsunami in Sri Lanka discussed previously, knowing that Muslim minorities live close to the shore gives specific information relative to that population that leads to specific plans for that community. With vulnerability maps, analysis can help illustrate where the greatest needs may be after disaster.

By placing a variety of different overlays of data in a geographic information system (GIS), or mapping software, we can actually understand and recognize the added vulnerabilities of minority groups. For example, known flood zones can be integrated with census data to understand whether racial and ethnic minorities are more likely to be at flood risk. Similarly, data can be integrated to analyze whether shelters and emergency transportation routes meet the needs of minority populations. Housing density data for areas where minorities live may also lead to a variety of changes in how we plan for and respond to disaster.

Part of understanding the community is learning to ask the right questions. To know what those questions should be, emergency responders need to become active in their communities. This is particularly important in understanding minority populations. The issues will vary from community to community and country to country, and understanding these complexities may be aided by subscribing to community newspapers and newsletters that will help responders understand the specific social structure of their communities. For example, in south Florida there is a major difference between Cubans and non-Cuban Hispanics. In areas in the Pacific Northwest, understanding Asian American issues may be key to reducing vulnerability. In areas of the Middle East, understanding the dynamics between majority and minority religious groups may be the key. Through this involvement, not only do emergency managers learn more about their communities, but communities also get the opportunity to meet and engage with emergency managers. For marginal populations who often feel on the fringe, direct involvement with emergency personnel helps build trust that may play an important role during the warning and evacuation phase of a disaster. In addition to building trust, emergency managers should engage minority populations as active members in the planning process so that they can contribute to their own resiliency.

By effectively using the human and cultural capital of minority community members, we can develop plans that take into account specific cultural issues often not considered. Minority groups often are excluded in disaster planning and preparation processes (Bolin and Bolton 1986; Aguirre 1988; Phillips 1993), and as a result, risk increases for these groups. A good example of this is evident in our previous discussion of what occurred during Hurricane Andrew with a sect of Orthodox Jews. Even though Miami Beach was under a mandatory evacuation order, this sect refused to evacuate because their leader in Israel felt they would be safe remaining in their homes. Before the evacuation call, no one in emergency management knew that this sect would seek guidance from their spiritual leader in Israel, and thus with the storm approaching, there was little that could be done to motivate evacuation compliance.

If Hurricane Andrew had stayed on its original predicted path, Miami Beach would have received a direct hit by the storm's eye and the accompanying storm surge. Luckily for this group, the storm tracked about 25 miles to the south. In the years following Hurricane Andrew, considerable effort was made to develop a relationship with this group. Ultimately, this effort paid off and led to the development of an evacuation plan that met both the needs of the group and the county. The heightened risk this sect experienced during Andrew would have been diminished had members of this community been part of the planning process in the first place. This example highlights the importance of incorporating minority leaders into emergency management advisory boards. Diverse advisory boards create environments where both the special needs and talents of underrepresented populations can be heard and utilized. In addition, initiatives to help employ people from minority groups also help to increase diversity within emergency management organizations, which will keep minority issues in the forefront.

Members of minority communities will know the best ways to engage with their citizens and will be aware of different cultural events that serve as ideal venues for community outreach. To help promote hazard awareness, emergency organizations can take advantage of strong traditions and institutions within these minority communities, such as religious organizations and cultural events. For example, in the United States, in some areas Cinco de Mayo festivals are ideal ways to reach Hispanics, and partnerships with black churches lend themselves to be conduits for reaching black citizens. To reach minority populations, emergency managers must not assume that one channel of communication will reach all citizens. Proactively engaging minority leaders in the process helps create a symbiotic relationship between emergency personnel and community members, where both are assisting the other to develop culturally appropriate and successful hazard planning.

5.8.3 PUBLIC EDUCATION

Recognizing that effective information varies based upon the target audience, we need to develop appropriate materials and delivery systems. Programs targeted toward racial and ethnic minorities must be a priority for emergency managers in all communities. Pamphlets and materials need to represent minority members through the use of minority actors in ad campaigns and appropriate language. Educational materials must focus on the information minorities most need to reduce their exposure. Information such as who needs to evacuate, transportation options, and shelter locations best serves minority populations. In conjunction with the materials, delivery methods geared toward minority populations are vital. In some countries and locations, hazard information is disseminated to the public at major grocery store chains. During specific periods of time, campaigns can be designed to reach the general public through a mechanism that they frequently use, for example, printing hazards information on grocery bags.

The problem with such campaigns for minorities is that the large grocery chains that participate in these programs often do not exist in minority neighborhoods. Small, independently owned grocery stores are more likely to be in minority neighborhoods, and such stores do not necessarily have the resources to engage in hazard education campaigns. As a result, minorities are less likely than others to receive the information. To reach minorities, then, emergency managers must think beyond traditional educational campaigns. Options include programs in adult education venues as well as public schools. Partnering with public schools in inner cities, for example, emergency managers can help develop materials that provide hazards education while fulfilling other academic requirements. Students can develop their reading, for example, with age-appropriate hazards stories. History and science lessons can likewise integrate information focusing on hazard mitigation and preparedness. Young minority children, then, are exposed to the language of hazards and methods of preparedness from a young age; it becomes part of their culture. They bring the information home to their parents, but more than that, they become adults who are aware of dangers and of ways to reduce their risk. While such programs are important for all, they are particularly important for minorities who have limited access to other types of programs and information. To ameliorate vulnerability, education programs are particularly effective during the warning/evacuation/response phase. Other programs need to be developed to reduce the effects of vulnerability during other disaster stages.

5.8.4 PLANNING WITH MINORITY COMMUNITIES

Education clearly reduces the probability of increased damage and mortality; however, it does not eliminate the increased risk of minority citizens. Time and time again, we see that plans often fail to recognize the needs of the community. Among the things that are often overlooked are plans for short- and long-term sheltering and displacement. The majority of high-level planners are part of the racial and ethnic majority, and plans are often based on their experience. As a result, the importance of friend and kin networks of some racial and ethnic groups is not recognized. This is particularly important during large-scale disasters where populations are displaced. Hurricane Katrina highlights the significance of this failure

Racial and ethnic minorities are often more connected to each other than those in the majority (Morrow 1997). They are more likely to be part of the informal economy, and thus be tied to their fellow community members in ways that often are not recognized. Displacing people, without understanding their social landscapes, results in additional trauma. Moving Hispanic families, for example, to locations with little Latino culture fails to recognize the importance of not only language, but the richness of their specific ways of life. After the 1972 Buffalo Creek flood in West Virginia, the U.S. Department of Housing and Urban Development (HUD) responded by setting up mobile homes in the hard-hit area. However, when placing families in this temporary housing, they failed to understand the importance of social networks among the population, and as a result, families were displaced from their usual social networks, which caused additional trauma during the recovery period (Erikson 1976).

One of the things displaced New Orleans residents miss the most is the food. While it seems like a trivial issue in the big picture, for those experiencing long-term displacement from their homes, these seemingly unimportant things make a huge difference in the quality of their "new" lives.

Displacing people long term reshapes their social landscapes. The social networks they relied on for transportation, child care, and entertainment, to name a few, are now gone (Litt 2008). Where people are relocated and how they are accepted in their new communities is a critical, and often forgotten, aspect of emergency planning. Displaced whites tend to move to communities where people look like them and accept them. This is not always the case for minorities. In fact, many Katrina evacuees felt unwelcome in their new communities (Miller 2012). Cultural sensitivity embedded within plans can minimize the additive effects of poor plans on minority communities.

5.8.5 BUILDING CAPACITY

While it is extremely important for emergency managers to integrate minority leaders into planning and create education programs that target minority populations, it is even more crucial for minority leaders to help their own communities develop and build capacity. In conjunction with this, the key is developing ways in which communities themselves can build their own capacity from the ground up. While the prior discussion focuses on how community members can help emergency managers plan better, we can likewise see ways that minority communities can help themselves prepare better, thereby improving their own resiliency to disaster.

Minority communities can develop teams within their own communities that focus on emergency preparedness. By creating both informal and formal ties with each other, they can avoid problems that stem from not trusting external power structures. Imagine a situation where you have a minority leader involved with emergency preparedness. The leader learns that a flood warning is going to be issued to the community. The community can create a network where the leader contacts key citizens, and then those citizens alert others within their network. The idea is that those who are designated to communicate the information to the rest of the community are trained to give proper information and recommendations for response. Since minorities are more likely to use kin and social networks, training community members can mitigate the danger of passing on poor information. These trained community members become conduits of education as well. They can pass on information that is developed specifically for their community or information developed for their racial or ethnic group. Specific information geared toward their population group considers culture in its development, and as a result is more likely to be utilized. These types of capacity-building activities may be particularly useful in poor and/or rural at-risk communities where relying on technological solutions is not possible.

FEMA's Citizen Corps program promotes community-level training for citizens. For such programs to succeed in minority communities, minority leaders must embrace them and promote involvement. One final way to build capacity in minority communities is to teach people that emergency management is a viable career option. Universities that offer emergency management training should actively recruit from underrepresented populations. Graduating trained minority emergency management personnel will create an environment where needs are more readily met.

5.9 SUMMARY

One of the reasons that addressing issues of vulnerability connected to race and ethnicity is challenging is that minority status is often tied to issues of poverty and social class. In other words, separating the source of increased vulnerability is difficult. However, even with the complex nature of the problem, this chapter highlighted ways in which race and ethnicity generate vulnerability. At the root of the problem lie societal systems rife with racism and discrimination. This system creates a social structure in which racial and ethnic minorities are segregated and ghettoized onto marginal lands and into dangerous housing. Experiences of racism shape how minorities see the world, and thus these social lenses shape how hazard warnings are filtered and understood. Responses to warnings and thus evacuations, for example, are different. While poor whites in the United States have some similar problems, such as lack of resources for evacuation, minorities' experiences are different, as they struggle to garner not only monetary resources, but political resources as well in a system that historically marginalizes them. In locations across the globe, historical and long-lasting ethnic conflicts, racial oppression, and marginalization shape the social landscape throughout the disaster cycle. And while there seems to be little that can be done when the problem is rooted in the structure of society itself, there are some clear suggestions that can be implemented to reduce the increased risk of minorities. One of the most important things that must be done is for us to recognize the increased vulnerability of minority populations in the first place. With clear recognition, solutions to the problem can begin to be addressed. Without an understanding of the unique experience of racial and ethnic minorities, their vulnerability to disaster will continue.

DISCUSSION QUESTIONS

1. Explain why we argue that race and ethnicity are social constructions.
2. Why is the concept of race difficult to understand globally?
3. What is the racial and ethnic composition of the United States? How do the categories for the United States compare to other countries?
4. Why is race and ethnicity not the same across cultures?
5. How does racism affect whites or those in the majority?
6. Explain at least five ways that racism affects the vulnerability of racial and ethnic minorities to hazards.
7. Discuss ways in which race played a role in the Hurricane Katrina disaster and one other international disaster.
8. Develop a plan for addressing the social vulnerability of racial and ethnic minorities in your community.

ACKNOWLEDGMENTS

I would like to thank Dr. Betty Morrow for allowing me use of her original work, which she developed for the FEMA Higher Education Course on this topic. In addition, I would like to thank all the editors for their hard work and ever-present patience during this process.

REFERENCES

Aguirre, B. E. 1988. The lack of warnings before the Saragosa tornado. *International Journal of Mass Emergencies and Disasters* 6:65–74.
Alston, D., and N. Brown. 1993. Global threats to people of color. In *Confronting environmental racism: Voices from the grassroots*, ed. R. Bullard, 179–94. Boston: South End Press.
Benavides, A., and S. Arlikatti. 2010. The role of the Spanish-language media in disaster warning dissemination: An examination of the emergency alert system. *Journal of Spanish Language Media* 3:41–58.
Bolin, R. C. 1986. Disaster impact and recovery: A comparison of black and white victims. *International Journal for Mass Emergencies and Disasters* 4:35–50.
———. 1994. Household and community recovery after disaster. Monograph no. 56. Boulder: University of Colorado, Institute of Behavioral Science, Program on Environment and Behavior.
Bolin, R. C., and P. Bolton. 1986. *Race, religion and ethnicity in disaster recovery*. Boulder: University of Colorado Press.
Bolin, R. C., and L. Stanford. 1998. *The Northridge earthquake: Vulnerability and disaster*. London: Routledge.
Brookings Institute. 2005. New Orleans after the storm: Lessons from the past, plans for the future. http://www.brookings.edu/~/media/Files/rc/reports/2005/10metropolitanpolicy_fixauthorname/20051012_NewOrleans.pdf.
Brunkard, J., G. Namulanda, and R. Ratard. 2008. Hurricane Katrina deaths, Louisiana, 2005. *Disaster Medicine and Public Health Preparedness* 2 (4): 215–23.
Bullard, R. D. 2000. *Dumping in Dixie: Race, class and environmental quality*. Boulder, CO: Westview Press.

Center for Social Inclusion. n.d. Hurricane Katrina fact sheet: Promoting opportunity for all Americans. http://www.centerforsocialinclusion.org/PDF/katrina_fact_sheet.pdf.

Dash, N., W. G. Peacock, and B. H. Morrow. 1997. And the poor get poorer. In *Hurricane Andrew: Ethnicity, gender, and the sociology of disasters*, ed. W. G. Peacock, B. H. Morrow, and H. Gladwin, 206–25. New York: Routledge.

de Silva, M. W. A. 2009. Ethnicity, politics and inequality: Post-tsunami humanitarian aid delivery in Ampara District, Sri Lanka. *Disasters* 31 (2): 253–73.

Donner, W., and H. Rodriguez. 2008. Population composition, migration and inequality: The influence of demographic changes on disaster risk and vulnerability. *Social Forces* 87 (2): 1089–1114.

Drabek, T. E., and K. S. Boggs. 1968. Families in disaster: Reactions and relatives. *Journal of Marriage and the Family* 30:443–51.

Elder, K., S. Xirasagar, N. Miller, S. A. Bowen, S. Glover, and C. Piper. 2007. African Americans' decisions not to evacuate New Orleans before Hurricane Katrina: A qualitative study. *American Journal of Public Health* 97 (S1): S124–29.

Elliott, J. R., and J. Pais. 2006. Race, class and Hurricane Katrina: Social differences in human responses to disaster. *Social Science Research* 35 (2): 295–321.

Erikson, K. 1976. *Everything in its path*. New York: Simon and Schuster.

Fothergill, A., E. Maestas, and J. Darlington. 1999. Race, ethnicity and disasters in the United States: A review of the literature. *Disasters* 23 (2): 156–73.

Gaillard, J.-C., E. Clave, O. Vibert, D. Azhari, J.-C. Denain, Y. Efendi, D. Grancher, C. C. Liamzon, D. R. Sari, and R. Setiawan. 2008. Ethnic groups' response to the 26 December 2004 earthquake and tsunami in Aceh, Indonesia. *Natural Hazards* 47:17–38.

Gladwin, H., and W. G. Peacock. 1997. Warning and evacuation: A night for hard houses. In *Hurricane Andrew: Ethnicity, gender, and the sociology of disasters*, ed. W. G. Peacock, B. H. Morrow, and H. Gladwin, 52–74. New York: Routledge.

Harper, K., and S. R. Rajan. 2004. International environmental justice: Building the natural assets of the world's poor. Working Paper Series no. 87, Political Economy Research Institute, University of Massachusetts Amherst.

Humes, K. R., N. A. Jones, and R. R. Ramirez. 2011. Overview of race and Hispanic origin: 2010. 2010 Census Briefs. U.S. Census C2010BR-02. http://www.census.gov/prod/cen2010/briefs/c2010br-02.pdf.

Joint Center for Housing Studies of Harvard University. 2011. The State of the Nation's Housing. http://www.jchs.harvard.edu/research/publications/state-nation'shousing-2011.

Klinenberg, E. 2002. *Heat wave: A social autopsy of disaster in Chicago*. Chicago: University of Chicago Press.

Knabb, R. D., J. R. Rhome, and D. P. Brown. 2005. Tropical cyclone report: Hurricane Katrina 23–30 August 2005. National Hurricane Center, updated September 2011. http://www.nhc.noaa.gov/pdf/TCR-AL122005_Katrina.pdf.

Lee, C. 1987. *Toxic waste and race in the United States*. New York: United Church of Christ Commission for Racial Justice.

Liang, N. J., Y. T. Shih, F. Y. Shih, H. M. Wu, H. J. Wang, S. F. Shi, M. Y. Liu, and Bill Wang. 2001. Disaster epidemiology and medical response in the Chi-Chi earthquake in Taiwan. *Annals of Emergency Medicine* 38 (5): 549–55.

Lindell, M. K., J. E. Kang, and C. S. Prater. 2011. The logistics of household hurricane evacuation. *Natural Hazards* 58:1093–1109.

Litt, J. 2008. New Orleans: Gender, the meaning of place, and the politics of displacement. *National Women's Studies Journal* 20 (3): 32–48.

Logan, J. R., and H. L. Molotch. 1987. *Urban fortunes: The political economy of race*. Berkeley: University of California Press.

Mando, A. M., L. Peek, L. M. Brown, and B. L. King-Kallimanis. 2011. Hurricane preparedness and sheltering preferences of Muslims living in Florida. *Journal of Emergency Management* 9 (1): 51–64.

McKinnon, J. D., and C. E. Bennett. 2005. We the people: Blacks in the United States. Census 2000 Special Reports. U.S. Department of Commerce, Economics and Statistics Administration, U.S. Census. http://www.census.gov/prod/2005pubs/censr-25.pdf.

Mileti, D. S., T. E. Drabek, and J. E. Haas. 1975. *Human systems in extreme environments*. Boulder: University of Colorado, Institute of Behavioral Science, Program on Environment and Behavior.

Miller, L. 2012. Katrina evacuee reception in rural east Texas: Rethinking disaster "recovery." In *Displaced: Life in the Katrina Diaspora*, ed. L. Weber and L. Peek, 104–18. Austin: University of Texas Press.

Moore, H. E. 1958. *Tornadoes over Texas*. Austin: University of Texas Press.

Morning, A. 2008. Ethnic classification in global perspective: A cross-national survey of the 2000 Census Round. *Population Research Policy Review* 27:239–72.

Morrow, B. H. 1997. Stretching the bonds: Families of Andrew. In *Hurricane Andrew: Ethnicity, gender, and the sociology of disasters*, ed. W. G. Peacock, B. H. Morrow, and H. Gladwin, 141–70. New York: Routledge.

Peacock, W. G., and C. Girard. 1997. Ethnic and racial inequalities in hurricane damage and insurance settlements. In *Hurricane Andrew: Ethnicity, gender, and the sociology of disasters*, ed. W. G. Peacock, B. H. Morrow, and H. Gladwin, 171–90. New York: Routledge.

Peacock, W. G., and A. K. Ragsdale. 1997. Social systems, ecological networks and disasters: Toward a sociopolitical ecology of disasters. In *Hurricane Andrew: Ethnicity, gender, and the sociology of disasters*, ed. W. G. Peacock, B. H. Morrow, and H. Gladwin, 20–35. New York: Routledge.

Peguero, A. 2006. Latino disaster vulnerability: The dissemination of hurricane mitigation information among Florida's homeowners. *Hispanic Journal of Behavioral Sciences* 28 (1): 5–22.

Perry, R. W., and M. K. Lindell. 1991. The effects of ethnicity on evacuation. *International Journal of Mass Emergencies and Disasters* 9:47–68.

Perry, R. W., and A. H. Mushkatel. 1986. *Minority citizens in disaster*. Athens: University of Georgia Press.

Phillips, B. 1993. Cultural diversity within disasters: Sheltering, housing and long-term recovery. *International Journal of Mass Emergencies and Disaster* 11 (1): 99–110.

Rubin, C. 1985. The community recovery process in the United States after a major natural disaster. *International Journal of Mass Emergencies and Disasters* 3 (2): 9–28.

Rubin, C. B., and R. Palm. 1987. National origin and earthquake response: Lessons from the Whittier Narrows earthquake. *International Journal of Mass Emergencies and Disaster* 5 (3): 347–55.

South, S. J., and K. D. Crowder. 1997. Escaping distressed neighborhoods: Individual, community and metropolitan influences. *American Journal of Sociology* 102 (4): 1040–84.

Statistics Canada. 2006. 2006 Census of Population, Statistics Canada catalogue no. 97-562-XCB2006011 (Canada, Code01).

Stretesky, P., and M. J. Hogan. 1998. Environmental justice: An analysis of Superfund sites in Florida. *Social Problems* 45 (2): 268–87.

Sykes, B. 2001. *The seven daughters of Eve*. New York: W. W. Norton.

Uyangoda, J. 2005. Ethnic conflict, the state and the tsunami disaster in Sri Lanka. *Inter-Asia Cultural Studies* 6 (3): 341–52.

Wilson, N., L. T. Barnard, J. A. Summers, G. D. Shanks, and M. G. Baker. 2012. Ethnicity in 3 influenza pandemics over a century, New Zealand. *Emerging Infectious Diseases* 16 (1): 71–77.

Wisner, B., P. Blaikie, T. Cannon, and I. Davis. 2004. *At risk: Natural hazards, people's vulnerability and disasters*. London: Routledge.

Yelvington, K. 1997. Coping in a temporary way: The tent cities. In *Hurricane Andrew: Ethnicity, gender, and the sociology of disasters*, ed. W. G. Peacock, B. H. Morrow, and H. Gladwin, 92–115. New York: Routledge.

Zifa, W. 2008. A preliminary report on the Great Wenchuan Earthquake. *Earthquake Engineering and Engineering Vibration* 7 (2): 225–34.

RESOURCES

BOOKS

Dyson, M. E. *Come Hell or High Water: Hurricane Katrina and the Color of Disaster.* New York: Basic Civitas Books, 2007 (paperback).

Horne, J. *Breach of Faith: Hurricane Katrina and the Near Death of a Great American City.* New York: Random House Trade Paperbacks, 2008.

Peek, L. *Behind the Backlash: Muslim Americans after 9/11.* Philadelphia: Temple University Press, 2011.

FILMS

American Apartheid. Princeton, NJ: Films for the Humanities and Sciences, 1998 (37 min).

A Village Called Versailles. New Day Films, 2009 (67 min).

Race—The World's Most Dangerous Myth. New York: Insight Media, 1993 (59 min).

Understanding Race. Princeton, NJ: Films for the Humanities and Sciences, 1999 (52 min).

When the Levees Broke: A Requiem in Four Acts. HBO Documentary Films, 2006 (directed and produced by Spike Lee). http://www.hbo.com/docs/programs/whentheleveesbroke/index.html.

Websites

PBS. "What Is Race?" http://www.pbs.org/race/001_WhatIsRace/001_00-home.htm.
Social Science Research Council. Hurricane Katrina Research Hub. http://katrinaresearchhub.ssrc.org.
Understandingrace.org. "Race: Are We So Different?" http://www.understandingrace.org/.
U.S. Census. U.S. Census data in your area. http://www.census.gov/main/www/cen2000.html.

6 Gender

Jennifer Tobin-Gurley and Elaine Enarson

CONTENTS

6.1 CHAPTER PURPOSE

What does gender have to do with disaster? And why focus on women and girls? Are women's and men's lives so different in a disaster? If so, why is this, and what does it mean for emergency management? To help answer these questions, the chapter starts by defining major concepts that are useful for understanding gender dynamics. Next, a conceptual framework for gender analysis and a statistical snapshot of gender relations in the contemporary United States is provided. Then, gender concerns are examined through the life cycle of disasters, drawing primarily on events from the United States, with a few international examples. The chapter concludes with practical steps toward more effective and equitable emergency management.

6.2 OBJECTIVES

As a result of reading this chapter, the reader should be able to:

1. Understand how gender differs from sex and sexuality
2. Appreciate how gender relations affect people's everyday lives

3. Reflect on gender inequalities affecting women in disasters
4. Explain how gender relations affect women and men in disaster contexts
5. Relate gender to other social dynamics affecting disaster resilience
6. Understand the relevance of gender to a social vulnerability approach
7. Identify action steps for mainstreaming gender in emergency management

6.3 INTRODUCTION

So what does gender have to do with disasters? Everything. Gender is a powerful marker of inequality, as well as difference. Resources critical to people's ability to anticipate, prepare for, cope with, respond to, and recover from disasters, including transportation, safe housing, secure income, time, good health, and political voice (Wisner et al. 2004) are not equally available to women and men in any society. As in every society today, social power accrues more to men than to women, not because "biology is destiny" but because *gender stratification* distributes social rewards and power in ways that privilege most boys and men. This chapter draws from research showing how differently women and men are affected by disasters, reinforcing the need for a more multidimensional or intersectional approach to the study of gender and disaster.

6.4 DEFINITIONS AND CONCEPTS

Gender is shorthand for a very complex and changing set of factors based on difference and inequality with respect to biology (reproduction, health, sexuality), the gender identities to which we are socialized (personality, interaction, gender norms), and the dominant gender relations of the societies we inhabit (life chances, opportunities for personal security, achievement, self-determination). Though sex, sexuality, gender identity, and gender relations are distinct, all are powerful forces in our lives. Gender, like race, is a *master status* that cuts across all other areas of social life and trumps other role identities such as teacher, student, boss, or friend. Women's and men's different family and job responsibilities, how and when they use public spaces such as parks or city streets, their modes of transportation—these and a host of other gender patterns put women and men in different places at different times during the day and week. This is true in affluent societies and poorer nations, and cuts across all cultures, faiths, and social groups.

Arguably, sex and gender stereotypes are still such a strong part of advertising, schooling, and family discipline because these norms are not "natural" at all, but must be carefully taught, much as racial identity is. External pressures—along with one's internal sense of being male, female, both, or neither—form a person's *gender identity*. Each generation and culture has different expectations of women and men, boys and girls, just as they have different values and approaches to the natural and built environment. While *social relations* refer to the multiple processes that are historically relevant in shaping our patterned realities and gendered experiences (Anderson 1996), gender norms and *gender relations* are created from the interaction between women and men, and among women and men, and are often quite diverse in complex societies around the world. Relationships may also change or be challenged by crisis, as we see later in this chapter. Women and men may have very different degrees of comfort reaching out for help from a counselor, taking directions from a first responder, or speaking out in a community meeting about reconstruction. This can become even more complicated for individuals who are lesbian, gay, bisexual, transgender, or any other form of sexual or gender identity that is harshly criticized by the dominant culture. As D'Ooge (2008, 22) reminds us, "When speaking of the challenges 'women' face in post-Katrina New Orleans, there are two problematic underlying assumptions: that the category of woman is stable and coherent and that women are heterosexual."

Is gender really all about women's vulnerability? As we will see, gender can endanger the health and well-being of both women and men in disasters (see Mishra [2009] for an international perspective on men in disasters), but it can also contribute to their capacity for *resilience* (Enarson

2012). The concept of resilience has many definitions, but within the context of disaster research it is most frequently defined as "the capability of a community to face a threat, survive and bounce back, or perhaps more accurately, bounce forward into a normalcy newly defined by the disaster related losses and changes" (Cox and Perry 2011, 395). While gender is never irrelevant in human life, it is never by itself a determinative factor of disaster vulnerability or resilience, any more than ethnicity or age. All people are inescapably defined at once by their sex, sexuality, gender, age, race or ethnicity, and their physical bodies at any point in time. The concept of *vulnerability bundling* highlights intersecting cultural and social patterns that, taken together, increase or reduce people's relative vulnerability and capacity for resilience in the face of hazards and disasters. (For a synthesis of findings on this issue from Bangladesh, see Lovekamp [2008].)

Gender inequality persists around the globe, but in different ways, as each new report from the Gender Equity Index demonstrates with respect to economics, education, and political status (Social Watch Organization 2012). These come into play strongly in developing societies, where gender inequality, environmental risk, and political uncertainty may limit the autonomy, education, livelihood, heath, safety, and voice of women and girls. Drought provides just one example of how this further undermines people's capacity to cope with disasters and adapt to climate uncertainties. Women's time and the education of their daughters are lost to the increasing need to walk further for potable water, which also jeopardizes their personal safety and overall health. (Visit the website of the Gender and Water Alliance to learn more: www.genderandwater.org/.)

Gender can be a *root cause of social vulnerability* based on gender differences or inequalities or both (Bolin, Jackson, and Crist 1998; Enarson, Fothergill, and Peek 2006; Enarson and Phillips 2008). For example, women have specific needs and limitations during pregnancy; their domestic work is generally discounted; and they are at increased risk of abuse postdisaster. Men are at physical risk in male-dominated relief occupations (Photo 6.1) and may feel it "unmanly" to ask for counseling or seek appropriate care, and therefore may suffer the effects of unmanageable stress or substance abuse. Cultural context is vital, too (Enarson and Meyreles 2004). In many wealthy nations, poor women and others living at increased risk may nonetheless be more resilient to the effects of a disaster than either women or men in low-income developing nations. Practitioners and others should pay particular attention to how income, disability, violence, age, homelessness, single parenting, social isolation, minority status, immigrant status, and widowhood may affect women's differential vulnerability. Marginal or transitional sexualities and gender identities can be a source

PHOTO 6.1   Male-dominated professions may put men differentially at risk, as is the case with many first-responder professions. (*Source*: Leif Skoogfors/FEMA photo.)

of solidarity, but they can also increase vulnerability due to social exclusion in formal relief systems and/or interpersonal violence when emergencies thrust people into close proximity (Balgos, Gaillard, and Sanz 2012).

6.4.1 THEORETICAL FRAMEWORKS

Social vulnerability analysis directs our attention to change. Climate change is a powerful force bringing more extreme and uncertain weather events in its wake, and women and men are not exposed in the same ways or with the same effects. The same can be said of terrorism and such technological hazards as toxic contamination of water supplies. Household and family lives are also changing in the United States. The percentage of female-headed households continues to increase, and women who are heads of households experience higher poverty rates than male heads of households (38.5% vs. 23.7%, respectively); these women are also disproportionately from marginalized racial and ethnic groups (West Coast Poverty Center 2009). Owing to maternal poverty and related factors, the children from these homes often live in substandard housing with caregivers who may lack jobs with secure benefits, not to mention reliable transportation in a disaster. High rates of child poverty in the nation also mean that growing numbers of children lack health insurance and therefore are without regular health care, so they are often facing the uncertainties of hazards and disasters while in poor health. The national shift away from state-supported social services especially affects families that depend on the social safety net in the best of times. As described in the demographic section (Section 6.5), these and related trends and patterns are highlighted as factors affecting disaster vulnerability. Gender relations matter in disasters in subtle ways as well and throughout the life course of a disaster (Fothergill 1998). They are an important, if neglected, aspect of good vulnerability analysis (Laska and Morrow 2006).

Gender theory informs disaster work in many ways, though not always directly. The dominant perspective in the United States and similar countries remains *liberal feminism*, highlighting persistent opportunity gaps between women and men in emergency management contexts. Expanding women's presence in the field and ensuring that existing relief and recovery resources are available to women and men is the focus. But important insights can be gained from alternative perspectives that question inequalities embedded in the status quo and call attention to gender-based violence. Other theorists emphasize that *global development* patterns are closely intertwined with gender relations in every society, including the United States, and that women and men play distinct roles in the use of natural and cultural spaces and use environmental resources differently. Men, too, are rethinking notions of *masculinity* and diverse strategies of manliness (Connell 2005). Thinking about gender in our era also leads to more critical analysis of dominant "either/or" traps that do not allow for the everyday realities of *transsexual*, *intersex*, and *bisexual* people as they cope with flooding or fires (Pincha and Krishna 2008) any more than traditional perspectives on gender allowed gays and lesbians to claim social space.

6.5 DEMOGRAPHIC OVERVIEW

The World Economic Forum produces an annual Gender Gap Report based on such statistical indicators as employment status, education, health, and exposure to violence to capture these inequalities between women and men, and boys and girls, as they change. Despite women's increased access to college education, a (slowly) narrowing gender gap in electoral politics, or the access of women and men to occupations traditionally considered "wrong" for them, the report indicates that significant gender equality gaps persist in many areas around the world (World Economic Forum 2011).

The implications of sex and gender in disasters are difficult to capture statistically, especially when used simply to note the relative numbers of women and men, for example, in a workplace or in a census tract. Yet census data and other statistical indicators are indispensable tools for social vulnerability analysis. As seen in Box 6.1, many demographic indicators hint at broader social

BOX 6.1   GENDERED DEMOGRAPHIC PROFILE FOR THE U.S.

FAMILY

Percent of all households comprised of married couples: 49%[a]

Percent of older women (65+ years) who are married: 49.6% (vs. 52.4% male)[b]

Percent widowed (40% female, 13% male)[b]

There were over four times as many widows (8.9 million) as widowers (2.1 million) in 2009[b]

EMPLOYMENT AND INCOME

Percent of women in the labor force: 59% (vs. 70% male)[a]

Percent of employed women working full time in 2010: 73%[c]

Percent of women not in the civilian labor force: 21% (vs. 15% male)[a]

Female-to-male earnings ratio at the median for year-round, full-time workers in 2010: 73% (up by 5% since 1999)[a]

Compared to the earnings of fully employed non-Hispanic males, non-Hispanic women were paid 78%; Asian women were paid 80%; black women were paid 62%; and Hispanic women were paid 54%[c]

For female-headed families, the annual average unemployment rate grew from 11.5% in 2009 to 12.3% in 2010, while the rate for black women increased from 11.5% in 2009 to 12.8% in 2010, and the rate for Hispanic women increased from 10.6% in 2009 to 11.4% in 2010[c]

HOUSING

Percent of women 65 and older who lived by themselves in 1970: 32% (vs. 15% male), and in 2010: 19% (vs. 8%)[a]

Family households maintained by women with no husband present numbered 15.3 million, almost three times the number maintained by men with no wife present (5.8 million)[d]

Percent of families maintained by women without spouses who are homeowners: 19.7% (vs. 7.1% male)[a]

Of the people who are homeless with children, 35% are male, 65% are females; 67.5% of the single homeless population is male, and this single population makes up 76% of the total homeless population[e]

EDUCATION

Percent of women aged 25 years and older with a bachelor's degree or higher in 2010: 27.9% (vs. 28.5% male)[a]

POVERTY

The number of people in poverty in 2010 (46.2 million) is the largest number in the 52 years for which poverty estimates have been published[f]

Percent of women living below poverty in 2010: 8.4% (vs. 6.9 male)[a]

Women accounted for 14.2% of unrelated individuals in poverty in 2002[a]

Percent of women 75 and over living below the poverty line: 11.4% (vs. 6.9% male)[a]

Percent of African-American women ages 65 and older who are poor: 7.4%[a]; of elderly Hispanic women, 5%[a]

Percent of older Hispanic women living alone who are poor (44.6%) and black women who lived alone and are poor (33.0%)[b]

Percent female-headed families with children in poverty in 2010: 40.7% (vs. male-headed families 24.8% and married families 8.8%)[c]

Percent of black women in poverty in 2010: 25.6% (vs. Hispanic women 25.0% and Native-American women 26.4%)[c]

AGE

Sex ratio for older adults: 135 women for every 100 men; ratio of 114 for the 65–69 age group, and 216 for persons over 85[b]

From 2000 to 2010, the male population grew slightly faster than the female population, contributing to a smaller sex ratio and lower morbidity rates among men[g]

DISABILITY

Percent of the U.S. median income earned by women with physical disabilities: 53.8% in 2008[a]

Percent of women living with a disability or residing in a nursing home: 12.9% (20.2 million)[h]

[a] U.S. Census Bureau. 2010. American Community Survey Data 1-Year Estimates, B12002. http:// www.census.gov.

[b] U.S. Department of Health and Human Services, Administration on Aging. 2011. A profile of older Americans: 2011. Washington, DC. http://www.aoa.gov/aoaroot/aging_statistics/Profile/2011/5. aspx.

[c] U.S. Department of Labor. 2010. Women in the labor force in 2010. Women's Bureau. http://www .dol.gov/wb/factsheets/Qf-laborforce-10.htm.

[d] U.S. Census Bureau. Profile of general population and housing characteristics: 2010 demographic profile data DP-1.

[e] U.S. Conference of Mayors. 2007. Hunger and homelessness survey: A status report on hunger and homelessness in America's cities. usmayors.org/hhsurvey2007/hhsurvey07.pdf.

[f] U.S. Census Bureau. C. DeNavas-Walt, B. D. Proctor, and J. C. Smith. 2011. Income, poverty, and health insurance coverage in the United States: 2010. Current Population Reports. U.S. Department of Commerce, Economics and Statistics Administration.

[g] U.S. Census Bureau. Lindsay M. Howden and Julie A. Meyer. 2011. Age and sex composition: 2010. 2010 Census Briefs. U.S. Department of Commerce, Economics and Statistics Administration.

[h] U.S. Census Bureau. Census 2000 Summary File 1 (SF 1) 100-Percent Data, P038. http://www .census.gov.

dynamics that position women and men differently in disasters in the United States. For example, most women live longer than men and hence are more likely to experience physical limitations that matter in emergencies. Ethnicity and race also interact with sex, so census data regularly indicate higher levels of poverty in households headed by African-American women and women from other marginalized ethnic groups. Across ethnic groups, men are more likely than women to have access to resources that can be protective in disasters, such as home ownership and secure income. At the same time, men are more likely than women to be homeless and living on the street when emergencies or disasters occur. Many men, especially those in disadvantaged ethnic communities, also experience high levels of interpersonal violence, which can undermine their ability to access neighborhood resources in disaster contexts. Women's high exposure to domestic violence and sexual assault has the same effect. The historic trend toward increased female employment changes the family context in which emergencies unfold and raises pressing issues related to child care and the

competing responsibilities of dual-career couples. When preparing for the unexpected, and especially in the aftermath of disaster, the traditional caregiving responsibilities of women across the
life span should be especially noted by emergency planners.

One outcome of the most recent U.S. economic downturn was a substantial national increase in
poverty for women and their families. In fact, the poverty rate for all women in the United States
rose to 14.5% in 2010, which is the highest it had been in 17 years (National Women's Law Center
2011). Black and Hispanic women, as well as single mothers, experienced an even greater increase,
and childhood poverty rose to 22.0% in 2010, leaving more children and women vulnerable to
the effects of disaster (National Women's Law Center 2011). Internationally, women and girls are
disproportionately affected by the global economic crisis. Much of the industry in the developing
world relies on cheap labor in the informal sector, where the poorest women make up 75%–90% of
the workforce and are the first to be laid off in an economic downturn (Eilor 2009). With respect to
education, a recent U.N. Human Development Report (United Nations 2011) shows that, on average,
higher percentages of men around the world receive at least a secondary school education, but the
ratio varies considerably. In very highly developed nations, the female/male gap is quite small (82.0
vs. 84.6), but it is substantial in the world's poorest, least developed nations (18.7 vs. 32.4); the gap
in most countries falls between the extremes (United Nations 2011). Gender disparities in health,
education, political participation, economics, and other realms all come strongly into play in disasters. As you read on, you may reflect on how these and other demographic patterns and trends can
be captured statistically to guide emergency planners.

6.6 GENDER CONCERNS THROUGH THE DISASTER LIFE CYCLE

Today's emergency managers have gender-sensitive research to guide them rather than the kind of
"myths of male superiority" that Scanlon (1999) documented in his study of the 1917 explosion in
Halifax, Nova Scotia. In this section, we review some of the major empirical conclusions drawn
about gender relations in warning, evacuation, response, and recovery by researchers who have
studied recent U.S. and international disasters, drawing attention to the practical implications for
emergency managers.

6.6.1 Risk Communication and Warnings

Concern for the safety of their families is a strong motive underlying women's well-documented
involvement in environmental protection movements and neighborhood emergency-preparedness
campaigns (Erikson 1994; Krauss 1993; Neal and Phillips 1990). Even the best designed and delivered warnings come to "receivers" who are human and draw on their own judgment, experience,
and networks before responding—or not. Who is listening when emergency managers try to alert
the public, and who is more likely to act? This is a complex subject, but researchers have demonstrated that gender relations are one part of the answer (Cutter 1992). Men, on balance, are more
risk tolerant than women, which likely translates into being less prone to take self-protective action
in disaster contexts (Finucane et al. 2000).

Women's pivotal roles in family life and their extensive social networks based on neighborhood,
parenting, school, work, and faith put them at the center of the process of interpreting and assessing warnings. They are also key actors in mobilizing response to warnings, as families generally
take action as a unit; as household managers, women are instrumental in drawing the extended
family together to assess the credibility of warnings and determine a course of action. This is especially important when large ethnic families and complex multigenerational households must be
gathered to assess warnings, share information, and chart a course of action (Phillips and Morrow
2007). (See Litt, Skinner, and Robinson [2012] for information on African-American women's
networks post-Katrina.)

Women are strong risk communicators as volunteers and staff in local social service groups and community agencies, and they are active participants in community-based preparedness and mitigation campaigns (Luft 2012; Turner, Nigg, and Paz 1986). In her research on the People's Hurricane Relief Fund following Katrina, Luft (2012, 251) notes:

> Many of the responsibilities and skills that constitute "women's work"—such as organizing the food, shelter, and care necessary for daily survival (reproductive labor); maintaining ties (networking); and emotional labor (solidarity work)—are central to community organizing and other forms of movement building.

Women are also dominant figures in the everyday activities of most religions, supporting the call to communicate to vulnerable groups through faith-based organizations, for example, in the wake of Hurricane Katrina (Eisenman et al. 2007). Although men may find official warnings more credible and rely more on mass media than informal conversation (Major 1999), outreach through the workplace may reach men best.

Gender can also constrain women's access to emergency-preparedness information and critically needed warnings and forecasts (for international examples, see Fordham 2001). The "digital divide" in cyberspace (unequal access to computers and the Internet) is a limiting factor in many cultures, still including the United States in some respects (Papadakis 2000), and varying by ethnicity. Low-income women less familiar with the Internet or those with less time or access to computers are disadvantaged by Web-based awareness and preparedness campaigns. Similarly, deaf or blind women and non-English speaking women cannot be reached unless alternative media and languages are used to convey potentially lifesaving information. Women's neighborhood-based networks are significant here, as these social connections can help identify needs and capacities, including who may need the most help in an emergency situation (Morrow 2006). Therefore, a one-size-fits-all approach to emergency risk communications targeting "the public" with very general messages may miss both a male audience in need of persuasion and women who face specific barriers in their communication networks. Effective disaster risk communication means reaching out creatively to, and being in dialogue with, different subpopulations.

6.6.2 Evacuation

When waters rise or the air thickens with smoke, women are reportedly among the first to act. In some studies, men have interpreted this desire to act as "panic," and women report being frustrated by the lack of social power or funds to make decisions for the household. Gender is, indeed, a good predictor of evacuation behavior, especially when children are present (Gladwin and Peacock 1997). The differences in evacuation behavior between women and men could be drawn upon to specifically target women in preparedness training and evacuation messaging, which could result in more timely evacuations, ultimately saving lives (Richter 2011).

In addition to other factors at play, the lack of access to functional cars and money for gasoline forced many low-income New Orleans residents—many of them poor women—to stay, as interviewers learned when they queried survivors in a Houston shelter (Eisenman et al. 2007; Elder et al. 2007). The sheer capacity to leave cannot be overestimated, as one single mother explained: "You have to be able to feed your children when you leave. You have to be able to have a place to stay, you have to have gas money, you have to have rental car money. I couldn't afford to do that" (Eisenman et al. 2007, S112). When Hurricane Katrina struck in 2005, 26% of households in New Orleans did not have access to personal automobiles (Willinger and Knight 2012), leaving more than 100,000 people stranded.

Most families evacuate together, but it is not uncommon for the sons and fathers of families facing evacuation to resist due to a strong sense of self as family provider and in the hopes of safeguarding property (see, for example, Eisenman et al. 2007, S111). Women, too, may feel this pressure, making the same decision to remain, and pay with their lives; this is especially likely in developing nations, where women's livestock, household gardens, and fishing or farming and waged labor support their families (Ikeda 1995).

6.6.3 Impacts and Crisis Response

On balance, women's response to crisis is more inside and backstage, while men's is more outside and front stage (Alway, Belgrave, and Smith 1998; Enarson 2001; Fordham 1998). In the immediate aftermath of a disaster, early research found that men were free to make their way to the center of damage to assist strangers, while women tend to help family and kin first (Wenger and James 1994).

In disaster crisis response, men may be constrained by masculinity norms and stereotypes, such as manhood being associated with toughness, both physically and emotionally. Pacholok (2009) found that male firefighters grappled with feelings that they had "lost" when they were unable to control large wildfires in Canada in 2003. In addition, the dynamics of masculinity fueled the conflicts between firefighter groups, which were then compounded by the media's use of heroic masculinity in their reporting of the firefighters. In the aftermath of the tsunami in India, men also felt constrained by mainstream notions of masculinity, and many visitors and the media ignored men's emotional trauma and misunderstood their role in community work in the disaster aftermath (Mishra 2009).

Women's presence is hard to miss in the lower levels of all Red Cross disaster activities (Gibbs 1990) and other disaster relief agencies (Enarson, Fothergill, and Peek 2006). Even in societies such as Iran, with strict segregation of the sexes in rural areas, the Red Cross and Red Crescent Society employ women to reach out to other women in their community who are unable to move freely, but likely to be hard hit in an earthquake or flood (Oxlee 2000). Formal emergency response roles, however, are highly gendered and gender segregated around the world, as discussed later in the chapter.

6.6.3.1 Life, Safety, and Health

This chapter focuses primarily on how gender difference and inequality put women and girls at increased risk. Gender-disaggregated mortality data are scarce, even in the United States (Enarson 2012). Following the 2011 East Japan earthquake and tsunami, Saito (2012) reports that neglecting to gather routine gender data and statistics made it difficult to assess the full impact of the disaster on women. (See Sawai [2012] for a detailed discussion of mortality rates in Japan.) A recent report analyzing 18 maritime disasters found that contrary to the legacy of "women and children first," it is actually the men who have a survival advantage (Elinder and Erixson 2012). Yet, a study on the children of Katrina suggests that more boys than girls died (Zahran, Peek, and Brody 2008), echoing other evidence that elderly, poor, African-American men suffered disproportionately high fatalities in this storm relative to their presence in the population most affected (Sharkey 2007). These findings support Klinenberg's (2002) conclusion from his "social autopsy" of Chicago's 1995 heat wave that 80% of the unclaimed bodies were those of African-American men who were old, poor, and residing in a highly vulnerable neighborhood. Controlling for age, men were more than twice as likely to die in the same age group, a finding Klinenberg (2002) relates to "the gender of isolation," reflecting masculinity norms of detachment and independence that result in more tenuous ties to family. However, European heat-wave studies found that it was elderly, disabled, low-income women who were more likely to die (Ogg 2005).

In studies of major destructive events in the developing world, girls and women are highly vulnerable to the effects of environmental disasters and are the majority of those killed (Anderson 2000; Cutter 1995; Ikeda 1995; Rivers 1982). A recent statistical study of disaster-related gendered gaps in life expectancy concludes that women, more than men, die at an earlier age than would be expected in developing nations that are struck by natural disasters (Neumayer and Plümper 2007). In addition to family care, physical health, and reproductive status, the gendered division of labor is a powerful explanation, for this puts adult women and men in physically different locations. For example, when the extraordinarily powerful 2004 Indian Ocean tsunami wave came ashore in many

Sri Lankan villages, men out fishing survived more often than women waiting on the beach to pre-pare and market the day's catch (Oxfam International 2005).

Women's often tenuous *access to health care* before disasters can deteriorate further in the aftermath, as was reported of low-income Katrina survivors who depended upon diabetes clinics, maternal- and infant-care programs, and community clinics serving those living with HIV/AIDS or other chronic diseases (Jones-DeWeever 2007). After working with incoming Katrina evacuees in Colorado Springs, Colorado, one recovery worker explained (Tobin-Gurley 2008, 66):

> We had several ladies and they had asthma and were on oxygen and different things were going wrong with them. They couldn't get glasses, their glasses were broken and their dentures were gone. I mean all of the things that we take for granted, those people could not get.

Poor living conditions, overcrowding, lack of access to services, constraints on breast feeding, and limited access to birth control were among the problems for women noted by health researchers in the aftermath of Katrina (Callaghan et al. 2007). Without access to reliable birth control, women may be faced with unintended pregnancies, so resilient family planning services are essential. Indeed, in the first six months following Katrina, 17% of 55 young women (aged 16–24) in New Orleans told researchers they needed but were not able to obtain health care, a third found it difficult to practice their usual birth control method, and four in five had not used birth control (Kissinger et al. 2007).

The immediate needs of *pregnant women* should certainly be part of emergency planning. Zahran and others (2011) found that after Hurricane Andrew, pregnant women experienced higher rates of stress-related negative birth outcomes as compared to women who did not endure the storm. In Hurricane Katrina, more than 1.1 million women of reproductive age (15–44 years) resided in the affected areas, and they were disproportionately at risk of adverse outcomes related to poor nutri-tion, lack of services, and poverty before the storm; not surprisingly, the rate of low-weight births among the children they gave birth to after the storm was significantly higher than the U.S. norm (Callaghan et al. 2007).

Significant threats to the life and safety of women and girls also arise from *gender violence*, which is discussed further in Chapter 12. (See Box 6.2 on violence against women in Haiti's emergency shel-ters.) New research from Australia (Parkinson and Zara 2011) documents the struggle of women to be safe from, and understand, male violence in the aftermath of Victoria's 2009 Black Saturday bushfire.

Finally, the interaction of social class, life stage, family size, and family structure generally puts women at greater risk of *postdisaster stress*. A major review of this literature based on case studies from the United States, Mexico, and elsewhere (Norris et al. 2002) determined that being married is a risk factor for women, while being somewhat more protective for men. Studies from the *Exxon Valdez* oil spill point to more self-destructive coping strategies such as substance abuse or fighting among men (Palinkas et al. 1993), and after the 2010 BP/*Deepwater Horizon* oil spill, Gill, Picou, and Ritchie (2011) reported similar, and possibly more intense, effects for fishing families along the Gulf Coast. Coping with the emotional needs of male partners is an added challenge to women who are "shock absorbers" for so many of the effects of disasters. Acting as sounding boards for men may also be part of the job of women in first-responder roles, as this firefighter who responded to the World Trade Center recalled (Hagen and Carouba 2002, 179):

> Guys will come into my office and cry to me who aren't going in to the office and crying to my lieuten-ants. As women, I think we've got a big burden. The burden has always been on the women, because we're in a fishbowl.

6.6.4 Recovery

This section offers a short review of gender issues throughout the recovery process, with selected examples of how women individually and collectively step into action to help themselves, their

---

BOX 6.2   VIOLENCE AGAINST WOMEN IN HAITI'S EMERGENCY SHELTERS

Women and girls are the first to suffer in Haiti from environmentally induced conflicts and disasters.... For example, the issue of women, girls' and boys' security and gender-based violence is intricately connected to environmental and disaster risk mitigation. Increased security issues in camps have been correlated with lack of food, water, electricity, shelter and adequate bathrooms and showers. Women and young girls in particular are facing abuse, discrimination, harassment and rape in camps and temporary shelters where basic needs are not met and conditions are becoming desperate. Therefore, assessments and planning around issues of clean water, sanitation and waste management must inevitably include their effects on women and vulnerable populations.... A great majority of displacement camps have only 1 bathroom for every 100 to 150 people. As a result, women and girls have to travel long distances, sometimes late at night, to access facilities. A great number of assaults against women take place in and around bathrooms. Two key environmental conclusions can be drawn from this phenomenon. First, poor disaster and sanitation planning without sufficient consultation from women's groups has unintentionally led to an increase in gender-based violence. Second, the resulting behavioral responses have strong negative environmental repercussions. In light of the precarious security risks of utilizing public facilities, many women are opting to stay closer to home, even if facilities do not exist. This fact has strong health and environmental implications for overcrowded IDP [Internally Displaced Persons] camps in which disease can quickly spread.

Source: Haiti Gender Equality Collective (2010).

---

families, and their communities. One clear conclusion is that, whatever the contours or cultural location of the next disaster or catastrophe, women, too, will be leaders in the long walk forward to what the "new normal" may bring.

6.6.4.1   Shelter and Housing

When forced to relocate during the emergency period, affluent women across the globe have the resources to move their families to out-of-town cabins and second homes, fly to the homes of distant family members, or check into hotels instead of shelters. Strong credit records and savings help them recover, unlike displaced low-income women who have a much more difficult time accessing resources and securing stable housing after being displaced (Tobin-Gurley, Peek, and Loomis 2010). Following Hurricane Katrina in 2005, temporary shelters across the United States, which often housed displaced residents for months or even years, were rarely sited near major employers of women, public transportation lines, or child-care centers, making it difficult for women to earn income and help their families start anew (Tobin-Gurley, Peek, and Loomis 2010). Two years after the 2010 Haitian earthquake, it was largely poor women who remain in temporary camps with little access to resources (Horton 2012).

6.6.4.2   Care Work

The emotional and physical needs of male partners, children, aging relatives, the ill or disabled, and other dependents are met predominantly by women before, during, and after disasters. These responsibilities tend to increase dramatically, even as newer forms of disaster work arise and women seek income-generating jobs. This is especially true of low-income women unable to purchase such replacement services as child or elder care, restaurant meals, domestic help, or dry cleaning. Often, households expand in size as women able to do so offer space and personal services (cooking, laundry, child care, emotional support) to kin, coworkers, friends, and evacuated families not known to them personally. For example, Saito (2012) found that a disproportionate burden was placed on housewives after the 2011 East Japan disaster: They were expected to take on the responsibility of caring for displaced family members as well as their own. In Haiti, following the 2010 earthquake, poor women have been exposed to even higher rates of poverty due to increased caring for children, the elderly, and the disabled (Nadelman and Louis 2010).

During their long stays in various temporary accommodations, women's day-to-day efforts to cook, clean, and care for their families, often in combination with paid jobs and unpaid community work, are complicated by the physical limitations of the temporary accommodations, e.g., lack of privacy, few play spaces for children or activities for teens, insufficient laundry facilities, and social isolation. For instance, in evacuation shelters in Japan, traditional gender roles were reinforced when women were asked to prepare meals for free, while men were offered the paid jobs of collecting and removing debris (Saito 2012). The routine and exceptional demands of daily life are more time consuming and difficult in temporary accommodations, but also an essential part of rebuilding home and hearth (Fothergill 2004). Kin-related work such as celebrating birthdays, religious holidays, and anniversaries; home visits to older relatives; and care for the ill does not stop during relocation, and generally falls to the women of the family.

Caring for children in temporary housing, or in the homes of distant kin or host families, can be extremely difficult (Enarson and Scanlon 1999; Peek and Fothergill 2009). New child-care issues arise, including conflicts with grandparents, disrupted nursing schedules and toilet training, more sibling conflict, and unfamiliar child-care providers. Single mothers displaced by the Gulf Coast storms reported that parenting became much more complicated after moving away from the fathers of their children and extended family networks (Peek and Fothergill, 2009). Peek and Fothergill (2009, 86) reported:

> While a few of the single mothers spoke of "absent fathers," most of the single mothers in our study informed the researchers that their children's fathers had played important roles in their children's lives before the storm. In fact, many of the single mothers reported that even though they did not live together, these fathers still spent time with their children and shared in at least some parental duties.

Losing even minimal paternal support and the help of extended kin greatly impacted women, increasing their daily responsibilities and intensifying the psychological burden of disaster response and recovery.

6.6.4.3 Income-Generating Work

Temporary relocation (which may last a long time) impinges directly and indirectly on women's ability to earn income. After Hurricane Katrina in 2005, female labor-force participation rates in New Orleans declined along with their average wages, the opposite of men's experience; further, it is female-dominated sectors, such as service work, health care, and education, that decline most dramatically (Jones-DeWeever 2007). In New Orleans, over 7,000 schoolteachers, almost all women, found themselves out of work in the aftermath of Hurricane Katrina when the New Orleans public schools illegally fired their teachers (United Teachers of New Orleans 2007; Winter 2012).

Women's income declines due to secondary unemployment, too. Domestic workers, for instance, may well lose both homes and jobs when their middle-class employers either temporarily or permanently relocate. The financial fallout for women after the 1997 Red River flood meant downward mobility for many when women lost income due to business closures and cutbacks and increased debt (Fothergill 2004). Similarly, relocated mothers after Hurricane Katrina (Tobin-Gurley 2008) and displaced women looking for work after the 2011 East Japan disaster (Saito 2012) faced a loss of income due to lack of child care and access to jobs. More than two and a half years after Hurricane Katrina, just 117 child-care centers in New Orleans were operating compared to 275 before the storm, and only one fifth as many public buses were available for employed women without private transportation (Agenda for Children 2008; New Orleans Index 2008).

Women who work in agricultural jobs or are owner/operators of family farms suffer both income loss and severe degradation of the natural world around them, in rich and poor societies alike.

Women with *resource-dependent livelihoods* are impacted in complex ways when these resources are degraded. (See, among others, Alston [2006] and Stehlik, Lawrence, and Gray [2000] for studies of women and drought in Australia.) The diffuse effects on women's livelihoods in the face of global warming warrant much closer attention as snow decreases, species decline, variability in weather patterns increase, and related effects linked both to climate change and to women's health and sustainable livelihoods. (See Owens [2005] for a study from indigenous communities in Canada's North and Dankelman's [2011] compilation of case studies from developing nations.)

6.6.4.4 Help Seeking

Like the men in their families, women generally resist asking for emergency assistance from government and private relief agencies because of the "stigma of charity" (Fothergill 2004). A single mother who was displaced following Hurricane Katrina explained (Tobin-Gurley 2008, 115):

> I tried to go through state assistance and I appealed it for a year, food stamps and welfare office, because I have never been on any assistance. Of course it was a hurting thing to your pride, but after a year I just got tired of it. I did not want to be on the benefits because that was my mom's life and I did not want to repeat that cycle. You know, you are living on the first and fifteenth and looking for your food stamps, your welfare check. I hated that, so I worked two jobs to maintain [pre-Katrina].

Yet, they must put aside these feelings, for researchers around the globe find that the "second disaster" of paperwork (Weaver 2002, 40) falls disproportionately to them. Like so many others with family responsibilities, this Native-American mother of a young daughter in the 1997 Red River valley flood had no choice (Enarson 1998, 3):

> I had a hard time going to, like, Red Cross or anything like that. I had a very difficult time. And I don't know if it was a pride thing or what. My Dad would not go. [And your husband?] Oh, there's no way. No. And when we were [evacuated] out there, I had to go. I had nothing for my daughter.

Wives and daughters interviewed in case studies typically report that it is they who register the household for assistance before evacuation, deal in person and by telephone with a range of agencies to file damage claims, and pursue the frustrating search for any and all relief and recovery resources. Spending valuable hours on the phone or in long lines is a difficult process, and after disaster it is typically women who are expected to take on this responsibility, often with young children in tow (Tobin-Gurley 2008).

6.6.4.5 Relocation

Women's economic status and family roles are formidable barriers in the race for affordable housing, making women *more dependent on temporary accommodations*. Women are far more likely than men to be household heads who rely on their own low incomes or modest government assistance, so the national shortage of affordable housing (Joint Center for Housing Studies of Harvard University 2004) can become a personal crisis. More likely than men to be renters, women cannot afford escalating rental rates, for example, in New Orleans, where rents nearly doubled after Hurricane Katrina and 75% of the housing units destroyed were considered affordable or low-income housing (GAO 2009, 12). The intentional demolition of thousands of public housing units by the government (not the storm) helps explain why 83% of single mothers were still unable to return to their own communities two years after the storms: "The same people who were left behind during the storm have been left behind in rebuilding it. The elderly, the young, single mothers" (Jones-DeWeever 2007, 10).

Couples may also struggle with *conflicting priorities* when making decisions about whether, when, and where to relocate, and about repair and rebuilding priorities. Flood-affected women in the midwestern United States objected when men's interests took priority in home reconstruction, and repairs to laundry rooms, home offices, or play spaces used predominantly by women and children were delayed: "I was just furious," one woman who worked at home told an interviewer. "It was as if my work was worthless" (Fothergill 2004, 139).

6.6.4.6 Marginalization

Gender bias in *recovery programs* may also deter women's recovery. Childers's study (1999) of several flooded communities in Louisiana found that low-income elderly women were disproportionately in need of economic assistance but less likely to receive it. Women have also been denied small-business loans and access to federal disaster-relief programs for small businesses (Nigg and Tierney 1990; Staples and Stubbings 1998). If small-loan programs targeting women do not include feasibility studies, job training, and other social supports, they may sap women's resources without advancing their long-term recovery.

Barriers to gainful employment for women following disaster are often reported in developing nations (see Enarson and Chakrabarti 2009). After the 2010 Haitian earthquake, many women indicated that opportunities for work would be more valuable than other kinds of disaster aid (Nadelman and Louis 2010). In fact, one long-time union leader working with Haitian women noted, "I do not want to see women only supporting the reconstruction, cooking for or bringing water to the men who get the jobs working on construction projects. Women can learn how to do this work too" (Nadelman and Louis 2010, 7). It is critical that women be included in decision making and be offered equal access to jobs that are generated in the postdisaster context (Nadelman and Louis 2010).

In the United States, too, gender bias in disaster recovery arises from normative expectations about whose voice matters, how a "family" looks or acts, stereotypes about the passions and skills of women and men, and lack of knowledge about the challenges and dangers faced by girls and women. Targeting relief funds to male-dominated employment projects in construction, debris removal, or landscaping supports the economic recovery of teenaged and adult men, but it disadvantages working-class women and girls who also need income support. When good disaster relief jobs are available, they primarily hire middle-class women with formal credentials, job experience, and professional networks (Krajeski and Peterson 1997).

While *emergency management plans* often overlook underserved and marginalized communities, inequalities based on race, class, age, and gender (as a strictly female/male dichotomy) receive far more attention in documents than the planning for specific needs of lesbian, gay, bisexual, and transsexual (LGBT) communities (D'Ooge 2008; Gaillard 2012; Pincha 2007). Members of the LGBT community serve important roles after disaster, such as the personal care provided by third-gender *warias* in Indonesia following the 2010 eruption of Mt. Merapi (Balgos, Gaillard, and Sanz 2012). Members of the LGBT community also have specific needs that are not always reflected in preparedness plans. For instance, the *warias* were not accounted for in evacuation centers following the Mt. Merapi eruption because policy guidelines only required lists of women, men, girls, and boys (Balgos, Gaillard, and Sanz 2012). Another sexual minority group, the *arvavanis*, were excluded from temporary shelters and denied resources and housing following the 2005 Indian Ocean tsunami (Pincha 2007), and another, the *baklas,* experienced discomfort in crowded evacuation spaces and were frequently ridiculed for their personal grooming needs in the male washrooms that they were instructed to use (Gaillard 2012). Including the specific needs of marginalized communities in disaster plans can increase the safety of this community and help reduce postdisaster discrimination.

6.7 WOMEN WORKING COLLECTIVELY

Sometimes typecast as hapless victims, women are actively involved in resolving problems before, during, and after a disaster, largely contributing to community resilience. (See Box 6.3 for an example of Muslim women working together.) As mothers and wives, community volunteers, and social service workers, they secure and distribute much-needed disaster relief assistance and are the lifeline for the emotional recovery of children and other dependents. Mental health counselors, antiviolence crisis workers, primary school teachers, and personal care workers in nursing homes or

BOX 6.3   WOMEN ORGANIZING

Following the 2005 Pakistan earthquake that killed thousands, Muslim women came together to help:

> Nawaz and her friends began thinking about collecting supplies and raising disaster relief funds. They started recruiting new members to their group—which has no name as of yet—at local mosques, in their neighborhoods and during *iftar*, the communal meal at nightfall in which Muslims break their sacred fast. In the past two weeks, the group—whose core was made up of friends in the neighborhood—has since swelled to 36 women and now includes homemakers, students, teachers, doctors, and other professionals. The women have raised about $14,000 in all.

Source: Stevens (2005).

halfway homes for the disabled are among the legions of women drawn into recovery work by the nature of their professions. (See Enarson [2012] for an in-depth discussion of U.S. women's occupationally based efforts.) Additionally, many women work in their own homes to support formal disaster responders in need of relief. For example, one employed woman in the Red River valley who hosted flood workers in her home (Enarson 1998, 4) explained:

> I never knew when I walked in my door who was coming out of my shower, who was using my laundry, or how many people I was going to feed that night when I came home. I had people in and out. . . . [The men] were tired by the time they came back, so I always had the meals ready to go, not knowing what time they were coming—and I never knew when they were going to be there.

At another level, women are highly involved in emergent postdisaster organizations. For instance, following Hurricane Katrina, many women who were community activists prior to the storm stepped into advocacy roles for equity in disaster relief and recovery (Jenkins 2012). From the ashes of the Berkeley/Oakland fires, women architects formed a women's group that met for over three years, providing "so much courage it saw almost full attendance every Monday night for three years" (Hoffman 1998, 60). In Miami, too, women built their own relief group (Enarson and Morrow 1998) when the male-dominated group distributing relief monies failed to address the needs of women and children. Women Will Rebuild, a coalition of over 40 women's organizations, mobilized for a place on the executive board and urged that 10% of all donated funds be redirected to women's economic recovery, antiviolence services, youth recreation, child care, and affordable housing. After the attacks of September 11, 2001, women family members led survivor groups seeking redress; six years later, their interfaith responses have been documented (Radcliffe Institute for Advanced Study 2007). After the 2005 hurricanes in the Gulf Coast of the United States, women's groups swung into action (Pyles and Lewis 2007), with local antiracist activities often in the forefront (Jenkins 2012; Luft 2008).

Community celebrations of survival and resilience are critical to recovery. Haitian women in Miami, for instance, organized a spring cultural celebration six months after Hurricane Andrew devastated their Miami neighborhood (Morrow and Enarson 1996). Quilters, artists, musicians, and writers used the arts to help others make sense of the 1997 Red River flood (Enarson 2000) just as the women from the Berkeley/Oakland hills that lost their homes "tatted back neighborhoods like so much lace" (Hoffman 1998, 61).

Women's collective recovery work in the United States parallels international organizing for sustainable mitigation and recovery, for example through grassroots women's networks (Yonder, Ackar, and Gopalan 2005) and women's labor unions (Lund and Vaux 2009). Recently, a network of women's organizations, called Rise Together for Women in East Japan Disaster, united to promote the rights of women and other vulnerable populations who were affected by the "triple disaster" of earthquake, tsunami, and nuclear meltdown in 2011. Following the 2011 Canterbury earthquakes in New Zealand, one woman began creating and gathering cloth hearts from around the world to give to survivors as a symbol of support and caring. More than 4,000 hearts became an exhibit at the Canterbury Museum and later were given to individual disaster survivors to inspire hope. The solidarity these groups demonstrated is their legacy to disaster resilience for women in hazard-prone areas around the world.

6.8 WORKING WITH WOMEN TO BUILD COMMUNITY RESILIENCE: STRATEGIC AND PRACTICAL STEPS

In an era of climate change and increasing hazards and disasters, gender sensitivity is not a luxury but an essential quality of effective disaster risk management. In this section, we discuss some of the practical implications of the preceding discussion, and frame specific initiatives for gender-inclusive emergency management.

6.8.1 DEVELOPING PARTNERSHIPS TO BUILD CAPACITY

Partnering with women's groups and agencies that know both the needs and capacities of local women opens new possibilities to increase community resilience in the postdisaster context and reinforce permanent networks of women engaging in local and national advocacy (Horton 2012). *Capacity building* is needed for crisis shelters, family assistance centers, community clinics, childcare centers, and other organizations that will be called upon by those least able to help themselves. This may include direct assistance to help low-budget agencies develop and test tailor-made emergency preparedness plans and help them secure the resources needed to implement these. Pilot programs can be funded and then scaled up to help foster a gender-sensitive culture of prevention at the grassroots level. Regional or national templates for capacity building in women's agencies can be developed and circulated using culturally specific approaches appropriate to different organizational environments. Training workshops bringing emergency-management issues into the forefront of operational planning in grassroots women's groups is essential, as is including these organizations, coalitions, and groups in scenario-based exercises. These organizations are a critical *social* infrastructure in all communities, so enhancing organizational resilience is an important investment in public safety. Bringing women's and community groups into the mainstream of emergency management as valued and long-term stakeholders and partners is the foundation for asking and answering the right questions about sex and gender in disaster contexts (see Photo 6.1).

6.8.2 RISK MAPPING

Gender-sensitive risk mapping is vital. Multidimensional risk maps now show at a glance which population groups are most exposed to particular hazards, and where critical facilities and lifelines are located. The complexities of gender identity and gender relations cannot be mapped in any simple way as a ratio of women to men in a given census block or year, but the statistical profile developed in the demographic section of this chapter suggests important indicators of vulnerability and capacity to monitor.

Practitioners should use census data if possible, but they should also ask community-planning agencies to gather or provide gender data directly or solicit this information directly from nonprofit organizations serving women and other high-risk populations or local universities and colleges. In the process, they will forge new links with future disaster researchers and volunteers and potential new emergency managers. Planners will learn about gender as a planning issue by connecting with women's groups across cultural and age groups, and by asking such questions as:

- What are the employment patterns and poverty rates of women and men who live here? What proportion of single mothers/fathers live below the poverty line?
- How many older women and men live alone, and at what income level? How many children are in the sole care of grandmothers on low incomes?
- How many women are living here, and with what kinds of disabilities? How many are employed in caregiving roles?
- What proportion of women in this community rents or owns their own homes? How many live in public-housing units, and where can homeless women and men be found in the event of an emergency?
- What are the comparative literacy rates of women and men, and do differences exist in the primary language or media they use?
- How many family child-care associations, women's business networks, women's trade union groups, service clubs, faith-based auxiliaries, youth agencies, and similar organizations exist here, and where are they located?
- Where are the child-care centers, schools, health-care facilities, parks, community centers, domestic-violence shelters, homeless shelters, adult day-care homes, halfway homes, and other places where outreach to women could be effective?

6.8.3 GENDER-SENSITIVE PROGRAMMING AND PLANNING

Gender-sensitive programming should include specific gender indicators, benchmarks, and targets in all aspects of project design, implementation, monitoring, and evaluation. Policy reviews are useful for identifying systemic gender bias that may disadvantage women or men, respectively, for example, in the design of psychosocial services or economic recovery programs. It is also vital that the public face of local, state, and national emergency management reflect the "gendered terrain of disaster" in website content and illustration, public education materials, emergency-management conference planning, and community outreach. (For recommended action steps from a Canadian perspective, see Enarson [2008]; see Box 6.4 for recommendations for gender mainstreaming.)

BOX 6.4   MEN AND GENDER MAINSTREAMING

Men participating in a break-out session of the 2004 Gender Equality and Disaster Risk Reduction Workshop in Honolulu made these strategic recommendations for change.

- Men need to advocate for gender equality.
- Men need to deliver gender-mainstreaming messages to other men.
- Men need to be full partners in gender sensitivity training.
- Men as leaders need to be committed to bringing gender equity results within their own organizations.
- Men need to confront gender stereotyping, and create opportunities for personal and institutional transformation.
- Men need to recognize that women have many personal knowledge and skills in coping with disasters, and that more women need to be trained as first responders.
- Tools are needed to sensitize and empower men to implement gender equality.
- A separate workshop on men's role in gender equality/gender mainstreaming is needed, and sessions should be held at upcoming meetings.
- The Gender and Disaster Network should be used to share ideas, tools, and best practices.

Source: Gender Equality and Disaster Risk Reduction Workshop (2004).

Guidelines for gender-sensitive planning are readily available through international sources. (Visit the Gender and Disaster Resilience Alliance as listed in the Resources section.)

Gender-sensitive awareness campaigns are equally important. Risk communicators should determine what television stations or community language radio stations are most popular with high-risk women and men, and plan how to reach the hard-to-reach, whether these are women lacking easy access to the Internet or male farmers unlikely to seek out postdisaster counseling. Every community is different, so risk communication projects must include messaging and outlets suitable to reach women in a Mennonite community, a mobile-home park dominated by seniors, Aboriginal youth living off reservation, or the personal-care attendants of people living with disabilities. Consulting with local women journalists and communications experts is a good beginning. Students can be enlisted to evaluate existing materials and propose alternatives. Local media contact sheets should also include newsletters and occasional publications put out by women's and community groups. Partnering with minority ethnic women's networks provides important communication avenues for two-way communication about the concerns of marginalized women and how they can protect themselves.

Implementing gender guidelines, many developed and tested by humanitarian relief agencies, save emergency managers' time. The resource section of this chapter includes websites that offer, among other tools, gender-sensitive risk-mapping templates; self-assessment guides for women's organizations about emergency preparedness; self-assessment guides for emergency management agencies about gender; sector-based guidelines for responding to women and men, boys and girls; and emergency-preparedness guides for domestic-violence shelters. Gender-sensitive steps toward disaster recovery, for instance, might include:

- Consulting with local women's groups to plan and evaluate recovery services, including opportunities for affected women to fully participate in decision making
- Building community capacity for continuous, affordable, and culturally appropriate child care and dependent care
- Giving priority to high-risk women seeking affordable and appropriate low-cost permanent housing, including rental rebates and loan assistance
- Providing continuous accessible health-care facilities, including mobile reproductive services and infant and maternal care
- Building community capacity for timely and culturally appropriate mental health services with sensitivity to the specific challenges faced by women and men, boys and girls
- Collaborating with women's antiviolence agencies to support their efforts to prevent and respond to abuse or assault in the aftermath of disasters

Gender-based assessments of emergency plans relating to particular issues are also needed. For example, a Canadian study found nurses were critical frontline responders to severe acute respiratory syndrome (SARS) when this public health threat shut down Toronto-area hospitals and brought international travel to a standstill in Canada (Amaratunga and O'Sullivan 2006). But these predominantly female nurses also described pressure from their own family members to not report to their hospitals. When they did choose to work, some reported feeling ostracized by others later, potentially deterring them from making the same decision in the future, which would ultimately undermine the surge capacity of hospitals. Much more attention to work and family conflicts is warranted. While the traditional family support system helped past generations put work first in an emergency, this cannot be assumed in the context of dual-career families and women's entry into first-response professions. (See Box 6.5 for more on the changing role of gender in the field of emergency management.) Dual-career families raise special concerns for emergency management agencies, principally around child care. As Scanlon (1998) notes, access to emergency child care needs to be incorporated into emergency plans, especially for parents who are both expected to respond to an emergency situation, such as a police officer and a nurse.

BOX 6.5   WORKING IN A MAN'S WORLD?

The Coordinator for the Emergency Planning and Preparedness Program, Joanne Sheardown, discusses the changing role of gender in the field of emergency management:

> I am often asked about working in a "man's world." I believe it is not a man's world but the world you make it out to be. The emergency management "world" encompasses not only the traditional first responder roles—police, fire and emergency medical services—but also the military, volunteer agencies, government departments and industry. Traditionally, female emergency managers have been represented in the health care, social service and educational agencies, while male managers have represented the police, fire and emergency medical services agencies. However, I have noticed that when municipalities move from using traditional first responder agencies such as fire and police for their municipal emergency managers to hiring a civilian emergency manager, a woman is often the successful candidate. As well, there seem to be more men in health care emergency manager positions in the last few years. The message? Emergency managers should not be defined by gender, but by the education and experience they bring to the job.

Source: Sheardown (2005).

Provisions for protecting reproductive health should also be in place for both women and men in planning responses to hazardous-materials events. Human resource policies and procedures should be reviewed to identify family needs and potential conflicts, and internal human resource management strategies revised as needed. Plans should also be reviewed with sensitivity to gender concerns during daytime and nighttime events.

Assessing emergency plans for gender sensitivity can become a routine part of organizational self-assessments. Planners might consider, for instance, whether or how well they have connected with women's networks to reach families with information about household preparedness, cleanup, and repair, and how likely their emergency warnings are to reach men who may be at risk yet unlikely to evacuate or otherwise protect themselves. How reliable are the caregiving support systems in place to help women and men access relief services, and how is the agency connected to women's and men's community organizations perhaps needing assistance with their own emergency planning? Are women from diverse cultural, age, and income groups integrated into emergency management activities in your community?

6.8.4   INTEGRATING WOMEN INTO EMERGENCY MANAGEMENT

Build a stronger organization with a broad base that reflects the diversity of the nation and its future. It is essential to actively recruit women who may not have considered jobs in emergency management at high levels or in nontraditional roles. The professionalization of emergency management will open the door to highly educated women, but recruiting and mentoring women and men whose life experiences have taught them about social vulnerabilities and the hazards of everyday life is equally important. Emergency managers can invite high school students to job-shadow emergency managers in nontraditional roles, and mentor young women and men who first enter the organization as student interns and temporary hires from underrepresented groups. Recruiting through an expanded and grassroots stakeholder network will encourage applications from Native-American, Asian, Latina, and African-American women; women with connections to different disability communities; older women with years of volunteer experience; and low-income women knowledgeable about handling crises. Outreach to students of environmental studies, ethnic studies,

PHOTO 6.2   Volunteers working on installation of a playground after Hurricane Ivan and Tropical Storm Arlene. (*Source*: Leif Skoogfors/FEMA photo.)

gerontology, social work, and gender studies is another important step. Targeted emergency management internships or study grants can be created to increase interest among women in studying emergency management and among men in studying disaster-relevant fields such as social work and psychology. Organizational self-assessments should be routinely used to monitor race, class, and gender patterns of employment, training, and promotion. In-house training programs presenting gender and diversity as positive organizational development should be part of the learning curve in every private and public agency that contributes in some way to building community resilience to disaster. (See Photo 6.2.)

6.9   LOOKING FORWARD

Gender concerns may begin with individual or group vulnerabilities based on sex, gender, and/or sexuality, but they are much more, extending to institutionalized gender practices, the informal cultures around us at work and at play, and of course to patterns of environmental, social, and political development.

Looking forward, it is imperative that the positive life experiences and assets of all people be brought to bear if we are to meet the challenges of a changing climate in the future. Signs of progress are evident. Compilations of "good practice" are available around disaster risk reduction and also climate change adaptation (see Gender Perspectives under Training and Practice Guides at the end of the chapter). The resources at the end of this chapter provide numerous other examples, including new global practice guides for integrating gender holistically, new ways to train women as risk communicators and disaster responders, and new reports from global workshops with concrete recommendations for change. These are important landmarks in the long road toward reducing risk and coping with hazards in sustainable, just, and gender-inclusive ways. In the United States, gender is increasingly salient in research, as demonstrated in this chapter, and in women's self-organization. New organizations now give voice to women emergency managers, and new training manuals and tools are available to help reduce and respond to gender violence and reproductive health risks. If the U.S. Girl Scout Organization is any guide to the future, the girl scouts who worked with women emergency managers to produce and star in their own public service announcement about emergency preparedness should give us heart (http://www.youtube.com/watch?v=TEwwAJR_ilo). The concerted efforts of all are needed in the years to come, and we are off to a good start. (See Photo 6.3.)

PHOTO 6.3 Visually impaired women in a workshop to empower themselves to cope with disasters. (*Source*: Ranjeet Kumar, courtesy of Flickr, http://www.flickr.com/photos/amcentermumbai/5567026240/in/ photostream. With permission.)

6.10 SUMMARY

This chapter began by inviting attention to how sex and gender interact with other social dynamics in our everyday lives, often to increase vulnerability but also as a foundation for resilience. Gender concerns through the disaster life cycle were illuminated through reports from many of the most destructive recent natural disasters, including those based on the division of labor and differences in risk perception and those based on gender power and the gender-based inequalities that jeopardize the safety and well-being of women and girls especially. Practical issues arising for women and men during preparedness, evacuation, emergency response, and recovery were discussed with attention to livelihood, housing, violence, and possible gender bias in programming. This led to a concluding section with action steps to more fully integrate gender into the routine practices and the overarching policies of emergency management.

The stories in this chapter have illustrated the ways in which women's and men's lives are disproportionately affected when disaster strikes. It is a top priority that communities, emergency management agencies, disaster relief organizations, and governments continue to increase the incorporation of women into planning for each stage of the disaster life cycle. As this chapter suggests, there are many areas where this is already happening, including an increase in gender-sensitive research, women's involvement in environmental protection and neighborhood emergency-preparedness campaigns, using women's skills in prevention and relief work, increased attention to gender-based violence after disaster, hospice nurses stepping up in a crisis, and women organizing collectively for social justice in disaster recovery. As disasters become more frequent and intense, and as climate change continues to disproportionately impact communities around the world, gender-sensitive planning will be crucial to securing the safety and livelihoods of women, men, girls, and boys.

DISCUSSION QUESTIONS

1. Take the role of any emergency manager or first responder you have seen in your favorite disaster movie and reverse the gender. What difference do you think it would make if this person were a woman (or man) instead, and why? Think about other practitioners, members of the public, family members, elected officials, etc.

2. Do you think men's or women's lives change more during a disaster? In what ways and why? What about in the recovery period?

3. Is it the job of an emergency manager to consider "private" issues such as domestic violence, sexual preference, child-care arrangements, or relationship stress? Why or why not?

4. Thinking of any emergency or disaster you have been involved with, what did you observe about the behavior of women and men? What do you think explains this?

5. What are the three most significant barriers to community resilience that gender inequalities or differences raise, in your view? How might each be addressed and minimized?

6. What do you think are the most significant barriers to girls or women on the basis of their sex and gender identity? What about boys and men?

7. How could a disastrous flood, fire, explosion, or health emergency in your community be a catalyst for change in family, community, or emergency organizations during the postevent "window of opportunity"?

8. What obstacles to gender mainstreaming have you identified through personal experience in emergency management? What changes have you seen in this respect in workplace cultures today?

ACKNOWLEDGMENTS

It is a pleasure to recognize the women and men who have helped develop and strengthen these ideas. Jennifer would like to dedicate a special thanks to Lori Peek, Michelle Lueck, and Chris Emrich for their assistance and helpful recommendations for this chapter. Elaine would also like to thank her colleagues who collaborated on the original FEMA Higher Education Project course and others known to her only virtually. We thank you all for helping us think through these issues and for prompting new questions.

REFERENCES

Agenda for Children. 2008. Greater New Orleans Community Data Center. "Open child care facilities in Orleans Parish as of April 28, 2008." http://www.gnocdc.org/.

Alston, M. 2006. "I'd like to just walk out of here": Australian women's experience of drought. *Sociologia Ruralis* 46 (2): 154–70.

Alway, J., L. L. Belgrave, and K. Smith. 1998. Back to normal: Gender and disaster. *Symbolic Interaction* 21 (2): 175–95.

Amaratunga, C., and T. O'Sullivan. 2006. In the path of disasters: Psychosocial issues for preparedness, response, and recovery. *Prehospital Disaster Medicine* 21 (3): 149–55.

Anderson, C. 1996. Understanding the inequality problematic: From scholarly rhetoric to theoretical reconstruction. *Gender and Society* 10 (6): 729–46.

Anderson, W. 2000. Women and children in disasters. In *Managing disaster risk in emerging economies*, ed. A. Kreimer and M. Arnold, 85–90. Washington, DC: World Bank.

Balgos, B., J. C. Gaillard, and K. Sanz 2012. The Warias of Indonesia in disaster risk reduction: The case of the 2010 Mt. Merapi eruption in Indonesia. *Gender and Development* 20 (2): 337–48.

Bolin R., M. Jackson, and A. Crist. 1998. Gender inequality, vulnerability and disaster: Issues in theory and research. In *The gendered terrain of disaster: Through women's eyes*, ed. E. Enarson and B. H. Morrow, 27–44. Westport, CT: Greenwood Publications.

Callaghan, W., S. Rasmussen, D. Jamieson, S. Ventura, S. L. Farr, P. D. Sutton, T. J. Mathews, et al. 2007. Health concerns of women and infants in times of natural disasters: Lessons learned from Hurricane Katrina. *Maternal and Child Health* 11:307–11.

Childers, C. 1999. Elderly female-headed households in the disaster loan process. *International Journal of Mass Emergencies and Disasters* 17 (1): 99–110.

Connell, R. W. 2005. *Masculinities.* 2nd ed. Berkley and Los Angeles: University of California Press.

Cox, R., and K. M. Perry. 2011. Like a fish out of water: Reconsidering disaster recovery and the role of place and social capital in community disaster resilience. *American Journal of Community Psychology* 48 (3): 395–411.

Cutter, S. 1992. Engendered fears: Femininity and technological risk perception. *Industrial Crisis Quarterly* 6:5–22.

———. 1995. The forgotten casualties: Women, children, and environmental change. *Global Environmental Change* 5 (3): 181–94.

Dankleman, I., ed. 2011. *Women and climate change: An introduction.* London: Earthscan.

D'Ooge, C. 2008. Queer Katrina: Gender and sexual orientation matters in the aftermath of disaster. In *Katrina and the women of New Orleans,* ed. B. Willinger, 22–23. New Orleans: Tulane University, Newcomb College Center for Research on Women.

Eilor, E. A. 2009. Emerging issue: The gender perspectives of the financial crisis. Commission on the Status of Women, fifty-third session. United Nations Interactive Expert Panel, New York, 2–13 March.

Eisenman, D., K. M. Cordasco, S. Asch, J. F. Golden, and D. Glik. 2007. Communication with vulnerable communities: Lessons from Hurricane Katrina. *American Journal of Public Health* 97 (S1): S109–15.

Elder, K., S. Xirasagar, N. Miller, S. A. Bowen, S. Glover, and C. Piper. 2007. African Americans' decisions not to evacuate New Orleans before Hurricane Katrina: A qualitative study. *American Journal of Public Health* 97 (S1): S124–29.

Elinder, M., and O. Erixson. 2012. Every man for himself: Gender, norms and survival in maritime disasters. Working paper, Uppsala University, Sweden. http://www.nek.uu.se or http://swopec.hhs.se/uunewp/.

Enarson, E. 1998. Women, work, and family in the 1997 Red River valley flood: Ten lessons learned. Unpublished community report. http://www.cridlac.org/digitalizacion/pdf/eng/doc13585/doc13585.htm.

———. 2000. Gender and natural disasters. International Labour Organization, InFocus Programme on Crisis and Reconstruction, working paper no. 1. http://www.ilo.org/public/english/employment/recon/crisis/gender.htm.

———. 2001. What women do: Gendered labor in the Red River valley flood. *Environmental Hazards* 3 (1): 1–18.

———. 2008. Gender mainstreaming in emergency management: Opportunities for building community resilience in Canada. Paper prepared for the Public Health Agency of Canada. http://www.gdnonline.org/.

———. 2012. *Women confronting natural disaster: From vulnerability to resilience.* Boulder, CO: Lynne Rienner Publisher.

Enarson, E., and P. G. Chakrabarti, eds. 2009. *Women, gender, and disasters: Global issues and initiatives.* New Delhi, India: SAGE Publications.

Enarson, E., A. Fothergill, and L. Peek. 2006. Gender and disaster: Foundations and possibilities. In *Handbook of disaster research,* ed. H. Rodriguez, H. L. Quarantelli, and R. Dynes, 130–46. New York: Springer.

Enarson, E., and L. Meyreles. 2004. International perspectives on gender and disaster: Differences and possibilities. *International Journal of Sociology and Social Policy* 14 (10): 49–92.

Enarson, E., and B. H. Morrow. 1998. Women will rebuild Miami: A case study of feminist response to disaster. In *The gendered terrain of disaster: Through women's eyes,* ed. E. Enarson and B. H. Morrow, 185–200. Westport, CT: Greenwood Publications.

Enarson, E., and B. Phillips. 2008. Invitation to a new feminist disaster sociology: Integrating feminist theory and methods. In *Women in disaster,* ed. B. Phillips and B. H. Morrow, 41–74. Bloomington, IN: Xlibris Publications.

Enarson, E., and J. Scanlon. 1999. Gender patterns in a flood evacuation: A case study of couples in Canada's Red River valley. *Applied Behavioral Science Review* 7 (2): 103–24.

Erikson, K. 1994. *A new species of trouble: The human experience of modern disasters.* New York: W. W. Norton.

Finucane, M., P. Slovic, C. K. Mertz, J. Flynn, and T. Satterfield. 2000. Gender, race, and perceived risk: The "white male" effect. *Healthy Risk and Society* 2 (2): 159–72.

Fordham, M. 1998. Making women visible in disasters: Problematising the private domain. *Disasters* 22 (2): 126–43.

———. 2001. Challenging boundaries: A gender perspective on early warning in disaster and environmental management. Paper prepared for the Expert Working Group meeting, Ankara, Turkey, 6–9 November. UN Division for the Advancement of Women. www.un.org/womenwatch/daw/csw/env_manage/documents.html.

Fothergill, A. 1998. The neglect of gender in disaster work: An overview of the literature. In *The gendered terrain of disaster: Through women's eyes*, ed. E. Enarson and B. H. Morrow, 11–25. Westport, CT: Greenwood Publications.

———. 2004. *Heads above water: Gender, class and family in the Grand Forks flood*. Ithaca, NY: SUNY Press.

Gaillard, J. C. 2012. *People's response to disasters: Vulnerability, capacities and resilience in Philippine context*. Angeles City, Philippines: Holy Angel University Press.

GAO, 2009. Disaster housing: FEMA needs more detailed guidance and performance measures to help ensure effective assistance after major disasters (GAO-09-796), Washington, DC.

Gender Equality and Disaster Risk Reduction Workshop. 2004. Executive summary. http://www.ssri.hawaii.edu/research/GDWwebsite/pages/exec_summary.html.

Gibbs, S. 1990. *Women's role in the Red Cross/Red Crescent*. Geneva, Switzerland: Henry Dunant Institute.

Gill, D. A., S. Picou, and L. A. Ritchie. 2011. The *Exxon Valdez* and BP oil spills: A comparison of initial social and psychological impacts. *American Behavioral Scientist* 56 (1): 3–23.

Gladwin, H., and W. G. Peacock. 1997. Warning and evacuation: A night for hard horses. In *Hurricane Andrew: Ethnicity, gender and the sociology of disasters*, ed. W. G. Peacock, B. H. Morrow, and H. Gladwin, 52–74. New York: Routledge.

Hagen, S., and M. Carouba, eds. 2002. *Women at Ground Zero: Stories of courage and compassion*. Indianapolis, IN: Alpha Books.

Haiti Gender Equality Collective. 2010. Ensuring Haitian women's participation and leadership in all stages of national relief and reconstruction. A Gender Shadow report of the 2010 Haiti PDNA. http://www.haiti-equalitycollective.org/2010/03/gender-shadow-report-on-haiti-pdna.html.

Hoffman, S. 1998. Eve and Adam among the embers: Gender patterns after the Oakland Berkeley firestorm. In *The gendered terrain of disaster: Through women's eyes*, ed. E. Enarson and B. H. Morrow, 55–61. Westport, CT: Greenwood Publications.

Horton, L. 2012. After the earthquake: Gender inequality and transformation in post-disaster Haiti. *Gender and Development* 20 (2): 295–308.

Ikeda, K. 1995. Gender differences in human loss and vulnerability in natural disasters: A case study from Bangladesh. *Indian Journal of Gender Studies* 2 (2): 171–93.

Jenkins, Pam. 2012. Gender and the landscape of community work before and after Katrina. In *The women of Katrina: How gender, race, and class matter in an American disaster*, ed. E. David and E. Enarson, 169–78. Nashville, TN: Vanderbilt University Press.

Joint Center for Housing Studies of Harvard University. 2004. The state of the nation's housing. http://www.jchs.harvard.edu/research/publications/state-nations-housing-2004.

Jones-DeWeever, A. 2007. Women in the wake of the storm: Examining the post-Katrina realities of the women of New Orleans and the Gulf Coast. Institute for Women's Policy report briefing, Part 3. http://www.soroptimist.org/pdf/women_in_the_wake.pdf.

Kissinger, P., N. Schmidt, C. Sanders, and N. Liddon. 2007. The effect of the Hurricane Katrina disaster on sexual behavior and access to reproductive care for young women in New Orleans. *Sexually Transmitted Diseases* 34 (11): 883–86.

Klinenberg, E. 2002. *Heat wave: A social autopsy of disaster in Chicago*. Chicago: University of Chicago Press.

Krajeski, R., and K. Peterson. 1997. "But she is a woman and this is a man's job": Lessons for participatory research and participatory recovery. *International Journal of Mass Emergencies and Disasters* 17 (1): 123–30.

Krauss, C. 1993. Women and toxic waste protests: Race, class and gender as sources of resistance. *Qualitative Sociology* 16 (3): 247–62.

Laska, S., and B. H. Morrow. 2006. Social vulnerabilities and Hurricane Katrina: An unnatural disaster in New Orleans. *Marine Technology Society Journal* 40 (4): 16–26.

Litt, J., A. Skinner, and K. Robinson. 2012. The Katrina difference: African-American women's networks and poverty in New Orleans after Katrina. In *The women of Katrina: How gender, race, and class matter in an American disaster*, ed. E. David and E. Enarson, 130–41. Nashville, TN: Vanderbilt University Press.

Lovekamp, W. 2008. Gender and disaster: A synthesis of flood research in Bangladesh. In *Women and disasters: From theory to practice*, ed. B. Phillips and B. H. Morrow, 99–116. Bloomington, IN: XLibris.

Luft, R. E. 2008. Looking for common ground: Relief work in post-Katrina New Orleans as an American parable of race and gender violence. *NWSA Journal* 20 (3): 5–31.

———. 2012. Community organizing in the Katrina diaspora: Race, gender, and the case of the People's Hurricane Relief Fund. In *Displaced: Life in the Katrina diaspora*, ed. L. Weber and L. Peek, 233–54. Austin: University of Texas Press.

Lund, F., and T. Vaux. 2009. Women building resilience: The case of self-employed women in India. In *Women, gender and disaster*, ed. E. Enarson and P. G. Dhar Chakrabarti, 212–23. Delhi, India: Sage Publications.

Major, A. M. 1999. Gender differences in risk and communication behavior: Responses to the New Madrid earthquake prediction. *International Journal of Mass Emergencies and Disasters* 17 (3): 313–38.

Mishra, P. 2009. Let's share the stage: Inclusion of men in gender risk reduction. In *Women, gender and disaster: Global issues and initiatives*, ed. E. Enarson and P. G. Dhar Chakrabarti. Delhi, India: Sage Publications.

Morrow, B. H. 2006. Women: An organizational resource. *Emergency Management Canada* 4:40–41.

Morrow, B. H., and E. Enarson. 1996. Hurricane Andrew through women's eyes: Issues and recommendations. *International Journal of Mass Emergencies and Disasters* 14 (1): 1–22.

Nadelman, R. H., and S. Louis. 2010. Women in Haiti after the January 12, 2010, earthquake. Huairou Commission: Women, Homes, and Community. http://ijdh.org/archives/12795.

National Women's Law Center. 2011. Poverty among women and families, 2000–2010: Extreme poverty reaches record levels as Congress faces critical choices. http://www.nwlc.org/resource/poverty-among-women-and-families-2000-2010-extreme-poverty-reaches-record-level-congress-fa.

Neal, D., and B. Phillips. 1990. Female-dominated local social movement organizations in disaster-threat situations. In *Women and social protest*, ed. G. West and R. Blumberg, 243–55. New York: Oxford.

Neumayer, E., and T. Plümper. 2007. The gendered nature of natural disasters: The impact of catastrophic events on the gender gap in life expectancy, 1981–2002. *Annals of the Association of American Geographers* 97 (3): 551–66.

New Orleans Index. 2008. Tracking recovery of New Orleans and the metro area. http://www.brookings.edu/~/media/research/files/reports/2011/8/29%20new%20orleans%20index/200908_katrina_index.

Nigg, J., and K. Tierney. 1990. Explaining differential outcomes in the small business disaster loan application process. Preliminary paper #156. Newark: University of Delaware, Disaster Research Center.

Norris, F., M. Friedman, P. Watson, C. M. Byrne, E. Diaz, and K. Kaniasty. 2002. 60,000 disaster victims speak: Parts 1 and 2. *Psychiatry* 65 (3): 207–60.

Ogg, J. 2005. *Heat wave*. London: Young Foundation.

Owens, S. 2005. Climate change and health: A project with women of Labrador. Santé Communautaire. MSc thesis, Université Laval, Quebec.

Oxfam International. 2005. Gender and the tsunami. Oxfam briefing note. http://www.oxfam.org/en/policy/bn050326-tsunami-women.

Oxlee, C. 2000. Beyond the veil: Women in Islamic national societies. *IFRC Magazine* 1. http://www.redcross.int/EN/mag/magazine2000_1/voile_en.html.

Pacholok, Shelley. 2009. Gendered strategies of self: Navigating hierarchy and contesting masculinities. *Gender, Work and Organization* 16 (4): 471–500.

Palinkas, L., M. A. Downs, J. S. Petterson, and J. Russell. 1993. Social, cultural, and psychological impacts of the *Exxon Valdez* oil spill. *Human Organization* 52 (1): 1–13.

Papadakis, M. 2000. Complex picture of computer use in the home emerges. Division of Science Resources Studies, NSF issue brief. http://www.nsf.gov/statistics/issuebrf/sib00314.htm.

Parkinson, D., and C. Zara, eds. 2011. *Beating the flames: Women escaping and surviving the Black Saturday*. Wangaratta, Victoria, Australia: Women's Health Goulburn North East. http://trove.nla.gov.au/work/157014364?selectedversion=NBD47778253

Peek, L., and A. Fothergill. 2009. Parenting in the wake of disaster: Mothers and fathers respond to Hurricane Katrina. In *Women, gender and disaster: Global issues and initiatives*, ed. E. Enarson and D. Chakrabarti. Delhi, India: Sage Publications.

Phillips, B., and B. H. Morrow. 2007. Social science research needs: Focus on vulnerable populations, forecasting, and warnings. *Natural Hazards Review* 8 (3): 61–68.

Pincha, C. 2007. *Understanding gender differential impacts of tsunami and gender mainstreaming strategies in tsunami response in Tamil Nadu, India*. Boston: Oxfam America.

Pincha, C., and H. Krishna. 2008. Aravanis: Voiceless victims of the tsunami. *Humanitarian Exchange Magazine* no. 41. http://www.odihpn.org/humanitarian-exchange-magazine/issue-41/aravanis-voiceless-victims-of-the-tsunami.

Pyles, L., and J. Lewis. 2007. Women of the storm: Advocacy and organizing in post-Katrina New Orleans. *Affilia: Journal of Women and Social Work* 22 (4): 385–89.

Radcliffe Institute for Advanced Study. 2007. Women's interfaith initiatives after 9/11. http://www.pluralism.org/events/womeninterfaith/index.php.

Richter, Roxanne. 2011. Disparity in disasters: A frontline view of gender-based inequities in emergency aid and health care. In *Anthropology at the front lines of gender-based violence*, ed. J. R. Wies and H. J. Haldane, 19–28. Nashville, TN: Vanderbilt University Press.

Rivers, J. P. W. 1982. Women and children last: An essay on sex discrimination in disasters. *Disasters* 6 (4): 256–67.

Saito, F. 2012. Women and the 2011 East Japan disaster. *Gender and Development* 20 (2): 265–79.

Sawai, M. 2012. Who is vulnerable during tsunamis? Experiences from the Great East Japan Earthquake 2011 and the Indian Ocean Tsunami 2004. United Nations Economic and Social Commission for Asia and the Pacific. http://e.unescap.org/idd/working%20papers/IDD-DRS-who-is-vulnerable-during-tsunamis.pdf.

Scanlon, J. 1998. The perspective of gender: A missing element in disaster response. In *The gendered terrain of disaster: Through women's eyes*, ed. E. Enarson and B. H. Morrow, 45–51. Westport, CT: Greenwood Publications.

———. 1999. Myths of male and military superiority: Fictional accounts of the 1917 Halifax explosion. *English Studies in Canada* 24:1001–25.

Sharkey, P. 2007. Survival and death in New Orleans: An empirical look at the human impact of Katrina. *Journal of Black Studies* 37 (4): 482–501.

Sheardown, J. 2005. International Association of Emergency Managers. Special focus issue: Women in emergency management. *IAEM Bulletin* 22, no. 9.

Social Watch Organization. 2012. Gender Equity Index 2012. http://www.socialwatch.org/node/14372.

Staples, C., and K. Stubbings. 1998. Gender inequality in business recovery following the Grand Forks flood. Paper presented to the Midwest Sociological Society, Kansas City, MO.

Stehlik, D., G. Lawrence, and I. Gray. 2000. Gender and drought: Experiences of Australian women in the drought of the 1990s. *Disasters* 24 (1): 38–53.

Stevens, Allison. 2005. Quake relief brings U.S. Muslim women together. Womensenews.org.

Tobin-Gurley, Jennifer. 2008. Hurricane Katrina: Single mothers, resource acquisition, and downward mobility. Master's thesis, Colorado State University.

Tobin-Gurley, Jennifer, Lori Peek, and Jennifer Loomis. 2010. Displaced single mothers in the aftermath of hurricane Katrina: Resource needs and resource acquisition. *International Journal of Mass Emergencies and Disasters* 28 (2): 170–206.

Turner, R. H., J. M. Nigg, and D. H. Paz. 1986. *Waiting for disaster: Earthquake watch in California*. Berkeley: University of California Press.

United Nations. 2011. Human Development Report 2011. Sustainability and equity: A better future for all. http://hdr.undp.org/en/reports/global/hdr2011/.

United Teachers of New Orleans, Louisiana Federation of Teachers, and the American Federation of Teachers. 2007. No experience necessary: How the New Orleans school takeover experiment devalues experienced teachers. New Orleans, LA: United Teachers of New Orleans.

Weaver, J. D. 2002. Disaster mental health: Trauma relief, concepts, and theory. In *Children and disasters: A practical guide to healing and recovery*, ed. W. N. Zubenko and J. A. Capozzoli, 34–71. New York: Oxford University Press.

Wenger, D., and T. James. 1994. The convergence of volunteers in a consensus crisis: The case of the 1985 Mexico City earthquake. In *Disasters, collective behavior, and social organization*, ed. R. Dynes and K. Tierney, 229–43. Newark: University of Delaware Press.

West Coast Poverty Center. 2009. Poverty basics. University of Washington. http://depts.washington.edu/wcpc/Family.

Willinger, B., and J. Knight. 2012. Setting the stage for disaster: Women in New Orleans before and after Katrina. In *The women of Katrina: How gender, race, and class matter in an American disaster*, ed. E. David and E. Enarson, 55–75. Nashville, TN: Vanderbilt University Press.

Winter, Michael. 2012. Judge: New Orleans teachers fired illegally after Katrina. *USA Today*, June 20.

Wisner, B., P. Blaikie, T. Cannon, and I. Davis. 2004. *At risk: Natural hazards, people's vulnerability and disasters*. 2nd ed. London: Routledge.

World Economic Forum. 2011. Global gender gap report. http://www.weforum.org/en/initiatives/gcp/Gender%20Gap/index.htm.

Yonder, A., S. Ackar, and P. Gopalan. 2005. Women's participation in disaster relief and recovery. Pamphlet #2, SEEDS. http://www.popcouncil.org/pdfs/seeds/Seeds22.pdf.

Zahran, S., L. Peek, and S. D. Brody. 2008. Youth mortality by forces of nature. *Children, Youth and Environments* 18 (1): 371–88. http://www.colorado.edu/journals/cye.

Zahran, S., L. Peek, J. Snodgrass, S. Weiler, and L. Hempel. 2011. Abnormal labor outcomes as a function of maternal exposure to a catastrophic hurricane event during pregnancy. *Natural Hazards* 17:1–16.

RESOURCES

WEBSITES

Disaster Watch. International website featuring grassroots women's organizations active in disasters. http://www.disasterwatch.net/.

Empower. Emergency management professional organization for women (U.S.). http://www.empower-women.com/mc/page.do?sitePageId=46823&orgId=emp.

Gender and Disaster Resilience Alliance (GDRA), http://www.usgdra.org. Voluntary organization working in the United States and sister network to the global *Gender and Disaster Network* (GDN), http://www.gdnonline.org.

TRAINING AND PRACTICE GUIDES

Gender Mainstreaming in Emergency Management: A Training Module for Emergency Planners. 2009. E. Enarson. http://www.gdnonline.org/resources/GEM_MainFINAL.pdf.

Gender Notes. 2009. E. Enarson for the GDN (Glossary; the Hyogo Framework for Action; Mitigation; Men and Masculinities; Abilities and Disabilities; Risk Communication). www.gdnonline.org/wot_keyresources.php.

Gender Perspectives: Integrating Disaster Risk Reduction into Climate Change Adaptation. 2008. ISDR. http://www.uneca.org/acpc/about_acpc/docs/Gender_Perspectives_Integrating_DRR_CC_GoodPractices.pdf.

Guidance Note on Recovery: Gender. 2010. UNDP-India and IRP. http://www.unisdr.org/files/16775_16775guidancenoteonrecoverygender1.pdf.

Prairie Women Prepared for Disaster. An Emergency Planning Guide for Women's Community Organizations. 2009. E. Enarson. www.pwhce.ca/program_gender_disaster_I.htm.

Reproductive Health Assessment after Disasters: Toolkit for Public Health Departments. 2011. University of North Carolina, Center for Public Health and Centers for Disease Control and Prevention. www.cphp.sph.unc.edu/reproductivehealth/.

Sex and Age Matter: Improving Humanitarian Response in Emergencies. 2011. D. Mazurana et al. Feinstein International Center, Tufts University. http://www.care.org/careswork/whatwedo/relief/docs/sex-and-age-disag-data.pdf.

Sexual Violence in Disasters: A Planning Guide for Prevention and Response. A. Klein for The Louisiana Foundation against Sexual Assault and the National Sexual Violence Resource Center (NSVRC), (English/Spanish). http://www.nsvrc.org/publications/nsvrc-publications/sexual-violence-disasters-planning-guide-prevention-and-response.

Working with Women at Risk: Practical Guidelines for Assessing Local Disaster Risk. 2003. E. Enarson et al., (English/Spanish). www.gdnonline.org/resources/WorkingwithWomenEnglish.pdf.

VIDEOS

Still Waiting: Life after Katrina, independent film by K. Brown and G. Martin. www.stillwaiting.colostate.edu/.

Sisters on the Planet. Vignettes from the United States, United Kingdom, Australia, Bangladesh, Carteret Islands, and Uganda. https://www.oxfam.org.au/explore/climate-change/what-oxfam-is-doing/sisters-on-the-planet/.

7 Age

Lori Peek

CONTENTS

7.1   CHAPTER PURPOSE

The length of time that someone has lived can significantly affect that person's ability to prepare for, respond to, and recover from disaster. Indeed, age is correlated with a number of factors associated with one's likelihood of withstanding a disaster event. For example, age in many ways influences cognitive development, physical ability and mobility, socioeconomic status, access to resources, assumed responsibility for disaster preparedness and response activities, and levels of social integration or isolation. Thus, it is clear that age alone does not make a person vulnerable. Instead, age interacts with many other factors to result in the increased vulnerability of some population groups, particularly the very young and the old. As such, this chapter focuses specifically on the vulnerabilities of children and the elderly in disaster.

7.2   OBJECTIVES

At the conclusion of this chapter, readers should be able to:

1. Offer definitions for "children" and "the elderly" based on chronological age
2. Explain why it is important to understand the distinctions between different groups of children (e.g., infants, very young children, young children, and youth) and the elderly (e.g., young old, aged, oldest old, and frail elderly)
3. Provide demographic overviews of the youth and elderly populations globally and in the United States
4. Understand the specific risks that children face across the disaster life cycle, and identify the factors most likely to increase their vulnerability during the warning, evacuation, response, impact, and recovery phases
5. Understand the specific risks that the elderly face across the disaster life cycle, and identify the factors most likely to increase their vulnerability during the warning, evacuation, response, impact, and recovery phases
6. Describe several possible approaches for addressing the vulnerability and increasing the resilience of children and the elderly before and after disaster

7.3   INTRODUCTION

Social definitions for both childhood and the elderly vary considerably across cultures, and contexts and are only loosely linked with chronological age (Boyden 2003; Friedsam 1962). However, for the sake of clarity, in this chapter I refer to children as those individuals age 18 or younger, although of course the diversity of young people must be recognized and captured in age-disaggregated data. For that reason, and where possible in this chapter, I distinguish between infants (0–1 year); very young children, preschool-aged children, and/or toddlers (2–4 years); young children (5–12 years); and adolescents, youth, and/or teens (13–18 years).

An elderly person typically is defined as someone who is 65 years of age or older. Further distinction is made between the "young old" (65–74 years of age), the "aged" (75–84 years of age), the "oldest old" (85 years of age or older), and the "frail elderly" (65 years of age or greater, with physical and/or mental infirmities) (He et al. 2005; Ngo 2001). It is important to understand the distinctions between these age groups because there are clearly differences *among* the elderly, as well as differences *between* older and younger persons in terms of health, function, and interaction in society (Friedsam 1962; Ngo 2001).

7.4   DEMOGRAPHIC OVERVIEW

On October 31, 2011, the world's population reached 7 billion (UN Population Fund 2011). With 2.2 billion young people under the age of 18, and 810 million people aged 65 and over, there are more children and more older persons living across the globe than at any other point in recorded history (ibid.). However, children and the elderly are distributed unevenly across developed and developing countries. In most high-income countries, children and youth make up about 20%–25% of the total population; in developing countries, they represent nearly half or even a majority of the population (Bartlett 2008). In absolute numbers, there are more elderly living in developing countries, but the elderly compose a larger proportion of the population in developed countries (HelpAge International 2012).

As of 2010, an estimated 308 million persons lived in the United States, making it the third most populous and one of the most diverse nations in the world. Almost one-quarter, or 24%, of the U.S.

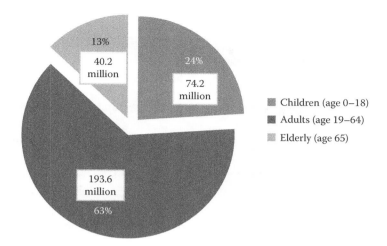

Children (age 0–18)
Adults (age 19–64)
Elderly (age 65)

FIGURE 7.1 U.S. population by age, 2010.

population is made up of children age 18 or younger, while persons age 65 and over represent about 13% of the total population (see Figure 7.1) (U.S. Census Bureau 2010).[*]

In this chapter, I offer a brief overview of some of the key demographic characteristics of American children and the elderly, with a specific focus on sex, racial and ethnic diversity, and poverty rates. It is important to consider the intersections between age and other characteristics because these factors all influence experiences in disasters, as will be further considered in later sections of this chapter and in other chapters of this book.

7.4.1 Children in the United States

In 2010, 74.2 million children lived in the United States. These children were divided proportionately by age group, with about one-third of the child population in each of the infant and very young (0–4 years), young (5–12 years), and adolescent (13–18 years) categories. There was a close to even distribution of boys and girls across each age category.

Children in the United States are actually more racially and ethnically diverse than their adult counterparts. Just over 54% of American children are non-Hispanic white,[†] while 23% of children are Hispanic or Latino, 14% are African American, 4% are Asian, Native Hawaiian, or Pacific Islander, and 5% are "all other races." The child population is a reflection of the growing diversity of the American population, as well as an indicator of the almost certain further diversification of the nation over the next several decades.

The number of children living in poverty in the United States grew steadily throughout the first decade of the twenty-first century. About 15.5 million American children live in families with incomes below the federal poverty level, which in 2011 was $22,350 for a family of four. A higher percentage of children (22%) in the United States live in poverty than any other age group. These numbers do not bode well for the future of many of America's youth, and they are even more troubling given that the federal poverty measure is widely viewed as a flawed metric of economic hardship. Research consistently shows that families need an income of about *two to three times* the federal poverty level to make ends meet. An additional 22% of the nation's children live in so-called "near poor" households (see Figure 7.2). These children and their families are often overlooked and are not eligible to receive

---

[*] Unless indicated otherwise, all figures included in this section of the chapter come from 2010 U.S. Census Bureau data, which are available online at: http://www.census.gov/.

[†] This can be compared with the overall U.S. population, which is about 72% non-Hispanic white. The term *non-Hispanic white* is used to refer to people who report being white and no other race and who are not Hispanic.

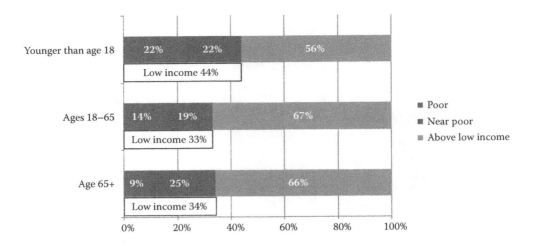

FIGURE 7.2   Family income by age, 2010.

public assistance, yet like their impoverished counterparts, they live in highly precarious situations nonetheless (Newman and Chen 2007). Poor and near-poor children, for example, are much more likely to experience food insecurity, lack health insurance and access to regular health care, struggle as a result of unaffordable housing costs, and attend lower quality schools and thus experience lower educational attainment (Fass and Cauthen 2007; Kozol 1991, 2005).

In 2010, 64% of black children (6.5 million), 63% of American Indian children (0.4 million), 63% of Hispanic children (10.7 million), 31% of Asian children (1 million), and 31% of white children (12.1 million) lived in low-income families (Addy and Wight 2012). Having immigrant parents increases a child's chances of being poor, with approximately six in ten children with immigrant parents living in poverty.

Family structure affects access to resources and economic well-being for children as well. Single-parent families are more than twice as likely to be low income as two-parent families. Nationally, 59% of single-parent families are low income, compared to just 23% of two-parent families.

The percentage of children living below the federal poverty level also varies by geographic location, with higher concentrations of poverty in the southern United States. Areas with the highest rates of child poverty include Mississippi (33%), the District of Columbia (30%), New Mexico (30%), Alabama (28%), Arkansas (28%), Louisiana (27%), Kentucky (26%), South Carolina (26%), Tennessee (26%), and Texas (26%). These figures can be compared to states with much lower child poverty rates, such as New Hampshire (10%), Maryland (13%), Connecticut (13%), and Alaska (13%).

7.4.2   Elderly in the United States

In 2010, about 40.2 million Americans were age 65 or older, representing just over 13% of the total population. Among the older population, approximately 21.7 million were aged 65–74 years, 13 million were aged 75–84 years, and 5.5 million were 85 and older. According to U.S. Census Bureau projections, the older population will continue to burgeon between 2010 and 2030 as the baby boom generation (people born after World War II and between 1946 and 1964) reaches age 65. The older population is projected to grow to 72.1 million, or 19.3% of the total population, by 2030 (see Figure 7.3). Significantly, the oldest-old population—those aged 85 and above—is also projected to double over the next several decades, to 9.6 million by 2030, and to double again to 20.9 million by 2050 (He et al. 2005, 6).

There is more sex ratio imbalance between older adults than among the rest of the population, with women comprising 57% of the elderly and men representing only 43% of those over 65 years of age. This is largely because women live longer, on average, than men. Older men are much more

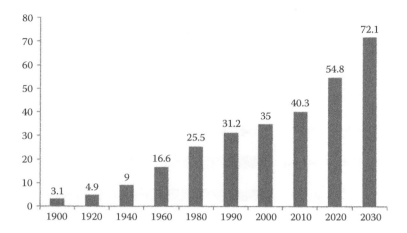

FIGURE 7.3   Number of persons 65 and older, 1900–2030 (numbers in millions). (*Source*: Administration on Aging [2011]. With permission.)

likely to be married than older women—72% of men versus 42% of women. The proportion of elderly people living alone has soared since 1950. Almost one in three, or 10.6 million, noninstitutionalized older persons live alone, and half of all women over the age of 75 live alone. A relatively small number (about 2 million) and percentage (5%) of persons over age 65 lived in nursing homes in 2010. However, the percentage increases with age, with about 1.4% of the young old, 4.7% of the aged, and 24.5% of the oldest old living in nursing homes.

The distribution of older persons varies considerably by state. Over half (56.5%) of persons 65 and older lived in 11 states: California (4.3 million), Florida (3.3 million), New York (2.6 million), Texas (2.6 million), Pennsylvania (2 million), and Ohio, Illinois, Michigan, North Carolina, New Jersey, and Georgia each had well over 1 million elderly residents (Administration on Aging 2011). Most older persons in the United States live in metropolitan areas, and the elderly are less likely to change residence than other groups (Administration on Aging 2011; He et al. 2005).

Older persons are less racially and ethnically diverse than other segments of the American population. However, the elderly population is expected to grow more diverse over the next several decades, largely reflecting demographic changes in the U.S. population as a whole. In 2010, the elderly population was 80% non-Hispanic white, 8.4% African American, 6.9% Hispanic (of any race), 3.5% Asian or Pacific Islander, less than 1% American Indian or Native Alaskan, and 0.8% of the elderly identified as some other race.

The median income of older persons in 2010 was $25,704 for males and $15,072 for females (Administration on Aging 2011). Major sources of income for older persons were: Social Security (reported by 87% of older persons); income from assets (reported by 53%); private pensions (reported by 28%); earnings (reported by 26%); and government employee pensions (reported by 14%). About 3.5 million older adults were living in poverty in 2010, which was lower than the national average. People aged 65–74 had a poverty rate of 9%, compared with 12% of those aged 75 and older. Older women were more likely than older men to live in poverty (13% compared to 7%). Elderly non-Hispanic whites (8%) were less likely than older blacks (24%) and older Hispanics (20%) to be living in poverty. Among older women living alone in 2003, poverty rates were 17% for non-Hispanic white women and about 40% for black women and Hispanic women (He et al. 2005).

Limitations of mobility and chronic poor health are difficulties common to older people around the world (IFRC 2007). In the United States, about 80% of seniors have at least one chronic health condition, and 50% have at least two (He et al. 2005). Arthritis, hypertension, heart disease, diabetes, and respiratory disorders are some of the leading causes of activity limitation among older people (He et al. 2005), and these health conditions are exacerbated by poverty and lack of access to

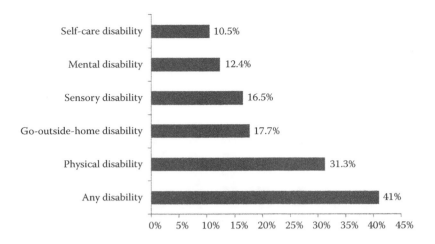

FIGURE 7.4   Disability characteristics among persons 65 and older, 2006. (*Source*: U.S. Census Bureau [2006].)

affordable and reliable health care. In 2006, 41% of the elderly, representing more than 14.5 million persons, had some type of disability, and many seniors reported having two or more disabilities (see Figure 7.4). (For related information, see Chapter 8 on Disability.) Older women (43%) were more likely than older men (38.2%) to experience disability. And, the disabled elderly were more likely to be living in poverty than their nondisabled counterparts.

7.5   VULNERABILITY ACROSS THE DISASTER LIFE CYCLE

Recent disaster events in the United States and around the globe tragically illustrate the vulnerability of children and the elderly during times of disaster. The 2004 Indian Ocean earthquake and tsunami claimed the lives of at least 60,000 children, most of whom lived in the hardest hit regions of Indonesia, Sri Lanka, India, and Thailand (Oxfam International 2005). Over 18,000 children perished in the 2005 Pakistan earthquake, largely as a result of the collapse of more than 10,000 school buildings (Hewitt 2007). In 2008, a deadly earthquake struck Sichuan Province in China and caused an estimated 10,000 child fatalities. Schools where predominantly poor children attended were especially hard hit, and many of the youngest victims died in their classrooms (Jacobs 2008). Following Hurricane Katrina, over 160,000 children from Louisiana and Mississippi were displaced from their homes and schools, and this population has subsequently suffered from high rates of emotional and behavioral problems, chronic health conditions, and poor access to medical care (Abramson and Garfield 2006; Abramson et al. 2007; Lauten and Lietz 2008).

Old age was the single most important factor in determining who died in Hurricane Katrina. Among the over 1,300 persons who perished in New Orleans, 67% were at least 65 years old, although this group represented only about 12% of the prestorm population (Sharkey 2007). The 1995 Chicago heat wave claimed more than 700 lives, and 73% of the heat-related deaths were among persons over 65 years of age (Klinenberg 2002). The 2003 European heat wave resulted in more than 52,000 deaths, most of which were concentrated among the elderly (Larsen 2006). In the 1995 Kobe earthquake, 53% of the fatalities were among older persons (Hewitt 2007). Similarly, the elderly in Japan were yet again among the hardest hit in terms of deaths and injuries in the 2011 Tohoku earthquake and tsunami (Associated Press 2011).

When certain segments of the population suffer disproportionately during times of disaster, it is important to consider what factors place these groups at particular risk before, during, and after the event. The following sections attempt to do just that by drawing on published research literature and agency reports that address the experiences of children and the elderly in disaster. The sections are organized by three major stages of the disaster life cycle: (1) warnings, evacuation, and response;

(2) impacts; and (3) short- and long-term recovery (see Fothergill 1996; Fothergill, Maestas, and Darlington 1999; Fothergill and Peek 2004). I begin by discussing issues that children face across the disaster life cycle. Then I consider factors that contribute to the vulnerability of older persons. The chapter concludes with a discussion of the implications of these findings for reducing vulnerability and increasing resilience.

7.5.1 Children—Warnings, Evacuation, and Response

This phase of the disaster life cycle entails receiving formal warning signals, such as emergency broadcasts and flood sirens or other risk communication of an immediate danger, and taking action with some type of response to the warning, such as evacuating or sheltering in place. To date, very little social science research has focused on how children receive, interpret, or respond to forecasts and warnings (Phillips and Morrow 2007). Dominant models of risk communication do not include youth as either sources or recipients of risk information (Mitchell et al. 2008). Instead, it is commonly assumed that parents will inform, warn, and protect their children in the event of a disaster (Adams 1995). The lack of focus on children's understanding of risk and warnings represents a serious gap in knowledge considering that: (1) children are often separated from their parents, such as when they are in school, in child care, or with their friends; (2) there are an estimated 1 million homeless and street youth in the United States who totally lack familial support (Unger, Simon, and Newman 1998); and (3) more than 1.6 million American children are home alone every day each year (Phillips and Hewett 2005).

Although children can contribute in meaningful ways during the warning and emergency-response phase of disasters, it is important to acknowledge that they do not have the same level of independence or resources available as adults (Mitchell et al. 2008). In homes, child-care centers, and schools, for example, adults are primarily responsible for making evacuation decisions, providing vital resources, securing shelter, and establishing routine (Peek and Fothergill 2008). Moreover, children and adolescents often turn to the important adults in their lives to help them understand and make sense of uncertain or frightening situations (Prinstein et al. 1996). According to Phillips and Morrow (2007), children model their behavioral response to disaster on the reactions of adults around them. Parents, teachers, and child-care workers give useful clues on how to respond given that children lack a behavioral repertoire or even a reference framework for disaster situations (ibid., 63).

A number of studies have examined the effect of having children on the evacuation decisions of adults. This work reveals that adults with children are more likely to respond to disaster warnings and evacuation messages than people without children (Carter, Kendall, and Clark 1983; Dash and Gladwin 2007; Edwards 1993; Fischer et al. 1995; Houts et al. 1984; Lindell, Lu, and Prater 2005). This suggests that parents and other caregivers of children would be receptive to hazards education materials that highlight the age- and hazard-specific risks children face, particularly if these materials draw on the principles of sound risk communication and include clear, consistent, and precise messages that are delivered through multiple channels (Mileti and Darlington 1997; Mileti and Fitzpatrick 1992; Mileti and O'Brien 1992).

While adults with children are more likely to respond to evacuation orders, a lack of resources may hinder the ability of low-income families to take recommended protective measures (Dash and Gladwin 2007). In Hurricane Katrina, poor and working-class mothers who were not able to leave New Orleans before the levee system failed faced dangerous and stressful evacuations with their children, as they were forced to wade through the floodwaters or be rescued by helicopter or boat (Fothergill and Peek 2006). In some cases, young people assisted directly with the evacuation of elderly and disabled family members by placing them on mattresses and helping them to float through the flooded city (Kirschke and van Vliet 2005).

Families with pets may also face particular challenges in evacuation. A study by Heath, Voeks, and Glickman (2000) explored evacuation and pet rescue in two communities: one in California that was under an evacuation notice due to flooding, and a second community in Wisconsin that evacuated in response to a hazardous chemical spill. Approximately 20% of pet-owning households in the California disaster and 50% of pet-owning households in the Wisconsin disaster evacuated without their pets. An estimated 80% of persons who reentered the evacuated areas did so to rescue their pet, and attempts to rescue a pet were most common among households with children. The authors posit that children may have become distressed over the abandonment of a pet and, therefore, put pressure on their parents to rescue it. This study demonstrates that pet rescues can endanger the health and well-being of animals and families, especially families with children.

The limited research available on children and emergency response primarily focuses on the household context and the decisions that adults make. But what happens when children are not at home when disaster strikes? Or when parents are separated from their children? Are schools and child-care centers adequately prepared? What factors shape evacuation planning and decision making among school administrators and child-care staff? These questions certainly warrant further consideration. On any given weekday during the academic year, there are approximately 55 million children in public and private schools across the United States (U.S. Census Bureau 2006). In addition to school-age youth, millions more infants and very young children are cared for in licensed child-care centers and in-home child-care settings.

Research on emergency response has highlighted the importance of household members being able to account for one another before taking recommended protective actions such as sheltering in place or evacuating (Tierney, Lindell, and Perry 2001). Parents, in particular, are highly unlikely to leave a threatened area until they are reunited with their children or certain that their children have been safely evacuated (Ronan and Johnston 2005). Research conducted in the aftermath of the 9/11 attacks emphasized the many problems that parents with children attending schools in lower Manhattan faced (Bartlett and Patrarca 2002). For example, because phone service was limited or nonexistent, parents were unable to contact the school to learn more about the situation or their spouses to coordinate who was picking up the child. In several cases, parents could not access their children's school because of the shutdown of public transportation services and street closings, which led to a delay in reuniting families.

Some research has focused on the ability or willingness of teachers and other school personnel to participate in the evacuation of students in the event of an emergency. Johnson (1985) surveyed 232 teachers at 29 public schools located near a nuclear power plant in California. Nearly one-third of the teachers indicated that they would not assist in an evacuation effort in the event of a radiological emergency, owing largely to a strong sense of obligation to their families and concerns for personal safety. An additional 10% of teachers qualified their responses by stating that their participation in evacuation efforts would be contingent upon being able to contact their own family members by telephone, limited to a specified length of time, or restricted to the evacuation of their class only. A survey of bus drivers in Suffolk County, New York, indicated that 66% would not report promptly to transport school children to destinations outside of the designated danger zone in the event of a nuclear accident (cited in Johnson 1985, 88). Bus drivers most often specified concern for family as the reason why they would not fulfill their duties. It is important to note that both of the aforementioned studies—of teachers in California and bus drivers in New York—were based on hypothetical incidents. Nonetheless, this research raises important questions about the role conflict that school personnel are likely to face as they attempt to care for the children in their schools while also trying to ensure the safety of their own families. Bartlett and Patrarca (2002) and Johnson (1985) recommend that school districts recruit back-up emergency personnel who could assist in the event of a major crisis.

Only three studies have explored preparedness and response capabilities among child-care centers. Olympia and colleagues (2010) distributed questionnaires to child-care centers in Pennsylvania to determine preparedness levels to respond to emergencies and disasters. The research team found that of those 496 centers that returned the survey, 99% had a written emergency plan, and 85% practiced that plan periodically throughout the year. About 77% of the centers in the study required at least one staff member to have first-aid training, and 33% required CPR training.

Wilson and Kershaw (2008) surveyed child-care providers in hurricane-prone regions of Florida. Most of the 67 child-care centers included in the sample had experienced a hurricane (83%) or had closed due to hurricane-related concerns (92%) over the past five years. Despite the high-risk area in which these centers were located, only about two-thirds of the respondents indicated that their center had a written hurricane response plan (and in about half of these cases, the plans were not frequently reviewed by center staff). Roughly 70% of respondents were either in the process of or had completed assembling a "hurricane kit" (including vital contact numbers, business papers, insurance, and medications). The authors also found that about 40% of the centers had a contingency plan in place in the event that their facility became uninhabitable following a hurricane.

Junn and Guerin (1996) examined levels of earthquake preparedness among child-care centers in a seismically active region of Southern California. They found that over half of the 25 centers studied did not have an earthquake plan on file; those that did often failed to share their plan with teachers, staff, parents, or local emergency-response agencies. Almost half of the centers lacked basic essentials, such as food or water, which would be necessary to cope comfortably in the aftermath of a major earthquake. In addition, approximately one-third of the center directors believed incorrectly that emergency-response agencies would evacuate children from child-care facilities for relocation within 24 hours after a disaster. The authors conclude that, at best, only half of the child-care facilities they studied were even minimally equipped to handle the crises associated with a major earthquake.

When evacuation is necessary, families typically seek refuge in the homes of relatives or friends or stay in hotels (Tierney, Lindell, and Perry 2001). Children who do stay in shelters may face special risks, and there is evidence that the United States is ill-prepared to handle disasters that involve large numbers of injured or displaced children (Markenson and Redlener 2004). When shelters first open, they may not have necessary supplies such as diapers, baby wipes, formula, soap, or prescription medicines to support the health and well-being of children, and infants may be especially vulnerable (Garrett et al. 2007). Also, children with disabilities or chronic health conditions may be particularly prone to adverse effects of evacuation and disruption of support systems and routines (Peek and Stough 2010; Rath et al. 2007). Brandenburg and colleagues (2006) identified numerous child injury hazards at a National Guard center in Oklahoma that had been converted to a temporary shelter for Katrina evacuees. Risks to children resulted from both preexisting conditions of the facility (e.g., open electrical outlets, lack of smoke detectors, insecure window screens) and hazards created as a result of the relief efforts and influx of evacuees and volunteers (e.g., unsafe toys, open containers of chemicals and cleaning materials, open tubs of water). Children are also at higher risk of acquiring respiratory and gastrointestinal diseases due to unsanitary conditions in shelters (Garrett et al. 2007), and this is especially true in developing countries (Bartlett 2008).

Shelter workers and local volunteers often play crucial roles in helping to minimize the threats to children's physical safety and emotional well-being. For example, Fothergill and Peek (2006) found that after Hurricane Katrina, shelter workers organized tutoring programs, play areas, and child drop-off locations that helped children stay active while giving parents the opportunity to rest or to take care of other important responsibilities (see Photo 7.1). The Church of the Brethren Children's Disaster Services program trains and mobilizes volunteers in the immediate aftermath of disaster and provides free child care to families affected by disasters of all types (Peek, Sutton, and Gump 2008). After the 2007 California wildfires, Save the Children partnered with Children's Disaster Services and the American Red Cross to set up "Safe Spaces" in evacuation centers (Smith 2008). The goal of "Safe Spaces" was to allow children to play in a secure and structured environment. Save the Children also recently implemented a program in evacuation centers called "Resilient and Ready." This program, which is workshop-based, allows children an opportunity to discuss their feelings of worry or concern, and also teaches them what to do in an emergency situation. After the children complete the workshop, they are given a backpack with emergency evacuation supplies.

PHOTO 7.1 Petionville, Haiti (February 22, 2010). Haitian children enjoy jumping rope under the shelter of a tarp in their temporary neighborhoods. (*Source*: U.S. Navy photo by Senior Chief Mass Communication Specialist Spike Call. Released.)

7.5.2 Children—Impacts

Over the past three decades, an increasing amount of scholarly attention has been devoted to the psychological impact of disasters on children. This literature examines children's responses to natural and technological disasters, as well as to terrorism and other forms of violent conflict (Weissbecker et al. 2008). The most widely studied reaction to disasters has been that of posttraumatic stress disorder (PTSD) or related symptoms (La Greca et al. 2002; Norris et al. 2002). This work has shown that a significant proportion of children show reactions following exposure to disasters that can substantially interfere with or impair their daily living and can cause distress to them and their families (La Greca et al. 2002). In their review of the literature on the psychosocial consequences of disaster, Norris and colleagues (2002) found that youth were more likely to be severely affected by disasters than adults, with 48% of school-age samples suffering from moderate postdisaster impairment and 52% experiencing severe or very severe effects in communities that had suffered a major natural disaster. Udwin (1993, 124) notes that there is a growing body of evidence to show that most children react adversely after exposure to traumatic events, and that a significant proportion of child survivors of disasters (possibly 30%–50%) are likely to develop PTSD symptoms, which may persist for long periods of time.

Disaster impacts on children vary by age group, prior experiences, and stage of physical and mental development. For very young children, problems include clinginess, dependence, nightmares, refusing to sleep alone, irritability and temper tantrums, aggressive behavior, incontinence, hyperactivity, and separation anxiety (Norris et al. 2002). Older children may exhibit marked reactions of fear and anxiety, increased hostility with siblings, somatic complaints, sleep disorders, problems with school performance, social withdrawal, apathy, reenactment through play, PTSD, and anxiety (Mandalakas, Torjesen, and Olness 1999). Adolescents may experience decreased interest in social activities and school, rebellion and other behavioral problems, sleep and eating disorders, somatic complaints, increased or decreased physical activity, confusion, lack of concentration, and a decline in responsible behaviors. As a consequence, they are more likely to engage in risk-taking behaviors, suffer from PTSD, and be at increased risk for alcohol or drug misuse after disaster (Mandalakas, Torjesen, and Olness 1999; Reijneveld et al. 2005; Shannon et al. 1994).

Several factors influence children's psychological and emotional reactions to traumatic events (Green et al. 1991; La Greca, Silverman, and Wasserstein 1998; Vernberg et al. 1996). One of the most critical predictors of children's postdisaster distress is the *extent and intensity of exposure* to the traumatic event. Children who experience life threat, become separated from family members, lose a loved one, suffer extensive damage to their homes and communities, or witness scenes of disaster destruction either directly or through media intake are at particular risk for developing PTSD, anxiety, or depression (Lengua et al. 2005; McFarlane 1987; Pfefferbaum et al. 1999; Saylor et al. 2003; Shannon et al. 1994). The *characteristics of the child,* including demographic characteristics and predisaster functioning, also influence children's reactions to disaster. Girls, racial and ethnic minorities, and children from lower-socioeconomic backgrounds seem to be at increased risk for psychological impairment after disaster, although results are not always consistent (Lonigan et al. 1994; Shannon et al. 1994; Vogel and Vernberg 1993). Children with poorer behavioral and academic functioning prior to disaster are also likely to suffer higher rates of postdisaster impairment (La Greca, Silverman, and Wasserstein 1998). *Characteristics of the postdisaster environment,* including parental distress, lack of access to social support, and the occurrence of additional life stressors (abuse, poverty, divorce, death or illness of a family member) have been linked to children's adverse mental health outcomes and behavioral problems in the aftermath of disaster (Maida, Gordon, and Strauss 1993; Stuber et al. 2005; Swenson et al. 1996; Warheit et al. 1996; Wasserstein and La Greca 1998). Finally, the *coping skills of the child* and the *coping assistance received* also influence children's ability to adapt and respond to highly traumatic events (Jeney-Gammon et al. 1993; Prinstein et al. 1996).

Compared to the number of studies that examine the mental health effects of disasters on children, much less research has explored children's risk for physical injury or loss of life in disasters of various types. The research that is available has examined the rates of injuries and fatalities among children in particular disaster events (Glass et al. 1977; Ikeda 1995; Parasuraman 1995; Ramirez et al. 2005). Most of this work has focused on developing countries because they are much more prone to large-scale natural catastrophes that cause extensive loss of life. In contrast to developing countries, the risk of child mortality by forces of nature in the United States is relatively low. The Centers for Disease Control and Prevention (2004) recorded 6,108 deaths caused by natural disaster events between 1999 and 2003. Of the persons killed, 530 were children and youth between the ages of 0 to 24 years.

Researchers have identified several social and environmental factors that contribute to children being at risk for death or injury in disaster. These include residing in poorer countries and communities (Sapir and Lechat 1986), living in and going to school in substandard structures (Hewitt 2007; Parasuraman 1995), losing a parent or becoming separated from family members (Sapir 1993; Sapir and Lechat 1986), and experiencing malnutrition and poor diet (Webster 1994; Young and Jaspars 1995) or artificial feeding (i.e., bottle feeding) (Kelly 1993). Female children are at higher risk of death (Ramirez et al. 2005; Rivers 1982; Sapir 1993), at least in developing nations. However, research by Zahran, Peek, and Brody (2008) shows that in disasters in the United States, the death rate for male children and youth is higher than the death rate for female children and youth across all age cohorts. There is no consensus in the literature on the age at which children are most at risk for death or injury in disasters, largely because different types of disaster seem to differentially impact children of various ages. For example, Zahran and colleagues (2008) found that in the United States, infants and very young children age 0–4 are most likely to die of exposure to extreme heat, 5–14 year-olds are most likely to die in cataclysmic storms and flood events, and adolescents and young adults age 15–24 are most likely to die of excessive cold.

Increased rates of physical abuse may also contribute to children's vulnerability in the aftermath of disaster. In one of the first attempts to empirically examine whether or not child abuse escalates after natural disasters, Curtis, Miller, and Berry (2000) discovered statistically significant increases in child abuse reports in the first six months following Hurricane Hugo and the Loma Prieta earthquake, but found no statistically significant change in abuse rates following Hurricane Andrew.

Keenan and colleagues (2004) examined whether there was an increase in traumatic brain injury (TBI, commonly referred to as shaken baby syndrome) among children 2 years old or younger after Hurricane Floyd. The results showed an increase in the rate of inflicted TBI in the most affected counties for six months following the disaster, possibly reflecting increased injury risk due to prolonged stress among caregivers.

Following the 2004 Indian Ocean tsunami, the media and advocacy organizations drew attention to the risks of sexual violence and human trafficking that children, and especially girls, faced in displaced-person camps (Enarson, Fothergill, and Peek 2006). Drawing on interviews with women's advocacy organizations, Fisher (2005) documented incidents of rape, molestation, and physical abuse perpetrated against women and girls in the tsunami aftermath. Over 2,000 sex offenders were lost in the chaos of the Hurricane Katrina evacuation, giving rise to reasonable fears about child predators in and around shelters (Lauten and Lietz 2008). After Katrina, some efforts were enacted to identify children separated from their legal guardians, to help thwart abductions, and to prevent child physical and sexual abuse (Brandenburg et al. 2007; National Center for Missing and Exploited Children 2006). However, the mere size of the mass shelters that opened after Katrina—as many as 60,000 people sought refuge at the Louisiana Superdome, with up to 25,000 at the nearby New Orleans Convention Center—exposed children to potential violence and compromised the ability of parents to establish a sense of safety for their families (Peek and Erikson 2008). These security threats continued as Katrina evacuees were moved into trailer parks, where almost half of the residents did not feel safe walking in their community at night and 45% did not feel comfortable letting their children play in the trailer parks during the day (International Medical Corps 2006). These settings were enormously stressful for the parents as well as for the children themselves (Fothergill and Peek 2012).

The impact of disasters on children's academic progress and educational outcomes is another area that has received increasing, although still insufficient, attention in the research literature (see Peek 2008). Disasters often destroy school buildings, especially in locations where engineering standards and building codes are not enforced or where buildings are of less structural integrity: Hewitt (2007) inventoried tens of thousands of schools that collapsed in earthquakes over the past two decades in several developing countries. The loss of schools may leave surviving children with few alternatives for an adequate education. Following Katrina, displaced students, many of whom were already behind their peers in reading and math, suffered significant challenges (Casserly 2006; Children's Defense Fund 2006). Vital records were lost in the storm, which resulted in delayed enrollment for some youth (Picou and Marshall 2007). Although getting children back into school was a top priority among parents (Fothergill and Peek 2006), many families did not immediately enroll their children in new schools because they were unsure how long they would be staying in their new community, and others simply did not want to let their children out of their sight (Casserly 2006). Some students were forced to enroll in several different schools as families moved across state lines in search of employment and affordable housing (Abramson and Garfield 2006; Picou and Marshall 2007). One study found that children experienced between 1 and 11 school changes over a three-month period following the storm, with an average of three moves per child (Lauten and Lietz 2008).

7.5.3 Children—Short- and Long-Term Recovery

Much of the literature available on children and recovery is geared toward adults and the ways that they can help children in the disaster aftermath. Parents are often recognized as the single most important source of social support for children following disaster (Prinstein et al. 1996). Parents provide material and emotional support, give comfort and nurturance, and offer a sense of physical safety. In addition to parents, other individuals such as teachers, peers, school counselors, psychologists, pediatricians, disaster relief volunteers, and shelter workers have been identified as playing key roles in reestablishing normalcy, allowing children to express their emotions, and assisting in coping efforts (Barrett, Ausbrooks, and Martinez-Cosio 2008; Johnston and Redlener 2006; Peek and Fothergill 2006; Peek, Sutton, and Gump 2008; Shen and Sink 2002). Indeed, Fothergill and Peek (2006, 122) argue that these various "support agents" play different, but vitally important, roles in the short- and long-term postdisaster recovery of children.

Some scholars have underscored the importance of encouraging traumatized children to express their feelings—verbally, in written form, and through art and play—to begin healing and recovery (Fothergill and Peek 2006; Looman 2006; Peek, Sutton, and Gump 2008; Raynor 2002). These different outlets may help children to articulate their sadness, fears, anxieties, most pressing needs, and hopes for the future. As Looman (2006) notes, however, the age of the child will likely determine the preferred mode of expression: Younger children tend to want to draw about their experiences, while adolescents prefer to talk or write about what happened to them in a disaster.

The importance of reopening schools and child-care centers quickly after a disaster has also been highlighted as essential to the successful recovery of children, families, and communities (U.S. GAO 2006; Wilson and Kershaw 2008). Indeed, schools are central to children's return to routine and normalcy. However, when a disaster causes widespread infrastructure damage and leads to the loss of teachers and other critical personnel, school reopening may be significantly delayed. Reopening schools may also be complicated by the presence of evacuated residents and emergency response personnel, since schools are often used as shelter facilities in disasters.

School-aged children who are displaced to new schools may face particular challenges in the recovery process. Picou and Marshall (2007) found that students who were displaced to Alabama following Katrina lacked reliable access to transportation and experienced unstable living situations, which led to attendance problems and negatively impacted academic performance. Moreover, families of displaced students suffered severe financial burdens that manifested in a lack of financial support for the daily needs of many displaced students. The rapid influx of new students also created challenges among peers and for teachers, school staff, and administrators. Children who were displaced after Katrina were sometimes teased or bullied by students in the receiving schools (Fothergill and Peek 2012; Peek 2012). Teachers had to go to great lengths to ensure that the emotional and academic needs of evacuee children were met, while also balancing the demands of the rest of the students in the class. Barrett, Ausbrooks, and Martinez-Cosio (2008) surveyed displaced middle and high school students who evacuated to Texas after Katrina. They found that nine months after the storm, there were few differences between the relocated Katrina evacuees and their peers in their new schools in terms of emotional well-being. However, evacuee youth were more prone to participate in risky behaviors and fewer protective behaviors (such as school sports or other extracurricular activities) than their non-evacuee peers. The findings indicate that the youths who built positive relationships with their new school, and those who had garnered positive support from adults (especially with their teachers), were managing better than those without a positive source of social support.

Children are at special risk for adverse psychological responses to disaster, but symptoms typically decrease rapidly, and recovery is generally complete by 18 months to 3 years postevent (Vogel and Vernberg 1993). Some children suffer longer-term impairment, however. Children most at risk for protracted psychological reactions and delayed recovery include those who experienced: highly stressful disasters that involved direct life threat; significant loss; separation from parents; and intense parental stress reactions (Garrett et al. 2007; Vogel and Vernberg 1993). Chemtob, Nomura, and Abramovitz (2008) explored the long-term emotional and behavioral consequences of the 9/11 terrorist attacks for 116 children who were 5 years old or younger and living or going to preschool in Manhattan at the time of the disaster. Nearly one-fourth of the children in the study were exposed to high-intensity events, such as seeing the World Trade Center towers collapse, seeing injured people or dead bodies, or witnessing people jump out of buildings. The study found that children exposed to such traumatic events were nearly five times more likely to suffer from sleep problems and almost three times more likely to be depressed or anxious than children who were not exposed to the attacks. In a follow-up study to the Buffalo Creek flood, Green and colleagues (1991) evaluated child survivors 17 years postevent when they were adults (the participants were first evaluated in 1974, two years after the disaster). The findings show that the survivors experienced a general decline in impairment over time, suggesting that most of the participants had indeed recovered from the disaster.

The long-term physical health effects for child disaster survivors are complex and not well understood. In the aftermath of 9/11, children in Manhattan were exposed to high levels of contaminants in the air as a result of the dust and debris generated by the collapse of the twin towers and other surrounding buildings (Bartlett and Patrarca 2002). Experts testified that the clouds of dust contained benzene, mercury, dioxins, fiberglass, and asbestos, among other substances, and that children could potentially face long-term health issues as a result of exposure (ibid., 9). Tens of thousands of Gulf Coast children who lived in Federal Emergency Management Agency (FEMA)-issued trailers after Katrina may experience lifelong health problems due to the formaldehyde present in the units (Gonzales 2008). Children, as well as adults, suffered ear, nose, and throat irritation, nausea, severe headaches, and asthma, and could potentially develop cancer as a result of the exposure to formaldehyde. The World Health Organization (WHO 2005) reports that an increasing number of children are becoming physically disabled due to an increase in sudden-onset disasters, malnutrition, chronic illness, war and other forms of violence, accidents, and environmental damage.

Some studies have explored whether children may recover at differential rates than their peers and even their family members, and what this may mean for designing postdisaster research and policy interventions. One such study of adjustment processes among persons who were displaced to Colorado after Hurricane Katrina found that children and their parents moved through four different stages of family adjustment: (1) family unity stage; (2) prioritizing safety stage (parents) and missing home stage (children); (3) confronting reality stage (parents) and feeling settled stage (children); and (4) reaching resolution (Peek, Morrissey, and Marlatt 2011). This research illustrates that parental and child adjustment trajectories are dynamic and may vary over time, thus underscoring the importance of considering the perspectives of both adults *and* children in long-term postdisaster research.

7.5.4   ELDERLY—WARNINGS, EVACUATION, AND RESPONSE

The ultimate goal of communicating warnings is to motivate individuals to take appropriate protective actions in the event of an impending threat. Yet few studies have explored ways to most effectively warn or communicate risk to the elderly. This means that we know very little about how older people prefer to receive warnings or how they interpret that information (Phillips and Morrow 2007). Mayhorn (2005) draws upon the aging literature to illustrate how documented normative age-related changes in perception, attention, memory, text comprehension, and decision making all may affect the processing of hazard-related risk and warning messages. Based on this information, Mayhorn asserts that when developing messages for older adults, designers should tailor the characteristics of the messages to compensate for age-related declines in visual and auditory perception and should take account of different types of memory limitations. With the rapid advent of new communication technologies—such as email, social networking websites, cell phone text messaging, and automatic telephone alert notification systems—it has become increasingly important to consider the ways that an older person's age and related physical and cognitive abilities, as well as their income, prior experience, social conditions, and educational backgrounds, might affect their capabilities to access and utilize these technologies.

Early studies on the elderly and disaster suggested that older persons are less likely to receive warnings than younger persons. Isolated living arrangements, diminished social networks, lower rates of information-seeking behavior, and limited physical and mental capacities were all identified as possible obstacles to the receipt of warning messages among seniors (Friedsam 1962; Perry 1979). Klinenberg's (2002) research on the 1995 Chicago heat wave, where almost three-fourths of the fatalities were among the elderly, revealed that city agencies and the media delayed warning the public about the imminent heat wave. Hundreds of the most vulnerable were dead before officials activated the city's heat emergency plan. When volunteers and city workers began canvassing neighborhoods to warn people of the dangers of the heat, many Chicago seniors refused to open their doors out of fear. Others were unable to engage in recommended protective actions (such as turning on fans or air conditioners or walking to air-conditioned public spaces) due to financial constraints and physical limitations.

The research available on warning response among the elderly is conflicting. Some of the first studies on this topic characterized older persons as a population in need of special attention among emergency managers because of their noncompliance to warnings and unwillingness to cooperate with authorities (Perry 1990). Possible explanations for elderly warning noncompliance included social isolation among some members of the population, inflexibility, a strong sense of independence, refusal to be separated from normal surroundings, limited mobility and higher degrees of physical infirmity, and fears of being mistreated by authorities (Friedsam 1962; Turner 1976). More systematic research by Perry and Lindell (1997), however, has challenged these assumptions about the elderly (also see Hutton 1976). Specifically, Perry and Lindell evaluated warning response among older persons across a variety of natural and technological disaster events, and found that citizens aged 65 and older who received warning messages were no less likely to comply with warnings and evacuation orders than their younger counterparts. In some cases, the elderly were actually more likely to comply. The authors conclude that while age alone is not a useful predictor of warning compliance, age is clearly an important variable in the warning phase to the extent that related physical, psychological, financial, and social conditions impact such things as the probability of receiving a warning, understanding it, and taking action based upon it (ibid., 264).

Although evacuation—which entails moving citizens from a place of danger to a place of relative safety—has long been used as a protective mechanism when disasters threaten (Perry 1990, 94), seniors often face additional challenges in the evacuation process. For instance, evacuation potentially entails significant financial (e.g., use of automobile, fuel, hotel stay, etc.), emotional (e.g., fear of the unknown, reluctance to leave pets, property, or possessions, etc.), and social (e.g., reliance on relatives, stigma, mistreatment, etc.) costs that may be exacerbated for elderly populations (IFRC 2007; Mayhorn 2005). Low-income seniors, the homebound, and those with physical or cognitive disabilities face compounded barriers that often make self-evacuation highly unlikely or impossible. For the frailest seniors, the risks of leaving must be balanced with the risks of staying. For example, when Hurricane Rita threatened the Gulf Coast, 2.5 million people evacuated the region, largely motivated by fears of another Katrina-like catastrophe (Garrett et al. 2007). Of the 111 storm-related deaths in Rita, 90 were due to the evacuation process itself as gridlock on the highway and oppressive heat took their toll on the chronically ill and elderly (ibid., 192). As Moody (2006, 14) notes, on the one hand, leaving the home in which an elder has lived for years can provoke "transfer trauma" and even cause death. On the other hand, simply leaving individuals alone to risk death is tantamount to abandonment of the weakest members of our society.

Nine out of ten, or 90%, of elderly Americans live at home, and an increasing number of these individuals live alone (U.S. Census Bureau 2006). Even when early warnings (as with a slow-rising flood or hurricane) are issued hours or days before a disaster occurs, few communities have plans in place to identify and reach out to older adults most likely in need of evacuation assistance (Wilson 2006). For many older adults, especially those with disabilities or who require special medical equipment, exiting their homes can be a great challenge when evacuation is required (McGuire, Ford, and Okoro 2007). Yet the responsibility to evacuate is placed on these individuals and their loved ones, which is particularly problematic in the United States, where people move frequently, families are often spatially dispersed, and it is common for seniors to lose valuable sources of social support as they age (Klinenberg 2002). Seniors who live at home may be at even greater risk when a disaster strikes with little or no warning (as with an earthquake, industrial accident, and terrorist attack). After the 9/11 attacks, a number of older adults and persons with disabilities were left for three days in buildings in lower Manhattan that had been evacuated, which highlights the pressing need to identify vulnerable people who are not in institutional settings or connected to community service agencies (O'Brien 2003).

Most emergency evacuation planning for seniors has actually been geared toward nursing homes and other assisted-living facilities (Lafond 1987), even though less than 10% of elderly adults in the United States actually live in these settings. Nursing-home residents are generally frail and at risk of rapid medical decline in the absence of continuous care (Laditka et al. 2007), and thus the stresses of evacuation can be particularly challenging for this population. However, the burden to evacuate is not placed upon each resident because long-term care establishments ostensibly have disaster and evacuation plans. The facility decides whether to evacuate, selects and arranges the mode of transportation, and plans appropriate temporary lodging (McGuire, Ford, and Okoro 2007). Yet, this certainly does not guarantee the safety and survival of residents, as was widely acknowledged after Hurricane Katrina. The owners of St. Rita's Nursing Home in St. Bernard Parish, just outside of New Orleans, were charged with the deaths of 35 elderly patients who drowned after the owners decided not to evacuate the facility. What received less attention from the media, however, was that of the approximately 60 nursing homes directly affected by Katrina, only 21 evacuated before the storm (Hull and Struck 2005). A number of these nursing-home facilities, which are obviously located in an extremely hazardous region, did not even have an evacuation plan on file (Wilson 2006).

Prior studies have identified numerous problems encountered in evacuating nursing-home residents during emergencies and disasters, including: (1) the absence of specific evacuation plans; (2) an insufficient number of vehicles that can accommodate walkers, wheelchairs, and other specialized medical equipment; (3) transportation delays and the resultant length of time required to move nursing-home residents to their designated shelters; (4) elevated stress and discomfort among the elderly as they wait for transport; (5) staff not being permitted to pass through police checkpoints after being called in to assist with an evacuation; (6) lack of adequate staff and high staff-client ratios; (7) large numbers of frail elderly and persons in need of specialized medical attention; (8) communication system disruption; and (9) lack of water, food, medicine, and other essential supplies (Elmore and Brown 2007; Mangum, Kosberg, and McDonald 1989; Vogt 1991; Wilson 2006). Vogt (1991) discovered that preparing for emergencies is a low priority within most nursing homes and related health-care organizations, and that too often these organizations utilize fire drills to prepare for all types of emergencies when the majority of events are not fire related. There is some evidence, however, that the catastrophic consequences of Hurricane Katrina have caused at least some long-term care facilities and nursing homes to reconsider their disaster preparedness and evacuation plans (Hyer et al. 2006; Laditka et al. 2007).

Most elderly, like other members of the population, do not evacuate to public shelters but instead relocate to the homes of relatives or friends (Tierney, Lindell, and Perry 2001). However, elderly adults who do utilize public shelters may encounter settings—such as churches and public schools—that are difficult to navigate because the facilities are located on more than one level (Vogt 1991). The elderly often evacuate without medications, eyeglasses, and other supplies, and thus may arrive at shelters without necessary provisions or knowledge of the whereabouts of their doctors (Ketteridge and Fordham 1998). Nursing-home residents are frequently evacuated to other nursing homes or to hospitals, where the professional staff can relatively easily care for their needs. In some mass evacuations, however, nursing-home residents end up in settings that were never intended to accommodate physically or mentally impaired persons. This creates numerous challenges related to feeding, cleaning, dressing, providing medications, and caring for these vulnerable individuals (Mangum, Kosberg, and McDonald 1989; Wilson 2006).

Sheltering in place during an emergency, either as a recommended action or because of a lack of other viable options, can lead to potentially life-threatening situations for the elderly. After 9/11, service personnel lacked access to older and frail residents living in the area surrounding Ground Zero where the twin towers collapsed. Essential services such as meals for the homebound and home health care were not delivered because staff had no official authorization to carry out their responsibilities. In some cases, elderly and disabled persons were left alone for days with no electricity (and therefore no television, lights, elevators, or refrigerators), no running water, and no information about what was happening (O'Brien 2003).

7.5.5   ELDERLY—IMPACTS

When disaster does strike, older adults are among those most likely to perish (Bourque et al. 2006). In the United States, the Centers for Disease Control and Prevention (2004) recorded 6,108 deaths caused by natural disaster events between 1999 and 2003. Over 40% (2,670) of those who died were persons 65 years of age and above, although the elderly represent only about 12% of the entire population. Research has also shown that the proportion of elderly injured in disasters is higher than would be expected based on the population distribution of this age group (Eldar 1992).

A number of factors place the elderly at increased risk for disaster-related injuries, mortality, and morbidity. Many older adults, and especially elderly women of color, live in socially and economically marginalized positions prior to a disaster. Low-income seniors may be unable to increase their preparedness for disasters—by storing food, purchasing emergency first-aid equipment, stockpiling medicines, or upgrading their dwellings—which puts them at special risk in times of disaster. Sensory impairment, resulting from vision or hearing loss, may reduce the likelihood than an older adult will receive, accurately perceive, or appropriately act on hazard warnings (Eldar 1992; Mayhorn 2005). Age-related mobility problems make it more difficult for some older adults to escape during times of disaster. For instance, some seniors are physically incapable of walking to an evacuation point in the event of a tsunami warning or hiking up a hillside in a flash flood, both of which are recommended protective actions obviously aimed at more able-bodied persons. Reduced thermoregulatory capacity in the elderly, combined with a diminished ability to detect changes in their body temperatures, may partly explain their higher susceptibility to death from extreme cold and extreme heat (Medina-Ramón et al. 2006).

For the growing number of older persons who suffer from chronic ailments, the shock of a disaster may further exacerbate poor overall health and could lead to premature death (Medina-Ramón et al. 2006). Seniors are also more vulnerable because they typically have a lower injury threshold and a decreased ability to survive injury once it has occurred (Eldar 1992). A disaster can force individuals to go for extended periods of time without adequate food, water, shelter, or access to regular medications, and the elderly are among those who have the hardest time withstanding these sorts of conditions. Older adults who take refuge in public shelters may suffer additional trauma and stress from the lack of privacy, crowded and noisy environments, uncomfortable sleeping arrangements, and lack of assistance with the activities of daily living (HelpAge International 2005). Older people with ailments such as diabetes or cancer may face difficulty in resuming life-sustaining treatment due to lost medical histories, lack of health insurance, or insufficient financial resources. Disasters can result in disabling conditions for some elderly, as they are forced to go without eyeglasses, hearing aids, walkers, and other devices that assist their daily living (Eldar 1992). These persons, who may have been relatively independent before the disaster, could become totally reliant on others.

Where the elderly live also puts them at risk for financial loss, death, or injury in disasters. A substantial proportion of older adults in the United States are concentrated in some of the most hazard-prone states. In fact, the four states with the highest number of federal disaster declarations—Texas, California, Florida, and New York—also happen to be the four states with the largest number of elderly residents (FEMA 2008; U.S. Census Bureau 2006). Older persons who live in low-cost housing are exposed to greater risks because of the lower-quality construction of these buildings, which may be particularly susceptible to floods, fires, tornadoes, or earthquakes (Fothergill and Peek 2004). Elderly persons who live in high-crime, high-poverty neighborhoods that are run-down and lack viable public spaces are more likely to suffer from social isolation and to receive insufficient assistance in a disaster (Klinenberg 2002).

Increased rates of elder abuse may contribute to the physical and emotional vulnerability of some older persons in communities struck by disasters, although this is a largely unexplored topic. After the *Exxon Valdez* oil spill in Alaska, community leaders responding to a survey reported an 11% increase in elder abuse (Araji 1992). The stresses of living in a postdisaster environment often strain family relationships (Morrow 1997), and individuals may become overwhelmed as they attempt to cope with their own or their family members' traumatic reactions to disaster, the loss of material possessions and valued family memorabilia, financial difficulties, and increased demands for care work between adults and their elderly parents. All of these factors could contribute to a higher incidence of elder abuse in the aftermath of disaster.

Although older persons are at greater risk for death or physical injury, available research suggests that they are actually less likely than their younger counterparts to suffer adverse psychological impacts in the aftermath of natural and human-made disasters (Ngo 2001). In their extensive review of the disaster mental health literature, Norris and colleagues (2002) report that negative psychological responses to disaster decline with age, and that middle-aged adults are actually most likely to be adversely affected. Greater chronic stress and additional demands related to providing care and support for dependent relatives may explain why being middle-aged is a risk factor for postdisaster distress (Bolin and Klenow 1988; Thompson, Norris, and Hanacek 1993). The elderly seem to be more psychologically resilient because of the greater life experience, maturity, and fewer obligations and responsibilities that come with age (Ngo 2001; Norris et al. 2002). In addition, the lower psychological vulnerability of older adults might be attributed to previous disaster exposure and related improved preparedness and positive coping skills (Bell, Kara, and Batterson 1978; Huerta and Horton 1978; Lawson and Thomas 2007; Ngo 2001; Norris and Murrell 1988).

While older adults as a whole may exhibit lower rates of postdisaster distress, they are still at risk for adverse psychological outcomes after exposure to natural disaster. Indeed, a number of studies have confirmed that the elderly have suffered from anxiety, depressive symptoms, and considerable physical and mental distress for months or even several years in the aftermath of disaster (Krause 1987; Melick and Logue 1985; Ollendick and Hoffmann 1982; Phifer 1990). Furthermore, rates of psychological distress tend to vary significantly among the elderly, as some segments of the older adult population are more vulnerable than others to disaster. In particular, predisaster characteristics and conditions of the elderly (e.g., socioeconomic status, race, gender, marital status, family size, available support networks, prior traumatic experiences) and disaster impacts (e.g., severity of exposure, financial and material loss, displacement) all influence mental health outcomes in the immediate and longer-term aftermath of disaster (Bolin and Klenow 1988; Ngo 2001; Norris et al. 2002; Tracy and Galea 2006).

One consistent finding in the literature is that low-income seniors are often most vulnerable to adverse psychological outcomes. This differential vulnerability may be directly related to associated deficits in coping tactics and low social-support resources (Phifer 1990). While some research has found that men exposed to disaster exhibit higher rates of stress and may engage in negative coping behaviors (e.g., alcohol abuse) (Phifer 1990), numerous studies have shown that older women are more vulnerable to the effects of stress than older men (see Fothergill 1996; Ollenburger and Tobin 1999). Older women, and especially older minority women, are more likely to be unmarried, to live alone, to have more caretaking roles, and to have fewer socioeconomic resources, which puts them at risk for stress-related illness after disaster (Ollenburger and Tobin 1999). However, older women typically have more social support, which suggests that their superior support networks may help them cope more effectively than men (Klinenberg 2002; Krause 1987; Tyler 2006).

Even though the elderly exhibit less postimpact psychological disruption than younger cohorts, they tend to experience greater proportional dollar losses (Bell 1978; Bolin and Klenow 1983; Kilijanek and Drabek 1979; Poulshock and Cohen 1975). These higher losses have been attributed to the elderly living in hazardous areas and residing in housing less resistant to forces of nature, although more systematic research across time, place, and disaster type is necessary to better understand the actual extent of losses suffered by the elderly (Ngo 2001). Early research by Friedsam (1961, 1962) and Bolin and Klenow (1983) discovered that older citizens were more likely to report greater material losses, despite indications that damages were evenly distributed across age groups. However, work by Huerta and Horton (1978) found no pattern of overreporting among the elderly. One thing that is certain is that those who have lived the longest often are at the greatest risk of losing the accumulated assets of a lifetime. Indeed, as a group, the elderly tend to lose more

PHOTO 7.2   Banda Aceh, Sumatra, Indonesia (January 14, 2005). An elderly woman collects bowls for washing and cooking, near her home, which was devastated by the December 26 tsunami. (*Source*: U.S. Navy photo by Photographer's Mate 3rd Class Tyler J. Clements. Released.)

irreplaceable items, and it is the loss of these possessions that often causes great distress among older persons (Huerta and Horton 1978; Ketteridge and Fordham 1998; Kilijanek and Drabek 1979). (See Photo 7.2.)

7.5.6   ELDERLY—SHORT- AND LONG-TERM RECOVERY

The stress confronted by disaster survivors is multifaceted, involving not only immediate loss and trauma but also a continuing requirement to adapt to a changing environment during the disaster recovery period (Norris and Hutchins 1989, 34). The research evidence available suggests that seniors often face financial, physical, and emotional obstacles as they struggle to recover and rebuild after a disaster. However, older adults who suffer less severe disruptions and have access to sufficient resources and sources of social support are able to cope effectively in the short- and longer-term aftermath of disaster.

As described previously, several studies have found that older citizens tend to experience greater proportional dollar losses in disasters. Yet many seniors, and especially elderly women, have inadequate savings or insurance coverage to help begin the process of disaster recovery (Bolin 1982; Childers 1999; Morrow-Jones and Morrow-Jones 1991). Moreover, relative to younger groups, the elderly are less likely to qualify for low-interest loans (Bolin 1982; Bolin and Klenow 1988). In an examination of the disaster loan process following the 1995 flooding in New Orleans, Childers (1999) found that poor elderly women were five times less likely than other elderly households, and almost six times less likely than younger people, to be approved for a loan. This is despite the fact that these low-income elderly women were overrepresented in the population applying to FEMA for loans.

Many aid agencies incorrectly assume that generalized emergency and recovery aid will reach older people or that family members will look after their interests (IFRC 2007). This assumption is especially problematic in light of past research that has documented that older adults are among those least likely to take advantage of aid (in the form of food, shelter, health care, or mental health services) or cash assistance from government or private sources (Poulshock and Cohen 1975). In their study of the long-term impacts of a tornado disaster on the elderly, Kilijanek and Drabek (1979, 559) argued that seniors and their families suffered from a "pattern of neglect." Of nine categories of potential help sources—including (1) relatives, (2) friends, (3) religious organizations, (4) Red Cross, (5) Salvation Army, (6) other voluntary organizations, (7) governmental agencies, (8) strangers, and (9) employers—survivors over 60 years of age received aid from all categories less frequently than did younger survivors. Furthermore, nearly 20% of older citizens who suffered the most extensive damage received no aid whatsoever from any of the nine sources.

The elderly may not receive adequate recovery assistance for several reasons.

1. Discrimination against the elderly by government agencies, humanitarian organizations, and communities may limit their access to vital postdisaster aid (HelpAge International 2005; IFRC 2007).
2. Overly bureaucratic agency procedures may discourage the elderly from applying for assistance. A number of scholars have noted that the elderly tend to feel confused, intimidated, and frustrated by complicated claim forms and procedural regulations (Bell, Kara, and Batterson 1978; Huerta and Horton 1978; Phillips and Morrow 2007). FEMA no longer requires that disaster victims travel to an application center and wait in line to fill out myriad forms (Childers 1999), a process that was particularly problematic for older persons who required additional support or transportation assistance to leave their homes (Poulshock and Cohen 1975). However, new technologies, including voice-prompt telephone systems and Internet-based aid applications, may be similarly inaccessible to certain segments of the elderly population.
3. The elderly, especially those with limited social networks, may lack the necessary information and support mechanisms to navigate increasingly complex recovery-aid application processes (Childers 1999).
4. A generational emphasis on self-sufficiency and independence may lead some elderly to fear that accepting aid will leave them dependent (Bell, Kara, and Batterson 1978; Ngo 2001).
5. Related to the previous point, the perceived stigma attached to accepting "welfare" may discourage the elderly from requesting any type of assistance (Huerta and Horton 1978; Poulshock and Cohen 1975).

Some studies have found that the elderly tend to suffer serious long-term health effects after disaster, including persistent depressive symptoms and perceived deterioration of physical health (Friedsam 1962; Melick and Logue 1985; Phifer 1990; Takeda, Tamura, and Tatsuki 2003; Tyler and Hoyt 2000). Yet other research suggests that older persons do not suffer lasting negative physical or mental health impacts (Hutchins and Norris 1989; Kilijanek and Drabek 1979), and that they actually rebound at equal rates or more quickly than younger persons (Bell, Kara, and Batterson 1978; Bolin and Klenow 1988; Miller, Turner, and Kimball 1981). In fact, some research has shown that the elderly experience positive impacts such as strengthened familial relationships and an increase in civic mindedness (as evidenced by higher rates of volunteerism and community involvement) during the recovery period (Bell, Kara, and Batterson 1978; Takeda, Tamura, and Tatsuki 2003).

Resource and social support differentials may help explain these conflicting findings regarding the long-term effects of disasters for elders (Takeda, Tamura, and Tatsuki 2003; Tyler 2006). Following a major tornado in Paris, Texas, Bolin and Klenow (1988) compared the psychosocial recovery of black and white elderly and nonelderly disaster victims. They discovered that elders within each racial group were more likely to be psychosocially recovered than were the younger disaster survivors in the sample, although a significantly higher proportion of white elders were fully recovered at eight months postimpact than were black elders. A number of characteristics had a positive effect on psychosocial recovery for both black and white elderly disaster survivors, including higher socioeconomic status, being married, having adequate insurance and sources of federal aid, and experiencing fewer postdisaster moves while in temporary housing. This study clearly indicates that the black and white elderly survivors who recovered the fastest had more financial, social, and emotional resources available to help them in coping with the numerous demands of the postdisaster environment.

The lasting effects of disaster and prospects for recovery among the elderly may also be shaped by the severity of the event. Disasters that cause more severe losses, trauma exposure, and ongoing displacement are especially stressful for the elderly and subsequently lead to slower recovery (Miller, Turner, and Kimball 1981). For example, post-Hurricane Katrina, seniors suffered more serious health declines in much greater numbers than younger storm survivors (Spiegel 2006). In addition, in the year following Katrina's landfall, Stephens and colleagues (2007) observed a significant increase in the proportion of deaths (43% increase over baseline) among current and former New Orleans residents. The researchers argue that the excess mortality, especially among the elderly and other vulnerable groups, demonstrates the enduring health consequences of a major natural disaster. They also suggest that the indirect deaths largely resulted from a virtually destroyed public health infrastructure. Sanders, Bowie, and Bowie (2003) interviewed elderly African-American public housing residents who were forcibly relocated from their homes when Hurricane Andrew struck Florida. They found that the seniors suffered from various physical and mental health conditions, but only about one-fourth of the older adults had their health-care needs met during the relocation. The physical and emotional challenges that the elderly faced were exacerbated by their separation from family, friends, former health care providers, and various community support services.

7.6 FUTURE RISK AND IMPLICATIONS FOR ACTION

Disaster risk is on the rise in the United States. Over the past five decades, the number of major federal disaster declarations has increased substantially (see Figure 7.5). The economic losses, damage to the built and natural environment, and human costs of these major disasters have been severe. Adjusting for inflation, natural disasters resulted in approximately $387 billion in property losses and over $85 billion in crop losses in the United States from 1960 to 2005. During the same time period, disasters claimed the lives of nearly 19,000 Americans and injured over 170,000 more (SHELDUS 2005).

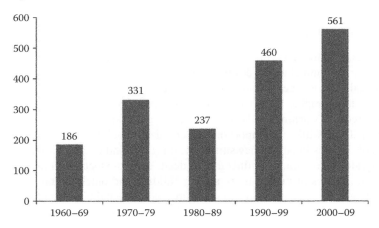

FIGURE 7.5 Number of U.S. federal major disaster declarations, 1960–2009. (*Source*: FEMA [2012].)

Beyond better tracking and reporting, the increase in the number of disaster events may be attributed to various demographic, socioeconomic, environmental, and technological factors. The U.S. population more than tripled from 1900 to 2010, placing more people in harm's way. The growing population has been accompanied by greater diversity, longer life expectancies, and more significant gaps between high- and low-income populations. Climate change, coastal land loss, and environmental degradation have resulted in more extreme weather events and have impacted fragile ecosystems. In addition, increased urbanization, infrastructure decay, and unsustainable development in hazard-prone areas such as floodplains, coastal regions, and earthquake fault zones have contributed to rising disaster losses.

Most experts agree that the financial and human tolls of disasters will continue to increase throughout the twenty-first century (Mileti 1999). Without a significant change in practice and policy, children and the elderly will also continue to be among those most affected when disaster strikes. Therefore, this final section presents some possible approaches for addressing the vulnerability of children and the elderly before and after disaster.

7.6.1 RECOGNIZE THE VULNERABILITY OF CHILDREN AND THE ELDERLY

A first step in reducing the vulnerability of children and the elderly involves recognition that these groups often have fewer resources and limited capacity to prepare for disaster, may suffer disproportionate losses when disaster strikes, and tend to face barriers in the recovery process. Available research evidence in the United States and in international contexts shows that children and the elderly are among those most at risk for death and injury in disaster, they may experience both short- and longer-term psychological impairment in the aftermath of disaster, they often suffer increased risk in shelters due to poor design and planning decisions, and they may require additional emotional, financial, and/or educational support during the recovery period. Volunteers, emergency managers, and other professionals who assist with disaster preparedness, response, and recovery activities must be encouraged to consider the elevated risks that children and the elderly face across the disaster life cycle. Moreover, these professionals should be taught to recognize the *root causes*—from increased exposure to hazards to unequal access to resources—that contribute to the vulnerability of the very young and the very old.

A growing number of research studies, policy briefings, and field reports focus on the experiences and needs of children and older persons in disasters. This information should be integrated into higher-education curricula for emergency managers, disaster planning and training exercises, emergency-response protocols, shelter planning activities, and community preparedness and education materials. A sustained focus on the special needs of children and the elderly will help to ensure that these groups are not rendered invisible in disaster planning and postdisaster resource allocation.

7.6.2 ACKNOWLEDGE DIFFERENTIAL VULNERABILITY AND TARGET RESOURCES ACCORDINGLY

In the United States, children and the elderly have very different pre- and postdisaster experiences on the basis of their age and stage of development, income and access to resources, race, gender, physical and mental abilities, geographic location, housing situation, and family structure. These critical social and demographic factors influence whether young people and older adults will prepare for disaster, receive warnings, take recommended protective actions, access aid, or recover fully from trauma. Thus, while it is important to recognize that children and the elderly are among the most vulnerable groups in emergency situations, it is also vital to acknowledge that not all children and not all elderly are equally vulnerable. Indeed, age intersects with many other factors to determine differential rates of vulnerability among children and older adults. For instance, a poor elderly African-American woman living alone in substandard rental housing is at increased risk for death or physical injury in a sudden-onset disaster. This is largely due to what Phillips and Morrow (2007, 63) refer to as the "clustering" of vulnerability factors that ultimately leads to amplified risk in disaster for the most marginalized members of society.

TABLE 7.1

Indicators of Increased Vulnerability among Children and the Elderly

Children	Elderly
Very young (0–5 years of age)	Oldest old (85 years of age or older)
Live in a single-parent household	Frail elderly
Homeless youth	Poor
Poor	Chronically ill
Mentally or physically disabled	Mentally or physically disabled
Occupy older or less-stable housing	Experience sensory or mobility limitations
Racial or ethnic minorities	Live alone
Pet owners	Socially isolated
Attend inadequately prepared child-care centers or schools	Renters
Lack access to social support	Occupy older or less-stable housing
Have limited coping resources	Live in inadequately prepared nursing homes or senior living facilities
Reside in a hazard-prone area	Racial or ethnic minorities
	Pet owners
	Reside in a hazard-prone area

Resources for disaster preparedness, emergency response and sheltering, and long-term recovery should be allocated in such a way that acknowledges that some children and some older adults are more vulnerable to the harmful impacts of disaster and thus require greater assistance. Of course, determining the relative vulnerability of children and the elderly and identifying those most at risk before and after a disaster can be challenging. However, emergency management agencies and community organizations can work together to develop means to find and work with the most vulnerable groups of children and the elderly (see Table 7.1).

7.6.3 MANDATE INSTITUTIONAL PREPAREDNESS

The limited research evidence available suggests that child-care centers, schools, nursing homes, and other institutions that serve the needs of children or the elderly are often not prepared for disasters. These institutions should be required to: (1) stockpile food, water, medications, and other necessary emergency supplies; (2) upgrade their dwellings (for example, structures in earthquake zones should be retrofitted, and heavy items such as bookcases should be bolted down); (3) develop emergency warning systems, emergency response guidelines, and evacuation plans in consultation with local emergency management agencies; and (4) review emergency plans on a regular basis with staff and parents of children or family members of the elderly.

Private and public child-care centers, schools, nursing homes, senior living facilities, and other institutions may require financial support to carry out various preparedness activities that would help increase the safety of the populations they serve. This means that local, state, and federal government entities must commit the necessary resources to ensure that these organizations can appropriately prepare for a disaster and can reopen in a timely manner in its aftermath.

7.6.4 BUILD CAPACITIES AND INVOLVE CHILDREN AND THE ELDERLY

Children and the elderly represent over one-third of the entire U.S. population. Beyond their sheer numbers, both children and older adults have considerable strengths that could serve as a significant resource for families, communities, and organizations attempting to prepare for, respond to, and recover from disasters. Rather than excluding their voices, children and the elderly should be actively encouraged to participate in disaster planning and relief efforts. I offer here just a few examples of ways that children and the elderly have contributed in meaningful ways to vulnerability reduction efforts.

An increasing number of children are learning about hazards in schools, on the Internet, and through popular media (Wachtendorf, Brown, and Nickle 2008; Wisner 2006). Children can draw on their newly acquired knowledge to help their families assemble emergency supply kits and develop household evacuation plans. Adolescents across the United States are becoming involved in Teen School Emergency Response Training (Teen SERT) programs, which help students to learn basic preparedness and response skills so that they can handle emergency situations. Bilingual children may translate disaster warnings and other materials for non-English-speaking adults in their families and communities (Mitchell et al. 2008). During the emergency response phase of disaster, children may actively engage in search-and-rescue activities and assist less able-bodied family members with evacuation (Kirschke and van Vliet 2005). Children often express a strong desire to be involved with postdisaster community rebuilding efforts, and they have contributed to reconstruction planning and design, assisted with clean-up activities, and helped to rebuild houses and schools (Peek 2008).

The elderly have a wealth of knowledge and experience accumulated over a lifetime. Older persons know the history of their community, and their experiences and memories of past disasters can assist in planning and risk-mitigation activities. The elderly are aware of the unique needs of older adults, and they can articulate those needs to emergency managers and other professionals. Shelter planning committees and local emergency management agencies could include members of the elderly community on decision making and advisory bodies such as disaster preparedness committees. Given that the elderly population of the United States is projected to double in coming decades, and that an increasing number of seniors live alone, the elderly can play an active role in identifying and reaching out to the most vulnerable members of the community. Building these types of social networks with elders could ultimately save the lives of those who are socially isolated or have mobility impairments (Klinenberg 2002). The elderly already comprise a large percentage of volunteers in nongovernmental organizations and in disaster relief and recovery (Lafond 1987; Lueck and Peek 2012). They should be acknowledged for their myriad contributions and encouraged to continue serving in this important capacity.

7.7   SUMMARY

As this chapter has demonstrated, children and the elderly are often among the most vulnerable to natural and human-made hazards. Yet, the vulnerability of these groups is neither inherent nor inevitable. Because vulnerability is rooted in social, economic, and cultural processes, it is possible to reduce many of the risks that children and the elderly face in disasters. Like other forms of social change, however, reducing vulnerability among these groups will require a sustained commitment from families, communities, emergency management agencies, disaster relief organizations, and all levels of government.

DISCUSSION QUESTIONS

1. In what ways do race, class, gender, physical and mental ability, and age interact and influence the experiences of children and the elderly in disaster?
2. What challenges does growing diversity among both youth and elderly populations pose for disaster planning and response? What opportunities for reducing vulnerability may emerge as a result of increasingly diverse younger and older populations?
3. How does unequal access to resources influence the experiences of children and the elderly before and after disaster?
4. How can organizations active in disaster planning, emergency management, and long-term recovery be more responsive to the specific needs of children and the elderly?

5. How can families and communities be more responsive to the specific needs of children and the elderly?
6. In what ways could the research findings detailed in this chapter be applied to emergency preparedness, response, or recovery activities?
7. Although an increasing number of studies have focused on the experiences of children and the elderly in disaster contexts, important gaps in knowledge remain. What do you see as the most pressing research needs in this subfield of disaster research?
8. What do you view as the greatest strengths of children and the elderly, especially as they relate to potential contributions to disaster planning and response?
9. How could children and the elderly be more actively engaged in disaster planning and response?

ACKNOWLEDGMENTS

Dr. Alice Fothergill and Dr. Bill Lovekamp offered feedback on earlier drafts of this chapter, which is gratefully acknowledged. I would also like to thank Dr. Brenda Phillips for initially inviting me to write this chapter and Dr. Deborah Thomas for her steadfast support and clearheaded advice.

REFERENCES

Abramson, D., and R. Garfield. 2006. *On the edge: Children and families displaced by Hurricanes Katrina and Rita face a looming medical and mental health crisis.* New York: Mailman School of Public Health, Columbia University.

Abramson, D., I. Redlener, T. Stehling-Ariza, and E. Fuller. 2007. *The legacy of Katrina's children: Estimating the numbers of hurricane-related at-risk children in the Gulf Coast states of Louisiana and Mississippi.* New York: Mailman School of Public Health, Columbia University.

Adams, J. 1995. *Risk.* London: UCL Press.

Addy, Sophia, and Vanessa R. Wight. 2012. *Basic facts about low-income children, 2010: Children under age 18.* New York: National Center for Children in Poverty, Mailman School of Public Health, Columbia University.

Administration on Aging. 2011. *A profile of older Americans: 2011.* Washington, DC: U.S. Department of Health and Human Services.

Araji, S. 1992. The *Exxon-Valdez* oil spill: Social, economic, and psychological impacts on Homer. Unpublished final report to the community of Homer, Department of Sociology, University of Alaska.

Associated Press. 2011. Japan earthquake 2011: Elderly hard hit as hope for missing fades. http://www.huffingtonpost.com/2011/03/17/japan-earthquake-2011-elderly-hard-hit_n_837117.html.

Barrett, E. J., C. Y. B. Ausbrooks, and M. Martinez-Cosio. 2008. The school as a source of support for Katrina-evacuated youth. *Children, Youth and Environments* 18 (1): 202–36.

Bartlett, S. 2008. The implications of climate change for children in lower-income countries. *Children, Youth and Environments* 18(1): 71–98.

Bartlett, S., and J. Patrarca. 2002. *Schools of Ground Zero: Early lessons learned in children's environmental health.* Washington, DC: American Public Health Association and Healthy Schools Network.

Bell, B. D. 1978. Disaster impact and response: Overcoming the thousand natural shocks. *The Gerontologist* 18:531–40.

Bell, B. D., G. Kara, and C. Batterson. 1978. Service utilization and adjustment patterns of elderly tornado victims in an American disaster. *Mass Emergencies* 3:71–81.

Bolin, R. 1982. *Long-term family recovery from disaster.* Boulder: Institute of Behavioral Science, University of Colorado.

Bolin, R., and D. J. Klenow. 1983. Response of the elderly to disaster. *International Journal of Aging and Human Development* 16 (4): 283–96.

———. 1988. Older people in disaster: A comparison of black and white victims. *International Journal of Aging and Human Development* 26 (1): 29–43.

Bourque, L. B., J. M. Siegel, M. Kano, and M. M. Wood. 2006. Morbidity and mortality associated with disasters. In *Handbook of disaster research,* ed. H. Rodríguez, E. L. Quarantelli, and R. R. Dynes, 97–112. New York: Springer.

Boyden, J. 2003. Children under fire: Challenging assumptions about children's resilience. *Children, Youth and Environments* 13 (1). http://www.colorado.edu/journals/cye/.

Brandenburg, M. A., M. B. Ogle, B. A. Washington, M. J. Garner, S. A. Watkins, and K. L. Brandenburg. 2006. "Operation Child-Safe": A strategy for preventing unintentional pediatric injuries at a Hurricane Katrina evacuee shelter. *Prehospital and Disaster Medicine* 21 (5): 359–65.

Brandenburg, M. A., S. M. Watkins, K. L. Brandenburg, and C. Schieche. 2007. Operation Child-ID: Reunifying children with their legal guardians after Hurricane Katrina. *Disasters* 31 (3): 277–87.

Carter, M. T., S. Kendall, and J. P. Clark. 1983. Household response to warnings. *International Journal of Mass Emergencies and Disasters* 9 (1): 94–104.

Casserly, M. 2006. Double jeopardy: Public education in New Orleans before and after the storm. In *There is no such thing as a natural disaster: Race, class, and Hurricane Katrina*, ed. C. Hartman and G. D. Squires, 197–214. New York: Routledge.

Centers for Disease Control and Prevention. 2004. Compressed mortality file: Underlying cause of death. http://wonder.cdc.gov/mortSQL.html.

Chemtob, C. M., Y. Nomura, and R. A. Abramovitz. 2008. Impact of conjoined exposure to the World Trade Center attacks and to other traumatic events on the behavioral problems of preschool children. *Archives of Pediatrics and Adolescent Medicine* 162 (2): 126–33.

Childers, C. D. 1999. Elderly female-headed households in the disaster loan process. *International Journal of Mass Emergencies and Disasters* 17 (1): 99–110.

Children's Defense Fund. 2006. *Katrina's children: A call to conscience and action*. Washington, DC: Children's Defense Fund.

Curtis, T., B. C. Miller, and E. H. Berry. 2000. Changes in reports and incidence of child abuse following natural disasters. *Child Abuse and Neglect* 24:1151–62.

Dash, N., and H. Gladwin. 2007. Evacuation decision making and behavioral responses: Individual and household. *Natural Hazards Review* 8 (3): 69–77.

Edwards, M. L. 1993. Social location and self-protective behavior: Implications for earthquake preparedness. *International Journal of Mass Emergencies and Disasters* 11 (3): 293–303.

Eldar, R. 1992. The needs of elderly persons in natural disasters: Observations and recommendations. *Disasters* 16 (4): 355–58.

Elmore, D. L., and L. M. Brown. 2007. Emergency preparedness and response: Health and social policy implications for older adults. *Generations* Winter: 66–74.

Enarson, E., A. Fothergill, and L. Peek. 2006. Gender and disaster: Foundations and directions. In *Handbook of disaster research*, ed. H. Rodríguez, E. L. Quarantelli, and R.R. Dynes, 130–46. New York: Springer.

Fass, S., and N. K. Cauthen. 2007. Who are America's poor children? The official story. New York: National Center for Children in Poverty, Mailman School of Public Health, Columbia University.

FEMA (Federal Emergency Management Agency). 2008. Declared disasters by year or state. http://www.fema.gov/disasters.

Fischer III, H. W., G. F. Stine, B. L. Stoker, M. L. Trowbridge, and E. M. Drain. 1995. Evacuation behavior: Why do some evacuate while others do not? A case study of Ephrata, Pennsylvania (USA) Evacuation. *Disaster Prevention and Management* 4 (4): 30–36.

Fisher, S. 2005. Gender based violence in Sri Lanka in the aftermath of the 2004 tsunami crisis: The role of international organizations and international NGOs in prevention and response to gender based violence. PhD dissertation, University of Leeds.

Fothergill, A. 1996. Gender, risk, and disaster. *International Journal of Mass Emergencies and Disasters* 14 (1): 33–56.

Fothergill, A., E. Maestas, and J. Darlington. 1999. Race, ethnicity, and disasters in the United States: A review of the literature. *Disasters* 23 (2): 156–73.

Fothergill, A., and L. Peek. 2004. Poverty and disasters in the United States: A review of the sociological literature. *Natural Hazards* 32:89–110.

———. 2006. Surviving catastrophe: A study of children in Hurricane Katrina. In *Learning from catastrophe: Quick response research in the wake of Hurricane Katrina*, ed. Natural Hazards Center, 97–130. Boulder: Institute of Behavioral Science, University of Colorado.

———. 2012. Permanent temporariness: Displaced children in Louisiana. In *Displaced: Life in the Katrina diaspora*, ed. L. Weber and L. Peek, 119–43. Austin: University of Texas Press.

Friedsam, H. J. 1961. Reactions of older persons to disaster-caused losses. *The Gerontologist* 1:34–37.

———. 1962. Older persons in disaster. In *Man and society in disaster*, ed. G. W. Baker and D. W. Chapman, 151–82. New York: Basic Books.

Garrett, A. L., R. Grant, P. Madrid, A. Brito, D. Abramson, and I. Redlener. 2007. Children and megadisasters: Lessons learned in the new millennium. *Advances in Pediatrics* 54:189–214.

Glass, R. I., J. J. Urrutia, S. Sibony, H. Smith, B. Garcia, and L. Rizzo. 1977. Earthquake injuries related to housing in a Guatemalan village. *Science* 197:638–43.

Gonzales, J. M. 2008. Kids in Katrina trailers may face lifelong ailments. *Denver Post*, May 28.

Green, B. L., M. Korol, M. C. Grace, M. G. Vary, A. C. Leonard, G. C. Gleser, and S. Smitson-Cohen. 1991. Children and disaster: Age, gender, and parental effects on PTSD symptoms. *Journal of the American Academy of Child and Adolescent Psychiatry* 30 (6): 945–51.

He, W., M. Sengupta, V. A. Velkoff, and K. A. DeBarros. 2005. 65+ in the United States: 2005. U.S. Census Bureau, Current Population Reports. Washington, DC: U.S. Government Printing Office.

Heath, S. E., S. K. Voeks, and L. T. Glickman. 2000. A study of pet rescue in two disasters. *International Journal of Mass Emergencies and Disasters* 18 (3): 361–81.

HelpAge International. 2005. *The impact of the Indian Ocean tsunami on older people: Issues and recommendations.* London: HelpAge International.

———. 2012. *Global ageing: Its implications for growth, decent work, and social protection beyond 2015.* London: HelpAge International.

Hewitt, K. 2007. Preventable disasters: Addressing social vulnerability, institutional risk, and civil ethics. *Geographischs Rundschau International Edition* 3 (1): 43–52.

Houts, P. S., M. K. Lindell, T. W. Hu, P. D. Cleary, G. Tokuhata, and C. B. Flynn. 1984. The protective action decision model applied to evacuation during the Three Mile Island crisis. *International Journal of Mass Emergencies and Disasters* 2 (1): 27–39.

Huerta, F., and R. Horton. 1978. Coping behavior of elderly flood victims. *The Gerontologist* 18 (6): 541–46.

Hull, A., and D. Struck. 2005. At nursing home, Katrina dealt only the first blow: Nuns labored for days in fatal heat to get help for patients. *Washington Post*, September 23.

Hutchins, G. L., and F. H. Norris. 1989. Life change in the disaster recovery period. *Environment and Behavior* 21 (1): 33–56.

Hutton, J. R. 1976. The differential distribution of death in disaster: A test of theoretical propositions. *Mass Emergencies* 1: 261–66.

Hyer, K., L. M. Brown, A. Berman, and L. Polivka-West. 2006. Establishing and refining hurricane response systems for long-term care facilities. *Health Affairs* 25: w407–11.

IFRC (International Federation of Red Cross and Red Crescent Societies). 2007. *World disasters report 2007: Focus on discrimination.* Bloomfield, CT: Kumarian Press.

Ikeda, K. 1995. Gender differences in human loss and vulnerability to natural disasters: A case study from Bangladesh. *Indian Journal of Gender Studies* 2 (2): 171–93.

International Medical Corps. 2006. *Displaced in America: Health status among internally displaced persons in Louisiana and Mississippi travel trailer parks.* Santa Monica, CA: International Medical Corps.

Jacobs, A. 2008. Parents grief turns to rage at Chinese officials. *New York Times*, May 28.

Jeney-Gammon, P., T. K. Daugherty, A. J. Finch Jr., R. W. Belter, and K. Y. Foster. 1993. Children's coping styles and report of depressive symptoms following a natural disaster. *The Journal of Genetic Psychology* 154 (2): 259–67.

Johnson, J. H. 1985. Role conflict in a radiological emergency: The case of public school teachers. *Journal of Environmental Systems* 15 (1): 77–91.

Johnston, C., and I. Redlener. 2006. Critical concepts for children in disasters identified by hands-on professionals: Summary of issues demanding solutions before the next one. *Pediatrics* 117 (5): 458–60.

Junn, E. N., and D. W. Guerin. 1996. Factors related to earthquake preparedness among child care professionals: Theory and policy implications. *International Journal of Mass Emergencies and Disasters* 14 (3): 343–59.

Keenan, H. T., S. W. Marshall, M. A. Nocera, and D. K. Runyan. 2004. Increased incidence of inflicted traumatic brain injury in children after a natural disaster. *American Journal of Preventive Medicine* 26 (3): 189–93.

Kelly, M. 1993. Infant feeding in emergencies. *Disasters* 17 (2): 110–21.

Ketteridge, A., and M. Fordham. 1998. Flood evacuation in two communities in Scotland: Lessons from European research. *International Journal of Mass Emergencies and Disasters* 16 (2): 119–43.

Kilijanek, T. S., and T. E. Drabek. 1979. Assessing long-term impacts of a natural disaster: A focus on the elderly. *The Gerontologist* 19 (6): 555–66.

Kirschke, J., and W. van Vliet. 2005. "How can they look so happy?" Reconstructing the place of children after Hurricane Katrina: Images and reflections. *Children, Youth and Environments* 15 (2): 378–91.

Klinenberg, E. 2002. *Heat wave: A social autopsy of disaster in Chicago.* Chicago: University of Chicago Press.

Kozol, J. 1991. *Savage inequalities: Children in America's schools.* New York: Crown Publishers.

———. 2005. *The shame of the nation: The restoration of apartheid schooling in America.* New York: Crown Publishers.

Krause, N. 1987. Exploring the impact of a natural disaster on the health and psychological well-being of older adults. *Journal of Human Stress* 13 (12): 61–69.

Laditka, S. B., J. N. Laditka, S. Xirasagar, C. B. Cornman, C. B. Davis, and J. V. E. Richter. 2007. Protecting nursing home residents during emergencies and disasters: An exploratory study from South Carolina. *Prehospital and Disaster Medicine* 22 (1): 42–48.

Lafond, R. 1987. Emergency planning for the elderly. *Emergency Preparedness Digest* 14 (3): 15–21.

La Greca, A. M., W. K. Silverman, E. M. Vernberg, and M. C. Roberts. 2002. Introduction. In *Helping children cope with disasters and terrorism*, ed. A. M. La Greca, W. K. Silverman, E. M. Vernberg, and M. C. Roberts, 3–8. Washington, DC: American Psychological Association.

La Greca, A. M., W. K. Silverman, and S. B. Wasserstein. 1998. Children's predisaster functioning as a predictor of post-traumatic stress following Hurricane Andrew. *Journal of Consulting and Clinical Psychology* 66 (6): 883–92.

Larsen, J. 2006. *Setting the record straight: More than 52,000 Europeans died from heat in summer 2003.* Washington, DC: Earth Policy Institute.

Lauten, A. W., and K. Lietz. 2008. A look at the standards gap: Comparing child protection responses in the aftermath of Hurricane Katrina and the Indian Ocean tsunami. *Children, Youth and Environments* 18 (1): 158–201.

Lawson, E. J., and C. Thomas. 2007. Wading in the waters: Spirituality and older black Katrina survivors. *Journal of Health Care for the Poor and Underserved* 18:341–54.

Lengua, L. J., A. C. Long, K. I. Smith, and A. N. Meltzoff. 2005. Pre-attack symptomatology and temperament as predictors of children's responses to the September 11 terrorist attacks. *Journal of Child Psychology and Psychiatry* 46:631–45.

Lindell, M. K., J. Lu, and C. S. Prater. 2005. Household decision making and evacuation in response to Hurricane Lili. *Natural Hazards Review* 6 (4): 171–79.

Lonigan, C. J., M. P. Shannon, C. M. Taylor, A. J. Finch Jr., and F. R. Sallee. 1994. Children exposed to disaster: II. Risk factors for the development of post-traumatic symptomatology. *Journal of the American Academy of Child and Adolescent Psychiatry* 33 (1): 94–105.

Looman, W. S. 2006. A developmental approach to understanding drawings and narratives from children displaced by Hurricane Katrina. *Journal of Pediatric Health Care* 20 (3): 158–66.

Lueck, M. and L. Peek. 2012. Disaster social service volunteers: Evaluation of a training program. *Journal of Applied Social Science* 6 (2): 191–208.

Maida, C. A., N. S. Gordon, and G. Strauss. 1993. Child and parent reactions to the Los Angeles area Whittier Narrows earthquake. *Journal of Social Behavior and Personality* 8:421–36.

Mandalakas, A., K. Torjesen, and K. Olness. 1999. How to help the children in complex humanitarian emergencies: A practical manual. http://www.childwatch.uio.no/research/children-in-emergencies/Lancet,%20 Children%27s%20rights%20in%20emergencies%20and%20disasters.pdf.

Mangum, W. P., J. I. Kosberg, and P. McDonald. 1989. Hurricane Elena and Pinellas County, Florida: Some lessons learned from the largest evacuation of nursing home patients in history. *The Gerontologist* 29 (3): 388–92.

Markenson, D., and I. Redlener. 2004. Pediatric disaster terrorism preparedness national guidelines and recommendations: Findings of an evidence-based consensus process. *Biosecurity and Bioterrorism* 2 (4): 301–14.

Mayhorn, C. B. 2005. Cognitive aging and the processing of hazard information and disaster warnings. *Natural Hazards Review* 6 (4): 165–70.

McFarlane, A. C. 1987. Family functioning and overprotection following a natural disaster: The longitudinal effects of post-traumatic morbidity. *Australian and New Zealand Journal of Psychiatry* 21:210–18.

McGuire, L. C., E. S. Ford, and C. A. Okoro. 2007. Natural disasters and older U.S. adults with disabilities: Implications for evacuation. *Disasters* 31 (1): 49–56.

Medina-Ramón, M., A. Zanobetti, D. P. Cavanagh, and J. Schwartz. 2006. Extreme temperatures and mortality: Assessing effect modification by personal characteristics and specific cause of death in a multi-city case-only analysis. *Environmental Health Perspectives* 114 (9): 1331–36.

Melick, M. E., and J. N. Logue. 1985. The effect of disaster on the health and well-being of older women. *International Journal of Aging and Human Development* 21 (1): 27–37.

Mileti, D. S. 1999. *Disasters by design: A reassessment of natural hazards in the United States.* Washington, DC: Joseph Henry Press.

Mileti, D. S., and J. D. Darlington. 1997. The role of searching in shaping reactions to earthquake risk information. *Social Problems* 44:89–103.

Mileti, D. S., and C. Fitzpatrick. 1992. Causal sequence of risk communication in the Parkfield earthquake prediction experiment. *Risk Analysis* 12 (3): 393–400.

Mileti, D. S., and P. W. O'Brien. 1992. Warnings during disaster: Normalizing communicated risk. *Social Problems* 39:40–57.

Miller, J. A., J. G. Turner, and E. Kimball. 1981. Big Thompson flood victims: One year later. *Family Relations* 30 (1): 111–16.

Mitchell, T., K. Haynes, N. Hall, W. Choong, and K. Oven. 2008. The role of children and youth in communicating disaster risk. *Children, Youth and Environments* 18 (1): 254–79.

Moody, H. R. 2006. The ethics of evacuation. *The Public Policy and Aging Report* 16 (2): 14–15.

Morrow, B. H. 1997. Stretching the bonds: The families of Andrew. In *Hurricane Andrew, ethnicity, gender, and the sociology of disaster*, ed. W. G. Peacock, H. Gladwin, and B. H. Morrow, 141–70. London: Routledge.

Morrow-Jones, H. A., and C. R. Morrow-Jones. 1991. Mobility due to natural disaster: Theoretical considerations and preliminary analysis. *Disasters* 15:126–32.

National Center for Missing and Exploited Children. 2006. National Center for Missing and Exploited Children reunites last missing child separated by Hurricane Katrina and Rita. Press release, National Center for Missing and Exploited Children, Alexandria, VA.

Newman, K. S., and V. T. Chen. 2007. *The missing class: Portraits of the near poor in America*. Boston: Beacon Press.

Ngo, E. B. 2001. When disasters and age collide: Reviewing vulnerability of the elderly. *Natural Hazards Review* 2 (2): 80–89.

Norris, F. H., M. J. Friedman, P. J. Watson, C. M. Byrne, E. Diaz, and K. Kaniasty. 2002. 60,000 disaster victims speak: Part I. An empirical review of the empirical literature, 1981–2001. *Psychiatry* 65 (3): 207–39.

Norris, F. H., and G. L. Hutchins. 1989. Life change in the disaster recovery period. *Environment and Behavior* 21 (1): 33–56.

Norris, F. H., and S. A. Murrell. 1988. Prior experience as a moderator of disaster impact on anxiety symptoms in older adults. *American Journal of Community Psychology* 16: 665–83.

O'Brien, N. 2003. *Emergency preparedness for older people*. New York: International Longevity Center-USA.

Ollenburger, J. C., and G. A. Tobin. 1999. Women, aging, and post-disaster stress: Risk factors. *International Journal of Mass Emergencies and Disasters* 17 (1): 65–78.

Ollendick, D. G., and M. Hoffman. 1982. Assessment of psychological reactions in disaster victims. *Journal of Community Psychology* 10:157–67.

Olympia, R. P., J. Brady, S. Kapoor, Q. Mahmood, E. Way, and J. Ayner. 2010. Compliance of child care centers in Pennsylvania with national health and safety performance standards for emergency and disaster preparedness. *Pediatric Emergency Care* 26 (4): 239–247.

Oxfam International. 2005. Back to work: How people are recovering their livelihoods 12 months after the tsunami. Briefing paper, Oxfam International, London.

Parasuraman, S. 1995. The impact of the 1993 Latur-Osmanabad (Maharashtra) earthquake on lives, livelihoods, and property. *Disasters* 19 (2): 156–69.

Peek, L. 2008. Children and disasters: Understanding vulnerability, developing capacities, and promoting resilience. *Children, Youth and Environments* 18 (1): 1–29.

———. 2012. They call it "Katrina fatigue": Displaced families and discrimination in Colorado. In *Displaced: Life in the Katrina diaspora,* ed. L. Weber and L. Peek, 31-46. Austin: University of Texas Press.

Peek, L., and K. Erikson. 2008. Hurricane Katrina. *Blackwell encyclopedia of sociology*, ed. G. Ritzer. Oxford, UK: Blackwell.

Peek, L., and A. Fothergill. 2006. Reconstructing childhood: An exploratory study of children in Hurricane Katrina. Quick response report #186, Natural Hazards Center, University of Colorado, Boulder.

———. 2008. Displacement, gender, and the challenges of parenting after Hurricane Katrina. *National Women's Studies Association Journal* 20 (3): 69–105.

Peek, L., B. Morrissey, and H. Marlatt. 2011. Disaster hits home: A model of displaced family adjustment after Hurricane Katrina. *Journal of Family Issues* 32 (10): 1371–96.

Peek, L., and L. M. Stough. 2010. Children with disabilities in disaster: A social vulnerability perspective. *Child Development* 81 (4): 1259–69.

Peek, L., J. Sutton, and J. Gump. 2008. Caring for children in the aftermath of disaster: The Church of the Brethren Children's Disaster Services program. *Children, Youth and Environments* 18 (1): 408–21.

Perry, R. W. 1979. Evacuation decision making in natural disasters. *Mass Emergencies* 4:25–38.

———. 1990. Evacuation warning compliance among elderly citizens. *Disaster Management* 3 (2): 94–96.

Perry, R. W., and M. K. Lindell. 1997. Aged citizens in the warning phase of disasters: Re-examining the evidence. *International Journal of Aging and Human Development* 44 (4): 257–67.

Pfefferbaum, B., S. J. Nixon, P. M. Tucker, R. D. Tivis, V. L. Moore, R. H. Gurwitch, R. S. Pynoos, and H. K. Geis. 1999. Post-traumatic stress responses in bereaved children after the Oklahoma City bombing. *Journal of the American Academy of Child and Adolescent Psychiatry* 38:1372–79.

Phifer, J. F. 1990. Psychological distress and somatic symptoms after natural disaster: Differential vulnerability among older adults. *Psychology and Aging* 5 (3): 412–20.

Phillips, B. D., and P. L. Hewett. 2005. Home alone: Disasters, mass emergencies, and children in self-care. *Journal of Emergency Management* 3 (2): 31–35.

Phillips, B. D., and B. H. Morrow. 2007. Social science research needs: Focus on vulnerable populations, forecasting, and warnings. *Natural Hazards Review* 8 (3): 61–68.

Picou, J. S., and B. K. Marshall. 2007. Social impacts of Hurricane Katrina on displaced K-12 students and educational institutions in coastal Alabama counties: Some preliminary observations. *Sociological Spectrum* 27:767–80.

Poulshock, S. W., and E. S. Cohen. 1975. The elderly in the aftermath of a disaster. *The Gerontologist* 15 (4): 357–61.

Prinstein, M. J., A. M. La Greca, E. M. Vernberg, and W. K. Silverman. 1996. Children's coping assistance: How parents, teachers, and friends help children cope after a natural disaster. *Journal of Clinical Child Psychology* 25 (4): 463–75.

Ramirez, M., M. Kano, L. B. Bourque, and K. I. Shoaf. 2005. Child and household factors associated with fatal and non-fatal pediatric injury during the 1999 Kocaeli earthquake. *International Journal of Mass Emergencies and Disasters* 23 (2): 129–47.

Rath, B., J. Donato, A. Duggan, K. Perrin, D. R. Bronfin, R. Ratard, R. VanDyke, and M. Magnus. 2007. Adverse health outcomes after Hurricane Katrina among children and adolescents with chronic conditions. *Journal of Health Care for the Poor and Underserved* 18 (2): 405–17.

Raynor, C. M. 2002. The role of play in the recovery process. In *Children and disasters: A practical guide to healing and recovery*, ed. W. N. Zubenko and J. Capozzoli, 124–34. New York: Oxford University Press.

Reijneveld, S. A., M. R. Crone, A. A. Schuller, F. C. Verhulst, and S. P. Verloove-Vanhorick. 2005. The changing impact of a severe disaster on the mental health and substance misuse of adolescents: Follow-up of a controlled study. *Psychological Medicine* 35:367–76.

Rivers, J. P. W. 1982. Women and children last: An essay on sex discrimination in disasters. *Disasters* 6 (4): 256–67.

Ronan, K. R., and D. M. Johnston. 2005. *Promoting community resilience in disasters: The role for schools, youth, and families.* New York: Springer.

Sanders, S., S. L. Bowie, and Y. D. Bowie. 2003. Lessons learned on forced relocation of older adults: The impact of Hurricane Andrew on health, mental health, and social support of public housing residents. *Journal of Gerontological Social Work* 40 (4): 23–35.

Sapir, D. G. 1993. Natural and man-made disasters: The vulnerability of women-headed households and children without families. *World Health Statistics Quarterly* 46:227–33.

Sapir, D. G., and M. F. Lechat. 1986. Reducing the impact of natural disasters: Why aren't we better prepared? *Health Policy and Planning* 1 (2): 118–26.

Saylor, C. F., B. L. Cowart, J. A. Lipovsky, C. Jackson, and A. J. Finch Jr. 2003. Media exposure to September 11: Elementary school students' experiences and post-traumatic symptoms. *American Behavioral Scientist* 46 (12): 1622–42.

Shannon, M. P., C. J. Lonigan, A. J. Finch Jr., and C. M. Taylor. 1994. Children exposed to disaster: I. Epidemiology of post-traumatic symptoms and symptom profiles. *Journal of the American Academy of Child and Adolescent Psychiatry* 33 (1): 80–93.

Sharkey, P. 2007. Survival and death in New Orleans: An empirical look at the human impact of Katrina. *Journal of Black Studies* 37 (4): 482–501.

SHELDUS (Spatial Hazards Events and Losses Database for the United States). 2005. 2005 U.S. hazards losses. http://webra.cas.sc.edu/hvri/products/sheldus.aspx.

Shen, Y., and C. A. Sink. 2002. Helping elementary-age children cope with disasters. *Professional School Counseling* 5 (5): 322–31.

Smith, F. 2008. The smallest victims of California wildfires are often forgotten. *Crisis and Emergency Management Newsletter* 14, no. 1. http://www.seas.gwu.edu/~emse232/february2008_7.html.

Spiegel, A. 2006. Katrina's impact on elderly still resonates. *National Public Radio*, March 1.

Stephens, K. U., D. Grew, K. Chin, P. Kadetz, P. G. Greenough, F. M. Burkle Jr., S. L. Robinson, and E. R. Franklin. 2007. Excess mortality in the aftermath of Hurricane Katrina: A preliminary report. *Disaster Medicine and Public Health Preparedness* 1 (1): 15–20.

Stuber, J., S. Galea, B. Pfefferbaum, S. Vandivere, K. Moore, and G. Fairbrother. 2005. Behavior problems in New York City's children after the September 11, 2001, terrorist attacks. *American Journal of Orthopsychiatry* 75 (2): 190–200.

Swenson, C. C., C. F. Saylor, P. Powell, S. J. Stokes, K. Y. Foster, and R. W. Belter. 1996. Impact of a natural disaster on preschool children: Adjustment 14 months after a hurricane. *American Journal of Orthopsychiatry* 66 (1): 122–30.

Takeda, J., K. Tamura, and S. Tatsuki. 2003. Life recovery of 1995 Kobe earthquake survivors in Nishinomiya City: A total-quality-management-based assessment of disadvantaged populations. *Natural Hazards* 29:565–83.

Thompson, M. P., F. H. Norris, and B. Hanacek. 1993. Age differences in the psychological consequences of Hurricane Hugo. *Psychology and Aging* 8:606–16.

Tierney, K. J., M. K. Lindell, and R. W. Perry. 2001. *Facing the unexpected: Disaster preparedness and response in the United States.* Washington, DC: Joseph Henry Press.

Tracy, M., and S. Galea. 2006. Post-traumatic stress disorder and depression among older adults after a disaster: The role of ongoing trauma and stressors. *Public Policy and Aging Report* 16 (2): 16–19.

Turner, R. 1976. Earthquake prediction and public policy. *Mass Emergencies* 1 (3): 179–202.

Tyler, K. A. 2006. The impact of support received and support provision on changes in perceived social support among older adults. *International Journal of Aging and Human Development* 62 (1): 21–38.

Tyler, K. A., and D. Hoyt. 2000. The effects of an acute stressor on depressive symptoms among older adults: The moderating effects of social support and age. *Research on Aging* 22:143–64.

Udwin, O. 1993. Annotation: Children's reactions to traumatic events. *Journal of Child Psychology and Psychiatry* 34 (2): 115–27.

Unger, J. B., T. R. Simon, and T. L. Newman. 1998. Early adolescent street youths: An overlooked population with unique problems and service needs. *Journal of Early Adolescence* 18 (4): 324–48.

UN Population Fund. 2011. State of the world population 2011: People and possibilities in a world of 7 billion. http://foweb.unfpa.org/SWP2011/reports/EN-SWOP2011-FINAL.pdf.

U.S. Census Bureau. 2006. 2006 American Community Survey Data. Washington, DC: U.S. Census Bureau. Retrieved February 1, 2008 (http://www.census.gov/).

U.S. Census Bureau. 2010. 2010 U.S. Census data. http://www.census.gov/.

U.S. DHHS (Department of Health and Human Services). 2012. The 2012 Health and Human Services poverty guidelines. http://aspe.hhs.gov/poverty/12poverty.shtml.

U.S. GAO (Government Accountability Office). 2006. *Lessons learned for protecting and educating children after the Gulf Coast hurricanes.* http://www.gao.gov/new.items/d06680r.pdf.

Vernberg, E. M., A. M. La Greca, W. K. Silverman, and M. J. Prinstein. 1996. Prediction of post-traumatic stress symptoms in children after Hurricane Andrew. *Journal of Abnormal Psychology* 105 (2): 237–48.

Vogel, J. M., and E. M. Vernberg. 1993. Part 1: Children's psychological responses to disasters. *Journal of Clinical Child Psychology* 22 (2): 464–84.

Vogt, B. M. 1991. Issues in nursing home evacuations. *International Journal of Mass Emergencies and Disasters* 9 (2): 247–65.

Wachtendorf, T., B. Brown, and M. C. Nickle. 2008. Big Bird, disaster masters, and high school students taking charge: The social capacities of children in disaster education. *Children, Youth and Environments* 18 (1): 456–69.

Warheit, G. J., R. S. Zimmerman, E. L. Khoury, W. A. Vega, and A. G. Gil. 1996. Disaster related stresses, depressive signs and symptoms, and suicidal ideation among a multi-racial/ethnic sample of adolescents: A longitudinal analysis. *Journal of Child Psychology and Psychiatry* 37 (4): 435–44.

Wasserstein, S. B., and A. M. La Greca. 1998. Hurricane Andrew: Parent conflict as a moderator of children's adjustment. *Hispanic Journal of Behavioral Sciences* 20 (2): 212–24.

Webster, C. 1994. Saving children during the Depression: Britain's silent emergency, 1919–1939. *Disasters* 18 (3): 213–20.

Weissbecker, I., S. E. Sephton, M. B. Martin, and D. M. Simpson. 2008. Psychological and physiological correlates of stress in children exposed to disaster: Review of current research and recommendations for intervention. *Children, Youth and Environments* 18 (1): 30–70.

WHO (World Health Organization). 2005. *Disability, including prevention, management, and rehabilitation.* Geneva, Switzerland: World Health Organization.

Wilson, N. 2006. Hurricane Katrina: Unequal opportunity disaster. *Public Policy and Aging Report* 16 (2): 8–13.

Wilson, S. L., and M. A. Kershaw. 2008. Caring for young children after a hurricane: Childcare workers reflect on support and training needs. *Children, Youth and Environments* 18 (1): 237–53.

Wisner, B. 2006. *Let our children teach us! A review of the role of education and knowledge in disaster risk reduction.* Bangalore, India: Books for Change.

Young, H., and S. Jaspars. 1995. Nutrition, disease, and death in times of famine. *Disasters* 19 (2): 94–109

Zahran, S., L. Peek, and S. D. Brody. 2008. Youth mortality by forces of nature. *Children, Youth and Environments* 18 (1): 371–88.

RESOURCES—CHILDREN AND YOUTH

VIDEOS

Children on the Frontline. http://www.oneplanetpictures.co.uk/catalogue/on-the-front-line/children-on-the-frontline.

China's Unnatural Disaster: The Tears of Sichuan Province. http://www.hbo.com/documentaries/chinas-unnatural-disaster-tears-of-sichuan-province/index.html.

Katrina's Children: A Documentary. http://www.katrinaschildren.com/.

Through a Child's Eyes: September 11, 2001. http://www.hbofamily.com/parent_handbook/through-a-childs-eyes-september-11.html.

KEY WEB SITES

American Red Cross Masters of Disaster Program: http://www.redcross.org/disaster/masters/.

Children, Youth and Environments (special issue on children and disasters) 18, no. 1 (2008). http://www.colorado.edu/journals/cye/18_1/index.htm.

Church of the Brethren Children's Disaster Services. http://www.brethren.org/cds/.

Plan International. http://plan-international.org/.

Save the Children. http://www.savethechildren.org/.

RESOURCES—ELDERLY

VIDEOS

Emergency Planning for People with Access and Functional Needs. http://emc.ornl.gov/training/emergency-planning/emergency-planning.html.

Preparing Makes Sense for Older Americans. http://www.ready.gov/seniors.

KEY WEB SITES

Administration on Aging. http://www.aoa.gov/.

Gray Panthers. http://www.graypanthers.org/.

HelpAge International. http://www.helpage.org/.

National Organization on Disability. http://www.nod.org/.

8 Disability

Elizabeth A. Davis, Rebecca Hansen, Maria Kett,
Jennifer Mincin, and John Twigg

CONTENTS

8.1   CHAPTER PURPOSE

This chapter addresses the inclusion of disability issues into all phases of disaster management and presents promising best practices that have emerged over the last few decades. In addition, remaining challenges are identified and discussed along with ways to include the disability community. The authors consider the current state of disability and disasters, legal and policy mandates, gaps and challenges, as well as providing U.S.-based and international examples. As these issues gain more attention globally, our goal is that this chapter will contribute to a growing body of knowledge in this field.

8.2 OBJECTIVES

As a result of completing this chapter, the reader will be able to:

1. Identify specific factors that may make people with disabilities vulnerable in times of disaster
2. Recognize theoretical concepts and terms about disability in the context of emergency management
3. Understand critical disability issues in the disaster cycle, including but not limited to communications, sheltering, evacuation, and related planning concepts
4. Utilize strategies and resources to increase resiliency within the disability community
5. Understand how to improve the capacity of emergency planners and managers to support people with disabilities before, during, and after disasters

8.3 INTRODUCTION

Disability is part of the human experience and impacts nearly everyone at some point in her/his life, either personally or through living with or caring for someone with a disability. In the last several decades, great strides have been made throughout the world in protecting the human and civil rights of people with disabilities, allowing for greater equality, accessibility, self-determination, and independence. It is absolutely imperative that this approach be extended to the field of emergency management: that in all phases—mitigation, planning, response, and recovery—the issues of disability be fully integrated and that people with disabilities be involved in the process.

There is some evidence, based primarily on disaster fatality statistics, that specific segments of the population are disproportionately affected by disasters (Knowles and Garrison 2006). People with disabilities, as well as older people, experience this disparity to an even greater degree, with higher rates of loss of life and greater exclusion and challenges during the recovery period (Tokesky and Weston 2006; HelpAge International and Handicap International 2012). For instance, a 2010 study revealed that the needs of older people are not adequately being met by response and humanitarian efforts (HelpAge International and Handicap International 2012). In addition, disasters can increase a person's susceptibility to becoming disabled. Worldwide, each year an estimated 7 million children become disabled, in one way or another, as the result of disasters (Peek and Stough 2010). Further, early estimates after the 2004 Asian tsunami indicated that the number of people with disabilities may have increased by as much as 20% in the affected countries (Alexander 2011).

Many factors contribute to increased vulnerability of people with disabilities. These may include lack of access to and equal opportunity for: employment, transportation, health care, education, and housing (see next section on demographic statistics for more detailed information). Factors that contribute to the social vulnerability of persons with disabilities persist in a disaster. Further, they will be compounded by the "new realities" that the disaster brings, including: loss of housing; injury or death of loved ones; injury or medical complications; limited access to clean water, food, roadways, and transportation, as well as social services; loss of equipment; and/or disruption of care. In addition, there are other factors that overlay with disability, including poverty, race, gender, age, and socioeconomic status, to list a few. Taken together, this can all affect a person's ability to access resources and participate in society.

Stereotyping and biased attitudes of others create barriers that prevent people with disabilities from achieving independence, equal access to resources, and meaningful engagement in society. Historically, disability was seen through the medical lens. A person with a disability often was treated as someone who was sick and needed specific medical interventions. Whereas anyone without a disability was seen as a "whole" person, a person with a disability was seen as "not whole," or special. Mistaking a disability for a problem or sickness not only fails to respond to a person's needs, it perpetrates a negative stereotype and an assumption that the person can and should be "cured" (Access Board n.d.a).

This viewpoint diminishes the contributions and capacities of an individual in favor of highlighting limitations. This understanding of disability at the individual and/or community level leads to many kinds of assumptions and misconceptions. A person's disability might be perceived as the individual's dominant characteristic or so-called master identity, relegating the person to a marginal role in society as an "invalid" or "handicapped" person. It may also be assumed that people with disabilities are entirely dependent on other people and institutions and not necessarily contributing members of society. Many might assume that people with disabilities have medical conditions and/ or are sick or that accommodating people with disabilities is cost prohibitive. Most importantly, people do not bring their disabling condition upon themselves and are not responsible for it; this is also true for people with mental health conditions. Unfortunately, many erroneously view that people with disabilities have brought the condition upon themselves, immediately limiting full inclusion.

The U.S.- and the U.K.-based disability rights movement, including the passing of the Americans with Disabilities Act (ADA) in the United States in 1990, has done much to shift these pejorative and paternalistic views toward a more inclusive and accurate functional model (see Section 8.5.2). Through the disability awareness movement, attention to how we discuss issues of disability and persons with disabilities has changed for the positive. Using language that put the person first has now been integrated into popular thinking. Rather than saying "disabled person," it is more common to hear "person with a disability," or "woman who is blind," or "student who uses a wheelchair." The idea is to place the person first in the view of society, emphasizing that the disability is a part, but not the total identity, of the person (Leeds 1990). The movement, and subsequent civil rights and legal authorities, recognize people with disabilities as contributors to society and continue to advocate for the full engagement and equal access for people with disabilities in all aspects of society. The effects of utilizing an archaic and traditional approach, focused on individual limitation, has led to the belief in "disabled people's vulnerability to natural hazards as tragic yet unavoidable" (Hemingway and Priestly 2006).

This chapter addresses the necessity of applying social/political and functional frameworks to disability for all phases of the emergency management cycle. As discussed in greater detail in Section 8.5, these models empower the entire community to address barriers and make improvements allowing for greater access throughout the emergency management cycle. The field of emergency management is very much at a dynamic stage in terms of integrating disability into core programs, policy, and practices. In the United States and internationally, significant movement has occurred; awareness is growing among emergency manager practitioners and organizations; and new and innovative practices that integrate disability into emergency programs are being established that allow for adaptation and replication in other places. Policies and practices addressing and incorporating people with disabilities will be explored in this chapter, as well as some of the more difficult challenges that still persist.

8.4   DEMOGRAPHIC OVERVIEW

8.4.1   Prevalence of Disability

Disabilities are widespread in societies, but the prevalence of disability in a given society may be difficult to measure, for several reasons: People with disabilities are diverse and heterogeneous; disability can be understood and defined in different ways (see Section 8.5); data collection methods vary and give different results; the social stigma of disability discourages people from identifying themselves as disabled. Accurate data are often lacking in low-income countries, which also tend to underreport disability because they collect data through censuses rather than surveys or focus on a narrow choice of impairments (WHO 2011).

Nevertheless, the World Health Organization (WHO) estimates there were around 785 to 975 million persons 15 years and older living with one or more disabilities in 2010. Of these, around 110 to 190 million experienced significant difficulties in functioning. Including children, over a billion people (or about 15% of the world's population) were estimated to be living with one or more disabilities (WHO 2011). See Box 8.1.

8.4.2 Social Consequences of Disability

Many people with disabilities have prospered and thrived in a variety of occupations. Almost all jobs can be performed by someone with a disability, and most people with disabilities can be productive, given the right environment. Yet, evidence from across the world shows that they and their families are more likely to experience economic and social disadvantage because of their disability. The onset of disability may also result in adverse impacts on education, employment, and earnings. Children with disabilities are less likely to start school, have higher dropout rates, and complete fewer years of education than children without disabilities. Household surveys in Malawi, Namibia, Zambia, and Zimbabwe have shown that between 24% and 39% of children aged 5 years or older with a disability had never attended school, compared to between 9% and 18% of those without a disability (WHO 2011).

Persons with disabilities are more likely to be unemployed and to earn less when employed; they also find it harder to obtain credit. Data from the WHO's World Health Survey of 51 countries (2002–2004) shows employment rates of 52.8% for men with disability and 19.6% for women with disability, compared with 64.9% for nondisabled men, and 29.9% for nondisabled women. Individuals with mental health difficulties or intellectual impairments are generally less likely to find employment (WHO 2011). Disability may also result in additional costs associated with medical care or assistive devices, or the need for personal support, and often require more resources to achieve the same outcomes as people without disabilities.

Demographic data from the United States starkly outlines the relationship between disability and lower socioeconomic status. The equalization of resources remains a struggle, and people with

---

BOX 8.1   PREVALENCE OF DISABILITIES IN THE UNITED STATES

According to the U.S. Census's 2009 American Community Survey (ACS), approximately 12.0% of noninstitutionalized, male or female, all ages, all races regardless of ethnicity, with all education levels in the United States reported a disability (Erickson, Lee, and von Schrader 2011). However, most disability organizations place the number higher, at closer to 20%, because the census does not take into account unreported disabilities and those living in institutions, among other factors (NOD n.d.).

Disability rates increase significantly with age: According to the 2009 ACS, 37.4% of noninstitutionalized, male or female, ages 65+, all races regardless of ethnicity, with all education levels in the United States reported a disability. Nearly 14 million Americans over 65 have one or more disabilities (Erickson, Lee, and von Schrader 2011). In comparison, just over 5.1 million American children between the ages of 5 and 15 report having a disability; and just over 18 million people aged 16–64 report having a disability (Erickson, Lee, and von Schrader 2011).

Veterans comprise a significant portion of people with disabilities; approximately 16.9% of veterans aged 21–64 report having a Veterans Administration (VA) service-connected disability, or nearly 2.2 million veterans (Erickson, Lee, and von Schrader 2011). As of January 2010, over 30,000 U.S. soldiers have been wounded in the Iraq War, with injuries including loss of limbs and posttraumatic stress syndrome (Brookings Institution 2008; EEOC 2008).

disabilities are disproportionately experiencing economic conditions such as poverty, low income, and low employment rates. According to the U.S. Census Bureau in 2010, nearly 28% of people with disabilities aged 18 to 64 live in poverty, compared to their counterparts without disabilities at 12.5%. Even among those who are not living in poverty, the census data shows that median earnings for men with disabilities were about $41,500, compared to $48,000 for those without, and this is similar for women, though overall women's median income is lower than men's (both disability and without disability) (Heasely 2011). According to the National Council on Disability, as a result of this pay disparity, an estimated 14.4 million households with at least one person with a disability cannot afford their housing—this is 41% of all households with disabilities (NCD 2010).

Over the last few decades, the trend of deinstitutionalization—moving people from institutional settings to integrated and less restrictive community settings—has taken hold. More and more, people with disabilities are living independently in communities of their choice. However, there are still many barriers to the availability of accessible, affordable, and integrated housing because of the "interaction of poverty, inaccessibility, and funding rules related to acquiring supportive services," as well as a disability policy system that is rooted in segregating people with disabilities (NCD 2010). Further, the reliance on community-based supportive services has increased. Services such as personal aids to support activities of daily living, home health aides, nurses, Meals on Wheels programs, and transportation services, for example, have become increasingly essential for the option to maintain and live independently within the community by self-determination.

Assistive technology is essential for more than a third of disabled Americans to permit self-care at home. This technology can range from a walker to a sophisticated computer controlling many household functions. While social service agencies can provide some of this equipment at low or no cost, they usually cannot pay for its continued maintenance and repair. Obviously, a person's income affects the ability to purchase and keep such items well maintained (Disability Funders Network n.d.).

People with disabilities experience significant health disparities compared to people without disabilities. Higher medical costs and ability to access insurance programs also impact overall health, income, and living conditions of people with disabilities. According to NCD (2009b), people with disabilities experience specific problems in accessing appropriate health care, including preventive programs. The report indicated that people with disabilities also often lack health insurance or coverage for necessary services such as specialty care, long-term care, care coordination, prescription medications, medical equipment, and assistive technologies. In fact, in the United States, Medicaid is the largest single source of health insurance and long-term care and the largest source of public financial support for people with disabilities. Seniors and people with disabilities comprise 24% of all Medicaid enrollees but account for 70% of program spending (NCD 2009b).

While many people with disabilities are employed, there is still a large gap between the numbers of people employed with disabilities compared to those without disabilities. A 2010 Kessler/National Organization on Disability (NOD) survey found that two in ten working-age people with disabilities were employed, compared to roughly six in ten without disabilities (Kessler Foundation/NOD 2010). It is estimated that over 65% of working-age adults with disabilities are unemployed (Disability Funders Network n.d.). The ADA itself specifically addresses in great detail how it is unlawful to discriminate in employment practices against a qualified individual with a disability. Many barriers have been identified preventing people with disabilities from either seeking employment, getting hired, or retaining a job once hired. A large survey of people with disabilities found that barriers include: no appropriate jobs available; family responsibilities; lack of accessible transportation; no appropriate information about jobs; inadequate training; fear of losing health insurance or Medicaid; and even discouragement from family and friends (Urban Institute 2001). Other barriers include employers' incorrect perception that hiring a person with disabilities will be more costly than an employee without disabilities (which has been disproved through many studies). Further attitudes within the workplace, such as unwarranted stereotypical thinking, impact the chances of someone getting hired and subsequently remaining in the position. Several organizations at the national and local levels focus efforts on employment for people with disabilities, as this is a complex issue that persists as a fundamental issue for this community.

8.5 DEFINITIONS AND CONCEPTS

8.5.1 DISABILITY RIGHTS

Active global campaigning and advocacy resulted in the United National Convention on the Rights of Persons with Disabilities (CRPD), established in 2008. The CRPD reinforces the intention that persons with disabilities are protected under the same legal frameworks and conventions as everyone else. As of 2011, there are 153 signatories and 112 ratifications of the convention. The United States signed the convention in 2009, but when put to a vote in December 2012, the U.S. Senate failed to obtain the required votes to ratify the CRPD. While the CRPD is not a panacea to eliminate discrimination or exclusion of persons with disabilities, it does provide a useful framework from which to ensure that national legislation is upheld and that disabilities are accounted for in risk reduction activities. Article 11 of the CRPD (situations of risk and humanitarian emergencies) states:

> States Parties shall take, in accordance with their obligations under international law, including international humanitarian law and international human rights law, all necessary measures to ensure the protection and safety of persons with disabilities in situations of risk, including situations of armed conflict, humanitarian emergencies and the occurrence of natural disasters.

In the United States, disability rights are based in a civil rights framework. This is embodied in the Americans with Disabilities Act of 1990 and now in its successor, the Americans with Disabilities Act Amendments Act (ADAAA) of 2008. This federal legislation defines disability, distinguishes disability as a protected class, and provides broad nondiscrimination protections and rights to people with disabilities. The ADA also establishes design requirements for the construction and alteration of facilities in the private and public sectors. These requirements are known as the ADA Accessibility Guidelines (ADAAG). The guidelines establish the minimum requirements for accessibility in buildings and facilities and in transportation vehicles subject to the Title II and Title III regulations (Access Board n.d.b).

There were several precursors to the ADA in the United States, including the 1973 Rehabilitation Act, which was the first U.S. law to prohibit discrimination on the basis of disability. Section 508 of the Rehabilitation Act, as amended, includes requirements that federal agencies ensure that electronic and information technology is accessible to employees and the public to the extent that access does not pose an "undue burden" (Access Board n.d.b). Box 8.2 describes ways in which the ADA is applied in emergency management.

However, it cannot be assumed that legislative change will translate easily and quickly into change on the ground; in fact, it may be many years before this happens. For example, India's Persons with Disabilities Act of 1996 failed to produce a noticeable change after the 2004 Asian tsunami. Planning and designs for post-tsunami housing and reconstruction programs in India largely ignored access and other disability issues. It was similar in Indonesia. The 1997 Act Concerning People with Disabilities was not implemented during the predisaster planning stage, nor was it necessarily utilized post-tsunami (IDRM 2005). Even when changes are applied, implementation will not be perfect. For instance in Japan, every municipality is required to produce its own master plan for supporting people with disabilities in a disaster. As of April 2011, 77% had completed such a plan, 53% had completed a database of people with disabilities who would need such support, and 83% were involved in identifying and assigning local residents or helpers to assist them in the event of evacuation. This is a considerable achievement, although the March 2011 earthquake and tsunami exposed a number of operational weaknesses, most obviously regarding shelter provision (Tatsuki and Comafay 2012).

BOX 8.2   APPLICATION OF THE U.S. ADAAA TO THE
PRACTICE OF EMERGENCY MANAGEMENT

Though the ADA does not specifically discuss the issue of compliance in emergency planning and response, it mandates compliance with public- and private-sector facilities and programs (Davis and Sutherland 2005).

The application of the ADAAA to the practice of emergency management is evolving. The U.S. Department of Justice (DOJ), responsible for enforcing the ADAAA, has produced guidance (described below). However, the requirements continue to be shaped as several lawsuits and DOJ settlements are occurring throughout the country, specifically challenging local jurisdictions on the accessibility of their emergency management programs. There continues to be much discussion about how the ADAAA can be applied in a disaster environment—where landscapes change, people's needs change, and facilities are damaged and destroyed. The following information describes the current situation, but we expect that there will be more development in this area over the next few years.

In 2007, the U.S. DOJ issued a guide for state and local governments (see *DOJ Best Practices Toolkit for State and Local Governments* in Resources) to offer an interpretation of the ADA as it applies to emergency management (DOJ 2007). It was intended to assist practitioners in making their emergency preparedness and response programs accessible to people with disabilities (Jones 2006). The DOJ guidance declares that, essentially, people with disabilities must have access to and cannot be excluded from emergency plans and programs. This interpretation is increasingly recognized in the emergency management community:

> While not specifically articulated within many of the authorities mentioned [in the ADA], in a post–September 11 United States, the interpretations are now shaped by a "big picture" approach and extend the rights of people with disabilities to share in access to services and programs, to include emergency preparedness planning and response. (Davis and Sutherland 2005)

Additionally, the guidance provides the ADA Checklist, based on ADAAG standards, which is to be used to support state and local efforts when surveying shelters and assessing accessibility. This was the first time that the DOJ offered this kind of interpretation in the emergency management field.

In addition to the toolkit, through their Project Civic Access, DOJ has also assessed and challenged ADAAA compliance among multiple local jurisdictions throughout the United States. The DOJ has found that many of the emergency management programs they have reviewed are not in compliance. The settlements detail tasks and time frames for remediation of the elements found to be noncompliant.

Finally, civil lawsuits occurring in local jurisdictions in states such as California, Florida, and New York have been filed citing lack of ADA compliance in emergency management programs. As these individual cities work through the settlement process, they are required to take steps to remediate the described inefficiencies. Within the last 3–5 years, several of these lawsuits have occurred, and different settlement agreements and approaches implemented in impacted cities (Sherry and Harkins 2011). Still, today many of these lawsuits are ongoing and the outcomes not yet realized. These lawsuits and those to come will impact how the ADA is applied to emergency management.

The discussion here refers specifically to government functions and accessibility, but the same is true for private business as well. The circuit court in Montgomery County, Maryland, endorsed the notion that the ADA Title III should be interpreted to mean that places of common access such as a department store and a mall need to take into account people with disabilities in their facility emergency plans (*Savage v. City Place Ltd. Partnership*, 2004 WL 3045404 [Md. Cir. Ct. 2004]).

8.5.2 Conceptual Models of Disability

A shift from the medical to the social model of disability is underpinned by an increased focus and awareness of the rights of persons with disabilities, moving away from a charity model of intervention to an increased awareness that persons with disabilities are entitled to enjoy the same rights as all other citizens.

8.5.2.1 The Medical Model

The medical model offers a framework in which disability is viewed as the disease, trauma, or health condition that disrupts what is considered to be "normal" functionality: physically, mentally, or socially (Veenema 2013, scheduled 3rd ed.). In the United States, social problems have historically been seen through the medical lens and perceived as "deviant" behaviors that were pathologized (Eitzen and Zinn 2003) as well as seen as individuals departing from what the dominant culture deemed to be social norms and societal contributions (Feagin and Feagin 1997, 16). Within this model people with disabilities are offered medical and/or technical solutions to alleviate their impairment. This was the dominant model of approaching disability in the nineteenth and twentieth centuries. The medical model treats the person as the illness rather than looking at the whole person and the circumstances of that person (Mincin 2012). This model does not consider how society deals with or perceives people with disabilities and perpetuates the societal barriers, stereotypes, misconceptions, and prejudices that prevent people with disabilities from fully integrating (Mincin 2012). The model is limiting because it does not allow for self-direction, self-determination, or the inclusion of the abilities people with disabilities possess, especially during disasters.

Often, society makes assumptions about people with disabilities, including levels of independence and dependence. For example, people with disabilities are often labeled "handicapped" based on visible characteristics, though these may not in fact be disabling (Tierney, Petak, and Hahn 1988). How society constructs "disability" has, in many ways, hindered how people with disabilities have been integrated into society. According to Hemingway and Priestly:

> The traditional view within social science and rehabilitation was to view the disadvantage associated with disability as an individual problem caused by impairment. From this perspective, the most appropriate response was either to correct the impairment or to help the person "come to terms" with it, by negotiating different (less valued) social roles. By contrast, social interpretations of disability have shown how people with similar impairment characteristics become more or less "disabled" in different environments and social circumstances. (Hemingway and Priestly 2006, 4)

8.5.2.2 The Sociopolitical Model

In recent years, and with the advent of the Disability Rights Movement/Independent Living Movement, societal norms have been challenged, and people with disabilities are advocating for a mainstream approach. The sociopolitical approach, also referred to as the rights-based model, moves beyond the individualized perspective and looks at how society and policies have defined disability. Generally, society disables people vis-à-vis a lack of access to structures, programs and services, and employment, for example. Focus is on societal prejudice, environmental factors, and that people with disabilities are an oppressed group within society. Disability, therefore, arises from oppression of society rather than the individual with the "defect" or disability (Shakespeare and Watson 2002). The sociopolitical model advocates for social change and the "total transformation of society" in regard to disability (Shakespeare and Watson 2002). According to Hubbard (2004):

> The sociopolitical model views disability as a policy and civil rights issue, not as a health impairment or a diagnosis-related funding issue. Individuals with disabilities are considered an oppressed minority faced with architectural, sensory, attitudinal, cognitive, and economic barriers, who are treated as second-class citizens, facing daily prejudice and discrimination.

The sociopolitical model is more of an empowerment model. Rather than "blaming the victim," the sociopolitical model states that it is society and its barriers that adversely affect people with disabilities, not the disability itself (Hubbard 2004). For example, if a workplace is not wheelchair accessible, a person in a wheelchair, who may be highly qualified, will not be able to physically access the building; hence that person cannot work there. This type of barrier is created by socially structuring the workplace to include some and exclude others (Hubbard 2004). "Technology, law, public policies, organizational practices, and the attitudes of other members have an impact on the extent to which physical impairments limit activity and constrain role performance" (Tierney, Petak, and Hahn 1988, 11).

The sociopolitical model also allows for a better understanding that not all persons with disabilities need care and support or, in disaster terms, are more vulnerable. As described previously, a person's vulnerability is dependent on a number of factors, including age, sex, social support, and context. Therefore, given the right support and adequate resources, the resilience and capacity of persons with disabilities can be promoted.

This model is very useful for an emergency management practitioner. For example, working with the disability community, the emergency manager can identify existing barriers within an emergency management program, such as shelter facilities, information, and/or evacuation policy/ protocols that are not accessible, and begin to implement appropriate change and solutions.

8.5.2.3   The Functional Model

The functional model, also taking hold in the mid to late twentieth century, views people with disabilities as a heterogeneous rather than homogeneous group. The functional model of disability moves the discussion from one of exclusivity to one of inclusivity, and has evolved into other theories such as sociopolitical, socioeconomic, and human rights approaches, especially considering that the functional model has roots in the Civil Rights Movement. This model ignores the medical and/or behavioral causes of disability and instead focuses on the resulting abilities and limitations. This approach helps to identify appropriate resources and practical solutions that will support individuals. The functional model operates off of the premise that contrary to stereotypes often portrayed, people with disabilities are a vital, significant, and contributory part of the population, with each person having a range of abilities and accomplishments. Further, the functional model asserts that disability is not a homogeneous population, but rather a diverse group of people offering various skills and requiring different types of accommodations (Tierney, Petak, and Hahn 1988). People may acquire a disability in many ways as well, including by birth, through illness or an accident, or from lack of access to social and health-care services.

Similar to the medical model, the functional model has practical applications. However, in contrast to the medical model, the functional model embraces a fuller range of applications beyond individual treatment. The functional model grew out of the Independent Living Movement and resulted in its own critical piece of civil rights legislation, the Americans with Disabilities Act of 1990 (ADA). While the functional model is tied to other models, like the human rights and sociological (environmental) approach, its origins were rooted in basic human dignity rights.

This model is also useful for an emergency manager. Within this framework, planners will work with service providers and individuals with disabilities to identify both their probable disaster-related needs and realistic strategies to meet those needs at each stage of the emergency. The best plans will emerge from a mutually respectful relationship among emergency managers, advocates, and members of the disability communities.

As an example, individuals living with multiple sclerosis (MS) may require some level of assistance during emergencies. MS is a chronic condition that will impact people differently, depending on the type of MS they have, and so the level of independence, need for assistance, etc., can vary greatly. But heat is something that aggravates the condition, creating a critical problem for people standing unprotected from sunlight or humid weather in long lines to obtain information, food, or other assistance at a recovery center. Therefore, it is more useful for a planner to utilize the functional model to identify the likely needs of individuals with MS, rather than to focus only on the fact that an individual is living with MS. It is the need beyond an individual's ability that is important in this specific scenario under this model rather than the condition and medical label.

8.5.3 Terminology

Terminology and definitions are different across the globe. As such, there are slight variations and nuances in perspective or emphasis. Further, some terminology carries the weight of a legal or statutory definition, while other terms represent a community's preference and identification. The World Report on Disability defines disability as an interaction:

> Disability is the umbrella term for impairments, activity limitations and participation restrictions, referring to the negative aspects of the interaction between an individual (with a health condition) and that individual's contextual factors (environmental and personal factors). (WHO 2011)

In the United States, the Americans with Disabilities Act Amendments Act of 2008 (ADAAA) provides a definition and terminology in terms of disability (see Box 8.3). In addition, under the Obama administration and the leadership of the U.S. Federal Emergency Management Agency's (FEMA) administrator Craig Fugate, FEMA has introduced new terminology that promotes an inclusive and functional approach within the context of emergency management. To promote the idea of inclusive emergency management, FEMA widely uses the term *whole community*, and defines it as "a means by which residents, emergency management practitioners, organizational and community leaders, and government officials can collectively understand and assess the needs of their respective communities and determine the best ways to organize and strengthen their assets, capacities, and interests" (FEMA 2011). Great efforts have been made in documents, presentations, and policy to explicitly include people with disabilities as essential partners within the "whole community."

FEMA, through the newly created Office of Disability Integration and Coordination, has also introduced the use of the terminology "People with Disabilities and Others with Access and Functional Needs" and defines this within a functional framework. At this time, this term has not been adopted in the Federal Response Framework, but it is strongly being promoted by FEMA and the U.S. Department of Justice (DOJ). The term *disability* is defined in the ADAAA. The *access and functional needs* term is intended to include people who have functional needs related to maintaining independence, communication, transportation, supervision, and medical care.

In recent years, jurisdictions in the United States have replaced *disability* with the terms *special needs*, *specific needs*, or *vulnerable population*. However, whereas *disability* is defined in federal law and regulation, *special needs*, *vulnerable*, or other similar terminology has no such legal definition. Since *special needs* and/or other similar terms continue to be used as a term by emergency practitioners, a debate has continued for some time now among professionals in the emergency management, health care, and disability advocacy communities as to its validity. *Special needs populations* can range from a single group to multiple, even overlapping populations. This might include documented or undocumented people in the country, low-income, non-English speaking, and/or pregnant women. When we use terms that are broader and not specific to protected classes, it can confuse issues and competing needs and demands.

The use and distinctions among these terms are important to consider. For instance, confusion over the definition of special needs during the 2007 California wildfires reportedly hindered response and recovery efforts because certain jurisdictions had different definitions of *special needs* (California Office of Emergency Services 2008). It is important that each jurisdiction clearly identify and articulate its special-needs populations.

BOX 8.3 THE ADA DEFINITION OF DISABILITY

The Americans with Disabilities Act of 1990 (ADA) codified a legal definition for the term *disability*, and created a protected class of persons with disabilities who can use the statute as legal authority to enforce civil rights. According to the ADA, an individual is defined as someone with a disability if he or she

1. Has a physical or mental impairment that substantially limits a major life activity
2. Has a record of such an impairment
3. Is regarded as having such an impairment

Types of disabilities as defined under the ADA (including the age spectrum from pediatric to geriatric) are

1. Physical (e.g., people with severe arthritis or spinal cord injuries, people who use wheelchairs, people with multiple sclerosis)
2. Sensory (e.g., people who are blind, deaf, hard of hearing)
3. Cognitive (e.g., people with mental illness, learning disabilities, mental retardation, developmental disabilities)

The Americans with Disabilities Act Amendment Act, passed in 2008, retains this basic definition of disability, but it also broadens the definition by modifying key terms of that definition by

- Expanding the definition of "major life activities"
- Redefining who is "regarded as" having a disability
- Modifying the regulatory definition of "substantially limits"
- Specifying that "disability" includes any impairment that is episodic or in remission if it would substantially limit a major life activity when active
- Prohibiting consideration of the ameliorative effects of "mitigating measures" when assessing whether an impairment substantially limits a person's major life activities, with one exception

Source: DOL (n.d.).

8.6 RELEVANCE TO THE PRACTICE OF EMERGENCY MANAGEMENT

The catastrophic events of September 11, 2001, and Hurricanes Katrina and Rita in 2005 served as an impetus for addressing disability in emergency management and resulted in new federal mandates in the U.S. Executive Order 13347, signed in 2004, intended to strengthen emergency preparedness with respect to individuals with disabilities in the federal arena (DHS 2006). This executive order directs the federal government to address the safety and security needs of people with disabilities in emergency situations, including natural and human-made disasters. To this end, the executive order created an Interagency Coordinating Council on Emergency Preparedness and Individuals with Disabilities (ICC), chaired by the Department of Homeland Security (DHS) and comprising several federal agencies as members. In the aftermath of Hurricane Katrina, Congress made significant changes to FEMA's enabling legislation, the Stafford Act, including the incorporation of disability and special-needs issues. The new law, entitled the Post-Katrina Emergency Management Reform Act of 2006, included provisions for: the inclusion of people with disabilities in every phase of emergency management at all levels of government; requirements for plans for the provision of postdisaster case-management services to victims and their families; requirements for accessible temporary and replacement housing; nondiscrimination in services on the basis of disability; and establishment of a national disability coordinator within DHS (currently located within FEMA).

With the emergence of new federal mandates and guidance, including the U.S. Department of Justice Toolkit (DOJ 2007), emergency managers in the United States are increasingly implementing inclusive emergency management programs that integrate disability-related issues in planning, response, recovery, and mitigation efforts. As states and local planners begin to utilize national guidance, familiarizing themselves with the latest opinions on these issues, they are bound to make major contributions with local solutions and resources.

By taking disability into account in emergency programs, emergency managers can address issues, put plans in place, and work with communities to increase resilience and decrease vulnerability to disasters. For instance, if the local emergency management office has a system for notifying the public during severe weather and includes utilizing accessible methods, different modalities, and existing organizational communication channels within the disability community, the chances are greater that people with disabilities (e.g., people who are deaf, hard of hearing, and/or with low or no vision) can receive and act upon the information, thus increasing their ability to take self-determined and -directed actions to protect life and property of themselves and family. In far too many cases, emergency notifications have not been accessible to people with disabilities, resulting in slow or no reaction time, thereby increasing the chances for death, injury, and/or property damage/loss.

These kinds of examples exist throughout the emergency management cycle. By including a disability perspective in developing recovery programs, services can be made more practical, helpful, and address real needs. For example, consider an individual who is able to return to her home after a flood, with only minimal damage to the home because it was located on a hill. Although not impacting her home, the flood has potentially impacted businesses, hospitals, roadways, schools, transportation, and service provision organizations (disruptions to their service delivery or inability to reach a location). If this person is reliant on home-based care, on dialysis treatments, on public transportation, or on food delivery, how will that person reasonably be able to sustain and live independently in that home? How can that person return to that home? Are there solutions such as neighboring communities and services that may be available? Is it more appropriate for the person to remain in interim housing until more of the community itself is restored? What will the impact be if she remains: deteriorating health and inability to live independently? Understanding the critical role that supportive services play in providing people with disabilities the ability to live independently is relevant to how recovery policies and procedures are approached and even prioritized. The illustration demonstrates how applying a disability lens to practice and policy greatly changes a person's chances to take appropriate action during a disaster, and also recover from a disaster.

U.S. state and federal policies and mandates regarding inclusion of disability along with fear of lawsuits or court action often create conflicted reaction to addressing disability and cause many to feel there is no clear direction. Without training and resources, emergency managers may not fully understand how to apply directives and successfully meet legal obligations. Limited staff, funding, and expertise, as well as competing interests, may make it difficult to access emergency managers or keep them from focusing on disability. Many are also frustrated because they feel that they cannot get disability groups to participate.

On the other side of the coin, some people with disabilities may be reluctant to participate and fully engage with emergency management, arising from deep-rooted distrust of the government, failure to understand emergency management and how they fit in, frustration with trying to get involved as emergency managers, as well as competing organizational interests. In Section 8.7.5, Implications for Action, we address specific solutions and give some examples for creating strong and effective partnerships between emergency management and the disability community.

8.7   VULNERABILITY ACROSS THE DISASTER CYCLE

This section discusses ways in which people with disabilities experience vulnerability across the disaster life cycle. Also included are some suggestions and examples of ways to remove barriers, implement disaster risk-reduction activities, and increase disaster resiliency. People with disabilities, their caregivers, emergency response personnel, and the overall community will benefit when including disability-related issues in all phases.

A study released by the General Accounting Office (GAO) that examined the National Response Plan and FEMA's coordination with nongovernmental organizations (NGOs) found that while some strides were made regarding mass-care needs and people with disabilities, many gaps still exist. The study focused on mass-care services more generally, FEMA's coordination with NGOs (national voluntary organizations active in disaster or NVOADs), and Red Cross's role in disaster relief. However, disability issues were included and examined. Most of the gaps identified focused on planning efforts for mass care on the federal level. Inadequacies around planning efforts, definitions of disability, support and guidance to the states, lack of use of subject-matter experts, lack of coordination for mass care for the disabled, and that certain requirements of the law have not been met (GAO 2008).

An important aspect to coordination of services is ensuring that there are enough resources and funding to provide services. Relationship building becomes even more valuable during the planning phase. According to the NCD quarterly report:

> It is critical that organizations and agencies, both NGOs and government entities, collaborate prior to, during and after a disaster. In addition, people with disabilities should be included in the collaborative efforts as volunteers, staff, planners, and organizations. Government agencies are especially helpful in terms of working with NGOs to gain access to areas where access would be prohibitive. For example, government entities can assist with ordering and loading trucks with necessary items, transportation of these items, and coordination. Since most government agencies are connected with emergency operations, they have direct access to many resources as well as the ability to deploy and coordinate as requested and necessary. Again, as mentioned earlier, VOAD organizations are also focused on greater collaboration among organizations in planning for disasters. (NCD 2008)

8.7.1   WARNINGS AND NOTIFICATION

It is critical that emergency warnings and notifications be disseminated in a timely manner to the public in order for risk-reducing actions to be undertaken. The United Nations emphasizes the need for "people centered" early warning systems that "empower individuals and communities" to take appropriate and timely protective action, with warnings and messages tailored to the specific needs of those at risk (UNISDR 2006).

Prior to identification of persons with disabilities along with their needs and capacities, preparedness planning is essential for organizing an effective and inclusive warning system. This can be done through methods such as vulnerability assessments or creation of special-needs registries. Importantly, people with disabilities should also be involved in developing warning systems and testing them (Handicap International Nepal 2009).

However, traditional notification systems have not taken people with disabilities into account (DOJ 2007). If information is not provided in multiple methods that are accessible and/or use available assistive technologies, it does not afford an individual with a disability, or family member, or caregiver, the opportunity to take actions in preserving their own lives and property. Further, if information is not clearly stated (orally or graphically), if it is too complex, or if it does not address specific information needs of the targeted recipients, these too will serve as barriers to taking necessary action.

In order to reach the broadest group of people, including people with disabilities, officials should utilize multiple methods. Broadcast and cable television, radio, sirens, flashing lights, and other similar methods have traditionally been used over the last decade, but additional methods have become commonplace. In the United States, many jurisdictions utilize the Internet, automatic-dialing systems, and/or registration-based alert systems that will send emergency messages to home phones, cell phones, email, smart phones, and other such technology. While these technologies benefit the whole community, they also benefit people with disabilities, many of whom rely on such advances in technology. However, with the introduction of these types of services, officials must also prepare individuals to understand that they will receive alerts or, if necessary, that they need to register for the services. These registration processes must also be accessible and should offer multiple ways to register (i.e., accessible website and by phone). Several U.S. cities are using 311 or 211 call centers, available to provide information and services to the public, to help support this effort to register people who cannot access a computer or the registration online.

In the United States, there are regulations in place that require emergency information to be accessible. The Federal Communications Commission requires broadcasters, cable operators, and satellite TV providers to make local emergency information accessible to persons who are deaf or hard of hearing, and to persons who are blind or have visual disabilities. Thus, emergency information must be provided both aurally and in a visual format (FCC n.d.). Details on accessibility are available in the FCC Consumer Guide. Additionally, other standards, such as Section 508 of the Rehabilitation Act apply to the accessibility of all types of electronic and information technology in the federal sector but are also generally applied to accessibility at other levels of government and in the private sector.

Additionally, in the United States in 2006, the Public Alert and Warning System Executive Order was signed, kicking off a national effort to improve rapid dissemination of emergency messages to as many people as possible over as many communications devices as possible. To do this, the project office of the Integrated Public Alert and Warning System (IPAWS) is planning to expand the traditional Emergency Alert Service (EAS) to include more modern technologies. At the same time, FEMA is upgrading the alert and warning infrastructure so that no matter what the crisis, the public will receive life-saving information. This effort is led by FEMA, DHS, the FCC, and several public and private stakeholders. The IPAWS project also specifically mandates that the public alert and warning system have the "capability to alert and warn all Americans, including those with disabilities and those without an understanding of the English language" (FEMA n.d.).

Though there is great progress being made, there is still work to be done. Evidence shows that government entities still struggle to provide accessible information to people with disabilities. For example, the National Organization on Disability (NOD) conducted a study in the United States in 2005 and found that just over four out of ten emergency management officials (42%) reported having conducted public information campaigns specifically targeted at people with disabilities. Of these, only 16% said the outreach campaign was available in accessible formats (NOD 2005a).

There are many ways officials can integrate accessible methods and assistive technologies in their notification plans and systems. The best way to start is to work directly with people with disabilities as well as the entities responsible for issuing alerts and notification. For example, officials can work with the disability community to identify some of the greatest gaps that are experienced within their community and appropriate/preferred solutions. Also working closely with mainstream media as well as disability and ethnic media entities, jurisdictions can work to correct problems and identify available, accessible, alternative solutions.

Some examples of accessible methods that can be integrated into different aspects of notification/ alert systems include:

- *Technology*: Closed or open captioning; video description; relay and video relay services; accessible websites and publications; smart phones, cell phones, and text messaging; weather radios with assistive components; radios with captioning; social media outlets such as Facebook and Twitter.

- *Interpreters*: Sign-language interpreters (shown on television, on the Web, at press conferences) and language interpreters (available by phone for rapid communication in many different languages).
- *Written communications*: Enlarged font and plain language styles in written and spoken language, communication boards that utilize pictorial illustrations of various words and phrases, and Braille printed material.
- *TTY/TDD (TeleTYpewriter/Telecommunication Device for the Deaf)/Relay*: Many jurisdictions are starting to utilize automated telephone dialing services or reverse 911-like systems that should include the capability for TTY/TDD messaging, relay services, and Internet protocols. Hotlines established by government or different agencies must include TTY/TDD numbers and operators as well as relay messaging options.

In countries or places without sophisticated communications technologies, simpler methods will be needed that will rely on people rather than automation. For example, Handicap International Nepal (2009) suggests the use of sirens, bells, and drums as auditory signals; flags, posters written with large characters, pictures that are color-contrasted, or turning lights off and on frequently as visual signals; clear and brief announcements to those who may have difficulty in understanding; and door-to-door notification and assistance for identified vulnerable people. In America Samoa, the method of banging large hanging canisters is used to spread the warning of a possible tsunami and to signal direction to move to higher ground. (See Photo 8.1.) This method is used in addition to other more technologically advanced siren systems, as demonstrated by American Samoa Office of Emergency Management personnel during a meeting.

PHOTO 8.1 Low-tech solutions are still relied upon worldwide to effectively warn the community. (Photo taken in American Samoa in 2007 by E. Davis. With permission.)

Additionally, officials should specifically target alerts/notifications to organizations and entities that work directly with and/or serve people with disabilities and other access and functional needs. These approaches may range from somewhat unsophisticated methods, such as a phone-tree system, to a more sophisticated technologically based system such as a computerized callout system. For example, many emergency officials are working with service organizations and networks to relay emergency information to their constituents. This is being done at the New York City Office of Emergency Management through their Advanced Warning System (AWS), which utilizes this automated system to send out preparedness information, real-time alerts, and recovery information to registered nonprofits and community-based service providers supporting people with "special needs" (NYC OEM n.d.). Organizations, when alerted, may also establish call-down systems or email to make consumers and families aware of the emergency information. They may also encourage forming personal support networks—made up of the service organizations, family, and friends—who have agreed to contact and share information during an emergency. The types of previously identified communication systems are strong and should always be part of any notification system.

Another strategy to target alerts/notifications is to develop mechanisms to directly alert individuals. Several jurisdictions in the United States, for example, have established registries that are targeted to people with disabilities or other access and functional needs who will need some assistance in an emergency (registries are discussed further in Section 8.7.5.2). And yet another example is the Oklahoma WARN system: a pager weather notification system in place targeted to people who are deaf or hard of hearing (see Section 8.8 as a best practice).

There is no one-size-fits-all solution to alert/notification. The best approach is to always consider low- and high-technology options to maximize resources that are available, engage the community, ensure that multiple methods are used, and utilize accessible and assistive technology methods.

8.7.2 Evacuation

As the 2004 Asian tsunami in India, Sri Lanka, and Indonesia showed, people with disabilities are more likely to be killed or injured in some rapid-onset disasters because they fail to understand the need to evacuate, are physically unable to evacuate without assistance, or cannot evacuate quickly enough (Alexander 2011). This is a devastating finding, but one that points to specific aspects of evacuation that can be improved through planning to increase overall resiliency and reduce risks for people with disabilities.

Emergency alerts and information are critical to an effective evacuation. When information is provided in a timely way and it is accessible (see Section 8.8), many people with disabilities can evacuate on their own or with the support of family or friends. However, others, whether living alone or in a group setting, will require some level of assistance. A U.S.-based survey conducted in 2005 by AARP found that 15% of adults age 50 or older, and 25% over the age of 75, require assistance from another person to evacuate from their home. This survey also revealed that of the approximately 13 million persons age 50 and older who will need help, about half will require aid from someone outside their household (Gibson and Hayunga 2006). Assistance may be available through family, neighbors, caregivers, service agencies, emergency responders, or some combination of these.

A primary concern in the planning process is to identify a means to evacuate. Most guidance tells individuals/families to identify transportation they will use to evacuate: private vehicles, rides from family/friends, public transportation, or specialized evacuation routes that will be established. For people with disabilities who require accessible transportation features, identifying transportation options becomes more difficult. Emergency planners have to make accessible transportation options available to the public as part of the evacuation plan. In the United States, accessibility of the overall vehicle stock within a jurisdiction's public transportation system, which will include paratransit, is already required. Although this is in place, existing systems will likely fall short, as there may not be enough accessible seating options or vehicles readily available (and consider if vehicles are damaged/destroyed as a result of the event). Therefore, what jurisdictions in the United States have been successful at doing is identifying nontraditional transportation providers not usually thought of in a response function and including them in evacuation plans, such as private bus/van companies and service organizations that maintain an accessible vehicle fleet. However, the coordination and dispatch of these resources, establishing memorandums of understanding (MOUs), the identification of their authority to be on the road during a disaster, and clearly establishing how these resources will be applied will all be critical to avoid an overdependency by multiple entities on the same vehicles.

Planners also have to consider options for providing assistance to people to help them leave their residence to even access transportation. In many cases, caregivers can help transfer people from home to transportation, but this may not always be possible or available at the time needed. Individuals may be living in a domicile that is not accessible or with multiple barriers that prevent them from self-evacuating. Other health- or disability-related issues may also prevent an individual from being able to self-evacuate. The reality is that there will be some percentage of a given population who will need this level of assistance, and planners need to address this proactively (NYC OEM 2007). Therefore, planners need to consider how people who need additional assistance can notify officials of this need, and then how and what resources can be deployed to provide this level of assistance. The response to this was seen during Hurricane Irene, when NYC OEM activated elements of its Homebound Evacuation Operation and instructed people in need of evacuation assistance to make themselves known through the established helpline system (Maniotis 2012).

During evacuation, people with disabilities are all too often separated from critical equipment and support that they rely on daily. Therefore, as part of preparedness messages, planning, and training, the need to keep this kind of support with the individual should be emphasized. This may not always be possible, and so messages about carefully labeling equipment and planning for ways to reunite people postevacuation is critical. Unfortunately, this was not the case during the Hurricane Katrina evacuation, when hundreds of people with disabilities were separated from critical equipment, such as customized electric wheelchairs. As a result, those authorizing moving and receiving evacuees had to provide individual support and replace highly specialized and expensive equipment, which was often not readily available (NOD 2005b). Many people with disabilities rely on caregivers to provide various levels of support, from a few hours a week to round-the-clock service. Caregivers are a heterogeneous group of people who make up a wide spectrum of people in any given community. There are more informal caregiving relationships, including family members or friends caring for other family members or friends in their homes, such as an older spouse caring for his or her spouse debilitated by stroke; family members caring for a child with a disability; or, increasingly common today, adult children caring for elderly parents. It also includes more formal caregivers from outside the family/friend network as well, such as paid home health-care providers and personal-care assistants or professional caregivers.

The importance of keeping people with disabilities together with their support network cannot be overemphasized. With a support network in place, individuals may be able to sustain more easily on their own through the phases of a disaster. Many times, people may be separated due to circumstances or policy. People may have no time to evacuate together, and individuals who require accessible transportation often are unable to travel with others in their support network. Every effort should be made to prevent this or reduce the amount of time that this occurs.

Additionally, the increased vulnerability to disaster among people with disabilities and their caregivers became dramatically evident during the evacuation of New Orleans during Hurricane Katrina. The *Washington Post*, Kaiser Family Foundation, and Harvard School of Public Health (2005) conducted interviews of displaced survivors in Houston, finding that over 40% of those who did not evacuate in a timely manner were either physically unable to leave for lack of transport or were caring for a disabled person. While the discussion thus far has focused on the importance of the caregiver for the individual with a disability, the reality is that many factors combine to make caregivers nearly or equally vulnerable in disaster. The very act of assisting their client may endanger the caregivers' safety. Paid helpers can be torn by obligation to their own family and the client, pressures that may push them to take unreasonable risks. These intersecting obligations have the power to sap their resilience precisely when it is most needed. Clearly, the role of caregivers during disaster is essential, and it is no overstatement to say that the caregiver may mean the difference for the client with a disability between life and death. Emergency managers have increasingly come to understand the importance of caregivers and the need for strategies to ensure that they are considered and incorporated into plans.

The importance of this caregiving relationship highlights the need for emergency planners to emphasize personal preparedness within the disability community. People with disabilities and their caregivers need to have strong communication, evacuation, shelter options, and other aspects of their emergency plans put together. Caregivers need to ensure that their own personal interests (i.e., small children or other family members) are part of the plan, and that each person has reasonable expectations for the support that the caregiver can provide during any phase of a disaster.

8.7.2.1 Congregate Care Settings

In addition to addressing the needs of people with disabilities living independently in the community, planners also have to take people permanently or temporarily residing in congregate-care facilities. Congregate-care settings can vary widely with different levels of regulation. For emergency planners, this is a separate and complex part of the evacuation plan, but it must be integrated and the resources coordinated here as well.

A jurisdiction may order an evacuation, but hospitals and nursing homes are sometimes exempted. In such cases, decision-making authority lies with the facility administrator to evacuate or shelter in place (GAO 2006). Administrators have to consider in-house resources and arrival of potential assistance against the risks of moving large numbers of people, which can be especially dangerous for frail patients or residents. When administrators choose to evacuate, they must consider availability of alternative sites, transportation resources, and movement of equipment, records, and staff. Whenever feasible, communication throughout the operation with residents, families, and staff alleviates stress and promotes cooperation.

Most residents will fare better in a like-to-like transfer, in which they are relocated to a facility with the same or higher-skilled staffing and care capabilities. Unfortunately, too often residents are brought to shelter locations that do not have adequate care levels or are not designed for higher medical-care capacity. While discussions about antidumping laws have been ongoing since Hurricane Andrew hit Florida in 1992, more recently it was reported that on a smaller scale, this occurred during Hurricane Irene, and the New York City Office of Emergency Management (NYC OEM) responded by permitting the residents into the Special Medical Needs Shelters, though the shelters were not intended for that purpose (Maniotis 2012).

"Transfer trauma" may occur when moving individuals whose age, disability, and/or medical condition has left them particularly frail. The actual evacuation itself can result in both physical and emotional trauma. Trauma can present as disorientation, advancing if untreated to serious deterioration of health or condition, further injury, or even death. Nursing homes and other critical care facilities must be especially aware of transfer trauma, conducting evacuations carefully to avoid or reduce it (Fernandez et al. 2002). Transfer trauma is typically associated with the period immediately preceding or following a disaster. In addition, frail or disabled survivors may face physical and emotional trauma for a long period after the disaster.

8.7.2.2 Workplaces and Residential Units

In the United States, many buildings with multiple units, such as offices, apartments, or condominiums, have a fire safety plan; however, these plans often fail to specifically take into account people with disabilities or place the responsibility to remedy an issue on the individual and not the building owner or management. This deficiency creates a possibly dangerous environment for people with disabilities, others who work or live in the building, and responding emergency personnel as well. After examining this issue, FEMA and the U.S. Fire Administration (USFA) developed excellent planning guides (FEMA 2010). At a minimum, facility safety plans should include: voluntary

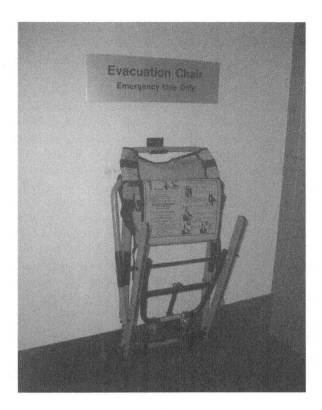

PHOTO 8.2 Located in the Austin Convention Center in Texas, an evacuation device is prominently located at every point of egress. (Photo by E. Davis. With permission.)

identification of people who may need assistance and the type of assistance required; accessible emergency notification and signage; purchase of and training on evacuation equipment designed for use by persons with disabilities; designation of areas of rescue assistance for people who cannot use the stairways or designated emergency exits; unobstructed paths of egress from the building; and drills and exercises on procedures for all affected individuals (JAN n.d.). See Photo 8.2.

8.7.3 Sheltering

A public emergency shelter is any building or facility used for the purpose of sheltering large numbers of people during and after emergencies, be it purpose-built or taken over at times of crisis. During or after a disaster, a critical number of community residents, including people with disabilities, may take refuge in a shelter. Shelters may be seen as a lifeboat on land, offering basic provision—food, water, a place to rest, and first aid at best. They may be managed by official or nongovernmental agencies. In the United States, many institutions traditionally have relied on and partnered with the American Red Cross, the Salvation Army, and other volunteer groups and faith-based organizations to manage and operate preidentified shelters.

Several elements of good disability practice in public emergency-shelter management exist (Twigg et al. 2011). The shelters must ensure equal access, including accessible parking, exterior routes, entrances, interior routes to the shelter area, and toilets serving the shelter area. Shelter staff, both professional and volunteer, should be trained in meeting the needs for people with disabilities. As an extension, sufficient medical and volunteer assistance must be available, including families, personal support networks, and where appropriate care animals (the presence of family and friends familiar with the individual's needs provides valuable support and reduces their trauma). The type of food available should include special diets. To accommodate adequately for people with disabilities, appropriate technical support (e.g., access to electricity for medical and mobility devices and refrigeration for medication) must be part of the shelter. The shelter should promote and sustain independence and safety as well as the use of appropriate methods of communication (visual, audio, and interpreters). To achieve shelters that are more inclusive and accommodating, shelter planning should involve people with disabilities, and shelter activity and practice require monitoring and reevaluation. Importantly, shelters should provide assistance for returning home, or provision of assistance in finding temporary accommodation for those unable to return to their homes immediately after an event.

Many shelter shortfalls are directly attributed to limitations in staffing and management. The global evidence also demonstrates: an acute shortage of shelter personnel trained in planning for people with disabilities; a lack of coordination and communication between emergency managers and between shelters regarding special needs, referrals, and acquisition of additional specialist human and material resources; failure to survey shelter sites with accessible features in mind and staff not trained to assess shelters for accessibility; and a lack of engagement with disabled people's organizations (DPOs) and other specialist disability organizations, both in disaster planning and during events, to understand disability-related needs and provide support. Good organization and planning are essential elements in shelter access and provision for people with disabilities at both the strategic and operational levels (Twigg et al. 2011).

There is no shortage of technical guidance on public emergency-shelter design, and in some countries, clear disability design standards are set. In the United States, the ADA under Title II and III interpretation requires shelters to be accessible and to otherwise accommodate persons with disabilities. In July 2007, the U.S. Department of Justice (DOJ) released guidance to state and local governments establishing these standards (DOJ 2007). In 2010, FEMA also published the "Guidance on Planning for Integration of Functional Needs Support Services in General Population Shelters" (FEMA 2010), which provides guidance on how to integrate accessibility and support services throughout shelter programs. While governments are slowly but steadily becoming aware of these requirements, shelters still fall short of basic ADA standards (e.g., an accessible route into the site location and accessible bathrooms). It is much easier to remedy these deficiencies when shelters are preselected in advance of a disaster, and it becomes much more problematic during the spontaneous identification of shelters.

One effective strategy begins with the identification by emergency managers of facilities that are both likely to be accessible and known or frequented by the community. The Senior Center Safe Center programs in Alabama and Florida are founded on this concept. Local governments either build new senior centers or retrofit existing facilities for dual use as shelters. These centers offer activities and services in the community every day, are outside the floodplain, and are built to withstand hurricane- and tornado-force winds. In addition to being accessible, they are equipped with generators, extra wall outlets, and satellite telephones. The roofs of these facilities are painted bright colors for easy recognition during flyovers and rescue operations (Alabama Department of Social Services 2006). The Adopt-a-Shelter program in Duval County, Florida, is a partnership between the county administration and local hospitals and medical supply companies to ensure that designated special-needs shelters are fully stocked prior to disasters, have developed inventories, and can provide resources in an emergency (NCD 2006).

Effective sheltering begins at the door of the shelter. Without a shelter intake process that is sensitive to the needs of people with disabilities, many problems may go unidentified. Shelters need to capture information on how to meet functional needs. While the process must allow an individual the right not to divulge his or her status, a lack of inclusiveness can cause hardship to both the individual and staff during the shelter stay. Therefore, if needs are acknowledged at intake, an opportunity is created early in what might become a prolonged stay to offer possible accommodation or to determine the need to relocate the person and his/her family in a different setting with a more appropriate level of care (e.g., medical-needs shelter, hospital, or nursing home).

In addition to being physically accessible, general-population shelters should be equipped with (and shelter staff trained to provide) accommodations for people with disabilities. These may include programmatic accommodations, the use of sign-language interpreters, or providing assistance with minimal activities of daily living (ADL), such as help with eating, ambulating, and grooming for individuals who require it. Service animals must always be allowed in shelters—this is mandated by law in the United States—and should not be separated from their owners.

Resource allocation and distribution is a shelter issue that can adversely impact people with disabilities. As was mentioned previously (Section 8.7.2 on evacuation), for a variety of reasons, people may arrive at shelters without medication, assistive devices (eyeglasses, canes, walkers, etc.), and durable medical equipment (oxygen machines and tanks). Planning for this reality will minimize the impact of such losses and permit individuals to maintain an equal or similar level of independence to their experience before the event. First and foremost, jurisdictions should educate the public about the importance of bringing necessary items with them. Planners should also identify sources of medical equipment and assistive devices that are likely to be needed in a shelter (e.g., oxygen-tank refill capability, manual wheelchairs, walkers). Establishing partnerships with medical equipment suppliers, pharmacies, disability agencies, and other related retailers will help tremendously in identifying supplies. Also necessary is the understanding of rules and regulation. For example, in Florida, only certain certified professionals can refill oxygen tanks. Thus, it may be necessary to build in a legislative waiver under emergency conditions or have certain staff always present.

In an attempt to serve evacuees with more consideration, and to reduce stress on hospitals, some jurisdictions in high-income countries have practiced the establishment of special/medical-needs shelters to provide a higher level of care, skilled staff, and equipment. These shelters are intended for people who have medical or care requirements beyond those that can be met at a general-population shelter facility, which in most cases is at a first-aid level of care. This approach has generated considerable debate: Opponents criticize it for separating or segregating disability and special-needs populations from the larger community. However, harsh reality finds emergency planners struggling to find adequate resources, so it may make sense to pool assets to support this level of sheltering. An abundance of resources is required to support such a shelter, including skilled medical and paraprofessional staffing, specialized equipment, uninterrupted power generation, abundant medication supplies, and the like. Emergency managers are increasingly attempting to colocate special/medical-needs shelters within or near general-population shelters. Undoubtedly, they face a struggle, since many jurisdictions are encountering shortages in the very resources needed to support general-population facilities.

After Hurricane Katrina, one city mayor designated a convention center as a general shelter and ensured that it had all relevant elements for people with disabilities, such as interpreters for the deaf, accessible shuttle services, a large number of volunteers to assist, and information on how to find accessible housing. Although the center was not run by experienced emergency managers, the city was able to successfully accommodate people with disabilities through an attitude of inclusiveness and making accessibility a priority (NOD 2005b). Similarly, a study of three emergency rest centers in the United Kingdom during floods in 2007 found that the rest-center workers and volunteers displayed a good knowledge of access issues for people with disabilities, which made them a valuable resource in the operation of the centers, despite the fact that most of them had limited emergency management training prior to the flooding event (Kipling, Newton, and Ormerod 2011).

Sadly, the belief that a shelter will be unable to accommodate their specific needs may make people with disabilities reluctant to evacuate in response to warnings. Where evacuation is frequent, in response to seasonal hazards, previous unpleasant experience of evacuation shelters may make people with disabilities reluctant to venture into them again. Changing these views will take explicit attention and work. The improvements and changes discussed will not all come overnight, but there must be a standard we can look to as we proceed to change the role of persons with disabilities in emergency management planning.

8.7.4   SHORT- AND LONG-TERM RECOVERY

After a disaster, people's needs include reentry issues, housing, and other types of longer-term disaster human services. In recent years, social sciences have begun to look at how disasters affect people who are considered more vulnerable than the general population, as well as an increased interest in how vulnerable populations recover postdisaster. However, findings in a review of the literature indicate that there simply is not enough research in the areas of disability and disaster recovery and provision of services (Mileti 1999). The literature reveals particular gaps of understanding in terms of the disability community and disaster recovery and in the provision of needed services. These include deficiencies in access to resources and to physical and mental health care, discrimination, aid organizations lacking understanding, and poverty issues.

While there are few empirical studies regarding disability and recovery, some recent disasters offer lessons learned regarding preparedness and response and the disability population. In 2009, the National Council on Disability (NCD) published a study on disability and all four phases of emergency management. According to the report, "Key findings remain scant because of the absence of empirical work in this area" (NCD 2009). The NCD (2009a) also reports the following types of long-term recovery issues of high concern for people with disabilities:

1. Temporary and long-term housing
2. Access to health care and mental health services
3. Jobs
4. Transportation
5. Rebuilding the community so that it is accessible to all

These topics are similar to the themes that emerge in the broader literature about vulnerable populations.

The recovery process of cleaning debris, restoring transportation routes and utilities, and repairing houses severely impacts people with disabilities and their capacity to return safely home. No one who relies on electricity to sustain life, such as people who use oxygen or ventilators, can return to an apartment or house without assurance of uninterrupted power. The lack of transportation services (especially accessible transportation), combined with the usual problems of postevent road access, can severely limit a person's ability to resume health-care services, work, and school.

Lack of suitable accessible housing is a major obstacle to getting people with disabilities to return to the community or to be resettled elsewhere. Many cities and towns have a shortage of accessible housing before a disaster event occurs. After a disaster occurs, demand for long-term, permanent housing rises precisely as resources become more scarce. As national and state rebuilding programs are established during the recovery phase, emergency management and the disability community together must advocate for inclusion of accessible housing and accommodation rights as an integral part of these proposed programs. Federally funded housing programs, such as those administered by the Department of Housing and Urban Development (HUD), include requirements in accordance with the ADA, Uniform Federal Accessibility Standards (UFAS), and other regulations mandating that a certain percentage of all construction must meet accessibility standards. As homes are being repaired or rebuilt with federal money, it is vital to consider accessibility requirements for individual homeowners or potential renters. Further, jurisdictions should consider encouraging or mandating the utilization of universal design concepts in all new construction and urban planning to ensure at least minimal accessibility, as this opportunity to design access during the rebuilding phase can be a positive outcome from a devastating event.

Temporary housing, such as the travel trailers and mobile homes FEMA often provides, also falls short of meeting accessibility requirements (Advocacy Center 2007). In fact, the problem became so dire in Louisiana and Mississippi after Hurricanes Katrina and Rita that an advocacy organization filed and won a lawsuit against FEMA on behalf of 11 Katrina and Rita evacuees with disabilities (Advocacy Center 2007). After the hurricanes, it was noted that, although approximately 25%

of Katrina evacuees had disabilities, only 1%–2% of such people from Louisiana and Mississippi received accessible trailers. On September 26, 2006, the Federal District Court for the Eastern District of Louisiana approved a settlement to ensure that FEMA will provide accessible trailers to people with disabilities. FEMA has continued to work toward a more appropriate solution as evidenced in the release of the 2008 Disaster Housing Plan (FEMA 2008).

In addition to ensuring that temporary housing is accessible to people with disabilities, long-term (permanent) housing needs to be accessible as well. Retrofitting houses so that people with physical disabilities can have a permanent home is not only an important step in helping victims of disaster rebuild their lives, it is an important step in rebuilding the devastated community. When homes are rebuilt that are accessible, it encourages all buildings in the community to be rebuilt per laws and regulations. This can have an overall beneficial effect on the entire community in many ways. The National Council on Disability (NCD 2008) asserts:

> The entire community benefits as access to public works and structures will increase access to the employment, healthcare, and independence for people with disabilities. We must ensure that the federal, state, and local authorities who operate public buildings will fill their obligation to comply with the laws; the cost of complying with the relevant laws later will undoubtedly exceed that of getting it right the first time.

Until services such as home-based care, health clinics, hospitals, and schools are restored, many people with disabilities may not be able to return. Without the proper support, they may not be able to function independently or safely. Service providers can also play a big role during recovery in helping clients to understand the aid available through federal and state government programs, private grants and foundations, and traditional disaster relief organizations, such as the American Red Cross. The National Council on Disability (NCD 2008) reported that many disability advocates believed that a majority of people with disabilities had not returned to New Orleans nearly three years after the storm because of lack of social and health services as well as accessible housing and other public facilities.

Through coordination with aid organizations, service providers can communicate benefit opportunities and eligibility requirements to their clientele, as well as determine their own internal policy and items for which they may apply. Too often, services are duplicated among agencies, while others are ignored or forgotten. Through a more coordinated effort, the needs of disaster victims can be met with greater effectiveness and efficiency.

8.7.5 IMPLICATIONS FOR ACTION

This section of the chapter demonstrates ways in which emergency programs can integrate disability awareness and planning into all phases. The engagement of the disability community in all parts of the emergency cycle is critical to empowering and strengthening resiliency of people with disabilities. It also improves the community response by ensuring that disability-related needs are identified and addressed before, during, and after emergencies. It cannot be reasonably expected that one agency or organization can effectively integrate disability planning into all aspects of an emergency program. Stakeholders from the community must be part of the planning process and work actively with emergency managers, public safety officials, and others responsible for emergency planning.

8.7.5.1 Stakeholder Involvement

People with disabilities and their organizations have repeatedly insisted on their right to be active stakeholders in emergency planning. This point is made emphatically in the 2007 Verona Charter on the rescue of persons with disabilities, for example (Verona Charter 2007). Policy makers are beginning to acknowledge this.

Many disabled persons organizations (DPOs) and disability organizations are involved in emergency response and providing relief. For example, they were quick to provide funds and material support after the 2004 Asian tsunami and Hurricane Katrina (Hemingway and Priestley 2006). After the 2008 Sichuan earthquake in China, associations of people with disabilities used mobile phones to provide information and social support to their members who were affected (Alexander 2011). In 1996–1997, a group in Los Angeles called Disabled People and Disaster Planning (DP2) produced a series of guidance notes on preparedness and response for emergency managers and people with disabilities drawing on lessons from the 1994 Northridge earthquake (see Resources). However, such initiatives are often spontaneous and not necessarily planned, coordinated, or replicated. Indeed, there is some evidence that disability organizations and support groups are often not sufficiently prepared themselves for emergencies (White et al. 2007), and many do not know how to link with the emergency management system (Twigg et al. 2011).

When stakeholder involvement is integrated in preparedness, response, recovery, and mitigation, communities are better able to accurately assess vulnerabilities, needs, and identify capabilities and resources that may not have been recognized. In the United States, FEMA promotes a "whole community" involvement and approach to emergency management, which includes people with disabilities, but also includes other segments of the community such as business, schools, health, faith-based organizations, social service agencies, and others (FEMA 2011). A similar approach to community resilience is now being promoted in the United Kingdom, but this is less explicit about the engagement of people with disabilities, which increases the risk of their being marginalized in emergency planning and response (Cabinet Office 2011a, 2011b).

There is great diversity among organizations and entities that provide services to people with disabilities. Some represent the broad spectrum of disability, while others may concentrate their services to certain segments of the disability community (i.e., people with developmental disabilities; people who are blind or have low vision). Others may not even have a specific disability mission. For example, a faith-based organization may have a mission to provide food services, but it is likely that a percentage of their population will have one or more disabilities. When bringing stakeholders into the planning process, it is important to have representation that reflects the diversity of the disability community and the service community.

Service providers or advocacy agencies that work directly with disability populations are well informed through their experience about the needs of the community. Many also have established and maintained trusted relationships with their consumers over extended periods of time. As a result, these entities are predictably expected to experience high call volumes and direct requests for assistance during disasters because they already have connections to individuals, families, and the community at large. Emergency management agencies will look to service providers to assist with identifying populations and conducting needs assessments, coordinating resources, and, if at all possible, enhancing everyday services to include additional assistance or to incorporate more people who have been made eligible for their services because of disaster.

Internationally, civil society groups, such as disabled people's organizations (DPOs), have a role to play: Some register members and collect information about specific requirements in disasters, and others work directly with other service providers on training and understanding the needs of persons with disabilities in local communities.

Emergency officials also have much to offer stakeholders in terms of providing information on emergency plans, integrating them in emergency protocols, and providing assistance in improving preparedness and resilience. This may include identifying hazard vulnerabilities; assisting them to develop a continuity-of-operations plan to improve their capability of continuing operations throughout the incident; and informing them of federal and state aid for which they may be eligible, and the details of the application process (Fernandez et al. 2002). It is a mutually beneficial relationship that, once established, will enhance capabilities and assistance to the disability community prior to, during, and after emergencies. Partners working with people with psychiatric disabilities should also be included (see Box 8.4).

8.7.5.2   Assessment and Identification

Warning and evacuation, as well as recovery efforts, are more effective if targeted at people known to have disabilities. Identification of people with disabilities can be done through social vulnerability assessments (see Chapter 16). However, there is evidence to suggest that people with disabilities are often overlooked when assessments are carried out. Their active involvement in assessing vulnerability (and capacity) is key to ensuring that they are made visible to planners and that their needs are identified and given sufficient priority. There should also be better registries of their locations, their needs, and the resources that can be called upon to assist during disaster.

This effort must be collaborative, incorporating multiple sources of information to obtain the most accurate picture. It will prove easier to identify people with disabilities who are affiliated with a service or advocacy agency than those who are not. Working with an inclusive disabilities planning group, as mentioned previously, will be an extremely helpful source of data, and will allow needs assessors to drill down beneath the standard demographic information collected. Information that is particularly useful includes:

- Individuals with disabilities who will require assistance during emergencies and what level of assistance actually is required
- Caregivers and support networks
- Resource capacities and limitations
- Locations of clusters of people with specific disabilities (e.g., school for the blind or deaf, congregate care facility, etc.)
- Targets for individual preparedness programs
- Community-based resources previously unknown or unavailable to emergency management, such as private fleets of accessible vehicles

Geographical information systems (GIS) technology can also be applied to this task (Enders and Brandt 2007). In Kobe, Japan, a comprehensive survey and mapping project has been undertaken to identify people with physical disabilities in hazard-prone environments (including factors such as housing condition and social isolation) and raise communities' and disaster planners' awareness of their situation and needs (Tatsuki and Comafay 2012).

To overcome the challenge of identifying those who require assistance (whether for notification or evacuation, etc.) and what form that assistance might take, some jurisdictions utilize a registry system. Though registries differ in purpose and operation, generally they comprise a database of people with various needs (eligibility determined by jurisdiction) who voluntarily register. Since registries are by legal interpretation voluntarily joined, it must be expected that they will not capture all those requiring assistance; the registry is instead one tool among many others for consideration.

Registries, when effectively in place, provide a variety of information, depending on the design by the jurisdiction. Common data found in a registry include the basic identification information, reason or level of assistance needs, and specific critical data, for example. Registries can assist managers to target preparedness materials and messages, and to streamline emergency communications. Florida has mandated the creation of a special-needs registry by all 67 counties, while most other states leave such action to the discretion of local authorities. Registries can be of enormous help to the emergency manager, but they come with a number of issues that should be carefully examined pre-implementation.

Registries are one of several possible tools a jurisdiction may use to identify people with disaster-related needs. That said, caution should be taken when planning a registry system. Several issues exist that complicate administering registries. There is a need to have a centralized dispatching system for disseminating the secure registry information to the right people under the right circumstances. During the first few days of the 2003 California wildfires, the registry lists were locked in secure locations in local fire stations, and could not be used for the intended purpose. The state did not have a centralized dispatching system to coordinate efforts among the communities, which curtailed the ability to ensure that everyone was notified (California State Independent Living Council 2004). Registries must have a mechanism for updating that includes financial and personnel resources; otherwise they can quickly become outdated, for example from death or relocation. Expectations about services must be clear, describing exactly what individuals can expect as a result of returning the registration form. In this way, unfounded expectations will be avoided and minimize the belief that by registering people will automatically receive assistance from the jurisdiction (which may not be the case). Residents may rely too much on having registered rather than taking the time to work up a personal preparedness plan. Those who refused to register prior to an emergency might clog the agency's phone lines at the last moment of a mandatory evacuation, expecting that they can register and be rescued. Importantly, confidentiality laws and obligations may impact the registry negatively, and these should be fully explored and understood prior to taking any other action to implement such a list. For example, the Health Insurance Portability and Accountability Act (HIPAA), Public Law 104-191, and other privacy laws may affect the type of information or the collection method allowed. Refugees with disabilities are often under unidentified (see Box 8.5).

It is also important to note that in many local jurisdictions and countries, registries do not exist. Even where they do, authorities should also be aware that persons with disabilities may not wish to register, as this may draw unwanted attention to themselves and create stigmatization and discrimination if there are no resources or support structures in place to benefit them. People will often refuse to sign up for the registry because they are unclear about how the information will be used or if it will be secured. Emergency managers often become frustrated with the registry, because only a small percentage of the eligible population needing assistance actually gives out their names and addresses (White et al. 2007), but this may be for some very valid reasons.

8.7.5.3 Training

Addressing underlying institutional weaknesses is essential for achieving widespread and lasting changes in operational practice. The most commonly advocated approach is to sensitize emergency management organizations and their staff through training, guidelines, and other technical resources. It has been suggested that such training should be made a prerequisite for career progression in emergency management (White et al. 2007).

Training press officers, outreach teams, shelter staff, and first responders on disability issues will help enhance communication with the disability community as well as increase awareness on better response methods during evacuations and rescues. Disability service providers, in coordination with emergency management, can assist in the training of press officers and other outreach workers to ensure that they are attuned to disaster-related needs issues. Training should focus on modality, i.e., different methods for relaying information and content, evaluation of effectiveness, and coordination of dissemination.

Outreach teams working in the community to help people prepare or to provide postdisaster recovery information should also be trained on disability issues. For example, after the World Trade Center attacks in New York City on September 11, 2001, outreach teams were trained on general recovery information as well as on disability awareness. They learned to identify communication and service needs while working in the field, and they received specific demographic information on the targeted area and guidance about interfacing with disability organizations (Mackert and Davis 2002).

Shelter staff, largely composed of volunteers, must receive training on how to work with people with disabilities. Minimally, this instruction should address sensitization to the issues, to intake processes, and to dealing with accommodation requests. Disability service agencies should be involved in the design and conduct of the training, whether held in advance of an occurrence or spontaneously just after an event.

Many first responders and other emergency management personnel are not trained in and lack basic understanding of emergency-related disability issues (White et al. 2007). Conversely, many disability organizations and individuals with disabilities know little about emergency management.

Cross training that brings together these two distinct communities has proven to be highly effective. There are now free, cost-sharing, and for-fee training packages available to states and localities. Examples can be found in the Resources section.

8.7.5.4 Outreach and Personal Preparedness

Building capacity within the disability community so that individuals are more prepared and better able to respond during disasters is a key concept that emergency managers should incorporate into planning and outreach efforts. There are several ways to accomplish this, including working through networks and providing accurate and timely information.

One of the greatest resources any individual possesses is his or her ability to self-prepare. An increasing amount of emergency preparedness information is now available and targeted to people with disabilities and seniors who frequently have disabling conditions. The primary source of this information is the Internet, as there are several websites being dedicated to this issue. However, millions of Americans are still computer illiterate or do not own a system, while in many other parts of the world, Internet access is much more restricted because of poverty and infrastructural limitations. Many who use computers may not be aware that the guidance is available. There are no filters to distinguish valid and useful information (see Resources section) from sites created essentially to sell a product. Further, some persons with disabilities will need assistance or assistive technologies to understand the necessary steps to be prepared for disasters.

In order to ensure that people with disabilities are aware of and have access to preparedness information, jurisdictions can work through social networks, community-based service organizations, and home health-care agencies. In addition to distributing the information, staff members of such organizations, when properly trained, can discuss the material with their clients or patients and assist them in taking the recommended steps for greater preparedness.

Persons who are blind will require accessible formats. In many cases, the issue of access has been resolved by the development of reader software that enables the text on the monitor screen to be transmitted audibly. For those not yet comfortable with mouse and keyboard, brochures and pamphlets can be recorded on cassette tape or DVD or printed in Braille. Several organizations have created model preparedness information directed at people with cognitive disabilities or who can understand only very basic ideas or who benefit from pictorial and graphic representations.

Support groups, self-help networks, or buddy systems can play an invaluable role in developing the capacity of people with disabilities to prepare for and respond to an emergency: These typically consist of two or three people—friends, colleagues, neighbors, or family members—who agree and plan to assist in times of emergency. In the United States, guidance on how to create personal support networks has been promoted for a number of years (e.g., American Red Cross 1997; Kailes 2002).

8.7.5.5 Continuity of Operations Planning

Social service agencies should develop continuity of operations plans (COOP). Indeed, there is some evidence that disability organizations and support groups are often not sufficiently prepared themselves for emergencies (White et al. 2007), and many do not know how to link with the emergency management system (Twigg et al. 2011).

All such agencies, private or public, struggle to find the funding and staff to develop such plans. At a minimum, the COOP plan should indicate a source of backup for essential functions and resources such as equipment, staffing, record keeping, facilities, and means of service delivery. These types of services are essential in order to implement recovery operations and move people back into their homes. Without these types of support services in place, many individuals will need to seek alternative locations to live, and many may not be able to self-sustain, resulting in placement in a congregate care facility.

Congregate and residential care facilities must also develop COOP plans. The U.S.-based Joint Commission on Accreditation of Healthcare Organizations (JCAHO) accredits eight different types of health-care facilities, the most relevant to emergency management being hospitals, long-term care facilities, behavioral health-care clinics, and ambulatory care institutions. In early 2008, JCAHO released a detailed standard for business continuity planning for these facilities, including procedures for operational interruptions, developing a backup system, and testing of those systems.

8.7.5.6 Exercises and Drills

Exercises and drills, which include key stakeholders representing disability populations as well as the individuals themselves, will provide valuable practical information to improve emergency plans. Persons with disabilities should be involved in all phases of this activity, including exercise and drill design, implementation, and evaluation. Experience has demonstrated that participation by people with disabilities brings out new and unexpected issues, which were either planned for inadequately or never considered seriously, if at all.

The unexpected outcome much earlier from the Interagency Chemical Exercise in New York City in 1998 showed that responders did not have training or experience in decontaminating people with auxiliary aids (i.e., wheelchairs, walkers, canes, glasses, hearing aids, etc.), with service animals, or with attached medical supports such as insulin pumps and cochlear implants. The "cold zone" became compromised for the original victims, all aid workers, and the second wave of first responders as a result of passing those people through when unsure how to deal with encountering an unfamiliar circumstance (Byrne and Davis 2005). This is consistent with some of the findings from the 2005 Department of Homeland Security's (DHS) third national Top Officials (TOPOFF3) drill with regard to disabilities. Facilities need to be accessible, and information should be provided in alternative forms (including closed-captioned). People with disabilities were inadequately represented during the drill, and planning for these diverse groups should explicitly be included in the exercise plan (Davis and Mincin 2003).

8.8 EXAMPLES OF SUCCESS AND BEST PRACTICES

8.8.1 Incorporating the Emergency Management Assistance Compact in Gulf States, U.S.

The Emergency Management Assistance Compact (EMAC) is an agreement used in emergency management among states in the United States outlining emergency services and resources that can be extended from states not impacted to states impacted by disaster. Until 2005, EMAC was not applied to the disaster-related needs of people with disabilities. However, following Hurricane Katrina, the U.S. Administration on Aging utilized EMAC to bring in social workers, case managers, and service providers from other states into the Gulf Coast with specific training in elder-service delivery to assist elderly disaster victims (Tokesky and Weston 2006). Utilizing this approach built the capacity of the impacted area to address the needs of the senior population. This approach can be replicated in future disasters and expanded beyond seniors into the larger disability community.

8.8.2 Disability Organization Planning Directly with Local Fire Department in New York City, U.S.

An example of a success story regarding the identification of a specific-needs group working together with first responders can be illustrated by both terrorist attacks, in 1993 and 2001, on the World Trade Center. The Associated Blind, an advocacy organization that also has people who are blind and with other disabilities on staff, was located right near the World Trade Center. After the 1993 bombing, the Associated Blind worked closely with the Fire Department of New York (FDNY) on emergency preparedness, planning, and effective evacuation routes for staff as well as rescue techniques for the firefighters. The plans were tested and staff practiced drills. As a result, all staff safely and independently evacuated their building during the 2001 terrorist attacks (NOD n.d.). This is a powerful example of how lives can be saved by identifying special-needs populations and working with them before the disaster hits.

8.8.3 STAKEHOLDER INITIATIVE IN LONDON, U.K.

When Full of Life, a self-help group of parents of children with disabilities in London, U.K., discovered that standard public information material distributed by the local emergency planning authorities in 2011 did not address disability issues, the parents sought out and collected guidance from elsewhere in the United Kingdom and the United States. After discussing these and the information they contained, the group bought "grab bags" for the families and prepared its own list of essential items to go in them to support the disabled children in an emergency.

8.8.4 INNOVATIVE NOTIFICATION SYSTEM IN OKLAHOMA, U.S.

The Oklahoma WARN (OK-WARN) is a pager weather-notification system for Oklahomans who are deaf or hard of hearing. Created after the 1999 tornado season with funding from the state school for the deaf, it provides notification and warning together with life-saving information on such quickly arising weather events as flash floods. It was created by meteorologist Vincent Wood, who recognized that people who are deaf or hard of hearing have limited access to emergency information. The OK-WARN requires that a person already have a vibrating pager, but this technology is relatively inexpensive and has been adopted enthusiastically throughout the nation by individuals who are deaf or hard of hearing. Participants receive alerts from the National Weather Service only a minute or two after they reach weather radios. The program was piloted in 2001 and was so successful that it is still currently in place. In 2008, OK-WARN was awarded the prestigious Alan Clive Service and Spirit Award, presented every year at the National Hurricane Conference. (See more in Chapter 18.)

BOX 8.4 INADEQUACIES IN ADDRESSING PSYCHIATRIC DISABILITIES

The National Council on Disability (NCD) outlined how the government failed to assist people with psychiatric disabilities during Hurricanes Katrina and Rita, identifying major violations of the law on several accounts during evacuations, including discrimination (NCD 2006). Specifically, some individuals with psychiatric disabilities "had difficulty comprehending the evacuation messages and other essential communications and some were treated roughly because they could not follow the instructions" (NCD 2006). According to the report:

> Disaster response plans often did not include protocols to evacuate people with psychiatric disabilities. During evacuations, emergency officials physically lost residents of group homes and psychiatric facilities many of who are still missing. Others have not or cannot return home because essential supports have not been restored or because the cost of living has increased too much. When people with psychiatric disabilities arrived at evacuation locations—ranging from state parks to churches—those locations often were not prepared to meet the medical and mental health needs of the evacuees with psychiatric disabilities. Many people with psychiatric disabilities never made it to evacuation shelters because they were inappropriately and involuntarily institutionalized. Some of these people still have not been discharged, despite evaluations that indicate they should be. (NCD 2006)

The Inter-Agency Standing Committee (IASC) issued guidelines to enable humanitarian actors to plan, establish, and coordinate a set of minimum multisectoral responses to protect and improve people's mental health and psychosocial well-being in the midst of an emergency (IASC 2007).

BOX 8.5   REFUGEES WITH DISABILITIES

In June 2008, the Women's Commission on Refugee Women and Children (WCRWC) released a limited, qualitative report that outlined the critical need for better understanding of the needs of people with disabilities and how to incorporate those needs (WCRWC 2008). According to the report, "Too often invisible, too often forgotten and too often overlooked, refugees with disabilities are among the most isolated, socially excluded and marginalized of all displaced populations" (WCRWC 2008, 1). The study included five refugee camps in Nepal, Thailand, Yemen, Jordan, and Ecuador (WCRWC 2008). These five countries currently receive thousands of refugees from neighboring countries that are experiencing conflict and war.

According to the National Emergency Management Resource Center (NEMRC), which summarized pertinent findings from the WCRWC report, the results of this limited qualitative study include the following findings:

- People with disabilities were not accurately and properly identified prior to conflict and in refugee camps.
- People with mental and cognitive disabilities were less likely to be identified and provided services than people with physical and sensory disabilities.
- Camps lacked accessible information, facilities, and services.
- The needs of people with disabilities are not fully understood; prejudice is pervasive.
- People with disabilities are often neglected and not considered.
- Services after a conflict are better than services provided prior to the conflict.
- There was a lack of expert workers in the field and on a policy level.
- There was a lack of a comprehensive, inclusive definition that nations can agree upon that does not fall under the "medical" model.
- There was a lack of resources specific to the needs of people with disabilities pre- and postconflict/disaster.

Broadly, report recommendations for the establishment and ongoing management of refugee camps included the following:

- *Accessibility*: This includes physical structures such as shelters and actual refugee camps as well as information and services.
- *Data collection*: Statistical information needs to be gathered from people with disabilities who enter camps.
- *Tolerance and greater understanding*: It is critical that misconceptions and myths related to disability be debunked both among workers and societies in general.
- *Targeted services*: In addition to ensuring that *all* services, facilities, and information are accessible, there are issues specific to the disability community that need to be addressed.
- *Disability coalition building*: Local disability organizations need to be incorporated into relief efforts.
- *Worker materials and guidance*: Update field manuals, guidance documents, and training materials to reflect current disability issues and how to work with the disability community during conflict and disaster.

During one of the interviews for the WCRWC study, a disability aid worker was quoted as saying,

In all wars and disasters, it is persons with disabilities that are first to die; persons with disabilities that are the first to get disease and infection; and it is persons with disabilities who are the last to get resources and medicines when they are handed out. They are treated as the bottom of the pile. (WCRWC 2008, 6)

8.9 SUMMARY

In conclusion, anyone involved in emergency planning, response, or recovery issues with the disability community needs to keep several points in mind. The issues that present will be labor intensive, costly, and time consuming. They will be ongoing and are best approached in partnership with the stakeholders directly. This ensures appropriateness of the plans, includes community buy-in, brings new information and resources into the equation, and leads to sustainability over time.

To truly maximize efforts given these points, the goal should be to "universalize" as often as possible. Just like the point made previously about incorporating the concepts of universal design and access when redesigning or rebuilding a community post disaster, so can we borrow that term in other ways. The use of open captions at the bottom of the television image may have been done with the needs of the deaf and hard of hearing in mind, but the written word available to reinforce the spoken message can be a benefit to persons with learning disabilities or to those for whom English is not their proficient first language and for everyone in a loud environment. Just as the assurance that the designated shelter or temporary housing unit have an access ramp leading into it may have been done with a wheelchair user in mind, so can that benefit an older person with an unsteady gait or even a mother of very young children in a stroller. If many types of needs for many people can be addressed simultaneously and with slight variations, the limited disaster resources will be maximized and leveraged. This will reduce individual needs as well as impacts on volunteers and staff.

Further, when an empowerment model is applied to the concept of emergency preparedness, it is consistent with the social and political movements in the disability community. It enables people with disabilities to become active and informed consumers of emergency information and to take their survival into their own hands to the best of their abilities rather than be passive victims waiting for help from others. For all the reasons stated in this chapter, that has a lasting impact on the system as well as the community.

DISCUSSION QUESTIONS

1. What key agencies or organizations in your community need to be working together?
2. Is there a way to "universalize" solutions to meet the needs of the targeted populations and the general populations?
3. How can a community maximize limited resources and staff, and address them in the face of diminished funds?
4. What attitudes on both sides need to be addressed in order to move a partnership forward?
5. Are there creative funding streams or ways of work as a consortium to put certain more costly measures in place?
6. What nontraditional resources do both emergency planners and disability organizations bring to the table?

REFERENCES

Access Board. n.d.a ADA Standards homepage. http://www.access-board.gov/ada/.

Access Board. n.d.b Frequently asked questions about ADAAG. http://www.access-board.gov/adaag/html/adaag.htm.

Advocacy Center. 2007. FEMA trailer lawsuit update. http://www.advocacyla.org/index.php/about-advocacy-center.html.

Alabama Department of Senior Services. 2006. Alabama breaks ground for the first safe center for senior citizens. http://www.highbeam.com/doc/1P3-999762881.html.

Alexander, D. 2011. Disability and disaster. In *Handbook of hazards and disaster risk reduction*, ed. B. Wisner, J. C. Gaillar, and I. Kelman, 384–94. London: Routledge.

American Red Cross. 1997. *Disaster preparedness for people with disabilities*. Washington, DC: American Red Cross.

Brookings Institution. 2008. Iraq index: Tracking variables of reconstruction and security in post-Saddam Iraq, January 28. http://www.brookings.edu/saban/iraq-index.aspx.

Byrne, M., and E. A. Davis. 2005. Preparedness for all: Why including people with disabilities in drills is a learning tool: Interagency Chemical Exercise (I.C.E.). *IAEM Bulletin*, April.

Cabinet Office. 2011a. Strategic National Framework on community resilience. London: Cabinet Office. http://www.cabinetoffice.gov.uk/sites/default/files/resources/Strategic-National-Framework-on-Community-Resilience_0.pdf.

———. 2011b. Preparing for emergencies: Guide for communities. London: Cabinet Office. http://www.cabinetoffice.gov.uk/sites/default/files/resources/PFE-Guide-for-Communities_0.pdf.

California Office of Emergency Services. 2008. After action report—October 2007 wildfires: City of San Diego County response. http://www.sandiego.gov/mayor/pdf/fireafteraction.pdf.

California State Independent Living Council. 2004. The impact of Southern California wildfires on people with disabilities. Sacramento, April.

Davis, E., and J. Mincin. 2005. Incorporating special needs populations into emergency planning and exercises. Research and Training Center on Independent Living, University of Kansas.

Davis, E., and D. Sutherland. 2005. It's the law: Preparedness and people with disabilities. *International Association of Emergency Managers Bulletin* 22, no. 3.

DHS (U.S. Department of Homeland Security). 2006. About the Interagency Coordinating Council. *Emergency Preparedness Now*, no. 2 (Spring). http://www.dhs.gov/xlibrary/assets/icc-0506-progressreport.pdf.

DisabilityFundersNetwork.n.d.Disabilitystatsandfacts.http://www.disabilityfunders.org/disability-stats-and-facts.

DOJ (U.S. Department of Justice). 2007. ADA best practices toolkit for state and local governments. 7th installment of the toolkit. http://www.ada.gov/pcatoolkit/toolkitmain.htm.

DOL (U.S. Department of Labor). n.d. The ADA Amendments Act of 2008: Frequently asked questions. http://www.dol.gov/ofccp/regs/compliance/faqs/ADAfaqs.htm.

EEOC (U.S. Equal Employment Opportunity Commission). 2008. Veterans with service-connected disabilities in the workplace and the Americans with Disabilities Act (ADA). http://www1.eeoc.gov/facts/veterans-disabilities-employers.html.

Eitzen, D. S., and M. B. Zinn. 2003. *In conflict and order*. 10th ed. Boston: Allyn and Bacon.

Enders, A., and Z. Brandt. 2007. Using geographical information system technology to improve emergency management and disaster response for people with disabilities. *Journal of Disability Policy Studies* 17:223–29.

Erickson, W., C. Lee, and S. von Schrader. 2011. Disability statistics from the 2009 American Community Survey (ACS). Cornell University Rehabilitation Research and Training Center on Disability Demographics and Statistics (StatsRRTC), Ithaca, NY. http://www.disabilitystatistics.org.

FCC (U.S. Federal Communications Commission). n.d. FCC emergency communications guide. http://www.fcc.gov/guides/emergency-communications.

Feagin, J., and C. B. Feagin. 1997. *Social problems: A critical power-conflict perspective*. Upper Saddle River, NJ: Prentice Hall Publishing.

FEMA (Federal Emergency Management Agency). n.d. IPAWS: Access and functional needs. http://www.fema.gov/access-and-functional-needs-organizations.

———. 2008. 2008 Housing plan. http://www.catastrophereadinessclearinghouse.org/pdf/FEMA_dhp_08.pdf.

———. 2010. Guidance on planning for integration of functional needs support services in general population shelters. http://www.fema.gov/pdf/about/odic/fnss_guidance.pdf.

———. 2011. A whole community approach to emergency management: Principles, themes, and pathways for action. http://www.fema.gov/library/viewRecord.do?id=4941.

Fernandez, L. S., D. Byard, C. Lin, S. Benson, and J. A. Barbera. 2002. Frail elderly as disaster victims: Emergency management strategies. *Prehospital and Disaster Medicine*, April–June. http://www.gwu.edu/~icdrm/publications/67-74_fernandez.pdf.

GAO (U.S. Government Accountability Office). 2006. Disaster preparedness: Preliminary observations on the evacuation of hospitals and nursing homes due to hurricanes. http://www.gao.gov/new.items/d06443r.pdf.

———. 2008. National disaster response: FEMA should take action to improve capacity and coordination between government and voluntary sectors. http://www.gao.gov/new.items/d08369.pdf.

Gibson, M. J., and M. Hayunga. 2006. We can do better: Lessons learned for protecting older persons in disasters. AARP Public Policy Institute. http://assets.aarp.org/rgcenter/il/better.pdf.

Handicap International Nepal. 2009. Mainstreaming disability into disaster risk reduction: A training manual. Handicap International Nepal, Katmandu.

Heasley, S. 2011. More than 1 in 4 people with disabilities live in poverty. Disability Scoop. http://www.disabilityscoop.com/2011/09/14/more-1-in-4-poverty/13952/.

HelpAge International and Handicap International. 2012. A study of humanitarian financing for older people and people with disabilities, 2010–2011. Published by HelpAge International, London, and Handicap International, Lyon. http://www.helpage.org/what-we-do/emergencies/a-study-of-humanitarian-financing-for-older-people-and-people-with-disabilities/.

Hemingway, L., and M. Priestley. 2006. Natural hazards, human vulnerability and disabling societies: A disaster for disabled people? *Review of Disability Studies* 2 (3): 57–67.

Hubbard, S. 2004. Disability studies and health care curriculum: The great divide. *Journal of Allied Health*, (Fall).

IASC. 2007. IASC guidelines on mental health and psychosocial support in emergency settings. http://www.who.int/hac/network/interagency/news/mental_health_guidelines/en/index.html.

IDRM. 2005. IDRM regional report of Asia. http://www.ideanet.org/cir/uploads/File/CIR_IDRM_Asia_05.pdf.

JAN (Job Accommodation Network). n.d. http://www.jan.wvu.edu/.

Jones, N. 2006. CRS report for Congress: The Americans with Disabilities Act and emergency preparedness and response. http://www.fas.org/sgp/crs/homesec/RS22254.pdf.

Kailes, J. I. 2002. Emergency evacuation preparedness: Taking responsibility for your safety—A guide for people with disabilities and other activity limitations. Center for Disability and the Health Professions, Western University of Health Sciences, Pomona, CA.

Kessler Foundation/NOD. 2010. Kessler Foundation/NOD survey of employment of Americans with disabilities. http://nod.org/assets/downloads/01-2011_Exec_Summary.pdf.

Kipling J., R. Newton, and M. Ormerod. 2011. Accessing emergency rest centres in the UK: Lessons learnt. *International Journal of Disaster Resilience in the Built Environment* 2 (1): 47–58.

Knowles R., and B. Garrison. 2006. Planning for the elderly in natural disasters. *Disaster Recovery Journal* 19(4).

Leeds, M. H. 1990. *Rights and responsibilities: People with disabilities in employment and public accommodations.* New York: Mark H. Leeds, Esq.

Mackert, R., and E. Davis. 2002. Report on special needs: Issues, efforts and lessons learned. FEMA (February).

Maniotis, D. 2012. NYC Coastal Storm Shelter Plan: Hurricane Irene preparation and response. Presented at the National Hurricane Conference on March 29, 2012.

Mileti, D. 1999. *Disasters by design: A reassessment of natural disasters in the United States.* Washington, DC: Joseph Henry Press.

Mincin, J. 2012. Strengths and weakness of the U.S.-based refugee resettlement program: A survey of International Rescue Committee employee perceptions. UMI Dissertation Services Publishing.

NCD (National Council on Disability). 2006. The impact of Hurricanes Katrina and Rita on persons with disabilities: A look back and remaining challenges. National Council on Disability, Washington, DC. http://www.ncd.gov/publications/2006/Aug072006.

———. 2008. Quarterly meeting report: People with disabilities and emergency management. http://www.ncd.gov/publications/2008/08082008.

———. 2009a. Effective emergency management: Making improvements for communities and people with disabilities. http://www.ncd.gov/publications/2009/Aug122009.

———. 2009b. The current state of health care for people with disabilities. http://www.ncd.gov/publications/2009/Sept302009.

———. 2010. The state of housing in America in the 21st century: A disability perspective. http://www.ncd.gov/publications/2010/Jan192010.

NOD (National Organization on Disability). n.d. Emergency preparedness initiative's guide on the special needs of people with disabilities for emergency managers, planners, and responders. http://www.nod.org/index.cfm?fuseaction=Feature.showFeature&FeatureID=1034.

———. 2005a. Emergency preparedness survey report, Nov. 30. http://nod.org/about_us/our_history/annual_reports/2005_annual_report/.

———. 2005b. Report on special needs assessment for Katrina evacuees (SNAKE) project. September. http://www.nod.org/Resources/PDFs/katrina_snake_report.pdf.

Peek, L., and L. M. Stough. 2010. Children with disabilities in the context of disaster: A social vulnerability perspective. *Child Development* 81 (4): 1260–70.

Plan International. 2010. Child-centred disaster risk reduction: Building resilience through participation. Lessons from Plan International. Plan UK. *Savage v. City Place Ltd. Partnership*, 2004 WL 3045404 (Md. Cir. Ct. 2004).

Shakespeare, T., and N. Watson. 2002. The social model of disability: An outdated ideology? *Journal of Research in Social Science and Disability* 2:9–28. http://www.leeds.ac.uk/disability-studies/archiveuk/Shakespeare/social%20model%20of%20disability.pdf.

Sherry, N., and A. M. Harkins. 2011. Leveling the emergency preparedness playing field. *Journal of Emergency Management* 9 (6): 11–16.

Tatsuki, S., and N. Comafay. 2012. Counter disaster measures for people with functional needs in times of disaster in Japan: Achievements and challenges before and after the great east Japan earthquake and tsunami disaster. *Journal of Disaster Management* 1 (1): 35–60.

Tierney, K. J., W. J. Petak, and H. Hahn. 1988. *Disabled persons and earthquake hazards*. Boulder: Institute of Behavioral Science, University of Colorado.

Tokesky, G., and M. Weston. 2006. Impacts and contributions of older persons in emergency situations: A case study of Hurricane Katrina in the United States of America. Unpublished report. World Health Organization, Geneva.

Twigg, J., M. Kett, H. Bottomley, L. Tan, and H. Nasreddin. 2011. Disability and public shelter in emergencies. Environmental Hazards 10 (3–4): 248–61.

UNISDR. 2006. Developing early warning systems: A checklist. United Nations International Strategy for Disaster Reduction, Bonn, Germany. www.unisdr.org/2006/ppew/info-resources/ewc3/checklist/English.pdf.

Urban Institute. 2001. Barriers to and supports for work among adults with disabilities: Results from the NHIS-D. http://www.urban.org/UploadedPDF/adultswithdisabilities.pdf.

Veenema, T. G., ed. 2013. Identifying and accommodating high-risk and high-vulnerability populations. Chapter 16 in *Disaster nursing and emergency preparedness for chemical, biological and radiological terrorism and other hazards*. Scheduled 3rd ed. New York: Springer.

Verona Charter. 2007. "Verona Charter" on the rescue of persons with disabilities in case of disasters: Declaration of the participants in the Consensus Conference held in Verona on 8–9 November 2007. http://www.eena.org/ressource/static/files/Verona%20Charter%20Endorsement%20form.pdf.

The Washington Post, Kaiser Family Foundation, and Harvard University. 2005. Survey of Hurricane Katrina evacuees. www.kff.org/newsmedia/upload/7401.pdf.

White, G. W., M. H. Fox, C. Rooney, and A. Cahill. 2007. Assessing the impact of Hurricane Katrina on persons with disabilities. Center on Independent Living/National Institute on Disability and Rehabilitation Research, University of Kansas.

White, G. W., M. H. Fox, C. Rooney, and J. Rowland. 2007. Final report findings of nobody left behind: Preparedness for persons with mobility impairments research project. Research and Training Center on Independent Living, Lawrence, KS. http://www.nobodyleftbehind2.org/~rrtcpbs/findings/.

WHO. 2011. World report on disability. World Health Organization, Geneva. http://www.who.int/disabilities/world_report/2011/en/index.html.

Women's Commission on Refugee Women and Children, June 2008. Disabilities among Refugees and conflict-affected populations. Accessed on December 3, 2012 at http://womensrefugeecommission.org/programs/disabilities/supporting-the-voices-of-refugees-with-disabilities.

RESOURCES

- Working with People with Disabilities. This is a training by the Baltimore County Fire Department and the Baltimore County Commission on Disabilities and is available on DVD. It is aimed at helping organizations work more effectively and compassionately with persons with disabilities. http://www.baltimorecountymd.gov/Agencies/fire/fire_academy/communityoutreach/DisabilitiesGuide.html.

- Community Emergency Preparedness Information Network (CEPIN) has been a FEMA training partner since 2004, developing and delivering U.S. Department of Homeland Security (DHS) certified courses on emergency and disaster preparedness for the deaf, hard of hearing, and deaf-blind. They offer additional information and services at http://www.cepintdi.org/.

- The Communication Picture Board was designed to help bridge the communication gap between emergency first responders and people who are deaf. The picture board is proven to also effectively enhance the communications needs between first responders and non-English speaking populations, children, people with developmental disabilities, as well as those impacted by a traumatic event. These boards are helpful in a variety of settings: in the field, on an ambulance, in a shelter, at an assistance center, etc. http://www.eadassociates.com/products.html#cpb.
- EAD & Associates, LLC Readiness Wheels designed to help seniors and people with disabilities get better prepared for all kinds of disasters. Also offer wheels on family and pet preparedness. The two-sided emergency preparedness wheels are sturdy, easy-to-use, and magnetized. They provide guidance on getting prepared and how to respond when a disaster occurs. http://www.emergencywheels.com.
- FCC Consumer Guide: Emergency Video Programming Accessibility to Persons with Hearing and Visual Disabilities. http://www.fcc.gov/guides/emergency-video-programming-accessibility-persons-hearing-and-visual-disabilities.
- Fire Safety for Staff Working with Individuals with Development Disabilities is a DVD/DC-ROM workbook set developed by the NYC Fire Department and the YAI Network. https://secure2.convio.net/yai/site/Ecommerce/1266361297?VIEW_PRODUCT=true&product_id=2101&store_id=1781.
- International Disability and Development Consortium (IDDC) aims to promote inclusive development worldwide. It has a focal point on conflict and emergencies, and publishes reports and guidance. http://www.iddcconsortium.net/joomla/.
- Job Accommodation Network (JAN) is a service of the Office of Disability Employment Policy (ODEP) of the U.S. Department of Labor. It is a free consulting service designed to increase the employability of people with disabilities by providing individualized worksite accommodations solutions, providing technical assistance regarding the ADA and other disability-related legislation, and educating callers about self-employment options. http://www.jan.wvu.edu/.
- Language Guidelines for Inclusive Emergency Preparedness, Response, Mitigation, and Recovery. The Office of Disability Integration and Coordination at FEMA provides guidance on utilizing inclusive language. http://www.fema.gov/office-disability-integration-coordination/office-disability-integration-coordination/office-1.
- National Center for Accessible Media—The Access to Emergency Alerts project unites emergency-alert providers, local information resources, telecommunications industry and public broadcasting representatives, and consumers in a collaborative effort to research and disseminate replicable approaches to make emergency warnings accessible. The website provides information on developments and resources in this topic area. http://ncam.wgbh.org/invent_build/analog/alerts/.
- National Fire Protection Association (NFPA) is the world's leading advocate of fire prevention and an authoritative source on public safety. NFPA develops, publishes, and disseminates more than 300 consensus codes and standards intended to minimize the possibility and effects of fire and other risks. General website is found at http://www.nfpa.org/index.asp?cookie%5Ftest=1. In addition, the NFPA has a newsletter, e-Access, designed to help reduce the worldwide burden of fire and other hazards on the quality of life for people with disabilities, which can be found at http://ebm.e.nfpa.org/r/regf2?aid=272412627&n=300&a=0.
- Nobody Left Behind Materials: Disaster Preparedness for People with Mobility Disabilities provides in-depth research, information, and resources designed for both consumers and emergency planners. http://www.nobodyleftbehind2.org/.
- The American Red Cross website provides preparedness information geared toward people with disabilities. http://www.prepare.org/home/.

- U.S. FEMA's preparedness website includes specific information and guidance on getting prepared for disasters that includes families, pets, and businesses. www.ready.gov.
- Resources on Emergency Evacuation and Disaster Preparedness is provided by the United States Access Board, which provides guidelines for facilities that address means of egress that are accessible to persons with disabilities. This website presents an overview of these design requirements. Also included are links to information developed by other organizations on evacuation planning and disaster preparedness. http://www.access-board.gov/evac.htm.
- Tips for First Responders is a computer application that provides guidance to first responders for providing service and assistance to people with disabilities. http://disabilitytips.tamu.edu/. Also available in hard copy through the University of New Mexico's Center for Development and Disability (who first developed the concept) at http://cdd.unm.edu/dhpd/tips.asp.

9 Health

*Deborah S. K. Thomas, Mary Shannon Newell,
and Debra Kreisberg*

CONTENTS

9.1   CHAPTER PURPOSE

As a fundamental human right, a healthy quality of life translates to safety and well-being throughout the disaster life cycle. In this chapter, health is treated as a broad concept that extends beyond the existence of disease and considers its implications for emergency management. In one respect, health is a condition that is superimposed upon other characteristics, such as gender, age, race, or class, but it is also an indicator of vulnerability. Additionally, health status is also linked to the health-care and public health systems, both of which also act as critical infrastructure and are directly relevant to a discussion of vulnerability. This chapter explores these relationships to further an understanding of the health aspects of vulnerability.

9.2   OBJECTIVES

As a result of this chapter, you should be able to:

1. Understand and identify issues specific to health and how they relate to vulnerability
2. Define terms used during disasters by the health community and understand the relevance of those definitions in the context of emergency management and disasters
3. Critically assess traditional emergency management approaches to addressing health during disasters
4. Understand health as a factor of resiliency
5. Describe strategies for integrating health concerns throughout all phases of emergency management
6. Discuss ways to conduct community outreach with health stakeholders

9.3   INTRODUCTION

Health as a condition is yet another factor contributing to and illuminating social vulnerability, both prior to and after an event. Health status reveals much about susceptible populations, as well as potential special-needs groups. Unlike many of the other characteristics discussed so far, however, it also has other dimensions that directly affect keeping people safe and increasing resilience. Disease can increase vulnerability, but as an agent it can also act as an event causing an outbreak of a deadly infection (a public health emergency). Additionally, the health-care and public health systems are critical infrastructure, the viability of which directly increases or decreases people's vulnerability. As a consequence, this chapter will address a slightly broader set of issues than other topical chapters, while still following the same overall format. After setting the context, the discussion will turn to health across the disaster cycle using an all-hazards approach, followed by some ideas for strategies and solutions for increasing capacity and resilience.

9.4   DEFINITIONS AND CONCEPTS

Health is perhaps not as easy to define as one might at first assume. Consider for a moment how people would answer if asked whether they felt healthy and what it means to be healthy. Some people might respond that they are a little sick with a cold or even are extremely tired. Others might say they feel healthy even though they have a chronic illness, such as high blood pressure, arthritis, asthma, or diabetes. Still others might mention happiness. The wide range of potential subjective interpretations captures the many facets of health and the challenges for assigning strict meaning related only to disease.

The World Health Organization's definition adopted in 1948 stands as a comprehensive and accepted definition: "Health is a state of complete physical, mental and social well-being and not merely the absence of disease or infirmity" (WHO 1948). This encompasses many aspects of health in addition to sickness, illness, or injury and embodies a broad set of considerations, implying that treatment of the individual alone is not the only solution to achieve healthy people and communities. Yet, even until the late 1970s, the Western paradigm emphasized the absence of disease and injury, a perspective that in some regards persists today if the focus does not extend beyond personal, clinical, or medical treatment.

Boorse (1977) argues that defining health by the absence of disease is particularly problematic because definitions of disease can be expanded almost infinitely so that everyone would really have some deficiency. Further, everyone will have some form of illness, probably numerous times, throughout a lifetime. However, this does not necessarily translate to a disability or even limited functionality. Having the common cold each year, or even multiple times a year, would not be considered a chronic illness, but certainly translates to a person being unhealthy for that period of time and possibly (or not) missing work or school and potentially requiring some medications. In other words, health as a condition encompasses both acute (rapid onset and progression) and chronic illness (persists for a long period of time and may have continued progression), as well as daily conditions of well-being. As a consequence, it is challenging to discern when everyday experiences transform from healthy to unhealthy.

In addition to taking an unnecessarily narrow view of absence of disease to mean health, its assessment based on averages or norms can be equally as limiting. Society determines what is normal, both cognitively and physically. As such, healthy versus unhealthy is commonly delineated by an average of occurrence or a judgment of what is functionally normal in a given setting or by a particular group (see Chapter 8 on disabilities, which emphasizes a functional approach). While it is important to have culturally specific definitions of health, just because a certain condition is prevalent, pervasive, and common does not mean that health should be measured from this statistical average. Janzen uses the example of malnutrition to illustrate this point; "if a society has widespread malnutrition the statistical norm for height and weight might not be healthy if a cross-society measure or norm is used" (Janzen 2002, 69). Having said this, utilizing statistical measures, with explicit consideration for appropriateness within the context, is incredibly useful for evaluating and understanding health. (See Section 9.5, which uses some measures to illustrate health status, especially as it relates to vulnerability.)

In 1978, the WHO reaffirmed the 1948 broad definition of health in the Alma Ata Declaration, which extended health as a "fundamental human right" that is "a most important world-wide social goal whose realization requires the action of many other social and economic sectors in addition to the health sector" (WHO 1978, Article 1). Thus, health also relates directly to a certain quality of life and a standard of living, not just to an individual's disease and injury characteristics or to biological considerations. While some argue that this definition is too broad, it does capture vital aspects for appreciating how we come to understand health and health outcomes.

Not all health status is attributable to our genetic makeup, our individual characteristics, or even behavior; evidence and research increasingly point to social contributors and conditions as well. In other words, our health is a function of our individual traits along with the types of places and conditions in which we live, as well as our standing in society. In short, genetics and individual characteristics alone do not determine the likelihood of developing a particular disease; many contextual variables directly affect the level of health as well. For example, nonhealth infrastructure also keeps people healthy. As an illustration, in most parts of the United States people can drink clean tap water delivered directly to homes, and sewage systems minimize human contact with wastewater. These basic services are not necessarily considered part of the health infrastructure (indeed, they are part of the urban infrastructure), yet they save thousands of lives and reduce illness significantly by decreasing the spread of disease that would otherwise occur through contaminated water supplies. In fact, health "is maintained by a cushion of adequate nutrition, social support, water supply, housing, sanitation, and continued collective defense against contagious and degenerative disease" (Feierman and Janzen 1992, xvii).

These relationships are captured by the ecological model of health, which acknowledges and incorporates the many dimensions, interrelationships, and influences that contribute to health. Health professionals, particularly in public health, require a fundamental understanding of this approach (Gebbie, Rosenstock, and Hernandez 2003). Biological risk factors, including the biology of disease and individual traits, are embedded within broader environmental, social, and behavioral factors and influences. In other words, we exist within a series of social, political, and economic networks and systems, all of which contribute to our well-being and health. Further, health requires treatment of individual conditions, but also attention to population and community health, as well as the social, economic, and political structures that directly affect health. According to Janzen (2002), understanding health should "include alongside the factors in the ecology of health the impact of household budget priorities, larger economic factors, and above all social and political institutions and forces" (Janzen 2002, 80). While genetics, our immediate environment, and individual behavior and characteristics certainly contribute to our health status, social conditions and structural considerations also come to bear on how healthy we are (see discussion of structure and agency in Chapter 2).

9.5 DEMOGRAPHIC OVERVIEW

A brief review of some statistics begins to illuminate how health is a condition that should be considered in emergency management, as well as how diseases themselves can act as a disaster. Importantly, disease burdens are not the same among all groups of people across social or economic conditions, revealing disparity that is not just linked to biology or risk. Health disparity is also a reflection of quality of life considerations linked to differential health and vulnerability status. Examining the leading causes of mortality worldwide and in the U.S. provides a backdrop to delve into further detail about the interrelationship between health, vulnerability, and disasters.

Globally, a distinct difference exists in the leading causes of death between high-income and low-income countries (Table 9.1). Overall, many more people die from infectious diseases and at younger ages in low-income counties. Surprising to some, the burden of chronic disease in low-income countries is also quite high, with heart disease and stroke taking millions of lives. High-income countries, on the other hand, experience mortality primarily from chronic diseases, and populations are often aging. In fact, the geographic variation is just as revealing (Figure 9.1), with the shortest life expectancies in sub-Saharan Africa and Afghanistan, ranging from 47 to 58 years, ages still considered quite young in many developed countries, which have life expectancies into the late 70s and early 80s. China has quite long life expectancies (86 and 80 for women and men, respectively), while Russia is somewhat lower than might be expected, particularly for men at 63 (women are at 75).

While it is true that everyone will die of something, the stark differences in causes of death do speak to the realities of life in these places. For example, taking just one example off of the list of leading causes of mortality, diarrhea kills more than 1.9 million children a year, mostly from resulting dehydration (WHO 2011). This is highly treatable with oral rehydration salts for a cost of only about 10 cents (WHO 2006), and so while more than a million children are saved each year and programs are expanding, millions are still dying, mostly in low-income countries. An inexpensive treatment exists; thus, the reason millions still die cannot be attributed to the lack of a medical intervention. Instead, the challenges revolve around availability, access, awareness and education, distribution, and acceptability, all of which are embedded in cultural, social, and economic systems as linked to health.

TABLE 9.1
Worldwide Leading Causes of Mortality

Ranking	Low-Income Countries	High-Income Countries
1	Lower respiratory infections (1.05 or 11.3%)	Ischemic heart disease (1.42 or 15.6%)
2	Diarrheal diseases (0.76 or 8.2%)	Stroke and other cerebrovascular diseases (0.79 or 8.7%)
3	HIV/AIDS (0.72 or 7.8%)	Trachea, bronchus, lung cancers (0.54 or 5.9%)
4	Ischemic heart disease (0.57 or 6.1%)	Alzheimer and other dementias (0.37 or 4.1%)
5	Malaria (0.48 or 5.2%)	Lower respiratory infections (0.35 or 3.8%)
6	Stroke and other cerebrovascular diseases (0.45 or 4.9%)	Chronic obstructive pulmonary disease (0.32 or 3.5%)
7	Tuberculosis (0.40 or 4.3%)	Colon and rectum cancers (0.30 or 3.3%)
8	Prematurity and low birth weight (0.03 or 3.2%)	Diabetes mellitus (0.24 or 2.6%)
9	Birth asphyxia and birth trauma (0.27 or 2.9%)	Hypertensive heart disease (0.21 or 2.3%)
10	Neonatal infections (0.24 or 2.6%)	Breast cancer (0.17 or 1.9%)

Source: WHO (2011).

Note: The number in parentheses is the number of deaths in millions. Income categories are based on 2008 groupings, and middle-income countries are not represented.

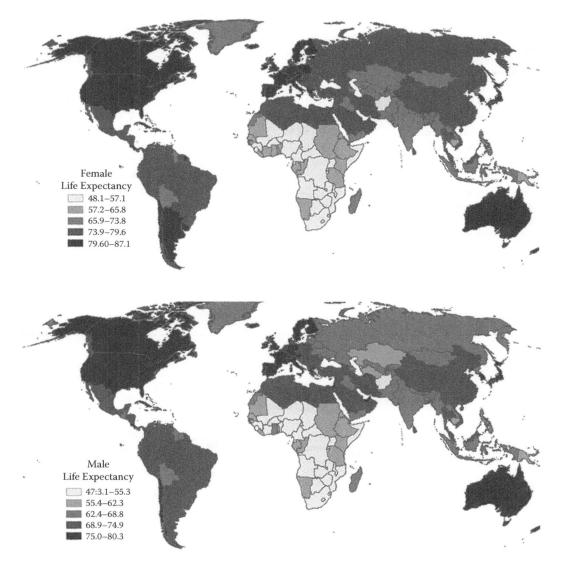

FIGURE 9.1 Global life expectancy at birth. (*Source*: United Nations, Department of Economic and Social Affairs, Population Division [2011], World Population Prospects: The 2010 Revision. http://www.un.org/esa/population/unpop.htm.)

In the United States, the leading causes of mortality are similar to high-income countries with some notable differences, partly due to consolidating all types of cancer into a single category (Table 9.2). However, a significant number of deaths are attributable to accidents, more aligned with low-income countries. Importantly, the causes of death are not quite the same for all segments of the population. The numbers are presented by gender and for whites and blacks to illustrate the point that overall numbers can mask the experiences of subpopulations. The graph of longevity across the United States also reveals stark regional variation (Figure 9.2), with the shortest life expectancies for black men and the longest for white women. Overall, life expectancies have increased over time for all groups, with the gap between the longest and shortest decreasing. Life expectancy varies for men and women with a difference of about 12 years between the shortest life expectancy for men in Mississippi (70.4 years of age) and the longest for women in Hawaii (82.5 years of age).

TABLE 9.2
CDC Leading Causes of Death, 2008

Cause of Death	All	Male	Female	White	Black
Diseases of heart	1 (25.0%)	1 (25.4%)	1 (24.5%)	1 (25.1%)	1 (24.5%)
Malignant neoplasms (cancer)	2 (22.9%)	2 (24.1%)	2 (21.7%)	2 (22.9%)	2 (22.1%)
Chronic lower respiratory diseases	3 (5.7%)	4 (5.5%)	4 (5.9%)	3 (6.1%)	6 (3.0%)
Cerebrovascular diseases (stroke)	4 (5.4%)	5 (4.4%)	3 (6.5%)	4 (5.3%)	3 (5.8%)
Accidents (unintentional injuries)	5 (4.9%)	3 (6.4%)	6 (3.5%)	5 (5.0%)	4 (4.3%)
Alzheimer's disease	6 (3.3%)	9 (2.0%)	5 (4.6%)	6 (3.6%)	—
Diabetes mellitus	7 (2.9%)	6 (2.9%)	7 (2.8%)	6 (2.6%)	5 (4.2%)
Influenza and pneumonia	8 (2.3%)	8 (2.1%)	8 (2.5%)	8 (2.3%)	—
Nephritis, nephritic syndrome, and nephrosis (kidney disease)	9 (2.0%)	10 (1.9%)	9 (2.0%)	9 (1.8%)	7 (3.0%)
Intentional self-harm (suicide)	10 (1.5%)	7 (2.3%)		10 (1.5%)	—
Septicemia			10 (1.6%)		9 (2.2%)
Assault (homicide)					8 (2.9%)
Human immunodeficiency virus (HIV) disease					10 (2.0%)

Source: Heron (2012).
Note: Percentages represent total deaths in that group due to the cause indicated.

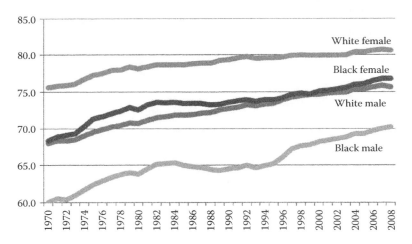

FIGURE 9.2 U.S. expectation of life at birth, 1960–2008. (*Source*: U.S. National Center for Health Statistics, National Vital Statistics Reports [NVSR], Deaths: Preliminary Data for 2008, Vol. 59, No. 2, December 9, 2010.)

Focusing on the direct impacts of disasters as a cause of death also highlights variation in vulnerability. Stark regional patterns exist globally (Figure 9.3). Capturing a global pattern of vulnerability, the OFDA/CRED International Database compiles current and historical information on disaster impacts around the world based on a standardized data collection methodology (EM-DAT 2012). Importantly, these only represent relatively large events, ones that kill more than 10 people, affect 100 people, have a declaration of a state of emergency, or have a call for international assistance. As such, this is not a complete depiction and is further limited because no details about the types of people affected (gender, age, or minority status) are compiled, mostly because this information is not commonly reported. Still, general trends can be detected, giving some insights into vulnerability and establishing further questions for investigation.

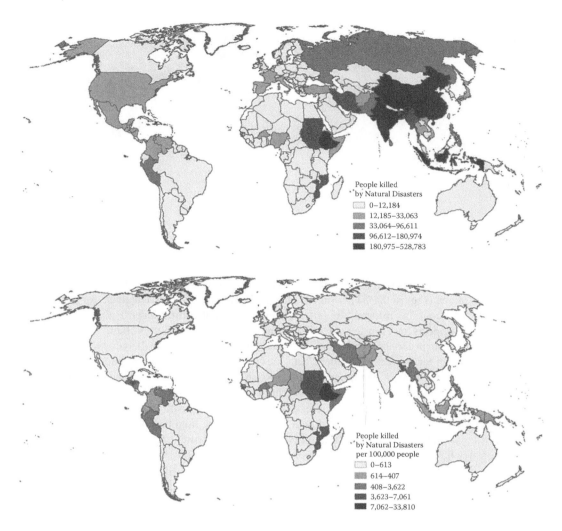

FIGURE 9.3 Worldwide disaster fatalities from natural disasters, 1970–2011. Natural events include: drought, earthquake, epidemic, extreme temperature, flood, insect infestation, mass movement dry, mass movement wet, storm, volcano, and wildfire. (*Source*: EM-DAT: The OFDA/CRED International Disaster Database. www.emdat.be. Université Catholique de Louvain, Brussels, Belgium.)

During the time period from 1970, earthquakes killed the most people (1,305,269), followed by storms (792,058), drought (677,621), and floods (266,427), and then epidemics (217,744). Asia and Africa have the highest numbers of deaths from natural disasters regionally, but the types of events are different. Focusing on the countries in the highest two categories, China, Indonesia (the 2000 tsunami), and Iran experience significant fatalities from earthquakes, with flooding also of importance in China. By contrast, in Sudan and Ethiopia in Africa, deaths stem from drought and epidemics. Indian disaster fatalities result from earthquakes and flooding, while in Bangladesh most people perish from storms (typhoons) and flooding, as well as epidemics. Overall, lower-income countries have much higher death rates from disasters than higher-income countries. Of the more than 3 million people who died from disasters during this period as recorded in EM-DAT, only 15,729 occurred in the United States, a lower figure in alignment with other high-income countries. Those regions of the world that have the shortest life expectancies experience the highest fatalities from natural disasters per 100,000 people.

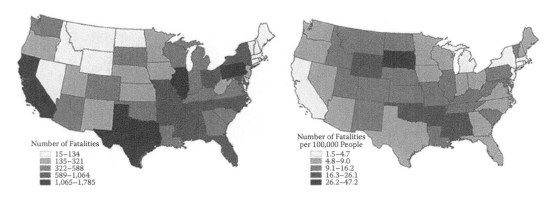

FIGURE 9.4 U.S. hazard fatalities for U.S. lower 48 states, 1970–2011. (*Source*: Hazards & Vulnerability Research Institute. 2012. The spatial hazard events and losses database for the United States [SHELDUS], version 9.0 [online database]. http://webra.cas.sc.edu/hvri/products/sheldus.aspx.)

A different database allows a more detailed picture of hazard fatalities at the subnational level for the United States (Figure 9.4). The Spatial Hazard Events and Losses Database for the United States (SHELDUS) contains information on 18 different types of natural hazards that caused more than $50,000 in property or crop loss or at least one death (Hazards and Vulnerability Research Institute 2012). Not surprisingly, deaths and injuries are not uniformly distributed, either regionally or by hazard type. In terms of raw numbers, fatalities are concentrated in the South/Southeast, the Great Lakes, and California. When taken as a proportion of the population, the pattern shifts to the Midwest and Intermountain West and is even further concentrated in the deep western Gulf States and along the Mississippi River Valley. Interestingly, flooding, heat, and winter weather caused the most fatalities, distinctive from the international experience. One might assume the variation exists because particular hazards occur less frequently. However, the United States does not necessarily experience fewer hazard types or events per area, but rather the interaction of social vulnerability with hazards is different. For example, in the case of earthquakes, California did experience major events in populated areas, in Loma Prieta in 1989 and again in Northridge in 1994, neither of which resulted in substantial deaths, unlike some international experiences with earthquakes that have killed tens of thousands of people in recent decades. Consequently, evidence again points to social vulnerability as driving factors for this disparate outcome.

This overview highlights some key issues around health and vulnerability, illustrating how they are intrinsically linked, both in terms of the direct effects on people's lives and the association between disparities in health outcomes and vulnerability. Additionally, while these data can suggest patterns and relationships, the importance of delving further into aggregate numbers is clearly demonstrated: A pattern at the global level may or may not persist at finer scales, or overall rates may not be applicable to subgroups or equivalent between groups. Monitoring and assessing health and vulnerability requires standardized data collection in disaggregate form, but information is not always collected, recorded, and/or disseminated by various population groups' stratifications. This brief review demonstrates the relevance and necessity of integrating the health topic into emergency management planning and response processes.

9.6 RELEVANCE

The discussion around health likely resonates with the constructs of social vulnerability presented in previous chapters, particularly Chapters 1 and 2. A stream of research in health, in fact, parallels that of vulnerability science, and is concerned with quite similar factors in the exploration of the determinants of health: those underlying characteristics, circumstances, and situations that contribute to health outcomes (Lindsay 2003). Social determinants of health broadly include social, economic, and environmental conditions affecting health. Evidence points to a wide range of community characteristics that directly link to health status, such as the configuration of the built environment, access to quality and appropriate health-care services, transportation systems, accessibility to quality food sources, economic opportunities, and environmental quality (Berkman and Kawachi 2000). Social determinants are a relatively recent acknowledgment within the health community, recognizing that there are significant influences in addition to health factors (personal health practices and behaviors, genetics, and medical care coverage). These are often beyond an individual's control and are potentially more influential in determining the health experience of a person across the life course. For example, simply being born in a poor and less educated family forms "a dynamic process that affects lifetime opportunities," such as educational opportunities, and contributes to the increased likelihood of becoming obese or a smoker (Marmot and Wilkinson 1999, 47). In addition to both social determinants and health factors, there are subpopulation groups that disproportionately bear the burden of poor health outcomes based upon another set of considerations, known as health disparities.

Health disparities are typically identified by inequities in mortality and morbidity rates, quality of life, and life expectancy that are stratified by population characteristics such as race, ethnicity, religion, gender, age, sexual orientation, and geography (Carter-Pokras and Baquet 2002; Colorado Department of Health and Human Services 2010). All of these characteristics contribute to what is known as health equity (Braveman and Gruskin 2003). Unfortunately, like with data challenges for the examination of disaggregate effects and outcomes from disaster impacts, data limitations also exist in health records and surveillance systems for fully documenting and assessing inequities in health status and outcomes (Ver Ploeg and Perrin 2004). In order to reduce these, a research agenda must be established around detecting, understanding, and reducing disparities (Kilbourne et al. 2006), an approach necessary for decreasing social vulnerability and increasing resilience as well. In 2008, the WHO published recommendations to improve the conditions that foster health inequity. These include: (1) improving daily living conditions that emphasize early childhood development, health-care access, and economic security; (2) addressing inequities in the distribution of political power and resources; and (3) developing and implementing surveillance systems and ways to measure these inequalities (WHO 2008a). While these are broad goals reflective of world conditions, there certainly remain elements of these challenges within both geographical locations and population groups in United States. These international recommendations complement the U.S. Institute of Medicines health-care-specific goals to reduce health inequities (Institute of Medicine 2003). Ultimately, disasters exacerbate these preexisting imbalances in health, often making it impossible for certain groups to recover from a severe event.

Building on the health ecology model, Figure 9.5 illustrates the interplay between contextual factors and the individual that affect vulnerability as associated with disasters as well as health status. Individual traits and characteristics contribute to health status and vulnerability, as do the capital investments (presented in Chapters 2 and 3) that support and influence a person. In this way, a person who has individual characteristics that might suggest high vulnerability or poor health status may actually have access to resources and infrastructure that could improve overall level of health and increase resilience. Additionally, this model recognizes structural influences that exist at larger scales, often beyond an individual's control (see discussion of agency and structure in Chapter 2), but which affect one's circumstances. Health and vulnerability do not just result from one single aspect of these interrelationships, but rather interactions among them at and between levels/scales.

In essence, this all means that the social, economic, and environmental circumstances of a place have direct and indirect effects on individual and community health (Brennan Ramirez, Baker, and Metzler 2008). By extension, because these conditions vary significantly, they likely play a part in explaining observed differences in health outcomes across various populations and places (Braveman and Gruskin 2003). Even though significant numbers of studies have started to establish the multilevel influences on health, these linkages and influences are not always well understood,

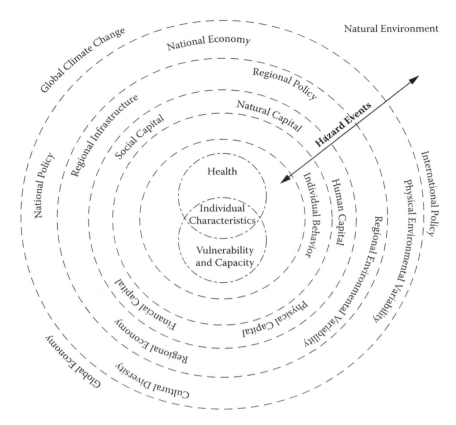

FIGURE 9.5 Model of factors contributing to vulnerability and health. (*Source*: Thomas, D, J. Scandlyn, J. Brett, and K. Oviatt. With permission.)

requiring additional inquiry. Like vulnerability expressing itself differentially throughout subpopulations and, as a consequence, hazards impacting various groups disproportionately, the existence of health disparities is well established (Ver Ploeg and Perrin 2004; Marmot 2005). Continuing to find mechanisms by which to accurately measure these differences and develop interventions that reduce them, particularly where they have implications for disaster mitigation, remains a global imperative for improving population health for its own sake and also for reducing the impacts of disasters.

9.7 VULNERABILITY ACROSS THE DISASTER LIFE CYCLE

Health and vulnerability are integrally related on many levels, including similarities in streams of research into underlying factors; disparities that exist between groups, creating differential experiences; and the link between agency and structure. Keeping people healthy and safe during and after an event is crucial, which requires planning in advance and considering the current state of health. In addition, health itself can be the source of a disaster, such as a disease outbreak or through bioterrorism. As such, understanding and addressing the interrelationships between health and vulnerability is vital for emergency management. The next part of this chapter directly addresses emerging issues related to health across the disaster life cycle, reviewing the following areas:

1. Health as a reflection of vulnerability
2. International health experiences and humanitarian assistance
3. Current health challenges in the United States

4. The integration of public health and health-care sectors with emergency management
5. Health impacted by disasters and considerations for evacuation, warning, and response
6. Health as part of the recovery process

9.7.1 HEALTH AS A REFLECTION OF VULNERABILITY

Those characteristics and factors that create differential exposure to, and experiences with, hazards are often the very same as those identified in considering social determinants of health and health disparities. As a consequence, not only is health an overlay with other characteristics, such as gender, age, or income status, that must be considered for disaster planning, it is also a reflection of underlying factors that contribute to vulnerability.

Utilizing health data to support public health and health-care preparedness, response, and recovery (see Section 9.7.3 for discussion of these sectors in the United States) is a process that is becoming more readily used for disaster vulnerability assessments. For example, Holt et al. (2008) illustrated the use of the Centers for Disease Control (CDC)'s Behavioral Risk Factor Surveillance System (BRFSS) to assess health status along with the American Hospital Association Annual Survey Database to establish health-care resources in a geographic information systems (GIS) environment for response planning. (See Chapter 16.9 for a brief review of these technologies for vulnerability assessment.) Established in 1984, the BRFSS is "a state-based system of health surveys that collects information on health risk behaviors, preventive health practices, and health care access primarily related to chronic disease and injury" (CDC 2008a), which can provide insights into community health not otherwise available. Thus, these types of data, along with other innovative health information sources, can aid in incorporating health concerns into emergency management and public health preparedness.

A portion of an assessment conducted in 2006 of patient need and gaps in service for Salud Family Health Centers (Salud) illustrates this association (de Jesus Diaz-Perez, Thomas, and Farley 2007). Salud is a federally qualified community and migrant health center system providing services in six counties in northeastern Colorado to indigent, uninsured, underinsured, migrant, and seasonal farmworker populations. Part of the evaluation involved developing a description of health-care need in the region based on a set of variables and approaches defined by previous research (Wang and Luo 2005; Luo and Wang 2003). While this study is embedded within an evaluation of various aspects of health-care access, the purpose here is to illustrate similarities between defining health-care need and understanding vulnerability. (See Chapter 14 for a more detailed discussion of vulnerability assessment.)

To define populations with higher needs, data from the U.S. Census were compiled based on broad categories and then statistically analyzed using a factor analysis, which combines data and condenses variables into similar groupings. The analysis condensed 13 census variables into three broad categories: sociocultural barriers, socioeconomic disadvantages, and isolation (Figure 9.6). From these, a composite score was calculated to determine health-care need based upon output from the statistical analysis; a block group with no scores (factor loadings) for the three broad categories in the upper quartile was considered low need, and block groups were defined as high if at least one score was in the upper quartile and none were in the lowest. The composite map displays areas with an aggregate of conditions and characteristics converging to reveal health need. The results can then inform health policy and even aid in locating additional health services.

So, while this evaluation of social indicators was developed to inform health policy and health-care delivery explicitly tied to health equity, similar approaches can also be used for incorporating vulnerable populations into emergency and disaster planning. Illustrating this association, a statewide cultural vulnerability analysis was conducted for Colorado in 2011, identifying vulnerable populations for hospital disaster preparedness planning (Kreisberg et al. 2011).

Data from the 2010 U.S. Census and American Community Survey (see Chapter 16) were compiled based on broad categories (Table 9.3). These data were then aligned with the location of hospital trauma centers to inform hospital cultural competencies for disaster preparedness planning.

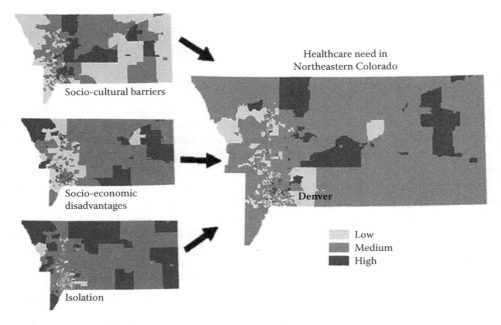

FIGURE 9.6 Health needs in northeastern Colorado. (*Source*: de Jesus Diaz-Perez, Thomas, and Farley [2007]. With permission.)

TABLE 9.3
Variables Compiled from the U.S. 2010 Census and American Community Survey

Category	Variable from 2000 U.S. Census at Tract Level	Denominator
Groups in high need of services	Seniors (age 65+)	Total population
	Children (age 0–14)	Total population
	Women of reproductive age (age 14–44)	Total population
	People living in group quarters	Total population
Socioeconomic status	Poverty (families and nonfamilies below poverty)	Families
	Female-headed households	Households
	Home ownership	Homes
	Median income	None
Indicators of deprived environment	Households with more than one occupant per room	Households
	Housing without basic amenities	Homes
Indicators of cultural and linguistic barriers and awareness	Population without high school diploma	Total population
	Linguistically isolated households	Households
	Hispanic population	Total population
	Non-white minority	Total population
Transportation mobility	Households without vehicles	Households

Ninety-three trauma centers were utilized based upon an inventory maintained by the Colorado Department of Public Health and the Environment (CDPHE 2012). Geographic service areas were calculated for each trauma center through a network analysis in the GIS, each one reflecting the shortest distance from a given location to a trauma center based on the physical location of the facility and the Colorado road network. Once the service areas were derived, the social vulnerability indicators were reaggregated to them to more adequately inform hospital emergency planners about the characteristics of the population that might need services in the time of disaster. As an example

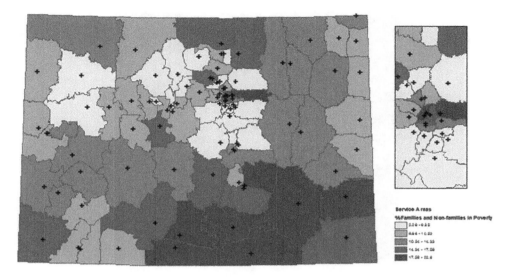

FIGURE 9.7 Families and households living in poverty by hospital service area in Colorado. (Created by Deborah Thomas and Eben Dennis. *Source*: Kreisberg et al. [2011].)

of one of the data variables, the percentage of people living in poverty is shown in Figure 9.7, revealing strong regional patterns and differences between hospital trauma center service areas.

9.7.2 INTERNATIONAL CONTEXT

> The earthquake was another reminder of the weakness of Haiti's public institutions and the vulnerability of its population without any kind of safety net. Into the breach have come humanitarian groups . . . but whether such goodwill can be converted into substantial reconstruction projects that grow the Haitian economy . . . remains to be seen. (Paul Farmer 2011, 139)

According to PAHO (2000), all disasters (in developing and developed countries) have common health challenges, including social reactions, communicable diseases, population displacements, climatic exposure, food and nutrition, water supply and sanitation, mental health, and damage to the health infrastructure. Unfortunately, many disaster myths are perpetuated that are, on the whole, not true and are detrimental to preparedness and response efforts (de Ville de Goyet 1999, 2000; Eberwine, D. 2005). For example, when an event occurs, it is entirely normal to have both individual and social reactions; however, this generally does not result in panic or shock, but rather people spontaneously organizing to address local needs. Additionally, disasters generally do not bring out the worst in human behavior and do not usually result in looting or rioting. It is important to recognize that people may have conflicting responsibilities, say to children, family and work, but this is not a deviant behavior.

In terms of health impacts, mass disease outbreaks and epidemics in the aftermath of an event are not inevitable. Most disease transmission can be attributed to fecal contamination of water and food, so ensuring a source of clean drinking water and mechanisms for sanitation is essential. Disruptions to water supply and sanitation systems pose serious health risks. Food shortages can be quite common, resulting from destruction of the actual food supply or the food distribution system.

Often, outbreaks are attributable to population density and displacement, and so refugees or people living in camps are potentially at greater risk (see Photo 9.1). In fact, refugee and migrant populations are a particularly vulnerable population for a variety of reasons. For example, violence against women often increases in refugee camps. Thus, disaster evacuation and population displacement requires careful emergency response attention, and disaster preparedness for refugee camps is even more vitally needed because of the vulnerable nature of these populations.

PHOTO 9.1   Haiti: aerial view of camp/shelter site after the 2010 Haiti Earthquake. (*Source*: http://gemini.info.usaid.gov/photos/displayimage.php?pos=-2864.)

Since health is such an immediate concern following any disaster, nations without a robust medical or health-care system significantly tax both that nation's and the international response capabilities. Damage to the public health and health-care infrastructure can have extensive and long-lasting impacts; a community cannot return to "normal" without these in place during the recovery process. The World Health Organization (WHO 2008b) launched the "Hospitals Safe from Disasters" strategy in 2008 to place a global emphasis on increasing the resilience of hospitals and other elements of a nation's health-care infrastructure. This strategy aims to build and reinforce hospitals that are more capable of withstanding a disaster based upon the hazard risk, the functionality of hospitals' systems and infrastructure following a disaster, and risk reduction mechanisms. Still, hospitals globally are not particularly prepared for disasters.

Communities need support in areas where they do not have the resources (not any and all assistance); assistance should be contextually appropriate and wanted. The evaluation of international disaster relief efforts has revealed that disaster response and recovery efforts must be tied to development efforts (Paul 2006). Just as preexisting health conditions are exacerbated by disasters, so too are the weaknesses in a nation's government, health, and infrastructure system revealed. Simply providing resources to nations during the immediate response to a disaster is not an effective strategy for international disaster relief. Instead, coupling disaster planning with sustainable development strategies offers greater opportunities. Further, ensuring that resources are available for recovery that rebuilds with mitigation in mind is just as important as response and relief efforts.

Disasters often highlight resource and health disparities between nations, and following disasters, this exposed need often prompts an influx of international relief aid, particularly to developing countries. However, despite the existence of organizations, such as the USAID, the International Red Cross/Red Crescent, Doctors Without Borders, and numerous other organizations dedicated to international disaster response, finding an efficient, effective, and appropriate process for assisting a nation in need remains a challenge.

9.7.3 THE STATE OF HEALTH CARE IN THE UNITED STATES UNDERLYING DISASTER PLANNING

The previous section also alludes to several other relevant health issues that directly affect vulnerability, including both access to health care and then, by extension, the complexity of the systems that address health in the United States. Access is a function of availability, both in terms of types of services and openings, in a reasonable proximity with appropriate transportation, as well as economically obtainable, either through payment or insurance. Unfortunately, both aspects pose challenges for many people in the United States.

According to the CDC (Cohen, Ward, and Schiller 2011), 18.2% of people under the age of 65 and 7.8% of children under 18 years of age were uninsured (no public or private insurance) in 2010. The good news is that the number and percentage of uninsured children declined from 1996 to 2010, probably mostly from an increase in the numbers and percentages covered by public health insurance, which increased to 27.4%. However, these numbers conceal disparities. For instance, Hispanics, people without a high school diploma, those in the West and South regions, and those aged 19–25 were less likely to have public or private insurance. For some without private insurance, health coverage is available through Medicaid for qualified low-income individuals and families through state-administered programs. Medicare health insurance is provided for people 65 years of age and older, people under 65 with certain disabilities, and all people with permanent kidney failure (CDC 2008b). Additionally, the federal government provides health services to higher-need populations through the Federally Qualified Community Health Centers program, which supplies primary care to over 16 million individuals nationally each year (HHS 2008a). While universal health insurance does not exist in the United States and the mechanisms for gaining coverage remain disparate, it is possible that the Affordable Care Act, which was signed into law in 2010, may close the gap in some health-care access. Still, access to health care through insurance remains a challenge, and certainly contributes to social vulnerabilities.

The health-care system is complex and is dominated by private insurance, with additional care provided by nonprofit organizations, private and public health providers, and public health agencies. Additionally, advocacy groups also play a role. Hospitals, clinics, pharmacies, nursing homes, primary care physicians, specialty doctors, nursing, physical therapy, mental health services, ambulance response, fire and police, community organizations, among many, many others are components of the health system, one that has several exemplary elements to it, but also is not equally accessible to all because of limited availability in many places and high cost. While the debates persist as to the cause and mechanisms for correcting this shortfall, there is little doubt that a health-care crisis exists in the United States, where the U.S. infant mortality rate ranks 29th internationally (CDC 2008b) and the per capita expenditure in 2006 was $7,026 per person, or 16% of the U.S. Gross Domestic Product, more than any other nation (HHS 2008b).

This discussion of the health system and accessibility issues all points to three major challenges for incorporating health into emergency management:

1. People without access prior to a disaster will not have improved opportunities for addressing health issues after an event.
2. A health-care system in crisis will not perform better in the face of a disaster.
3. The health-care and public health systems are intricate and multifaceted, making the linkages to emergency management, while necessary, complicated.

9.7.4 HEALTH CARE, PUBLIC HEALTH, AND EMERGENCY MANAGEMENT SYSTEMS

Health is an intricate arrangement of individual, community, and structural considerations. As a consequence, improving health ultimately requires a systems and policy approach, not just individual-level interventions and treatment. Not surprisingly, multiple approaches exist for addressing health needs and improving health status. These models, as they relate to segments of the health system, also perform associated functions in U.S. disaster and emergency management systems.

Health care/medicine and public health differ in focus and approach, although they are clearly interrelated and complement one another. A medical model (reviewed in Chapter 8 with regard to disabilities) drives health care, which emphasizes the treatment of individuals for particular diseases, conditions, and/or injuries. In this way, a person is diagnosed, and then appropriate treatment is administered at an individual level. The ecological model of health (described in Section 9.4) guides public health, which focuses on populations (rather than individuals), drawing from multiple social science and natural science disciplines with prevention, rather than treatment, as the overarching goal. This approach consists of the established core areas of "epidemiology, biostatistics, environmental health, health services administration, and social and behavioral science, but . . . it also encompass[es] eight critical new areas: informatics, genomics, communication, cultural competence, community-based participatory research, policy and law, global health, and ethics" (Gebbie, Rosenstock, and Hernandez 2003, 1). Major priorities (Public Health Functions Steering Committee 1994) include:

1. Prevention of epidemics, spread of disease, and injury
2. Protection against environmental hazards
3. Promotion of healthy behaviors
4. Responding to disasters and assisting communities in recovery
5. Assuring the quality and accessibility of health services

Divisions between the medical approach and public health are not necessarily black and white (many studies, researchers, and practitioners bridge the two), and research from one area frequently informs the other. Yet they are "distinct fields with separate infrastructures and financing mechanisms, unique perspectives, and a divergent, sometimes, tumultuous history" (Salinsky 2002, 3). Adding emergency management to the equation with a different history, emphasis, and approach, one that has tended to use top-down driven planning, requires significant organizational and interagency planning and coordination across diverse systems. In fact, while medicine and public health have clearly interfaced with disasters for a long time, it has not been until recently that research and practice in these fields have become integrated into multidisciplinary disaster management and response (Shoaf and Rottman 2000). To illustrate this point, the American Academy of Disaster Medicine (AADM) was organized in 2006 to promote education in disaster medicine and provide a mechanism for assessing physician qualifications in this area (the American Board of Physician Specialities n.d.), and CDC's Preparedness and Emergency Response Learning Centers (PERLC) (formerly known as Centers for Public Health Preparedness program) came online in 2010 to "strengthen terrorism and emergency preparedness by linking academic expertise to state and local health agency needs" (CDC 2011a). Perhaps because of this recent coupling, and differences in historical development and frame of reference for these three essential systems, improved integration of public health, health-care infrastructure, and emergency management remains a priority (Hooke and Rogers 2005).

Identifying ways to "standardize and codify the profession of disaster medicine and public health preparedness" continues to be the primary means for integrating health care and public health systems (Subbarao, Dobalian, and James 2011). Developing measurable objectives to guide disaster preparedness and response practice for both public health and health-care organizations that are nested within the construct of the emergency management system brings a common language to disaster management and will aid in synchronizing these three areas essential to health preservation during disasters. The importance of developing an "integrated, all-of-Nation, capabilities-based approach to preparedness" was emphasized by President Obama in Presidential Directive-8, in which he directed the development of the National Preparedness Goal (Obama 2011; DHS n.d.). This goal continues to refine the process for integrating the roles of the medical system, public health, and emergency management in disaster preparedness and response.

The common thread that connects each of these systems' effectiveness in executing their combined role in disaster preparedness and response is the concept of community resilience in its ability to increase community capacity for enduring disasters (Burkle 2011; Bush 2007). Finding ways to measure resilience is in itself a challenging endeavor; directing and designing processes and policies to effect positive change upon a community's resilience continues to be a work in progress. The most recent research in community resilience identified five elements important to disaster planning that influence a community's level of resilience. These factors are (Chandra et al. 2010):

1. Physical and psychological health
2. Social and economic equity/well-being
3. Effective risk communication
4. Integration of organizations (government and nongovernmental)
5. Social connectedness

Developing mechanisms and approaches that address these community components is perhaps the next step in integrated disaster planning.

9.7.4.1 Considerations for Public Health and Medical and Emergency Management Response

The association between emergency management, public health, and environmental health and safety may not be obvious, but in the most basic sense, disasters are extreme environmental events (Logue 1996). Additionally, technological events have direct environmental health impacts, and in the United States, the Environmental Protection Agency (EPA) is designated to prepare for and respond to oil, hazardous substance, pollutant, or contaminant emergencies, also working with other agencies within the context of a natural disaster. Natural events themselves can cause contamination and affect water supply and waste disposal, solid-waste handling, food handling, vector control, and/or home sanitation (PAHO 2000). Occupational health and safety are also important aspects of environmental health and disasters, as these involve keeping workers safe. Hurricane Katrina demonstrates the connection; the environmental health impacts of Hurricane Katrina were far-reaching, including power, natural gas, vector/rodent/animal control, contamination from underground storage tanks, food safety, drinking water, wastewater, road conditions, solid waste/debris, sediments/soil contamination (toxic chemicals), and housing (e.g., damage and mold) (CDC and EPA 2005). EPA responded to chemical and oil spills, collected abandoned chemical containers, coordinated recycling of damaged appliances, and collected and recycled electronic waste (GAO 2007). In terms of environmental monitoring, EPA also conducted air, water, sediment, and soil sampling; helped assess drinking water and wastewater infrastructures; and issued timely information to the public on a variety of environmental health risks. (See Box 9.1.)

Because of the configuration of the public health system and the nature of dealing with health concerns, the issues of federalism, privacy, and fairness in allocating resources have implications for public health emergency response (Hodge, Gostin, and Vernick 2007). The previous discussion on the response systems for public health and medical services centered on national organization and coordination. However, much of public health practice (like emergency management) occurs at the state and local level, where funding and divisions of efforts between levels of government vary greatly (Hodge, Gostin, and Vernick 2007; Salinsky 2002). This has implications across the entire disaster life cycle in terms of quality, continuity, capabilities, and even resources. Ultimately,

BOX 9.1   LONG-TERM HEALTH EFFECTS OF HURRICANE KATRINA

Hurricane Katrina has had far-reaching health consequences, particularly on the most vulnerable, stemming from a compromised health-care system, long-term displacement of people from their homes and communities, and environmental contamination. Not only was the health-care system compromised, its fragility continues to affect recovery; hospital capacity remains diminished, with some of the hospitals having never reopened (Charity Hospital as a notable example), particularly those serving lower income, vulnerable populations (Eaton 2007). But, it is not just about hospitals as institutions; the story includes individual people. Nurses, physicians, pharmacists, among all others, were also among the evacuees, some of whom have not returned and who were also among the populations who lost houses. Physicians have had to struggle to rebuild practices with little federal assistance and populations who have returned slowly, which has particularly affected pediatricians (Needle 2008). Further, without jobs, people lose insurance, which also affects the ability of the health-care system to rebound. However, without an intact and healthy infrastructure, how do people return, especially those who rely on this system for regularly monitored treatment for any chronic condition, including mental health, diabetes, heart disease, or numerous other serious ailments? Ultimately, the result is quite a conundrum: many people not being able to return without a functioning health system and resources, but the health-care system needing human resources and patients to operate. The bottom line is that recovery depends on a functioning health infrastructure.

Women and children have particularly suffered. In one longitudinal study of 1,082 randomly selected displaced Gulf Coast households, the Gulf Coast Child and Family Health (CAFH) study has reported some disturbing findings regarding the physical and mental health of children and mothers, as well as living conditions (Redlener, DeRosa, and Hut 2008). For example, "Almost half of parents reported that one or more of their children showed signs of new emotional or behavioral difficulties that did not exist prior to Hurricane Katrina" (Redlener, DeRosa, and Hut 2008, 9). A mother's health status also directly affects her child's and is illustrated by another finding: "Symptoms of depression among mothers were high, and their children were two and a half times more likely to have an emotional or behavioral problem than children of mothers who did not show signs of depression" (Redlener, DeRosa, and Hut 2008, 9). Given that other studies have found that women's health has suffered severely in the aftermath of the hurricane as well (Jones-DeWeever 2008), this does not bode well for the suffering of people in post-Katrina Louisiana and Mississippi.

this translates to the need for significant interjurisdictional coordination, which is usually not easy. Additionally, high-quality response and recovery are also linked to the strength of the public health infrastructure at the state and local level, a system that is understaffed and underfunded (Trust for America's Health 2008). Similar to the health-care system generally, the public health system cannot realistically be expected to perform at a level higher than it exists at a baseline.

Another extremely sensitive topic of concern is information sharing. As required by the Health Insurance Portability and Accountability Act of 1996 (HIPAA), health-care plans, clearinghouses, and providers must adhere to the Standards for Privacy of Individually Identifiable Health Information (the Privacy Rule) (HHS 2002). Essentially, this means that health information must be protected and treated as private unless an individual has consented to access, and information cannot be released or shared outside of the defined criteria and guidelines. In terms of disaster response, the guidance published by HHS (2005) with regard to Hurricane Katrina states that health-care providers can share individual health information for treatment when imminent danger to a person or the public exists; and for the release of information on whether a person is in a facility and that person's condition. Additionally, entities not covered by the Privacy Rule, such as the American Red Cross, can share patient information. So, for all intents and purposes, HIPAA does not really apply in the disaster context, but it is not clearly defined, and there is no other legislation that covers this privacy protection (Hodge, Gostin, and Vernick 2007). All in all, the acquisition, analysis, and dissemination of public health information are clearly necessary for quality public health preparedness and response, but privacy issues should be addressed.

Another consideration and challenge during the health response to disasters is maintaining standards of care to which both patients and medical professionals are accustomed. To standardize expectations during these circumstances, in 2009 the Institute of Medicine developed criteria and protocols for "crisis standards of care" (Altevogt et al. 2009). This guidance visualizes a delivery of care during dire circumstances that is equitable, is fair, includes community and provider collaboration to establish these standards, and is supported by the rule of law. In most states, crisis standards of care would only be authorized by the expressed approval and signatory authority of the governor.

In summary, new national legislation is fostering a climate where emergency management, public health, and medical systems must work to integrate and coordinate effectively to address both public health emergencies as well as natural, technological, and human-induced events. National efforts offer a framework defining roles and responsibilities, and both public health and medicine offer significant resources, foundations of knowledge, and opportunities for improving preparedness, response, recovery, and mitigation and for protecting the well-being of individuals and communities.

9.7.4.2 Public Health and Medical Services Response System in the United States

The National Response Framework (NRF) identifies key principles, roles, and structures organizing the national response to all hazards, including natural and technological disasters, major transportation accidents, and acts of terrorism (DHS 2008). It is important to recognize that emergency response is a complex relationship between local, state, and federal agencies, with local jurisdiction retaining primary responsibility for response, the intricacies of which are not discussed here. Instead, this overview focuses on the relevance of the NRF to health. The priorities for public health and medical services in the NRF include saving lives and protecting the health and safety of the public, responders, and recovery workers, as well as protecting critical resources and facilitating the recovery of individuals, families, governments, and the environment (DHS 2008, HHS 2007).

The NRF organizes the national response to disasters into functional areas designated as Emergency Support Functions (ESF). Emergency Support Function #8 (ESF #8) is specifically aimed at federal public health and medical services coordinated by the Department of Health and Human Services (HHS). These include "behavioral health needs consisting of both mental health and substance abuse considerations for incident victims and response workers and, as appropriate, medical needs groups defined . . . as individuals in need of additional medical response assistance, and veterinary and/or animal health issues" (DHS 2008, HHS 2007).

In support of ESF #8, the National Disaster Medical System (NDMS) is in place to supplement medical response to a disaster and includes Disaster Medical Assistance Teams (DMAT), Disaster Mortuary Operational Response Teams (DMORT), National Veterinary Response Teams (NVRT), National Nurse Response Teams (NNRT), and National Pharmacy Response Teams (NPRT) as well as Federal Coordinating Centers for recruitment and coordination of hospitals to receive evacuated patients. All of these teams comprise people with expertise in defined specialty areas and are deployed in the event of a designated, declared disaster. Priority areas include interoperable communication systems, bed tracking, personnel management, fatality management planning, and hospital evacuation planning. Other activities involve bed and personnel surge capacity, decontamination capabilities, isolation capacity, pharmaceutical supplies, training, education, and drills and exercises. HHS also established the Metropolitan Medical Response System (MMRS) in 1996 in response to the increased threat of biological and chemical terrorism, as demonstrated by the sarin gas attacks in Tokyo (Titan Corp. 2005). In 2003, the MMRS was transferred to the Department of

Homeland Security due to organizational realignment. Currently, over 124 U.S. cities are enrolled in this system, which is designed to coordinate response capabilities within highly populated areas for disasters involving the use of weapons of mass destruction or other similar acts of terrorism. (See Photo 9.2.)

In 2006, The Pandemic and All-Hazards Preparedness Act (PAHPA) was enacted into law to further define the role of public health and medical services. PAHPA's purpose is "to improve the Nation's public health and medical preparedness and response capabilities for emergencies, whether deliberate, accidental, or natural" and has attempted to streamline the federal public health response (U.S. Congressional Record 2006). The PAHPA also created the Office of the Assistant Secretary for Preparedness and Response (ASPR) within the U.S. Department of Health and Human Services (HHS) to provide a lead agency to coordinate a growing body of national programs and resources that support state and local efforts related to health and disasters. PAHPA addresses national surveillance methods and systems, surge capacity (personnel, facilities, and equipment), and vaccine development and distribution.

Through PAPHA, ASPR developed the inaugural National Health Security Strategy. This strategy defines the national vision for health security and "is achieved when the Nation and its people are prepared for, protected from, respond effectively to, and are able to recover from incidents with potentially negative health consequences" (HHS 2009). This vision, which recognizes the linkages between homeland security objectives and the responsibilities placed upon the health-care sector for disaster preparedness and response, is accomplished through the attainment of two goals: (1) building community resilience throughout the nation and (2) strengthening health systems' abilities to mitigate and respond to disasters. Ultimately, "achieving national health security requires better coordination between the health system and the emergency response system" in addition to the cooperation and participation of the private sector and the individual citizen (HHS 2009, 3).

To achieve these goals, the CDC developed two sets of systems-based core competencies: one for public health organizations and one for the health-care sector. While these capabilities are developed with the specific considerations and unique dynamics of each system in mind, there is appropriately much similarity between the two sets. The 14 functional health-care capabilities focus largely upon increasing the capacity and ability of the medical system to respond to disasters that precipitate the need to surge medical assets and respond to mass casualty incidents (CDC 2012). The 15 functional

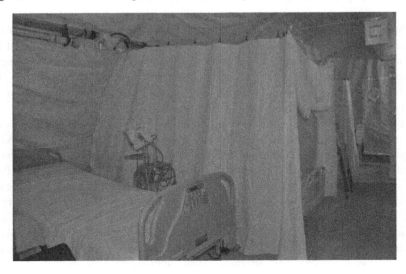

PHOTO 9.2 Joplin, MO, August 23, 2011—St. John's mobile hospital tent units continue to serve patients after EF-5 tornado destroyed St. John's Regional Medical Center on May 22, 2011. (Photograph by Elissa Jun for FEMA.)

public health preparedness capabilities, which are aligned with both the 10 essential public health services and the target-capabilities list, provide planning guidelines to state and local public health agencies to better prepare their respective communities for disasters (CDC 2011b). Importantly, these sets of capabilities are a significant step toward providing a framework for both private and public health systems for preparedness planning and activities, as these sets explicitly identify where such systems overlap and diverge, thereby facilitating joint planning and collaboration.

This type of cooperative planning between the public and private health sectors is demonstrated in the Healthcare and Public Health (HPH) Sector-Specific Plan, an annex to the National Infrastructure Protection Plan. HPH is critical infrastructure at approximately 16% of GDP (HHS 2010). As such, this document devises a plan for comprehensively establishing goals, identifying and prioritizing assets, assessing risk, implementing protective programs, and developing mechanisms to evaluate these programs (HHS 2010). The plan identifies four HPH sector goals—service continuity, workforce protection, physical asset protection, and cyber security—to frame the development of supporting objectives.

9.7.5 MENTAL HEALTH

Mental health effects of disasters in the population are generally not acute, but this depends on the type of event and the experiences, and events can have long-lasting effects on various aspects of mental health. Norris et al. (2002a), in an analysis based in a review of 20 years of literature, found that youth more than adults who were from developing rather than developed countries, or who experienced mass violence, were more likely to have adverse outcomes (posttraumatic stress, depression, and anxiety, as well as posttraumatic stress disorder, major depression disorder, generalized anxiety disorder, and panic disorder). For adults, more severe exposure, females, middle age, ethnic minority status, secondary stressors, prior psychiatric problems, and weak or deteriorating psychosocial resources increased the likelihood of adverse outcomes (Norris et al. 2002a). Interestingly in this study, rescue and recovery workers showed remarkable resilience, but this should not deter from providing mental health services to responders. Based on the overall findings from the first phase of the study, the team recommended "early intervention following disasters, especially when the disaster is associated with extreme and widespread damage to property, ongoing financial problems for the stricken community, violence that resulted from human intent, and a high prevalence of trauma in the form of injuries, threat to life, and loss of life" (Norris et al. 2002b). When planning for public health disaster response, addressing these broad public health concerns, while not falling for the myths, is vital for the best outcome.

9.7.6 HEALTH CONSIDERATIONS FOR EVACUATION, WARNING, AND RESPONSE

The health considerations for evacuation, warning, and response revolve around individual needs and then the extending effects on disaster operations. During both advanced-warning events as well as sudden-impact events, individuals need to bring personal medications during any relocation, which should be labeled with the identified dosage and interval. Additionally, a person should keep a backup prescription (although for some medications this is not possible) in order to obtain a refill in the event of lost medication or if the time away from home extends beyond the amount filled. Ideally, an individual should have additional refills already in possession, but again there may be limitations placed on the amount that can be obtained at a given time, either because of the type of medication, insurance restrictions, or lack of money to pay for a double prescription. Complications further arise from medications that need refrigeration (such as insulin), and so this simple measure would require attention in shelters or in the selection of a place to stay. Beyond medications, some people also require medical treatment, such as dialysis, radiation or chemotherapy, methadone maintenance, or mental health visits. Additionally, if the evacuation is longer term, a person may not have access to a physician for continued treatment or prescription refill. Further, if the health-care system itself is compromised because the effects of a disaster are so extensive, a person may not be able to continue treatment simply because the health resource is no longer available. In short, a person who is dependent on a particular medication or treatment of a chronic (or acute) condition should carefully plan to the best degree possible in consultation with the health-care provider prior to any event. This should also include support systems and networks (friends and family), as well as plans for home, work, and school.

In terms of hospitals, shelters, and other health-care providers, health has implications for operations. Shelters can become quickly strained if they are responsible for a continuum of care exceeding their capabilities, but the reality is that the population comes as it comes, and it will likely be reflective of the preexisting vulnerable populations. The expectation is that hospitals will stay open, but they will likely not be able to provide elective services or even attend to nonpriority cases; typical ailments still need treatment, but the capacity may not exist. And, in some instances, hospitals themselves must be evacuated. Overall, hospitals must be reserved for care and not

---

**BOX 9.2 A CASE STUDY OF TWO HOSPITALS IN
NORTHERN HAITI AFTER THE 2010 EARTHQUAKE**

One might question what the role of an already-fragile health system could or would be during response and recovery in the face of such an extensive catastrophe, especially with most Ministry of Health functions and other resources concentrated in the devastated region. The underdeveloped nature of the health system might support an argument for top-down response from international sources, particularly in the absence of leadership from the Haitian government or Haitian disaster management structures, and yet opportunities likely exist for incorporating bottom-up approaches.

This case study, which focused on the two main hospitals in the northern region of Haiti, provides an interesting comparison, not just because of their location at the periphery of the seismically affected areas, but also because one is a private and the other a public institution. Justinian Hospital in Cap-Haitien, the second largest city in Haiti on the north coast, is a public hospital that falls under the Haitian Ministry of Health. It is the largest health-care provider in northern Haiti, with 250 beds serving an estimated population of 850,000. Sacre Coeur Hospital, on the other hand, is a private Catholic facility and is located in the town of Milot, 70 miles south of Cap-Haitien. It is a 73-bed hospital and is the largest private hospital in northern Haiti.

Several themes emerged from the surveys and the interviews taken together. In terms of challenges, these included: inadequate hospital capacity, overall poor coordination (although many examples described instances of ingenuity and adjustment), the need for a model for integration of international efforts into local structures and organizations, and an urgent need for disaster training. Despite all of the challenges, there were also many very positive and encouraging elements of the response. First and foremost, the medical, nursing, and support staff had an extremely high level of dedication to serving the victims. And while there were many challenges with international organizations and individuals integrating into the Haitian system for various reasons, there were also several positive examples.

As the memories of the earthquake recede in the "international consciousness," international health advocates must maintain the focus on the dire state of health care in Haiti. This cannot just be an international effort, as the local health authorities and the Haitian government have a significant role to play. Many places, though perhaps not quite as extreme as Haiti, also do not have the necessary resources (financial, educational, etc.) to carry out effective disaster planning in the health sector, and so basic guidelines are needed for these settings (Thomas et al. 2011).

become unplanned shelters. Home health care can also become disrupted during a disaster. Cross-jurisdictional care can also be problematic. Thus the medical and public health response planning is extremely important, particularly for those with a health condition, which includes workforce emergency response training.

9.7.7 SHORT- AND LONG-TERM RECOVERY

In terms of short- and long-term recovery, efforts should involve ensuring that a recovery plan is in place with agreed-upon goals specific to health. The greatest challenge for health is likely ensuring that the public health and health-care infrastructure is returned to a pre-event level. However, this likely will not return to something better than was in place, though this perhaps would be desirable. If the system was inadequate before the disaster, then it will likely still not meet the needs even if returned to that status. In this instance, aiming to improve the infrastructure would be a laudable goal. For example, if a clinic was deteriorated prior to an event and then incurred damage, would it be logical to rebuild it to previous conditions? Ensuring that health services returned and environmental conditions are safe (debris removal, contamination cleanup, road repair, utility repair, and sanitation and clean water availability) is a priority for recovery because it would be extremely difficult for individuals to return for the longer term without these resources, particularly if they had diminished health conditions. Additional recovery efforts include providing long-term follow-up to those affected, both the population and responders, and ensuring that postevent assessments on successes and failure are conducted that can guide future planning.

9.7.8 CLIMATE AND HEALTH

Increasing recognition and interest in the health effects of climate change have emerged in recent years, and so necessitates at least mention of this topic, especially given the relationship to hazards as well as public health preparedness activities. Broad consensus exists that the climate is warming, with many environmental, social, and economic implications. The relationship between climate and health is essentially linked to weather-related climate events and shifting patterns of disease (Relman et al. 2008; Shea 2007). While there is little doubt that climate change has an effect on health, the complexity of the interaction is not well understood beyond generalizations and studies on specific types of hazards, for example heat waves or droughts, but the full range of effects is only beginning to be established. Climate change will likely pose new health challenges, although many of the functions already performed by public health, particularly within the context of preparedness, are applicable to understanding the health effects of climate change (Frumkin et al. 2008). Public health systems are in the process of developing strategies for mitigating and adapting to climate change. "Identifying vulnerabilities, tracking disease and environmental conditions, and educating the public on the individual ways they can prepare themselves and their families for climate change" remain the primary ways in which public health is approaching strategy development for this complex issue (APHA 2011, 67). Clearly, coordination and planning across many sectors will be necessary in the future to work toward reducing the effects of climate change on populations throughout the world.

9.8 STRATEGIES FOR SUCCESS

This chapter has emphasized the need for integration and coordination of planning and response between public health and emergency management systems. Integration and coordination of these systems remain central in efforts to reduce disaster loss while ensuring that vulnerable people are explicitly included in dialogue about disaster planning. Beyond coordination, each of these systems has much to learn from one another due to the focus of each—as well as their historical development. Public health emphasizes prevention rather than response, while disasters are the purview of emergency management.

Public health has a great deal of experience in the communication of health risks, which are generally focused at creating healthy behaviors and lifestyles. In many cases, this most directly aligns with mitigation due to the prevention orientation of the messages. Emergency communication, however, has a greater sense of urgency, may be more incomplete, and can change as an event unfolds (Hooke and Rogers 2005). The audience is of extreme importance when creating a message, and any risk communication should really be designed for multiple audiences to include diverse populations. Risk communication involves working with the media and having a lead spokesperson so that messages are not confused. The bottom line is that effective communication between all stakeholders will only improve emergency response efforts.

Community preparedness is essential for effectively addressing health issues in emergency management, and community-based approaches provide an effective mechanism for involving stakeholders and empowering communities. (See Chapter 16 for a discussion of the use of a participatory, community-based approach for vulnerability assessment.) This process establishes relationships and builds trust, in addition to giving the community a voice in setting priorities for disaster planning. Additionally, education occurs throughout as well.

Two examples derive from a focus on reducing health disparities and improving community health. Even though the focus is health specifically, the efforts can certainly inform vulnerability reduction efforts at the community level. The toolkit for health and resilience in vulnerable communities (THRIVE) is a community assessment designed specifically to improve health outcomes and reduce disparities (Davis, Cook, and Cohen 2005). Using a resilience approach to community health in order to evaluate risk as well as resources, the assessment included built-environment factors, services and institutions, and structural considerations in a community-engagement process. The second example provides guidance for selecting from several models and approaches, simply laying out a process for helping communities address social determinants of health (Brennan Ramirez, Baker, and Metzler 2008). After presenting several case studies as examples of products from completed and ongoing processes, guidelines for adapting the social determinants of health to any neighborhood are supplied. The general elements include:

1. Enlisting participation
2. Methods for assessing the social determinants of health
3. A process for building community capacity
4. Approaches for focusing the initiative
5. Development and implementation of an action plan
6. Assessment of progress
7. Recommendations for maintenance

Both of these efforts present exciting opportunities for focusing on community assets as well as risk based in an action approach that can be an impetus for change.

9.9 SUMMARY

Health as a basic human right by extension equates to equal access to safety and well-being as the cornerstone to reducing vulnerability and increasing resilience. In its association with vulnerability, it is an overlay of other characteristics, and it is also a reflection of the fragility or vitality of a community. In many ways, we are concerned with the effects of disasters because of the ways they impact people's well-being. As a consequence, health captures many elements that place it at the center of considering vulnerability, capacity, and resilience. An unhealthy community with a broken public-health and health-care system would likely not weather a disaster without significant loss.

DISCUSSION QUESTIONS

1. What types of nonhealth infrastructure directly affect the health status of a community?
2. In further consideration of the data tables and maps presented on disease and disaster mortality, what additional underlying factors may lead to the patterns? How are these related to vulnerability?
3. What is the relationship of individual characteristics and structural considerations? What contributes to your health?
4. In using health as an indicator of vulnerability, what types of variables would you like to examine?
5. What are the functions of public health, and how do they contribute to an understanding of vulnerability and improve emergency management capabilities?
6. When considering the health-care and public health systems, what considerations affect their functioning for emergency response?
7. Public health focuses on prevention, and so how does this relate to emergency management?
8. In terms of health, how can this be incorporated into emergency management as an overlay of vulnerability?
9. How does a community-based approach strengthen a community's resilience for addressing two social determinants: health and vulnerability?

ACKNOWLEDGMENTS

Sincere thanks go to Jean Scandlyn, Ronica Rooks, and Sharry Erzinger, who are not only dear friends, but also treasured colleagues who selflessly provided invaluable advice on this chapter. And our sincere gratitude goes to Brenda Philips for her words of encouragement, insights, friendship, and patience. The authors also acknowledge and thank Elizabeth Davis and Alan Clive for their contributions to the chapter that appeared in the first edition of this book. Alan Clive's tenacity and spirit will be remembered, and it is with gratitude and fondness that we continue to dedicate this chapter to him. This chapter represents the writing of the present authors and does not necessarily reflect those of previous authors.

REFERENCES

Altevogt, B., C. Stroud, S. Hanson, D. Hanfling, and L. Gostin. 2009. *Guidance for establishing crisis standards of care for use in disaster situations.* Washington, DC: The National Academies Press. http://www.nap.edu/catalog/12749.html.

American Board of Physician Specialities n.d. http://www.aapsga.org/academies/disaster-medicine/index.html.

American Board of Physician Specialties. n.d. Disaster Medicine. http://www.abpsus.org/disaster-medicine.

APHA (American Public Health Association). 2011. Climate change: Mastering the public health's role. http://www.apha-environment.org/pdf/APHA_ClimateChg_guidebook.pdf.

Berkman, L. F., and I. Kawachi, eds. 2000. *Social epidemiology.* New York: Oxford University Press.

Boorse, C. 1977. Health as a theoretical concept. *Philosophy of Science* 44:542–77.

Braveman, P., and S. Gruskin. 2003. Defining equity in health. *Journal of Epidemiology and Community Health* 57:254–58.

Brennan Ramirez, L. K., E. A. Baker, and M. Metzler. 2008. Promoting health equity: A resource to help communities address social determinants of health. U.S. Department of Health and Human Services, Centers for Disease Control and Prevention, Atlanta. http://www.cdc.gov/nccdphp/dach/chaps/.

Burkle, F. 2011. The limits to our capacity: Reflections on resiliency, community engagement and recovery in 21st-century crisis. *Disaster Medicine and Public Health Preparedness* 5:S176–81.

Bush, G. W. 2007. Homeland Security Presidential Directive/HSPD-21: Public Health and Medical Preparedness. http://www.fas.org/irp/offdocs/nspd/hspd-21.htm.

Carter-Pokras, O., and C. Baquet. 2002. What is a health disparity? *Public Health Reports* 117 (5): 426–34.

CDC (Centers for Disease Control and Prevention). 2008a. About the BRFSS. http://www.cdc.gov/BRFSS/about.htm.

———. 2008b. National Center for Health Statistics. Topics: Medicare program–general information and Medicaid program–general information. http://www.cms.hhs.gov/home/medicare.asp.

———. 2011a. *Centers for public health preparedness.* http://www.cdc.gov/cphp/centers.htm.

———. 2011b. Public health preparedness capabilities. http://www.cdc.gov/phpr/capabilities/.

———. 2012. *Healthcare preparedness capabilities: National guidance for healthcare system preparedness.* http://www.phe.gov/Preparedness/planning/hpp/reports/Documents/capabilities.pdf.

CDC (Centers for Disease Control) and EPA (U.S. Environmental Protection Agency). 2005. Joint Taskforce. Hurricane Katrina response, initial assessment. http://www.epa.gov/katrina/reports/envneeds_hab_assessment.html.

Chandra, A., J. Acosta, L. Meredith, K. Sanches, S. Stern, L. Uscher-Pines, M. Williams, and D. Yeung. 2010. Understanding community resilience in the context of national health security. Working paper. RAND Health, Washington, DC.

Chu, M. C., and J. A. Rhoades. 2008. The uninsured in America, 1996–2007: Estimates for the U.S. civilian noninstitutionalized population under age 65. Statistical Brief #214. Agency for Healthcare Research and Quality, Rockville, MD. http://www.meps.ahrq.gov/mepsweb/data_files/publications/st214/stat214.pdf.

Cohen, R. A., B. W. Ward, and J. S. Schiller. 2011. Health insurance coverage: Early release of estimates from the National Health Interview Survey, 2010. *Division of Health Interview Statistics, National Center for Health Statistics, Centers for Disease Control.* http://www.cdc.gov/nchs/data/nhis/earlyrelease/insur201106.pdf.

Colorado Department of Public Health and Environment, Health Equity. n.d. An explanatory model for conceptualizing the social determinants of health. http://www.cdphe.state.co.us/opp/resources/Health%20Equity%20Framework%20.pdf.

Colorado Department of Public Health and Environment (CDPHE), Health Equity. 2010. An explanatory model for conceptualizing the social determinants of health. http://www.chd.dphe.state.co.us/HealthIndicators/Documents/Resources/Social%20Determinants%20of%20Health%20Packet.pdf.

Davis, R., D. Cook, and L. Cohen. 2005. A community resilience approach to reducing ethnic and racial disparities in health. *AJPH* 95 (12): 2168–73.

de Jesus Diaz-Perez, M., D. Thomas, and T. Farley. 2007. *Assessing gaps in service for a community health center system.* 2007 Annual Meeting of the Association of American Geographers, San Francisco, California Online Program. http://meridian.aag.org/callforpapers/program/AbstractDetail.cfm?AbstractID=13398.

de Ville de Goyet, C. 1999. Stop propagating disaster myths. *Prehospital Disaster Med.* 14:213–14.

———. 2000. Stop propagating disaster myths. *Lancet* 356 (9231): 762–64.

DHS. n.d. National Preparedness Guidelines: Introduction. http://www.dhs.gov/national-preparedness-guidelines

DHS (U.S. Department of Homeland Security). 2008. National Response Framework: Overview. http://www.fema.gov/emergency/nrf/.

Eaton, L. 2007. New Orleans recovery is slowed by closed hospitals. *New York Times*, July 24.

Eberwine, D. 2005. Disaster myths that just won't die. *Perspectives in Health* 10 (1). http://www.paho.org/English/DD/PIN/Number21_article01.htm.

EM-DAT (Emergency Events Database). 2012. EMDAT: The OFDA/CRED international disaster database. Université Catholique de Louvain, Brussels, Belgium. www.emdat.be.

Farmer, Paul. Haiti After the Earthquake. 2011. New York, Public Affairs.

Feierman, S., and J. M. Janzen, eds. 1992. *The social basis of health and healing in Africa.* Berkeley: University of California Press.

Frumkin, H., J. Hess, G. Luber, J. Malilay, and M. McGeehin. 2008. Climate change: The public health response. *American Journal of Public Health* 98 (3): 435–45.

GAO (U.S. Government Accountability Office). 2007. Report to congressional committees, Hurricane Katrina, EPA's current and future environmental protection efforts could be enhanced by addressing issues and challenges faced on the Gulf Coast. http://www.gao.gov/new.items/d07651.pdf.

Gebbie, K., L. Rosenstock, and L. M. Hernandez, eds. 2003. *Who will keep the public healthy? Educating public health professionals for the 21st century.* Committee on Educating Public Health Professionals for the 21st Century, National Academy of Sciences. Washington, DC: National Academies Press.

Hazards and Vulnerability Research Institute. 2012. The spatial hazard events and losses database for the United States (SHELDUS), version 9.0, online database. Columbia: University of South Carolina. http://webra.cas.sc.edu/hvri/products/sheldus.aspx.

Heron, M. 2012. Deaths: Leading causes for 2008. *National Vital Statistics Reports* 60 (6). http://www.cdc.gov/nchs/data/nvsr/nvsr60/nvsr60_06.pdf.

HHS (U.S. Department of Health and Human Services). 2002. Modifications to the standards for privacy of individually identifiable health information—Final rule. http://www.hhs.gov/ocr/privacy/hipaa/administrative/privacyrule/privruletxt.txt.

———. 2005. HIPAA privacy rule compliance guidance and enforcement statement for activities in response to Hurricane Katrina. Hurricane Katrina bulletin #2. http://www.hhs.gov/ocr/privacy/hipaa/understanding/special/emergency/enforcementstatement.pdf.

———. 2007. Public health emergency response: A guide for leaders and responders. http://www.phe.gov/emergency/communication/guides/leaders/Pages/default.aspx.

———. 2008a. Primary Health Care: The Health Center Program. Health Resources and Services Administration. http://bphc.hrsa.gov/.

———. 2008b. National health expenditure data highlights. Centers for Medicare and Medicaid Services. http://www.cms.hhs.gov/NationalHealthExpendData/02_NationalHealthAccountsHistorical.asp#TopOfPage.

———. 2009. *National Health Security Strategy of the United States of America*. Washington, DC: Government Printing Office.

———. 2010. Healthcare and public health sector specific plan: An annex to the National Infrastructure Protection Plan. http://www.phe.gov/Preparedness/planning/cip/Pages/ssp.aspx.

Hodge, J. G. Jr., L. O. Gostin, and J. S. Vernick. 2007. The pandemic and all-hazards preparedness act: Improving public health emergency response. *JAMA* 297 (15): 1708–11.

Holt, J. B., A. H. Mokdad, E. S. Ford, E. J. Simoes, G. A. Mensah, and W. P. Bartoli. 2008. Use of BRFSS data and GIS technology for rapid public health response during natural disasters. *Prev. Chronic Disease* 5 (3): A97.

Hooke, W., and P. G. Rogers, eds. 2005. Roundtable on Environmental Health Sciences, Research, and Medicine, National Research Council. *Public health risks of disasters: Communication, infrastructure, and preparedness*. Washington, DC: National Academies Press.

Institute of Medicine. 2003. Board on Health Sciences Policy. Committee on Understanding and Eliminating Racial and Ethnic Disparities in Health Care. Smedley, Brian D. Adrienne Y. Stith, and Alan R. Nelson (editors). The National Academies Press: Washington, DC. http://www.iom.edu/Reports/2002/Unequal-Treatment-Confronting-Racial-and-Ethnic-Disparities-in-Health-Care.aspx.

Janzen, J. M. 2002. *The social fabric of health: An introduction to medical anthropology*. Boston: McGraw Hill.

Jones-DeWeever, A. A. 2008. *Women in the wake of the storm: Examining the post-Katrina realities of the women of New Orleans and the Gulf Coast*. Washington, DC: Institute for Women's Policy Research.

Kilbourne, A. M., G. Switzer, K. Hyman, M. Crowley-Matoka, and M. J. Fine. 2006. Advancing health disparities research within the health care system: A conceptual framework. *American Journal of Public Health* 96 (12): 2113–21.

Kreisberg, D., D Thomas, M. Valley, C. Sasson, E. Janes, M. S. Newell, and C. Little. 2011. Integrated emergency preparedness planning for vulnerable populations. University of Colorado Center for Integrated Disaster Preparedness. CIDP Report #3. August. http://www.ucdenver.edu/academics/colleges/medicalschool/departments/EmergencyMedicine/DisasterHealthPrepare/Pages/default.aspx.

Lindsay, J. R. 2003. The determinants of disaster vulnerability: Achieving sustainable mitigation through population health. *Natural Hazards* 28:291–304.

Logue, J. N. 1996. Disasters, the environment, and public health: Improving our response. *American Journal of Public Health* 86 (9): 1207–10.

Luo, W., and F. H. Wang. 2003. Measures of spatial accessibility to health care in a GIS environment: Synthesis and a case study in the Chicago region. *Environment and Planning B—Planning Design* 30 (6): 865–84.

Marmot, G. 2005. Social determinants of health inequalities. *Lancet* 365:1099–1104.

Marmot, G., and R. G. Wilkinson. 1999. *Social determinants of health*. Oxford, U.K.: Oxford University Press.

Needle, S. 2008. Pediatric private practice after Hurricane Katrina: Proposal for recovery. *Pediatrics*. 122 (4): 836–42.

Norris, F. H., M. J. Friedman, P. J. Watson, C. M. Byrne, E. Diaz, and K. Kaniasty. 2002a. 60,000 disaster victims speak: Part I. An empirical review of the empirical literature, 1981–2001. *Psychiatry* 65 (3): 207–39.

———. 2002b. 60,000 disaster victims speak: Part II. An empirical review of the empirical literature, 1981–2001. *Psychiatry* 65 (3): 240–60.

Obama, B. 2011. Presidential Policy Directive/PPD-8: National preparedness. http://www.dhs.gov/xabout/laws/gc_1215444247124.shtm.

PAHO (Pan American Health Organization). 2000. Natural disasters: Protecting the public's health. Scientific Publication No. 575. Washington, DC: Pan American Health Organization, Pan American Sanitary Bureau, Regional Office of the World Health Organization.

Paul, B. 2006. Disaster relief efforts: An update. *Progress in Development Studies* 6 (2): 211–23.

Public Health Functions Steering Committee. 1994. Healthy people in healthy communities. http://www.health.gov/phfunctions/public.htm.

Redlener, I., C. DeRosa, and R. Hut. 2008. Legacy of shame: The on-going public health disaster of children struggling in post-Katrina Louisiana. The Children's Health Fund and the National Center for Disaster Preparedness, Columbia University Mailman School of Public Health. http://www.childrenshealthfund.org/sites/default/files/BR-White-Paper_Final_REV1-12-09F.pdf.

Relman, D. A., M. A. Hamburg, E. R. Choffnes, and A. Mack. 2008. *Global climate change and extreme weather events: Understanding the contributions to infectious disease emergence.* Workshop summary. Washington, DC: National Academies Press. http://www.nap.edu/catalog/12435.html.

Salinsky, E. 2002. Public health emergency preparedness: Fundamentals of the "system." National Health Policy Forum background paper. NHPF, Washington, DC.

Shea, K. M. 2007. Global climate change and children's health. *Pediatrics* 120 (5): e1359–67.

Shoaf, K. I., and S. J. Rottman. 2000. The role of public health in disaster preparedness, mitigation, response, and recovery. *Prehospital and Disaster Medicine* 15 (4): 144–46.

Subbarao, I., A. Dobalian, and J. James. 2011. Reflections on the discipline and profession of disaster medicine and public health preparedness. *Disaster Medicine and Public Health Preparedness* 5:S168–69.

Thomas, D., R. A. King, S. Montas, P. Minn, D. Varda, C. Sasson, and S. N. Ansari. 2011. *Local health capacities in northern Haiti response and recovery. Presented at AAG Annual Meeting.* http://meridian.aag.org/callforpapers/program/AbstractDetail.cfm?AbstractID=38964.

Titan Corp. 2005. *History of the Metropolitan Medical Response System: The First Decade.* Reston, VA: Titan Corp.

Trust for America's Health. 2008. Issue report: Shortchanging America's Health 2008, a state-by-state look at how federal public health dollars are spent. http://www.healthyamericans.org/reports/shortchanging08/.

Ursano, R., C. Fullerton, and A. Terhakopian. 2008. Disasters and health: Distress disorders and disaster behaviors in communities, neighborhoods, and nations. *Social Research* 75 (3): 1015–28.

U.S. Congressional Record. 2006. Pandemic and All-Hazards Preparedness Act (PAHPA). Public Law No. 109-417, 109th Congress. http://frwebgate.access.gpo.gov/cgi-bin/getdoc.cgi?dbname=109_cong_public_laws&docid=f:publ417.109.pdf.

Ver Ploeg, M., and E. Perrin, eds. 2004. *Eliminating health disparities: Measurement and data needs.* Panel on DHHS Collection of Race and Ethnic Data, National Research Council. Washington, DC: National Academies Press.

Wang, F., and W. Luo. 2005. Assessing spatial and nonspatial factors for healthcare access: Towards an integrated approach to defining health professional shortage areas. *Health Place* 11:131–46.

WHO (World Health Organization). 1948. Preamble to the constitution of the World Health Organization as adopted by the International Health Conference, New York, 19–22 June 1946; signed on 22 July 1946 by the representatives of 61 states (Official Records of the World Health Organization, no. 2, p. 100) and entered into force on 7 April 1948.

———. 1978. Declaration of Alma Ata, Article 1. http://www.who.int/social_determinants/tools/multimedia/alma_ata/en/index.html.

———. 2006. Improved formula for oral rehydration salts to save children's lives. http://www.who.int/mediacentre/news/releases/2006/pr14/en/index.html.

———. 2008a. Closing the gap in a generation: Health equity through action on the social determinants of health. Final Report of the Commission on Social Determinants of Health. http://www.who.int/social_determinants/thecommission/finalreport/en/index.html.

———. 2008b. Hospitals safe from disasters: Reduce risk, protect health facilities, save lives. www.who.int/hac/techguidance/safehospitals.

———. 2011. Top 10 causes of death. Fact sheet no. 310. http://www.who.int/mediacentre/factsheets/fs310/en/index.html.

RESOURCES

American Academy of Pediatrics. Children's health topics: Disaster preparedness. http://www2.aap.org/disasters/index.cfm.

American Journal of Disaster Medicine. http://www.pnpco.com/pn03000.html.

Centers for Disease Control (CDC). Emergency preparedness and response. http://emergency.cdc.gov/.

Centers for Disease Control (CDC). Coping with a disaster or traumatic event, trauma and disaster mental health resources. http://www.bt.cdc.gov/mentalhealth/.

Centers for Disease Control (CDC). Public health preparedness: Mobilizing state by state. A CDC report on the public health emergency preparedness cooperative agreement. http://emergency.cdc.gov/publications/feb08phprep/.

Centers for Public Health Preparedness (CPHP)program. http://www.cdc.gov/phpr/cphp/centers.htm.

Disaster Medicine and Public Health Preparedness. http://www.dmphp.org/.

Environmental Protection Agency (EPA). Emergency management. http://www.epa.gov/oem/content/er_cleanup.htm.

International Journal of Disaster Medicine. http://informahealthcare.com/journal/sdis.

International Strategy for Disaster Reduction. 2008. ISDR-biblio 3: Health, disasters and risk. Geneva: UN/ISDR-12-2008.

Journal of Prehospital and Disaster Medicine. The Official Medical Journal of the World Association for Disaster and Emergency Medicine. http://pdm.medicine.wisc.edu/.

Pan American Health Organization (PAHO). Disasters: Preparedness and mitigation in the Americas. News and Information for the international community. http://new.paho.org/disasters/newsletter/index.php.

Titan Corp. 2005. *History of the Metropolitan Medical Response System: The First Decade.* Reston, VA: Titan Corp.

U.S. Department of Health and Human Services, Agency for Healthcare Research and Quality (AHRQ), Public Health Emergency Preparedness. http://www.ahrq.gov/prep/.

U.S. Department of Health and Human Services, Assistant Secretary for Preparedness and Response, Office of Preparedness and Emergency Operations. http://www.hhs.gov/aspr/opeo/index.html.

U.S. Department of Homeland Security. 2011. National Preparedness Goal. Washington, DC: Government Printing Office.

U.S. Food and Drug Administration. Drug Preparedness and Response to Bioterrorism (FDA/CDER) http://www.fda.gov/Drugs/EmergencyPreparedness/BioterrorismandDrugPreparedness/default.htm.

World Health Organization. 2002. Gender and health in disasters. Geneva, Switzerland: World Health Organization.

World Health Organization. Humanitarian health action: Health emergency and disaster risk management. http://www.who.int/hac/techguidance/preparedness/en/index.html.

10 Language and Literacy

Jenniffer M. Santos-Hernández and Betty Hearn Morrow

CONTENTS

10.1 CHAPTER PURPOSE

Language and literacy are important social vulnerability factors. The inability to openly communicate, to thoroughly assess a situation, and to make (often quick) informed decisions affects the capacity of individuals to mitigate, prepare for, cope with, respond to, and recover from emergencies or disasters. Literacy is not just an indicator of the cognitive skills of an individual to read and write. Literacy is also an indicator of the situated tools that allow us to engage in society, access knowledge, and form our perception. Literacy is vital during crisis events and is important to understand how we can better reach those groups that are often marginalized because of language and literacy limitations. This chapter focuses on how language and literacy informs emergency preparedness and disaster experiences. The chapter intends to provide the readers with ideas and tools that seek to enhance their capacity to reach targeted audiences.

10.2 OBJECTIVES

As a result of this chapter, you should be able to:

1. Discuss the evolving meaning of literacy and different types of literacy and their relevance for emergency management, including: document literacy, prose literacy, quantitative and financial literacy, information literacy, media literacy, health literacy, computer and digital literacy, cultural literacy, visual literacy, legal literacy, and environmental literacy.

2. Review research studies that examine how language proficiency and literacy may impinge upon the capacity of diverse groups to receive and evaluate emergency or disaster-related information.
3. Provide an overview of current demographic patterns and their implications for emergency and disaster practitioners.
4. Present strategies to assess the reading level of disaster-related materials and to develop programs and systems that reach community members.
5. Develop an international perspective that allows you to recognize cultural differences and to effectively address literacy challenges.

10.3 INTRODUCTION

On a daily basis, many groups, including elders, individuals with impaired cognitive functions, individuals with physical disabilities, ethnic minority groups, the poor, migrants and their children, and those displaced by environmental degradation, experience language and literacy challenges. Literacy can be defined as "the ability of people to listen, speak, read, write, and think" (Cooper et al. 2012), whereas language can be defined as "a system of shared symbols that includes speech, written characters, numerals, symbols, and non-verbal gestures and expressions" (Witt 2009). Nevertheless, language and literacy extend beyond the mere ability to listen, read, write, speak, and think. Instead, they are tools that enable people to fully engage in society and to choose and secure a livelihood that can allow them to maintain, improve, and secure their lives and the lives of their children.

To better capture a more comprehensive view of how literacy affects life chances and outcomes, the definition of literacy has evolved. A more critical definition of literacy provides a more comprehensive understanding of the context in which the ability to listen, read, write, speak, and think is developed and how it affects the capacity of people to function in society. The study of literacy has become central for understanding the capacity of individuals to freely choose, achieve, and secure a sustainable livelihood. As such, exploring the implications of language and literacy in the context of social vulnerability to disasters is very important. The ability to access, interpret, share, and act upon emergency information during a moment of crisis can be vital. Being able to understand the symbols used to transmit emergency information to a diverse audience is key for public and personal safety. Beyond the ability to understand risk information, literacy deals with the ability of individuals to function in society. This chapter explores a comprehensive definition of literacy and language, how these can contribute to social vulnerability, and elaborates on its implication for emergency management.

10.4 THE EVOLVING MEANING OF LITERACY AND NEW TYPES OF LITERACY

Although the immediate thought when literacy is mentioned may be the ability to read and write, there are many types of literacy that facilitate our relationships with others and with the world around us. Some types of literacy are functional literacy, document literacy, prose literacy, computer literacy, cultural literacy, visual literacy, and quantitative literacy, among others. Literacy is an evolving concept, and it is much more comprehensive than just reading and writing.

The definition of literacy has evolved from one focused on communication to one that considers elements such as culture, politics, economics, religion, and race (Street 2011). Researchers have increasingly focused on understanding how literacy serves as a source of power that informs social exchanges or interactions among different members of society. Disaster practitioners can and must identify individuals and groups with literacy limitations during nonemergency times and develop capacity-building strategies that are appropriate to the needs of the population under consideration.

As the world has changed and as society has adopted new ways of structuring interactions, new forms of literacy have become important in ensuring that individuals can fully participate in society (Figure 10.1). Those "ways of structuring" are defined ways of achieving certain goals, for

FIGURE 10.1   Literacy types.

example, finding a job, filling a flood damage declaration, voting, and applying for preparedness programs. Different types of literacy can be perceived as "competencies" that individuals may utilize to fully engage in modern society. There are several forms of literacy, and because society is constantly changing, new "ways of structuring" social life or new forms of "literacy" are expected to emerge. Some traditional forms of literacy included document literacy, prose literacy, and visual literacy. Other more recent forms of literacy discussed are health literacy, legal literacy, cultural literacy, media literacy, digital literacy, environmental literacy, and financial literacy. What all types of literacies have in common is that they focus on evaluating our capacity to identify, access, analyze, evaluate, and use different social resources that allow an individual to participate and benefit from society.

   Document literacy consists of the ability to find information through documents, to complete a form, and to comprehend noncontinuous text. **Prose literacy** is the ability to read, analyze, comprehend, and synthesize information found in continuous texts, such as stories, news, and novels. **Visual literacy** consists of the ability to comprehend ideas and information transmitted through the use of images, figures, and forms. (See Photo 10.1.)

   Cultural literacy focuses on understanding the values, morals, long-standing concerns, and traditions that constitute the dominant culture and other subcultures. **Health literacy** consists of the ability to access, understand, analyze, interpret, and express health-related matters. **Media literacy** entails the ability to access, analyze, evaluate, use, and create different types of media. **Environmental literacy** is an emerging type of literacy that explores our understanding of topics such as air pollution, food production, energy, water, and waste management. **Digital literacy** consists of the ability to access and use different forms of digital technology. In addition, digital literacy includes the ability to locate, analyze, evaluate, and use information that is available through the use of digital technology. The emergence of new forms of digital technology has led to the creation and adoption of new ways to share and collect disaster- and emergency-related information (see Chapter 18).

PHOTO 10.1 An example of document literacy. These are forms used by a church after Hurricane Katrina to keep track of the distribution of food. (Photo by Jenniffer M. Santos-Hernández. With permission.)

   The development of smart-phone applications and tools opens a new set of possibilities for users and can serve as an example to understand the challenges of emerging forms of literacy (see also Di Maggio 2001). As the digital revolution advances, less than 3% of the people living in developing countries have access to a computer and even fewer have access to the Internet. In the United States, it is estimated that approximately 25% of households do not have Internet at home, a statistic perhaps surprising to some (U.S. Census of Population and Housing 2010). Table 10.1 illustrates the increasing access to computers and the Internet. Importantly, Internet use varies by demographic group (age, income level, etc).

   Smart phones offer more advanced computing capabilities and connectivity than preceding cell phones. However, in order to use a smart phone, the potential user is required to, first, have the economic resources to obtain one, and then to be literate in the use of digital devices. The user must become familiar with different applications and know ways to identify new ones in order to fully derive the benefits of having access to that type of digital device. While new ways of accessing information emerge, traditional ones do not necessarily disappear. Therefore, in some ways, the emergence of new technology not only creates new ways to share information, but also increases the complexity associated with that task. This challenge is particularly important for emergency management. While we may be inclined to seek new ways of sharing information through the use of new technology, we must first understand how the residents of a jurisdiction receive information. Before we identify and examine other ways to reach our constituents, we must have a clear under-standing of what sources of information are preferred by the public, why some sources are preferred over others, what kind of information they seek during an emergency, and what the main challenges in reaching certain groups or communities are.

   Beyond information sources, it is important to understand the culture of those whom we are trying to reach. Different groups have different systems of meanings and behaviors that define the way that routine and nonroutine tasks and events are done and interpreted. An example of cultural literacy

TABLE 10.1

Computer and Internet Access in the United States (in thousands)

Year	Households (total)	Household with computer at home (%)	Household with Internet use at home (%)
2010	119,545	76.7	71.1
2009	119,296	(x)[a]	68.7
2007	117,840	(x)	61.7
2003	113,126	61.8	54.7
2001	109,106	56.3	50.4
2000	105,247	51.0	41.5
1997	102,158	36.6	18.0
1993	98,736	22.9	(x)[b]
1989	94,061	15.0	(x)

Source: U.S. Census Bureau, Current Population Survey (CPS), October 1984, 1989, 1993, 1997, 2000, 2001, 2003, 2007, 2009, 2010.

[a] In 2007 and 2009, the CPS did not ask about computer access.

[b] Beginning in 1997, the CPS started asking questions about the Internet. Additionally, question wording regarding both computer use and Internet access differed from year to year.

PHOTO 10.2 The image on the door says "Public Health, Not Migration" at the local hospital of Jimani, Dominican Republic, after the 2010 Haiti earthquake. The sign is an example of lack of cultural literacy. In addition to the language barrier, since Haitians are generally not fluent in Spanish, a better sign would provide information on how to obtain immigration-related information for those Haitians who crossed the border into the Dominican Republic seeking medical attention. (Photo by Jenniffer M. Santos-Hernández. With permission.)

is the ability to recognize that different cultures have different rituals for handling the death and for mourning the loss of a member of their group. Another example could be the concern of some migrants for accessing information about their place of origin or for knowing the status of services to send or to receive money from their families in the aftermath of a disaster (see Photo 10.2). It is important for emergency personnel to be aware of those rituals, needs, concerns, and behaviors stemming from cultural values so that they can be taken into account during crisis events. (See Box 10.1.)

BOX 10.1   APPROPRIATE LANGUAGE WARNING MESSAGES

A case study of tsunami preparedness efforts in Puerto Rico illustrates the importance of care-fully selecting language(s) for evacuation warnings. The National Weather Service developed the TsunamiReady Program to help communities reduce tsunami-related impacts (NOAA 2012). Tsunami preparedness programs have brought many benefits for the local communi-ties, including the installation of monitoring systems, the installation of warning systems, and the development of response plans.

As specified by the TsunamiReady Program guidelines, depending on the size of the popu-lation served, a number of requisites must be met to be designated as a TsunamiReady com-munity. Standard requisites for all communities include:

- Having a 24-hour warning point, an emergency operations center (EOC)
- Having the standard National Weather Service (NWS) specific area receivers in public facilities
- Establishing a communication network between communities and counties, desig-nating safe zones and tsunami shelter areas
- Providing tsunami response materials to the public
- Encouraging hazard-related curriculum at schools
- Having a tsunami hazard operations plan
- Holding a meeting between the National Weather Service office and the emergency manager in charge twice every year
- Having an NWS official visit the community at least every other year

There are currently over 20 coastal municipalities in Puerto Rico that have been recognized as tsunami ready. As part of this program, an evacuation exercise was conducted at schools located close to the shore in western Puerto Rico. During the tsunami exercise, the National Weather Service emergency alert system was activated, and warnings were also emitted using recently installed sirens. These sirens have the capacity to emit a voice message, which may help reduce potential uncertainty when sirens are used for multiple hazards that require dif-ferent protective actions. However, the sirens that were installed at one of the schools emit the voice message in English. Even though English is an official language in Puerto Rico, the vast majority of the population communicates in Spanish, the other official language.

During the 2012 North Atlantic Tsunami Exercise in Puerto Rico, referred to as the LANTEX 2012 exercise, several schools were evacuated. The warning emitted during the evacuation was for a shooting. Nevertheless, students continued the evacuation. While it is hard to determine that language was the only reason why students continued the evacuation process, when participants were informally asked about whether they understood the message being transmitted, they usually claimed that they were just participating in the preplanned exercise and that they did not understand the English message being transmitted through the loudspeakers. This highlights the need to better understand the characteristics of the popula-tion we are trying to serve, and the need to internally and externally assess the implementation of preparedness efforts aimed at enhancing the warning communication and public response processes. The fact that the warning system transmits voice messages in English raises the concern as to whether the targeted audience will understand the message, and whether the message will elicit the intended action. While the new speakers may allow residents to more easily receive a message in an English-speaking locality, these technological improvements are likely not terribly effective in a Spanish-speaking locality.

(*Source*: Research conducted by Jenniffer Santos-Hernández as part of her dissertation data collection.)

10.5   LITERACY AND LANGUAGE PROFICIENCY

The inability to speak the language of the place where we live or are visiting can exacerbate our vulnerability to disasters. Perry (1987) found that people are more likely to hear a warning message if it is delivered in the language that they speak. People who do not speak the language of the place where they are located when a disaster occurs may experience numerous difficulties. For example, when focusing on the experiences of undocumented Latino workers after Hurricane Katrina, Santos-Hernández (2006) found that undocumented migrants who did not speak English often failed to understand the risk that the hazard represented to their lives and decided to stay in areas that were exposed to storm surge. Their vulnerability arising from language limitations was compounded by their migratory status and the fear of deportation.

Research on language and literacy is somewhat limited and mostly found within the literature devoted to risk communication and public response to warnings (Bolin 2006; Fothergill et al. 1996; Lindal et al. 2004; Peacock et al. 1997). For instance, Aguirre (1988) studied the 1987 tornado that struck the town of Saragosa, Texas, where 29 people died. He found that, although the vast majority of the residents were Spanish speakers, the message was not transmitted through the local Spanish television channel. A translation of the NWS warning message was transmitted through a local Spanish radio station, but residents failed to recognize its urgency because it was not followed by information through their other sources of information.

The increase in population displacement as a result of climate extremes also raises the importance of paying attention to language and literacy proficiency. Because of language limitations, evacuees often miss important information, ranging from everyday needs like the availability of services for personal care to long-term needs like reconstruction assistance (Subervi, F. 2010). Evacuees with limited language proficiency could enter an agreement without fully understanding, may be hesitant or unable to ask their questions or to express their situation, may not be aware of assistance services available, may receive erroneous information from others, and may risk their lives and their property because they are not able to fully understand the language and culture of their new location.

10.6   CURRENT DEMOGRAPHIC PATTERNS

In 2001, with the slogan of "Literacy as Freedom," the United Nations declared the years 2002 to 2012 as the U.N. Literacy Decade. The main goal of the U.N. Literacy Decade was to achieve access to basic education for all individuals by 2015 and to reduce illiteracy by 50% (UNESCO 2005). Basic education is a right entitled to all human beings in the Universal Declaration of Human Rights. Nevertheless, that right continues to be denied to over 776 million people who are considered illiterate, and two-thirds of those are women (United Nations Development Fund for Women 2008). Moreover, over half of those considered illiterate speak a language that is different from the one of instruction at their country of residence (UNESCO 2011).

The official language of instruction is often a source of conflict and disadvantage. In countries like Zimbabwe where multiple languages are considered as official, the language of instruction predominantly used in advanced education is not necessarily the most widely used language. In the case of Zimbabwe, English is considered the official language. However, the vast majority of Zimbabweans, speak Shona, Ndebele, and other Bantu languages. In many developing countries, the official language is a source of contention because it is tied to colonial political arrangements. With the exception of a few cases, not speaking the main language of instruction also means that you do not speak the official language of the country where you live.

Other countries, such as the Republic of Ireland, have a national language (Irish), but English is the main language used on an everyday basis. At the same time, English is often referred to as the "international business language." The shift toward a global economy has imposed the need for many countries to adopt English as the standard language for international communication. As developing countries adopt English as the language for international business, employees in those

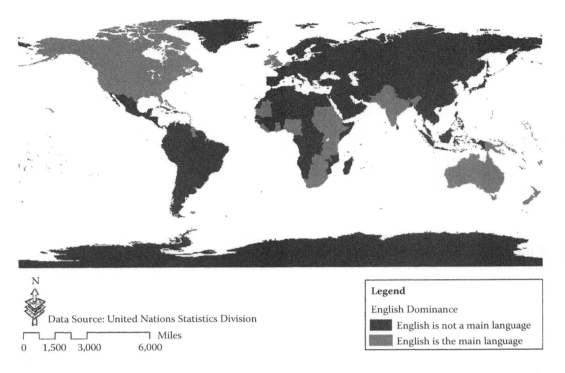

N

Data Source: United Nations Statistics Division

Miles

0   1,500   3,000   6,000

Legend
English Dominance
■ English is not a main language
■ English is the main language

FIGURE 10.2 Countries in which English is not the main language used by the population language or is an official language.

areas are forced to learn English to secure their current employment or to seek new opportunities in emerging employment sectors. Figure 10.2 shows countries where English is not the language used by the majority of the population.

The Literacy Decade was particularly important because it was crucial for an evolving definition of literacy by the international community and by national governments. The U.N. recognized that the skills required and the demands placed to fully engage in modern society extend beyond the traditional view of literacy, which focused on the ability to read, write, and communicate. This approach to literacy acknowledges that the definition of literacy is one that is evolving because is tied to a world that is constantly changing, hence the emergence of new types of literacy. In addition, it highlights the need to pay attention to the social context, the different ways of learning, and the sources of literacy inequality, such as gender, race, and religion, among others.

In the United States, the U.S. Census Bureau collects data on the ability of people to speak English and offers four categories to choose from—very well, well, not well, and not at all—as part of the American Community Survey (Shin and Kominski 2007). The data is grouped into four main language groups: Spanish, other Indo-European, Asian and Pacific Island, and all other languages. Twenty percent of the U.S. population five years and older speak a language other than English at home, and a quarter of those who speak a language other than English at home described their ability to speak English as "not well" or "not at all" (U.S. Census 2011a; Ryan and Siebens 2012)). While the distribution of the population among the four main language groups seems relatively even, Hispanics are overrepresented in the category of those who don't speak English at all. Table 10.2 presents illiteracy rates for the top countries sending immigrants to the United States through visas.

As shown in Table 10.2, women in immigrant populations are likely to be less literate. This is a serious issue for emergency managers, considering that women usually have primary responsibilities for household preparedness, caregiving, and recovery. Women in general tend to take hazard warnings more seriously, and thus are an important conduit to their families (Bateman and

TABLE 10.2

Illiteracy Rates for Countries with the Highest Number of Immigrants Entering the United States with Visas

Country of Origin	Number of Immigrants (2011)	Male Illiteracy	Female Illiteracy
Canada	12,800	1.0%	1.0%
Mexico	143,446	5.6%	8.2%
China	87,016	2.9%	8.7%
India	69,013	24.8%	49.2%
Philippines	57,011	5%	4.2%
Dominican Republic	46,109	10.6%	10.3%
Cuba	36,452	0.17%	0.18%
Vietnam	34,157	4.7%	8.9%
South Korea	22,824	0.1%	0.1%
Colombia	22,635	6.7%	6.6%
Haiti	22,111	46.7%	55.4%
Iraq	21,133	14%	29.4%

Source: U.S. Department of Homeland Security, the 2011 Yearbook of Immigrant Statistics.

Edwards 2002; Fothergill 1996; Sorenson and Mileti 1989). In fact, evacuation behavioral studies have revealed that men are less likely to evacuate (Morrow and Gladwin 2005). Women also tend to have heavy responsibilities for seeking relief supplies and assistance for the household after an event. The language and literacy problems of immigrant or poorly educated women can increase the challenges associated with getting help for their families from a system that tends to place women at a disadvantage.

10.7 COMPOUNDED VULNERABILITIES

Groups who have problems with English are likely to have other characteristics limiting their ability to respond to an emergency or disaster. Overrepresented in the "Below Basic" category in the National Assessment of Adult Literacy (NAAL) are people with multiple disabilities, the elderly, blacks and Hispanics, and those with less than a high school education (NAAL 2006). As previously mentioned, female immigrants are more likely to lack literacy, thus compounding other gender inequalities. Even documented workers may be wary of government authorities due to negative experiences with authorities in their home countries. Both recent immigrants and foreign workers are liable to have limited education and low literacy rates in their own languages. Tourists, international business representatives, and foreign exchange students may not speak English or be familiar with the area.

People who have language and literacy issues are also likely to be unfamiliar with the local culture of their current place of residence (Rogers 1992). They may be relatively new to the area, such as recent immigrants, migrants, foreign or guest workers, and be unfamiliar with local hazards and conditions. They are more likely to be located in rural or isolated areas. They often lack resources, including transportation, to respond without assistance. They may not have family and social connections in the community to consult in an emergency. Other vulnerability factors likely to be associated with limited language proficiency are poverty, race, and ethnicity (discussed in other chapters). Young children may only know their native language. These vulnerable groups will be especially dependent upon emergency managers and responders, making it essential that disaster professionals collect data on their conditions and location.

In the next section we discuss the imprtance of working with vulnerable groups prior to a disaster.

10.8   SOLUTIONS AND STRATEGIES

Effective emergency managers know the populations they serve and plan their programs accordingly. Paying special attention to those at highest risk is not only altruistic, it is good management practice. In the end, it can make the job easier. In fact, it is the responsibility of emergency managers and responders to take whatever measures necessary to reach everyone within their regions of responsibility. Any program receiving U.S. federal assistance must meet the requirements of an executive order that requires "meaningful access" to services for those with limited English proficiency (DOJ 2008). Including people of all language and literacy levels, defined in the broad sense, and tailoring educational and response plans accordingly can produce outstanding results. This section presents reading assessment methods, strategies for targeting specific groups, and a cautionary note on disaster policy transfers and the importance of internal and external policy assessments.

10.8.1   Become Literate about Our Communities

Emergency managers and practitioners are being required to become increasingly prepared to address the challenges posed by the uncertainty of a changing climate and new threats resulting from our evolving modernization (see Photo 10.3). Thus, it is important to provide them with the best training and tools that can allow them to address existing needs, prepare for unexpected situations, learn about the culture of those living in their jurisdiction, and achieve their ultimate goal of ensuring public safety. The tasks at hand are not easy ones, and this section is intended to provide the readers with some ideas and methods that can enhance their capacity to reach a diverse society.

10.8.2   Reading Level Assessment

There is little evidence of major systematic efforts to write emergency- and disaster-related printed materials at appropriate literacy levels. In some instances, the use of jargon makes it more difficult for people who are already under stress to understand instructions. The following quotation provides

PHOTO 10.3   A group of local and international assistance personnel having an ad hoc operations and international coordination meeting at a shelter in Jimani, Dominican Republic, after the 2010 Haiti earthquake. (Photo by Jenniffer M. Santos-Hernández. With permission.)

an example from the *Plain Language at Work Newsletter* (Impact Information Plain-Language Services 2006). Instructions from a post-Katrina state website:

> The Assistance Centers will help mitigate the potential for misunderstanding and abuse by providing standardized, structured, and guided relationships between homeowners and service providers. In addition, the Assistance Centers will maintain registries of professional service providers and building contractors. Through the Solicitation for Offer, Assistance Centers will be directed by the selected management firm and staffed by contracted experts, which may include non-profit organizations specializing in providing advisory services to homeowners (78 words, 39 difficult words, 16th-grade reading level).

This can just as easily be put as:

> Use the Assistance Centers if you have problems with builders or other services. These centers also keep lists of approved builders and services. We will attempt to select companies and non-profit groups who can best run these centers (38 words, 6 difficult words, 8th-grade reading level).

Emergency- and disaster-related materials, such as this chapter, tend to be written at high reading levels. For example, the average person may have difficulties in reading this chapter or in understanding the difference between risk and vulnerability and other conceptual terms and debates. Even before using any emergency and disaster materials available from state and national sources, it is a good idea to check their readability. In many communities, hazards materials need to be adapted to the lower language and literacy skills to better reach residents. There are several options for assessing the appropriateness of text materials. While these methods provide some guidance in terms of how to design materials for a general audience, many factors affect the readability of text, including sentence length, word choice, layout, tone, organization, use of illustrations, and appeal to the reader (Osborne 2000). While formulas are useful for a rough assessment, it is important to look at the material as a whole and to examine whether it includes information that is relevant and uses a language that is understood by those we are trying to reach. Using plain language and keeping an eye out for regional language variations is vital, as this will likely affect how the message being transmitted is interpreted by those we are trying to reach. Therefore, the methods available are useful for initial efforts, but constant collaboration between emergency managers and communities is the best way of ensuring that materials accurately represent and address the needs of the targeted audience.

Two of the most common methods of assessing readability are the Flesch-Kincaid Formula and the Simplified Measure of Gobbledygook (SMOG) developed by McLaughlin (1969). The Flesch-Kincaid Formula was created by Rudolf Flesch in the 1940s and later enhanced by John P. Kincaid (Kincaid et al. 1975). It is used by the U.S. Department of Defense as a standard test. It rates text on a 100-point scale: The higher the score, the easier it is to read the document. For most standard documents, a score of approximately 60 to 70 is accepted. However, for many targeted groups, a higher score is suggested. The Flesch-Kincaid Formula allows us to estimate the reading grade level and the reading age level. The reading grade level indicates the education required to easily understand a text. The formula for calculating the reading grade level is as follows:

$$0.39\left(\frac{\text{Total Words}}{\text{Total Sentences}}\right) + 11.8\left(\frac{\text{Total Syllables}}{\text{Total Words}}\right) - 15.59$$

The reading age indicates the minimum age for which a written material is appropriate. The formula to calculate the reading age level is:

$$0.39\left(\frac{\text{Total Words}}{\text{Total Sentences}}\right) + 11.8\left(\frac{\text{Total Syllables}}{\text{Total Words}}\right) - 10.59$$

Word-processing software (e.g., Microsoft Word, Open Office, among others) offers the Flesch-Kincaid assessment tool as part of the software package; the readability test toolbox is usually found under the Spelling and Grammar functions. Step-by-step instructions on how to use the Flesch-Kincaid tool in different word processing and office productivity platforms can be found using online search engines.

Another tool for evaluation the reading level of text is the Simplified Measure of Gobbledygook, often referred as SMOG, which is used to obtain a rough SMOG assessment (Table 10.3). The process for obtaining an approximate grade level using the McGraw SMOG conversion table consists of counting the number of words that contain three or more syllables in a chain of 30 consecutive sentences. Once the number of polysyllabic words (three or more syllables in a chain of 30 sentences) is counted, this number is looked up on the SMOG conversion table. For example:

This short sentence probably needs a reading grade level of less than nine.
This longer sentence, which contains an adjectival clause and polysyllabic words, probably has a reading age of more than sixteen years or grade level.

As a general rule, it can be assumed that people who are

- At a Grade 3 or lower will not be able to read most low-literacy materials and will need repeated oral instructions, materials composed primarily of illustrations, or audio or video messages
- At Grades 4–7 will need low-literacy materials
- At Grades 7–8 will struggle with most materials, but will not be offended by low-literacy materials

Developing simple materials that clearly explain the situation and specify the actions needed is vital in order to reach those with lower levels of literacy.

10.8.3 TARGETING HARD-TO-REACH GROUPS

Targeting hard-to-reach groups can be perceived as an overwhelming task. As we discussed in the previous section, materials that are available through government organizations do not always

TABLE 10.3
Simplified Measure of Gobbledygook (SMOG) Conversion Table

Total Polysyllabic Word Count	Approximate Grade Level (±1.5 grades)
0–2	4
3–6	5
7–12	6
13–20	7
21–30	8
31–42	9
43–56	10
57–72	11
73–90	12
91–110	13
111–132	14
133–156	15
157–182	16
183–210	17
211–240	18

Source: Developed by Harold C. McGraw, Office of Educational Research, Baltimore County Schools, Towson, Maryland.

integrate the needs of the population we are trying to reach. As a consequence, materials need to be adapted and innovative strategies have to be devised. Marginalized communities and disadvantaged groups often feel misrepresented, and the first step to connect with a hard-to-reach group is to engage them in the planning effort from early on. When communities identify themselves with the programs that are being offered to them, they engage in their implementation and adopt them more easily. One of the challenges when dealing with marginal communities is that they are often historically disenfranchised communities that do not trust government assistance programs. Therefore, clearly delineating the goals of any capacity-building program before reaching a community is vital for the establishment of a trustworthy relationship from the onset. It is important for emergency managers to clearly convey how a policy is relevant to the specific group, and what adaptations can and cannot be made to integrate other needs in addition to the ones specified by the policy. Having a clear and common understanding of the scope and limitations of a specific policy is vital for its success and for establishing long-term relationships with those communities.

10.8.4 Disaster Policy Transfers

When discussing disaster policy transfers, Aguirre (1992) stresses that the effectiveness of international emergency management programs depends on the sociocultural isomorphism of programs themselves, and how well they match the society hosting the policy. Sociocultural isomorphism refers to cultural similarities or uniformities among societies, groups, and subgroups. The increasing connections among different societies, a process referred to as globalization, has led to the formation of a world culture, or as some scholars argue, globalization has facilitated the diffusion or transference of a standardized Western culture.

Meyer et al. (1997) studied the process of globalization, specifically international isomorphism or the standardization of social structures in different societies. They argue that global models and standard organizational forms increasingly inform spheres or institutions such as the economy, politics, religion, the family, and others creating a world culture. Education is one of those institutions that is being transformed by globalization.

A similar pattern to that observed in social institutions is often observed in emergency management. In an effort to increasingly protect citizens, countries often adopt new technologies. In the developing world, the adoption of emergency management technologies and policies from developed societies often creates a paradox in which, although they may offer emergency managers opportunities, they do not fully meet their needs. For example, the adoption and implementation of an imported policy may allow emergency managers to secure funding for the purchase of more advanced communication devices. However, the devices capable of meeting the policy requirements may not be available in the new country, and they may need to be ordered from another country. The imported devices, in turn, may be designed for a different set of users, such as those who speak a language different from the one where the resources are now going to be used. The same can be the case for a community capacity-building program. Effective disaster-reduction and capacity-building programs are driven by the community. For disaster-reduction programs to be effective, they must not simply attempt to integrate and gain the support of the community, but recognize their importance as active contributors of local knowledge and information (Mercer et al. 2010).

The importance of the integration of community and scientific knowledge is recognized by the Hyogo Framework for Action, which was a result of the World Conference on Disaster Reduction held at Hyogo, Japan, in 2005. The use of participatory approaches affords an opportunity for people-centered capacity-building programs in which regular interactions between organizational representatives and community members are fostered. Although imported policies may contribute to increased professionalization in emergency management, to the adoption of standardized procedures, or to highlight the importance of mitigation initiatives, they may also fail to fully and effectively address the needs of the communities they intend to serve. This is because those policies where created for different users, stakeholders, or beneficiaries who may have different needs, perceptions, attitudes, and motives. The adoption of imported policies sometimes is the result of what disaster and public policy researchers refer to as "focusing events." Focusing events are those that provide advocacy and policy groups with the rhetorical tools to seek change (Birkland 1998).

In other situations, foreign technologies or management strategies enter host countries through international assistance. When different countries assist others affected by hazards, they do so because the organizational and social features of the affected society have provided the stage for a disaster or catastrophic event to take place. Some of the material resources transferred include food, water, medicines and health-care materials, educational materials, construction materials, and volunteer services. Some of the nonmaterial resources transferred include ideas or ways of managing crisis situations. When material resources are transferred, it is important to examine whether they are appropriate for their intended use. For example, in the aftermath of the Indian Ocean tsunami, delegations from several countries coordinated the donation of very sophisticated camping tents. However, concerns were raised regarding the camping tents as an environmental adaptation because of the high temperatures in the region; instead, makeshift tarp tents with cross-ventilation were preferred by local residents (Rodriguez et al. 2006).

While learning from the disaster experience of other communities is vital for risk reduction, adopted policies must be translated and adapted to the needs of the people they intend to serve. To do so, it is important to provide all stakeholders that may be affected by those policies with opportunities to evaluate their specific needs. External assessments are also very valuable because they may provide decision makers, the organizations implementing policies, and the communities being served with a fresh and systematic analysis that can allow them to identify challenges and seek appropriate and sensible changes.

10.9 SUMMARY

As society has evolved, it has become increasingly evident that the world is connected and increasingly integrated. The United States is also an increasingly diverse nation. Hispanic and Asian populations are expected to triple, and non-Hispanic whites will make up only one-half of the total population by 2050 (U.S. Census 2011b). While some regions will be impacted more than others, it would be rare to find a community in which there were not some people without English language proficiency, whether resulting from English not being their first language or from limited education, and thus low reading ability. English is also increasingly being used for international business and will increasingly reach areas dominated by other languages. These changes highlight the importance of working collaboratively and the need to ensure representation of all groups in decision making at different levels.

The aforementioned changes have critical implications for emergency management and disaster planning. Those with English limitations are also likely to have other qualities that can lead to response difficulties. It can be said that a community is only as resilient as its weakest link. Highly vulnerable populations are likely to suffer disproportional impacts from a hazard and to have the most difficulty during recovery. It is essential that we:

- Know our communities, including the locations of high-risk groups
- Use our communities, including local leadership of both genders
- Develop programs and materials to reach targeted populations in effective ways
- Understand the organizational elements that mediate the capacity of emergency managers to regularly work with vulnerable groups.

Spending time and effort up front can have a large payoff from a management perspective. The result will be better communication, better relationships, more effective partners, and safer communities. And from a social justice standpoint, empowering those to whom disasters are more pervasive is our obligation as fellow citizens.

DISCUSSION QUESTIONS

1. What are some specific case studies from past disasters where literacy or language barriers hampered access to emergency or disaster information and services? Are they still occurring?
2. How can formal and informal sources of information about limited-English-proficiency populations in local communities be used to improve safety and services?
3. What are some common trends in literacy rates related to gender and countries of origin? What are the implications for your community?
4. Find an example of disaster or emergency text that is difficult to read and/or understand. Rewrite it in plain English.
5. Explain one way to analyze the reading level of text materials. Practice with materials from the Web sites of major response agencies or from your own community.
6. What are some strategies for delivering messages to targeted audiences that may have limited English proficiency? What can be done to be sure that high-risk populations are not left out with increased use of new technologies? How can technology be beneficial and prejudicial at the same time?
7. How can the development of special materials for those with limited language and literacy skills also enhance emergency management programs in other ways?
8. How can better disaster-related policies be developed and implemented? How can emergency managers better prepare for reaching marginalized communities?

REFERENCES

Aguirre, B. E. 1988. The lack of warnings before the Saragosa tornado. *International Journal of Mass Emergencies and Disasters* 6 (1): 65–74.

———. 1992. Disaster programs as technology transfers: The case of Puerto Rico in the aftermath of Hurricane Hugo. *International Journal of Mass Emergencies and Disasters* 10 (1): 161–78.

Bateman, J., and B. Edwards. 2002. Gender and evacuation: A closer look at why women are more likely to evacuate for hurricanes. *Natural Hazards Review* 3:107–17.

Birkland, T. 1998. Focusing events, mobilization, and agenda setting. *Journal of Public Policy* 18 (1): 53–74.

Bolin, B. 2006. Race, class, ethnicity, and disaster vulnerability. In *Handbook of disaster research*, ed. H. Rodriguez, E. L. Quarantelli, and R. R. Dynes. New York: Springer.

Cooper, J. D., N. D. Kiger, M. D. Robinson, and J. A. Slansky. 2012. *Literacy: Helping students construct meaning*. Belmont, CA: Wadsworth, Cengage Learning.

DiMaggio, P. 2001. From the digital divide to digital inequality: Studying Internet use as penetration increases. Center for Arts and Cultural Policy Studies, Working Paper #15. Princeton University, Princeton, NJ.

DOJ (U.S. Department of Justice). 2008. Executive Order 13166: Improving access to services for persons with limited English proficiency. http://www.usdoj.gov/crt/cor/Pubs/eolep.htm.

Education for All Global Monitoring Report. 2011. The hidden crisis: Armed conflict and education. Paris, France: United Nations Educational, Scientific, and Cultural Organization (UNESCO).

Fothergill, A. 1996. Gender, risk and disaster. *International Journal of Mass Emergencies and Disasters* 14 (1): 33–56.

Fothergill, A. E., G. M. Maestas, and J. DeRouen Darlington. 1999. Race, ethnicity and disasters in the United States: A review of the literature. *Disasters* 23 (2): 156–73.

Impact Information Plain-Language Services. 2006. Post-Katrina jargon: Just what hurricane victims don't need. *Plain Language at Work Newsletter* 27, September 7. http://impact-information.com/impactinfo/newsletter/plwork27.htm (accessed December 12, 2012).

Kincaid, J. P., R. P. Fishburne Jr., R. L. Rogers, and B. S. Chissom. 1975. Derivation of new readability formulas (Automated Readability Index, Fog Count, and Flesch Reading Ease Formula) for Navy enlisted personnel, Research Branch Report 8-75, Millington, TN: Naval Technical Training, U. S. Naval Air Station, Memphis, TN.

Lindell, M. K., and R. W. Perry. 2004. *Communicating environmental risk in multiethnic communities*. Thousand Oaks, CA: Sage.

McLaughlin, H. 1969. SMOG grading: A new readability formula. *Journal of Reading* 22:639–46.

Mercer, J., I. Kelman, L. Taranis, and S. Suchet Pearson. 2010. Framework for integrating indigenous and scientific knowledge for disaster risk reduction. *Disasters* 34 (1): 214–39.

Meyer, J., J. Boli, G. M. Thomas, and F. Ramirez. 1997. World society and the nation state. *American Journal of Sociology* 103 (1): 144–81.

Morrow, B. H. 1999. Identifying and mapping vulnerability. *Disasters* 23:1–18.

Morrow, B. H., and H. Gladwin. 2005. Final report: *Hurricane Ivan Behavioral Analysis*. Submitted through Dewberry to U.S. Corps and FEMA. August. http://www.iwr.usace.army.mil/nhp/index.cfm?pgid=90&navid=48.

NAAL (National Assessment of Adult Literacy). 2006. A first look at the literacy of America's adults in the 21st century. http://nces.ed.gov/NAAL/PDF/2006470.pdf.

NOAA (National Weather Service). 2012. TsunamiReady Program. http://www.tsunamiready.noaa.gov/.

Osborne, H. 2000. In other words...Assessing readability...Rules for playing the numbers game. *Boston Globe. On Call.* December.

Peacock, W., B. Morrow, and H. Gladwin, eds. 1997. *Hurricane Andrew: Ethnicity gender and the sociology of disasters*. London: Routledge.

Perry, R. W. 1987. Disaster preparedness and response among minority citizens. In *Sociology of disasters*, ed. R. R. Dynes, B. DeMarchi, and C. Pelanda, 135–51. Milan, Italy: Franco Angeli Libri.

Rodriguez, H., T. Wachtendorf, J. Kendra, and J. Trainor. 2006. A snapshot of the 2004 Indian Ocean tsunami: Societal impacts and consequences. *Disaster Prevention and Management* 15 (1): 163–77.

Rogers, G. O. 1992. Aspects of risk communication in two cultures. *International Journal of Mass Emergencies and Disasters* 10:437–64.

Ryan, C. I., and J. Siebens. 2012. Educational attainment in the United States: 2009. Current Population Reports, U.S. Census Bureau.

Santos-Hernández, J. 2006. Losing everything: Undocumented Latino workers and Hurricane Katrina. In *Learning from catastrophe: Quick response research in the wake of Hurricane Katrina*. Natural Hazards Center, Special Publication #40. Boulder: University of Colorado.

Shin, H., and R. A. Kominski. 2010. Language use in the United States: 2007. American Community Survey Reports. U.S. Census Bureau.

Sorensen, J. H., and D. S. Mileti. 1989. Warning systems for nuclear power plant emergencies. *Nuclear Safety* 30 (3): 358–70

Street, B. V. 2011. Literacy inequalities in theory and practice: The power to name and define. *International Journal of Education Development* 31:580–86.

Subervi, F. 2010. An Achilles heel in emergency communications: The deplorable policies and practices pertaining to non-English speaking populations. Unpublished manuscript. Center for the Study of Latino Media and Markets, School of Journalism and Mass Communication, Texas State University–San Marcos.

UNESCO. 2005. Aspects of literacy assessment: Topics and issues from the UNESCO Expert Meeting, 10–12 June 2003, Paris.

United Nations Development Fund for Women. 2008. UNIFEM annual report. New York: United Nations.

U.S. Census. 2011a. Native North American languages spoken at home in the United States and Puerto Rico: 2006–2010, American Community Survey Briefs. http://www.census.gov/prod/2011pubs/acsbr10-10.pdf.

———. 2011b. 2010 Census shows America's diversity. http://www.census.gov/newsroom/releases/archives/2010_census/cb11-cn125.html.

U.S. Census of Population and Housing. 2010. Computer and Internet use in the United States. http://www.census.gov/hhes/computer/publications/.

Witt, J. 2009. *SOC 2009*. New York: McGraw-Hill.

RESOURCES

Citizens Corps Resources in Additional Languages. http://www.citizencorps.gov/resources/catalogue/language.shtm.

Limited English Proficiency: A Federal Interagency Website. Provides guidelines, tools, and materials for the implementation of language proficiency. http://www.lep.gov/.

National Resource Center on Advancing Emergency Preparedness for Culturally Diverse Communities. http://www.diversitypreparedness.org/.

U.S. Department of Homeland Security. 2011. *2011 Yearbook of Immigrant Statistics*. http://www.dhs.gov/sites/default/files/publications/immigration-statistics/yearbook/2011/ois_yb_2011.pdf (accessed December 12, 2012).

11 Households and Families

Tricia Wachtendorf, Mary M. Nelan, and Lynn Blinn-Pike

CONTENTS

11.1 PURPOSE

Disasters affect a wide range of units. Individuals experience differential impacts, sometimes influenced by their social characteristics—such as age, gender, race or ethnicity, ability, education level, or economic class—and always influenced by how they are embedded in their physical and cultural landscapes. There are, of course, other units of analysis affected by disaster events, including communities that may or may not be bounded by geography. This chapter, however, takes a close look at households and families as a unit of analysis, and considers the particular ways in which strengthening capacities in households may ultimately reduce vulnerability. Relevant content for our consideration of families and disasters that significantly overlaps with other chapters in this volume (e.g., violence, gender, age, ability) are not treated in depth in this chapter. Rather, readers are encouraged to consult those chapters directly.

11.2 OBJECTIVES

As a result of this chapter, readers should be able to:

1. Define and explain key terms that are used to understand household and family composition
2. Describe current household and family composition patterns in the United States and globally

3. Understand the relationship between household and family characteristics and warning, evacuation, response, disaster impacts, and the ability to recover from and disasters
4. Understand how households and families experience emotional/psychological, social, economic, and physical disaster impacts
5. Understand factors affecting economic and emotional recovery from disasters, as well as ways families cope
6. Explain strategies for action that emergency managers can take to reduce disaster vulnerability for households

11.3 INTRODUCTION

This chapter is divided into four sections. The first section (11.4) defines terms and concepts such as *household* and *family*. In addition, we provide a description of the current status of households and families and then highlight relationships between household composition, family and social networks, and the ability to respond to and recover from disasters. The second section (11.5) explains the relevance of understanding family and disaster research for the practice of vulnerability reduction. This section focuses on the disaster life cycle of warning/evacuation/response; impacts; and short- and long-term recovery. A third section (11.6) highlights renters as a particularly vulnerable household when disaster strikes. A fourth section (11.7) provides implications for action and outlines strategies for reducing vulnerability in disaster contexts, particularly for high-risk households. Across all of the sections, we offer examples of the effect country and culture may have on how families mitigate, prepare for, respond to, and recover from emergencies and disasters.

11.4 DEFINITIONS AND TRENDS

This section looks at key words and defines them for use throughout the chapter. After distinguishing between household and family, the section then looks at trends that influence these social units as they prepare for and respond to disaster. Due to the significant complexity in censusing families globally in a single chapter, this section necessarily focuses on U.S. census data to demonstrate areas relevant to disaster time periods.

11.4.1 DEFINITIONS AND CENSUS

What is a household? What is a family? How we define and understand these terms has real consequences in our ability to make sense of them in a disaster context. Indeed, most people respond to hazards and experience disasters as household members, be it as a single person living alone or as one with two or more members. The U.S. Census Bureau (2010a) defines a household as including all persons who occupy a housing unit, with one person in each household designated as a "householder." Likewise, the Census Bureau defines a family as a group of people living in the same household related by birth, marriage, or adoption. Most households are composed of families—people related by blood or marriage or who consider themselves to be family—but that is not necessarily the case. The U.S. Census Bureau defines a nonfamily household as "a householder living alone (a one-person household) or where the householder shares the home exclusively with people to whom he/she is not related" (U.S. Census Bureau 2012a). People at the household level make decisions related to insurance, housing mitigation, preparation, evacuation, response, and recovery. Their decisions, and the limits that families and households may face in making them, carry serious implications for exposure to hazards.

Although less true today than perhaps 50 years ago, the U.S. family has typically consisted of a nuclear family, that is, both parents and their children (Schwede 2007). Multigeneration families that include an elder adult are not uncommon, particularly among minorities, where families with more than one nuclear unit, such as two brothers and their families, are also sometimes found (U.S.

Census Bureau 2012b). Fields (2004) identified an increase in adult children returning to live with their parents, sometimes as single adults and other times as divorced adults with their own children. In some countries, the nuclear family may vary from the U.S. norm. For example, some nations practice arranged marriages such as in areas within Pakistan and China. Such practices still exist in many areas around the world, with the support of other social institutions (religion, politics) and as a reflection of cultural traditions. Still, concern exists that some arranged marriages are forced. In the aftermath of the 2004 Indian Ocean tsunami, the loss of spouses led to rapidly arranged marriages in some areas. With four times as many women dying as men, concern arose over rapid marriages for teenaged brides (Mulligan and Shaw 2011). Scholars have noted similar examples in disasters of conflict (e.g., war in Bangladesh, see Wahra 1994) and disasters of consensus (e.g., earthquake in Pakistan, see Sayeed 2009).

With respect to households in disasters, whether or not those living under the same roof are able and willing to pool their resources and make important decisions together becomes a critically important consideration for preparedness, mitigation, response, and recovery. At the same time, family networks frequently extend beyond the household to include other relatives. These nonhousehold kin networks and resources can play a role in how a household copes with emergencies and disasters, as we will learn more about later in this chapter. In 2010, about half of all U.S. households were composed of married couples with or without children (48%); 27% were composed of adults living alone; 13% were made up of individuals who were related; and 12% contained members who were not related.

11.4.2 TRENDS

U.S. government data show seven recent trends that point to the importance of considering both households and families when dealing with disasters (U.S. Census Bureau 2002, 2003, 2004, 2006, 2010a, 2012a, 2012b). First, the popularity of marriage is declining. In 1970, 68% of adults were married; in 2002 that number had declined to 60%, and in 2010 it was 48%. A second, and related, trend is that the age when people do marry is increasing. In 1960, the median age for marriage was 22.8 years for men and 20.3 years for women. In 2002, the numbers had changed to 27.1 and 25.3 years, respectively. In 2010, the numbers were 28.2 and 25.9, respectively. Also related to popularity of marriage is a third social trend involving the growing acceptance of couples living together outside the institution of marriage. The approximate number of cohabiting couples since 1960 has increased with time: 1960 (0.5 million), 1980 (1.75 million), 2000 (5.8 million), 2006 (6.4 million), and 2010 (7.5 million). In addition, in 2010, 22% of first births were to cohabiting couples, up from 12% in 2002.

The fourth trend relates to the greater diversity of families and households. The U.S. Census Bureau survey (2010b) asked citizens about 14 different relationships, including living with a husband or wife, in a nonfamily household, or in an unmarried-partner household. Comparing the data on these three household types in 2000 and 2010, family households decreased from 68% to 64% while nonfamily households increased from 32% to 34%, and unmarried-partner households increased from 5% to 7%.

Acquiring accurate data on the prevalence of same-sex couples is quite challenging. In all cases, states vary in how they define and count these relationships for same-sex couples, and additional changes may occur even between the writing and publishing of this chapter. Some states have legal definitions that award same-sex couples the same rights as heterosexual couples; other states offer only partial rights or do not recognize these unions at all. In 2010, there were 131,729 same-sex married couple households and 514,735 same-sex unmarried partner households in the United States. Beyond same-sex couples (lesbian or gay), people who live in bisexual or transgendered relationships remain undercounted both in the United States and worldwide. What is clear is that little research and few policies address the concerns of LGBT (lesbian, gay, bisexual, transgendered) families and households vis-à-vis disaster impacts.

A fifth trend relates to divorce rates, which have remained relatively high, although they have decreased slightly since the 1990s. In the United States, 1990 saw 4.7 divorces per 1,000 population; 2000 saw 4.1 divorces per 1,000 population, with additional declines in 2009 to 3.4 divorces per 1,000 population. Fewer divorces per 1,000 individuals in the United States reflects the previously described family and household trends concerning marriage: fewer marriages, later age of marriage, increased cohabitation, increased unmarried partner households (both same-sex and opposite-sex couples), etc.

Sixth, there is an increase in the number of minority groups in the U.S. population. The percent of minorities in the U.S. population increased from 31% in 2000 to 36% in 2010. From 2000 to 2010, the specific changes in the U.S. population were as follows: Hispanics/Latinos (12.5% to 16.3%), Asians (3.6% to 4.7%), blacks (12.1% to 12.2%), and whites (69% to 63.7%). In addition, it is important to note that different racial/ethnic groups tend to have different marriage rates. For example, in 2010, the following represents the percentages of married couples among all couples by ethnic group: white (81%), Asian (80%), Hispanic (55%), and African-American (48%). White and Asian couples are more likely to be married, and minority families are more likely to live in multigenerational households. This trend has also resulted in increased numbers of interracial/interethnic individuals, families, and households. From 2000 to 2010, the number of interracial/interethnic married couple households in which one person was multiracial increased from 16% to 17%, and those in which both persons were multiracial increased from 6% to 10%. In 2010, 9.5% of U.S. households were made up of opposite-sex married couples, each with a different race or Hispanic origin. The figures for unmarried households were: opposite sex (18.26%) and same sex (20.65%).

A seventh trend involves an increase in households with only one person, which is likely due to a combination of factors, including delayed marriage, increased numbers of childless couples, divorce, and increased longevity. The percentages of individuals living alone in various years were approximately: 1940 (8%), 1970 (15%), 2000 (25%), and 2010 (27%). A particularly interesting trend in highly developed nations occurs among older residents often living alone in households, particularly those over the age of 85. Disasters, such as heat waves, put elderly people living alone at particularly high risk of death, as seen after the 1995 Chicago and 2003 European heat waves (Klinenberg 2002; Larsen 2006). Given the fact that disability increases with age, concern for these presumably higher risk households should become more prevalent.

The bottom line is that only about one-quarter of U.S. households now include nuclear families, or, in other words, two heterosexual parents and their biological children. We will examine, in the following sections, the ways in which household composition influences disaster vulnerability and capacity, how families and households experience disaster events, and how emergency managers can better consider the needs and strengths of family and household units. (See Photo 11.1.)

11.5 VULNERABILITY ACROSS THE DISASTER LIFE CYCLE

Access to political, economic, and social capital affects the extent to which households experience greater vulnerability and the extent to which households are resilient. Whether expressed as capital (e.g., Aldrich 2011; Dynes 2005; Tierney, Lindell, and Perry 2001) or capacities (Anderson and Woodrow 1990), families and households have an advantage if they have: the ability to exert political will on key decision makers; access to financial and other material resources to aid in mitigation, preparedness, response, and recovery; and connection to others in social networks that can mobilize to provide help. Poor households; single-female-headed households; households with a member who is elderly or who has a disability; and lesbian, gay, bisexual, or transgender (LGBT) households experience greater vulnerability in particular phases of the disaster life cycle (see Chapters 4, 6, 7, 8). Minority households and families with lower incomes are also at higher risk for injury, death, or property loss (Fothergill, Maestas, Darlington 1999; Sharkey 2007).

PHOTO 11.1   Pumpkin Town, WV, 8/7/2001—A family of flood survivors stands with their belongings in a small community near McGraws. Left to right: David Trump, Wendy Trump, Minnie Trump holding her 3-week-old granddaughter Sarah, and Birchie Blankenship. FEMA has provided aid for the family. (FEMA News Photo by Leif Skoogfors.)

Disaster researchers and emergency managers often use the life-cycle approach to organize findings and plan services (Neal 1997). Here, given the structure of other chapters in the text, we divide the life cycle into three phases to facilitate discussion:

1. Warning/evacuation/response
2. Impacts
3. Short- and long-term recovery

We include evacuation in the warning phase, although some discussion as it relates to evacuation or sheltering in place is noted in the section on impacts, and sheltering is also treated in the section on recovery. Our division into distinct phases serves to focus our discussion, yet as Neal (1997) notes, the life cycle of disaster is based on ideal types, where in fact issues tend to blur or span across particular phases of disaster. In practice, however, vulnerability in one phase frequently closely connects to other phases, as illustrated in our discussion of renter households (see Section 11.6).

11.5.1   WARNING, EVACUATION, AND RESPONSE

Households and families generate internal resources and skills that can be helpful in a disaster context. For example, the presence of multiple households and family members increases the number of people available to mitigate disaster, such as when storm shutters need to be installed. Family members living outside of a disaster area can also provide a place to evacuate that is more comfortable and has more access to resources than a public shelter. Similarly, social networks can provide valuable emotional and financial support during a prolonged recovery period. Disruptions to these social relationships can undermine resilience in the face of disaster (Norris, Friedman, and Watson 2002; Norris et al. 2002). This section looks at warning, evacuation, and response by examining factors that influence these sociobehavioral responses.

11.5.1.1   Social Influences

What compels families and households to evacuate? Burnside, Miller, and Rivera (2007) found that family and friends have the greatest influence (e.g., compared to media) over evacuation behavior in hurricanes. Mikami and Ikedo (1985) confirmed these findings when they studied a devastating flood in 1982 in Nagasaki, Japan. For this event, Japanese families underestimated the possibility of a disaster and then made every effort to contact and be with their family members. According to Mikami and Ikedo (1985), in both pending floods and earthquakes, Japanese would return to their homes to check on the well-being of other family members. After Hurricane Katrina, respondents ranked being able to keep family members together as the third most important factor in future evacuation decisions. Only being able to track the hurricane and knowing its intensity were rated as more important (Morrow and Gladwin 2006). Given that hundreds of children became separated from family members during the evacuation of New Orleans (Osofsky et al. 2009), this concern is not unfounded. Separation can be profound and traumatic during major events. During the 2004 Indian Ocean tsunami, thousands of children experienced separation from their families or became orphaned. Governments, often with the assistance of nongovernmental organizations (NGOs), placed many of these children with family or foster families within one year of the tsunami (Nwe 2005). Agencies also worked diligently on reports of child abduction and human trafficking (Fisher 2009), a situation also found after a cyclone damaged West Bengal (Sinha and Bhattacharyya 2009). Clearly, advance warning and assistance with evacuation resources may be necessary to preserve and protect families, particularly children. As households and families increasingly go their separate ways each day to jobs, schools, and other activities, understanding that households evacuate as social units becomes important to emergency managers. (See Box 11.1.)

11.5.1.2 Social Networks

Marital status, one type of social and legal relationship, seems to influence family and household disaster experiences. Social isolation tends to be associated with slower warning receipt and inclination to evacuate, particularly among the elderly with health problems. Rosenkoetter et al. (2007) studied the perceptions of older adults regarding evacuation in a natural disaster. Their study found that living alone, coupled with health problems that decreased mobility and lack of transportation, influenced elderly individuals' receptivity to evacuation. Following Hurricane Katrina, elderly men died in numbers disproportionate to their population across New Orleans (Sharkey 2007). In contrast, nonelderly in committed partnerships and marriages appear to be more likely to prepare for disaster, to want to mitigate their risks, and to evacuate (Rosenkoetter et al. 2007).

Family members connected by social networks can also help with advice and resources. Interviews with families affected by massive flooding in Denver in 1965 showed that families evacuated as units

---

BOX 11.1 SURVIVAL VERSUS STAYING BEHIND TO HELP

Japan is no stranger to the devastating effects of tsunamis. Over time, Japan has developed a culture of *tsunami tendenko*. Those in threatened areas are taught to focus on running as fast as they can, without concern for others. They are encouraged explicitly to save themselves rather than returning to their homes, looking for loved ones, and remaining with those who are evacuating at a slower pace. There is a strong element of trust in others in this statement, which might not be immediately apparent to those unfamiliar with the culture. The trust lies in individuals taking responsibility for themselves: If everyone does their best to run to higher ground, at least some of the family members may survive. If everyone looks for others and delays evacuation, no one from the family may survive. Researchers who studied the effects of the 2011 Tohoku Japan tsunami found repeated reference to *tsunami tendenko*, although some people did opt to stay behind with family members who could not evacuate easily or nearly perished while helping a family member. Others expressed guilt for not helping others, even though they knew it would have meant losing their own lives.

Source: Chang et al. (2011) and SEEDS (2011).

and took refuge in the homes of relatives rather than in official centers (Drabek and Boggs 1968). Interaction between relatives during the warning period increased the likelihood that relatives' homes would be selected as evacuation points. Younger and older families, compared to middle-age families, were more likely to seek help from and to evacuate with extended family members.

Climate change is also directly affecting communities worldwide. For example, Allen (2006) examined the processes of community-based disaster preparedness and climate adaptation in the Philippines. Here, extended family structures (e.g., social capital) strengthen access to resources, especially if family members migrated to other communities and created bonds between communities.

11.5.1.3 Family and Household Composition

Multigenerational households are more likely to evacuate as a unit, and gathering family members takes time (Drabek and Boggs 1968). Household size also appears important with respect to evacuation destination. During the 2004 hurricane season in Florida, larger families were less likely than smaller families to move in with other family or friends during an evacuation (Smith and McCarty 2009). The authors found that host families generally have a hard time accommodating many visitors, particularly for extended time periods. A larger family, therefore, may more often need to seek shelter in public shelters or expend financial resources to stay in hotels. In general, about 20% of evacuating households will arrive in public shelters (Drabek 1986), though this finding probably holds true for some areas more than others. Areas of reduced income, such as developing nations or pockets of inner-city poverty, will likely generate greater need for relief efforts, including sheltering. Large-scale catastrophes, such as seen in the 2004 Indian Ocean tsunami or the 2010 Haiti earthquake, can also increase the numbers of displaced households. Even at the one-year mark, the massive destruction in Port-au-Prince (the capital of Haiti) had left close to 1 million survivors struggling to resume normal household activities while living in tent cities (Farmer 2011).

11.5.1.4 Income

Access to economic resources cannot be ignored as an important influence on the ability to mitigate against and prepare for disasters, or to take appropriate action in response to disaster warnings. Poverty increases vulnerability, and with 15% of the United States population below the poverty line in 2010 (U.S. Census Bureau 2011), a disaster further decreases their abilities to provide for members of their households and families. For those living in urban areas or dependent on public transportation, evacuation may be difficult to nonexistent. At least 120,000 residents in New Orleans (based on 2.4 persons × 51,000 housing units) did not have a vehicle available for evacuation purposes (Laska 2008). People affected by hurricanes, droughts, or famine in developing nations may lack resources to leave isolated or unsafe locations. Gaillard, Liamzon, and Villanueva (2007) examined the causes of the 2004 typhoon that devastated eastern Luzon, Philippines. They found that based on family size and socioeconomic status, poorer and larger families were relegated to living in dangerous areas in order to make a living. As a result of increased population and population density, individuals migrated to dangerous areas (e.g., flood plains, river deltas, and volcano slopes) to provide food for their families. Their lack of economic resources pushed them to areas where they were at greater risk. Their lack of economic resources also left them unable to take appropriate protective action in these hazardous areas.

Lower income levels are also linked to concerns about particular households and families, such as single parents, recent immigrants, senior citizens, and development status. Indeed, it is the intersection of these factors (income, gender, age, social isolation) that increases family and household vulnerability. To illustrate, low-income, female-headed households are particularly vulnerable in disaster contexts. After an earthquake in Bhuj, India, in 2001, efforts to offer relief focused on helping widows and their children (Lund and Vaux 2009). Nongovernmental organizations seeking to help women and children in Turkey established microscale economic efforts that transformed into small factories run by widows (Yonder, Akcar, and Gopalan 2009).

In short, plans that rely on personal responsibility to evacuate often overlook the real ability of many households to comply, particularly when access to public transportation leading up to and during the event is scarce. Further, assumptions made about why people do or do not leave also ignore the very real consequences of such evacuation choices. The impacts of those choices can be significant.

11.5.1.5 Age

Households with children have a higher probability of perceiving risk associated with disasters (Riad and Norris 1998). Consequently, families and households with children are more prone to evacuate; in contrast, families and households with elderly experience more difficulty in evacuating (Gladwin, Gladwin, and Peacock 2001). These studies clearly tell us that many families make their preparation and evacuation decisions as a unit, and will wait for all family members before leaving, a pattern particularly common in minority and intergenerational households. To illustrate, Drabek and Boggs (1968) reported on a study of Denver families who experienced relocation as a result of the massive flood of 1965. They described (a) the families' responses to initial warnings as disbelief, (b) their preferences to evaluate as a unit, and (c) their desires to take refuge in the homes of relatives rather than in official shelters. (See Photo 11.2.)

11.5.1.6 Minority Families and Households

Several studies have examined warning perception and evacuation compliance for minority families, suggesting that perceptions of the information and language barriers can leave these families at risk when disaster threatens their community. Perry and Greene (1982) studied the responses of Mexican-American families when they were warned of a pending flood in the western United States in 1978. The flood eventually resulted in over $6 million in damages and the evacuation of 1,200 people. The authors reported that the Mexican-American families, compared to white non-Hispanic families who lived in the same danger zone, were more skeptical about the warnings and perceived themselves to be in less danger. Consequently, they were less likely to evacuate, and continued with their daily routines.

PHOTO 11.2 Houston, TX, 9/5/2005—Thomas John and baby brothers were among the 18,000 Hurricane Katrina survivors who were housed in the Red Cross shelter at the Astrodome and Reliant center after evacuating New Orleans. (FEMA photo by Andrea Booher.)

Although Perry and Greene's 1982 study is several decades old, more recent research suggests that the relationship between minority status and evacuation delay/noncompliance remains a relevant concern in the United States. Approximately 100,000 poor and African-American residents did not evacuate the greater New Orleans area prior to when Katrina made landfall (Nigg, Barnshaw, and Torres 2006). Eisenman et al. (2007) and Fothergill, Maestas, and Darlington (1999) suggested that minorities living in the United States were at greater risk for not responding to disaster warnings due to language barriers, distrust of governmental authorities, preferences for seeking information from family or relatives (versus other official sources), and lack of transportation and economic resources. Others suggested that "cultural ignorance, ethnic insensitivity, racial isolation, and racial bias" resulted in these households being less prepared, having fewer resources for evacuation, and lacking access to relief and recovery services (Fothergill, Maestas, and Darlington 1999, 169). A study of flooding in Fiji revealed that internal cultural and religious differences required varying and culturally sensitive relief and recovery efforts (Gillard and Paton 1999). Vulnerability of minorities in disasters is addressed in more detail in Chapter 5 of this text; however, it is important to note that the findings on minorities are equally relevant to the behavior and experience of minority families. (See Box 11.2.)

11.5.1.7 Pets

The choice to evacuate, or the extent to which warnings are taken seriously, is not always predictable. For example, there is some evidence that the more pets in a household or family, the higher the risk of noncompliance in household evacuation. In a study by Heath et al. (2001), many residents explained that they failed to evacuate because they owned multiple pets, owned outdoor dogs, or did not have a cat carrier. This study reinforced that human–pet bonds influence family emergency evacuation. Heath et al. (2001) concluded that predisaster planning should place a high priority on facilitating pet evacuation through predisaster education of pet owners and emergency management personnel. (For more information on the relationship between pet attachment and family evacuation, see Chapter 14 on animals in disaster.) In addition, it is important for mental health professionals who work in disaster preparation and response to comprehend the importance of this human–pet bond. Similar outcomes in evacuation noncompliance by pet owners resulted in federal mandates for state emergency plans to take pets into account in evacuation and sheltering (Congressional Research Service 2006; Pets Evacuation and Transportation Standards Act 2006).

In sum, the issues that concern households and families will vary, depending on the country and region in which their members live and the threats they face. Their ability to mitigate against and prepare for disasters, as well as respond to warnings, will depend on the economic, political, social, cultural, and geographic circumstances in which they find themselves at the time. (See Box 11.3.)

11.5.2 IMPACTS

Different types of households experience different challenges after disaster strikes. This next section highlights just a few of the ways that the family and household characteristics can influence

---

BOX 11.2   TRUST AND HOUSEHOLD MITIGATION

Sources of trusted information likely affect which mitigation measures are taken. Peguero (2006) was interested in Latino disaster vulnerability and the dissemination of hurricane mitigation information among Florida's homeowners. In this study, Latino homeowners relied on family (and friends) for information on disaster mitigation. Immigration status was not asked of respondents, but the findings could also suggest that family networks among illegal or recent immigrants are a vital source of information on mitigation practices.

BOX 11.3   PREPAREDNESS

Concerns about disaster threats vary considerably worldwide. While residents in areas along the American Southeast and Gulf Coast worry about hurricanes, communities in the Midwest worry about tornadoes, and communities along the West Coast worry about earthquakes. Fung and Loke (2010) found that infectious disease, e.g., severe acute respiratory syndrome (SARS), was the largest disaster concern among families with children under the age of 15 in Hong Kong. This was especially so given the crowded conditions that are typical in that city. Unfortunately, lack of household preparedness is fairly common worldwide. Among Hong Kong families with children under 15, approximately half were sufficiently prepared for a disaster (i.e., having three days of supplies). Less than half were confident in their government's response to disasters (Fung and Loke 2010). In New South Wales, Australia, only 23% of households reported being prepared (i.e., a flashlight, "battery-operated radio, appropriate batteries, mobile phone, emergency contact list and first aid equipment") prior to a severe storm that resulted in 10 deaths (Cretikos et al. 2008, 195). In 2005, 55% of New York residents stated that they felt well informed of how to react in the event of an emergency; however, only 14% stated that they had a household emergency plan in place, and only 36% of those surveyed stated that they had the proper supplies to prepare for an emergency (i.e., "three days of water and nonperishable food, a first-aid kit, flashlight, battery-operated radio, and personal hygiene items") (Citizen Preparedness Research 2005, 8). Approximately half of the parents surveyed stated that their children are aware of how to behave in the event of an emergency if their parents are absent, and approximately the same percentage reported past conversations with their children about emergency plans.

disaster vulnerability. We will also suggest ways in which breakdown of the family structure and other factors can exacerbate household and family stress in the postdisaster environment.

11.5.2.1   Family and Household Characteristics

When we take a close look at several household examples, each of which includes composition of different family members with unique needs and circumstances, we can begin to appreciate the wide range of concerns facing households and families in the postdisaster milieu. In this section, we look at three types of compositions that matter for families impacted by disaster: same-sex couples, families with members who have disabilities, and those affected by language barriers.

Little evidence has been gathered to date about the experiences of LGBT families and households. What is clear is that the impacts are influenced by policies that fail to consider basic human rights such as visitation of loved ones who were hospitalized, survivors' rights, or abilities to comfort each other in public. Stigma still associated with sexual orientation and gender identification can generate hardships in the postdisaster environment, and legal constraints imposed on same-sex couples can exacerbate obstacles they routinely encounter. Stigma against same-sex relationships can make it difficult or even dangerous for LGBT couples to comfort each other in public settings, for example, or disclose their relationship to public officials while seeking household assistance. In countries—such as Kenya, Kuwait, Saudi Arabia, Iran, and Burma—where homosexuality is still considered illegal, same-sex couples may face additional threats to personal safety or even an increase in hate crimes (see Chapter 12 on violence; see also Eads 2002; D'Ooge 2008).

Households that comprise members with disabilities may face particular hardships in the aftermath of disasters. People with disabilities may rely on assistive technologies and durable medical equipment. This necessary equipment may be left behind during a hasty evacuation or may be lost or damaged. These family members with disabilities are consequently left more dependent on others, which can be challenging if they are separated from their family and others in their social support network. These circumstances can also increase the burden on family members, even when the person with the disability would otherwise be relatively independent. Loss of a walker or wheelchair can suddenly leave a family member dependent on others for mobility and functional access. Loss of a hearing device suddenly leaves a person who is hard of hearing dependent on family members for information and communication. Loss of critical medication suddenly leaves a person dependent on family to regularly procure this critical necessity (National Council on Disability 2009; see also Chapter 8 on disability).

Likewise, language and immigration status can leave a household differentially at risk. Recent immigrants, in particular, require targeted outreach because of their lack of familiarity with types of disasters and appropriate protective measures. According to estimates by the 2010 American Community Survey, in the United States, 4.6% of households do not have a household member 14 years old or older who speaks English only or very well. For households speaking Spanish or an Asian/Pacific Island language, 24%–27% of households do not have a member 14 years or older who speaks English only or very well (U.S. Census Bureau 2010b). The diversity of languages present within the United States is also found in other nations. In Pakistan, people speak Urdu, Pushto, and other regional languages associated with various tribes—a reality also found in Kenya, India, and other nations. In addition, those who use American Sign Language practice regional variations in their signs, and people who sign in other nations do so with local colloquialisms and jargon. Outreach, education, and assistance leading up to, during, and after a disaster must, therefore, be multilingual and consider spoken and signed languages as well as literacy levels. (Also see Chapter 10 on language and literacy.)

An example of a positive approach to reaching out to non-English speakers occurred after the September 11, 2001, terrorist attacks. The airplane that struck the World Trade Center in the United States killed thousands of people, many of whom had family connections around the world. The Federal Emergency Management Agency (FEMA) issued disaster information in dozens of languages across the affected region and through organizations interacting with the family members of the missing. Such outreach must continue in the postdisaster environment when helping organizations may claim that second-language responses are challenging to provide. Santos-Hernandez (2006), for example, visited a shelter in operation after Hurricane Katrina struck the U.S. Gulf Coast. Spanish-speaking shelter occupants were unaware of resources and shelter rules, which shelter personnel had posted in English, and had no way to communicate with the English-speaking staff. Phillips et al. (2012) found similar challenges among providers who sheltered Vietnamese-American and Cajun (i.e., French-speaking) families.

11.5.2.2 Types of Impacts

Table 11.1 shows that disasters can impact households and families in four ways: economic, emotional/psychological, physical, and social. No household or family is affected in exactly the same way, and many face different combinations of these four impacts. In our treatment of household and family impacts, we weave back and forth between the various effects as the economic, physical, and social effect are often closely linked to increases in emotional stress for the family.

As demonstrated throughout this volume, disasters affect populations and even geographic regions differently. The Indian Ocean tsunami killed between 200,000–300,000 people in 2004; the same year, almost 80,000 people died in the Kashmir, Pakistan, earthquake. Cyclone Nargis killed over 100,000 people in Myanmar in May 2008, the same month that approximately 70,000 perished in the Sichuan China earthquake. Haiti's devastating earthquake in 2010 claimed at least 200,000 lives. Add in fatalities from disease, heat waves, famines, occasional flooding, and other events that strike around the world, we begin to recognize the high cost of disasters to human life.

Although costs to families and households are high in all settings, the economic demands of disasters may vary, depending on whether the location is a developed or emerging country. In most disasters, the high costs pertain primarily to housing and property losses, job losses, and needed resources (Comerio 1998). In emerging countries, scarce federal, state, and local funds that were

TABLE 11.1

Four Ways Disasters Can Impact Households and Families

Economic	Uninsured home and property losses
	Temporary or permanent loss of employment
	Loss of resources used for household or income generation
	Higher living costs, including transportation
Emotional/psychological	Role overload, conflict, or inadequacy
	Overworked parents and bored children
	Stress in intimate and partner relationships
	Family violence and human trafficking
	Behavioral problems in children
	Loss of pet
Physical	Loss of family members and/or friends
	New disabilities from disaster injuries
	Destroyed or damaged homes
	Loss of possessions including personal treasures
	Loss of environment and tools for everyday living
	Temporary or permanent dislocation
	Longer commutes to work or school
	Loss of local businesses, services, schools, recreational programs, etc.
Social	Loss of neighborhood
	Loss of social networks, institutions, and services
	Expanded roles for both women and men
	Becoming an orphan or widow/er
	Community impacts including migration

Source: Based in part on FEMA (2003).

previously targeted for growth and development may be reallocated to pay for relief and reconstruction. Predisaster conditions also set the stage for postdisaster effects on the family. For example, prior to the 2008 China earthquake, many of the men had migrated to the cities for work and were not present during the disaster (Tomlinson 2010). Women took on family responsibilities as the main caregivers prior to, during, and after the earthquake. In addition, women prioritized family well-being, which meant that they primarily worked in the home and did not seek outside employment to provide income for the family (Tomlinson 2010).

When a disaster hits, some individuals are less affected, or may even benefit, while other individuals may suffer significant or even catastrophic losses, depending on where they live. While economic losses might be large in areas of high risk, some of those affected may benefit from safety nets such as insurance and additional financial resources to absorb and recover from the loss. Thus, vulnerability to natural disasters is a combined function of exposure (risk of experiencing a disaster event) and the ability to cope (Masozera, Bailey, and Kerchner 2007).

Losses associated with family and household units include work locations. One might lose an income due to a factory or office being destroyed or because a small or home-based business was lost. Raising livestock and crops is prevalent in agricultural areas and serves as a primary source of income and food for families worldwide. The death of that livestock may lead to economic hardship for families following disasters. Mallick, Rahaman, and Vogt (2011) reported that none of the families in their study group had planned to save their livestock from the resulting floods from Cyclone Alia, which struck India and Bangladesh in 2009. Consequently, livestock died, and much of the surviving livestock was sold off or died following the flood due to the lack of usable drinking water. Women and children who were tasked with finding drinkable water had to travel 2.5 hours further each day. This additional distance led to higher dropout rates in schools because of the time necessary for water collection (Mallick, Rahaman, and Vogt 2011). In this case, we can see how economic losses not only affect family resiliency but also family responsibilities and long-term education for children within the household. Decimation of cattle in rural Alberta, Canada, in 2003, resulting in the inability to sell Canadian beef to the United States given discovery of bovine spongiform encephalitis (BSE) in other provinces, not only wrought economic hardships, but increased stress levels significantly, particularly among women. To respond, women altered household spending habits, increased their work time, and decreased leisure time (Reinsch 2009).

Not all effects of disasters are negative for families. Lindgaard, Iglebaek, and Jensen (2009) examined changes in family functioning in the aftermath of the 2004 Indian Ocean tsunami. In a study of Norwegian families who had been traveling in Southeast Asia during the tsunami, they found that those families reported increased cohesion among family members who had also experienced the event. In other words, these Norwegian family members shared the disaster experience. Rather than feel their disaster experience was isolating and that no one else understood what they had gone through, these Norwegian families were able to bond through the experience. Notably, however, these Norwegians families were tourists in Southeast Asia when the tsunami struck. The families were able to leave the affected areas and return to their homes that were left unscathed, unlike families residing in the impact-zones, who suffered widespread losses and would face the challenges associated with community recovery. Indeed, other studies of disaster survivors who lived where the event had occurred reported a breakdown of the family support system (Babugura 2008; Rofi, Doocy, and Robinson 2006).

Interestingly, even within the same study, a small group of parents who felt distant from their spouses reported more arguments, particularly about the tsunami itself. Some children were afraid to leave their parents and preferred to sleep with them at night. This observation points to the important role parents play in providing comfort to young members of the family after a disaster event (Lindgaard, Iglebaek, and Jensen 2009).

Sometimes, disaster survivors invent their own kinship relationships to at least temporarily compensate for those compromised by the event. For example, Blinn-Pike, Phillips, and Reeves (2006) found that Katrina evacuees formed bonds with the other residents in their shelters and formed what they described as "family" units that provided important temporary and short-term support.

Disaster impacts can include significant changes in family structure. Rofi, Doocy, and Robinson (2006) studied the tsunami mortality and displacement in Aceh Province, Indonesia, where more women than men died. Gender roles (see Chapter 6 in this volume) increased female vulnerability, as women were more likely to be home during the tsunami, often with their dependent children (Nishikoiri et al. 2006). Similar patterns exist with the elderly, who are often home when disasters strike, as was the case with the Japanese earthquake and tsunami of 2011. In the case of the Indian Ocean tsunami, children lost mothers, and husbands became widowers (Rofi, Doocy, and Robinson 2006). Wachtendorf et al. (2006) reported a similar finding from the same event in India and Sri Lanka. Given the clearly defined gender roles in the villages they visited, many widowers reported concerns about how they would become the primary caregiver to children, particularly if many women in their extended family also perished in the disaster. Men were left contending with unfamiliar roles and expressed concern that they would prove inadequate as caregivers (Wachtendorf et al. 2006; Kumaran and Torris 2011). (See Photo 11.3.)

Gendered changes in families seem common, with considerable impacts on women. Following Hurricane Andrew in Miami in 1992, women worked together to advocate for their families (Enarson and Morrow 1998). Women increased responsibilities for their personal lives (e.g., family, homes, employees, etc.) and engaged in advocacy for women in the broader community. Women experiencing the 1997 flooding in Grand Forks, North Dakota, U.S., shouldered tasks generally thought to be men's work (i.e., sandbagging) and redefined their community and family roles (Fothergill 2004). Other roles remained the same but increased with women continuing in the role of family caregiver, a finding reported as early as the 1964 Alaskan earthquake (Auf der Heide 2000). Daycares closed

PHOTO 11.3 Many widowers in India and Sri Lanka worried about their ability to take on new roles in child rearing after the mothers of their children perished in the 2004 tsunami. (Photo courtesy of the Disaster Research Center, with permission.)

down, with an increasing burden typically placed on women. These types of gendered impacts on families are common worldwide, including leading efforts to secure relief supplies. (See Photo 11.4.) In some events (e.g., the 2010 Haiti earthquake), though, women and girls have experienced harassment and violence while waiting for food and water (Farmer 2011). Extended family networks proved useful for many women in such cases, from day care to personal protection. When those networks were unavailable, young children and youth were at risk to sexual violence when older family members left the household to acquire aid or employment (Farmer 2011). In some cases, women earned higher positions following the Grand Forks flood, and earned more money as a result (Fothergill 2004).

Post-disaster convergence of people is well-documented in the literature (Kendraand Wachtendorf 2003; Heath et al. 2001; Wenger and James 1994; Scanlon 1991; Fritz and Mathewson 1957). Among these convergers, the anxious include families trying to find missing loved ones, including pets. For example, after the 2008 Wenchuan, China earthquake, family members converged on the last known locations of loved ones. Families may experience considerable stress trying to locate loved ones.

Family-assistance centers play critical roles in helping people find out about their loved ones and supporting them during a stressful period. For example, after the 2001 terrorist attacks in New York City, which left thousands of people unaccounted for, family and friends plastered the city with photos of missing loved ones. The city quickly established a family-assistance center in midtown Manhattan and later expanded their effort to a larger shipping pier facility along the Hudson River. The assistance center provided counseling services and served as a convenient, one-stop facility to submit DNA samples, apply for financial assistance, make free national and international phone calls, receive first aid, have a meal, and connect with other families (Kendra and Wachtendorf 2003). Even during smaller events, such as airline crashes, family-assistance centers provide important services and information dissemination. (See Box 11.4.)

Helping families may not be a simple or straightforward task, and it certainly is one that requires cultural sensitivity. Wachtendorf et al. (2006) studied the impacts and consequences of the December 2004 Indian Ocean tsunami in India and Sri Lanka. In one community, donated tents meant to serve as temporary shelters in India went unused by displaced survivors. Survivors

PHOTO 11.4 Concrave, Haiti, 2/4/2010—Haitian women and children queue to receive humanitarian aid rations distributed by sailors assigned to the amphibious dock landing ship USS *Carter Hall* (LSD 50). *Carter Hall* is conducting humanitarian and disaster relief operations as part of Operation Unified Response after a 7.0-magnitude earthquake caused severe damage in and around Port-au-Prince, Haiti, January 12. (U.S. Navy photo by Mass Communication Specialist 1st Class Monique Hilley/Released.)

BOX 11.4   INTERNET AND SOCIAL MEDIA CONNECTIONS

More recently, the Internet has begun to play a critical role in disaster response. For example, the American Red Cross has established a Safe and Well online registry, where disaster survivors can register to note their well-being. Family in or outside the disaster-affected area can search for the names from anywhere they have Internet access. After the 2007 Virginia Tech University shooting in the United States, students encouraged their peers to update their Facebook status with "I'm ok" and created a Facebook page, "I'm ok at VT" (Vieweg et al. 2008). Following the 2010 Haiti earthquake, the 2011 New Zealand earthquake, and the 2011 Japan tsunami, the online search company Google launched a people-finder service to enable loved ones to search for the status of those in the impact zone (L.A. Times 2011). Social-media technologies offer new options for family members seeking information about their loved ones, particularly for families at great distance from the disaster itself who might not otherwise be able to access a physical location for a family-assistance center. These technologies offer alternative means for communication, including in remote areas of developing nations. Nevertheless, the "digital divide" remains a significant barrier for many. What is key, though, is that social units (families and households) will use social-media tools to reestablish or maintain social relationships.

---

said that the tents felt like ovens in the hot day sun, which proved particularly problematic, as their campsite was in an area without shade. But the tents also did not take into account family structure. Barely able to accommodate four people, the donated tents were ill-suited to large families with many children and extended kin. The families improvised ad hoc tents that allowed in the sea breeze to cool occupants and open their tents to many family members. Another critical household matter emerged when residents realized that relief packages distributed by the Indian government did not account for varying sizes of household units. Again, families adapted creatively. Households with fewer members bartered their extra items for other goods they needed.

Research demonstrates that families and household units provide critical social support in coping with disaster impacts. Social units can respond creatively and effectively to the stress associated with disaster impacts, even when government and nongovernment organizations fail to understand their needs. By understanding and applying the research, we can not only explain the impacts of disasters on families, but identify practical solutions as well.

11.5.3 SHORT- AND LONG-TERM RECOVERY

Recovery is the least-researched phase of disasters. Existing research points to the role of both family and community-level factors in determining the effectiveness of short- and long-term recovery efforts. Here, we discuss economic recovery and emotional recovery together, given that both are so closely linked in the research.

11.5.3.1 Economic and Emotional Recovery

Just as households and families are different and are affected by disasters in different ways, they also recover in different ways. What determines the degree of continuing vulnerability from a disaster? What accounts for two families from the same area, both left homeless, coping very differently one year after the disaster? Family 1 may experience increased family stress, depression, and child behavioral problems, while Family 2 may keep an optimistic outlook and draw closer to family, friends, and spiritual beliefs to get through this critical time. Family 1 could be described as being more vulnerable, while Family 2 could be described as more resilient.

At the community level, perceived availability of assistance and resources is one of the most important factors in short-term family recovery (Bolin 1981). Accessing those resources may be difficult, depending on one's socioeconomic circumstances. Sociopolitical ecology theory, for example, predicts that competition will erupt, with some groups securing more resources than others (Peacock and Ragsdale 1997). (See Box 11.5.)

Predisaster socioeconomic status is a critical factor for household recovery, as those with preexisting resources, such as savings and insurance, may more readily have access to support in order to begin the recovery process. Employment continuity is critical here as well. If a disaster

---

BOX 11.5 RECOVERY CHALLENGES FOR SAME-SEX COUPLES

In the United States, the availability of resources and services for short- and long-term recovery varies by state for families consisting of same sex-couples. Households composed of LGBT couples are thus at a political, social, and economic disadvantage in those states that do not recognize the legitimacy of such unions, where they are denied access to household assistance, have no legal basis to justify shared household accommodations, and have no right to request information about family members who do not meet the state's definition of "family." China, Haiti, and Japan do not recognize same-sex unions, and therefore families composed of same-sex couples would not have been eligible for comparable assistance as heterosexual couples after the respective 2008, 2010, and 2011 disasters in these countries. However, the lack of systematic research in this area leaves many questions unanswered about the experience of these households. Nevertheless, the inability of same-sex couples to marry adversely affects their ability to access resources directed toward spouses and legally recognized family members (Broderick 2011). In contrast, countries that recognize same-sex marriages—such as Canada, the Netherlands, and Sweden—provide comparable short- and long-term assistance to households, regardless of the sexual orientation or gender of the couple.

compromises household income, the ability to recover may stall. Larger families may require more space; families with young children may require easy access to schools, while families with elderly members may require housing proximate to care facilities; and households comprised of family members with disabilities may require specialized housing, supplies, and careful case management (Stough and Sharp 2008). An Earthquake Engineering Research Institute team of social scientists and emergency managers traveled Japan after the 2011 Tohoku catastrophe and found that while prefectures were giving priority for temporary housing to families with small children or the elderly, housing units were not necessarily near public transportation or the types of services these families would need (Chang et al. 2011). Those without sufficient preexisting economic resources (that remained available after the disaster) were more reliant on government assistance—including temporary housing and transportation—than those who were able to draw on their own resources, resources from family, or insurance.

Bolin (1981) studied families one year after two tornadoes hit Wichita Falls, Texas. The tornadoes left more than 18,000 people homeless, 900 injured, and 47 dead. He concentrated on predictors of emotional and economic recovery. The best predictors of long term *emotional* recovery included fewer housing and relocation issues; more informal aid from kin and the mainstream community; younger age of adult(s) in the family; less damage to the home; and more and better insurance coverage. While the predictors of *economic* recovery are similar to those listed for emotional recovery, he found two additional predictors of economic recovery: religiosity and previous disaster experience. Religiosity may reflect active church involvement, thereby increasing access to social networks and sources of aid. Religious families may also rely on their faith as a coping strategy (see Chapter 13).

Researchers have assessed family adaptation to crisis by examining physical and mental health, feelings of well-being, level of family unity, and quality of marital and parenting relationships (Pakenham, Samios, and Sofronoff 2005). As might be expected, strained family relationships are common during disasters and long-term recovery periods. Bolin (1982) identified a number of persistent psychosocial effects among tornado victims, including strained family relationships, separation anxieties among children, sleep disturbances, and anxieties over disaster recurrence. Socially isolated households, such as elderly living alone, may require additional support. After the 1994 Kobe, Japan, earthquake, nursing school students and faculty volunteered to visit with seniors after realizing that *kodokushi* or suicide had increased (Kako and Ikeda 2009). As mentioned previously, temporary housing for displaced victims tends to be crowded, socially isolating from familiar networks, in an unfamiliar location, and often culturally inappropriate. Not surprisingly, levels of stress are associated with the number of moves necessary before reestablishing permanent housing, and by the length of time spent in temporary shelters. The more moves (three moves was the critical number above which stress effects were clear) and the greater the amount of time spent in temporary shelters, the greater was the incidence of persistent negative psychosocial effects. This research suggests that emergency shelters and temporary housing programs can have long-term effects on victims' recoveries (Bolin 1982).

Examples from recent disasters around the world point to the additional complexities in considering long-term recovery. For example, Babugura (2008) explored the vulnerability of children and youth in drought disasters through a case study in Botswana. Results showed that family relationships became strained over economics, and children were forced to adopt adult roles. Children grew aware of the stress, in some cases blaming themselves for the family's hardship. Older children took on adult roles, such as taking care of siblings while parents migrated for work. Moreover, family relationships became conflicted and kin networks grew stressed. Economic difficulties that required family loans resulted in severed relationships when families could not repay the amounts.

Of course, support from family members outside the household can prove a critical determinant in recovery (Bolin 1982). One study of a flood in Lagos, Nigeria, found that family support was essential: 75% of poor urban households reported receiving assistance from family and friends (Adelekan 2010). And these findings are not only limited to Africa. Dawe, Moya, and Valencia (2009) found that Filipino farming families confronting drought supplemented their income through loans and support from family members. As found with the Canadian cattle example mentioned previously, Filipino households reduced their expenses, but unlike the Canadian example, they did so through lower rates of food consumption. This put children in the family at risk of long-term malnutrition and strained family relationships.

Whittle et al. (2010) examined local recovery following the floods of June 2007 in Hull, U.K. They found that families and communities became socially isolated, which disrupted important support systems. Relationships among spouses varied in how they responded to the floods. Some women were responsible for the flood recovery in their homes because their husbands worked daily. This caused tension in the relationship. However, other couples found that, after surviving the flood and the resulting arguments, their relationships were stronger. Overall, parents felt that they had failed their children by not being able to protect them from the aftermath of the flood. In addition, children lost some contact with their grandparents as a consequence of the flood, either because they relocated too far away or the damage to their homes prevented invitations for grandparents to visit. If terms such as *stress*, *roles*, and *economics* seem familiar from the section on impacts, they should be, as there is a clear link between disaster impacts and recovery.

Individuals who are sources of support can also be sources of stress, particularly if there are intense frequent contacts and inequality in the relationships. In a study after Hurricane Andrew, people were asked how much more stress they felt in their relationships with others (Morrow 1997). The results showed that they felt increased stress, in decreasing order, with their partners (56%), among other adults in the household (47%), between adults and children (46%), among children (43%), with relatives (30%), with neighbors (30%), and with friends (16%). Stress, particularly economic stress (including that induced by disaster impacts) can lead to familial changes. When researchers compared divorce rates in U.S. counties that did and did not experience major natural disasters (flood, tornado, and earthquake) over time, one found no long-term differences (Aguirre 1980). In contrast, two studies reported an increase in divorce rates (Morrow 1997; Cohan and Cole 2002). There is some indication that marriages that were strong prior to the disaster got stronger, and marriages that were weak got weaker (Davis and Ender 1999; Harvey et al. 1995; Dash et al. 2007).

Research further suggests that how families adjust over the long term—their outlook, their interpretation of their circumstances, and their interaction with each other—is an important consideration in determining recovery. In 1983, bushfires devastated a major part of Southeast Australia. Fourteen people died, including a mother and her four children, who were trapped in their car as they tried to reach safety. McFarlane (1987) assessed the long-term impact of the bushfires on the patterns of interaction in families by comparing a group of disaster-affected families with families that had not been exposed to the disaster. Eight months after the disaster, the disaster-affected families showed increased levels of conflict, irritability, and withdrawal compared to the nonaffected families. Maternal overprotection and negative changes in parenting behaviors were also common in the affected families.

Harvey et al. (1995) studied people's accounts of loss and recovery from the 1993 flooding in the states of Illinois, Iowa, and Missouri. Forty-five individuals who had experienced very serious losses, including homes, jobs, and property, provided extensive, written narratives about their losses and how they coped. Respondents reported in their narratives that marriages and close relationships that were problematic before the flooding often became more problematic as the flooding worsened. The relative power of the members of a given household or family can be an important factor in whether they get needed help and resources, particularly where domestic violence may be present (see Chapter 12 in this volume). In some cases, disasters are associated with family violence. In 2007, in Bangladesh, two severe floods struck the country. Biswas et al. (2010) reported an increase in domestic violence within families, where 70% of mothers and 40% of fathers reportedly emotionally or physically abused their children or withheld food. In addition, 86% of women reported spousal abuse. Socioeconomic status did not spare victims, with reports of violence occurring across all income levels. These findings point to the need for additional research in this area, and particularly focusing on cohabiting and LGBT relationships, where there is a dearth of data.

Vigil and Geary (2008) studied how family coping affected displaced adolescents living in a post-Katrina relocation center. Adolescents whose parents depended more on nonfamilial and community-provided support had lower self-esteem and more symptoms of distress and depression, which increased family stress. Although using community resources may be necessary for families, it also tended to make adolescents more aware of their homelessness, to generate memories of the hurricane experience, and to feel socially stigmatized.

Months after Hurricane Katrina, over 770,000 people remained displaced. Family members were scattered across the country, and more than 4,500 families from the Gulf Coast ended up in Colorado (Montero 2006). In 2005 and 2007, Peek, Morrissey, and Marlatt (2011) interviewed 23 families (adults and children) displaced to the state of Colorado after Hurricane Katrina. Their data generated a four-stage model showing how parent and child adjustment evolved. Family members initially attempted to maintain family unity. After this first stage, parents and children adjusted differently. In the second stage, parents made safety a priority; conversely, children dealt with missing their homes. Parents then moved on to confronting reality as children began to settle into their new environment. Finally, family members eventually became resolved with their circumstances

Although a good deal of research focuses on preparedness and response, significantly more research is needed in the broad area of recovery. This assertion holds true for research on family recovery from disaster. More long-term systematic research would help to identify the commonalities and differences across household type, as well as provide a lens into the different ways households around the world cope in the long term after disaster recovery.

11.6 TYPES OF VULNERABLE HOUSEHOLDS: RENTERS

Clearly, different types of households embody different types of vulnerabilities and capacities across the disaster life cycle. This section will highlight the particular issues that renters face as a way to illustrate how social vulnerability in one period is deeply connected to the extent to which vulnerability exists in other disaster periods.

11.6.1 VULNERABILITY ACROSS THE DISASTER LIFE CYCLE: RENTERS

According to Burby and Steinburg (2002), renters have less control over preparedness and mitigation activities such as damage-prevention initiatives (e.g., installing storm shutters) as well as property maintenance and upkeep. Rather than being able to directly influence their risks, renters must rely to some extent on landlords for such protective measures. Renters are at risk of being displaced from their homes after a disaster if one or more of several conditions are present. First, if their rental housing does not have hazard-mitigation measures in place—such as shutters (for hurricane), elevations (for hurricane or flooding), tie-downs or retrofitting (for seismic hazards)—the renter may find that the unit receives too much damage to return to immediately after the disaster or even after some time has passed. Second, the owner of the rental housing may not have funds to repair or rebuild the unit after the disaster has struck, may use insurance payouts for purposes other than rebuilding the rental property, or may decide to improve the property and raise the rent to above pre-event levels. In all three cases, the renters may find that they no longer have an inhabitable unit to return to (or at least not one that they can afford) and discover that they must join others in similar circumstances vying for now-limited affordable housing. Third, like private housing, rental housing may become part of a government buy-out mitigation program. In these cases, renters may similarly find themselves without a home to return to. Finally, in some cases, property owners cannot be located, which may delay efforts to repair or rebuild the property. For example, regulations may require that all the owners of multiunit condominium properties be contacted to give permission before rebuilding occurs. Delays in locating one or more owners in a disaster aftermath may result in delays for units, even where owners have given permission to have repairs done.

A very important factor affecting the number of homeless families after a disaster is whether mitigation occurred, such as shutters and earthquake-minimizing measures, on public and subsidized housing units. Such housing units have less control over recovery capacity related to housing insurance, repairs, and reconstruction (Burby and Steinburg 2002). Most renters do not have insurance on their personal property, even though such policies are relatively inexpensive. Thus renters, not surprisingly, comprise a high proportion of displaced families who end up in tent cities and temporary housing after an event. Families and households who rent through public assistance programs are particularly at risk. Hurricane Andrew dislocated families from every public housing unit in south Miami-Dade County. Most of these families spent the next year or more in tent cities and FEMA trailers (Morrow 1997).

Because renters live in buildings owned by someone else, they are at risk for long-term displacement in a disaster situation. The 1994 Northridge earthquake, for example, severely affected renters. Los Angeles County declared that 27,000 multifamily buildings, or 84% of the damaged homes, were uninhabitable. Many renters went into other nearby rental units. However, a number of initiatives and partnerships were required to rebuild rental units (Comerio 1998). The economic recession, coupled with few apartment owners holding earthquake insurance, meant that funds for rental recovery would be meager. Moreover, many apartment buildings were owned by multiple landlords, which complicated the process of rebuilding. Finally, the recession also meant that there would be minimal cash flow for their collective efforts to rebuild, thus undermining their ability to secure government disaster loans.

Clearly, the challenges renters face is not only limited to those in the United States. Whittle et al. (2010) conducted a real-time study of local recovery following the floods of June 2007 in Hull, U.K. Compared to homeowners, families who rented were more vulnerable because they were removed from damaged homes without knowing if they could return. In addition, following the event, rental prices increased, leaving families who couldn't afford them with few options. Renters were at the whim of landlords, who could decide when to start the repairs as well as what to repair. The authors noted reports of families living in damaged homes and still paying rent for months after the flood.

11.6.2 Disaster Policies: Renters

A close treatment of disaster policies and assistance programs seems to suggest that homeowners benefit more when compared to renters. When disaster strikes, the first place for survivors to start in the United States is to apply for a Small Business Administration (SBA) loan. SBA provides low-interest disaster loans to homeowners, renters, businesses of all sizes, and private, nonprofit organizations to repair or replace real estate, personal property, machinery and equipment, inventory, and business assets that have been damaged or destroyed in a declared disaster. Renters may apply for a personal property loan, which cannot exceed $40,000. Acceptable items that can be covered include furniture, clothing, and cars damaged by the disaster (SBA 2012).

The Federal Emergency Management Agency (FEMA) in the United States provides other kinds of assistance for renters and homeowners. Coverage includes costs associated with debris removal, crisis counseling, medical services, funeral costs, transportation, and fuel, among other items. People must apply for that assistance, have FEMA inspectors confirm the legitimacy of their application, and then document their expenses. In previous disasters, such as the 1989 earthquake in Loma Prieta, California, renters and others successfully sued FEMA over "head of household" issues, where, in some cases, the first person to apply for federal assistance within the affected rental unit secured the funds. However, the reality is that many renters erroneously assume that they do not qualify for federal assistance.

11.6.3 Assisting Renters

A number of disaster organizations assisted Northridge, California, renters after the earthquake. Up to 160,000 residents received help from approximately 450 voluntary organizations. For renters, applying for assistance through voluntary organizations may be a particularly helpful route. However, even experienced disaster organizations tend to favor homeowners over renters. Disaster organizations that focus on rebuilding, for example, typically select low-income homeowners to assist. Renters who live in multifamily households, public housing, or in rental homes usually remain at the mercy of landlords or governmental agencies. Displacement can be considerable, as has been the case in Louisiana after Hurricane Katrina. Public-housing units were condemned across multiple parishes. New units were being rebuilt in mixed-income complexes. Meanwhile, community members (residents, housing advocates, neighborhood associations, nonprofit organizations) worried that low-income households and families might experience permanent displacement as a result—a reality that played out. In a controversial decision, the New Orleans City Council voted to demolish 4,529 apartments in four public housing complexes. Three of the buildings returned as a mixed-income design, but "with only 807 of them affordable to former residents, they constitute a serious reduction in the overall number of homes serving displaced residents" (Rose 2011).

To rebuild rental units, the City of Los Angeles secured $10,641,000 in funding for both single-family and multifamily housing. The U.S. Department of Housing and Urban Development (HUD) provided funds from its Community Development Block Grants (CDBG) and Home Investment Partnership Funds. The state convinced some lenders to forgive loans and late payments. Los Angeles donated funds to repair 12,000 rental units. By 1997, three-fourths of the units were repaired to some degree (Comerio 1998). Meanwhile, renters had relocated to new places, farther away from friends, social resources, and work than before.

Communities can assist renters in several ways. After the Loma Prieta earthquake, for example, Santa Cruz, California, built the Neary Lagoon Housing Cooperative with a mix of predisaster and disaster funds. The Co-op set aside 25% of its units for earthquake victims, to insure that those directly affected did not lose rental housing permanently. The city also sustained damage to three of four single-room-occupancy (SRO) hotels that provided affordable, convenient rentals to seniors and low-income households. Efforts were enacted to ensure that the rebuilt units remained affordable. Temporary housing was secured in a previously abandoned nursing home. Some SRO residents stayed there until they were able to return to the downtown SROs. Rental prices in those units increased less than $100. After Hurricane Katrina, though, rental prices increased as much as 25% in some rental units (Phillips 1998).

Other strategies are critical for renters to reduce their household vulnerability. For example, mitigation programs that target renters, in addition to landlords, can help renters (particularly long-term renters) decide on ways to make their housing units more disaster resistant. Campaigns that promote renters' insurance can leave these households better prepared when disaster strikes. Strengthening local ordinances that govern landlord responsibility for disaster-mitigation strategies could further reduce disaster vulnerability for renters and generate a more consistent standard across rental properties. Community-wide efforts, particularly in the postdisaster environment, that promote the protection of affordable rental housing as a recovery priority could protect households that relied on rental units prior to the disaster or those who newly find themselves relying on rental units as a result of the disaster. After a 5-year conflict between state government and housing advocates, the state of Mississippi reached a post-Katrina agreement to provide assistance to households "with unrepaired wind damage, residents seeking to permanently occupy cottages, and very low-income renters" (Morse 2011, 141). Less than three months after the decision, 17,000 households applied for aid.

11.7   IMPLICATIONS FOR ACTION

Table 11.2 notes some of the activities that households can take in building a disaster supply kit. The resources section at the end of the chapter directs readers to a variety of sources that provide information for households. The research in this chapter points to a number of areas where emergency managers, public officials, and nongovernmental organizations can take steps to reduce disaster vulnerability. Based on this research and that noted in the rest of this volume, the following recommendations for action emerge.

11.7.1   IMPLICATIONS FOR EMERGENCY MANAGERS AND SOCIAL SERVICE AGENCIES

Outreach is a first step for action. Many emergency management agencies around the world, as well as national and international disaster-response organizations, have developed websites and materials to help households and families reduce their vulnerability (see Resources section in this chapter for suggestions). A number of additional outreach strategies could help reach households in their communities. Reaching families and households in the context of their daily lives is crucial, as

TABLE 11.2
Building a Household Disaster Supply Kit

Basic Supplies	Additional Emergency Supplies	First-Aid Supplies	Supplies for Unique Needs
• Water (3-day supply of one gallon per person per day)	• Prescription medications and glasses	• 2 pairs of sterile gloves	Babies:
• Food (3-day supply of nonperishable food)	• Infant formula and diapers	• Sterile dressings	• Formula
• Radio: battery powered or hand crank	• Pet food and water for pet	• Soap and antibiotic towelettes	• Diapers
• Flashlight	• Money (cash, traveler checks, change)	• Antibiotic ointment	• Bottles
• Extra batteries	• Important family documents (in a waterproof container)	• Burn ointment	• Powdered milk
• Whistle	• Emergency reference information	• Adhesive bandages (different sizes)	• Medications
• Dust mask, plastic sheeting, and duct tape	• Blanket or sleeping bag for each person	• Eye wash	• Moist towelettes
• Personal sanitation supplies	• Change of clothing	• Thermometer	• Diaper rash ointment
• Wrench or pliers	• Household bleach and medicine dropper	• Prescription medications and medical supplies	Adults:
• Can opener (manual)	• Fire extinguisher	• Nonprescription drugs, such as pain relievers, anti-diarrhea medication, antacid, laxatives	• Denture needs
• Local maps	• Matches in waterproof container	• Scissors	• Contact lenses and supplies
• Cell phone and charger (inverter or solar charger)	• Personal hygiene items (including feminine supplies)	• Tweezers	• Extra eye glasses
	• Supplies for food and drink	• Lubricant (e.g., petroleum jelly)	Cold climate:
	• Paper and pencil		• Jacket or coat
	• Books, games, puzzles, activities for children		• Long pants
			• Long-sleeve shirt

Source: FEMA (2012).

disasters are simply not salient events for many (Tierney, Lindell, and Perry 2001). Most households fail to prepare or simply cannot afford to do so (Tierney, Lindell, and Perry 2001). To overcome these challenges, organizations could distribute free pamphlets and materials in public places, such as schools, recreation locations, libraries, and supermarkets. Some organizations have set up disaster information booths at key events. Agencies in the state of Delaware in the United States, for example, held a preparedness day at a minor-league baseball game in 2012. In the late 1990s and early 2000s, a national mitigation program known at the time as Project Impact promoted disaster mitigation at NASCAR racing events. Kobe, Japan, created an interactive earthquake museum that not only tells the story of the Great Hanshin earthquake that devastated the city in 1995, but also educates children and adults about the earthquake hazard. These are family events where all members of a household might have access to important information.

Outreach strategies should include making full use of public media. This might include local newsletters and radio stations serving audiences that represent different segments of the community, including minority groups and non-English speakers. But with heightened use of social media, families may increasingly look to more ephemeral Internet-based sites for information. Community groups, agencies, and faith-based institutions may provide the key in helping keep emergency managers aware of important sources that constituents look to for information, as well as serving as a point for distributing information from the emergency managers themselves. Materials should target particular groups, helping to ensure that information is accessible to all household members. Some household members may require large-print pamphlets or pamphlets in multiple languages. Children may best absorb information written in story form with a lot of pictures and simple language. Family members with varying levels of literacy or cognitive functioning might benefit from visually oriented materials as well. Households and families represent ready units for outreach. Because many people tend to live in these collective units, it is possible to maximize public funds to conduct public education efforts.

Facilitating the reopening of schools and child-care programs quickly is a second step that can help both children as well as their caregivers. Sometimes this requires ensuring that transportation and school uniforms are provided as well. Following the Indian Ocean tsunami in 2004, Wachtendorf et al. (2006) interviewed mothers who were quite concerned about their children's ability to get to school safely, since they could no longer afford to pay for transportation. In the post-disaster environment, children will be bored and parents stressed. Schools are often used as shelters, but shelter operators should avoid using them as temporary housing in the aftermath. Informal child-care operators, such as family caregivers, provide a valuable service that needs support in order to get parents back to work and to keep children safe, yet they rarely are considered as part of the recovery effort. Formal day-care operators are critical as well. Parks and recreational programs should have high priority in the recovery process. Children and youth need to be kept occupied during long recovery periods to avoid boredom, depression, and behavioral problems.

A third, and central, strategy that cannot be understated is the importance of keeping family and social groups together when assigning shelter space or temporary housing. Grouping households and kin networks together enables them to provide each other with emotional and physical support, such as child care.

Fourth, emergency managers, social service agencies, and disaster organizations must consider the diversity of households and family structures in order to address and reduce vulnerability. Labels are important. Definitions of family should expand to include culturally diverse and marginalized groups when designing assistance programs. There are many examples in past disasters where nonfamily households, such as two unrelated individuals living together, have experienced difficulty in getting appropriate joint assistance. In the process of policy development and implementation, remembering that families are diverse and therefore have diverse needs can help guide disaster response and recovery in ways that benefit a range of family types.

Of course, there is diversity between families, but also within families. Peek, Morissey, and Marlatt's (2011) study on displaced Hurricane Katrina families noted that children and parents experience and perceive their recovery differently. This research suggests that disaster researchers and policy makers need to consider both parent and child perspectives when learning about and making decisions regarding household recovery needs.

Households and families are multifaceted. Multigenerational households may also contain elderly members. Senior citizens do respond to evacuation messages when they are received, but they may require transportation assistance. In a survey conducted by AARP (American Association of Retired Persons), approximately 13 million persons over the age of 50 reported that they would need assistance in an evacuation (Krisberg 2007). Because disabilities increase with age, households with people who are disabled may not be able to evacuate easily. In households and families where a caretaker is present, that person may delay or resist evacuation because of the difficulties in doing so.

Understanding household and family situations enables practitioners to design specific efforts for their respective risks. By understanding the situational realities of today's households and families, we can design improved evacuation protocols. With increasing numbers of minority families and households across the United States, more attention needs to be paid to social, political, and cultural complexities associated with their disaster experiences. (For specific details on racial and ethnic minorities, see Chapter 5.) Good emergency management practice involves knowing the extent to which high-risk households and families live in each community—as well as the situations in which they tend to be concentrated—prior to disaster.

11.8 SUMMARY

This chapter highlighted the various ways that families and households are affected by disasters. It stressed the diversity of households across the United States and internationally while, at the same time, pointing to common challenges faced by households as they prepare for, respond to, and attempt to recover from disasters.

DISCUSSION QUESTIONS

1. Think of the composition of different types of households and families in the United States and globally. In what ways do these different households experience unique vulnerabilities?
2. If households and families are so diverse, how can emergency managers adequately address the needs of all households?
3. What can a community do to assist renters and landlords to mitigate and respond to disasters?
4. What strategies can emergency managers and responders take to help households and families cope and reduce stress?
5. Compare and contrast how a household in the United States, Canada, India, Haiti, and Japan might experience similar or different vulnerabilities, depending on their family composition. Consider all phases of the disaster life cycle.
6. Consider the *tsunami tendenko* culture mentioned in Box 11.1. How might this approach to tsunami evacuation prove beneficial to households and families? What problems for different types of households or families could you anticipate?
7. Consider different types of families in your community. How might you opt to design disaster information material and programs differently to best reach each audience? What distribution venues might prove most effective and why? You may wish to consider LGBT households, families with children or elderly members, households with members who don't speak the dominant language in your community, and nonfamily households, among other household types.

ACKNOWLEDGMENTS

This material is partially based upon work supported by the National Science Foundation under Grant No. 0826832. Any opinions, findings, and conclusions or recommendations expressed in this material are those of the authors and do not necessarily reflect the views of the National Science Foundation.

REFERENCES

Adelekan, I. O. 2010. Vulnerability of poor urban coastal communities to flooding in Lagos, Nigeria. *Environment and Urbanization* 22 (2): 433–50.

Aguirre, B. E. 1980. The long term effects of major natural disasters on marriage and divorce: An ecological study. *Victimology: An International Journal* 5:298–307.

Aldrich, D. P. 2011. Institutional and local responses to the 2011 Tohoku disaster: Social capital and recovery. Natural Hazards Center Quick Response Report #225. http://www.colorado.edu/hazards/research/qr/.

Allen, K. M. 2006. Community-based disaster preparedness and climate adaptation: Local capacity-building in the Philippines. *Disasters* 30 (1): 81–101.

Anderson, M. B., and P. J. Woodrow. 1990. Capacities and vulnerabilities analysis. In *Disaster and development workshops: A manual for training*, 7–14. Cambridge MA: IRDP, Harvard University.

Auf der Heide, E. (2000). *Disaster response: Principles of preparation and coordination*. http://coe-dmha.org/Media/Disaster_Response_Principals.pdf.

Babugura, A. A. 2008. Vulnerability of children and youth in drought disasters: A case study of Botswana. *Children, Youth, and Environments* 18 (1): 126–57.

Biswas, A., A. Rahman, S. Mashreky, F. Rahman, and K. Dalal. 2010. Unintentional injuries and parental violence against children during flood: A study in rural Bangladesh. *Rural and Remote Health* 10 (1): 1199.

Blinn-Pike, L., B. Phillips, and P. Reeves. 2006. Shelter life after hurricane Katrina: A visual analysis of evacuee perspectives. *Journal of Mass Emergencies and Disasters* 24 (3): 303–31.

Bolin, R. C. 1981. Family recovery after disaster: A discriminant function analysis. Paper presented at the annual meeting of the American Sociological Association, San Antonio, TX.

———. 1982. *Long-term family recovery from disaster*. Boulder: University of Colorado.

Broderick, J. 2011. The biopolitics of desire: Exploring the axis of sexuality during the 2004 Indian Ocean tsunami in Thailand. First Place Undergraduate Paper at the Annual Hazards and Disasters Student Paper Competition.

Burby, R., and L. Steinburg. 2002. In the shadow of a refinery: Preparedness of vulnerable populations exposed to disasters. Paper presented at the International Sociological Association, Brisbane, Australia.

Burnside, R., D. S. Miller, and J. D. Rivera. 2007. The impact of information and risk perception on the hurricane evacuation and decision-making of Greater New Orleans residents. *Sociological Spectrum* 27 (6): 727–40.

Citizen Preparedness Research. 2005. Methodological considerations and key findings in preparedness research. *Citizen Preparedness Review* 1. http://www.ready.gov/research/citizen-preparedness-research.

Chang, S., D. Aldrich, R. Eisner, L. Johnson, T. Norton, K. Tierney, T. Wachtendorf, et al. 2011. The March 11, 2011, Great East Japan (Tohoku) earthquake and tsunami: Societal dimension. EERI Special Earthquake Report, August. http://www.eqclearinghouse.org/2011-03-11-sendai/files/2011/03/Japan-SocSci-Rpt-hirez-rev.pdf.

Cohan, C. L., and S. W. Cole. 2002. Life course transitions and natural disaster: Marriage, birth, and divorce following hurricane Hugo. *Journal of Family Psychology* 16 (1): 14–25.

Comerio, M. 1998. *Disaster hits home: New policy for urban housing recovery*. Berkeley: University of California Press.

Congressional Research Service. 2006. Federal emergency management policy changes after Hurricane Katrina: A summary of statutory provisions. Washington, DC.

Cretikos, M., K. Eastwood, C. Dalton, T. Merritt, F. Tuyl, L. Winn, and D. Durrheim. 2008. Household disaster preparedness and information sources: Rapid cluster survey after a storm in New South Wales, Australia. *BMC Public Health* 8:195–203.

Dash, N., B. H. Morrow, J. Mainster, and L. Cunningham. 2007. Lasting effects of Hurricane Andrew on a working class community. *Natural Hazards Review* 8 (1): 13–21.

Davis, K. M., and M. G. Ender. 1999. The 1997 Red River Valley flood: Impact on marital relationships. *Applied Behavioral Science Review* 7 (2): 181–88.

Dawe, D., P. Moya, and S. Valencia. 2009. Institutional policy and farmer responses to drought: El Nino events and rice in the Philippines. *Disasters* 33 (2): 291–307.

D'Ooge, C. 2008. Queer Katrina: Gender and sexual orientation matters in the aftermath of the disaster. In *Katrina and the women of New Orleans*, ed. B. Willinger, 22–24. Executive report and summary of findings. New Orleans: Newcomb College Center for Research on Women, Tulane University.

Drabek, T. E. 1986. *Human system responses to disaster: An inventory of sociological findings*. New York: Springer.

Drabek, T. E., and K. S. Boggs. 1968. Families in disaster: Reactions and relatives. *Journal of Marriage and the Family* 30 (3): 443–51.

Dynes, R. R. 2005. Community social capital as the primary basis for resilience. Preliminary paper #344. University of Delaware Disaster Research Center.

Eads, M. 2002. Marginalized groups in times of crisis: Identity, needs and response. Natural Hazards Research and Applications Information Center, University of Colorado, Boulder.

Eisenman, D., K. Farmer, K. M. Cordasco, S. Asch, J. F. Golden, and D. Glik. 2007. Disaster planning and risk communication with vulnerable communities: Lessons from Hurricane Katrina. *American Journal of Public Health* 97 (S1): S109–15.

Enarson, E., and B. H. Morrow. 1998. Women will rebuild Miami: A case study of feminist response to disaster. In *The gendered terrain of disaster*, ed. E. Enarson and B. H. Morrow, 185–99. Miami, FL: Praeger.

Farmer, D. B. 2011. Mothers and daughters of Haiti. In *Haiti: After the earthquake*, ed P. Farmer, 282–95. New York: Public Affairs.

FEMA. 2003. A social vulnerability approach to disasters. FEMA Emergency Management Institute, Higher Education Project. http://www.training.fema.gov/EMIWeb/edu/sovul.asp.

———. 2012. Basic disaster supplies kit. http://www.ready.gov/basic-disaster-supplies-kit.

Fields, J. 2004. America's families and living arrangements: 2003. *Current populations reports*, ser. P-20, no. 553. U.S. Government Printing Office, Washington, DC.

Fisher, J. 2009. *Human trafficking: Law enforcement resource guide*. Supply, NC: Coastal Books.

Fothergill, A. 2004. *Heads above water: Gender, class, and family in the Grand Forks flood*. Albany: State University of New York Press.

Fothergill, A., E. Maestas, and J. D. Darlington. 1999. Race, ethnicity and disasters in the United States: A review of literature. *Disasters* 23 (2): 156–73.

Fothergill, A., and L. Peek. 2004. Poverty and disasters in the United States: A review of recent sociological findings. *Natural Disasters* 32:89–110.

Fritz, C. E., and J. H. Mathewson. 1957. Convergent behavior in disasters: A problem in social control. Special Report for the Committee on Disaster Studies. National Academy of Sciences, National Research Council, Washington, DC.

Fung, O. W. M., and A. Y. Loke. 2010. Disaster preparedness of families with young children in Hong Kong. *Scandinavian Journal of Public Health* 38 (8): 880–88.

Gaillard, J., C. C. Liamzon, and J. D. Villanueva. 2007. "Natural" disaster? A retrospect into the causes of the late-2004 typhoon disaster in Eastern Luzon, Philippines. *Environmental Hazards* 7:257–70.

Gillard, M., and D. Paton. 1999. Disaster stress following a hurricane: The role of religious differences in the Fijian Islands. *Australasian Journal of Disaster and Trauma Studies* 2.

Gladwin, C., H. Gladwin, and W. G. Peacock. 2001. Modeling hurricane evacuation decisions with ethnographic methods. *International Journal of Mass Emergencies and Disasters* 19 (2): 117–43.

Harvey, J. H., S. K. Stein, N. Olsen, R. J. Roberts, S. K. Lutgendorf, and J. A. Ho. 1995. Narratives of loss and recovery from a natural disaster. *Journal of Social Behavior and Personality* 10 (2): 313–30.

Heath, S. E., A. M. Beck, P. H. Kass, and L. T. Glickman. 2001. Risk factors for pet evacuation failure after a slow-onset disaster. *Journal of the American Veterinary Medical Association* 218 (12): 1905–10.

Kako, M., and S. Ikeda. 2009. Volunteer experiences in community housing during the Great Hanshin-Awaji earthquake, Japan. *Nursing and Health Sciences* 11 (4): 357–59.

Kendra, J. M., and T. Wachtendorf. 2003. Reconsidering convergence and converger legitimacy in response to the World Trade Center disaster. In *New threats, new ideas*, ed. L. Clarke, 97–122. Vol. 11 of *Terrorism and disaster*. New York: Elsevier Science.

Klinenberg, E. 2002. *Heat wave: A social autopsy of disaster in Chicago*. Chicago: University of Chicago Press

Krisberg, K. 2007. *Emergency preparedness a challenge for older Americans: Better disaster plans needed for seniors*. London: Alpha International.

Kumaran, M., and T. Torris. 2011. The role of NGOs in tsunami relief and reconstruction in Cuddalore District, South India. In *The Indian Ocean tsunami: The global response to a natural disaster*, ed. P. P. Karan and S. P. Subbiah, 183–211. Lexington: University of Kentucky Press.

Larsen, J. 2006. Setting the record straight: More than 52,000 Europeans died from heat in summer 2003. Washington, DC: Earth Policy Institute. http://www.earth-policy.org/plan_b_updates/2006/update56.

Laska, S. 2008. What if Hurricane Ivan had not missed New Orleans? *Sociological Inquiry* 78 (2): 174–78.

Lindgaard, C. V., T. Iglebaek, and T. K. Jensen. 2009. Changes in family functioning in the aftermath of the 2004 tsunami in Southeast Asia. *Journal of Loss and Trauma: International Perspectives on Stress Coping* 14:101–16.

L.A. Times. 2011. Google deploys person finder after Japan earthquake, tsunami leave hundreds dead. March 11. http://latimesblogs.latimes.com/technology/2011/03/google-deploys-person-finder-after-japan-earthquake-tsunami-leaves-hundreds-dead.html.

Lund, F., and T. Vaux. 2009. Work-focused responses to disasters: India's self employed women's association. In *Women, gender and disaster: Global issues and initiatives*, ed. E. Enarson and P. Chakrabarti, 212–23. New Delhi, India: Sage.

Mallick, B., K. Rahaman, and J. Vogt. 2011. Coastal livelihood and physical infrastructure in Bangladesh after Cyclone Alia. *Mitigation and Adaptation Strategies for Global Change* 16 (6): 629–48.

Masozera, M., M. Bailey, and C. Kerchner. 2007. Distribution of impacts of natural disasters across incomes: A case study of New Orleans. *Ecological Economics* 3 (2–3): 299–306.

McFarlane, A. C. 1987. Family functioning and overprotection following a natural disaster: The longitudinal effects of post-traumatic morbidity. *Australian and New Zealand Journal of Psychiatry* 21 (2): 210–18.

Mikami, S., and K. Ikedo. 1985. Human response to disasters. *International Journal of Mass Emergencies and Disasters* 3:107–32.

Montero, D. 2006. Longing for a taste of home: Katrina evacuees struggle to adjust to life in Colorado. *Rocky Mountain News*, A-18.

Morrow, B. H. 1997. Stretching the bonds: The families of Andrew. In *Hurricane Andrew: Ethnicity, gender and the sociology of disasters*, ed. W. G. Peacock, B. H. Morrow, and H. Gladwin, 141–70. New York: Routledge.

Morrow, B. H., and H. Gladwin. 2006. Coastal Louisiana post-Katrina evacuation planning survey. Final Report submitted through Dewberry and Davis and URS to FEMA.

Morse, R. 2011. Come on in this house: Advancing social equity in post-Katrina Mississippi. In *Resilience and opportunity: Lessons from the U.S. Gulf Coast after Katrina and Rita*, ed. A. Liu, R. Anglin, R. Nizelle Jr., and A. Plyer, 131–47. Washington, DC: Brookings Institution.

Mulligan, M., and J. Shaw. 2011. Achievements and weaknesses in post-tsunami reconstruction in Sri Lanka. In *The Indian Ocean tsunami: The global response to a natural disaster*, ed. P. Karan and S. Subbiah, 237–60. Lexington: University of Kentucky Press.

National Council on Disability. 2009. Effective emergency management: Making improvements for communities and people with disabilities. Washington, DC: National Council on Disability. http://www.ncd.gov/publications/2009/10132009.

Neal, D. M. 1997. Reconsidering the phases of disaster. *International Journal of Mass Emergencies and Disasters* 15 (2): 239–64.

Nigg, J. M., J. Barnshaw, and M. R. Torres. 2006. Hurricane Katrina and the flooding of New Orleans: Emergent issues in sheltering and temporary housing. *Annals of the American Academy of Political and Social Science* 604 (1): 113–28.

Nishikoiri, N., T. Abe, D. G. M. Costa, S. D. Dharmaratne, O. Kunii, and K. Moji. 2006. Who died as a result of the tsunami? Risk factors of mortality among internally displaced persons in Sri Lanka: A retrospective cohort analysis. *BMC Public Health* 6:73–80.

Norris, F. H., M. J. Friedman, and P. J. Watson. 2002. 60,000 disaster victims speak, Part II: Summary and implications of the disaster mental health research. *Psychiatry* 65 (3): 240–60.

Norris, F. H., M. J. Friedman, P. J. Watson, C. M. Byrne, E. Diaz, and K. Kaniasty. 2002. 60,000 disaster victims speak, Part I: An empirical review of the empirical literature, 1981–2001. *Psychiatry* 65 (3): 207–39.

Nwe, Y. Y. 2005. Children and the tsunami: One year on. UNICEF. http://www.unicef.org/emerg/disasterinasia/files/WhatWorked.pdf.

Osofsky, H. J., J. D. Osofsky, M. Kronenberg, A. Brennan, and T. C. Hansel. 2009. Posttraumatic stress symptoms in children after Hurricane Katrina: Predicting the need for mental health services. *American Journal of Orthopsychiatry* 79 (2): 212–20.

Pakenham, K. I., C. Samios, and K. Sofronoff. 2005. Adjustment in mothers of children with Asperger syndrome: An application of the double ABCX model of family adjustment. *Autism* 9 (2): 212–20.

Peacock, W., and K. Ragsdale. 1997. Social systems, ecological networks and disasters: Toward a socio-political ecology of disasters. In *Hurricane Andrew: Ethnicity, gender, and the sociology of disasters*, ed. W. E. Peacock, B. Morrow, and H. Gladwin, 20–35. Miami: International Hurricane Center, Florida International University.

Peek, L., B. Morrissey, and H. Marlatt. 2011. Disaster hits home: A model of displaced family adjustment after Hurricane Katrina. *Journal of Family Issues* 32 (10): 1371–95.

Peguero, A. 2006. Latino disaster vulnerability: The dissemination of hurricane mitigation information among Florida's homeowners. *Hispanic Journal of Behavioral Sciences* 28 (1): 5–22.

Perry, R. W., and M. R. Greene. 1982. The role of ethnicity in emergency decision-making process. *Sociological Inquiry* 52 (4): 306–34.

Pets Evacuation and Transportation Standards Act. 2006. S. 2548—109th Congress. http://www.govtrack.us/congress/bills/109/s2548.

Phillips, B. D. 1998. Housing low income and minority groups after Loma Prieta: Some policy considerations. In the National Report to Congress on the Loma Prieta Earthquake. U.S. Geological Survey.

Phillips, B. D., T. Wikle, A. H. Hakim, and L. Pike. 2012. Establishing and operating shelters after Hurricane Katrina. *International Journal of Emergency Management* 8 (2): 153–67.

Reinsch, S. 2009. A part of me had left: Learning from women farmers in Canada about disaster stress. In *Women, gender and disaster: Global issues and initiatives*, ed. E. Enarson and P. Chakrabarti, 152–64. New Delhi, India: Sage.

Riad, J. K., and F. H. Norris. 1998. Hurricane threat and evacuation intentions: An analysis of risk perception, preparedness, social influence, and resources. Disaster Research Center preliminary paper #271, University of Delaware, Newark, DE.

Rofi, A., S. Doocy, and C. Robinson. 2006. Tsunami mortality and displacement in Aceh province, Indonesia. *Disasters* 30 (3): 340–50.

Rose, K. 2011. Bringing New Orleans home: Community, faith, and nonprofit-driven housing recovery. In *Resilience and opportunity: Lessons from the U.S. Gulf Coast after Katrina and Rita*, ed. A. Liu, R. V. Anglin, R. M. Mizelle Jr., and A. Plyer, 99–119. Washington, DC: Brookings Institution Press.

Rosenkoetter, M. M., E. K. Covan, B. K. Cobb, S. Bunting, and M. Weinrich. 2007. Perceptions of older adults regarding evacuation in the event of a natural disaster. *Public Health Nursing* 24 (2): 160–68.

Santos-Hernández, J. 2006. "Losing everything": Undocumented Latino workers and Hurricane Katrina. In *Learning from catastrophe: Quick response research in the wake of Hurricane Katrina*, 131–50. Boulder: Natural Hazards Center, University of Colorado.

Sayeed, A. T. 2009. Victims of earthquake and patriarchy: The 2005 Pakistan earthquake. In *Women, gender and disaster: Global issues and initiatives*, ed. E. Enarson and P. G. Dhar Chakrabarti, 131–42. New Delhi, India: Sage.

SBA (U.S. Small Business Administration). 2012. Disaster loans. Washington, DC.

Scanlon, T. J. 1991. *Convergence revisited: A new perspective on a little studied topic*. Boulder: Institute of Behavior Sciences, University of Colorado.

Schwede, L. 2007. A new focus: Studying linkages among household structure. Race ethnicity, and geographic levels with implications for census coverage. U.S. Census Bureau, Washington, DC.

SEEDS Asia. 2011. Damage/needs assessment in the affected area of the 2011 off the Pacific coast of Tohoku earthquake and tsunami, 11 April 2011. OYO International Corp. and Kyoto University.

Sharkey, P. 2007. Survival and death in New Orleans: An empirical look at the human impact of Katrina. *Journal of Black Studies* 37 (4): 482–501.

Sinha, S., and P. Bhattacharyya. 2009. Cyclone Aila in West Bengal: A report by Jamsetji Tata Centre for Disaster Management, TISS, July. Tata Institute of Social Science, Mumbai, India.

Smith, S. K., and C. McCarty. 2009. Fleeing the storm(s): An examination of evacuation behavior during Florida's 2004 hurricane season. *Demography* 46 (1): 127–45.

Stough, L., and A. Sharp. 2008. *An evaluation of the impact of the National Disability Rights Network participation in the Katrina Today project*. Washington, DC: The National Disability Rights Network.

Tierney, K. J., M. K. Lindell, and R. W. Perry. 2001. *Facing the unexpected: Disaster preparedness and response in the United States*. Washington, DC: John Henry Press.

Tomlinson, H. M. 2010. Perceptions of natural hazards in mountain landscapes: Awareness, anticipation and mitigation in post-earthquake Beichuan, China. Master's thesis, Durham University, England. http://etheses.dur.ac.uk/3198/.

U.S. Census Bureau. 2002. Washington, DC.

———. 2003. Washington, DC.

———. 2004. Washington, DC.

———. 2006. Selected social characteristics in the United States: 2006. Washington, DC.

———. 2010a. Income, poverty and health insurance coverage in the United States: 2009. Washington, DC.

———. 2010b. American community survey. Washington, DC.

———. 2011. Income, poverty and health insurance coverage in the United States: 2010. Washington, DC.

———. 2012a. Current population survey—Definitions. http://www.census.gov/cps/about/cpsdef.html.

———. 2012b. Households and families: 2010. Washington, DC.

Vieweg, S., L. Palen, S. Liu, A. Hughes, and J. Sutton. 2008. Collective intelligence in disaster: An examination of the phenomenon in the aftermath of the 2007 Virginia Tech shooting. In *Proceedings of the 5th International ISCRAM Conference*, May, Washington DC. http://www.jeannettesutton.com/uploads/CollectiveIntelligenceISCRAM08.pdf.

Vigil, J. M., and D. C. Geary. 2008. A preliminary investigation of family coping styles and psychological well-being among adolescent survivors of Hurricane Katrina. *Journal of Family Psychology* 22 (1): 176–80.

Wachtendorf, T., M. K. James, R. Havidan, and J. Trainor. 2006. The social impacts and consequences of the December 2004 Indian Ocean tsunami: Observations from India and Sri Lanka earthquake. *Spectra* 22 (S3): S693–714.

Wahra, G. 1994. Women refugees in Bangladesh. In *Women and emergencies*, ed. B. Walker, 45–49. Oxford, UK: OXFAM.

Wenger, D., and T. James. 1994. The convergence of volunteers in a consensus crisis: The case of the 1985 Mexico City earthquake. In *Disasters, Collective Behavior, and Social Organization*, ed. R. R. Dynes and K. J. Tierney, 229–43. Cranbury, NJ: Associated University Presses.

Whittle, R., W. Medd, H. Deeming, E. Kashefi, M. Mort, G. Walker, and N. Watson. 2010. After the rain: Learning the lessons from flood recovery in Hull. Final project report for Flood, vulnerability and urban resilience: A real-time study of local recovery following the floods of June 2007 in Hull. Working paper. Lancaster University, Lancaster, UK.

Yonder, A., S. Akcar, and P. Gopalan. 2009. Women's participation in disaster relief and recovery. In *Women, gender and disaster: Global issues and initiatives*, ed. E. Enarson and P. Chakrabarti, 189–211. New Delhi, India: Sage.

RESOURCES

ORGANIZATIONS

- Gender and Disaster Network, www.gdnonline.org
  The Gender and Disaster Network is an educational project initiated by women and men interested in gender relations in disaster contexts.
- National Council on Family Relations, www.ncfr.org
  The National Council on Family Relations provides an educational forum for family researchers, educators, and practitioners to share in the development and dissemination of knowledge about families and family relationships, establishes professional standards, and works to promote family well-being.
- Cooperative State Research, Education and Extension Service, www.csrees.usda.gov
  The Cooperative State Research, Education and Extension Service provides programs through partnerships with land-grant universities and cooperative extension faculty in every state. Programs that are supported include: communities at risk, housing and environment, leadership and volunteer development, financial security, public policy and rural and community development.
- Build Change, www.buildchange.org/
  Build Change is a U.S.-based organization that travels internationally to design earthquake-resistant homes and trains individuals (i.e., builders, engineers, homeowners, and government officials) to build the homes.
- Outreach International, http://www.outreach-international.org/
  Outreach International is an organization that focuses on sustainable solutions through education. They focus their work on impoverished communities and work toward providing individuals and families with clean water, nutrition, sanitation, and leadership training.
- Caritas Australia, http://www.caritas.org/
  Caritas Australia responds to disasters and crises in impoverished communities and works toward educating the population in sustainable methods. In the past, Caritas has provided sustainable agricultural solutions to farmers, provided water catchments so that communities have access to clean water, and have worked toward disaster risk reduction in communities.
- ShelterBox. http://www.shelterbox.org/

RESOURCE WEBSITES

- Family emergency preparedness plan from Ready America: http://www.ready.gov/.
- Basic emergency supply kit: http://www.ready.gov/.
- Protecting your property or business from disaster: http://www.fema.gov/plan/prevent/howto/index.shtm#4.
- FEMA library: http://www.fema.gov/library/index.jsp.
- Disaster planning for pets, family: http://www.humanesociety.org.
- Preparing for disaster in London: http://www.london.gov.uk/priorities/london-prepared/home.
- Emergency preparedness kit in Canada: http://www.redcross.ca/article.asp?id=33847&tid=001.
- Get ready for a disaster in New Zealand: http://www.getthru.govt.nz/web/GetThru.nsf.

12 Violence

Brenda D. Phillips and Pam Jenkins

CONTENTS

12.1   CHAPTER PURPOSE

The purpose of this chapter is to examine concerns about all kinds of violence in a disaster context. Sections examine the types of violence that appear in a disaster context and sensitize readers to the issues surrounding this difficult subject. The chapter concludes by outlining implications for action for emergency managers, nonprofit organizations, and others concerned with reducing injuries and deaths.

12.2   OBJECTIVES

As a result of reading this chapter, readers will be able to:

1. Identify and explain the various types of violence that exist across all societies
2. Explain why the concept of violence is relevant to an agency or organization responsible for disaster management
3. Give examples of the kind of violence that have occurred in various disasters around the world
4. Recognize the times during the life cycle of emergency management when people might be most at risk
5. Discuss why some populations may bear higher risk of exposure to violence during disaster times
6. Make clear why collaborative partnerships must occur across the affected area in order to reduce violence or address its consequences
7. Outline strategies for action that can reduce the likelihood of violence in disaster settings

12.3   INTRODUCTION

In most disasters the crime rate drops, a reality that often surprises people. For example, looting, defined as the theft of people's possessions in a disaster, is unusual, although media reports suggest otherwise (Fischer 1998). In reality, people arrested in a disaster area are often local residents going back for a pet, medicines, or possessions (Tierney, Lindell, and Perry 2001). However, despite the drop in the crime rate, some violent acts go unrecognized and unrecorded in disaster contexts. It may seem surprising that in a context where people turn out to help each other through tragedy, interpersonal and intentional violence may occur. Yet, repeatedly, reports and studies surface that violence does indeed occur along a continuum from public harassment of women and girls waiting in line for relief supplies to rape, human trafficking, and homicide. This chapter discusses these cases and presents implications for action.

Violence remains one of the least examined and least understood behaviors in disaster contexts, particularly after the alarming and largely untrue media reports during Hurricane Katrina (see Box 12.1). What has not been widely told about those days is the considerable level of prosocial behavior that saved lives, prevented harm, and demonstrated remarkable resiliency (Rodriguez, Trainor, and Quarantelli 2006). Despite the general good news about disaster and crime, it remains true also that disaster reveals deeply embedded social problems, including violence (Barton 1970; DOJ n.d.).

12.4   A VIOLENT SOCIETY

Advocates for those affected by violence suggest that our cultures and history demonstrate a high degree of tolerance for violence. From childhood on, families, the media, and other agents of socialization encourage children to live, play, and even work in a culture that does not acknowledge the pervasiveness or influence of violence. Those concerned point to toy and game producers that advertise violent options ranging from guns, bayonets, and tanks to graphic gaming software that awards points for brutal slayings and degrading interactions, particularly with women as the targets.

BOX 12.1   HURRICANE KATRINA: MYTH AND REALITY

A cliché in any disaster is that the event brings out the best and worst in people. As portrayed in the media, those affected by Hurricane Katrina appeared among the worst. We heard that they "were raping babies in the Superdome and Convention Center, guns were blazing in the Superdome, and helicopters were shot out of the sky as they tried to rescue people from roof tops." Very little of that proved to be true (Rodriguez, Trainor, and Quarantelli 2006). And the many acts of heroism, especially by African-American men, went unnoticed and undocumented.

Yet all violence did not disappear during Katrina. Gretna sheriffs shot their guns in the air to keep New Orleanians from crossing the Crescent City Bridge to higher ground. Seven New Orleans police officers were charged with first-degree and attempted first-degree murder in a shooting of unarmed storm victims on the Danziger Bridge in Eastern New Orleans. Seven years later, a federal jury convicted a number of these police officers for their actions and for the coverup. A local jazz singer was raped on a rooftop as she waited for rescue. People lacking transportation were left to die in their homes and on bridges and overpasses.

Efforts to evacuate women and children in domestic-violence shelters began on Friday before the storm came ashore late Sunday and early Monday (Jenkins and Phillips 2008). When the director of one shelter went to the bus station, the police had commandeered the station and no buses were leaving. The director eventually found keys to a church van and drove the residents to Baton Rouge herself. The storm and levee failures subsequently destroyed or severely damaged shelter locations across three parishes. Police and other rescue services normally involved in providing protection were compromised and are still struggling to redefine services and protection for battered women. In Louisiana, those who work to protect those at risk have been forced to reconfigure and reconceptualize the safety net not only for battered women and their children, but for those at risk for child and elder abuse as well. Crime rates in New Orleans have risen, including homicide, domestic violence, and rape. Hurricane Katrina and the levee failures that flooded 80% of the city destroyed important social networks and displaced social service organizations that would normally provide protection and support, and fostered a climate where violence has become a heightened concern.

Source: Pam Jenkins. With permission.

Worldwide, violence of all types has remained a concern. Distinguishing between disasters of consensus (floods, hurricanes, tornadoes) and disasters of conflict (genocide, terrorism) can provide further insight (Quarantelli and Dynes 1976). Disasters of consensus represent events where people come together to render aid. A high degree of cooperation tends to develop, coupled with an outpouring of aid and compassion. Nonetheless, observers and researchers have recorded instances of both individual and systematic violence, usually against the least powerful members of the affected society. Women and children are usually noted as those at highest risk, especially in societies that view women to blame for the event (their "sinful" action caused the earthquake). Still, even in nations that proclaim equality for women, violence remains problematic after disaster, but is usually hidden from view.

Disasters of conflict such as genocide, ethnic conflict, and terrorism inherently produce violence of all kinds. Not only are women and children at risk, but so are men. Complex humanitarian emergencies that compel people to make horrific decisions to survive, or that require people to migrate into unfamiliar or hostile environments, lie behind conditions that increase vulnerability. In these events, such as terrorism, perpetrators intentionally inflict violence to cause physical, psychological, and economic violence. People, including disaster professionals, often express surprise to learn that violence of other types occurs in disasters of consensus, such as earthquakes, hurricanes, or floods.

In disasters of consensus, people tend to come together to help with massive outpourings of donations and volunteer time. Such was the case in 2010, when a major earthquake destroyed much of Haiti's capitol, Port-au-Prince. Far less known, reports of harassment, assault, rape, and abductions of women and children took place within relief camps (Farmer 2011).

Perhaps what is most alarming is the near-complete failure to learn from the past—that violence will occur in disasters of both types. Evidence has been mounting that those tasked with relief and recovery efforts must heed. Planning for disasters must incorporate concerns about violence in order to protect those at risk and reduce human suffering.

12.5   THE EFFECTS OF VIOLENCE

In any society, violence occurs on several different levels. In this section, we review how people experience three forms of violence. We then turn to how fears of violence are often misplaced and how exposure to violence changes over time.

12.5.1   THREE FORMS OF VIOLENCE

Violence falls into three general categories. First, intentional violence includes that encountered at the individual level. Suicide serves as an example, even though social, economic, psychological, and medical conditions as well as despair caused by a disaster environment may influence this highly personal act (Durkheim 1897/1997). Other forms of intentional violence stem from interpersonal acts, including assault, hate crimes, abuse, and homicide (see Box 12.2). Intentional violence can occur at any age, in any population, or within any socioeconomic strata. Child, adult, or elder abuse can take multiple forms as well, including physical, psychological, verbal, sexual, or economic attack. Human trafficking, defined as abductions for purposes of physical and sexual exploitation, fits in this category.

A second form of violence is termed *structural violence*, wherein corporate and/or government policies make people less safe, secure, and healthy. Also described as *organized violence*

BOX 12.2   DOMESTIC VIOLENCE/SEXUAL ASSAULT ACROSS THE WORLD

- Violence by men in intimate partner relationships is widespread across the globe.
- The rates of reported violence vary tremendously, from 13% in Japan to 61% in provincial Peru.
- Sexual assault rates hold the same variance, with the lowest rate of 6% in Japan and the highest rate of 59% in Ethiopia.
- Though the rates of domestic violence vary, some of the patterns remain similar.
- If women have ever been a victim of domestic violence, it is likely that there will also be an event of severe violence.
- The acts of domestic violence against women are not an isolated event, but are part of a pattern of continuing abuse.
- In most of the settings across the world, the women most at risk are separated or divorced.
- Most of the women also reported emotional abuse and controlling behavior in their relationships.
- Situations of conflict, postconflict, and displacement (such as a disaster) may exacerbate existing violence and present new forms of violence against women.

Source: WHO Multi-Country Study on Women's Health against Women, summary of initial results on prevalence, health outcomes and women's response. 2005. Geneva: World Health Organization.

or *economic violence*, structural assault occurs when social policies operate to increase poverty, reduce life spans, and/or put people in dangerous spaces and situations. Corporate downsizing and federal policies for deinstitutionalization of mental health facilities, for example, have put people on the street in the United States, where the risk of violence increased dramatically (Wisner et al. 2005). In places like Haiti, overexploitation and exportation of local resources pushed people into urban areas searching for work. When the earthquake struck in 2010, at least 200,000 people died. Government lack of attention to building codes, coupled with an historically unstable political system, also compromised life safety. These types of structural violence, embedded systemically into social institutions or exploitative practices, put people differentially at risk.

Political violence comprises the third form of violence experienced in society. Such violence historically includes armed uprisings and riots or the response to protests, terrorist attacks (domestic and international), and even conscripted military service. Historically, a military conscription across North America required tens of thousands to fight in wars they did not support. Pacifists, including Quakers, Mennonites, and Amish men, have felt forced to choose between their religious beliefs, military conscription, or prison. U.S. pacifists during World War II could opt for civilian public service, which led directly to the development of the Mennonite Disaster Service in 1950. Conscientious objectors to military initiatives have fared similarly. Ethnic conflict in the 1990s generated a massive humanitarian crisis between Hutu and Tutsi tribes in Rwanda. People able to flee such political violence may linger for extended time periods in relief camps, where they may be subject to additional forms of exploitation and violence.

Terrorism represents a form of political violence experienced worldwide (Rubin and Renda-Tenali 2002). In Oklahoma City in the United States, for example, 168 people, including children in a day-care center, perished under a domestic attack in 1995. In 2001, over 3,000 people representing 23 nations died in the externally generated terrorist attacks on New York City and Washington, DC. Angry blaming erupted against Muslims, resulting in various forms of intentional violence (Peek 2011; Poynting 2004). Similar conflicts continue today as terrorist organizations seek to inflict damage in France, Indonesia, Germany, London, and other locations.

12.5.2 COUNTERTRENDS

Certainly, though, levels of violence vary by society, although no society is immune from violence. Sweden, for example, has drawn a line about parental violence, deeming spanking (corporal punishment) to be a crime. Parenting and educators' organizations in various nations have worked to label toys, music, and software with warnings of violent content. Television and Internet sites allow parents to block some images, though such an effort remains an uphill battle.

American public opinion is "strongly supportive of measures to register firearms, promote firearm safety and keep criminals from acquiring guns" by "large majorities" (Smith 2003, 2). Those most at risk seem most likely to support antiviolence efforts; for example, there is a gender gap, with women less likely to support military spending and more likely to encourage gun control.

Worldwide, social movements for peace and nonviolence have appeared to counter these violent trends. Awareness has developed gradually, primarily through the work of advocates for justice. In the 1960s, several nations launched anti-child-abuse movements, which led to restrictions ranging from child labor to physical child abuse. Medical professionals and teachers now must recognize and respond to harm against children. Social service agencies now exist to remove children from violent situations and protect them legally. However, such training and agencies have made little entrée into the field of disaster work until recently.

In the 1970s, campaigns called Take Back the Night emerged to protest rape and sexual assault. Stronger laws against domestic violence arose at the same time from the battered women's shelter movement (Schechter 1982). Efforts continue to this day to strengthen protective orders for women at risk in many nations. In the 1980s, outcry arose over "granny" or elder abuse, including sexual, physical, and financial forms of violence and exploitation. Concern for lesbians, gay men, bisexual, and transgendered (LGBT) people emerged from the gay rights movement during the same time period (Adam, Duyvandak, and Krouwell 1999). Penalties for hate crimes have stiffened, in part as a response to the gay rights movement as well as increased response to hate crimes based on race (Peek 2003, 2011; FBI 2008). Websites that proclaim "we are not afraid" in the aftermath of terrorism have been created. As a sign of resilience to the power of violence over our lives, tens of thousands of people turn out every year in Oklahoma City in the United States to remember those lost in the attack on the Murrah Federal Building. Through participating in an annual runner's marathon, they vow to never forget and never allow a repeat occurrence. The associated Oklahoma City National Memorial concentrates on teaching about the consequences of violence through their vision: "We come here to remember those who were killed, those who survived and those changed forever. May all who leave here know the impact of violence. May this memorial offer comfort, strength, peace, hope and serenity."

Other countertrends offer hope. In 2011–2012, a social movement dubbed "Arab Spring" arose in objection to regimes that practiced often brutal control politically and militarily. In Myanmar/ Burma, dramatic changes in 2012 led to the election of Aung San Suu Kyi (a former Nobel Peace Prize winner) to parliament. Previously imprisoned under house arrest, her decades-long peaceful protests demanding democracy finally resulted in significant internal change.

Countertrends specific to disaster impacts have also developed in recent years. The Gender and Disaster Network (www.gdnonline.org) has created and maintained downloadable materials (reports, brochures, checklists, guidance) on a range of concerns related to violence. In the aftermath of Hurricane Katrina in the United States and the Haiti earthquake, network members moved swiftly to alert the media, distribute materials, and advocate for survivors. After the 2004 Indian Ocean tsunami, those working with disaster relief in various affected nations (particularly Indonesia and Thailand) collaborated with anti-human-trafficking advocates to protect children from being abducted (Kara 2009).

12.6   DIFFERENTIAL EFFECTS OF VIOLENCE

A number of trends connect to the various forms of violence, often undermining multiple myths and beliefs about how violence occurs. These trends correspond to familiar issues raised throughout the text that link greater power to the influence of prejudice and discrimination. Those who reject these forces—in an effort to influence and control their individual lives and destinies—risk historic patterns of retaliatory violence. The amount of personal power that one possesses as a member of a given population makes a difference: Powerful groups tend to perpetrate violence.

12.6.1   RACE AND ETHNICITY

Historically, racist groups target those deemed inferior or those who threaten their power, control, or influence. In the United States, African-American men have been targeted historically for alleged attacks on white women. Such a false accusation led to the murder of 14-year-old Emmitt Till in rural Mississippi in 1955, an innocent child who may have only said hello to a white woman (Morris 1984). In fact, most intentional violence (e.g., rape, murder) occurs within rather than between racial and ethnic groups (South and Felson 1990).

Disasters of conflict routinely reveal historic tensions between rival groups, usually over the power to control one's destiny or over valuable resources in a given geographic location. In Rwanda, decades of conflict between Hutu and Tutsi tribes has generated massive needs for humanitarian relief. As the nation struggles to emerge from the conflict, and the people begin to heal, numerous external organizations have helped to rebuild every dimension of society from interpersonal trust to public infrastructure (Farmer 2011).

12.6.2 AGE

Age also matters. Youth tend to experience certain types of interpersonal violence more than other age groups, as victims and perpetrators, a trend especially true among males. Violence tends to decline as men age, although exceptions to that pattern do occur. Senior citizens experience other forms of violence at higher levels than those at younger ages, for example, forms of economic exploitation such as being targeted in scams for postdisaster roof repairs and building construction (Choi and Mayer 2000).

12.6.3 GENDER

Gender also differentiates trends in violence and represents the area in which the bulk of research has occurred specific to disasters. Within the family, family members commit the bulk of attacks on women and children. The range of violence to which women are exposed can be considerable, including harassment, physical attack, rape, forced prostitution, labor exploitation, and neglect (Watts and Zimmerman 2002). Young men, particularly African-American men in low-income neighborhoods, have higher rates of exposure suggesting that a link of age, race, and income increases exposure to violence. Such exposure has been linked to increased rates of posttraumatic stress disorder (PTSD), which can be further aggravated in disaster contexts (Fitzpatrick and Boldizar 1993).

12.6.4 DISABILITY

People with disabilities bear a disproportionate risk of violence, including sexual assault and financial exploitation. The American Bar Association (Petersilia 2000) reports that "studies from the U.S., Canada, Australia and Great Britain consistently confirm high rates of violence and abuse in the lives of persons with disabilities." Assault is particularly of concern for people with cognitive disabilities, with rates that may be four to ten times higher than for people without such circumstances. Children with disabilities are nearly twice as likely to experience both physical and sexual abuse as nondisabled children. Legal experts indicate that prosecution for people with disabilities, particularly those with cognitive or developmental disabilities, is particularly difficult.

12.6.5 OCCUPATION

Occupations and workplaces also expose some people to violence on a regular basis, such as service in the military, law enforcement agencies, and even first responders including firefighters, ambulance drivers, and paramedics. Political violence often affects occupational or social groups such as peace officers and political demonstrators, physicians and staff involved in reproductive services, and visible minorities subject to racial and ethnic profiling. Women in the military have begun to report assaults, with as many as one in four women reporting sexual harassment, rape, and unwanted sexual advances, but face retribution when they do (Sadler et al. 2003). Rates of intimate-partner violence appear to have increased in the workplace as well (Swanberg, Logan, and Macke 2005).

Violent outbreaks in school and university settings have claimed dozens of lives, such as the shootings at Virginia Tech University in the United States in 2007. A shooter who claimed ties to a terrorist organization murdered French soldiers and opened fire on a Jewish school in France in 2012. Continuing concern exists over improvised explosive devices (IEDs) that target the military and officials in varying countries. Incidents such as the sarin gas attack on the Tokyo subway in 1995 and the bombing of the London underground in 2005 seek to inflict violence on people simply going to work. Because occupations tend to be gender-segregated, disproportionate impacts can occur even in terrorist attacks in a public setting. The events of September 11, for example, claimed the lives of hundreds of police and firefighters in historically male-dominated occupations.

12.6.6 Homeless Populations

U.S. residents in highly stigmatized social groups may not be able to report violence to authorities. Homeless adults and teens living on the streets may fear encounters with the police or not merit local recognition as credible sources. Women, men, and youth working as prostitutes will not report crimes, assuming that they will be blamed for the assault due to the nature of their work. Undocumented workers fail to report crimes against them as well, out of fear of deportation, an anxiety that also affects legal immigrants as well. Undocumented or documented workers may expose family members to violence. Such a concern developed when temporary laborers camped in City Park in New Orleans, Louisiana, after Hurricane Katrina. Women living in the camps were subjected to a range of violence in an unsettled city.

12.6.7 Socioeconomic Status

Income also obscures the realities of violence. Interpersonal violence can take place at all socioeconomic levels; high incomes do not afford protection. In contrast, higher incomes mean that abusers may be more likely to hide their actions or to avoid prosecution or jail time. Studies clearly indicate that the lower the income or socioeconomic level of the neighborhood, the more likely that a crime will come to the attention of the police. In lower income areas, it is more likely that the perpetrator will go to jail and will be more likely to face capital punishment. The death penalty in particular has been critiqued as disproportionately affecting African-American men (Free 1996). Economic levels thus obscure violence by privileging those with higher incomes who can afford representation and lessen their rates of prosecution.

12.7 RELEVANCE TO DISASTERS

Disasters appear to increase people's exposure to violence and to heighten the fearful context in which they try to survive, live, and provide for their families. The picture, though, is complex because multiple conditions influence the context in which people experience violence. It is possible, for example, that the catastrophic context of Hurricane Katrina increased a number of factors that led to increased interpersonal violence. These factors include overcrowding in available housing and, on the other hand, isolation in areas where repopulation is slow. Survivors of the 2004 tsunami in Sri Lanka had to contend with a "poorly designed, gender-insensitive" set of interventions that left "women vulnerable to assault when accessing basic facilities such as bathing areas or when carrying out daily tasks, including water collection" (Fisher 2009, 235). Research in New Zealand found that domestic violence increased when "abusers fear they are losing control of their environment...an analysis easily transposed to circumstances following a disaster" (Houghton 2009, 101).

Disasters may also permit a context that increases other kinds of risk. After the 1994 Northridge, California, earthquake, household survey data did not find an increase in victimization across Los Angeles County. However, researchers did uncover a continuing risk for younger minority males and others already at risk (Siegel, Bourque, and Shoaf 1999). After the *Exxon Valdez* oil spill along the Alaskan coastline, native men were much more likely than others to report both increased substance abuse and "fighting" in their community, among their friends, and in their own family. Researchers reported that the spill, the response, and the recovery periods all created conflicts, including the distribution of cleanup jobs, increased concerns over threats to the subsidence life on which the local economy and culture were based, and undermined abilities to feed their families (Palinkas et al. 1993). Spousal and child abuse also appeared to increase in some areas affected by the oil spill. Elders in the community of Homer, Alaska, for example, reported an increase in violence (Aranji 1992). Similarly, domestic and sexual violence appear to increase in the wake of other disasters, sometimes as long as one year later (Enarson 1998). A study in postflood Bangladesh uncovered an increase of parental violence against children in conditions of geographic and social isolation within families subject to arduous economic circumstances (Biswas et al. 2010). Disaster contexts can disrupt important social networks that serve to protect those at risk. Children suffer when parents die or when they become separated from their parents. Women who lose a partner may be subject to rapid remarriage; in some areas after the 2004 tsunami, local customs pushed young girls into arranged "tsunami" marriages (Mulligan and Shaw 2011; Felten-Biermann 2006).

Because interpersonal, structural, and political violence disproportionately affect some social groups more than others, disaster managers and others need to understand their impact on the ability to prepare for, respond to, and recover from disasters. Disasters may also reveal violence or increase exposure as survivors come to the attention of officials tasked with relief and recovery efforts.

Historically, practitioners involved in emergency management lack awareness of violence issues. Their counterparts, agencies that advocate against violence and for survivors, typically fail to plan for disasters, including mitigating shelters, designing evacuation plans, and becoming involved in postdisaster case management and reconstruction.

Regardless of whether increased exposure is associated with higher stress, ineffective policies, failure to plan or cross-train, or a lack of understanding, we must be ready to protect children, people with disabilities, the elderly, racial and ethnic minorities, lesbians, gays, and others at risk. Addressing the realities of violence requires partnering with a wide array of those involved in risk reduction for both disasters and violence. Collaborations between law enforcement, social and health service providers, domestic-violence shelter staff, antiviolence programs, and advocates for social groups at risk, emergency managers, and others involved in postservice disaster delivery can result in appropriate and effective interventions.

In this section, we review violence in a disaster context specific to a particular population at risk. The purpose of this section is to reveal areas of concern for those involved in preparedness, response, and recovery efforts and to introduce proactive (rather than reactive) solutions. Section 12.8 then outlines general strategies for reducing vulnerabilities and exposure to violence before, during, and after a disaster event.

12.7.1 GENDER-BASED VIOLENCE

At any point in the emergency management life cycle, women may be in danger of losing their lives or sustaining serious injuries. Domestic assault in a nondisaster context is pandemic. Homicide remains one of the leading causes of death among women. In the United States, one-third of the female homicides are the result of a domestic-violence incident (Wells and DeLeon-Granados 2005; Tjaden and Toennes 2000).

Violence and homelessness are also related. For example, nearly half of women in homeless shelters are fleeing domestic violence (U.S. Conference of Mayors and Sodexho 2005). Violence also impoverishes women. Full shelters and lack of affordable housing before, during, and after disasters may force women back into dangerous living conditions. Poor women are much more likely to rely on overcrowded domestic-violence shelters than middle-class women with more resources. These circumstances render many women far less able to withstand the effects of disasters. Moreover, disasters often create economic difficulties for families in the short and long term. The result of the economic difficulty is that victims may find themselves unable to leave a situation or take legal action to keep themselves and their children safe. Disasters may also claim the lives of important advocates. The 2010 Haitian earthquake, for example, resulted in the deaths of three key feminist leaders (see Box 12.3). In other words, the disruption caused by the disaster can exacerbate potentially violent situations.

The aftermath of any disaster may increase the vulnerability of many who would be victims of interpersonal violence. First, evacuating from an area will place families and friends in housing situations that may create the opportunity for domestic violence, rape, and sexual assault. After Hurricane Katrina, for example, extended family members would stay with the one relative or friend who was in an evacuee city such as Baton Rouge, Dallas, or Atlanta. Sometimes, this would mean

BOX 12.3   HAITI EARTHQUAKE CLAIMS FEMINIST LEADERS

Disasters are clearly associated with concerns about violence of all kinds. In the aftermath of the 2010 Haiti earthquake, social media sites lit up with unexpected losses—the kinds of losses that could have made a difference in a postearthquake environment. Tragedy claimed the lives of three of Haiti's top feminist leaders, women who gave their time and talent to save the lives of others on a daily basis. Myriam Merlet had served as the chief of staff for the Haiti Ministry on Gender and Women's Rights. Her work concentrated on rape in a pre-disaster environment, with recent victories that laid a foundation for change before the earthquake. Anne Marie Coriolan, also a victim of the earthquake, had served as an advisor to the ministry. She also created an organization called Solidarity with Haitian Women. Coriolan's organization had given voice to marginalized Haitian women who looked to feminist leadership as advocates and agents of change. Magalie Marcelin, a lawyer and prominent activist on behalf of Haitian women, also perished in the quake. Marcelin had created an organization called Kay Fanm, devoted to reducing domestic violence against Haitian women. The Kay Fanm organization also provided micro-loans to Haitian women, an effort that would have been invaluable after the earthquake.

Their losses demonstrate several key points. First, women in marginalized circumstances need advocates and visionaries who will devote time to reducing the risks faced by other women. Second, these feminist leaders recognized the critical importance of empowering women to be active in their own lives through bringing charges against perpetrators and gaining access to secure livelihoods. Third, the loss of their lives demonstrate the critical importance of strong connections between antiviolence advocates and organizations and emergency management professionals. Fourth, organizations must work diligently to replace key leaders lost to tragedy. Fifth, organizations and agencies external to an affected area must find ways to enhance security of those at risk: Haiti could ill-afford to lose these women leaders, and the world should never face such a tragedy again.

Sources: Based on a variety of social media and traditional media accounts. For an illustration, see the article written by David Nasaw for *The Guardian*. http://www.guardian.co.uk/world/2010/jan/22/earthquake-kill-haiti-feminists.

that there would be 30 people or more in a single-family dwelling. The evacuation also meant that people lacked access to familiar support systems, including shelters, social service providers, health-care workers, and others who often observe and stand between those at risk and those who offend. Women and girls seeking relief supplies after the 2005 Pakistan earthquake experienced harassment and assault. Attempting to retain cultural values and to practice modesty, some women refused to go to medical tents that did not separate genders. Women's reasons for doing so included fear of exposure to harassment and assault. Similarly, they felt uncomfortable standing in lines for a latrine in close proximity to men. Sensitive attention to these cultural nuances resulted in altering locations to increase privacy and in relocating latrines (Sayeed 2009; Miller and Arquilla 2007).

What is clear is that violence against women and children (especially girls) has been and remains an issue before, during, and after disaster. To illustrate the problem, consider that a Santa Cruz battered women's shelter reported a 50% increase in temporary restraining orders after the 1989 earthquake. That same year, the *Exxon Valdez* oil spill was associated with increased domestic violence, including child neglect, elder and spouse abuse, child abuse, child sexual abuse, and rape. In 1992, post–Hurricane Andrew telephone calls for spouse abuse increased by 50% to the local community helpline. After the 1997 Grand Forks flood, counseling of domestic-violence clients climbed 59% (Enarson 1998; Fothergill 2004). Internationally, Hurricane Mitch in 1998 also increased violence rates for both women and men. After the Indian Ocean tsunami in 2004, reports of domestic violence and assault in refugee camps came into nongovernmental organizations (NGOs) attempting to support survivors (Enarson 2006; Fisher 2009). Comparable reports, including rape, resurfaced after the 2010 Haiti earthquake (Farmer 2011).

After Hurricane Katrina in 2005, domestic-violence shelter providers observed new problems (Jenkins and Phillips 2008; Brown, Jenkins, and Wachtendorf 2010). First, the hurricane destroyed shelters and programs in three parishes. Anticipating the destruction, shelter providers had to secure their own resources to transport women and children to safety in Baton Rouge and other locations. Second, at least half of the staff lost their own homes and had to relocate, resulting in considerable loss of key support for the previously sheltered women and children. Women with few housing options returned to their abusers, further exposing themselves and their children to risk. In other instances, abusers tracked down and moved in with their victims (Jenkins and Phillips 2008). When the population of Orleans Parish began to trickle back after the mandatory evacuation of the area, battered-women program staff at two locations reported that their clients were reporting more serious violence coming less gradually than before the storm (Jenkins and Davidson 2008). New Orleans three years after the 2005 storm remained an environment with serious safety issues. Police still operated out of temporary trailers, with few officers assigned specifically to domestic violence. Rates of homicide, assault, and rape rose as well as mental illness and suicide rates. Friends and other sources of social support remained in faraway cities, trying to rebuild their own lives. The city's public hospital and most of the public housing units have not reopened; these historically safer havens have fared badly, with serious consequences for those experiencing interpersonal violence (Jenkins and Phillips 2008). The long-term recovery of New Orleans created opportunities for change (the creation of the New Family Justice Center Alliance) and continuing high rates of interpersonal violence that dominate the New Orleans discourse.

Emergency managers, police, social service providers, community organizers and activists, and concerned citizens must take action to safeguard those at risk. Unfortunately, few jurisdictions and domestic-violence providers take such action. Emergency managers and others who routinely plan for disaster also routinely exclude domestic-violence providers. Those same providers often fail to prepare for disaster contexts, including evacuation of residents and staff, continuity of operations, and resumption of services. A significant disconnection exists between the two communities regarding the information, resources, and expertise needed to address the issue (Enarson 1998).

Further, as often happens with disasters, routinely awarded grants are redirected toward disasters, meaning that local social service providers struggle to meet local need. One study that examined 77 domestic-violence programs could not meet a demand for increased service (Enarson 1999). A clear problem exists when those at risk for violence continue to experience vulnerability from disaster. Because of a lack of planning for such circumstances, emergency managers and social service providers fail to reduce that risk.

12.7.2 AGE

As described in Chapter 7 on age, children and seniors may be at particular risk during disasters. Individuals separated from family members, children, and seniors with disabilities or frail medical conditions are likely to be particularly vulnerable.

12.7.2.1 Children

As a result of Hurricane Katrina, for example, children could and did become separated from family and guardians, rendering them potentially vulnerable to exploitation, abuse, or neglect. Though shelters established programs to assist unaccompanied children, the separation of children must be avoided at all costs in the future (Peek 2008; Peek and Fothergill 2006, 2008). Further, parents with limited custodial authority took children, sometimes resulting in protracted legal battles.

It should be noted, though, that much of the violence that children experience occurs within their family units. Consequently, even if families remain intact during a disaster, it is wise to train staff and volunteers working with survivors to identify children who may be in danger. Just as medical and educational professionals bear responsibility in many nations to recognize and report abuse, so should those operating in a disaster context. As in Hurricane Katrina, where family members were crowded together in shelters, family homes, and motels, the potential for abuse and neglect could increase. Coupled with isolation from protective social networks, violence in general will increase. Officials should assume that similar patterns could result in a disaster environment. Tent cities, trailer parks or caravans, and relief sites should include protective measures for children.

A number of key organizations represent partners in reducing children's risk to postdisaster violence. Those organizations include child protective services, homeless providers, organizations that address street violence (including child prostitution), disability organizations, law enforcement, educators, and recreational program staff. Careful cross-training should take place in order to prepare these organizations for the disaster time period. Organizations likely to become involved in disaster response should be trained in the language, content, and procedures common to response and even recovery time periods. Similarly, disaster response and recovery organizations should cross-train with children's advocate organizations in order to understand and benefit from their knowledge and perspectives. Predisaster programs designed to identify children at risk and move them into safe environments need to be designed, including those for children with prior abuse (such as screening for previous traumas likely to resurface during disaster), children separated from their families (e.g., shelter programs), and children with disabilities (who have a higher risk of exposure to violence). Key to assisting children, beyond providing a safe environment, is restoring structure and stability to their lives. Teachers, social service providers, and recreational staff can predesign programs that reintegrate children into social and educational opportunities that provide a framework in which children can rebound (as described in Chapter 7).

12.7.2.2 Seniors

Senior citizens are considered at risk for several forms of violence and abuse outside of the context of disasters. Those risks include sexual and physical violence, neglect (nutritional, medical, psychological), and financial exploitation. Frail elderly are particularly vulnerable because of being unable to easily access, manage, or control their health or resources. Even seniors in congregate care facilities have been exposed to assault and theft. Family members, friends, and even strangers may take advantage of their circumstances (National Research Council 2003).

The elderly present unique challenges for safety from abuse and from the effects of disaster. Those elderly whose living conditions before a disaster made them at risk for abuse may find those conditions exacerbated after a disaster (Fernandez et al. 2002; Evans 2010; Jenkins, Laska, and Williamson 2008). Agencies must construct outreach programs, particularly through senior programs that connect seniors with seniors (Friedsam 1961, 1962; Kilijanek and Drabek 1979).

Care must be taken, therefore, to ensure that appropriate planning and preparedness have taken place along with building adequate partnerships among relevant senior care agencies and organizations. Adult protective service organizations serve as a primary resource for assisting and supporting seniors at risk and should be brought in as key partners. Home health-care agencies and health providers that work with homebound seniors or frail elderly can be tasked to assess risk. Shelter providers must be trained to conduct careful intake procedures to determine if social support (family, friends) exists for elderly residents. Training of shelter workers should include teaching them to recognize signs of abuse or exploitation and how to report concerns. State legal offices, such as the attorney general, can develop task forces to safeguard the interests of seniors involved in rebuilding their homes so as to reduce the risk for fraud. Because disability prevalence increases with age, disability organizations should be integrated into a planning team as well (National Council on Disability 2009).

12.7.3 RACE AND ETHNICITY

Historic patterns of segregation and discrimination, as well as repetitive threats and acts of violence, have resulted in higher vulnerability among racial and ethnic minorities across the world. The global ethnic conflicts that dominate the latter part of the twentieth century and the early twenty-first century are often based in historical racial or ethnic antagonisms (Soeters 2005). All three types of violence (intentional, structural, and political) occur as part of racial and ethnic conflicts. These ongoing conflicts do not disappear during a disaster, but instead create further opportunities for violence.

Segregation patterns since emancipation, for example, have marginalized minority housing into floodplains and other hazardous areas (Cutter 2006). In Princeville, North Carolina, for example, freed slaves established the first town incorporated by African Americans in the United States. Originally known as "Freedom Hill," this location was along the Tar River, which repeatedly flooded. In the late 1990s, after a series of rain events, Princeville (named after a mayor who rescued people during a flood in the 1800s) flooded again, this time up to the rooftops. Princeville residents chose not to move despite a federal buyout offer. As described by locals, the community represented—among other things—a safe haven against the threat of attack by the Ku Klux Klan. Flood risk occurred because of a hazardous location, and people stayed in part because of violent threats. The threat of violence thus perpetuated risk, this time in a disaster context (Phillips, Stukes, and Jenkins 2012).

Similar circumstances lay behind patterns of neighborhood development in New Orleans, with the consequence that historically African-American areas such as the Lower 9th ward flooded (Cutter 2006). Racial and ethnic vulnerability in disasters includes disproportionate loss of life. This trend was seen as a result of Hurricane Katrina, where more African Americans died than individuals from other races, even when controlling for original population numbers. Such deaths were also disproportionately older and male (Sharkey 2007).

Violence remains a concern throughout many minority communities to this day. Young African-American males are far more likely to be exposed to violence than other races, with the consequence that symptoms of posttraumatic stress disorder (PTSD) rates are higher (Fitzpatrick and Boldizar 1993). Disasters produce further stress, though in general PTSD rates are lower than expected among most populations. The exception is among those exposed to trauma prior to the disaster. If that trauma has not been treated, the potential for PTSD among disaster survivors is much higher (Norris, Friedman, and Watson 2002; Norris et al. 2002). Racial and ethnic minorities that have sustained previous trauma, then, are more likely to be traumatized by a disaster event.

In an electronic discussion of the impacts of disasters on minority communities in the United States, FEMA's former associate director in the 1990s, Kay Goss (n.d.) said, "FEMA will do all it can to empower the African American community to fundamentally change the vulnerability of Black America to disasters." Doing so will require considerable attention from disaster managers and others dedicated to reducing not only the threat of disasters, but of violence, economic discrimination, housing segregation, and political marginalization. Social problems lie behind many of the forms of violence described in this chapter. Social problems require social solutions in which disaster managers and others concerned with vulnerability reduction must participate: "The more fundamental lesson of disasters, however, is that the social disadvantages that our society treats as ordinary and unremarkable become deadly in dramatic ways in the course of a disaster" (Farber n.d., 19).

12.7.4 DISABILITY

According to the American Bar Association, despite a decrease in crime over the past several decades in the United States, people with disabilities (especially developmental disabilities) "have not experienced greater safety" (Petersilia 2000). There's no doubt that the idea of someone with a disability suffering violent attacks, abuse, or exploitation is stunning. Further, the same social characteristics that predict violence in general exist for individuals with disabilities as well.

Worldwide, it is estimated that 10% or about 3.5 million people displaced by disasters of consensus or of conflict have disabilities (Wolbring 2011). The American Bar Association notes that poverty rates are higher among people with disabilities; consequently, protection of those living in dangerous areas, who use public transportation, or who are dependent on those who might exploit them is of concern (Petersilia 2000). Disability also increases with age, representing particularly challenging issues with the onset of new and unfamiliar conditions (National Council on Disability 2009). In developing nations, disabilities remain a particular problem with extremely limited resources for education and work. Forced to beg or endure homeless conditions, many people with disabilities experienced poorer health, diminished educational and economic opportunities, dependency, and acute poverty (World Health Report 2011). Conditions such as these are associated with increased mortality in disaster events.

Disasters also have the potential to create new disabilities. The 2010 Haiti earthquake represents one example. Crush injuries resulted in permanent disabilities for a significantly new portion of the population (Farmer 2011). Amputations of limbs, which saved lives, also presented new challenges in an environment difficult to navigate and a society not historically accessible. Prior to the earthquake, about 1 million people in Haiti had disabilities. Postdisaster, new numbers of people with disabilities required rugged wheelchairs and significant levels of external aid (Wolbring 2011). This new group of people with disabilities may require special attention to prevent exploitation. Those still lingering in relief areas and lacking social support networks represent a population of particular concern.

Studies on violence against people with disabilities create an alarming scenario for disaster contexts. One study found that 13% of women with physical disabilities reported physical or sexual abuse in the year preceding the survey. Perpetrators included husbands, partners, attendants, health-care providers, and strangers. Sexual abuse was more likely to be committed by strangers (Young et al. 1997), suggesting that the act of leaving familiar settings to go to shelters or temporary locations might be of concern. The Center for Research on Women with Disabilities in the United States (2000) reports that the disability type most likely to receive services from domestic-violence providers was an individual with mental illness; far fewer women with physical disabilities, developmental disabilities, or visual or hearing disabilities received services. Children with disabilities (especially developmental disabilities) bear a disturbing risk of sexual abuse (Wilgosh 1993). It is clear that many individuals with disabilities remain under the radar for antiviolence services, despite their risks (Young et al. 1997).

People with disabilities would benefit from preplanning that increases their safety in an unfamiliar environment. In addition, individuals with cognitive disabilities "often feel powerless to avoid painful or harmful experiences. According to the American Bar Association, when a person is dependent on another for food, clothing, shelter, and all social interaction, that dependency prevents him or her from resisting abuse" (Petersilia 2000). Consequently, outreach and efforts to assess and protect individuals in shelters, temporary housing, or other locations used in a disaster context would be crucial. Part of that would need to involve safety training (Petersilia 2000) that should include disaster preparedness. As with other areas of concern, it is necessary to build and work with a broad set of partners to address the issues of disabilities, disasters, and vulnerability. Likely partners would include judges, associations that work with and for people with disabilities, law enforcement, domestic-violence protection services, and social service providers. For example, Safe Place in Austin, Texas, provides free and confidential services, including staff who use American Sign Language and also offer a Disability Services Safety Awareness Program (www.safeplace.org). After the Haiti earthquake, responding organizations included Whirlwind Wheelchair International; Portlight Strategies, Inc.; Catholic Charities; and the Institute on Disabilities at Temple University (Wolbring 2011).

12.7.5 SEXUAL ORIENTATION AND VIOLENCE

Stigmatized groups of all kinds, including lesbians, gay men, and bisexual or transgendered individuals, are among those whose survival, safety, and well-being may be contingent upon finding safe space and sensitized emergency services. Interpersonal violence like hate crimes, including murders, rape, and physical assault, are particular concerns. Structural forms of violence include an "epidemic of homeless" among LGBT youth (Ray 2006). Intentional violence that occurs because of stigmatization, isolation, and marginalization includes higher rates of teen suicide.

Eads (2002) found that the needs of the LGBT community were not well met after September 11 in the United States. For example, supporting organizations reported knowing of individuals whose same-sex partner had been killed or injured. Yet these same organizations could not provide the healthy partner with information about the deceased or injured partner because they were not legal kin. Some LGBT individuals reported fear of requesting services, despite losing a job or experiencing damage to their home. Some who did attempt access reported traumatizing experiences related to their sexual identity. Fear of hate crimes, reprisals, and being singled out or denied aid all prevent people qualified for aid from seeking it out. The American Red Cross did provide funds and programming to same-sex partners from donated funds. Hurricane Katrina revealed holes in U.S. federal policies to serve LGBT communities (D'Ooge 2008). Anecdotal reports from Katrina report a rise in fears of public condemnation or hate crimes among those who traveled to public shelters. Loss of one's community and valuable social networks also increased reported fears of violence. Indonesia reported an increase in heterophobic responses among LGBT individuals after the 2004 tsunami (Liang 2010).

A number of organizations exist to provide support to LGBT individuals and to disaster managers seeking to create a safer, more humane environment before, during, and after disasters. PFLAG (Parents and Friends of Lesbians and Gays), for example, has chapters in many areas. Antiviolence initiatives, gay-rights organizations, faith-based communities, and others have stood by LGBT populations and can serve as sources of information, as conduits for aid and relief, and as partners in planning and in aid distribution systems.

12.7.6 SUICIDE

Postdisaster suicide rates among both sexes and all age groups were found to have increased four years after a major disaster had been declared (1982–1989) in a sample of U.S. counties, while rates in nonimpacted counties during the same time period did not increase (Krug et al. 1998).

Though mental health rates do not rise considerably after most disasters, there is potential for suicide to increase under some circumstances. For example, the magnitude and scope of the disaster could matter. Catastrophic events that tear apart the social fabric of a community produce isolating conditions that are associated with suicide (Durkheim 1897/1997). An event that involves loss of neighborhoods, social networks, and social support systems could increase the potential for suicide. Hurricane Katrina represents one example of an event of this magnitude: Suicide rates appear to have risen since then. Local social and mental health service providers indicated that one year after the storm, suicide rates had risen from 9 per 100,000 to 26 per 100,000 in New Orleans (Penix 2006).

Suicide may be more likely to increase during the recovery than the immediate relief period as people deal with the stresses and disruptions to medications, medical and psychological providers, and social networks. Regardless of the time period, disaster managers should work with suicide hotlines, psychological and social service providers, and medical professionals to design and offer appropriate suicide intervention procedures.

12.7.7 IMMIGRANTS AND RECENT ARRIVALS

Violence and associated emotional and cognitive reactions can interfere with people's willingness to listen to and follow those in authority positions. Those who have arrived in a host country from nations of political repression or communities with historically poor relations with police may not trust law enforcement or others in a crisis. The Loma Prieta earthquake of 1989 illustrates the unanticipated consequences of emergency management planning when "participation by citizens was missing" (Phillips 1993, 104). Fear of the uniformed National Guard troops—there to provide support—kept recent immigrants from moving to better shelters with food, medical care, and tents. Their fear stemmed from multiple negative, even deadly, encounters with the military in their countries of origin, including nations where missing family members became known as *los desparecidos* or "the disappeared," who never returned (Phillips 1993). Political refugees found the military-support option terrifying to the point of refusing to accept aid (Phillips 1993, 102–3):

> Victims' prior experience also hindered some outdoor sheltering attempts. To accommodate the outdoor campers, city and county officials persuaded the American Red Cross (ARC) to open Ramsey Park as an official shelter. To expedite this process, the National Guard erected tents inside fenced off areas of the park. However, Central American refugee families apparently found this image terrifying. Immigrants who had fled military and government-backed death squads in their native countries now faced similar imagery after disaster. What city, county, and ARC officials hoped would become appropriate shelter now became transformed into a symbolic concentration camp. Approximately three hundred campers refused to leave Callaghan Park for Ramsey Park—in part because of this horrific reminder.

Recent immigrants who experienced the 1994 Northridge earthquake in the United States avoided seeking assistance out of fear of deportation and possible violence (Bolin and Stanford 1998, 27):

> Indeed, an abrasive anti-immigrant discourse was (and continues to be) a prominent feature of the California political scene. FEMA, as part of a new federal law, requires all relief applicants to declare their residency status, a declaration subject to auditing by the Immigration and Naturalization Service. As one community worker in Ventura reported, "many Latinos around here think the federal government can just load them up in box cars and ship them off to Mexico, no matter how long they've lived here."

In subsequent disasters, immigrants also declined to visit relief centers despite promises from the federal government that basic humanitarian aid was free and did not require documentation. The risk of violence, exposure, or deportation due to having lost papers in the disaster overshadowed basic human needs for food, water, medical aid, clothing, and shelter.

12.8 IMPLICATIONS FOR ACTION

How can emergency managers, case managers, advocates, police, shelter providers, and others take steps to mitigate violence as a risk factor in disasters? In this section, we review practical strategies that can reduce the potential for violent impacts. The content that follows emanates from empirical research coupled with well-grounded practices that have worked in previous disaster contexts.

12.8.1 RESEARCH LOCAL PATTERNS OF VIOLENCE

A first step requires researching local patterns of violence as a part of vulnerability assessments. Agencies involved in disaster work should identify and understand local patterns of violence—the types, extent, and impact on certain groups. Even violence that occurred decades past, particularly if politically motivated, can linger to affect those living in the community today, such as the example from the Loma Prieta earthquake, where frightened immigrants chose not to enter safe locations. Which social groups are likely to be fearful of violence and which kinds of violence? How will those historic patterns affect people's willingness to listen to those in authority, to follow emergency recommendations, or to trust outside of their familiar social networks? Who knows and understands the local population? Who might be your collaborators in this emergency?

Violence data can be found through local sources such as police and domestic-violence programs, suicide hotlines, advocacy organizations, national clearinghouses, and government and nongovernmental organizations. Many community agencies prepare regular reports about violence, victims and survivors, trends, concerns, and patterns over time. Formal records, though, may not reflect the real rates of violence, as many victims fear reporting their assault. Some conservative nations blame women for their assault, and reporting an event may occur at the expense of one's life. Even in some nations where police have been tasked with protecting the public, rapes go unrecognized. Some locations, such as in Pakistan, report that women who go to police stations have been raped again by the police (Quraishi 1997). Pakistani response has been to open up female-only police stations with female officers. Since January 2009, nine such police stations have registered 11,789 cases of violence against women (VNC 2011).

12.8.2 Increase Knowledge about Barriers

A second step involves increasing the knowledge of the emergency manager, advocate, agency, or caseworker about barriers that limit residents' abilities to address risk in their lives. What kinds of barriers, for example, impede the ability of those at risk to move freely and safely about their community and at various times of the day? How, when, and where can those at risk—the homeless surviving under a bridge, children walking home from school, an individual with a mobility disability waiting for public transportation, seniors living independently, disaster survivors seeking latrines or clean water—access safe space? What kinds of barriers interfere with drawing on supportive interpersonal networks? By identifying those whom social groups trust, such as home health-care workers, pastors, neighborhood leaders, and educators, it may be possible to identify routes through which information can be transmitted about personal safety and disasters. Further, efforts to safeguard those at risk for increased violence can be developed at a programmatic level such as a neighborhood-watch type of program. By creating this program in a nondisaster environment, it can operate during and after disasters as well as reduce risks of violence. Relief camps that operated in the wake of the 2004 tsunami or the 2010 Haitian earthquake practiced the use of safety patrols and increased lighting. Women and girls walked to the latrine and medical clinics in groups to avoid harassment and assault.

In a disaster, staying free of violence will become less prioritized as people seek safety from the impending disaster. Yet, the risks to interpersonal violence do not go away during this time, and emergency managers need to prepare shelter workers, transportation providers, and first responders about how the issues of interpersonal violence may impede an individual's or family's ability to seek safety. For example, during Hurricane Katrina, some mothers felt compelled to evacuate with abusers in order to keep their children safe. In a number of cases, formerly abusive partners, who had custody for the weekend, evacuated with their children.

How can existing resources such as emergency preparedness information, shelters, relief assistance, and recovery assets be used to protect those at risk and facilitate their protection not only from violence, but also their recovery? Suggestions include the following:

- Key emergency preparedness materials should include information on where to seek safety from threats of violence and how to report such violence to authorities.
- Evacuation resources should be prioritized to include those at risk, such as residents in domestic violence, congregate-care settings, residential locations for those with developmental disabilities, domestic-violence shelters, or homeless shelters.
- Shelters can designate staff as liaisons to groups within a shelter and to their advocacy groups. While those at risk may not interact with shelter staff, they may do so with an advocacy group that visits the shelter on a regular basis.
- Care should be taken to accord confidentiality and privacy when people enter a relief setting or shelter. Intake procedures could allow people to self-identify issues of concern or to request that a particular organization be notified of their presence in the shelter.
- Transportation systems should include people present to monitor for violence, fraud, and exploitative behaviors, including economic exploitation and emotional manipulation.
- Law enforcement personnel and other first responders should understand that they may represent danger to some populations and to dress, act, and interact with people with

sensitivity. By working with advocacy groups and locally trusted leaders, it may be possible to provide support and assistance to those experiencing violence.

- Relief centers should widely disseminate information on how to reach safe locations should an individual be experiencing violence of any kind. Designated officials should be trained on how to recognize the signs of abusive relationships and how to intervene sensitively and safely for all concerned.
- Staff and personnel can be trained on how to watch for suicide, to monitor for hate crimes, and to work sensitively with traumatized (but often silent) populations.
- Websites and other social media can include links to advocacy and support organizations; information about violence, suicide, and hate crimes; and directions to places of safety.

12.8.3 KNOW YOUR COMMUNITY'S RESOURCES

Local networks and resources can assist and support the emergency management community about those at risk and help disseminate disaster information. A number of local or state agencies and organizations can become new partners in efforts to reduce violent exposure. Examples of such organizations might include:

- Institutional safe homes, victim services, community outreach programs
- Domestic-violence shelters
- Child and adult protective services
- Aging organizations and government agencies
- Suicide hotlines and counselors
- Judicial systems and advocates for victims of violence or intimidation
- Government agencies with antiviolence initiatives
- Nonprofit service and advocacy agencies
- Advocacy groups for those at risk, including seniors, people with disabilities, and lesbian, gay, bisexual, and transgendered individuals
- Nongovernmental organizations that bring in trained experts capable of recognizing problematic shelters and relief-camp layouts and of providing expertise
- Feminist organizations that advocate for women and children at risk
- Community networks, neighborhood collaboratives, and self-help groups

First steps include initiating local consultations with advocacy groups to learn about local problems and local resources. Building bridges of collaboration with facilities or organizations serving people who routinely live with fear and violence is crucial (see Box 12.4). This includes learning how populations at risk are affected in the local area and how organizations try to help street children, the homeless, battered women, gays and lesbians, undocumented immigrants, gang members, and seniors in high-crime areas. By inviting representatives from these groups or their representative organizations or advocates to the emergency management planning table, fresh perspectives and insights can be generated for disaster contexts. Next steps would invite these new partners to emergency management cross-training and exercises so that partners build relationships, learn each others' perspectives and language, and design practical plans that link well to create a new kind of safety net. An extremely important component of this is to help new collaborative partners learn about disaster practices. Agencies that seek to help those at risk for violence need to establish standard operating procedures for emergencies. They also need to mitigate their buildings structurally for local hazards and to design continuity-of-operations plans should their facilities and staff be affected.

BOX 12.4   2012 WINNER OF THE MARY FRAN MYERS AWARD: DAMAI PAKPAHAN, INDONESIA

Damairia (Damai) Pakpahan from Indonesia received the 2012 Mary Fran Myers Award from the Gender and Disaster Network. This award, established in memory of Myers's efforts to link gender with practice, recognizes individuals who integrate research with action. Ms. Pakpahan has worked diligently for decades in the area of gender justice and development, including work related to the 2004 tsunami as well as issues associated with climate change and earthquakes. She has personally trained over 500 civil servants on issues of gender, development, and disasters. Her work for the Aceh Tsunami Programme resulted in significant elevations in understanding issues of gender. Her résumé includes serving as program officer with Oxfam in Jakarta and as a key gender analyst for the Gender Working Group in the Indonesia Disaster Management Society. She is the cofounder of multiple organizations focused on human rights, justice, and democracy that focus on women's poverty, gender-based violence, street children, disabilities, land rights, and disaster concerns. She has published widely on issues of gender and disasters for women's studies journals and for the broader media. Her work includes advocacy for gender issues in the Indonesia National Disaster Management Law. As one nominator said of Ms. Pakpahan, she is the "perfect mixture of activism, feminism, journalist and intellectual with a strong passion for gender and disaster." Ms. Pakpahan's passion for and advocacy about women and children in a disaster context clearly marks her as this year's winner of the Mary Fran Myers Award.

Local agencies can serve as productive partners in new efforts to address fear and violence as vulnerability factors in disaster education. For example:

- After the 1989 Loma Prieta earthquake, the city of Santa Cruz, California, distributed "Holiday Help Lines" flyers alerting residents that holidays in the wake of a disaster can be extremely stressful and providing contact information for seven community-based anti-violence groups.
- Interagency networks with managers and residents in group shelters such as domestic-violence shelters, group homes for runaways, and halfway homes for ex-convicts can ensure their access to emergency assistance. The Emergency Network of Los Angeles (www.enla.org) is a community-based collaborative representing the needs and interests of recent immigrants and works closely with local emergency management authorities.
- After Hurricane Katrina, many nonprofits dealing with interpersonal violence created emergency plans. The New Orleans' Mayor's Task Force on Domestic Violence brought in disaster and domestic-violence speakers to inform and support efforts to rebuild the local safety net for those at risk. The state of Louisiana provided training on maintaining rape crisis programs in the context of disasters.
- The 2004 Indian Ocean tsunami brought together an array of nongovernmental organizations concerned with gender-based violence. In Sri Lanka, women's organizations responded quickly. The Coalition for Assisting Tsunami Affected Women funded member organizations, visited areas that had sustained damage, served as advocates, gathered data, and demanded action. The Women's Coalition for Disaster Management formed a gender-watch network in tsunami areas that assessed all elements of the recovery from relief distribution to lobbying against alcohol sales inside relief camps. Women in Need, an existing antiviolence against women organization, focused on trauma counseling (Fisher 2009).

12.8.4   MAKE THOSE AT RISK A PRIORITY

Both before and after disaster, planners should make those most at risk a priority:

- Include community agencies and organizations serving those affected by violence in all outreach efforts.
- Prioritize hazard mitigation, emergency preparedness outreach, assistance during evacuation, utility restoration, and financial relief to shelters housing people whose safety depends on these facilities.
- Give priority status to homeless shelters, domestic-violence shelters, and children's services.

By learning from previous events, we can improve future response. What Hurricane Katrina taught us is that the services for victims of domestic violence need to be mobile during evacuation, response, and recovery. Shelter residents need transportation resources and police protection during evacuation, shelter, and interim housing. People who are homeless or who work in occupations that place them at risk (e.g., prostitution) need to receive assistance to reach secure shelter as well. The traditional methods of helping victims of violence will not necessarily work after a disaster, especially if the agencies are impacted themselves. For example, Crescent House, the only shelter in Orleans Parish, was flooded and then caught fire (see Photos 12.1 and 12.2). The local YWCA was also flooded and never reopened.

Agencies and organizations that provide antiviolence training, places of refuge, alternative school programs to keep kids off the streets, senior centers, home health-care providers, and others in routine contact with those at risk must receive attention and priority for restoration of utilities, facilities, and funding.

12.8.5   ENHANCE CREDIBILITY AMONG AUTHORITY FIGURES

Researchers agree that credibility is key to motivating people at risk to heed warning messages and access aid. Efforts might avoid unnecessarily intimidating symbolism, including appearance,

PHOTO 12.1   Crescent House, a shelter for survivors of domestic violence in New Orleans, was destroyed by Hurricane Katrina-related flooding and fire in 2005. (Photo by Pam Jenkins. With permission.)

PHOTO 12.2 An empty lot stands as mute testimony to the difficulties of recovering from disaster. This location formerly held Crescent House, a center for survivors of domestic violence before Hurricane Katrina, and was not rebuilt. (Photo by Pam Jenkins. With permission.)

language, demeanor, and signage. After Hurricane Andrew, employees removed the word "Federal" from a FEMA sign in south Dade County (Phillips, Neal, and Garza 1994). The U.S. Army set up mobile kitchens, brought in Spanish-speaking soldiers, and invited immigrant women into the kitchens to prepare culturally familiar meals. All types of shelters and agencies need to think carefully about how they let victims know that services exist. For example, after Katrina, Crescent House provided brochures that featured Catholic Charities (their home agency) rather than services for domestic violence. Then, when someone would visit their table, they could pick up information without arousing suspicion from an offender. Often, the workers would meet with the women in the bathroom of the center to make a safety plan. Disasters, for those exposed to violence, are not business as usual. Practicing flexibility in the delivery of services and information may be necessary rather than attempting to reintegrate standard outreach strategies. Women affected in an earthquake in India came to rely on each other and on relationships that emerged through self-help sewing groups. Simple discussion among the women creating items to sell began to transform their sense of self and their power in affected villages (Lund and Vaux 2009).

Some strategies might include:

- Identifying in advance who the most credible authorities are to the specific population at risk and working with them on public outreach strategies.
- Offering information by people who are as familiar and similar to the affected population as possible. The principle of homogeneity means that we trust people like ourselves more than we do people we perceive as different. Seniors can speak to seniors; people with disabilities can connect with their peers; and even children can reach out to other children.
- Recruiting volunteers, students, and staff from groups at risk of violence, e.g., minority families in low-income neighborhoods.
- Working through trusted organizations and places, including worship locations. This is particularly important with extremely marginalized populations such as the homeless or in LGBT communities.

12.8.6 Publicize

Emergency managers, social service providers, antiviolence agencies, and advocates can capitalize on disaster events to integrate violence concerns into all aspects of local emergency management, for example, by

- Initiating student internships with local colleges and universities to study and analyze violence issues in disasters at the local level
- Disseminating preparedness, transportation, evacuation, protective action, and recovery information through agencies, organizations, program offices, and advocates to reach those historically at risk for violent exposure
- Conducting emergency preparedness training at places where those at risk may congregate, including homeless shelters, senior centers, recreational facilities, school programs, and domestic-violence shelters
- Involving civic and community organizations in developing emergency evacuation kits, first aid, and communication resources to be used during an event. (For examples of items in such kits, visit www.ready.gov, www.fema.gov, or www.redcross.org.)
- Increasing outreach to social groups at heightened risk of violence by publicizing updated contact information for relevant local and regional organizations (e.g., those working against intolerance and hate crimes, gang violence, violence against people with disabilities, and senior exploitation, as well as women's shelters)
- Participating in events to distribute information and enhance credibility among at-risk populations, including Domestic Violence Month, Sexual Assault Awareness Week, Take Back the Night marches, Disability Awareness Week, Hispanic Heritage Month, African American History Month, Women's History Month, Gay Pride/Coming Out Day, Grandparents' Day, ethnic festivals, and other local events

12.8.7 Planning

Planning for resumption of services to those at risk after a disaster is key. Every jurisdiction should have a plan dedicated to violence issues and should integrate key partners from across the community in order to build a working partnership. Central to any planning effort is

- Training social service providers on local hazards and assisting them with developing evacuation procedures, security needs, communication resources during disasters, and strategies for ensuring that services remain in place as needed during and after disaster. Appointing a staff member to be in charge of such training and planning is a first step.
- Training emergency management staff on local issues of violence within the community.
- Getting to know the service providers and key staff that take on the issue of violence, of all kinds, within the community.
- Integrating key community leaders into planning efforts in order to identify places where they can be of assistance and where they may need assistance themselves.
- Critiquing the existing plan for areas where violence issues have not been considered (for example, in disaster shelters or temporary housing) and, in concert with central partners, identifying solutions.
- Developing and maintaining updated phone call lists of organizations that are active participants in all phases of disasters from education through evacuation and relocation.
- Designing a communication system for participating organizations to stay in touch before, during, and after a crisis.
- Setting out a clear division of labor to identify and respond to those at risk for violence.
- Writing a formal memorandum of understanding regarding relationships and responsibilities.

- Designing plans for identifying those at risk for violence in open shelters and relief camps and ensuring that local camp/shelter layouts protect those at risk.
- Empowering local citizens to be active in their own safety, including training on disasters and on violence, and then implementing procedures to use these citizens for safety patrols and buddy systems.
- Ensuring that women and girls have access to sustainable livelihoods as part of their economic recovery (Klein 2008; Lund and Vaux 2009).
- Examining short- and long-term recovery scenarios from other disasters in order to identify potential places where recovery planning is needed to aid those at risk for violence, particularly service provision, temporary housing, temporary protection orders, hotlines, incarceration of offenders, and safe places.

12.9 SUMMARY

Some groups, such as senior citizens, children, survivors of domestic violence or hate crimes, homeless persons, people with disabilities, lesbians, gays, and others experience higher rates of exposure to violence outside the context of disaster. Studies suggest that exposure may increase after disaster as well. It is the work of emergency managers, social service providers, health-care workers, community and civic organizations, and advocates to partner with each other to educate and cross-train in each others' areas of expertise. By working together to understand the problem of violence and disaster vulnerability, it is possible to collaboratively share resources and address violence. A result of this collaboration will be strengthened programs for both violence prevention and disaster preparedness. Care must be taken to influence every dimension of the life cycle of emergency management, including reaching out to affected groups through providing preparedness information, emergency-response-period resources, and recovery aid.

DISCUSSION QUESTIONS

1. How is violence experienced differentially across populations?
2. How does a disaster context influence the potential for violence? What do you think are the most important issues raised by violence for emergency practitioners?
3. How does violence intersect with other patterns of vulnerability?
4. What emergency management policies could help to build strong human communities with reduced levels of violence and fear?
5. What is the role of the emergency manager in reducing vulnerabilities?
6. Briefly explain how hate crime, elder abuse, or domestic violence affects people's ability to anticipate, cope with, resist, and recover from a disaster.
7. Identify two patterns of violence you think call for special attention by emergency managers. Using a disaster event you have experienced or studied, illustrate how and why these patterns were significant.
8. What is meant by *structural violence*? How do you think it puts people at increased risk in disasters?
9. Design a job for researchers by drafting a "request for proposal" in the area of disasters and violence. What do you want to learn more about and why? What methodologies would you encourage and why? How do you expect the findings would impact your work as an emergency manager?
10. In your view, how does violence relate to other forms of social vulnerability?

ACKNOWLEDGMENTS

The authors acknowledge and thank Elaine Enarson for her contributions to the chapter that appeared in the first edition of this book. This chapter represents the writing of the present authors and does not necessarily reflect those of previous authors or contributors to the FEMA Higher Education project on social vulnerability to disaster.

REFERENCES

Adam, B., J. Duyvandak, and A. Krouwell. 1999. *The global emergence of gay and lesbian politics*. Philadelphia: Temple University Press.

Aranji, S. 1992. *The* Exxon-Valdez *oil spill: Social, economic, and psychological impacts on Homer*. Anchorage: University of Alaska.

Barton, Allan. 1970. *Communities in disaster: A sociological analysis*. Garden City, NY: Anchor Books.

Biswas, A., A. Rahman, S. Mashreky, F. Rahman, and K. Dalal. 2010. Unintentional injuries and parental violence against children during flood: A study in rural Bangladesh. *Rural and Remote Health* 10:1199.

Bolin, R., and L. Stanford. 1998. Cultural diversity, unmet needs, and disaster recovery: The Northridge earthquake. *Disasters* 22 (1): 21–38.

Brown, Bethany, Pamela Jenkins, and Tricia Wachtendorf. 2010. Shelter in the storm: A battered women's shelter and catastrophe. *International Journal of Mass Emergencies and Disaster* 28 (2): 226–45.

Center for Research on Women with Disabilities. 2000. Facts about programs delivering battered women's services to women with disabilities. http://www.bcm.edu/crowd/abuse_women/progfact1.htm.

Choi, N., and J. Mayer. 2000. Elder abuse, neglect and exploitation risk factors and prevention strategies. *Journal of Gerontological Social Work* 33 (2): 5–25.

Cutter, S. 2006. The geography of social vulnerability: Race, class and catastrophe. http://understandingkatrina.ssrc.org/Cutter/.

D'Ooge, Charlotte. 2008. Queer Katrina: Gender and sexual orientation matters in the aftermath of the disaster. In *Katrina and the women of New Orleans*, ed. Beth Willinger, 22–24. Executive report and summary of findings. New Orleans: Newcomb College Center for Research on Women, Tulane University.

Durkheim, E. 1897/1997. *Suicide*. New York: The Free Press.

Eads, M. 2002. Marginalized groups in times of crisis: Identity, needs and response. Quick Response Report #152, Natural Hazards Research and Applications Information Center. http://www.colorado.edu/hazards/.

Enarson, E. 1998. Battered women in disaster: A case study of gendered vulnerability. EIIP Virtual Library Online Presentation. http://www.emforum.org/vlibrary/libchat.htm.

———. 1999. Violence against women in disaster. *Violence against Women* 5 (7): 742–68.

———. 2006. Violence against women in disasters. http://www.gdnonline.org.

Evans, Jeff. 2010. Mapping the vulnerability of older persons to disasters. *International Journal of Older People Nursing* 5 (1): 63–70.

Farber, D. n.d. Disaster law and inequality. http://risk.berkeley.edu/papers/Disaster_Law_and_Inequality_Farber.pdf.

Farmer, P. 2011. Haiti after the earthquake. New York, NY: Public Affairs Perseus Group.

FBI (Federal Bureau of Investigation). 2008. Hate crime—overview. http://www.fbi.gov/about-us/investigate/civilrights/hate_crimes/.

Felten-Biermann, C. 2006. Gender and natural disaster: Sexualized violence and the tsunami. *Development* 49 (3): 82–86.

Fernandez, Lauren, Deana Byard, Chien-Chih Lin, Samuel Benson, and Joseph A. Barbera. 2002. Frail elderly as disaster victims: Emergency management strategies. *Prehospital and Disaster Medicine* 17 (2): 67–74.

Fischer, H. W. 1998. *Response to disaster*. 2nd ed. Lanham, MD: University Press of America.

Fisher, S. 2009. Sri Lankan women's organizations responding to post-tsunami violence. In *Women, gender and disaster: Global issues and initiatives*, ed. E. Enarson and P. Chakrabarti, 233–49. New Delhi, India: Sage.

Fitzpatrick, K., and J. Boldizar. 1993. The prevalence and consequences of exposure to violence among African-American youth. *Journal of the American Academy of Child and Adolescent Psychiatry* 32 (2): 424–30.

Fothergill, A. 2004. *Heads above water: Gender, class, and family in the Grand Forks flood*. Albany: State University of New York Press.

Free, M. D. 2002. Race and presentencing decisions in the United States: A summary and critique of the research. *Criminal Justice Review* 27 (2): 203–32.

Friedsam, H. J. 1961. Reactions of older persons to disaster-caused losses. *The Gerontologist* 1:34–37.

———. 1962. Older persons in disaster. In *Man and society in disaster*, ed. G. W. Baker and D. W. Chapman, 151–82. New York: Basic Books.

Goss, K. n.d. EIIP virtual forum. http://www.emforum.org/pub/eiip/lc991110.txt.

Houghton, Rosalind. 2009. Everything becomes a struggle, absolute struggle: Post-flood increases in domestic violence in New Zealand. In *Women, gender and disaster*, ed. E. Enarson and P. Chakrabarti, 99–111. New Delhi, India: Sage.

Jenkins, Pamela, Shirley Laska, and Gretchen Williamson. 2008. Connecting future evacuation to current recovery: Saving the lives of older people in the next catastrophe. *Journal of American Society on Aging* 31 (4): 49–52.

Jenkins, P., and B. Phillips. 2008. Battered women, catastrophe, and the context of safety after Hurricane Katrina. *NWSA Journal* 20 (3): 49–68.

Kara, S. 2009. *Sex trafficking inside the business of modern slavery*. New York: Columbia University Press.

Kilijanek, T., and Tom Drabek. 1979. Assessing long-term aspects of a natural disaster: A focus on the elderly. *The Gerontologist* 19 (6): 555–66.

Klein, Alisa. 2008. *Sexual violence in disasters*. Hammond: Louisiana Foundation against Sexual Assault. https://www.ncjrs.gov/App/publications/Abstract.aspx?id=245782.

Krug, E. et al. 1998. Suicide after natural disasters. *New England Journal of Medicine* 338 (6): 373–378.

Liang, Jamison. 2010. Inside Indonesia: Homophobia rising. http://www.asylumlaw.org/docs/sexualminorities/Indonesia063009.pdf.

Litaker, D. 1996. Preventing recurring injuries from violence: The risk of assault among Cleveland youth after hospitalization. *American Journal of Public Health* 86 (11): 1633–36.

Lund, F., and T. Vaux. 2009. Work-focused responses to disasters: India's self-employed women's association. In *Women, gender and disaster*, ed. E. Enarson and P. Chakrabarti, 212–23. New Delhi, India: Sage.

Miller, A., and B. Arquilla. 2007. Disasters, women's health and conservative society: Working in Pakistan with the Turkish Red Crescent following the South Asian earthquake. *Prehospital and Disaster Medicine* 22 (4): 269–73.

Morris, A. 1984. *Origins of the Civil Rights Movement*. New York: Free Press.

Mulligan, M., and J. Shaw. 2011. Achievements and weaknesses in post-tsunami reconstruction in Sri Lanka. In *The Indian Ocean tsunami: The global response to a natural disaster*, ed. P. Karan and S. Subbiah, 237–60. Lexington: University of Kentucky Press.

National Council on Disability. 2009. *Effective emergency management*. Washington, DC: National Council on Disability.

National Research Council. 2003. *Elder mistreatment*. Washington, DC: National Academies Press.

Norris, F. H., M. J. Friedman, and P. J. Watson. 2002. 60,000 disaster victims speak: Part II, Summary and implications of the disaster mental health research. *Psychiatry* 65 (3): 240–60.

Norris, F. H., M. J. Friedman, P. J. Watson, C. M. Byrne, E. Diaz, and K. Kaniasty. 2002. 60,000 disaster victims speak: Part I, An empirical review of the empirical literature, 1981–2001. *Psychiatry* 65 (3): 207–39.

Palinkas, L., M. Downs, J. Petterson, and J. Russel. 1993. Social, cultural and psychological impacts of the *Exxon Valdez* oil spill. *Human Organization* 52:1–13.

Peek, L. 2003. Community isolation and group solidarity: Examining Muslim student experiences after September 11th. In *Beyond September 11th*, ed. J. Monday, 333–54. Boulder: Natural Hazards Center, University of Colorado.

———. 2008. Children and disasters: Understanding vulnerability, developing capacities, and promoting resilience. *Children, Youth and Environments* 18 (1): 1–29.

———. 2011. *Behind the backlash: Muslim Americans after 9/11*. Philadelphia: Temple University Press.

Peek, L., and A. Fothergill. 2006. Reconstructing childhood: An exploratory study of children in Hurricane Katrina. Quick response report #186. Boulder: Natural Hazards Center, University of Colorado.

———. 2008. Displacement, gender, and the challenges of parenting after Hurricane Katrina. *National Women's Studies Association Journal* 20 (3): 69–105.

Penix, M. 2006. Post-Katrina depression triples suicide rate in New Orleans. http://lcmedia.typepad.com/katrina/2006/07/postkatrina_dep.html/.

Petersilia, J. 2000. Invisible victims: Violence against persons with developmental disabilities. *Human Rights* 27 (1): 9–12.

Phillips, B. 1993. Cultural diversity in disasters: Sheltering, housing, and long-term recovery. *International Journal of Mass Emergencies and Disasters* 11:99–110.

Phillips, B., D. Neal, and L. Garza. 1994. Intergroup relations in disasters: Service delivery barriers after Hurricane Andrew. *Journal of Intergroup Relations* 21:18–27.

Phillips, B., P. Stukes, and P. Jenkins. 2012. Freedom Hill is not for sale and neither is the Lower Ninth Ward. *Journal of Black Studies* 43 (4): 405–26.

Poynting, Scott. 2004. Living with racism: The experiences and reporting by Arab and Muslim Australians of discrimination, abuse and violence since 11 September 2001. Report to the Human Rights and Equal Opportunity Commission, Sydney.

Quarantelli, E. L., and R. Dynes. 1976. Community conflict: Its absence and its presence in natural disasters. *Mass Emergencies* 1:139–52.

Quraishi, Asifa. 1997. Her Honor: An Islamic critique of the rape laws of Pakistan from a women-sensitive perspective. *Michigan Journal of International Law* 18:287–320.

Ray, N. 2006. *An epidemic of homelessness.* Washington, DC: National Gay and Lesbian Task Force Policy Institute and National Coalition for the Homeless.

Rodriguez, H., J. Trainor, and E. L. Quarantelli. 2006. Rising to the challenge of catastrophe: Emergent and prosocial behavior following Hurricane Katrina. *Annals of Political and Social Science* 604 (1): 82–101.

Rubin, C., and I. Renda-Tenali. 2002. Disaster terrorism timeline. http://www.disaster-timeline.com/terrorismtl.html.

Sacks, R., J. Flattery, and R. Hut. 2004. Crisis of confidence. http://www.childrenshealthfund.org/media/mediakit/Maristsurvey_824.pdf.

Sadler, A., B. Booth, B. Cook, and B. Doebbeling. 2003. Factors associated with women's risk of rape in the military environment. *American Journal of Industrial Medicine* 43:262–73.

Sayeed, Azra Talat. 2009. Victims of earthquake and patriarchy: The 2005 Pakistan earthquake. In *Women, Gender and Disaster: Global issues and initiatives*, ed. Elaine Enarson and P. G. Dhar Chakrabarti, 131–42. New Delhi, India: Sage Publications.

Schechter, S. 1982. *Women and male violence.* Boston: South End Press.

Sharkey, P. 2007. Survival and death in New Orleans. *Journal of Black Studies* 37 (4): 482–501.

Siegel, J., L. Bourque, and K. Shoaf. 1999. Victimization after a natural disaster: Social disorganization or community cohesion? *International Journal of Mass Emergencies and Disasters* 17 (3): 265–94.

Smith, T. W. 2003. *Public opinion on gun control.* Chicago: National Opinion Research Center, University of Chicago.

Soeters, Joseph. 2005. *Ethnic conflict and terrorism: The origins and dynamics of civil wars.* Florence, KY: Routledge Press.

South, S., and R. Felson. 1990. The racial patterning of rape. *Social Forces* 69 (1): 71–93.

Swanberg, J., T. Logan, and C. Macke. 2005. Intimate partner violence, employment and the workplace. *Trauma, Violence and Abuse* 6 (4): 286–312.

Tierney, K., M. Lindell, and R. Perry. 2001. *Facing the unexpected.* Washington, DC: Joseph Henry Press.

Tjaden, Patricia, and Nancy Thoennes. 2000. Full report of the prevalence, incidence, and consequences of violence against women. Findings from the National Violence against Women Survey, 1–71. Washington, DC: U.S. Department of Justice, Office of Justice Programs, National Institute of Justice.

U.S. Conference of Mayors and Sodexho, Inc. 2005. Hunger and homelessness survey: A status report on hunger and homelessness in America's cities. http://usmayors.org/pressreleases/documents/hungerhomelessnessreport_121208.pdf

U.S. Department of Justice. n.d. Crime and victims statistics. http://bjs.ojp.usdoj.gov/.

VNC (Violence Is Not Our Culture Campaign). 2011. Women's police stations for gender based violence. http://www.violenceisnotourculture.org/node/1711.

Watts, C., and C. Zimmerman. 2002. Violence against women: Global scope and magnitude. *The Lancet* 359:1232–37.

Wells, William, and William DeLeon-Granados. 2005. An analysis of unexamined issues in the intimate partner homicide decline: Race, quality of victim services, offender accountability, and system accountability. National Criminal Justice Reference Service, Rockville, MD. https://www.ncjrs.gov/pdffiles1/nij/grants/196666.pdf.

Wilgosh, L. 1993. Sexual abuse of children with disabilities: Intervention and treatment issues for parents. *Developmental Disabilities Bulletin* 21 (2): 1–12.

Wisner, B., P. Blaikie, T. Cannon, and I. Davis. 2005. *At risk.* 2nd ed. London: Routledge.

Wolbring, G. 2011. Disability, displacement and public health: A vision for Haiti. *Canadian Journal of Public Health* 102 (2): 157–59.

World Health Report. 2011. *World report on disabilities.* Washington, DC: The World Bank.

Young, M., M. Nosek, C. Howland, G. Chanpong, and D. Rintala. 1997. Prevalence of abuse of women with physical disabilities. *Archives of Physical Medicine and Rehabilitation* 78 (Suppl.): S34–38.

RESOURCES

- Violence Is Not Our Culture; links to information about women's police stations in Pakistan. http://www.violenceisnotourculture.org/node/1711.
- The Gender and Disaster Network provides extensive sets of resources for a wide set of issues on violence. Visit www.gdnonline.org to search for violence against women, human trafficking, guidelines, checklists, reports, studies, and more. See the searchable Gender Sourcebook for broader information on training, planning, and relief and recovery efforts. The Gender and Disaster Network remains the single best source of information on issues and resources for women experiencing violence in a disaster context.
- Community Oriented Policing Services (COPS) office promotes community policing through hiring grants, promoting innovative approaches to solving crime, and training and technical assistance to implement and sustain community policing. The COPS site (http://www.cops.usdoj.gov) lists publications and multimedia products on topics of interest to communities, such as community partnerships, crime prevention, problem solving, school safety, and many more.
- The United Nations offers information and data on human trafficking. This website includes a case-law database. http://www.unodc.org/unodc/en/human-trafficking/index.html.
- The National Council of Churches continues to monitor postearthquake violence against women in Haiti. http://www.nationalcouncilofchurches.us/news/82966/.
- The National Network for Safe Communities "is an alliance of cities dedicated to advancing proven strategies to combat violent crime, reduce incarceration and rebuild relations between law enforcement and distressed communities. It brings together police chiefs, prosecutors, community leaders, service providers, mayors, street workers, scholars and others concerned about the impact of crime and current crime polic[i]es on communities. The National Network is designed to support its members by creating a national community of practice, raising the visibility of its members' work, offering them technical support, recognizing and helping others learn from their innovations, supporting peer exchange and education, and conducting research and evaluations." http://www.nnscommunities.org/pages/the_network.php.

Section III

Building Capacity and Community Resilience

13 Religion, Faith, and Faith-Based Organizations

Brenda Phillips and Michael D. Thompson[*]

CONTENTS

13.1 CHAPTER PURPOSE

The purpose of this chapter is to examine and understand the dual notions of vulnerability and resilience that exist and operate within various religious contexts. We can understand vulnerability by focusing on issues of concern, such as when people of faith experience negative repercussions during a disaster. Yet, considerable reservoirs of resilience exist within both individuals and their faith traditions. To understand better this dual reality, this chapter examines cases where religious groups have experienced differential levels of impacts from disaster events. From existing research,

---

[*] Personal correspondence with one of the author's contacts was, at times, conducted under conditions of requested anonymity. This was particularly true with aid workers operating in countries where differences between faiths could have compromised personal safety.

religious vulnerabilities clearly intersect with biased assumptions about race, ethnicity, gender, and sexual orientation.

To expand the reader's understanding, we also explore religion from a social-science perspective that defines, enumerates, and illustrates the roles and functions of various world religions. Examining the broader context of faith traditions and religious organizations reveals deep reservoirs of resources for supporting those at risk in disasters. The religious community offers tremendous capacities for rebuilding and restoring the built environment as well as the hopes of people who have experienced harm. Religion, revealed first as a potentially divisive condition, then emerges as a means for rebuilding fences across assumed differences.

13.2   OBJECTIVES

As a result of this chapter, readers should be able to:

1. Provide examples of religious groups that have experienced harm because of disaster events
2. Distinguish between disasters of consensus and disasters of conflict
3. Identify major world religions, their global geographic dispersion, and approximate numbers of adherents
4. Define religion from a social-science perspective and outline the main roles and functions of a religious institution in society
5. Understand the ways in which religious organizations can promote resilience and coping during disaster impacts
6. Present examples of best practices for the integration of religious organizations into risk-reduction activities
7. List strategies that provide for continuity of operations for religious organizations

13.3   INTRODUCTION

A worldwide, diverse array of faith traditions suggests considerable complexity in understanding how religious-affiliated groups experience disaster impacts. Furthermore, within any major faith— Christianity, Islam, Buddhism, Judaism, Confucianism, Taoism, and Hinduism (Smith 2009)—one can find considerable variation from orthodox to progressive or from inner-centered to outwardly focused. Each religion has also grown out of particular sociohistorical and political contexts. The Protestant Reformation of the 1500s, for example, generated multiple new faith traditions with complex histories of persecution and subsequent migration. Even today, governments may marginalize faith traditions, such as the political exclusion experienced by Tibetan Buddhists. These contexts influence the manner in which people experience their faith, their needs in a disaster context, and even the resources available to them individually and collectively.

A first step in understanding vulnerability experienced by religious populations, then, should be to grasp both the breadth and depth of a given faith tradition, its sociocultural context, and historical background. Doing so will provide insights not only for potential conflicts and issues that might arise, but will also inform practitioners on best practices for serving those affected. Imagine, for example, operating a shelter or relief camp with a diverse array of faith-related needs for food, hygiene, modesty, interaction, and worship. Attending to such basic human needs provides both physical and psychological comfort, and can lay a foundation for a more effective recovery.

Other factors place religious populations at risk as well, such as space and time (Neal 2012; Wisner, Blaikie, and Cannon 2004). The 2004 Indian Ocean tsunami, which claimed in excess of 8,000 lives along the southeastern coast of India (and approximately 300,000 across 13+ nations), caused significant losses among specific religious populations in southeastern India. The highest totals fell among Christian pilgrims taking a traditional beach walk on the day after Christmas. Further north along the shore, small communities of Buddhists faced near-annihilation when waves surged through their villages; in coming days, traditional cremations became problematic when survivors could not easily retrieve the bodies of loved ones. Further north, an Indian Islamic village, staggered by losses that morning, worked arduously to bury their dead before nightfall per religious custom (Phillips et al. 2008).

Furthermore, crisis occasions that incorporate both disasters of consensus (earthquakes, tsunamis) and disasters of conflict (terrorism, hate crimes, arson; e.g., see Quarantelli and Dynes 1976; Stallings 1988) reveal that some populations bear disproportionate consequences. Relying on Sorokin (1942), Quarantelli and Dynes (1976) explain that disasters of conflict in particular can polarize communities. A recent example stems from the well-documented backlash against Muslims after September 11th (Peek 2011). Yet, despite such obvious impacts across a range of hazards, it is clear that religion remains an underexamined area of inquiry when assessing vulnerability. Initiating such an effort has become a necessary task in understanding and addressing both vulnerability and resilience associated with faith.

Conversely, religion also emerges as a critical source of support (Smith 1978; Ross and Smith 1974; Ross 1980). Faith comes with a wide array of beliefs and practices that people can use to promote resilience. After this chapter addresses vulnerabilities associated with religion and disaster, the following sections reveal an array of resources offered by religious organizations. When used in concert with recommended best practices, faith traditions can generate tremendous healing. Faith-based organizations provide long-standing social structures and often deep resources for disaster times, with associated social rewards for adherents (Nelson and Dynes 1971). Faith-based volunteerism, perhaps the most well-known resource used in disaster times, is most common in religious communities with strong social networks (Becker and Dhingra 2001; Homeland Security Institute 2006). Spillover effects also benefit the broader society, with faith-based volunteers more likely to have a strong sense of community identity and civic participation (Park and Smith 2000; Ruiter and De Graaf 2006; Wilson 2000).

13.4   WHAT IS RELIGION?

For social scientists, religion is a social institution that forms an important foundation in most societies. Social scientists define institutions as social structures that function to stabilize society and maintain continuity across generations (Durkheim 1912; Ahler and Tamney 1964). Manifest functions of a religious institution include promoting solidarity and providing explanations or comfort in times of bereavement or distress, such as during disasters. Latent, or unintended, functions often operate alongside more manifest functions. For example, participating in rituals such as regular worship, communion, seders, or meditation can generate considerably strong social ties and meaningful connections to one's faith. The notion of the "heart" and the "hand" further exemplifies the latent function. Most religious people feel a clear and strong emotional attachment to their faith, an inner sense of "feeling" about what is believed. Out of their feeling grows a corresponding commitment to "action," to doing something that helps validate what they sense to be true and important (Dyner 1964; Pilarin and Chang 1990). What is felt in the heart results in what is done with the hand. A classic example comes from faith traditions that direct people to be the hands and feet of Jesus, the faith basis for organizations like Mennonite Disaster Service (Wiebe 1979). In contrast, dysfunctionality also occurs in all social institutions, such as when a belief system constrains an individual to the point that they become vulnerable to a disaster—and examples abound in locations that enforce gender-based seclusion.

Social institutions are further maintained through associated statuses and roles created and affirmed by members. Statuses, or social positions that we occupy, might include pastors, priests, rabbis, or imams or lay positions such as elder, deacon, or choir director. Their role, defined as the behavior attached to a status, is to provide leadership and to carry out the functions of the relevant social institution. By leading members through rites and rituals such as baptisms, bar or bat mitzvahs, or issuing a five-time daily call to prayer, rituals build commitment to the faith and generate certainty across the life cycle. As we shall see in an upcoming section, pastoral care and rituals can be tremendously important to those affected by disaster. To summarize, societies need institutions such as religion. Institutions function to afford some degree of predictability and to maintain social order. In the chaos of a disaster, returning to a source of solace can be extremely comforting. Faithful people who act on their beliefs can help to restore social order through missions and service, acts often directed at those affected by issues of social justice. Our starting point in understanding the role of religion in social vulnerability is to describe the diverse array of faith traditions worldwide.

13.5   A GLOBAL CENSUS OF RELIGIONS

To enumerate or census those who may be members of a particular religion is particularly thorny. A starting point for understanding religious diversity stems from counting people who commit to particular faith traditions. Yet doing so is not easy, as "membership" may be quite complex and range from ardent devotion to inactivity. Further, many religious organizations maintain even inactive members on an official membership roll. People may also vary in their participation from daily to weekly to annually—or may practice a more spiritual relationship unconnected to a worship location. Considering the complexity of completing a census of world religions, most attempts generate ballpark estimates of Christianity, Judaism, Buddhism, Islam, Hinduism, Confucianism, and Taoism (Smith 2009). This section summarizes briefly what is known about world faith traditions numerically.

Christians represent about 2.18 billion adherents worldwide. Catholics represent 50.1% of all Christians, followed by Protestants who fall at 36.7% of the total Christian population. Numbers of Christians have quadrupled in the last 100 years with widespread geographic dispersion. No single center of religious population concentration exists for Christians (PEW Forum 2011b). Globally, Christianity is distributed as follows: 37% live in the Americas (804,070,000); Europe ranks second with 26% of the world's Christians (565,560,000); sub-Saharan Africa follows closely with 24% (516,470,000), with 13% located in the Asian Pacific area (285,120,000), and 4% found in the Middle East/North Africa (285,120,000) (PEW 2011b). Historically, the bulk of faith-based organizations (FBOs) active in disaster have been Christian, which suggests that such organizations benefit from operating in an interfaith manner.

The most rapidly increasing religious population globally is Muslims (PEW Forum 2011a). From a base of 1.6 billion estimated to be present in 2010, projections suggest a 35% increase over the next 20 years to approximately 2.2 billion. To grasp the significance of this trend, consider that experts predict the growth rate of Muslims to be 1.5% from 2010 to 2030 compared to 0.7% for non-Muslims. The increasing prevalence of Muslims in the world suggests a clear need for disaster relief officials to become familiar with the practices and faith-based needs of Muslims in geographic regions both heavily and sparsely populated by followers of Islam.

Hindus, often identified as the world's oldest religion, includes an estimated 900–950 million followers, or about 14% of the world's population. Concentrated in nations such as India, Nepal, and Sri Lanka, disasters such as tsunamis, earthquakes, and floods regularly impact Hindus. The complexity of Hinduism is difficult to describe within a single chapter. For our purposes, some key beliefs and practices (which arise later in the section on coping) relate to one's actions and one's fate, including the belief in karma—that one's actions have consequences both positive and/or negative. How one behaves in a disaster thus carries implications for one's life here and after death (Smith 2009). Hindus also believe in the notion of reincarnation or rebirth, a conviction that has implications for postdisaster counseling and can offer solace during grief.

Buddhists, believed to number about 376 million, also believe in reincarnation and that people can be reborn multiple times (Smith 2009). Followers of the Buddha work toward a higher state of enlightenment. Key guidances direct them to not kill, steal, or lie. One state that Buddhists work toward is mindfulness, where they try to increase awareness of one's mind, body and feelings. An important practice associated with moving toward mindfulness is meditation, either individually or in a collective setting. Specific truths and practices guide followers as they seek to understand suffering, a core that could prove useful in leading people through disaster impacts.

In 2010, the Jewish Data Bank estimated world population numbers to be about 13.4 million. Jews have historically been the most migratory religious population worldwide. One in four Jews migrated, compared to 5% of Christians and 4% of Muslims, with a total of 3.6 million Jewish migrants dispersed worldwide (PEW Forum 2012). Although Israel contains the most concentrated population of Jews, those who come from this tradition of faith dwell worldwide. A basic understanding of rituals, practices, and beliefs—necessary for working with any faith tradition—would suggest that disaster managers should pay attention to food preparation in public shelters, to ensure the presence of faith leaders knowledgeable of the history and social connections of Jews, and to recognize the potential resources that can be brought through Jewish relief organizations.

13.6 DYSFUNCTIONAL ASPECTS OF RELIGION

The anti-Muslim backlash mentioned previously suggests that religion alone may not account for vulnerability to disasters of consensus or conflict. Indeed, various reports suggest that population-specific affiliation may nuance how people associated with particular religions experience disasters, including those that historically foster consensus (e.g., natural hazard events such as earthquakes). In digging into accounts of such events, it is clear that demographic factors further imperil those already at risk, including race/ethnicity, gender, and sexual orientation.

13.6.1 RACE, ETHNICITY, AND RELIGION

The clearest example combining racial and religious vulnerabilities arises out of disasters of conflict. Poynting (2004) found that racially based attacks occurred against those of Middle Eastern appearance during the 1991 Gulf War in Australia and again after September 11th. Attacks included social incivility (verbal abuse), threats, violence, media vilification, and racism institutionalized in police, security agency, and immigration agencies.

Peek (2011) confirmed similar findings in New York City and across the United States ranging from hate stares, intimidation, and assault to murder (see Box 13.1). Further, hate crimes continued across the United States in later years, influenced no doubt by strong feelings when some terrorist groups associated their acts with Islam. Lingering effects continue, with one study finding that 47.4% of Muslims felt less than comfortable going to hurricane shelters after 9/11 (Mando et al. 2011). Comfort levels increase when providers address issues of personal safety (see Box 13.2), cleanliness (essential for Islamic worship practices), access to prayer space (prayer occurs five times daily), and privacy (a specific practice often linked to values of modesty and gender concerns; see Mando et al. 2011).

BOX 13.1   SEPTEMBER 11TH AND THE MUSLIM-AMERICAN EXPERIENCE IN THE UNITED STATES

The consequences of postdisaster exclusion for this rapidly growing religious minority group in the United States were extensive. Peek (2011) writes that the most common interpretations of 9/11 "speak to one reality, a reality of social solidarity, of bravery, of good deeds, and of kindness. But a second powerful reality also exists that the very notion of a single, unified 'altruistic community' serves to obscure."

As the national mood swung from shock to outrage after 9/11, Muslim Americans experienced blame, scapegoating, and were ultimately excluded from the broader collective processes of grieving. The men and women whom Peek (2011) interviewed, without exception, wished to be a part of the so-called nation united. Instead, they found themselves on the outside, looking in. One young Muslim woman who is quoted in the book captures the feeling:

"I wanted to join those people who were volunteering downtown. . . . To me, that was the American community coming together and trying to do what they can. But I didn't feel like I could, for my own safety. I wear a headscarf. I wanted to be part of that community, but I'm not really."

The aftermath of September 11th—the most shocking and deadly terror attacks in the nation's history—precipitated the largest-ever rise in anti-Islamic hate crime:

- Following 9/11, the onset of hate crime activity was swift and the increase in recorded hate crimes substantial, with a 1600% recorded jump in anti-Islamic hate crime.
- The events of 9/11 have had an enduring effect on anti-Islamic hate crime, with increased numbers of recorded hate crime representing a "new normal" for Muslim Americans.
- While all types of hate crime surged after 9/11, crimes against Muslim persons were more common than crimes against their property.
- Intimidation, vandalism, and simple assault were the most common forms of hate crime directed at Muslim Americans.
- Prior to 9/11, anti-Islamic hate crime was primarily concentrated in large metropolitan regions with diverse populations. But after 9/11, anti-Islamic hate crime became much more geographically dispersed, with hate crimes occurring in large cities as well as in more remote regions and areas that had previously been unaffected by such crime.
- The overall risk of experiencing hate crime increased for all Muslims after 9/11, although the relative risk was much higher for those individuals living in countries with smaller Muslim populations.

Sources: Peek (2011); Peek and Lueck (2012).

BOX 13.2   PROTECTING MUSLIM-AMERICAN STUDENTS AT OSU ON SEPTEMBER 11, 2001

RESPONDING ON CAMPUS TO 9/11

It has now been over a decade since 9/11 took place. Horror, fear, uncertainty, sadness, and terror were just some of the words used to describe our feelings throughout that long day. Mind-numbing events continued to unfold: A second jet hits the South Tower; a plane hits the Pentagon; passengers force United 175 to the ground in Pennsylvania to prevent it from hitting another national target; the South Tower crashes to the ground, followed by the North Tower; hope of survival in the Towers diminishes, and many first responders, both police and firefighters are lost. As with most tragedies, almost immediately, stories of courage and extraordinary kindness began to emerge. These stories renewed our spirits. Our administration used a concentric-circle model of crisis management to determine what needed to be done and in what order. Our goal was to work with those most affected (the center) and work outward. Following are some of the decisions made and strategies employed in the subsequent hours and days after 9/11:

- We immediately established a large television viewing area in the Student Union with free water, coffee, and food.

- We assigned counseling staff to the area to help comfort students and identify students in crisis.
- We verified that no faculty or staff members were on official business in the impacted areas.
- We made inquiries to determine if any of our students, faculty, or staff members potentially had family involved in the tragedy and sent staff to them to offer assistance and support.
- Senior administration and student affairs staff helped identify subpopulations potentially at risk for violence (international students from the Middle East) that might surface as a potential target.
- We asked that city police monitor the area mosque and notify us of any issues.
- We met with campus leaders (students and staff) to plan a vigil on campus with area firefighters and first responders. Representatives from many faiths and local firefighters were asked to speak briefly at the vigil.
- We dealt with rumor control, including parental calls about alleged riots and flag burning. There were no such incidents on campus or in our community.
- We kept classes in session to keep students engaged.
- Several administrators participated in an impromptu prayer service on the library lawn on the evening of 9/11.
- We asked campus ministers to ride the campus bus lines that served both the campus and community and were heavily utilized by international students. They did so for the rest of the week. A schedule was devised and monitored by the group.
- We passed out cards to international and ethnic minority students describing how to report any bias-motivated incidents on campus, including key people on and off campus to call for assistance. These cards were developed well in advance of this incident but were redistributed to staff and students to remind them of our protocols.
- Our response was effective overall. We faced new challenges as they unfolded and did our best to focus on high levels of individual and community support.

Lee Bird
Vice president for student affairs, Oklahoma State University

13.6.2 Gender and Religion

The intersection of religion and gender can also place women and their children at higher risk, especially with disasters of conflict. September 11th manifested as a gendered experience of postdisaster violence, as the "brunt of racial attacks was disproportionately borne by Arab-background women, notably Muslim women and girls wearing the hijab" in Australia (Poynting 2004, 4; Newell 1990; Hage 1991). Peek (2011) found similar responses to Muslim-American women and girls who, upon leaving their homes to travel to worship, school, or stores, endured hate stares on subways, were spat upon, or experienced having their traditional head covering violently removed.

Gender, race, and religion may have also negatively influenced birth outcomes for Arabic-named women. Muslim women who reported increases in harassments and violence following September 11th experienced moderately increased chances of low birth weight or preterm delivery; researchers did not find such increases among comparison groups (Lauderdale 2006). Further, women who gave their children distinctive ethnic names experienced an even higher risk of low birth weight or preterm delivery, a finding consistent with studies that stronger ethnic identification and racially connected stress increase infant vulnerability (Lauderdale 2006).

Issues with disasters, gender, and religion also arise within faith traditions. For example, in societies where *purdah* (exclusion) is practiced out of conservative religious beliefs, women and their children waited in vain in Bangladesh for males or relatives to evacuate them while floodwaters rose. Gendered interpretations of disaster have also blamed women for earthquakes, tsunamis, and other natural hazard events, assuming that women who sinned somehow brought disaster to affected communities (Sayeed 2009). Such blaming occurred after a 7.6-magnitude earthquake struck the North-West Frontier Province of Pakistan in 2005, and women subsequently internalized the blame as their responsibility (Sayeed 2009). Religious adherents have also assigned the mark of transgression in nongendered explanations too, including those who saw Hurricane Katrina's destructive inundation as retribution for alleged immorality among New Orleans residents in the United States.

13.6.3 SEXUAL ORIENTATION, RELIGION, AND DISASTER

Little is known about sexual orientation in the context of disaster, with scant studies addressing only surface issues experienced within the lesbian, gay, bisexual, transgendered, and intersex-identified (LGBTI) communities (D'Ooge 2008; Eads 2002). Given disagreements among and within religions over LGBTI presence and acceptance, it makes sense that sexual orientation might serve as an additional factor differentiating vulnerability, including the imputation of transgression. The strong presence of faith-based organizations active during response and recovery time periods would certainly bring those with disparate perspectives into potential philosophical conflict.

During disasters, members of LGBTI communities might feel a need to become (further) closeted or to remain distanced when searching for services in shelters with pastoral counseling or with long-term rebuilding efforts. Given that many nations do not recognize gay or lesbian marriages, such couples likely do not qualify for federal disaster aid (D'Ooge 2008). People with unmet needs not served by government programs usually rely on nongovernmental or faith-based organizations to overcome disasters.

In a disaster relief context, religions that pull away from nonheterosexual relationships might experience cognitive dissonance around serving LGBTI persons. Locations historically at risk for disasters, such as Indonesia, have reported increasing homophobia arising from conservative Islamic groups (Liang 2010). Given findings that attribute disaster causes to women, one would suspect that members of LGBTI communities would also find disaster causes ascribed to one's sexual orientation.

In summary, it is clear that people may use religious beliefs to differentiate between people, with significant consequences for those affected by disaster. Research also demonstrates that such practices occur out of misperceptions of religion (such as attributions linking terrorism to specific faiths), within religions, and across faith traditions. These dysfunctional aspects of religion, however, can be countered dramatically and positively by those same faiths, suggesting the complexity of understanding the role of religion in disaster.

13.7 RELIGION IN DISASTER

The remainder of this chapter looks at the functions and roles of religion in a disaster context, beginning with a basic understanding of major faith traditions. Scant research exists to document the role of religion in disaster, though it is clear that religion is a powerful resource at the individual and collective levels. Given the number of followers documented previously in Section 13.5, faith-based organizations (FBOs) active in a disaster context clearly link those affected by disaster to enormous reservoirs of time, talent, and resources.

13.7.1 PHILOSOPHICAL BASES FOR RELIGIOUS-BASED DISASTER RELIEF

When disasters occur—whether caused by human action or myriad other factors—religious responses are varied and intriguing. Some people simply focus on survival or personal care. Others seem to need explanations, that is: Why did God allow this to happen? At their best, though, religious individuals and organizations have often taken initiative or joined with others in assisting those who need help. A fourth-century Christian historian named Eusebius provided a glimpse into both the spirit and substance of such efforts during the ravages of the plague in a rural portion of the Roman Empire:

> A great population [was] almost entirely wiped out, nearly all being speedily destroyed by famine and pestilence.... Some shriveled like ghosts of the departed, staggered about... until they fell down, and as they lay in the middle of the streets they would beg for a small scrap of bread and, with their last gasp, cry out that they were hungry—anything more than this anguished cry was beyond them.... No less horrible was the plague that infected every house, especially those that had survived the famine.... Death waging war with the two weapons of plague and famine, quickly devoured whole families, so that two or three bodies might be removed for burial in a single funeral procession.
>
> In this awful adversity they alone [the Christians] gave practical proof of their sympathy and humanity. All day long some of them tended to the dying and to their burial, countless numbers with no one to care for them. Others gathered together from all parts of the city a multitude of those withered from famine and distributed bread to them all. (Maier 1999, 328–29)

More than half of the world's population claims allegiance to three related religions, the so-called Abrahamic families of faith: Judaism, Christianity, and Islam. Those belief systems, though different at significant points, clearly reflect a strong adherence to ethical monotheism—the insistence that there is only one divine being and that actions are the clearest reflection of proper faith in God. As such, the three faiths provide a convenient starting point for examining religious responses to disaster.

While it is not surprising that these three religious groups, among others, respond to crisis situations, it is interesting to note the level of both commitment and organization that often exists, while at the same time recognizing some of the challenges and tensions. A brief appraisal of a few organizational mission statements from among the three suggest that some of the more effective relief efforts clearly find their chief motivation in the social teachings of their faith.

13.7.2 CHRISTIANITY

Two mission statements from Christianity—the largest of the world's religions—serve as pertinent examples, the first being from the mission statement of World Vision, the largest and probably best known of the Protestant ministries:

> World Vision is an international partnership of Christians whose mission is to follow our Lord and Savior Jesus Christ in working with the poor and oppressed to promote human transformation, seek justice, and bear witness to the good news of the Kingdom of God.

A further expansion of the mission statement speaks specifically to disaster relief.

> We are responsive to life-threatening emergencies where our involvement is needed and appropriate. We are willing to take intelligent risks and act quickly. (www.wvi.org 2012)

As its name indicates, Catholic Charities represents the largest body of Christians caring for a wide diversity of human need. Part of that task involves an understanding of its role in disaster relief, and a willingness to work with other like-minded individuals and groups.

> In times of disaster, Catholic Charities is prepared and ready to help. We recognize the value of coordinating disaster response and recovery through the sharing of resources, people, technical assistance, and other support. (catholiccharities.org)

Many Christian organizations and denominations have similar statements, all reflecting a commitment to Christ and to his teachings regarding service to those in need.

13.7.3 JUDAISM

Both Judaism and Islam also sponsor organizations designed for quick response to urgent need. The Jewish Coalition for Disaster Relief (JCDR), for instance, seeks to bring together "the experience, expertise and resources of Jewish organizations that assist victims of natural or man-made disasters on a non-sectarian basis." In recent decades, the JCDR has played an active role in crises in Central America, Kosovo, Turkey, Ethiopia, El Salvador, and India.

One member of the JCDR is the Union for Reform Judaism (URF), representing the largest group of Jews in America. The URF claims an impressive history of generosity in the face of devastating loss, including recent involvement in Haiti, with the Indonesian tsunami, and in Sudan. Philosophically, the Reformed Jewish community looks to the Hebrew scriptures for guidance about proper responses to human troubles, and is committed to aiding both Jews and non-Jews during crisis times. Midrash Tehillim 52:24, providing commentary and interpretation on the biblical message, sums up the issue succinctly: "What is might? When you see people about to fall and rescue them." Further, the famed Rabbi Hillel taught, "If I am not for myself, who am I? But if I am only for myself, what am I?" (see www.urg.org).

Among those in the line of influence from Hillel was Saul of Tarsus, a young Jewish leader who later became a follower of Jesus, and is better known to posterity by his Roman name—Paul. A planter of Christian churches and a writer of influential letters, at the heart of Paul's message remained his insistence—a legacy from Judaism—that true faith should result in service to others, a point he insisted upon with his converts.

13.7.4 ISLAM

For Muslims—those who comprise the third and youngest member of the Abrahamic faiths—a certain amount of generosity is viewed not as a simple request, but rather as one of the five fundamental pillars of Islamic practice. *Zakat*, translated as "that which purifies," and often understood simply as "alms," is the giving of a fixed portion of one's wealth to charity, and especially to the poor and needy.

Historically speaking, Islam's social focus has often tended to be an inward one, serving primarily those of the Muslim community. That reality has often drawn criticism from others. However, the picture seems to be changing a bit; Islamic Relief Worldwide (IRW), founded in the United Kingdom in 1984, has been broadening their organizational vision. Given a four-star rating by Charity Navigator, America's leading independent charity evaluator, IRW works in partnership with other international aid organizations, church groups, and local relief agencies, with part of the mission being a commitment to "enable communities to mitigate the effect of disasters, prepare for their occurrence and respond by providing relief, protection and recovery" (www.islamic-relief.com).

13.7.5 RESPONDING APPROPRIATELY

A particularly positive and commonly heard claim suggests that religious relief agencies are among the first to bring aid and are willing to stay the longest. Their volunteers tend to be highly motivated, well trained, and compassionate, and as a result have developed a quite positive reputation in recent decades. As one leader stated it, "Faith-based groups work from their hearts, and those they serve can sense that" (personal correspondence with author 2012).

Mennonite Disaster Service (MDS) is an excellent example of the heart–hand connection. Officially representing Mennonite churches in the United States and Canada, the staff and volunteers of MDS find their historical roots among the Anabaptists, one of the groups that emerged as a part of the Protestant Reformation in the sixteenth century (Grosh 2009). Often referred to as "radical reformers," Anabaptists sought to establish what they saw as a simple, biblical model of Christian faith. Their unyielding emphasis on peacefulness and service continues to characterize present-day Mennonites. That mindset is immediately evident in the response of MDS to both domestic and international crises. Their contribution goes far beyond initial acts of emergency care. Their reputation is one of a high level of competence in vital tasks, matched by the building of ongoing and meaningful relationships with those they serve. Any number of other groups advertise the same strengths through literature and websites, but MDS clearly and consistently delivers on the promise. They take very seriously the admonition of Paul's words in Galatians 6:2, "Bear one another's burdens, and in this way you fulfill the law of Christ." (See Box 13.3.)

Humanitarian assistance, though, can sometimes be accompanied by difficulties and controversy, and the three faith families of Abraham provide obvious examples. It is no secret, for instance, that some of the evangelical Christian groups hope for success through proselytizing. The Baptist General Convention of Oklahoma states in a promotional piece that "disaster volunteers become the hands and feet of Jesus, doing personal ministry in order to earn the right to share the gospel." In other words, physical assistance serves as a means to recruit new members through spiritual conversion.

Such a sentiment is understandably problematic in areas where the dominant religious faith is different from that of the aid workers, and where attempts to evangelize are not welcomed and may even be illegal. Muslim countries provide a prime example, where political and religious leaders

---

BOX 13.3   "BEST PRACTICES" FOR FAITH-BASED COMMUNITIES

In the United States and Canada, Mennonite Disaster Service (MDS, www.mennonite.mds. net) enjoys a strong reputation as an organization that works effectively with damaged local communities. Extolled by numerous directors of the U.S. Federal Emergency Management Agency, research reveals key strategies that enable the faith-based organization to work effectively. MDS, a predominantly Anglo and conservative organization, has enjoyed considerable success in working across cultural differences. Their strategies include the following:

- A low-key approach into a community to seek out community and faith leaders to introduce themselves and their services (An initial question asked is "What would be helpful to you?")
- Working with long-term recovery committees as partners in a collaborative process, allowing local leaders to identify clients and determine needs
- Identifying available facilities for housing long-term and short-term volunteers in a location that does not consume local resources or housing options for those who are displaced
- Buying groceries, tools, and other supplies via local stores when possible in a disaster zone
- Training long-term volunteers to the process of case-management work and interacting with local communities and diverse cultures
- Sensitizing volunteers to local cultures before their traditional one week of repair and reconstruction service and processing those experiences at evening meals
- Inviting clients to an evening meal to share their story at the MDS camp
- Staying on for the long term, well after other organizations have left the area
- Adhering rigidly to local building codes and creating effective relationships with officials tasked with such procedures
- Providing oversight and support from a binational office to volunteers working on local sites

Source: Phillips and Gaeddert (2012).

allow and even honor other faiths, but where attempts at making converts remain forbidden. At a time of crisis or disaster when various relief groups desire to enter the country, suspicion and distrust might preclude the possibility of the much-needed help, or bring danger to either the workers or to those with whom a divergent religious message is communicated. Such concerns prevented some religious groups from making entry into affected countries after the 2004 tsunami and prompted rapid response by countergroups as a visible demonstration of political authority and religious presence (Jasparro and Taylor 2011).

In Pakistan, for instance, Islam is clearly the dominant faith in terms of numbers and influence, and while other religions such as Christianity and Hinduism are allowed, the freedom to seek converts has traditionally been denied. One aid worker observed that the government officially allowed Christian missionaries to work only among relatively segregated Christian communities (primarily low-caste Hindus who converted before the partitioning of India and Pakistan in 1947). Though such a barrier might seem harsh, the aid worker had also observed that a number of missionary-minded staff members worked especially hard—under the "neutral" banner of a nongovernmental organization (NGO)—at seeking opportunities to evangelize (personal correspondence 2012). Pakistani leaders would obviously view such efforts as attempts to undermine both civil and religious authorities.

That controversial topic was center stage in a 2006 seminar setting in Indonesia, involving both Christians and Muslims. The Rev. Mark S. Hanson, presiding bishop from the Evangelical Lutheran Church in America (ELCA), stressed that both Christianity and Islam had a shared responsibility "to preserve life beyond the members of their own faiths." In the aftermath of the 2004 earthquake and tsunami disaster, he reassured Muslim participants that, in keeping with international standards for humanitarian assistance, Lutheran relief effort would not proselytize or try to convert disaster victims in need of assistance. In his words, "We are called to walk with people who are suffering, not to take advantage of their suffering" (Hanson 2006).

Another area of concern, of course, relates to the proper routing of relief funds. Religious organizations contribute a substantial portion of the money given in disaster response, and as with other donors, are concerned that recipients will use funds for designated purposes. Accountability is often a difficult task, and there have been unhappy incidents of misdirected money, often into the pockets of corrupt local officials. In one particularly poor country, a Muslim responded to a local disaster by funneling his generous gifts through a foreign NGO. Though the organization represented a different faith than his own, the man knew the past track record and believed that the funds were more likely to make it to the desired destination (personal correspondence with author 2012).

Political considerations also present a related challenge, especially when leaders view outside "assistance" as a potential threat. A case in point would be the well-documented hesitancy on the part of the military regime in Myanmar to accept foreign aid in the aftermath of repeated disasters during the last decade. While ruling over a decidedly Buddhist country, the main concern of the leadership seemed to be political rather than religious, fearing that outside influence—regardless of task or motive—might threaten the military's ability to exercise control over the country. One NGO leader offered the comment that the government tried to cover up or ignore the sad occurrences, denied broad media coverage, and was quite careful about permitting donations earmarked for relief. Aid workers, whether religious or not, were viewed suspiciously, with the result that desperately needed assistance was limited and in some cases denied altogether.

Positive intentions, sometimes religiously motivated, can be a bit unrealistic and as a result be a potential hindrance in responding to a disaster. In the immediate aftermath of the Vietnam War, the U.S. government was desperately trying to resettle hundreds of thousands of Vietnamese immigrants who had fled their home country and could not safely return. Many in the United States opposed the resettlement program for a variety of reasons, and one good-hearted religious group unwittingly contributed to the opposition through their undying, if naïve, faith in the good will of the North Vietnamese conquerors. "What we hope," they stated, "is that the refugees here, when they see things calm down over there, will go home to rebuild their lives" (Thompson 2010, 66).

That type of assessment did not grow out of a particularly informed view of the situation, and contributed to the anti-resettlement viewpoint.

While a bit difficult to assess, the picture is also potentially complicated by the theological or philosophical beliefs of those who are suffering. A disaster is often viewed simply as bad karma, or as evidence of some type of judgment due to divine displeasure. Where those convictions exist, a willingness to seek or receive assistance can be limited, or in some cases even opposed. One NGO staff member related the frustration she felt when both citizens and government officials in a Buddhist region slowed the process of direct aid by stating: "This is God's will and we accept it" (personal correspondence with author 2012). In a more pointed and sobering example, an earthquake of October 8, 2005, devastated portions of northern Pakistan. Some of the more conservative religious leaders attributed the disaster to the presence of western NGO personnel. The foreigners were seen as "working against Islam" and thus responsible for the resultant judgment of God. (For similar examples after the 2004 tsunami, see Jasparro and Taylor [2011].)

Reale (2010) examines the religious assistance question from another angle. Acknowledging that religious groups and organizations from the more developed countries are well equipped and highly committed to relief efforts, Reale suggests that those factors do not necessarily make them more effective. Citing specific examples from the aftermath of the 1998 tsunami in Papua New Guinea, the 2004 Indian Ocean tsunami, and the previously mentioned earthquake in Pakistan, Reale makes a strong case that local religious bodies are often in a better position to respond:

> These bodies are embedded in the local community, speak the local language and understand the local culture. They know who in the community is most vulnerable and what people and infrastructure is available to assist. Religious institutions often have their own facilities, such as a prayer space that can be used for shelter or the distribution of food. Local bodies are already on the ground and can respond immediately. They are also often still involved in helping a community recover long after outside NGOs and UN bodies have gone home. (Reale 2010, 2)

Reale further suggests that local religious leaders and institutions are often better able to respond than governments, and especially where public officials are distrusted or suspected of corruption.

In summary, major faith traditions generate and send forth numerous mission teams, servant volunteers, and faith-based organizations (FBOs) that can and do make a difference to those suffering from the consequences of disasters. The deep pockets, both financially and with human resources, that religions can generate mean that these social institutions provide significant and meaningful resources in times of disaster. The flexibility and speed at which they can act stands in contrast to sometimes overly bureaucratic, slow, insensitive, and policy-laden governmental structures. What remains critical, though, is the approach that such individuals and organizations take when responding to those harmed by earthquakes, terror, or hate crimes. Effective approaches stem from efforts that understand the importance of local faith traditions and actually use those beliefs to aid those who suffer from disaster impacts (Chester 2005).

13.8 RELIGION AS RESILIENCE

The most commonly investigated dimension of religious organizations active in disaster addresses what happens to faith in a disaster. Most writers on this subject start with the understanding that people base their belief in a benevolent deity on trust, which can be undermined in a disaster event. People may ask: "Why did a loving God allow this to happen?" Or, some may think, "Where is my God?" Faith can be shaken (Koenig 2006; Kraybill and Peachey 2002). Attempts to reconcile the image of a god that allows suffering with one that speaks of love are termed *theodicy* (Chester 2005).

Indeed, a common phrase heard after disaster is that the event was an "act of God," a phrase with which some may take exception. After the 1997 tornado outbreak in Arkansas in the United States, for example, elected officials drafted legislation to fund disaster relief efforts. Deeply religious, the governor refused to sign the bill, which described the event as an "act of God." Insurance providers use similar phrasing, often to delimit events that they are willing to cover. In 1972, a different governor blamed a dam collapse in Buffalo Creek, West Virginia, as an act of God. Angry survivors, along with a successful legal team, redirected blame to the coal company deemed responsible (Erikson 1976).

The attribution of a disaster to a deity seems somewhat common, as is questioning that deity for why an event occurred. Aborigines in Australia blamed a demon for the great 1921 mine disaster in Queensland (Piggin 2009). Some faiths, such as Islam, may attribute a natural event to the will of Allah/God. Such attributions frame how people view disasters and may impact mitigation, preparedness and even rebuilding measures, including rebuilding in the same location (Ensor 2003). It may be that such attributions are more likely in natural disasters, since technological events can be blamed on a specific actor.

However, as Schmuck (2000, 92) argues, such an attribution may be somewhat healthy in that "the religious explanation prevents those affected from literally wasting time and energy asking why disasters happen to them and not to others." For those who lack means to reduce their vulnerability, such an explanation may make sense and certainly reduces cognitive dissonance. Accepting an event as God's will also seems to be associated with giving survivors a sense of control and a belief that a purpose existed amid the devastation (B. Smith et al. 2000). Religious leaders appear to play a significant role in generating such explanations. In the absence of religious leaders identifying a cause, attribution to a deity may not develop (Kroll-Smith and Couch 1987). Area churches in one post-Katrina study indicated that they portrayed God positively and asked congregants to "trust God's will," a message consistent with existing research (Cain and Barthelemy 2008, 40).

Yet as this entire volume has made clear, vulnerability to disaster lies not in the presence or absence of a deity but in the social structures and systems of stratification that marginalize some and privilege others. Religious institutions often taken on these issues of social justice as the core of their disaster work and seek out those historically oppressed: "And if you give even a cup of cold water to one of the least of my followers, you will surely be rewarded" (Matthew 10:42, New Living Translation). This section thus examines: (1) what happens to faith in a disaster context and (2) the role of religious institutions in disaster events, particularly the leadership prompted by the statuses and roles associated with various faith traditions.

13.8.1   Faith as a Base for Resilience

As noted, questions about causation trouble those affected by disaster. The extent of that questioning is not clear. A study conducted on tornado survivors in 1965 in the United States found that naturalistic explanations were more common than supernatural (i.e., deity-associated, see Dynes and Yutzy 1965). Several supernatural attributions may be possible, including the event being caused by an angry god (demanding appeasement), by despair (a rare, existentialist perspective), as God's punishment, or as God's will (Dynes and Yutzy 1965). Regardless of explanation, "disasters of natural or human origin, violent crimes and acts of terrorism, military combat, and brutal accidents" represent "overwhelming life experiences." Such trauma "injures the inner, spiritual world and wounds the soul of the one who believes" and "faith oftentimes is broken" (Wilson and Moran 1998, 171).

For those who question why God has forsaken them, psychologists have found that many survivors use their faith as a coping mechanism. Giving oneself over to an omniscient being seems to help, lifting the burden of what happened and what must be faced. "Giving it to God" also seems to quell survivor guilt, including among those who made life and death decisions regarding loved ones after the 2004 tsunami (Koenig 2006).

Both formal and informal (lay) religious leaders participate in helping people to overcome disaster trauma. Pastoral staff members involved in providing disaster spiritual care have used listening as a way to help survivors process grief, fear, and guilt (Chinnici 1985; Jordan 1976; Roberts and Ashley 2008; see Photo 13.1). To help survivors who are grieving or depressed, psychologists recommend that such counselors should become familiar with specific religious beliefs. Native

PHOTO 13.1 Mennonite Disaster Service (MDS), U.S. Gulf Coast oil spill, Plaquemines Parish, Louisiana, 2010: "Listening." (Photo courtesy of Mennonite Disaster Service. With permission.)

Americans use sweat lodges, for example, which can aid in dealing with painful emotions (De Silva [2006] as based on Wilson and Moran [1998]). Buddhism promotes *annicca*, or the idea that every-thing is impermanent, as well as the idea of *karma*, that individuals will benefit from their actions (De Silva 2006).

Other individual-level responses include prayer, which can aid people psychologically (Smith et al. 2000). Studies have also coined prayer as a "hazard adjustment" used by clergy to help those affected to persevere and try to understand that their God had a plan (Mitchell 2003). People displaced by Hurricane Katrina also used prayer as a coping strategy as well as talking and staying informed (Spence, Lachlan, and Burke 2007). Some differences have been found in the use of prayer, with women more likely than men to use this practice. Further, nonwhites displaced by Katrina were more likely to pray than whites, and those with incomes less than $20,000 (U.S. dollars, considered poverty income in the United States) are also more likely to use prayer (Spence, Lachlan, and Burke 2007). Older black survivors of Hurricane Katrina not only used prayer, but also turned to reading the Bible and helping others during their emotional recovery. Researchers conclude that spirituality represents a form of cultural capital that should not be overlooked among the highly vulnerable (Lawson and Thomas 2007).

Those seeking to provide spiritual or psychological care can draw upon such concepts and prac-tices to help survivors understand the event, situate it within a context relevant to their identity, facilitate recovery, and encourage *karma* through postdisaster volunteerism (De Silva 2006; Lam 2002; Nelson 1976; Peek et al. 2008). By relying on local faith, those seeking to help disaster survi-vors can foster resilience more effectively than by imposing values that are external and unfamiliar.

Furthermore, religious rituals promote coping at either the group or individual level (Durkheim 1912; De Silva 2006). Funerals for people who died or for people whose homes were destroyed (Reed 1977), compassionate meals for the bereaved, and anniversary events (Eyre 2006) bring people together in quasi-therapeutic contexts. Buddhists, for example, give alms after a death typically at seven days, three months, and one year (De Silva 2006). It is clear that religion can make a difference for many people in the context of disasters and that both clerical and lay leadership is critical in mak-ing sure that such aid is offered in a culturally, socially, religiously, and politically sensitive context.

13.8.2 THE ROLE OF RELIGIOUS LEADERSHIP IN DISASTERS

When the 2004 Indian Ocean tsunami occurred, Buddhist monks were among those who knew what to do. On December 26, early in the morning, tsunami waves rushed into Seenigama Village, Sri Lanka, destroyed hundreds of houses, toppled a train crowded with families on holiday, and killed over 100 in the village proper. Monks urged people to higher ground, where temples were located, an act that saved many lives and reduced injuries (Yamazaki and Yamazaki 2011). Although those who faced the 2004 tsunami may not remember prior inundations, Sri Lanka has indeed experienced such disasters. Interestingly, the Kelaniya Temple (4.5 miles east of Colombo) contains a tsunami mural painted on its walls (Yamazaki and Yamazaki 2011). In this case, local religions retained historic information, with faith leaders taking on the role of life safety as part of their religious status.

Further north, the community of Vailankanni, India suffered extensive losses among pilgrims visiting the local Catholic Church during Christmas holidays. The near 40-foot tsunami claimed thousands along the southeastern shore of the state of Tamil Nadu, including hundreds of families walking the beach that morning. Waters pushed into town through a concentrated business district, destroying the marketplace and pushing toward the basilica. Given its location further inland at an uphill location, the church survived the tsunami intact and with only minor water intrusion (see Photo 13.2). Survival of the church and its pastoral leadership proved extremely important. The church attended to survivors, donated land for mass graves (of thousands), conducted burial ceremonies, hosted visitors from the Vatican who came to mourn, organized memorial masses, and counseled the grieving (Phillips et al. 2008). See Box 13.4 and Photos 13.3 and 13.4.

Hurricane Katrina in the United States displaced well over 1 million people in 2005. Sent across all 50 states, residents found shelter sometimes where their gas ran out and where faith-based groups opened places of worship, staffed convention centers, and renovated empty buildings (Phillips et al. 2012; Phillips and Jenkins 2009; Szabo 2007). The significant numbers of those displaced meant that many shelters opened with limited resources and lack of knowledge in how to help survivors, a problem particularly acute within the faith-based sector (Pant et al. 2008; Phillips

PHOTO 13.2   Vailankanni Church, India. (Photo by Brenda Phillips. With permission.)

BOX 13.4   THE 2004 INDIAN OCEAN TSUNAMI, VAILANKANNI CHURCH, INDIA

Documents obtained from the Vailankanni Church in southeastern India describe a sunny and breezy day on the day after Christmas in 2004: "There was no sign of havoc from the sea. . . . The course of water came to the front side of the Shrine straight from the sea." Waters that killed people bathing in the sea, walking along the shore, or shopping in the business sector failed to damage the shrine, a site of dedicated visitation among thousands on their annual pilgrimage. Water surrounded the shrine on all four sites, but a slightly uphill and elevated location, coupled with an external barricade, prevented further intrusion; local residents viewed the salvation of the church as a miracle. Four thousand pilgrims who had remained in the basilica following an earlier mass survived, but an estimated 700 pilgrims who had left, including entire families, perished. Even heavier loss of life occurred in villages slightly north, with an overall death toll officially exceeding 8,000 but locally estimated to surpass 10,000 and perhaps as high as 18,000.

Church administration stepped immediately into relief work, including the provision of food, shelter, and clothing for survivors. Schools, halls, church lodges, and even private residences of the church administration opened to the newly homeless as other religious and social organizations from the Tamil Nadu province brought forth additional aid. Youth associated with the church assisted with retrieving bodies of the deceased, using church vehicles and volunteers. Families searched for their loved ones; the church buried unidentified victims in a special location on church land. In the days following, shrine administrators worked with local social services to distribute basic needs including rice, wheat, oil, milk, power, and vegetables along with tar-mats, stoves, school uniforms, school books, and temporary sheds. Survivors could secure meals three times daily at the Shrine Community Hall for two months following the tsunami.

As the recovery progressed, religious clergy prepared worship materials, including a prayer recited at daily mass through January 31, 2005. Church leaders perceived the slow recovery as "a gradual and steady disappearance in the thoughts of people at Vailankanni about all the hardships, loss of lives and properties, mental anguish, physical setbacks, fear, anxiety and uncertainty about the future, the sun of hope, certainty, courage and joy has dawned over this international tiny town of Vailankanni." Higher church officials visited in the months that followed, holding special masses and prayers, visiting areas damaged on the coast, and thanking those who provided volunteer service. Special blessings were held for the foundation stone at the Tsunami Memorial Cemetery (see Photos 13.3 and 13.4).

Source: "Tsunami Hit at Vailankanni." Document provided courtesy of the Vailankanni Shrine Administration, Vailankanni, India.

PHOTO 13.3   Vailankanni Tsunami Memorial Site, India. (Photo by Brenda Phillips. With permission.)

PHOTO 13.4 Vailankanni Tsunami Memorial Shrine, India. (Photo by Brenda Phillips. With permission.)

et al. 2012). Those who arrived often came in without clothing or possessions, separated from loved ones, and experiencing acute losses of entire neighborhoods. Churches, temples, synagogues, and mosques offered meals, laundry service, reunion assistance, and help with finding jobs, new housing, and reconstruction (Phillips and Jenkins 2009; Cain and Barthelemy 2008; Farris 2006). Following the relief effort, dozens of faith-based organizations sent hundreds of thousands of volunteers to the U.S. Gulf Coast for over five years. For the poor, for those living in areas historically segregated by race and ethnicity, for the elderly, and for many single parents, a return home would not have been possible without this considerable backbone of volunteer assistance. FBOs helped to repair and rebuild houses, provide pastoral counseling, fund various initiatives, offer medical and dental aid, conduct case management, build long-term recovery committees, and more (Phillips and Jenkins 2009). Equally important, many faithful volunteers learned about unique ways of life, crossed racial and ethnic barriers, and returned home as advocates for the Gulf Coast (Evans, Kromm, and Sturgis 2008).

13.9 IMPLICATIONS FOR ACTION

Noah may have been the first emergency manager (Dynes 1989). Facing a global flood, he gathered up animals and willing people, moved them into the ark, and emerged as the hero of the day. Noah saw it coming, and unfortunately too many faith-based institutions fail to do the same.

13.9.1 MITIGATION AND PREPAREDNESS

Hurricane Katrina destroyed or heavily damaged most worship locations across the city of New Orleans. Historically, African-American areas were especially hard hit, with up to 15 feet of water filling sanctuaries in the Lower Ninth Ward. The Catholic church took a major hit as well, with extensive damage to most locations, two-thirds of which lacked insurance (Devore 2007). Rebuilding churches, synagogues, and temples would take considerable time, especially with clergy and lay leadership dispersed across the U.S. worship centers, and responding religious organizations would have to adapt, just as they did after the unexpected events and unforeseen needs created by September 11th (Sutton 2003). Circuit riders would emerge, with pastors traveling by car or by air back to congregations returning slowly and unevenly to urban neighborhoods (Phillips and Jenkins 2009). Some created virtual communities, using email and Internet sites to gather the missing members, stay in touch, and rebuild important social networks. Rebuilding churches in areas historically populated by racial and ethnic minorities would truly make a difference, as it returned local leadership, replaced a positive resource within a stricken community, and served as a base for community rebuilding efforts.

Mitigation standards for worship locations have not been well developed, but some guidance materials do exist (Church World Services n.d.). Worship locations should make efforts to

- Adhere to local building codes or, where those are lacking (e.g., the impact felt in Haiti), build to the strongest level possible given the history of area hazards.
- Add safe rooms in areas subject to high winds or tornadoes.
- Conduct a structural mitigation assessment for the full range of hazards in a given area and implement measures deemed essential, such as hurricane clamps on roofs, elevated portions to deter flooding (such as in sanctuaries), and barricades for intrusion.
- Conduct a nonstructural mitigation assessment to determine if insurance covers potential losses both for downtime (when services cannot be offered) and displacement (when the worship location must move temporarily or permanently).
- Conduct mitigation planning with members of the faith community to determine priorities and funding for initiatives that must be undertaken (such as the costs of structural mitigation measures or an increase in insurance coverage).
- Educate clergy, administrative staff, and lay leadership in spiritual care using established ethical standards for cultural and social diversity.
- Develop a plan for housing clergy, administrative staff, and lay leadership should their homes be destroyed or damaged, as these leaders will be needed after disaster strikes.
- Design and train staff and followers on evacuation procedures when an emergency strikes.
- Establish a rainy-day fund for when disaster does strike.
- Train disaster teams within existing, knowledgeable faith-based organizations with long-term experience in delivering effective and appropriate aid. Work with local partners like emergency managers and disaster organizations to cross-train, develop mutual aid agreements, and establish standard operating procedures. Connect with established faith-based organizations within the denomination or faith tradition to learn from and collaborate with these experienced partners.
- Conduct outreach assessments among followers to determine their susceptibility to disaster impacts. Strengthen their home-based resistance so they will be available to assist during disaster impacts.
- Use disaster recovery periods as a time to integrate mitigation measures, as this is the time when followers may feel most compelled to donate or participate in such efforts.
- Create materials in advance to offer spiritual care through both individual outreach and group rituals, such as home blessings and community memorials.
- Routinely back up critical records needed to continue normal operations.
- Develop an internal disaster plan and train a wide array of staff and followers on the procedures. Ensure that someone can step in to a critical role should the assigned person not be present.
- Pre-position critical supplies for first aid, fire suppression, and resuscitation and train a wide range of staff and followers on the use of such equipment.

13.9.2 EDUCATION AND CROSS-TRAINING

Religious organizations often shoulder responsibility for the well-being of their parishioners. Faith-based organizations concerned with disaster impacts have also taken on the task of developing curricula for disasters from terrorism to pandemics. Their efforts represent important steps forward in not only assisting members of congregations, but in producing materials for potential use in emergency management classrooms. To date, though, few educational institutions have integrated research on religion and disasters into courses or programs despite the significant role played by FBOs during relief and recovery efforts (Rowel, Mercer, and Gichomo 2011). Hesston College in Kansas, an institution affiliated with Anabaptist/Mennonite traditions, is an exception (www. hesston.edu). Their curriculum focuses on graduating students capable of providing leadership for Mennonite Disaster Service, with alumni also moving into construction industries and social services. Such efforts represent important steps forward toward integrating religious studies into disaster degree programs. Educational institutions and practitioners that do integrate the faith-based community can generate important social capital. Such collaboration "that engages faith-based leaders in local, state, and federal planning activities is essential if communities are to become disaster resilient" (Rowel, Mercer, and Gichomo 2011, 32; see Box 13.5). A common example of this collaboration occurs in the United States, as the American Red Cross routinely establishes agreements with faith-based locations as shelters.

BOX 13.5   TOWARD INTERNATIONAL COLLABORATION AMONG FAITH COMMUNITIES

A creative international collaboration was formed in May 2012 among La Iglesia Luterana Agustina de Guatemala (ILAG), Evangelical Lutheran Church in America (ELCA) Southeastern Synod, and the Global Mission Unit of the ELCA in the creation of a two-year appointment position: global mission associate, ILAG Disaster Ministry development assistant. This position was formed to aid the ILAG with the development and implementation of their disaster preparedness and response plan. The responsibilities of this position include

- Accompanying the ILAG pastoral team in development and implementation of a disaster program in various communities and congregations
- Assisting with the training of leaders and health promoters in areas of disaster preparedness and response
- Providing pastoral care and support to people in areas of disaster impact
- Connecting ILAG with (and being a liaison to) governmental agencies and NGOs/resources active in disaster response
- Working with ILAG youth in disaster preparedness
- Being a liaison to the ELCA Southeastern Synod Disaster Task Force for development of resources

This new disaster preparedness and response program within ILAG is an important part of the partnership developed by the ILAG in collaboration with the ELCA Southeastern Synod:

- To train local leaders in disaster preparedness and resiliency. Communities will be better prepared for and able to respond to disasters.
- To improve the lives of ILAG's brothers and sisters in a safe, sustainable way. Health promoters received training in congregational disaster preparedness and resiliency in June 2012. The training included building resiliency and an overview of disaster ministry. Health promoters completed an informational sheet of what region and

community they were from throughout Guatemala and what disaster risks were present in their communities. Also, each health promoter was handed an inventory sheet to document their skills and abilities in their respective communities. These health promoters will assist congregations with preparedness planning and disaster response within their communities.

Source: Sandra L. Braasch, a diaconal minister In the Evangelical Lutheran Church in America (ELCA), currently serving two years with the ELCA Southeastern Synod companion church, La Iglesia Luterana Augustina de Guatemala (ILAG), as a global mission associate: ILAG disaster ministry development assistant.

Just as educational degree programs need to incorporate religion and disaster studies, the faith-based community also needs to conduct appropriate training. Indeed, "training for leaders and lay-persons is essential" (Rowel, Mercer, and Gichomo 2011, 32). Evidence from studies of those who provided shelters after Hurricane Katrina (noted previously) suggest that while people of faith want to help, they do require additional training. Such training must be "culturally appropriate" (Rowel, Mercer, and Gichomo 2011, 32) in order to meet the diverse needs encountered across a multifaith community. Failure to do so may result in wasted efforts, lost resources, and prolonged suffering. Not understanding the political and cultural contexts in which disasters occur and relief efforts take place can bog down or deter aid delivery (Schreurs 2011). The "competitive compassion" triggered by the 2004 Indian Ocean tsunami demonstrated this problem when a massive outpouring of aid either failed to reach affected areas or was culturally inappropriate for the climate, culture, or faith traditions (Kumaran and Torris 2011; Jasparro and Taylor 2011; Sugimoto, Sagayaraj, and Sugimoto 2011).

And, while sympathetic listening can produce therapeutic effects, more structured psychological first aid from clergy and laity requires "specialized knowledge . . . in the aftermath of widespread trauma and mass casualty events" (McCabe et al. 2007, 171). A one-size-fits-all approach will not work, as differences within a given population need to be considered. In Fiji, for example, differences in relief aid experienced with Hindu and Muslim Indian groups may have impeded psychological recovery (Gillard and Paton 1999). Training, certification, and credentialing of those who work in disaster contexts is considered standard for most disaster organizations that provide mental health care, such as the Red Cross. Training specific to spiritual care for survivors deserves the same type of attention and should be integrated into seminaries and similar educational facilities. Some efforts have developed toward this end, such as the Lutheran Disaster Response, which trains chaplains for disaster work and offers online devotional guides (http://www.ldr.org/resources/). Similarly, Church World Services has developed a set of ethical standards for disaster spiritual care and professionalism (http://www.churchpandemicresources.ca/files/SpiritualCareStandards.pdf):

- Providing appropriate care in line with our capabilities
- Providing correct information to those who seek our care
- Making only promises we can fulfill an affirmative and respectful interfaith response
- Refraining from the distribution of unsolicited religious literature
- Refraining from all forms of proselytizing and sermonizing
- Honest, fair, direct, and impartial behavior
- Offering spiritual care to all, regardless of gender, age, national origin, sexual orientation, religious tradition, or political belief
- Preserving the integrity and confidentiality of the information of and about others
- Loyal and respectful service to a community impacted by disaster
- Respecting the various theologies, traditions, and values of each individual and faith group
- Valuing and respecting the variety of disciplines and capabilities present in the community

- Facilitating diverse participation in planning community services
- Working within a coordinated response
- Respecting the variety of disciplines engaged in a holistic broad-based approach to spiritual care (physical, psychological, emotional, intellectual, and relational)
- Referring survivors to other services when it is beneficial, appropriate, and accepted
- Carrying current credentials or validation from a sponsoring body

It should be clear that no governmental or nongovernmental organization—or faith-based organization—should operate independently. Emergency managers have knowledge that those in the faith-based community need to know about disaster relief and recovery. Similarly, the faith-based community has knowledge and resources that can be leveraged to relieve suffering and prompt recovery efforts. Training across each other's often separate areas of responsibility is absolutely necessary to leverage the human capital contained in each and make a difference in communities stricken by disaster impacts.

13.10 SUMMARY

Religion is a major social institution that operates in nearly every society. Religion functions to stabilize society and includes both manifest and latent functions. Manifest functions are the obvious ones that include promoting solidarity and explanations for events, such as those experienced in disasters. Latent functions, the unintended functions, exist as well and include the generous acts of volunteerism and service offered by faith-based organizations. Dysfunctional consequences can occur as well, including when faith is used to vilify people on the basis of presumed group membership or through blaming a faith (or subgroup) for the consequences of an event. Faith traditions associated with the religious institution vary widely in their beliefs and practices, all of which can influence disaster experiences and relief operations. What is also clear is that faith groups bring tremendous resources to disaster contexts, a form of human capital that can be leveraged widely to alleviate suffering, provide spiritual counseling, and focus on the social-justice needs of those historically marginalized and rendered vulnerable in disaster contexts.

DISCUSSION QUESTIONS

1. How do social scientists define religion? What is the role of religion in society?
2. Distinguish between manifest and latent functions of religious institutions.
3. What are some of the dysfunctional aspects of religion? Besides those mentioned here, what kinds can you uncover through a basic Internet search? Distinguish between those that are connected to disasters of consensus and disasters of conflict.
4. Discuss the numbers of adherents worldwide connected to various faith traditions and consider the amount of human resources or social capital that they can offer in a disaster context.
5. What are some of the major beliefs of various faith traditions and their relevance to disaster relief conditions?
6. What should religious organizations avoid doing in a disaster context to do no further harm? What are some good practices, as supported by research (e.g., coping and counseling), in which religious institutions can participate?
7. How should religious institutions integrate disaster management practices into their own continuity of operations plans? Look at a religious setting in your own community and, if possible, visit that location. What kinds of risks might exist there to threaten the location's participation as a resource in a disaster? How could they reduce impacts?

REFERENCES

Ahler, J., and J. Tamney. 1964. Some functions of religious ritual in a catastrophe. *Sociological Analysis* 25:212–30.

Becker, P., and P. Dhingra. 2001. Religious involvement and volunteering: Implications for civil society. *Sociology of Religion* 62 (3): 315–35.

Cain, D., and J. Barthelemy. 2008. Tangible and spiritual relief after the storm: The religious community responds to Katrina. *Journal of Social Service Research* 34 (3): 29–42.

Chester, D. 2005. Theology and disaster studies: The need for dialogue. *Journal of Volcanology and Geothermal Research* 146:319–28.

Chinnici, R. 1985. Pastoral care following a natural disaster. *Pastoral Psychology* 33 (4): 245–54.

Church World Services. n.d. *The religious community as disaster educator: Planning, prevention, and mitigation.* New York: Church World Services, Emergency Response Program.

De Silva, P. 2006. The tsunami and its aftermath in Sri Lanka: Explorations of a Buddhist perspective. *International Review of Psychiatry* 18 (3): 281–97.

Devore, D. 2007. Water in sacred places: Rebuilding New Orleans Black churches as sites of community empowerment. *Journal of American History* 94 (3): 762–69.

D'Ooge, C. 2008. Queer Katrina: Gender and sexual orientation matters in the aftermath of the disaster. In *Katrina and the women of New Orleans*, ed. Beth Willinger, 22–24. Executive Report and Summary of Findings. Newcomb College Center for Research on Women, Tulane University.

Durkheim, E. 1912. *The elementary forms of religious life.* New York: Oxford University Press.

Dynes, R. 1989. The symbolic uses of disaster and the lessons of disaster for individual and social potential. Preliminary Paper #142A. Newark: University of Delaware, Disaster Research Center.

———. 1994. Situational altruism: Toward an explanation of pathologies in disaster assistance. Preliminary paper #201. Newark: University of Delaware, Disaster Research Center.

Dynes, R., and D. Yutzy. 1965. Religious interpretations of disaster: Topic 10. *Journal of the Liberal Arts*, (fall): 34–48.

Eads, Marci. 2002. Marginalized groups in times of crisis: Identity, needs, and response. Quick Response Report #152. Boulder: University of Colorado, Natural Hazards Research and Applications Information Center. http://www.colorado.edu/hazards/qr/qr152/qr152.html.

Ensor, M. 2003. Disaster evangelism: Religion as a catalyst for change in post-Mitch Honduras. *International Journal of Mass Emergencies and Disasters* 21 (2): 31–49.

Erikson, K. 1976. *Everything in its path.* New York: Simon and Schuster.

Evans, D., C. Kromm, and S. Sturgis. 2008. *Faith in the Gulf: Lessons from the religious response to Hurricane Katrina.* Durham, NC: Institute for Southern Studies.

Eyre, A. 2006. Remembering: Community commemoration after disaster. In *Handbook of disaster research*, 441–456. New York: Springer-Verlag.

Farris, A. 2006. Katrina anniversary finds faith-based groups still on the front lines, resilient but fatigued. http://www.rockinst.org/about_us/faith-based/.

Gillard, M., and D. Paton. 1999. Disaster stress following a hurricane: The role of religious differences in the Fijian Islands. *Australasian Journal of Disaster*, no. 2: 2–9.

Grosh, J. 2009. How does MDS decide where to work? *Behind the Hammer*, (March): 4–5.

Hage, G. (1991). Racism, multiculturalism and the Gulf War. *Arena* 96:8–13.

Hanson, M. 2006. Resources for communicators (Internet blog). http://www.rfcnews.com/?p=166.

Homeland Security Institute. 2006. *Heralding unheard voices: The role of faith-based organizations and non-governmental organizations during disasters.* Arlington, VA: Analytic Services Incorporated.

Jasparro, C., and J. Taylor. 2011. Transnational geopolitical competition and natural disasters: Lessons from the Indian Ocean tsunami. In *The Indian Ocean Tsunami: The global response to a natural disaster*, ed. P. Karan and S. Subbiah, 283–300. Lexington: University of Kentucky Press.

Jewish Data Bank. 2010. World Jewish Population, 2010. http://www.jewishdatabank.org/Reports/World_Jewish_Population_2010.pdf.

Jordan, C. 1976. Pastoral care and chronic disaster victims: The Buffalo Creek Experience. *Journal of Pastoral Care* 30 (3): 159–70.

Koenig, H. 2006. In *The wake of disaster: Religious responses to terrorism and catastrophe.* Philadelphia: Templeton Foundation Press.

Kraybill, D., and L. Peachey, eds. 2002. *Where was God on Sept. 11? Seeds of faith and hope.* Scottdale, PA: Herald Press.

Kroll-Smith, J., and S. Couch. 1987. A chronic technological disaster and the irrelevance of religious meaning: The case of Central Pennsylvania. *Journal for the Scientific Study of Religion* 26 (1): 25–37.

Kumaran, M., and T. Torris. 2011. The role of NGOs in tsunami relief and reconstruction in Cuddalore District, South India. In *The Indian Ocean Tsunami*, ed. P. Karan and S. Subbiah, 183–212. Lexington: University of Kentucky Press.

Lam, P. 2002. As the flocks gather: How religion affects voluntary association participation. *Journal for the Scientific Study of Religion* 41 (3): 405–22.

Lauderdale, D. 2006. Birth outcomes for Arabic-named women in California before and after September 11. *Demography* 43 (1): 185–201.

Lawson, E., and C. Thomas. 2007. Wading in the waters: Spirituality and older Black Katrina survivors. *Journal of Health Care for the Poor and Underserved* 18:341–54.

Liang, J. 2010. Inside Indonesia: Homophobia rising. http://www.asylumlaw.org/docs/sexualminorities/Indonesia063009.pdf.

Mando, A., L. Peek, L. Brown, and B. King-Kallimanis. 2011. Hurricane preparedness and shelter preferences of Muslims living in Florida. *Journal of Emergency Management* 9 (1): 51–64.

McCabe, O., A. Mosley, H. Gwon, G. Everly, J. Lating, J. Links, and M. Kaminsky. 2007. The tower of ivory meets the house of worship: Psychological first aid training for the faith community. *International Journal of Mental Health* 9 (3): 171–90.

Meier, P. L. 1999. *Eusebius: The Church History*. Grand Rapids, MI: Kraegel Publications.

Mitchell, J. 2003. Prayer in disaster: Case study of Christian clergy. *Natural Hazards Review* 4 (1): 20–26.

Neal, D. M. in press. Disaster and social time. *International Journal of Mass Emergencies and Disaster* 30 (3).

Nelson, L., and R. Dynes. 1971. *Religious reality construction and helping action*. Working Paper #42. Columbus, OH: Disaster Research Center.

———. 1976. The impact of devotionalism and attendance on ordinary and emergency helping behavior. *Journal for the Scientific Study of Religion* 15:47–59.

Newell, P. 1990. *Migrant experience of racist violence: A study of households in Campbelltown and Marrickville*. Sydney, Australia: Human Rights and Equal Opportunities Commission.

Pant, A., T. Kirsch, T. Subbarao, Y. Hsieh, and A. Vu. 2008. Faith-based organizations and sustainable sheltering operations in Mississippi after Hurricane Katrina: Implications for informal network utilization. *Prehospital and Disaster Medicine* 23 (1): 48–54.

Park, J., and C. Smith. 2000. To whom much has been given: Religious capital and community voluntarism among churchgoing Protestants. *Journal for the Scientific Study of Religion* 29 (3): 272–86.

Peek, L. 2011. *Behind the backlash: Muslim Americans after 9/11*. Philadelphia: Temple University Press.

Peek, L., and M. Lueck. 2012. When hate is a crime: Temporal and geographic patterns of anti-Islamic hate crime after 9/11. In *Crime and criminal justice in disaster*, 2nd ed., ed. D. W. Harper and K. Frailing. Durham, NC: Carolina Academic Press.

Peek, L., J. Sutton, and J. Gump. 2008. Caring for children in the aftermath of disaster: The Church of the Brethren Children's Disaster Services Program. *Children, Youth and Environments* 18 (1): 408–21.

PEW Forum. 2011a. The future of the global Muslim population: Projections from 2010–2030. http://www.pewforum.org/Global-Muslim-Population.aspx.

———. 2011b. Global Christianity. http://www.pewforum.org/Christian/Global-Christianity-worlds-christian-population.aspx.

———. 2012. Faith on the move. http://www.pewforum.org/Geography/Religious-Migration-overview-of-migrants-origins-and-destinations.aspx.

Phillips, Brenda, and Russ Gaeddert. 2012. Entering and serving communities after disaster: Implications for service delivery. *Journal of Intergroup Relations* 39 (forthcoming).

Phillips, B., and P. Jenkins. 2009. The roles of faith-based organizations after Hurricane Katrina. In *Meeting the needs of children, families, and communities post-disaster: Lessons learned from Hurricane Katrina and its aftermath* ed. K. Kilmer, V. Gil-Rivas, R. Tedeschi, and L. Calhoun, 215–238. Washington, DC: American Psychological Association.

Phillips, B., D. Neal, T. Wikle, A. Subanthore, and S. Hyrapiet. 2008. Mass fatality management after the Indian Ocean tsunami. *Disaster Prevention and Management* 17 (5): 681–97.

Phillips, B., T. Wikle, A. Hakim, and L. Pike. 2012. Establishing and operating shelters after Hurricane Katrina. *International Journal of Emergency Management* 8 (2): 153–67.

Piggin, S. 2009. Religion and disaster: Popular religious attitudes to disaster and death with specific reference to the Mt. Kembler and Applin coal mine disasters. *Journal of Australian Studies* 5 (8): 54–63.

Piliavin, J., and H. Charng. 1990. Altruism: A review of recent theory and research. *Annual Review of Sociology* 16:27–65.

Poynting, S. 2004. *Living with racism: The experiences and reporting by Arab and Muslim Australians of discrimination, abuse and violence since 11 September 2001.* Sydney, Australia: Report to the Human Rights and Equal Opportunity Commission.

Quarantelli, E. L., and R. Dynes. 1976. Community conflict: Its absence and its presence in natural disasters. *Mass Emergencies* 1:139–152.

Reale, A. 2010. Acts of God: The role of religion in disaster risk reduction. *Humanitarian Exchange Magazine.* http://www.odihpn.org/humanitarian-exchange-magazine/issue-48/acts-of-gods-the-role-of-religion-in-disaster-risk-reduction.

Reed, J. 1977. The pastoral care of victims of major disaster. *Journal of Pastoral Care* 31 (2): 97–108.

Roberts, S., and W. Ashley. 2008. *Disaster spiritual care: Practical clergy responses to community, regional and national tragedy.* Woodstock, VT: Sky Lights Path Publishing.

Ross, A. 1980. The emergence of organizational sets in three ecumenical disaster recovery organizations. *Human Relations* 33:23–29.

Ross, A., and S. Smith. 1974. The emergence of an organizational and an organization set: A study of an interfaith disaster recovery group. Preliminary Paper #16. Newark: University of Delaware, Disaster Research Center.

Rowel, R., L. Mercer, and G. Gichomo. 2011. Role of pastors in disasters curriculum development project: Preparing faith-based leaders to be agents of safety. *Journal of Homeland Security and Emergency Management* 8 (1): 1–32.

Ruiter, S., and N. D. De Graaf. 2006. National context, religiosity, and volunteering: Results from 53 Countries. *American Sociological Review* 71 (2): 191–210.

Sayeed, A. 2009. Victims of earthquake and patriarchy: The 2005 Pakistan earthquake. In *Women, gender and disaster: Global issues and initiatives*, ed. Elaine Enarson and P. G. Dhar Chakrabarti, 131–42. New Delhi, India: Sage Publications.

Schmuck, H. 2000. An act of Allah: Religious explanations for floods in Bangladesh as survival strategy. *International Journal of Mass Emergencies and Disasters* 18 (1): 85–95.

Schreurs, M. 2011. Improving governance structures for natural disaster response: Lessons from the Indian Ocean tsunami. In *The Indian Ocean tsunami*, ed. P. Karan and S. Subbiah, 261–82. Lexington: University of Kentucky Press.

Smith, B., K. I. Pargament, C. Brant, and J. Oliver. 2000. Noah revisited: Religious coping by church members and the impact of the 1993 Midwest flood. *Journal of Community Psychology* 28 (2): 169–86.

Smith, Huston. 2009. *The world's religions.* New York: Harper.

Smith, M. H. 1978. American religious organizations in disaster: A study of congregational response to disaster. *Mass Emergencies* 3:133–42.

Sorokin, P. A. 1942. *Man and society in calamity.* New York: Dutton.

Spence, P., K. Lachlan, and J. Burke. 2007. Adjusting to uncertainty: Coping strategies among the displaced after Hurricane Katrina. *Sociological Spectrum* 27:653–78.

Stallings, R. 1988. Conflict in natural disasters: A codification of consensus and conflict theories. *Social Science Quarterly* 69:569–86.

Sugimoto, S., A. Sagayaraj, and Y. Sugimoto. 2011. Sociocultural frame, religious networks, miracles: Experiences from tsunami disaster management in South India. In *The Indian Ocean tsunami*, ed. P. Karan and S. Subbiah, 213–35. Lexington: University of Kentucky Press.

Sutton, J. 2003. A complex organizational adaptation to the World Trade Center disaster: An analysis of faith-based organizations. In *Beyond September 11th: An account of post-disaster research*, ed. J. Monday, 405–28. Boulder: University of Colorado, Natural Hazards Applications and Information Research Center.

Szabo, L. 2007. Faith rebuilds house and soul. *USA Today*, July 18.

Wiebe, K. 1979. *Day of disaster.* Scottdale, PA: Herald Press.

Wilson, J. 2000. Volunteering. *Annual Review of Sociology* 26:215–40.

Wilson, J., and T. Moran. 1998. Psychological trauma: Posttraumatic stress disorder and spirituality. *Journal of Psychology and Theology* 26 (2): 168–78.

Wisner, B., P. Blaikie, and T. Cannon. 2004. *At risk.* London: Routledge.

Yamazaki, K., and T. Yamazaki. 2011. Tsunami disasters in Seenigama Village, Sri Lanka, and Taro Town, Japan. In *The Indian Ocean tsunami: The global response to a natural disaster*, ed. P. Karan and S. Subbiah, 135–59. Lexington: University of Kentucky Press.

RESOURCES

- Church World Services offers webinar training for those involved in long-term disaster recovery. Previous webinars and available related content have focused on long-term recovery processes, organizational roles, case management, and disabilities. The present link is http://www.cwserp.org/.
- Church World Services also provides guidance on mitigation efforts that can be found at http://cwserp.fatcow.com/sitebuildercontent/sitebuilderfiles/6the_disaster_educator.pdf.
- Standards of spiritual care can be found at several locations. Church World Services offers this, http://march2recovery.org/wp-content/uploads/2012/05/Points-of-Consensus-Spiritual-Care.pdf, and Lutheran Disaster Response provides these guidelines, http://www.ldr.org/resources/.
- In the United States, the National Voluntary Organizations Active in Disaster (NVOAD) offers information on their website. Participating members include dozens of faith-based organizations. Information can be found at http://www.nvoad.org/.

14 Animals

Tamara Gull

CONTENTS

14.1 CHAPTER PURPOSE

This chapter introduces the reader to the needs of animals in disasters, their effects on human disaster survivors, and the existing plans and programs that can assist disaster planners in accommodating the needs of animals.

14.2 CHAPTER OBJECTIVES

As a result of reading this chapter, readers should be able to:

1. Recognize the emotional connection that exists between pet/livestock owners and their animals and how it may influence owner decisions and actions during disasters
2. Understand the dependence of animals on their human owners and how disasters can affect the ability of owners to provide for their animals as well as the behavior of the animals themselves
3. Identify the public health and humane concerns presented by animals and/or animal carcasses during disasters
4. Address specific needs of service animals and their humans during disasters
5. Outline challenges associated with disaster planning for animals (including livestock)
6. Know what steps individuals and communities can take to allow better care for animals involved in disasters
7. List and describe the various national-level organizations and policies that pertain to animal disaster management
8. Know where to find information on disaster planning for animals

14.3 INTRODUCTION

Regardless of where a disaster occurs, animals are likely to be involved. These animals can range from the pampered apartment pup in New York City to a farm hog in Iowa, and from a show horse in Oregon to zoo inhabitants in Texas. No matter the demographics of a population, humans and animals frequently share each others' lives. Disaster planning and response must take into account the numbers and types of animals likely to be encountered in the course of a disaster, as insufficient or inappropriate preparation for animals may directly impact the effectiveness of the plans in place for human victims.

Why is animal planning a concern? First, a large proportion of the human population owns animals. Best estimates state that approximately 60% of households have at least one small-animal pet, but many households have multiple pets. Second, owners have emotional attachments to their animals that can alter their responses during a disaster. Third, animals in disaster areas may behave differently than normal and even become a threat, such as the formation of packs of feral and aggressive dogs once their human caretakers are no longer present. Fourth, there are public health concerns regarding animals in disaster areas, as animals can carry disease and their carcasses can breed flies and other disease vectors. Fifth, there are humane concerns. No animals should be left to starve or die of dehydration because their human caretakers were not available. Finally, there are some animals that cannot or should not be separated from their owners, such as service animals (e.g., seeing-eye dogs, seizure-watch animals, and assistance primates), as that could adversely affect their owners' health and safety.

14.3.1 Pets and Human Relationships

Why do animal owners have emotional attachments to their animals? Only a few decades ago, dogs were usually kept chained outside to bark at strangers, and cats were tolerated only as long as they hunted and caught vermin. The position of the family pet has changed dramatically since then. In the past few decades, pets have become widely accepted as members of the family. Some owners even consider pets to be substitute children. Some persons cohabiting with animals consider themselves to be caretakers of the animals rather than owners, an acknowledgment of the changing perception of the pet as companion rather than property. In these situations, pets are frequently allowed inside the home, onto the couch, and into the owner's bed. Pet contact has been documented to reduce stress and have a calming effect on people, while loss or separation from pets can adversely affect the health of pet owners (Sofair 2002; Barker 1999). Plaintiffs in recent legal cases have won compensatory damages associated with injury to pets, where even two decades ago pets were considered to have no value other than their purchase price (*Leith v. Frost* 2008).

In the event of a disaster, many pet owners will expect to take their pets along and will strongly resist any suggestions to leave them behind. Retrieval of a pet is the most common reason for people to return to an evacuated area. As many as 20% of pet owners will refuse evacuation if their pets are not included (Heath, Voeks, and Glickman 2001). This is especially true of elderly pet owners, but children may also be extremely upset at leaving a family pet behind. Animal safety is of high importance to animal owners, second only to family safety and often superseding personal safety. Much of this is because pet owners recognize how dependent their pet is for the basic needs: food, water, and shelter. Most household pets would not be able to survive even if set free because of a lack of hunting skills, lack of acclimation to adverse weather, and predation. Community outrage occurs when media stories are broadcast of owners forcibly separated from their pets during evacuations, resulting in the death or loss of the pet.

There are many examples of the adverse social effects of separating owners from their animals during disasters as well as examples of potentially preventable animal deaths as a result of disasters. For instance, despite the efforts of multiple animal rescue groups, many pets died in the aftermath of Hurricanes Katrina and Rita in 2005 when owners were not able to return to retrieve pets left locked in houses with limited food and water (Anderson and Anderson 2006; Louisiana SPCA 2006). Other pets died or disappeared when turned loose by their owners or well-meaning others. Traumatized Katrina survivors are still looking for their pets seven years later, pets they thought they would only be separated from for a day or two. These owners may carry a significant guilt burden for their perceived failure to save their pet as well as feelings of loss or bereavement, even if the pet is not known to have died. People may also experience anger if forcibly separated from a pet, and this anger may be directed at disaster assistance workers, other evacuees, and even themselves. As might be expected, angry people are often uncooperative and may adversely affect the emotional state of others around them and increase the overall stress level in a shelter.

14.3.2 Consequences of Animal–Human Separation

Animal behavior is another consideration during disasters. Animals in disaster areas may behave differently than they would in their normal home situations, and this can pose a threat to rescuers as well as those returning to clean up and rebuild following a disaster. Dogs are naturally pack animals, and in the absence of their normal pack, represented by their human family, they may congregate into packs with other abandoned or freed dogs. Depending on the behaviors of individual dogs, these packs may be mere nuisances scavenging for food or they may become overt threats aggressive to humans. This is not dependent on the specific breeds of dogs present in a pack, but is instead dependent on the natural aggressiveness of the individual dogs in the pack.

Humane concerns may also contribute to the handling of animals during disasters. Over 1,000 dogs and cats were euthanized following Hurricane Andrew in Florida in 1992 (Irvine 2004). These animals were euthanized simply because there was no place to house them, no way to evacuate them, and they could not be left to drown or starve. No one wants to see livestock trapped in a pen or pasture consumed by a wildfire, or drowned as rising waters obliterate the high ground on which they have sheltered. Pets locked in homes may be similarly vulnerable to fire or drowning or even suffocation as mudslides engulf the building in which they are trapped. Abandoned confined animals may starve or die of dehydration. Starved omnivorous or carnivorous animals may engage in cannibalism or predation if no other options are available. Obviously, all of these situations present the potential for enormous animal suffering. Humans do not want to feel responsible for animal suffering, and many people feel anguish and guilt when hearing reports of animal suffering or unnecessary animal deaths, even if they were not in a position to prevent it. Appropriate disaster planning can decrease or eliminate the likelihood of animal pain and suffering.

14.3.3 LIVESTOCK

Livestock can also become more dangerous during a disaster, as they may feel more threatened or anxious due to the alteration of their normal environment. Herd bulls or alpha cows in particular may be quite aggressive even toward familiar people (Bassert and McCurnin 2010). Herds or flocks of livestock can panic and stampede easily when frightened, potentially causing severe injury to anyone in the way.

Public health concerns are also present with regard to animals in disasters. Normally well-cared-for animals can acquire diseases from which they would normally be protected. These include parasites as well as bacterial or viral diseases. Many animal species, both wildlife and domestic animals, can become infected with a bacterial disease known as leptospirosis. This organism survives well in stagnant water and can cause kidney and liver failure in humans. Multiple examples of human leptospirosis outbreaks have been reported in flooded areas, and untended animals can contribute to these. Naturally occurring anthrax is also more common in certain geographic areas following a flood, and infected livestock may represent a threat to humans. Additionally, animals in packs are more likely to spread diseases than animals kept segregated in homes; these diseases include minor ones like hookworm infestations and major ones such as rabies. Animal feces can contain bacteria that can make humans ill, and basic human sanitation and hygiene are often suboptimal in disaster areas. Thus potential exposure of humans to disease-causing organisms increases during disasters where animals are present. If significant numbers of animal carcasses are exposed following a disaster, such as the tens of thousands of hogs that drowned in North Carolina following Hurricane Dennis, these carcasses provide breeding grounds for disease-carrying vectors such as flies and may result in significant manure contamination of waterways (Mallin et al. 2002; Wing, Freedman, and Band 2002). While the carcasses themselves are not harmful, the odors generated by them are also exceedingly unpleasant.

14.3.4 SERVICE ANIMALS

Accommodation of service animals is also needed when planning for disaster management. "Service animals" usually refers to dogs, but both miniature horses and small primates are also employed as service animals for people with various medical conditions. Interestingly, the most recent Department of Justice update on the Americans with Disabilities Act acknowledges only dogs and miniature horses as potential service animals (DOJ 2010). This leaves those persons using primates as service animals in limbo regarding the ability of their animals to accompany them into public places.

Service animals must be evacuated with their owners, as separation from a service animal can have devastating consequences for the owner. While only a minuscule fraction of the population employs service animals, disaster planners should recognize that they may be faced with these situations. Another group of service animals are the working dogs that may accompany disaster relief personnel: search and rescue dogs, explosives-detection dogs, cadaver-finding dogs, and crisis-response dogs. If these dogs will be employed in a disaster-afflicted area, then accommodations must be made for their shelter and rations as well (Jones et al. 2004).

14.3.5 OTHER CONCERNS

Examples of animal involvement in disasters are widespread. The New Orleans Aquarium lost thousands of fish due to a generator failure during Katrina's aftermath (CNN 2005). Wildfires in Texas and Oklahoma in 2005 killed more than 5,000 cattle (Mutch and Keller 2010). During the 2011 tornado that devastated Joplin, Missouri, 3,000 turkeys were lost or killed (Associated Press 2011). Uncounted pets were lost during Hurricanes Katrina and Rita (Louisiana SPCA 2006).

The types of disasters that can affect animals are many and varied. We most commonly think of natural disasters: floods, tornadoes, wildfires, and mudslides. However, animals are equally as at-risk as humans from other types of disasters. Chemical spills from manufacturing plants or transportation vehicles have affected animals. Livestock are susceptible to starvation secondary to another factor that eliminates their forage diet: drought, fire, or plant diseases. Animals are also susceptible to some biological agents that can be acquired from humans, such as some of the influenza viruses. Animals are exquisitely susceptible to certain types of contagious bioterrorism attacks; because of the way we raise large numbers of livestock in small geographic areas, introduction of a livestock pathogen such as rinderpest or contagious bovine pleuropneumonia into a U.S. feed yard could have a truly devastating effect on the nation's food supply. Even a natural pandemic of a livestock pathogen could have dramatic effects on our animal populations, while humans may not be affected by these organisms. An example of this is the 2001 outbreak of foot-and-mouth disease in livestock in the United Kingdom: Many thousands of animals died, but millions more had to be slaughtered to prevent the spread of the virus (Defra 2004). Humans are completely unaffected by this disease. Any large-scale animal pandemic could result in the deaths or forced slaughter of uncounted numbers of food animals. Food insecurity caused by unavailability of animal protein and increased food costs can affect large segments of the human population and cause anxiety, apprehension, and social unrest.

Animals can also be affected by human strife: The Baghdad Zoo lost over 95% of its animals, mostly to starvation, in the months following the U.S. invasion of Iraq (Anthony and Spence 2007). Animals are sometimes more susceptible than humans to certain agents; one classic example is the sensitivity of bird species to carbon monoxide. Obviously, disasters do not necessarily affect animals and humans in the same way or on the same scale.

Why should we focus on animals during disasters? Because ignoring the animals can dramatically affect the success of disaster plans for humans. The emotional attachment as well as financial and humane concerns surrounding animals makes it dangerous to exclude them from disaster planning. In the following sections we will discuss many of the specific details of animals in disasters and will hopefully demonstrate their importance in disaster planning.

14.4 DEMOGRAPHIC OVERVIEW

Disaster planning for animals is complicated by the lack of accurate animal demographics. This can create a challenge for emergency preparedness personnel.

14.4.1 PETS

One very important question to answer when considering inclusion of animals into disaster plans is how many animals are there and of which species? Answering this question is far more difficult than it appears. For humans, census data are used to generate estimates for planning purposes. However, no comprehensive census exists for animals. Data must be extracted from many other sources, none of which are complete and many of which address only pets or only livestock. Most municipalities require dog and cat licenses for pets within the town; however, citizen compliance with required licensure is very poor, and city-issued pet licenses should not be relied upon for accurate data. Rabies tags issued by veterinarians would generate a far more accurate count of dogs and cats, but there is no central clearinghouse for that data except in retrospective format. The state veterinarian's office should be able to provide numbers of vaccinated animals by county, but the data may be several years old by the time it is collated. Additionally, some owners still fail to have their pets vaccinated for rabies. The American Veterinary Medical Association (AVMA) does conduct periodic estimates of pet ownership by household; in 2007 it published that 37% of households had dogs, 32% had cats, 4% had birds and 2% had horses, but no estimates were provided regarding the number of each species per household

(AVMA 2007). The AVMA's website does offer a calculator to estimate the number of pet-owning households in a community (http://www3.avma.org/reference/marketstats/ownership_calculator.asp).

14.4.2 LIVESTOCK

Livestock numbers are even more difficult to track down, as livestock are constantly bought, sold, and slaughtered. National-level initiatives to identify all livestock have been unsuccessful, and there are no required licenses for food-producing animals. Some vaccines such as brucellosis have associated numbered ear tags, but these vaccines are not given to all livestock and are less than optimally useful for animal enumeration or tracking. The best places to look for livestock and equine numbers would include the county agricultural extension services (which collaborate with the U.S. Department of Agriculture) or the American Veterinary Medical Association. Both of these agencies track animal demographics, but there is no mandatory reporting to either; numbers may be significantly inaccurate or outdated.

A challenge for the reader could be to try to determine the numbers of animals in your community. Contact your local city offices and county extension agent. Take those numbers as a start, but also determine which groups of animals are not included in the numbers you have been provided. Do they include zoos (public and private)? Are animal shelters and humane societies counted? Does your municipality track exotic species (reptiles, exotic hoofstock, big cats)? Do they track or license dangerous species such as venomous animals or large carnivores? Are there surveys of wildlife species in your area, especially threatened or endangered species? Trying to answer these questions just for your immediate area will give you an idea of the challenges involved in finding animal demographics for your disaster plans.

14.5   VULNERABILITY ACROSS THE DISASTER LIFE CYCLE

Proper preparation is crucial to an appropriate animal disaster response, as managing animals and their humans across the disaster life cycle is very different from handling humans alone. Animal-specific concerns must be addressed.

14.5.1 WARNINGS, EVACUATION, RESPONSE

Animals cannot respond by themselves to disaster warnings. It is the responsibility of human caretakers to pay attention to such warnings and to respond appropriately. Disaster planners must consider how best to disseminate animal-relevant information to animal owners, as much of this information may not be applicable to the general public. While pets are usually fairly easy to move, movement of horses and livestock can be extremely time consuming and fraught with risk. Both disaster planners and animal owners must consider well ahead of time the requirements for handling their animals during adverse events, whether the response is evacuation, shelter in place, or even slaughter. The specific responses depend on many variables, including emotional attachment, animal monetary value, logistics issues, and behavioral issues (Madigan and Whittemore 2000; Noah, Noah, and Crowder 2002; Hall et al. 2004; Irvine 2004, 2006; Nusbaum, Rollin, and Wohl 2007).

14.5.1.1   Small Animals

House pets such as dogs and cats are usually the easiest animals to deal with during disasters. There are normally one to a handful per household, and most are docile or even friendly. Many are used to riding in cars and in carriers. Their food is readily portable and widely available commercially. However, there are ways in which pets can also be difficult evacuees. Some are poorly socialized to other animals. Some may be overly protective of their people, of food, or of their kennels. Some may not be vaccinated against commonly transmitted diseases. Cat owners often do not have carriers big enough to accommodate a litter box, and dog owners may not have a kennel of sufficient size for prolonged residence. Many pets do not wear collars and are not microchipped for identification. See Box 14.1.

Many preparations may be made by disaster planners to accommodate pets, but much of the success of an endeavor will rely on the preparation of the owners themselves. Owners should make sure that they have appropriate crates or kennels for their pets: sturdy, well-ventilated crates that are sufficiently large for the dog to stand up, turn around, and lie down with legs extended. Cat carriers may be of a similar size, but for extended housing, cat cages should also have at least a 12" × 15" space to accommodate a litter box in addition to the sleeping space. Animals should be identified with both a microchip and a collar with tags that include the owner's name and cell phone number. A point of contact remote to the disaster location is also helpful in the event that cell phone towers are down or cell phones are lost or dead.

Owners should have in their possession the animal's current vaccination certificates, and animals should be vaccinated against rabies and the common viral diseases for their species. Vaccination against Bordetella (kennel cough) is preferred for both dogs and cats, as this disease is readily transmitted in kennels. Owners should carry photographs clearly showing them with their animal in the event owner and animal are separated; there have been cases of multiple owners claiming the same animal, so some form of photographic proof is desired. Several days' worth of food and any required medications should also be brought along with food and water bowls, leashes, a favorite toy, pet beds, and other accoutrements necessary for the pet's well-being. Box muzzles should be brought by owners of potentially aggressive dogs; such muzzles may be worn by the dog while walking and do not inhibit panting or drinking water. Muzzles that force the dog's mouth closed should never be left on for more than 5–10 minutes, especially in hot or humid conditions.

Owners who are evacuating to community-run shelters should be prepared to potentially be responsible for some of their animal's care if shelter staffing is insufficient. Owners whose communities have pet-friendly shelters may be required to preregister their pets for shelter admittance; this helps communities know how many animals they may need to shelter.

BOX 14.1   PREPARING YOUR PET FOR DISASTER: IF YOU EVACUATE, ALWAYS TAKE YOUR PETS!

Pet needs for admittance to most shelters:

- Your contact information (normal and emergency)
- Sturdy collar/harness and leash (with ID tags)
- Pet crate or carrier
- Pet medications and medical records
- Veterinarian's name and contact information
- Vaccination certificates and tags
- Photos and descriptions of your pet
- Food and water for 3+ days
- Food and water bowls, marked
- Information on feeding schedules and amounts
- Manual can opener
- Litter box, litter, and scoop for cats
- Pet beds and toys
- Grooming items
- Cleaning supplies and trash bags

Source: Extracted from HSUS pamphlet "Disaster Preparedness for Pets," 2001. Other resources available at Ready.gov.

Not all owners will choose to evacuate with their pets. Pet abandonment has been shown to be a major consequence when humans evacuate during disasters. Research has indicated that owners have several reasons for leaving their pets behind during an evacuation. Sometimes this is due to a simple lack of planning. Owners who have never before had to evacuate may not have made any accommodations for bringing a pet or have adequate supplies on hand. Lack of resources for pet transport may also induce an owner to abandon a pet, such as owners that do not have carriers or kennels for pets. Often this may be due to a lack of commitment to the pet, especially to animals kept outdoors. These animals may be expected to fend for themselves. Unfortunately, many people are not committed to the pet they adopt, treating the pet as a disposable commodity rather than a living creature. Owners who do not regularly visit a veterinarian, who fail to have their pet spayed or neutered, or who fail to have their pet vaccinated are more likely to abandon a pet during a disaster (Heath et al. 2001; Heath, Voeks, and Glickman 2001). Such owners are also more likely to relinquish a pet for other nondisaster-related reasons (moving, unemployment, etc.). Other owners abandon pets because they believe that aggressive pets will not be accepted at shelters (Heath et al. 2001), when in fact most shelters will make accommodation for all but the most aggressive dogs. And some owners leave pets in the care of someone who refuses to evacuate, which often ends badly in disasters with extensive home damage. There have also been instances where owners who have abandoned animals have been prosecuted for animal abandonment or neglect, so owners of animals should take responsibility for them to avoid potential legal consequences. Owners who abandon their pets when evacuating increase the workload and drain the resources of first responders and rescue workers in the disaster area, so owners should be encouraged to evacuate with their pets whenever a pet-friendly evacuation option is available.

14.5.1.2 Large Animals

Horses occupy an intermediate position in the spectrum between house pets and livestock. For many horse owners, the horse is a treasured pet and may have significant emotional value in addition to its intrinsic monetary worth. Many city-dwelling horse owners board their horses at a commercial care facility that may be distant from their homes, but nonetheless have significant emotional attachment to the horses. These owners may attempt to move into disaster-stricken areas to try to evacuate their animals, or may be reluctant to leave their homes unless they can contact the caregiver at the boarding barn to make sure their equine companion is safe. Few boarding facilities have disaster or evacuation plans, even those in areas at consistent risk of hurricanes or wildfires. Few horse owners who board their horses at commercial facilities own their own horse trailer. Few boarding facilities own sufficient horse trailers or trucks to evacuate all equine residents at one time, so either multiple trips or borrowing of more trailers may be required. Horses and livestock also require tremendous amounts of food and water: An average 1200-lb. horse needs approximately 25 lbs. of food per day just for maintenance; more is needed if the animal is sick, injured, or nursing young. As a result, considerable planning must go into determining whether to shelter in place or evacuate, as evacuation also means moving tons of food. Horses unfamiliar with each other may not be randomly housed with one another, as fighting will occur as a new dominance order is established. Stallions should never be housed together or even in stalls next to one another, as they will try to fight. Stallions should only be turned out alone or with mares already belonging to them in pens with tall sturdy fencing, as they will attempt to break down fences to get to another stallion or a mare in season. Stallions should also never be handled or led by inexperienced personnel, as they can be dangerous and should not be trusted. In short, moving large animals is difficult even with advance notice and planning. Rapid onset events, such as tornadoes, represent an even greater threat.

In addition, horses are prey animals and have a very strong flight response when they are frightened. They also readily sense when a human is anxious or apprehensive. Although most horses are not aggressive toward humans, fear-based responses by a horse may result in severe injury to inexperienced handlers. Frightened horses may also be very difficult to load onto a trailer, and blindfolding or chemical sedation may be required. Sheltering of horses is most often dependent on the resources of the horse owner, as states seldom have provisions for sheltering of large animals. Horse owners should have a personal disaster plan with prearranged transportation and shelter for their horses. Reciprocal agreements with other horse owners/barns distant to their town of origin are recommended. Horses should be identified with a tag or tape braided tightly into the mane or tail as well as a tag on the halter, as halters may come off. Horses may also be microchipped just like dogs and cats, or branded. Livestock crayons or spray paint can also be used in a pinch. Horse owners should have photographs of their horse with them, again preferably with the owner in the photo. Horse owners should also have the horse's most recent Coggins test (a test for the disease Equine Infectious Anemia) and vaccine records as well as registration certificates. Lead ropes and feed/water buckets should be provided by owners as well. Bedding (straw or wood shavings) is bulky to transport and may preferably be stockpiled at the intended shelter area or purchased at the destination. Horses produce large quantities of waste, but this waste may be easily composted (in contrast to dog and cat waste, which is more difficult to compost due to the potential pathogens found in it [Hawaii CES 1998]).

Livestock, including cattle, sheep, goats, swine, chickens and exotic livestock such as camelids or ratites (ostriches and emus), can also be affected by disasters in very large numbers. Many of these animals are kept at pasture and are most commonly threatened by disasters encompassing a large area, such as wildfires or floods. For example, over 123,000 cattle froze or drowned in North Dakota alone during the 1997 blizzards and floods that affected the north-central United States (ND-SWC 1997). Other types of animals, such as swine and chickens, are typically kept housed and may be affected by much smaller-scale disasters such as a building fire.

Livestock owners may be as reluctant to leave their animals as pet owners, though not necessarily for the same reasons. Many family farms do have an emotional attachment to their livestock, as they have raised the ancestors of their stock for many generations. Most farmers and ranchers are very respectful of their livestock and feel that they have significant responsibility toward seeing that they are well cared for, even that their animals trust them to take care of them. Many small farmers know each of their animals by personality, and many name them. Some livestock are very dear to the children of a household, as children often raise and train young livestock for 4-H, Future Farmers of America, or county and state fair programs. Many of these former show animals become prized breeding stock later in life. Many purebred livestock breeders have decades invested in improving the genetics of their stock, and loss of breeding animals can be an irrevocable personal as well as financial blow. Many livestock owners depend on their animals for their livelihood. Loss of their stock can be a devastating financial setback that will have effects long after the disaster situation is resolved, as many family farms cannot afford insurance against disaster losses. Commercial livestock-raising operations, on the other hand, have little if any emotional attachment to their animals. Instead, the animals are a commodity to be sold and slaughtered. These commercial operations will likely not make significant efforts at animal evacuation and will instead prefer to shelter in place, slaughter animals if severe injury or death seems imminent, or even simply abandon them. The commercial livestock-rearing operations usually have insurance to cover disaster losses, and so the financial blow may not be as severe. (See Photo 14.1.)

Unfortunately, most livestock owners and family farmers do not possess sufficient trailers to haul all their livestock at once. Commercial facilities may not own any trailers, instead contracting with commercial hauling agencies. Many trips may be necessary to transport stock to a safe location. Most livestock is neither tame nor trained to lead, and some livestock (adult bulls, cows with calves, ratites) may be extremely aggressive toward humans. Some stock cannot be commingled (e.g., adult bulls will fight and injure each other if confined together). Much livestock is maintained at pasture, and gathering of animals from pasture is never a quick process. In many situations, livestock must be rounded up by riders on horseback due to terrain and dispersal of the pastured animals.

Often, the most efficient solution to move pastured livestock away from a threatened area, such as a wildfire, is to cut fences and drive the animals toward safety. However, this bears its own risks as far as road crossings and trespassing or damage to private property en route to a safe location. In addition, if animals must be moved in this manner over any significant distance, then accommodations for feed and water along the route must be considered. An adult bovine ($\approx$1500 lbs.) will eat approximately 2%–3% of its body weight (30–45 lbs.) in forage each day. Often cattle may only be driven 5–10

PHOTO 14.1   St. Louis, Missouri, July 9, 1993. Many livestock and animals were rescued from high water levels. During a disaster, FEMA provides much-needed financial assistance and ensures that fresh water, food, shelter, and communications are available in the flood-stricken area. After the 1993 Midwest floods, a total of 534 counties in nine states were declared for federal disaster aid. As a result, 168,340 people registered for federal assistance. (Photo by Andrea Booher/FEMA Photo.)

miles in a day with experienced cowhands on horseback, especially in areas where road crossings or traffic are prevalent. Cattle and other hoofstock are herd animals. When moving an established herd, it is extremely helpful to identify the dominant animals in a herd and focus effort on convincing those animals to move in the desired direction; the rest of the herd will follow. In these situations, it is invaluable to have experienced livestock handlers/cowhands available, as inexperienced personnel will be ineffective at the task and highly likely to be injured by panicked livestock. If livestock cannot be moved due to logistic issues, field-expedient slaughter should be considered. Slaughter and euthanasia are discussed later in this chapter. One unique aspect of livestock should be noted with regard to movement: True ruminants such as cattle, sheep, and goats float relatively well for short periods and so may be able to cross waterways that are deep but slow moving. This is due to gas in the large digestive compartment called the rumen. Baby livestock do not float and swim poorly; they should be portaged across deep water by other means. Horses do not float but can swim short distances, while camelids such as llamas and alpacas do not float and cannot swim. None of these species are likely to enter water without a great deal of encouragement from experienced herders.

Many livestock do not have permanent identification of any kind. They may have numbered plastic ear tags, but each owner uses their own numbering system, and these tags are at high risk of loss. They may have brands, but these often only identify the ranch of origin and not the individual animal. Some cattle may have federally issued orange metal brucellosis ear tags; these do provide a unique identifier, but that information may be difficult to obtain during periods when computer support is unavailable. However, not all cattle are vaccinated for brucellosis; unvaccinated animals will not have orange tags. Small ruminants (sheep, goats, and camelids such as llamas and alpacas) and swine are even less likely to have permanent identification. Animals confined together will taste and remove most forms of temporary identification such as cardboard hang-tags or tape collars. Methods of temporary identification of livestock could include livestock crayons or spray paint, which may be applied to the haircoat, and glue-on numbered cardboard back tags such as those used in sale barns.

14.5.1.3 Sheltering

Many animal organizations provide guidance on disaster preparedness for animals for both animal owners and disaster planners. The Federal Emergency Management Agency (FEMA), the Humane Society of the United States (HSUS), the American Society for the Prevention of Cruelty to Animals (ASPCA), and the AVMA are all excellent resources for disaster planning. Part of disaster planning must include the establishment of temporary animal shelters, whether they will be housed in existing animal facilities, other brick-and-mortar buildings, or in temporary buildings or tents. Persons establishing a shelter should be trained in shelter management and be thoroughly familiar with the National Incident Management System, the Incident Command System, and the National Response Plan (Beaver et al. 2006). This will allow animal shelter managers to work effectively with other disaster responders and human shelter managers. Animal shelter managers must also be specifically trained in managing animals in disasters. All of this training is available through the FEMA website and should be completed well in advance of any disaster, as not only training but extensive prior planning is needed to establish a shelter. Shelter management should not be a task undertaken by untrained personnel, as operations are likely to be inefficient and disorganized and fail to work effectively within the larger disaster response organization. This can hinder shelter operations and directly affect the ability of the responders to provide care for the animals and reunite them with their owners. (See Box 14.2.)

BOX 14.2   PUPPIES, DOG DROWN WHEN BRADFORD ANIMAL SHELTER FLOODS

Alligator Creek flash flood waters poured into shelter despite sand bags, drainage trenches, and other precautions
Posted: June 25, 2012—4:42pm | Updated: June 26, 2012—7:19am
Copyright 2012, The Florida Times-Union. All rights reserved.

Four puppies and a young dog drowned when a flash flood triggered by rain from Tropical Storm Debby sent water from Alligator Creek pouring into the Bradford [FL] County Animal Control and Shelter in Starke. "We had moved the puppies up to the high end of the shelter, thinking they would be safe there," said Capt. Carol Starling of the Bradford County Sheriff's Office, who oversees the animal shelter. Personnel also had laid down sand bags and dug drainage trenches around the building as a precaution to protect animals inside. In addition county crews previously had cleaned out the creek in an effort to keep it running freely and within its banks, she said. "We all feel so bad. . . . We never expected the creek would rise this fast and this high and we really felt the ditches would handle it if it came out of the bank," Starling said.

All appeared fine late Sunday night [when] they last checked the shelter, which is within about 20 yards of the creek. In the wee hours of the morning, however, water breached the shelter. It rose nearly knee-deep inside where the animals were held, she said. The bull dog/house mix puppies that died were part of a large litter recently brought to the shelter along with their mother. The animals were waiting to be picked up by a rescue group, when they were caught in the flood, Starling said. It appeared that the mother dog had tried to save all her puppies but couldn't. Shelter staff discovered the flooded building shortly before 7 a.m., Starling said. The surviving animals—about 60 dogs, cats, and kittens—immediately were evacuated to safety on higher ground at the county fairgrounds by sheriff's deputies and animal control personnel, she said. The mother dog and surviving litter mates have been picked up by a rescue group. Other rescue groups arrived throughout the day to help and pick up animals, she said. The flooding destroyed much of the shelter's stock of dog food and cat litter. It would welcome donations of pet food as well as cat litter, clean towels and small bath rugs in good condition that can be used in the animals' pens, Starling said. As rain began falling about 4 p.m., Starling said it's likely the shelter animals will remain at the fairgrounds for about four or five days. Once it stops raining and the creek recedes, personnel will clean the shelter and make sure it is safe.

Source: Transcribed verbatim from http://jacksonville.com/news/florida/2012-06-25/story/puppies-dog-drown-when-bradford-animal-shelter-floods. Used with permission.

Experience has shown that animal shelters that are co-located with human shelters provide the best situation for pet owners (FEMA/DHS 2007). However, certain considerations must be taken into account when housing pets and owners in the same facility. Most human shelter plans will not allow pets to be housed in the same room with their owners due to concerns about both animal behavior and allergies in humans. However, sheltering animals in another part of the human shelter facility may be possible. Service animals, however, must be sheltered with their owners, as their presence is required for daily living tasks (FEMA 2010). Service animals often wear harnesses or vests that designate them as a service animal, but this is not required. Shelter managers may only ask an animal owner if the animal is a service animal and what tasks the animal is trained to perform in order to determine that the animal is permitted in a human shelter. Animal shelter managers will need to work with human shelter managers to ensure that the needs of service animals in the human shelter are met and that they do not get forgotten in the confusion of caring for pets. Among the other aspects of care that must be considered by shelter organizers will be ensuring that there is a dedicated area for dog walking (both pet and service dogs) that is a sufficient distance away from human living and dining areas. Such areas require picking up feces and hosing urine several times per day, depending on the number of animals present.

There are many additional considerations for animal sheltering (Hudson et al. 2001). Cats and dogs should be housed in acoustically separate locations if possible, as many cats become very stressed when there are barking dogs in the area. Shelter workers should have hearing protection, especially if the animals are sheltered indoors. An area for decontamination of animals caught in floodwaters or chemical spills may be necessary (Soric, Belanger, and Wittnich 2008). Cages or kennels should be placed on a surface that is easily cleaned and disinfected, as fecal and urine contamination will occur. Cages should not be stacked unless they have solid floors and can be secured in place; a kennel or cage can be easily tipped by the animal inside. Temperature control is important; dogs and cats have thick hair coats and regulate their temperature primarily by panting. They do not have many sweat glands and cannot cool by evaporative methods like humans can. Fans provide some relief, but not as much as experienced by humans. Storage areas for food are required, and these may need to be protected from vermin. Clean water is just as important for animals as it is for humans. Some means of keeping one animal's equipment separate from another's is also desirable, as is an area to wash bowls, bedding, and cages. All of these considerations mean that locations for temporary animal shelters must be scouted out well ahead of time and permission obtained from the facility owner. Organization and good recordkeeping are also paramount, since animals cannot tell you their story (FEMA/DHS 2007).

Shelter workers may also be faced with sheltering small exotic pets such as ferrets, hedgehogs, birds, reptiles, and rodents. Each of these species has particular needs, but most important is provision of a place to shelter with food and water. Small exotics should be housed separately (visual and acoustic) from dogs or cats, if possible. They are also exquisitely sensitive to cold temperatures and drafts, and some may become dormant if kept in too cold an environment. Reptiles in particular are cold-blooded and wholly dependent on environmental heat; reptile cages should be provided with heat lamps at one end if the ambient temperature is below $\approx85°F$. Owners will hopefully bring cages and prepared food for their small exotics, as their particular diets may not be widely available. Some species require fresh fruits and vegetables, or fresh meat (usually mice) in the case of some reptiles. In short-term shelters, a few days of deprivation should not be a major problem. However, sheltered exotic animals kept for more than a week will require their special diets or appropriate supplements. Most small exotics are not vaccinated for anything, but ferrets should be vaccinated for canine distemper. Small exotics are usually timid animals, but will bite if frightened or feeling cornered. Psittacine birds such as parrots have a very powerful bite, strong enough to amputate a finger if received from a large parrot. Shelters will need to determine if they are willing to accept venomous exotic species such as venomous snakes or lizards, keeping in mind that stressed owners may set the animals free if they cannot be sheltered.

Managing an animal shelter is a challenging task and not one that should be attempted by someone new to the process. Many animal organizations offer training in sheltering animals, and local disaster management groups should ensure that their staff or reliable volunteers are trained in shelter management. Having volunteered at a previous shelter is unlikely to be sufficient preparation for the management of a shelter. A number of resources for shelter setup and management are provided in the Resources section. (See Photos 14.2 and 14.3.)

14.5.2 IMPACTS

By now you have recognized that animals are as susceptible to disasters as humans, but not nearly so easy to organize and shelter. Animals may also suffer injuries and illnesses subsequent to disasters; some of these may be treated by the layperson, while many require veterinary intervention.

PHOTO 14.2   The Joplin, Missouri, AARC emergency animal shelter following the 2011 tornadoes. Note the solid barriers between cages and the veterinary treatment area. (Photo credit: Joplin Humane Society. With permission.)

PHOTO 14.3   Another photo of the Joplin, Missouri, temporary animal shelter following the 2011 tornadoes. (Photo credit: Joplin Humane Society. With permission.)

Some specific examples are covered in this section. Ideally, any rescued animal should be evaluated by a veterinarian or trained veterinary technician upon admission to a shelter, but often there are insufficient veterinary assets for this to occur.

14.5.2.1 Injuries

Dogs and cats tend to suffer many of the same injuries as the humans they stay with. They may receive crushing injuries from collapsing buildings or traumatic wounds from air-blown debris. However, pets do tend to suffer more than humans from heat injuries, mostly due to their limited ability to dissipate excess heat. Heat exhaustion and heat stroke are common conditions, especially in long-haired pets. The primary signs of heat injury in pets are a rectal temperature of >105°F, panting, weakness, and collapse. Animals with these conditions should be seen by a veterinarian, but immediate cooling measures should be taken: Bring the animal to an air-conditioned or shaded area and place ice packs wrapped in cloth to the major veins on the neck and between the hind legs and on the head. Stop active cooling measures when the animal's temperature gets down to 103°F. Pets with short muzzles such as pugs, bulldogs, and Persian cats may be more susceptible to heat injury since they cannot breathe as efficiently.

Paw-pad injuries are common in dogs as well, and are difficult to heal. Pad injuries should be gently cleaned and bandaged with gauze and a conforming bandage such as Kling. Adhesive tape does not stick well to fur, and neither do Band-Aids. A veterinarian should evaluate the injury to determine if further treatment is necessary. Eye injuries are also common and often simply due to blown dust. Eyes may be gently irrigated with saline solution for contact lenses or eye wash to see if that resolves the problem. Animals with injuries are often reluctant to leave bandages on and will also rub or lick injuries, so supervision may be required to prevent further damage.

Working animals can also suffer morbidities during disasters. Working animals are typically dogs used for search and rescue, explosives detection, or cadaver detection. Data collected from dogs used after the World Trade Center attacks in 2001 revealed that working dogs suffered gastrointestinal upset, pad injuries, fatigue, loss of appetite, dehydration, respiratory problems, heat exhaustion, and orthopedic problems (Slensky et al. 2004). Such conditions, while usually mild, cause discomfort to the dog and can affect the dog's ability to do its job. Accommodations for rest, feeding, and medical treatment of working dogs should be considered in a disaster plan. These animals should be housed separately from privately owned animals if possible, as they require a great deal of mental focus to perform their tasks (Jones et al. 2004), and pet shelters are frequently noisy and chaotic and prevent working dogs from obtaining rest.

Horses often injure themselves trying to escape a threat, so cuts from barbed wire and sheet metal are common. Horses are also extremely sensitive to smoke inhalation; a horse with no visible burns can still die following a fire. Horses are extremely susceptible to tetanus, so any penetrating wound on a horse should be treated by a veterinarian. Horses and large livestock have a great deal of blood in their bodies. An injury may result in several gallons of blood loss, yet this is not a significant problem for a previously healthy horse, despite what it looks like to us. Nonetheless, direct pressure should be applied to stop blood loss. Livestock are hardy but still prone to injuries from fencing materials such as barbed wire and blunt trauma from stampeding herdmates. Do not attempt to assist injured livestock without knowledgeable personnel and appropriate restraint, as humans are easily injured by hurt, frightened livestock. When livestock are injured, danger frequently applies to an entire herd or flock rather than individual animals due to their tendency to move as a herd unit.

14.5.2.2 Deaths

Animal deaths may also occur during and after disasters. The scope and number of such deaths vary depending on the type of disaster and the type of area affected. A disaster confined to a city such as the attack on the World Trade Center will have relatively few animal deaths, and those mostly of pets. In contrast, a disaster affecting an agriculture-intensive area may result in tens of thousands of animal deaths, even if the disaster area is relatively confined. There are hog farms and cattle feedlots that house more than 20,000 animals in a fairly small area, and a single chicken farm may have over 1 million birds. In these cases, disaster management may include not only euthanasia of severely injured animals, but also disposal of tons of animal carcasses. Animal disease outbreaks may require the deaths of many more animals. Over 4 million livestock were slaughtered during the 2001 foot-and-mouth disease outbreak in the United Kingdom (DEFRA 2004). Most of the animals did not have the disease but were slaughtered to prevent its spread. Not all of the animals were slaughtered at the same time or location, but the sheer number of animal lives lost was stunning.

First responders and others may feel compelled to euthanize an injured animal. However, euthanasia of animals is best carried out by experienced personnel. Training courses are available in appropriate and humane euthanasia techniques for various species, and the AVMA provides detailed guidelines for selecting an appropriate euthanasia method. The "bullet between the eyes" is seldom the best approach, as the brains of many animal species are not centered between the eyes, plus stray bullets or ricochets could potentially cause injury to others. The skulls of livestock in particular are very thick, such that a bullet fired at the wrong angle will bounce off the animal's head. Plus, shooting a cow between the eyes will only badly damage her sinuses, leaving her alive but in severe pain. For small animals, chemical euthanasia is best and usually consists of an overdose of an injectable barbiturate drug administered by a veterinarian. For livestock or horses, a captive bolt gun (a gun that fires a retractable metal rod rather than a bullet) is often the most efficient and humane method, but placement of the bolt varies by species and should be done by trained personnel.

The deaths of animals may be unavoidable during a disaster. Feelings of grief and bereavement may overwhelm animal owners, even owners of livestock. Non-animal-owners may not understand the depth of grief that can be induced by the death of a companion pet or a well-loved farm animal. Even other animal owners may belittle the feelings of the bereaved owners if they have never gone through the loss of a beloved pet. Studies have reported that one-third of dog owners felt closer to their dog than to any human family member (Barker and Barker 1988), so it is not surprising that grieving will occur. Emergency personnel should be prepared to deal with animal-loss grief in the same manner that would be used for the loss of a friend or relative. Pet owners will go through the same stages of grief for a deceased pet as they will for a deceased human, even if they had to make the decision to euthanize the pet. In some cases, the grief may be compounded if such a decision had to be made expeditiously due to an encroaching threat, especially if the animal might have been saved if there had been just a little more time. This may be particularly applicable to livestock owners, as much of society does not understand the level of attachment that farmers and ranchers have for their livestock (Hall et al. 2004; Nusbaum, Wenzel, and Everly 2007).

The deaths of animals require consideration of what should be done with the remains. The American Veterinary Medical Association determined in 2009 that animal carcasses in and of themselves do not present an imminent public health hazard (AVMA 2009). However, carcasses should be disposed of as expeditiously as possible, as these carcasses will rapidly decompose, contributing to flies, creating unwanted odors, and even potentially contaminating water sources used for humans or other animals. Disposal of large numbers of animal carcasses, which may number into the thousands, can be a logistic nightmare. Carcasses are often disposed of by pit burning followed by burial, although this requires large amounts of flammable fuel and heavy equipment. Pit burning also creates considerable amounts of smoke, the odor of which many people find unpleasant. Other options include composting and rendering, although this last option may not be available if carcasses are decomposed or the animals died or were euthanized due to infectious disease. If otherwise-healthy food animals are to be euthanized due to imminent starvation (due to isolation from blizzards or prolonged drought conditions) or inability to evacuate, some municipalities may allow the meat to be distributed to shelters, charities, or food banks. This may help in easing food crises following the disaster, especially if fresh food cannot readily be brought in due to road damage. If this is an option, animals should be humanely slaughtered and butchered by personnel experienced in these tasks. Ill or injured animals should never be used for human consumption unless the injury is acute and the animal slaughtered immediately thereafter (e.g., a steer that broke a leg in a stampede). Animals euthanized with chemical euthanasia solutions should never be used for human or animal consumption; there are many instances of dogs and wildlife dying of barbiturate overdose after scavenging from the carcass of an animal euthanized with barbiturates. Animals subjected to chemical euthanasia should be deeply buried, burned, or rendered to prevent such scavenging.

Although there is definitely public health concern following a disaster, animals appear not to contribute greatly to public health issues. There are potential hazards with food and water contamination by animal waste or decomposing carcasses, but these have not been seen to have any significant impact in North American disasters (Blake 1989). The same is true of fears of packs of free-roaming aggressive dogs and rabies outbreaks, as these have not been seen to happen to any extent. There have been noted increases in human cases of leptospirosis in tropical regions following tsunamis or floods (ProMED 2012), but it is unknown to what degree animals contribute to the increase.

Animal deaths do not always occur immediately during and after a disaster. A disaster may have long-lasting impact on animal species. For example, two years after the 2010 Deepwater Horizon oil spill in the Gulf of Mexico, there still appear to be effects evident in marine species (NOAA 2011; Mote 2012). Dolphin and sea turtle deaths have risen sharply, and several fish species are exhibiting abnormalities that may impact their long-term survival. It is not known whether the oil is the direct cause of these problems; research is ongoing in that regard. However, we do know that 20 years after the *Exxon Valdez* oil spill, some marine species have still not recovered to prespill numbers (National Wildlife Federation 2012). Disasters may have extreme impacts on endangered species whose habitat is confined to a localized geographic area. Examples of this are some of the endangered species found only on isolated atolls in the Pacific and Indian Oceans, or the giant kangaroo rat, which occupies an area of only five square miles in California. If a wildfire were to sweep through the Taft area of west-central California, the entire known population of this animal could be lost within a few years, even if a few individuals remain. The population could easily become unsustainable if too small a genetic pool remains, and the world could lose another animal forever. This would be a loss to the entire world, not just the local area affected by the fire.

14.6 RETRIEVING LOST ANIMALS

In addition to animal injuries and deaths, lost and missing animals are frequent occurrences during disasters. These might include a dog that escaped its yard due to a damaged fence or a sheep that became separated from its flock during fearful flight from a threat. Lost animals are often very difficult to reunite with their owners. This is often due to an inability to positively identify the owner or the animal. Far too many pet owners do not keep collars on their pets or have them microchipped, which prevent timely reuniting of pet with owner. As collars can be lost, microchipping is strongly encouraged for all pets, even those who wear collars. Microchips can be read with handheld scanners available at most veterinary offices and animal shelters, and owner information is easily obtained by calling the manufacturer of the chip and providing the chip number. Most microchip manufacturers also have a website at which chip numbers can be checked if Internet service is available. Chips are usually implanted between the shoulder blades of small animals.

Relatively few horses and livestock are microchipped. When they are, the chip is usually implanted into the crest of the neck on the left side. Most livestock and some horses carry only a brand. Brands can identify the farm of origin if the brand has been properly registered with the state board of agriculture or the county clerk. Brands can be hot-iron brands or freeze brands and may be almost anywhere on the animal's body, although the thigh or shoulder are the most common areas. Some breeds of horses, such as Arabians and Bureau of Land Management (BLM) mustangs, have freeze brands on their necks. Thoroughbred horses are not branded but may have a registration tattoo on the inside of the upper lip. Owners of Arabians and thoroughbreds with brands or tattoos may be identified through their breed registries: the Arabian Horse Association or the Jockey Club, respectively. BLM mustang adopters may be identified by contacting the Bureau of Land

FIGURE 14.1 Freeze brand interpretation for horses. (From the Bureau of Land Management website, http://www.blm.gov/wo/st/en/prog/whbprogram.html.)

Management (http://www.blm.gov/wo/st/en/prog/whbprogram.html). Registration freeze brands on the neck use special characters, as depicted in Figure 14.1.

Identifying the owner of an animal is only the first step in reuniting a lost animal with its owner. Following disasters, owners may not be contactable due to evacuation, power failures, lost or dead cell phones, downed phone or power lines, and various other reasons. Owners may also forget to update microchip information when they move to a new home; this is extremely common with military families and others who move frequently. Horse and livestock owners may have sold the animal carrying their brand to another person. Nonetheless, having a name will at least provide a starting point.

Lost animals, usually dogs or cats, may also be found and informally adopted by Samaritans who may or may not notify animal shelters or rescue organizations of their new pet. Lost livestock may join another herd or flock they encounter in their roaming and remain unnoticed for extended periods of time due to remote pastures and infrequent gathering of stock. Lost animals may roam a considerable distance away from their home following a disaster, especially since many familiar landmarks and smells may have been destroyed. A "found" animal should always be reported to the local animal shelter or animal welfare society as well as all rescue groups known to be operating in the area. Websites such as Petfinder.com, LittleLostDog, or LostFoundPets offer links to many local and national lost pet sites on which owners or finders can post information. Lost-and-found animals may also be posted on local Craigslist sites. However, during active disaster operations, shelter personnel may not have time or resources to post information on every pet in their custody, so visiting shelters may be necessary to ensure that the lost pet is not present. Seekers of lost pets should not rely too heavily on breed and color descriptions, as interpretation of those varies widely, especially for mixed-breed dogs. Instead, photos are far better tools.

Additionally, disasters in which multiple rescue organizations are involved often lack a centralized database of found animals; seekers of lost pets may have to personally call or visit each rescue's shelter. One thing that was learned during the aftermath of Hurricanes Katrina and Rita is that the chances of reuniting a pet with its owner are increased if the pet can be kept close to the disaster-affected area (Anderson and Anderson 2006). Many pets were sent to shelters many states away after the hurricanes, as closer shelters were overcrowded and arrangements for other close-by sites had not been made. The decisions to send pets to distant shelter were often made by desperate and overworked shelter managers, many of whom were untrained in shelter management, and often at the request of the distant shelters that wished to provide some form of assistance to rescued pets and overcrowded local shelters. The pets that traveled far away from Louisiana had a much lower rate of return to their owners (Anderson and Anderson 2006). This was possibly because animals were often sent far away in desperation to find them a place to stay, and records of where they were found were not effectively communicated (Louisiana SPCA 2006). Another reason could be that some owners lacked the resources to identify and claim pets that were far away from their location, keeping in mind that many hurricane evacuees were in temporary or makeshift housing for many months, often without Internet access. Sheltering animals close to the area affected seems to be the best practice.

14.6.1 ANIMAL RESCUE

Animal rescue has become a popular topic recently, especially since the Hurricanes Katrina and Rita disasters during which over 15,000 animals were rescued. Much of this animal rescue was necessary due to two conditions: First, many owners left their pets behind because they only anticipated a short absence. Second, most human shelters refused to accommodate pets, so owners were forced to abandon them. The toll that these conditions imposed on the New Orleans area shelter workers, pets, and pet owners has spurred dramatically increased interest in animal rescue, which has resulted in the development of many animal-focused programs and organizations. Many animal rescue organizations exist across the United States, both publicly funded and private. Some operate locally, while others will send personnel to remote locations. Some are highly trained, while others have only a great deal of enthusiasm and volunteers. Regardless of resources available, animal rescue is a physically and mentally demanding and strenuous task that can last far beyond the immediate postdisaster period and long after the emergency volunteers have gone home. (See Photo 14.4.)

For example, the Joplin Humane Society in Missouri took in over 1,300 animals following the 2011 tornadoes that devastated that city. While more than 500 of them were reunited with their owners shortly after the tornadoes, over a year later some animals are still awaiting homes and the shelter is at full capacity. Some pet owners remain in temporary housing that does not allow pets, so their pets also remain at the Humane Society. The full scope of animal rescue cannot be covered here (the interested reader is referred to the Resources section of this chapter), but anyone interested in animal rescue and animal sheltering should contact the Humane Society of the United States (HSUS), the American Society for the Prevention of Cruelty to Animals (ASPCA), the American Humane Association (AHA), or their local humane organization and inquire about training and opportunities. Untrained volunteers may be turned away during a disaster despite their enthusiasm, as experience has shown that untrained animal rescue workers can make the situation more difficult for the overall rescue effort and can endanger both themselves and the animals they are attempting to rescue (Irvine 2006; McConnico et al. 2007). It should be noted that some aspects of rescue, particularly large-animal rescue, may require a veterinarian. These aspects include examination and injury assessment, chemical restraint, and emergency treatment of wounds. Veterinarians are also required to determine if an injury is severe enough that humane euthanasia is required to prevent animal suffering. (See Box 14.3.)

PHOTO 14.4 Hackberry, Louisiana, October 3, 2005. Cattle, rescued from the flooded marshes of lower Cameron Parish, are brought to the high school's rodeo pens to await sorting and return to their owners. Several thousand cattle, belonging to an estimated 15 ranchers, are still lost in the marshes and are being rescued by cowboys on horseback. (Photo by Win Henderson/FEMA.)

BOX 14.3   THE FUKUSHIMA ANIMAL HOLOCAUST

Following the March 2011 earthquake and tsunami that hit Japan, many residents of Fukushima prefecture were forced to evacuate due to the damage to the Fukushima Daiichi nuclear power plant. However, multiple reports indicate that the government of Japan made no efforts to rescue animals from Fukushima Prefecture. Evacuees were forced to leave their pets behind, as they were not permitted on evacuation buses. Livestock owners were forced to kill their animals or leave them to starve, and accusations that government officials were using inhumane methods of euthanasia have been made. Pet owners evacuated from the area of the power plant were prohibited from reentering the 20-km exclusion zone around the power plant, even though their pets had been left with only a few days of food and water. Animal rescue efforts were undertaken surreptitiously by several animal rescue groups, but they were stopped on multiple occasions by police. The Japanese government has not been forthcoming with information on animal casualties and rescue efforts in the exclusion zone, and rescue workers have been turned away despite evidence of diminishing radiation levels. The Hoshi family of Fukushima prefecture and other rescue volunteers have been catching and feeding animals in the exclusion zone despite the fines and imprisonment that will be imposed if they are caught by police. Other animal rescue groups are operating outside the radiation exclusion zone and have had some success in reuniting or adopting found animals, but those animals inside the exclusion zone are dependent on those few people willing to brave the police and the threat of radiation. There are no estimates available of the numbers of animals killed or abandoned as a result of the tsunami, but it is likely that the numbers were in the tens of thousands overall.

Source: Compiled from Fukushima Animal Holocaust Report parts 1 and 2 (2011) and Guttenfelder and Zackowitz (2011).

14.7   RECOVERY

The recovery phase following a disaster may last for months to years for humans involved, and the same is true of the animal victims. Some Hurricane Katrina families are still living in trailers or with relatives, awaiting the opportunity to rebuild their destroyed homes. Similarly, some animals rescued during the aftermath of the Joplin tornadoes still languish in shelters, and some owners are still looking for their lost pets. Owners who find their pets may discover that their new living situations do not allow them to keep the pet. The pet may have injuries or illnesses caused by the disaster that require chronic care or even euthanasia. I personally know of several cats whose asthma was so worsened by smoke from the 2010 California wildfires that their disease became refractory to treatment and they had to be euthanized. Other pets may have permanent disabilities from injury: amputations, poorly healed fractures, and heart failure or lung disease secondary to heartworm infection have all been seen in rescued pets. I have treated horses for more than three years following barn fires, as these horses required multiple skin grafts as well as treatment for smoke-inhalation-induced respiratory disease. These horses were the lucky ones, as most of their stablemates died in the fire. Livestock may become unruly and difficult to handle as well as more prone to flight responses. Animals that were starved may exhibit food-protective behaviors, including rapid or compulsive eating, sometimes to the point of vomiting.

Some animals undergo personality changes, becoming fearful or aggressive. Posttraumatic stress disorder (PTSD) has been diagnosed in animals just as in people, with similar symptoms: hyperalertness, inappropriate responses, difficulty sleeping, mood changes, irritability, and more. PTSD is often seen in military working dogs returning from a combat zone as well as natural-disaster survivors. Behavioral changes in pets may be so severe that owners give them up as a result, particularly if there are small children in the household. Children often do not understand that their beloved pet is not the same as it was before the disaster and may be injured by a formerly harmless pet responding in a new way to a previously tolerated stimulus. Pet owners should observe their pets closely following rescue in order to identify any new behaviors.

14.7.1 REHABILITATION

It should be evident that some animals may require significant rehabilitation following rescue. This may be as simple as supervised leash walks until a dog becomes accustomed to his changed neighborhood. It may also be very complex and expensive, such as an animal with a poorly healed fracture that needs multiple surgeries and physical therapy to regain mobility. Rehabilitation may be distressing to owners, too. Although animals have no body image and are not humiliated or embarrassed by loss of a limb or an eye, owners often find it very difficult to accept a pet with an amputation or a lost eye. Horses with chronic injuries or illnesses may no longer be suitable for riding, forcing some owners to rehome or euthanize them, as they cannot support a horse that cannot work. Highly performing show horses may not regain their prior level of performance even if no physical cause can be found, and lengthy retraining may be necessary. (See Photo 14.5.)

14.7.2 REUNIONS AND REHOMING

Despite the efforts of animal rescue organizations, some animals will inevitably fail to find their owners following a disaster. Owners may have been injured or killed, or their personal situations may not allow them to care for a pet. They may be preoccupied with caring for the human members of their family, or they may simply make the decision to walk away from a pet. Some animals may have been stray or feral prior to the disaster. In large-scale disasters, owners may be unable to track down their pets due to dispersal of rescued animals to multiple temporary shelter locations, involvement of many diverse rescue groups, and lack of centralized animal cataloguing. Regardless, rescue workers should not expect to be able to find the owners for all rescued animals. Some sources estimate that owners will retrieve less than half of rescued animals, while others quote 10%–20% reunion rates (Anderson and Anderson 2006; Louisiana SPCA 2006). The animals not reunited with their owners will have to be placed with brick-and-mortar shelters as emergency or temporary

PHOTO 14.5 The Louisiana SPCA temporary shelter in New Orleans following Hurricanes Katrina and Rita. This was the shelter that the LA-SPCA moved into after the evacuation shelter at Lamar-Dixon was closed. The LA-SPCA's permanent shelter had been destroyed in the flooding. (Photo credit: Jackson Hill Photography. With permission.)

shelters are gradually closed down after a disaster. Once the immediate threat period is over, permanent animal shelters around the area should be prepared to handle an influx of animals well above normal levels. Shelters may fill rapidly. Once rescue animals are dispersed to brick-and-mortar municipality shelters, owners may have a limited amount of time to reclaim their pet before it is either euthanized or placed for adoption.

Municipality animal shelters are of two basic types: the so-called kill shelters that hold an animal for a predetermined amount of time and then euthanize the animal if an owner is not found, and no-kill shelters that will house animals indefinitely until they are adopted. No-kill shelters may still euthanize an animal if it is found to be aggressive or if it has a severe injury or illness from which it is unlikely to recover. Obviously the no-kill shelters would be a preferable choice for rescued animals, but these shelters may be choosy about the animals they will accept. No-kill shelters have individual policies, but many tend to accept mostly good-tempered animals that would be expected to have a difficult time being adopted from a kill shelter: older pets, those with chronic but manageable diseases, and pets with permanent injuries such as amputations. The reason for this is that these pets would be unlikely to be adopted when there are young, healthy pets available. Shelters that do engage in euthanasia after a set amount of time will often be able to find homes for the puppies, kittens, and dogs or cats that appear to be mostly purebred, but damaged pets may not find a home in the time allotted. Rescue shelters may need to negotiate with permanent shelters to have animals accepted into their facility, especially if the facility is a no-kill shelter.

Breed-rescue organizations are another option for placement of animals, particularly dogs that appear to be purebred. These volunteer organizations are usually findable on the Internet and tend to be extremely helpful, as their volunteers are very enthusiastic about their favorite breed of dog. Some breed rescues will also accept mixed-breed dogs that are recognizably mostly the breed of interest. Relatively few of these organizations have brick-and-mortar shelters; instead, most rely on a network of foster-care volunteers to care for pets until permanent homes can be found. Most breed-rescue organizations keep excellent records of people to whom animals are adopted, and most also use some sort of screening process to ensure that the animal is going to an appropriate home. Many breed-rescue organizations may be located some distance away from the site of the disaster, but most also have a network of volunteers who are willing to transport pets to breed shelters or foster homes. As such, breed-rescue organizations may be a viable option for pets whose owners fail to retrieve them following a disaster. During my tenure as a shelter veterinarian on a military base, I worked closely with both the local civilian no-kill shelter and with breed-rescue organizations to place as many animals as possible with them. My shelter was required to euthanize animals after just 72 hours if no owner could be found, so we were always working against the clock to find either owners, homes, or alternative placements for the animals. Most of the personnel who worked at the shelter had adopted at least one pet from the shelter rather than see it euthanized, myself included. It is common to see shelter workers and foster families adopt pets for which they are responsible, as familiarity with an animal often breeds attachment.

14.7.3 DISASTER BENEFITS FOR ANIMALS

Disasters may occasionally provide unanticipated benefits for animals. Animal shelters are chronically short of funds. Donations to animal rescue and animal welfare associations increase during disasters, sometimes (but not often) in excess of the funds needed for the immediate crisis. Visibility of animal shelters and rescue organizations increases in the community, which can stimulate an influx of volunteers both during and after the crisis. Perhaps most significant, animal organizations can use disasters as a lever to induce local change. Shelter organizations have been able to use public attention and community involvement to spur improvements in their facilities and operations. The Plaquemines Parish Animal Welfare Society in Belle Chasse, Louisiana, raised funds to build a state-of-the-art animal shelter in the years following Hurricanes Katrina and Rita. The facility is several times larger and far more efficient, attractive, and user friendly than the previous concrete-block building. It contains not only animal housing, but also exercise runs, rooms in which clients can meet potential pets, a spay-and-neuter clinic, and the local animal control facilities. This facility would have been impossible without the attention focused on south Louisiana following the hurricanes, as donations to Louisiana humane societies poured in from all over the country once the plight of the New Orleans pets was publicized. Louisiana animal shelters were also quick to take advantage of available federal funding. Not all donations are monetary: Del Monte Foods and Best Friends Animal Society donated 41,000 pounds of dog food that was distributed to families affected by the 2010 Deepwater Horizon oil spill, while the ASPCA, Best Friends, and others initiated the Gulf Coast Companion Animal Relief Program. This program provided free veterinary care to pets of families affected by the oil spill (Louisiana SPCA 2010). None of this would have been possible without the focus on the Gulf Coast region that followed the 2005 hurricanes.

14.7.4 HUMAN PSYCHOLOGICAL IMPACT

The recovery phase following a disaster must also consider animal caretakers and owners as well as their animals. Animal owners and workers often feel a great deal of responsibility toward the animals entrusted to them, and may feel guilt and sadness at their loss. This may be exacerbated if animal owners have no other remembrances of their pet such as photographs, which may have been destroyed in the disaster. Animal caretakers may find themselves in need of mental health assistance, particularly if animals were lost or euthanized. Grief counseling or support groups may be indicated for owners grieving a lost pet. For livestock owners, the grief over the loss of animal life may be compounded with fear and insecurity about their future livelihood. A research study documented multiple social and psychological effects on farm families who lost livestock during the 2001 United Kingdom foot-and-mouth disease outbreak (Nusbaum, Wenzel, and Everly 2007). These included grief over animal loss, distress over animal welfare, loss of sense of control, isolation from neighbors and governments, financial problems, increased suicidal tendencies, and trauma to children after witnessing animal slaughter and parental distress. Over 80 suicides actually occurred among farmers. Farming communities also suffered from financial losses and uncertainty and loss of community cohesion. Veterinary clinic personnel and shelter workers are also at high risk for mental health issues following a disaster: Caregiver fatigue may set in either during or after the disaster (Irvine 2010). Animal shelter workers forced to euthanize animals may also experience either grief or loss of empathy secondary to their disaster work (Hall et al. 2004). Following Hurricanes Katrina and Rita, 50 of the original 65 Louisiana SPCA personnel resigned due to professional and personal trauma. Only one of the original seven humane officers (rescuers) stayed with the agency, the others resigning due to physical and emotional trauma associated with animal rescue (Louisiana SPCA 2006). PTSD is also seen in disaster workers in any capacity, but especially those whose jobs require them to encounter dead bodies (human or animal). Mental health counseling should be sought if discussion with colleagues, support groups or other coping mechanisms are insufficient.

14.8 IMPLICATIONS FOR ACTION

14.8.1 HOUSEHOLD AND FAMILY LEVEL

It is ultimately the responsibility of animal owners to prepare their animals for disasters, although depressingly few owners do so. Do a quick survey of your pet-owning friends and family. How many of them have a pet emergency response kit? Would they take their pets with them if they had to leave their homes? If not, why not? Do they know if their pets are welcome at friends' or relatives' houses? People who might be evacuating to friends or relatives elsewhere may need to find an alternate evacuation site if the relatives will not take their pets as well. Increasing the commitment of owners to their pets may improve pet transport during evacuations and decrease the number of animals needing to be rescued after a disaster. This may be attempted by programs designed to promote responsible pet ownership during nondisaster times, such as free or low-cost spay-and-neuter and vaccine clinics, community dog training or socializing programs, dog parks, and community awareness activities. Neighbors looking after neighbors can also inquire about pet evacuation plans, as lack of foresight regarding pets may cause some owners to leave pets behind. Owners should begin preparing to evacuate as soon as the initial possibility of a disaster is announced. This may allow them to secure space at a boarding kennel or veterinarian's office before they fill up, or to contact multiple friends or relatives to ask if they might accommodate visitors with pets. Owners should have a pet emergency kit for each pet, including all the equipment, supplies, and documentation that would be necessary for their pet to be admitted to a shelter. All of this material should be stored together in a readily accessible space, not an attic or remote storage space.

Owners of service animals should be particularly vigilant about keeping a handy evacuation kit for both themselves and their animal. Human health-care or assistance providers should also be notified of the kit's location and contents. Users of service animals should also ensure they have plans for their own evacuation along with their animals, as special arrangements may need to be made for animal transport. Service-animal owners who fail to plan may find themselves deprived of more than just companionship if their animal cannot physically travel on the conveyance with them. While federal law requires that service animals be allowed in public buildings and transportation and in emergency shelters, service-animal owners may still find that their animal is uncomfortable or unable to assist them in such situations and may prefer to make their own arrangements. Persons with service animals should identify "pet-friendly" shelters or motels, as their animals may have more comforts and assistance there than at a human-only shelter or, worse, left if behind. Owners of service animals should also develop a support network of people and organizations on whom they can call for assistance. This could include veterinarians, shelters, humane societies, and pet foster homes in their area.

14.8.2 FARMING FAMILIES

Family farms create a special situation. Owners of food animals and livestock should carefully plan their responses in the event of a disaster. If all animals on the premises cannot be moved simultaneously in farm-controlled conveyances, a priority list should be made of which animals to evacuate first. Plans should be made for the animals to shelter in place if they cannot be moved, to include facilities like cattle pads on high ground for floods or covered barns or windbreaks for severe weather. Farmers should work with their neighbors in the event animals must be evacuated under their own power through adjoining property. Horse owners should ensure their horse will willingly enter a trailer without the need for extensive convincing or chemical restraint.

14.8.3 COMMUNITY ORGANIZATIONAL LEVEL

Communities bear a great deal of responsibility for their own disaster preparedness. Community animal agencies (animal control and shelters) should develop detailed disaster plans for their areas. Human medical facilities have been required to have disaster plans for years, but animal facilities often lag far behind. Communities should also verify that they have appropriate insurance coverage for animal-related losses or damage. Municipal or county animal shelters should expect to be involved in both local and regional disasters, as they have animal-capable facilities, personnel familiar with animal needs, and significant local knowledge. While community shelters obviously have limited space, community animal workers may have knowledge of other facilities that might be used to shelter animals, local animal demographics, and local veterinarians who might be willing to assist. Municipalities should also contact veterinary clinics in their area to determine what they might be willing to contribute during a disaster.

Communities should also be proactive about educating their citizens about options for pets caught in disasters. Information about pet-friendly shelters should be readily available on community websites and via posters in community centers or mass mailings. Such information should include requirements for pets and owners wishing to use the shelter and contact information for an individual knowledgeable about the shelter. Communities can also decrease animal abandonment and animal deaths during disasters through programs that encourage responsible pet ownership and commitment of owners to their animals. These programs may include free or low-cost veterinary care, dog parks, community-sponsored dog training and educational programs on community-access television, posters in municipal buildings, and features in the local print or Internet media. Use of social media such as Facebook may allow community organizations to reach large numbers of pet owners efficiently. While these programs may seem to have little to do with disaster preparedness, evidence has shown that owners with minimal commitment to their pets are more likely to abandon them during hard times. Communities with robust mass communication skills regarding their pet disaster options are likely to have better compliance than areas whose options are not widely disseminated.

Community shelters and rescue organizations can be of significant help even in disasters by which they are not affected. Animal shelters might contact a shelter in an affected area and volunteer to temporarily house shelter animals. This may be done even before a disaster strikes, so that shelter animals may be preemptively evacuated as was done in Houston prior to Hurricane Ike. That can free the donor shelter's staff to provide services elsewhere in their affected community or even take care of their own families. Community shelters may also maintain a list of volunteers willing to foster either shelter animals or privately owned animals in the event of a disaster; this can also be invaluable to anyone trying to get an animal out of a danger zone. Community shelters can certainly be involved in animal rescue efforts following a disaster as well, as many shelter employees and volunteers may already be trained in disaster response, may be familiar with animal behavior and be comfortable around a wide variety of animals, and may be able to handle aggressive animals. Some may also be trained in paraveterinary skills, similar to a veterinary technician. Shelters can volunteer to house rescued pets, but should keep careful track of who those pets were received from so that they have the best chance of being reunited with their owners.

14.8.4   Veterinarians

Veterinary practices and veterinarians can also play a significant role in disaster preparedness (Heath et al. 1997). Veterinary clinics and hospitals should each have a detailed emergency response plan for animals in their care, particularly since owners may not be reachable during an emergency. Owners are also likely to believe that a veterinary facility is one of the safest places their animal could be during a disaster. Practice disaster plans should ensure that sufficient personnel can remain at the practice who will not be distracted by family or personal concerns. Veterinary clinics also need to ensure their business continuity, such that they can be reached by clients and can access supplies, equipment, and medical records during an emergency. This may require the development of an extensive emergency kit and even offsite storage of electronic medical records. Veterinarians may wish to make prearrangements for an alternate clinic site if there is damage by a disaster; this information can be communicated to clients ahead of time. Local veterinarians are often extremely willing to volunteer time, services, and even facilities during times of need, as service to society is part of the Veterinarian's Oath (Nusbaum, Rollin, and Wohl 2007). Veterinarians may also be enlisted to assist in identifying evacuation sites and transport options for animals, particularly horses and livestock. Veterinarians can also be intimately involved in disaster preparedness through client education. Veterinarians are largely trusted by their clientele (more so than human physicians), and so may have significant influence on their clients. One-on-one client education, presentations at community or club forums, and media releases can all provide information to animal owners.

Private-practice veterinarians have always had a role in the control of contagious animal diseases and the protection of our food supply by acting as local eyes and ears for state and federal veterinarians (Wenzel and Wright 2007). Veterinarians in practice will be the first to notice increased incidences of animal diseases; early recognition of disease outbreaks can enhance response time and help limit the outbreak. Veterinarians who see an increase in disease incidence or suspect a case of a foreign animal disease should contact their state veterinarian immediately. Veterinarians should also communicate with their local or state public health officer with regard to zoonotic disease occurrence. All accredited veterinarians should familiarize themselves with the basics of the Incident Command System, as that will allow greater efficiency and understanding of the disaster response network. Veterinarians interested in deeper involvement with disaster response may consider volunteering for a Veterinary Medical Assistance Team (VMAT), discussed in the next section.

Veterinarians may also find themselves in the role of providing psychological assistance to clients who have lost animals. As veterinarians are intimately involved in animal care and agriculture, they are uniquely qualified to empathize with bereaved clients suffering from animal loss.

Community organizations and local veterinarians may find themselves collaborating with State Agricultural Response Teams (SARTs). SARTs are multiagency coordination groups built of both governmental and private entities whose purpose is to improve disaster capabilities in the animal and agricultural sectors in their state. Many SARTs are based in a nonprofit organization that allows the SART to seek funding from many sources. Not all states have SARTs, but if present they can be an excellent resource for emergency preparedness. Your community may also have or wish to participate in a County Animal Response Team (CART) to better focus on the animals in your immediate community. CARTs are prepared to assist with many aspects of animal disaster management, from public service announcements to shelter identification and setup to providing the local knowledge needed to state and national assistance agencies. (See Box 14.4.)

BOX 14.4   RESCUING ANIMALS IN DISASTERS: SMART PRACTICES SPOTLIGHT ON BURKE COUNTY, NORTH CAROLINA, AND LOS ANGELES COUNTY, CALIFORNIA

Summary: During an emergency or disaster, taking care of large animals requires advance planning and workers who know how to handle and move animals to safety. Burke County Emergency Services developed a rescue plan and sponsored training for emergency workers. In Los Angeles County in California, the Department of Animal Care and Control organized and trained the LA County Equine Response Team.

It happens every time there's a major disaster. Animals are left behind and their owners are desperate to save them. Many take their own lives in their hands to rescue their pets or evacuate their livestock, making response operations ever more difficult for emergency management and responders.

That's why state and local governments across the country are including animal rescue and evacuation operations in their disaster planning. Take North Carolina, for example. Thousands of animals died and hundreds of others had to be rescued as a result of the flooding caused by Hurricane Floyd in 1999. Randy McKinney, assistant director of Burke County Emergency Services, was part of a swift water rescue team that was sent in to work in that disaster. "After we finished rescuing people, they asked us to rescue animals," he said. "And we were at a loss. In a flood, you just don't put a large animal in the boat with you."

After Hurricane Floyd, McKinney said, the state asked all the counties to update their emergency operations plans to include policies and procedures for rescuing animals in disasters or emergencies. That meant identifying agencies that should be involved and who needed to be contacted, including a call-down list of veterinarians that work with large animals. Burke County Emergency Services decided to do more, organizing three days of large-animal rescue training for emergency workers. They learned about equipment needed to extricate animals from precarious situations, medications that can be utilized to calm traumatized animals and generally how to behave around animals in distress.

The Los Angeles County Department of Animal Care and Control established the LA County Equine Response Team, which is made up of experienced volunteers who are trained and ready to help the department evacuate large animals during emergency situations. Team members have to complete an extensive large animal handling training program and learn how to work with frightened animals in difficult situations. Putting together the Equine Response Team involved two years of intense development and the cooperation and involvement of staff not only from the Department of Animal Care and Control, but the Fire Department, the Sheriff's Department, Risk Management, the California Highway Patrol and county attorneys.

Source: Transcribed verbatim from http://www.fema.gov/emergency/managers/animalrescue.shtm

14.8.5 National Level

Although most of the programs and policies that affect animals in disasters are present at the community, county, or state levels, some federal programs exist that are designed to assist disaster operations affecting animals. The most significant of these is the PETS Act of 2006. The PETS Act (Pets Evacuation and Transportation Standards Act HR 3858) amends the Robert T. Stafford Disaster Relief and Emergency Assistance Act to require greater involvement of FEMA in animal disaster planning (Govtrack 2006). The act demands that FEMA verify that pets are covered in local and state disaster preparedness plans. It also allows FEMA to provide financial support such as grants to improve infrastructure such as animal evacuation shelters and to fulfill the fundamental needs of pets, including food, water, and shelter. Service animals are also included in the PETS Act, but horses and livestock are not. The same act also allows state animal agencies to be reimbursed for costs incurred in response to a federally declared emergency. If state and community animal organizations take advantage of the opportunities presented by the PETS Act, it could dramatically improve the handling of animals during disasters. Several states have also enacted "No Pet Left Behind" laws that complement the PETS Act. These laws mandate pet accommodations during disasters at the state level by allowing pets on public transportation and in other nonfederally controlled places during evacuations.

Other funds or equipment to improve local disaster preparedness may be obtained through solicitation of area businesses or various animal-related organizations. The HSUS maintains a financial assistance page that can guide interested municipal organizations in securing funding. Some of this funding may be available to nongovernmental community organizations as well.

The AVMA has published many documents and guidelines on animal disaster management. The AVMA also sponsors the Veterinary Medical Assistance Teams (VMATs). The VMATs are volunteer teams of veterinarians, veterinary technicians, and support staff whose assistance may be requested by a state afflicted with a disaster. VMATs are prepared to handle many of the veterinary or technical aspects of animal disaster management, including evaluation of disaster situations, assisting with proper sheltering of animals, providing preventive medicine services, performing water quality and sanitation inspections, and addressing environmental and agricultural issues. VMAT teams can also provide food inspections, emergency animal medical care, carcass disposal, wildlife rehabilitation, zoonotic disease control, and collection of laboratory samples, if needed. Obviously, one VMAT team cannot simultaneously perform all of these functions, but VMAT teams can complement the resources already available in the community. VMATs may also work hand-in-hand with the Army Veterinary Corps, as they did on the island of St. Thomas after Hurricane Louise in 1995. Other national-level nongovernmental organizations can also offer assistance. The HSUS sponsors DARTs, or Disaster Animal Rescue Teams, which are available to respond to any type of disaster, whether natural or human-induced. The ASPCA can deploy teams of trained personnel to assist in animal sheltering and rescue as well, as can other animal-welfare organizations

PHOTO 14.6 The ASPCA deployed an assistance team to Joplin, Missouri, following the 2011 tornadoes that devastated the city. (Photo credit: Joplin Humane Society. With permission.)

such as the American Humane Association, Code 3 Associates, and Emergency Animal Rescue Services. Community shelter managers and disaster planners are encouraged to enlist the assistance of these teams for any qualifying disaster. In addition to the obvious benefits to animals from having trained animal response teams present, there are likely also human psychological benefits from evacuees knowing that trained veterinary disaster-assistance specialty teams are operating in the area. When multiple animal rescue organizations are available, VMATs usually handle livestock while the others focus on small-animal rescue. (See Photo 14.6.)

14.9 SUMMARY

Disregard of animals during disasters has caused the loss or death of uncounted animals and commensurate human distress. Although special accommodations and plans are required to appropriately handle animals in disaster situations, implementing such plans will improve human compliance and reduce both human and animal distress before, during, and after a disaster. Animal disaster preparedness is complex and requires special training, but the success of animal disaster preparedness ultimately depends on the animal owner. Training and disaster assistance can be provided to individuals and organizations by multiple agencies, including FEMA, AVMA, HSUS, and ASPCA. Increasing attention is being paid to animal disaster preparedness through the implementation of state and federal legislation.

DISCUSSION QUESTIONS

1. Why are people so attached to their animals? Is this good or bad?
2. Why do humans experience guilt and sadness when confronted with animal suffering?
3. What are the animal demographics in your community? Use available resources to find estimated numbers for small animals, horses, livestock, and exotic animals in your town or county.
4. How could you personally assist with animal emergency preparedness?
5. What facilities in your area would be appropriate as emergency animal shelters? What factors do you think might be important in making such choices?

6. If you have animals, are you ready for an evacuation? What items do you think would be important to have in your animal emergency kit?

7. Does your veterinarian have a clinic disaster plan? To what location would your pet be evacuated if it were in the vet clinic at the time of a rapid-onset disaster?

REFERENCES

Anderson, A., and L. Anderson. 2006. *Rescued: Saving animals from disaster*. Novato, CA: New World Library.

Anthony, L., and G. Spence. 2007. *Babylon's Ark: The incredible wartime rescue of the Baghdad Zoo*. New York: Thomas Dunne Books/St. Martin's Press.

Associated Press. 2011. Report: Twisters that hit SW Mo. claim about 3K turkeys. *Joplin Globe*, May 27. http://www.joplinglobe.com/tornadomay2011/x320356571/Twisters-that-hit-SW-Mo-claim-about-3K-turkeys.

AVMA. 2007. U.S. pet ownership and demographics sourcebook. http://www.avma.org/reference/marketstats/sourcebook.asp.

———. 2009. Policy determination on animal carcass risk in natural disasters. http://www.avma.org/KB/Policies/Pages/Animal-Carcass-Risk-in-Natural-Disasters.aspx.

Barker, S. B. 1999. Therapeutic aspects of the human-companion animal interaction. *Psychiatric Times* 16:45–46.

Barker, S. B., and R. T. Barker. 1988. The human-canine bond: Closer than family ties? *Journal of Mental Health Counseling* 10:46–56.

Bassert, J. M., and D. M. McCurnin. 2010. Restraint and handling of animals. In: *Clinical textbook for veterinary technicians*. 7th ed. Philadelphia: W. B. Saunders Co.

Beaver, B. V., R. Gros, E. M. Bailey, and C. S. Lovern. 2006. Report of the 2006 National Animal Disaster Summit. *Journal of the American Veterinary Medical Association* 229 (6): 943–48.

Blake, P. A. 1989. Communicable diseases: The public health consequences of disasters, 1989. U.S. Department of Health and Human Services (Atlanta), 7–12.

CNN. 2005. Katrina kills most fish in New Orleans aquarium, September 9. http://articles.cnn.com/2005-09-07/tech/katrina.zoos_1_zoos-and-aquariums-american-zoo-aquarium-association-web-site?_s=PM:TECH.

DEFRA (Department for Environment, Food and Rural Affairs). 2004. U.K. FMD Data Archive. http://footandmouth.csl.gov.uk/secure/fmdstatistics/slaughtmonth.cfm.

DOJ (U.S. Department of Justice). 2010. ADA 2010 revised requirements for service animals. DOJ, Civil Rights Division, Disability Rights Section.

FEMA. 2010. Guidance on planning for integration of functional need support services in general population shelters, 28–29. Washington, DC: FEMA.

FEMA/DHS. 2007. Best practice shelter operations: Pet-friendly shelters. http://www.lsart.org/sites/site-1707/documents/ShelterOperations-PetFriendlyShelters2.pdf.

Fukushima Animal Holocaust. 2011. http://ireport.cnn.com/docs/DOC-708650.

Govtrack.us. 2006. HR 3858 (109th): Pets Evacuation and Transportation Standards Act of 2006. http://www.govtrack.us/congress/bills/109/hr3858.

Guttenfelder, D., and M. G. Zackowitz. 2011. Japan nuclear zone: The dogcatchers. http://ngm.nationalgeographic.com/2011/12/japan-nuclear-zone/guttenfelder-field-notes.

Hall, M. J., A. Ng, R. J. Ursano, H. Holloway, C. Fullerton, and J. C. Casper. 2004. Psychological impact of the human-animal bond in disaster preparedness and response. *Journal of Psychiatric Practice* 10:368–74.

Hawaii Cooperative Extension Service. 1998. Composted animal manures: Precautions and processing. http://www.ctahr.hawaii.edu/oc/freepubs/pdf/AWM-1.pdf.

Heath, S. E., A. M. Beck, P. H. Kass, and L. T. Glickman. 2001. Risk factors for pet evacuation failure after a slow-onset disaster. *Journal of the American Veterinary Medical Association* 218 (12): 1905–10.

Heath, S. E., J. Hooks, K. Marshall, R. Dorn, R. D. Linnabary, and J. Casper. 1997. Participation of veterinarians in disaster management. *Journal of the American Veterinary Medical Association* 210 (3): 325–28.

Heath, S. E., S. K. Voeks, and L. T. Glickman. 2001. Epidemiologic features of pet evacuation failure in a rapid-onset disaster. *Journal of the American Veterinary Medical Association* 218 (2): 1898–1904.

Hudson, L. C., H. M. Berschneider, K. K. Ferris, and S. L. Vivrette. 2001. Disaster relief management of companion animals affected by the floods of Hurricane Floyd. *Journal of the American Veterinary Medical Association* 218 (3): 354–59.

Irvine, L. 2004. Providing for pets during disasters: An exploratory study. Quick Response Report 171, Natural Hazards Center, University of Colorado.

———. 2006. Providing for pets during disasters, part II: Animal response volunteers in Gonzales, Louisiana. Quick Response Report 187. Natural Hazards Center, University of Colorado.

———. 2010. A thousand dogs barking. *Natural Hazards Observer* 34 (4): 1.

Jones, K. E., K. Dashfield, A. B. Downend, and C. M. Otto. 2004. Search-and-rescue dogs: An overview for veterinarians. *Journal of the American Veterinary Medical Association* 225 (6): 854–60.

Leith v. Frost. 2008. Appellate Court of Illinois, 4th District. http://www.animallaw.info/cases/causil2008 wl5473300.htm.

Louisiana SPCA. 2006. Hurricane Katrina: A Year in Review, 2006. http://la-spca.org/page.aspx?pid=297.

———. 2010. The Gulf Coast Companion Animal Relief Program. http://la-spca.org/gulfcoastrelief.

Madigan, J. E., and J. Whittemore. 2000. The role of the equine practitioner in disasters. *Journal of the American Veterinary Medical Association* 216 (8): 1238–39.

Mallin, M. A., M. H. Posey, M. R. McIver, D. C. Parsons, S. H. Ensign, and T. D. Alphin. 2002. Impacts and recovery from multiple hurricanes in a Piedmont-coastal plain system. *BioScience* 52:999–1010.

McConnico, R. S., D. D. French, B. Clark, K. E. Mortensen, M. Littlefield, and R. M. Moore. 2007. Equine rescue and response activities in Louisiana in the aftermath of Hurricanes Katrina and Rita. *Journal of the American Veterinary Medical Association* 231 (3): 384–92.

Mote Marine Laboratory. 2012. Two years after Deepwater Horizon: Mote's oil spill response. http://www.mote.org/index.php?src=news&srctype=detail&category=Newsroom&refno=595.

Mutch, B., and P. Keller. 2010. Case study: Lives lost, lessons learned—The victims and survivors of the 2005–2006 Texas and Oklahoma wildfires. Wildland Fire Lessons Learned Center. http://www.scribd.com/doc/39355558/Lives-Lost-Lessons-Learned-The-05-06-TX-and-OK-Wildfires.

National Wildlife Federation. 2012. Compare the *Exxon Valdez* and BP oil spills. http://www.nwf.org/Oil-Spill/Effects-on-Wildlife/Compare-Exxon-Valdez-and-BP-Oil-Spills.aspx.

ND-SWC (North Dakota State Water Commission). 1997. The floods of 1997: A special report. http://www.swc.state.nd.us/4dlink9/4dcgi/GetSubCategoryPDF/36/floodbk.pdf.

NOAA (National Oceanic and Atmospheric Administration). 2011. Gulf spill restoration damage assessment. http://www.gulfspillrestoration.noaa.gov/2012/03/study-shows-some-gulf-dolphins-severely-ill/.

Noah, D. L., D. L. Noah, and H. R. Crowder. 2002. Biological terrorism against animals and humans: A brief review and primer for action. *Journal of the American Veterinary Medical Association* 221 (1): 41–43.

Nusbaum, K. E., B. E. Rollin, and J. S. Wohl. 2007. The veterinary profession's duty of care in response to disasters and food animal emergencies. *Journal of the American Veterinary Medical Association* 231 (2): 200–2.

Nusbaum, K. E., J. G. W. Wenzel, and G. S. Everly. 2007. Psychologic first aid and veterinarians in rural communities undergoing livestock depopulation. *Journal of the American Veterinary Medical Association* 231 (5): 692–94.

ProMED archive (International Society for Infectious Diseases). 2012. Number 20120425-1113040.2012. Leptospirosis—Peru (Loreto) fatal. ProMED mail. http://www.promedmail.org/.

Slensky, K. A., K. J. Drobatz, A. B. Downend, and C. M. Otto. 2002. Deployment morbidity among search-and-rescue dogs used after the September 11, 2001, terrorist attacks. *Journal of the American Veterinary Medical Association* 225 (6): 868–73.

Sofair, J. B. 2002. Pet medicine. *Psychiatric Times* 21:35–36.

Soric, S., M. P. Belanger, and C. Wittnich. 2008. A method for decontamination of animals involved in floodwater disasters. *Journal of the American Veterinary Medical Association* 232 (3): 364–70.

Wenzel, J. G. W., and J. C. Wright. 2007. Veterinary accreditation and some new imperatives for national preparedness. *Journal of the American Veterinary Medical Association* 230 (9): 1309–12.

Wing, S., S. Freedman, and L. Band. 2002. The potential impact of flooding on confined animal feeding operations in eastern North Carolina. *Environmental Health Perspectives* 110:387–91.

RESOURCES

- American Red Cross. Pet Sheltering: Building Community Response. May 2007. https://www.llis.dhs.gov/member/secure/detail.cfm?content_id=26529.
- American Veterinary Medical Association. http://www.avma.org.
- American Veterinary Medical Association, Centers for Disease Control and Prevention. Interim Guidelines for Animal Health and Control of Disease Transmission in Pet Shelters. Oct 2005. https://www.llis.dhs.gov/member/secure/detail.cfm?content_id=19712.
- American Veterinary Medical Association. Development of State/Local Animal Care Plans. 19 April 2001. https://www.llis.dhs.gov/member/secure/detail.cfm?content_id=17416.

- FEMA: Rescuing Animals in Disasters. http://www.fema.gov/emergency/managers/animalrescue.shtm.
- Florida State Agricultural Response Team. Pets and Disasters: Identifying Community Bureau of Land Management Mustang and Burro Adoption Program. http://www.blm.gov/wo/st/en/prog/whbprogram.html.
- LLIS.gov: https://www.llis.dhs.gov/index.do contains over 2,000 documents related to animals in disasters. Registration is required.
- Louisiana Humane Society Hurricane Katrina Report. https://www.la-spca.org/hurricanekatrina.
- National Organization on Disability: For Owners of Pets or Service Animals. http://nod.org/research_publications/emergency_preparedness_materials/for_owners_of_pets_or_sevice_animals/.
- Ready.gov: http://www.ready.gov includes a Community Pet Preparedness Toolkit and other resources.

15 The Nature of Human Communities

Pam Jenkins

CONTENTS

15.1 CHAPTER PURPOSE

Disasters change communities. This chapter explores the complex dynamic between communities and disasters. In some disasters, communities are brought closer together, and in others, they lessen community ties and deepen existing inequalities. Additionally, the narratives that communities tell and that others tell about the disaster influence a community's ability to understand and recover. In the twenty-first century, how communities develop and how disasters occur has changed. This chapter reviews how a community can plan for a disaster by building on its strengths and strategizing for resiliency. This chapter also suggests that disaster professionals must be involved in the work of community building if they are to be successful at fostering long-term disaster preparedness and resiliency.

15.2   OBJECTIVES

As a result of reading this chapter, the reader should be able to

1. Explain how the term community is defined
2. Discuss the possible effects of the disaster on the community
3. Describe the characteristics of a resilient community and the challenges to long-term resiliency
4. Understand the role that disaster professionals have to play in developing resilient communities

15.3   INTRODUCTION

The complex effects of disaster on community offer an avenue to study the ways that communities work together and the ways that communities come apart. When a disaster happens, the world focuses on the dramatic moments of the event. These moments of crisis do not happen in a vacuum: Disasters happen in a context to specific individuals, families, and communities. To understand a disaster, scholars should also know the communities. Researchers are also members of communities, sometimes the ones dramatically affected by disasters (see Box 15.1).

BOX 15.1   MY COMMUNITY AND HURRICANE KATRINA

New Orleans is a community of neighborhoods. I grew up in a small town in the Midwest, and New Orleans had that same small-town sensibility. I could not go somewhere where I didn't run into someone I knew. My neighborhood was a walkable, friendly place to live. In many ways, New Orleans was the best of a small town, the closeness without provincialism. To be sure, it was a poor city with a high rate of interpersonal violence, not-so-good public schools, and other social problems. But living here, I was part of a rich culture where celebrating life through food, music, and friends was part of everyday life.

Living in New Orleans had all three aspects of community discussed in this chapter. We were a community of place with our own traditions unique to the American landscape. New Orleans was also a community of shared interests where people came together to work on the serious problems of the city. In this context of place and interest, we developed a wide and diverse attachment to others. It was never easy to live in New Orleans; the storm made it even harder.

The hurricane struck New Orleans on August 29, 2005. By August 31, 80% of the city was flooded, and 1,400 people had perished. Entire communities were washed away. We were unmoored, lost without the anchor of our neighborhoods. One by one, my neighbors and I returned to see our homes. Nearly everyone I knew had damage. Before the storm, we came together for many reasons, but after the storm we came together to throw out each other's belongings and tear out the walls and floors of our homes.

In my experience, my community (not necessarily the official response) became a therapeutic community. Our friendships deepened. Strangers came to help. There is something about having your taken-for-granted everyday life destroyed that puts into relief what we lost. The old New Orleans became so very precious to us. The recovery of New Orleans is uneven. Some neighborhoods are totally back; other neighborhoods may only, seven years later, have one house on a block rebuilt. But in each community, people who remain share how they came home and how they rebuilt. Neighborhood associations are thriving, and new people are moving in.

Yet, in this recovery, I know I stand in privilege. I had a job, insurance, friends, and family. Others did not recover in the same way; many of the social ills remain. Our ability to build community before Hurricane Katrina determines how New Orleans will fare in the future.

Most survivor narratives emphasize individual and small groups, but rarely take into consideration the history of a community. Contrasting Hurricane Katrina to the 2010 floods in Nashville, community members from Nashville stated that the floods (where 19 people lost their lives and there were $1 billion dollars in property damage) showed how the community could "take care of its own." Throughout the coverage, the narrative of the flood for residents of middle Tennessee was that they could manage this disaster. Country star Brad Paisley's statement shows this response to the flood, "I've never seen a community rally like this town has. There's been hardly any looting. There's been amazing stories of churches that flooded the streets like the river did and help people out. If there's a silver lining, it's that the world is getting to see Nashville at its best through this tragedy" (Daren 2010).

It is a badge of honor that communities can "pick themselves up," especially in contrast to the depiction of the survivors of Hurricane Katrina. These events in Joplin, Missouri, and Nashville, Tennessee, while devastating, do not compare to the lasting effects of the levee breaches in New Orleans and the hurricane damage to the Mississippi Gulf Coast. Reporting about disaster shows the public the event, the response and, sometimes, the recovery. What is consistently missing from the usual description of the disaster is an understanding of the social and economic conditions pre-event. What were the strengths of the community before the disaster? And, subsequently, what does the community become after a disaster? These key questions allow scholars to explore how communities can become prepared for a future acute crisis.

Disasters happen in the context of their communities. Hurricane Katrina and the subsequent levee breaches are examples of how the response did not know the community. The unique culture of New Orleans and the persistent inequality in New Orleans helped to create the conditions that produced the horrific aftermath of the levee breach. The Army Corps of Engineers' inattention to the levees resulted in the flooding, and the slow response of federal, state, and local governments to the disaster meant that people were abandoned and left on their own.

Although the city evacuation plan was one of the few in the country to include public transportation in its evacuation plans, officials (for a wide variety of reasons) failed to deploy public transportation before the storm (Litman 2005), even though the prior census showed that nearly one-fourth of the residents did not have their own transportation. As then-Senator Barack Obama (2005) noted,

> Whoever was in charge of planning was so detached from the realities of inner city life in New Orleans...that they couldn't conceive of the notion that they couldn't load up their SUVs, put $100 worth of gas in there, put some sparkling water [in] and drive off to a hotel and check in with a credit card...this other America was somehow not on people's radar screen.

National and state emergency planners did not take into consideration both the strengths and the challenges of New Orleans. Family ties are one of the strengths of a city like New Orleans. When people evacuated, they evacuated with their entire families, in caravans that included multiple generations. This community characteristic would have been useful in planning. Planning needed to reflect that people would be more likely to leave if they could take their families and could afford to go. The agony of neighborhood after neighborhood that struggled on their own to get people out and save each other became an important and continuing part of the Katrina story.

15.4 WHAT IS A COMMUNITY?

There is little agreement about what makes up a community. *Community* is a term used by politicians, scholars, and community organizers to denote many types of relationships. Communities, like disasters, are not static—they change over time. This clarion call for community input becomes a symbol for groups of people that share some similarities. Community can mean place; it can mean culture; it can mean shared interests or values. Most communities have borders, some of which are defined, and others have borders that cannot be seen. How human beings live together and build relationships is complex. Brint (2001, 1) describes the enduring qualities of community:

> It is not at all surprising that the idea of community retains its power as a symbol and an aspiration. The term suggests many appealing features of human social relationships—a sense of familiarity and safety, mutual concern and support, continuous loyalties, even the possibility of being appreciated for one's full personality and contribution to group life rather than for narrower aspects of rank and achievement.

We all want to belong to a community or think we do belong to a community or communities. We have our friends, families, church groups, or neighbors. In any emergency situation, we most often turn to our closest group first, but will turn to the larger community for help and information. Community is the subtext of our social life; it is not surprising it has many definitions. These definitions can and do overlap, which presents difficulties for both practitioners and scholars. The following three types of community are general categories that are not all inclusive, but give a broad view of this concept.

Community as place. The most common use of the word denotes a location. We think of community most often as a neighborhood or town. People choose to live in a particular location for a variety of reasons: There might be good schools; it is where they grew up; or, perhaps, it is all they can afford. During and after a disaster, the community of place is disrupted and can be destroyed.

Community as shared interests. This definition refers to those groups built by shared interests and culture. This group may reflect the church group one belongs to or the chess group from the weekend. It may also reflect political or economic interests that are shared. Whether the disaster affects this type of community depends on whether it is place-based or virtual. This type of community may provide some support after a disaster.

Communities as attachment. This community refers to those people in one's life linked by care. Family is the obvious example here as well as friends. In a disaster, if members of this community are not place-based, they can be support for those in the disaster area.

All types of these communities are undergoing change that will affect efforts to increase resiliency and also prepare for future storms. First, communities of place have undergone significant change (Warren 1963). These changes happen over time, and planning sometimes falls behind the new landscapes. Small towns and villages that defined the United States are disappearing, replaced by suburbs and metropolitan communities that flow into one another. The boundaries of many communities are no longer discrete, but continuous. These boundaries in communities become important during all phases of a disaster. Community boundaries can determine the order of evacuation and timing of return, and boundaries between regions also influence the ways that resources are shared and assistance provided.

All types of communities are affected by new technologies like Facebook, Twitter, blogs, and Google Earth. These virtual networks are used to keep track of family during a disaster and to let others know what is needed. They can also be used to disseminate warnings and information about danger, as well as to provide vital information during an event. During a California wildfire that destroyed more than 1,500 homes, social networking sites (like Facebook, Myspace, etc.) were used to keep the community apprised of the situation in real time (instead of waiting for daily press reports), and allowed anyone to share information. These new technologies have many implications for disaster response coordination. According to Eric Rasmussen, president and CEO of the nonprofit organization Innovative Support to Emergencies, Diseases, and Disaster:

> We can send an SMS [short message service/texting] message onto Google Earth in an emergency center, and it sees a dot with a color-coded response, with my name and date. Right underneath that, there's a button that

says reply, and aid workers can send a note that we have the resources you need 2 miles north. ... Suddenly there's a two-way conversation using nothing but a cell phone with one bar. (Olson 2008)

15.4.1 Sociological Understanding of Community

In sociology, community studies have been historically based on the concepts from Ferdinand Tonnies (1887/1963). *Gemeinschaft*: In this type of community, the social interactions emphasize the group interests over the individuals, a common language or culture, and social bonds that are based on tradition. Much of the writing about life in the rural United States used the concept of gemeinschaft as the basis of their studies. Gesellschaft, on the other hand, represents a greater difference in ways of life, including different beliefs and more distant interactions, with a greater sense of rules and regulations.

Other community scholars also note that multiple communities coexist and overlap in a "mosaic of communities" (Marsh and Buckle 2001). People living in the same geographic area can have vastly different values, sense of community, access to services, interests, religions, or sense of obligation to others. Even when people do share characteristics of a community, they may not realize that they are a community or act like a community. Community solidarity certainly does not emerge from simple geographical closeness, or even from shared interests or needs. Prior to effective community disaster work (education, risk analysis, mitigation, or response training), a sense of community bonding and obligation must exist.

Brint (2001) provides an overview of the difficulty of studying and operationalizing community. While he criticizes the term *community* and the ways in which community studies are conducted, he does argue that some communities are more suited for the modern world. He concludes that communities that are more loosely connected and activity based is where "the best hopes exist for bringing some of the virtues of community to the modern world, while at the same avoiding its characteristic vices and its purely mythical connotations" (Brint 2001, 20). Community is a construct with many meanings used in a variety of ways. While difficult, understanding communities is essential to prepare for and survive a disaster. Individual families may rebuild, but communities come back.

15.5 DISASTERS

Much of the earlier literature in disasters referred to natural disasters as "acts of God" and other types of disasters as human made. This dichotomy does not reflect the growing link between disasters that seem random (such as hurricanes or tornadoes), and the disasters that are caused by human-made actions. Hurricane Katrina epitomized this newer version of disaster (Brunsma and Picou 2008). Natech (natural disaster–triggered technological) disasters occur when natural disasters produce direct, indirect, and/or purposeful releases of toxic and hazardous materials into the biophysical environment (Brunsma and Picou 2008). Further, the intensity of the storm may have been enhanced by the global climate change, but the flooding that devastated New Orleans was due to failure in the levee system. This idea that disasters may be both natural and human made alters how to respond to the next event.

Since Hurricane Katrina, the earthquake in Haiti, and the Indian Ocean tsunami, social scientists have attempted to not only broaden the categories of disaster, but also to broaden how disaster researchers work. Tierney (2007, 520–21) states that disaster researchers must begin to think about disasters differently:

> Disaster researchers must stop organizing their inquiries around problems that are meaningful primarily to the institutions charged with managing disasters and instead concentrate on problems that are meaningful to the discipline. They must integrate the study of disasters with core sociological concerns such as social inequality, societal diversity and social change.

A broader understanding (Williams 2008) may be required so that these larger scale disasters can be analyzed and new policies developed.

The concept of community is one of those broad sociological concepts that are critical to any current study of disaster. The effects of disasters on communities are not time limited. The effects range from the short-term, immediate effects and then the longer-lasting effects that linger for years and sometimes decades. As we have seen so poignantly in Hurricane Katrina, the response can be as devastating as the event itself. First, there is some place disruption (Bruhn 2005). In a disaster, no matter how small, the physical landscape changes. In a tornado, such as in Joplin, Missouri, people emerge from a shelter to see their environment completely altered. The physical landscape is the most visually dramatic aspect of a disaster, but the social landscape may never be the same. People are killed and injured in the disaster. As well, people have mental and physical effects that last longer than the time it takes to repair the physical damage. In Erickson's (1978) study of the Buffalo Creek flood, he concluded that it was not so much the water, but that it was the separation from meaningful places and people that caused greater trauma. The process of recovery also adds to the stress and trauma. While the new Joplin or Nashville may look somewhat like the old places, people still remember what the old place looked like, and they remember the trauma of how the familiar was destroyed.

Inequalities in place before a disaster occurs are often reproduced after a disaster. In the early recovery of a disaster, it appears that people from all walks of life are working together for everyone. As the recovery continues, the inequalities prior to the disaster can reemerge. The inequalities (Lowe and Shaw 2009) can show up in every phase of the disaster, from response to preparedness. The Louisiana Road Home program (see Box 15.2) is a good example of the inequalities that resurfaced after a disaster. These inequalities are not just on an individual level, but a community and institutional level as well.

BOX 15.2   THE LOUISIANA ROAD HOME PROGRAM

Issues of race and class in recovery collide when evaluating the Road Home program implemented in Louisiana after Hurricane Katrina. The Road Home program, funded by the U.S. Department of Housing and Urban Development (HUD) for an estimated $10.5 billion, is the largest housing redevelopment program in the history of the United States. Road Home began solely as a program to help homeowners rebuild after the storm, but it was eventually extended to cover rental property. The purpose of the program was to supplement funds for recovery after the storm available to homeowners in addition to private insurance and federal flood insurance. The Road Home began accepting applications in July 2006 and stopped new applications on July 31, 2007. More than 186,000 homeowners applied for grants through the program (Eden and Boren 2008). The homeowner had three options in the application process for a grant: (1) monies for rebuilding, (2) funds to purchase a new home, and (3) a buyout by the state of the damaged home (Fletcher 2011).

The funds were channeled through the Louisiana Recovery Authority (LRA) to a private company, ICF International. LRA was established by the state to oversee administration of federal disaster funds. From the beginning, the program came under intense scrutiny. In addition, the LRA contracted with RAND to conduct their own evaluation that showed a flawed program that took months or years to bring relief to a homeowner (Eden and Boren 2008), if at all.

In 2008, the Greater New Orleans Fair Housing Action Center, National Fair Housing Alliance, and five African-American homeowners filed a class action lawsuit against HUD and the Louisiana Recovery Authority (LRA). The suit alleged that the LRA's Road Home program discriminates against African-American homeowners in New Orleans. The lawsuit was filed in the U.S. District Court for the District of Columbia.

The suit stated that the formula to calculate grants created by ICF (approved by the LRA and HUD) used the prestorm value of a resident's home rather than an actual estimate of rebuilding costs. As a consequence, black moderate- and low-income homeowners received less money than their counterparts, who were mostly white, living in comparably built and equally damaged but higher valued homes. The suit stated that the grants from Road Home should be based on rebuilding costs rather than the prestorm value of the homes. In July 2011, the federal government approved a settlement that awarded $62 million to Louisiana under its new Blight Reduction Grant Adjustment program. In addition, HUD and Louisiana changed the Road Home program grant formula to provide full relief to more than 13,000 homeowners. All eligible low- and moderate-income homeowners (mostly African Americans in New Orleans) received uncapped additional compensation grants (approximately $473 million), based on the estimated cost of damage to their homes and not the much lower prestorm market value of their homes (Fletcher 2011).

Using New Orleans as a case study, Adams, Van Hattum, and English (2009, 616) refer to the long-term effects on communities and individuals as "chronic disaster syndrome." This conceptualization is based on a multifaceted view of displacement. Displacement refers to those who were out of the city for years; displacement also refers to those who came back but were not able to return to their homes; and finally displacement refers to those who are permanently displaced (after Hurricane Katrina, nearly 100,000 people). They describe this syndrome as a confluence of three factors. They define chronic disaster syndrome as:

1. Individual suffering in the form of effects of chronic trauma and long-term displacement
2. The workings of disaster capitalism (as revealed in the case of Katrina's aftermath) tied to the undermining of public infrastructures of social welfare and their replacement with private-sector service provision through contracts with for-profit corporations
3. The ways that displacement functions within disaster capitalism as an ongoing, productive way of life

Klein (2008) refers to the shock doctrines that can occur in a disaster. This happens when the collapse is so severe after a disaster that a new government arrangement can occur between the state and private contractors. In these arrangements, a new plan to rearrange social institutions occurs that changes how services are provided. Two rearrangements from Hurricane Katrina illustrate these differences. First, the closure of the public schools immediately after the storm and their reopening as mostly charter schools is considered one of the largest education experiments in the history of the United States. At the same time, four of the largest public housing units were closed. This closure effectively delayed or prevented some people's return. (See Photo 15.1.)

Bruhn (2005, 108) states that disasters define communities; they put them "on the map." Cordova, Alaska, the Lower 9th Ward in New Orleans, and Kobe, Japan, all have had their senses of their communities changed by the disaster. Both outside and within the community, the community becomes known for the disaster. Nashville residents talked about themselves as heroes, while residents of New Orleans were portrayed as victims and even looters. This struggle for the narrative often leads some of the leadership to act reactively. After a disaster, a community and its leaders will want to return to the "way that it was." Smith (2011) writes that in the midst of the many tasks that must be completed, what he refers to as a "reactive approach" can be used to make decisions that may not move a community past the disaster.

PHOTO 15.1   Renew Hope. In May 2006, New Orleans residents are still gutting their homes 10 months after Hurricane Katrina. (Photo credit: Richard Babb. With permission.)

15.6   HOW A COMMUNITY RESPONDS TO DISASTER

The effect that disasters have on community structure is not static and can be both positive and negative. In some cases, disasters can strengthen a community structure (the "therapeutic community"), but more often disasters exacerbate existing community conflict (the "corrosive community").

15.6.1   THE THERAPEUTIC COMMUNITY

Disasters are often thought to pull communities together, although this shared unity is usually short-lived. The idea of the "therapeutic community" is that after a disaster the collective imagination of a community is activated like never before. A community once fractured by diverse interests and historic rifts can be turned into a united community of survivors with a shared history—because the process of response and recovery breaks old ways, promoting innovation and improvisation, changing traditional norms and roles, creating new communication across once-static social boundaries, and focusing diverse groups on common goals. Disasters can increase feelings of social bonding and group culture, and be "therapeutic" for a community. "The shared trauma of a disaster can create community . . . in the same way that common language and common cultural backgrounds can . . . [create] a common culture, a source of kinship" (Erickson 1994, 231; see also Quarantelli and Dynes 1976; Barton 1970; Fritz 1961, 685). The therapeutic community may exist for a short time after a disaster. (Recall the solidarity of New Yorkers after September 11th, or the immediate local response to the Chinese earthquakes. Or, recall how everyone suddenly talks to each other on the streets or on the bus after a huge snowstorm.) It may last longer for some subgroups within a community (for example, a particular neighborhood). But the collective mind of the "therapeutic" community does not usually last through the initial response phase. Soon after a disaster, the ordinary ways of thinking and interacting may come back, and life goes back to normal. In some cases, a "corrosive community" process replaces the "therapeutic community," wherein existing inequalities are exacerbated, different agendas and perceptions emerge, blame is assigned, and groups fight for resources.

15.6.2 THE CORROSIVE COMMUNITY

The "corrosive community" is characterized by a loss of trust in community—a perceived loss of charity, concern, empathy, and recovery resources; a fragmentation of community groups; and a breakdown of social relationships, both personal and institutional. As victims and survivors fight for scarce resources and debate recovery options, community conflict emerges.

Disasters do not create conflict; they amplify previously existing inequality within a community. Poor, young, elderly, and minority populations are most vulnerable every day, including during a disaster. Disaster tears the scab off a community to expose the persistent wound of conflict and vulnerability underneath. Some examples of community conflict and corrosion include:

- *Inadequate social infrastructure* (health care, housing, education, etc.): Before Katrina, one-third of New Orleans lived in poverty. The city had the highest murder rate in the United States, an infant mortality rate twice as high as Beijing's, and a bankrupt education system with the lowest paid teachers in the nation. The percentage of African Americans who did not own a car was 35%. The vulnerability of the population was very high before, during, and after the storm.
- *Race and class divisions*: The Chicago heat wave of 1995 killed African Americans at a higher rate than whites, because of higher social isolation in depopulated parts of town. Of all disaster deaths worldwide, 2% come from developed countries, and 98% come from less developed and developing countries. Hate crimes against Arab Americans increased after the World Trade Center was bombed. Racial tension soared after Hurricane Katrina, with victims blamed for their loss. Conflict can also emerge when some groups receive more aid or faster aid than others.
- *Corruption*: After the Chinese earthquake in 2008, locals protested shoddy school construction and rampant government corruption. Similar charges were made after Hurricane Andrew in Florida when newer houses failed and older ones remained standing.
- *Tension between outsiders and locals*: Tension can occur when local organizations are ignored or underfunded compared to outside organizations, when local businesses are undermined by overabundance of relief supplies, and when nonlocal urban planners have more voice than local citizens or planners. Concerns emerge that outside contractors, builders, and volunteer "trauma tourists" take recovery jobs of locals.
- *Land-use planning*: Conflict arises about the value of developing or restoring beaches, wetlands, floodplains, high wildland fire areas, earthquake faults, etc. What is the "highest" or "best use" of the land? And, without careful planning rules, gentrification can occur in the rebuilding phase, leaving poor people nowhere to live in the community.
- *Looting*: Social behavior after a disaster is overwhelmingly prosocial. However, a persistent stereotype of large-scale disasters is of rampant looting and lawlessness. In fact, "the mass media played a significant role in promulgating erroneous beliefs about disaster behavior" (Tierney, Bevc, and Kuligowski 2006). For example, after Hurricane Katrina there were reports of riots, murders, babies with their throats slit, an epidemic of rape, looting, carjacking, and shooting at rescue helicopters. Most of these reports turned out to be false or grossly inflated—few bodies, witnesses, survivors, or survivors' relatives could be found. In most cases there were other explanations. Most "looting" was of perishable food and drink. Most deaths were natural. People reported they fired shots to get noticed and be rescued. "Pro-social behavior (much of it emergent) was by far the primary response to Katrina, despite widespread media reports of massive antisocial behavior"

(Rodriguez, Trainor, and Quarantelli 2006). However, when lawlessness does occur after a disaster, it is most likely when the local police force is seen as corrupt or inefficient, people are extremely disadvantaged compared to others, unemployment is high, and high gang membership and crime rates existed before the disaster (Dynes and Quarantelli 1968; Quarantelli and Dynes 1976).

With so much destruction, conflict will occur in communities. Conflict can push groups of people to form alliances, articulate their concerns, and push for change. Organizations—from antiviolence against women groups to affordable housing groups to immigrant advocates to environmentalists—can find new voice for political mobilization of the marginalized, and disasters can create a new forum to critique the status quo (Olson and Drury 1997; Passerini 2000).

15.7 SUSTAINABILITY

The more sustainable a community is, the better it is able to both mitigate disasters before they happen and bounce back after a disaster with minimum impact.

15.7.1 THE SUSTAINABLE, DISASTER-RESILIENT COMMUNITY

Disasters by Design (Mileti 1999) and *Holistic Disaster Recovery: Ideas for Building Local Sustainability after a Natural Disaster* (Natural Hazards Research and Application Information Center 2001, 1–3) identify six principles of community sustainability.

1. Residents' quality of life is maintained and enhanced. For example, proactive initiatives to help the most vulnerable are secured; social safety nets are in place; venues exist for civic, sport, and artistic events; home ownership is high; and the community has agency and awareness of hazards and mitigation.
2. Local economic vitality is enhanced through reliable jobs, a diversified business pool, and a stable tax base. However, environmental interests are never subservient to business interests. In the best cases, business realizes it can save money and attract customers by not damaging the environment.
3. Social and intergenerational equity is ensured so that everyone is treated fairly in the current generation, and so that future generations do not pay for the mistakes and inaction of the current generation. This is often done by protecting the environment, the economy, and moving toward a more inclusive community of vast opportunities for everyone.
4. Environmental systems that protect a community from the impacts of disasters are maintained and enhanced by replacing local practices that are detrimental with those that allow ecosystems to continuously renew themselves. Sometimes this means protecting areas and creating parks and open space, and other times it means changing long-held patterns such as reductions in driving, sprawl, and pollution. Protecting environmental systems includes reducing CO_2 emissions to reduce the impact of global climate change.
5. Disaster resilience and mitigation are incorporated into everyday community decisions, which necessitate good coordination and networking between groups and organizations, as well as effective government that can coordinate across jurisdictions.
6. A consensus-building, participatory process is used to make decisions. Overt efforts to improve racial, class, or religious barriers to communication, cooperation, and compassion are implemented. Government represents diverse voices of the community, and there is strong leadership for building common goals.

15.7.2 RESILIENCY IN COMMUNITIES

As with many concepts, *resilience* is a term that can mean everything and nothing. Norris et al. (2008) refer to resilience as a metaphor, much like the concept of community. Everyone has an idea of what resiliency is, but no one can quite define it. *Resilience* is often used to describe individuals who bounce back from trauma or succeed in spite of living conditions that are very stressful. As discussed previously in this chapter, the focus is often on the individual's or the family's recovery rather than a community's resilience. On the other hand, the disaster literature has begun to apply resilience to communities that have suffered through some type of disaster. What makes one community better able to recover than others? (See Photo 15.2.)

One of the keys to recovery is the evacuation experience itself. Tobin and Whiteford (2002) note the experiences after the eruption of the Tungurahua volcano in Ecuador. They found that differing experiences of evacuation led to a variety of economic outcomes, as well as the community's perception of risk and health outcomes. Evacuation as part of the disaster event often leaves individuals and families at a loss. For those disasters where there is some notice, the uncertainty of evacuation will lead to decisions that put individuals and communities at risk.

Much has been written about the preexisting conditions of the community as a significant factor in resilience. As with community, cultural values can appear vague and difficult to define. However, it is possible to recognize and build upon unique cultural values that each community holds. For example, Helton and Keller (2010) identified cultural values that enhanced resiliency among Appalachian women. One of those cultural values revolves around the concept of *neighborliness*, which promotes care for others and develops a sense of safety. This value of neighborliness certainly plays out in disasters. The relationships made before a disaster will be important during a disaster and in recovery. In one neighborhood during Hurricane Katrina, it was the neighbors who were able to get one elderly immobile neighbor evacuated. They loaded her into the bed of a pickup truck and drove her to Baton Rouge, Louisiana. This sense of knowing your neighbors and helping them out can be recognized and should be part of any plan to enhance resiliency.

PHOTO 15.2 Broadmoor lives. In the first citywide planning meeting, the Broadmoor neighborhood in New Orleans was tentatively classified as a "green space." The neighborhood responded by building one of the strongest neighborhood associations in the city and galvanizing the residents to rebuild. (Photo credit: UNO/CHART. With permission.)

Community resilience has been framed (Norris et al. 2008, 127) as a process that links "a network of adaptive capacities (resources with dynamic attributes) to adaption after a disturbance or adversity." Norris et al. (2008) state that community resilience could be an "extraordinary" strategy for disaster readiness. From their perspective, community resilience is a complicated process that involves factors such as economic development, social capital, information and communication, and community competence. We list these because they illustrate the complexity of resilience:

1. *Economic development.* Resilient communities have the capacity to provide an economic climate for recovery. The first part of economic development is resource volume and diversity, which includes jobs, land use, housing, health services, and schools. The second part of this factor is how communities address resource equity and social vulnerability.
2. *Social capital.* In this factor, network structures and linkages, social support, and community bonds are included. Basically, the strength of community networks is a major part of this section. Social support focuses on the networks that might be available to people who need aid in a crisis. Community bonds include the larger networks that individuals have with agencies and organizations in their communities.
3. *Information and communication.* Systems and infrastructure for informing the public shape the capacity of a community to inform its citizens in both disaster and nondisaster time frames. How the narrative emerges during and after a disaster may be the key to the ability of a community to respond. In the early days after Hurricane Katrina, there was an emphasis on rescue, but as the rescue narrative was inadequate to explain what people were seeing, the emphasis in the media shifted to the narrative of law and order (Ya Salaam 2006).
4. *Community competence.* This factor involves how capable a community is to act collectively and its ability to make decisions. As well, it would also include the capacity of a community to create an atmosphere of trust, along with how able a community is to empower those who have least access to resources.

Elements of all four of these factors can be measured prior to an event as an ongoing process of disaster preparedness. Resilience is not, then, pulling yourself up by your boot straps, but a dynamic process of how a community survives. The problem of any discussion with resiliency is that the lack of resiliency can be viewed as the individual's or community's responsibility. "If someone had just tried hard enough, they would be okay by now." Or, "If the community would just have worked hard enough, all the homes would be rebuilt." The factors that determine resiliency occur in a larger context. The strategies that people employ to be resilient may still fail for reasons that are totally out of their control. For communities as well, the struggle to come back after a disaster may not be successful because of policies and resources beyond their influence. (See Photo 15.3.)

15.8   WHAT EMERGENCY MANAGERS AND PLANNERS CAN DO

Emergency planners need to be part of the everyday conversation in any community. If communities are more disparate and harder to identify and disasters are more frequent and more serious, emergency planners should have an increased role in the lives of their communities.

15.8.1   BE PART OF CREATING COMMUNITY KNOWLEDGE

Without local knowledge of the community, plans will fail. There are many strategies based on best practice, but those plans will work only if they are "fitted" to the local communities. For example, the Natural Hazard Mitigation Association is launching a special program entitled Resilient Neighbors Network (RNN) to link grassroots communities that will work to become safer, disaster resilient, and sustainable. The purpose of this program is to offer ideas and feedback to the Federal Emergency Management Agency (FEMA) on how the federal government can help increase

PHOTO 15.3 FEMA trailers in Hollygrove. As residents returned to neighborhoods such as Hollygrove, they reconstituted their community. Here, three FEMA trailers are on the same lot facing each other. (Photo credit: Pamela Jenkins. With permission.)

community resilience to natural hazards. This program and similar programs will allow local communities and then state and federal programs to adopt best practices and to develop unique resilient strategies (http://nhma.info/nhma-launches-resilient-neighbors-network). Kobe, Japan, is a good example of strategies that build on local knowledge. After the earthquake, the response changed Japanese society in several ways. There was an increase in the number of voluntary and nongovernment activities and a greater collaboration between local government and residents' associations (Shaw and Goda 2004). (See Box 15.3.)

15.8.2 BUILD PARTNERSHIPS THAT INCREASE KNOWLEDGE AND PARTICIPATION

Traditionally, emergency and disaster personnel have relationships with disaster relief agencies and other first responders. These partnerships have a long history with each other and may provide a certain level of comfort with their roles and responsibilities. The community is often seen as a place to reach out to rather than bringing members of the community to the table where planning for disasters occurs. For example, domestic violence programs across the nation have experience in managing personal crisis with vulnerable populations. Groups that work on a day-to-day basis with vulnerable populations have the capacity and the ability to plan for these groups in a larger disaster.

15.8.3 BUILD NEW NORMS AROUND DISASTER

Disaster work should no longer be separate from everyday community work. Disaster professionals can help build emergency management into existing community organizations and everyday routines by developing policies and practices that facilitate families and communities assisting each other. They can organize neighborhoods around hazard mitigation and help to coordinate communication between community groups.

15.8.4 INCREASE CIVIC PARTICIPATION IN DISASTER PLANNING

Emergency response teams and planning committees, for example, should be actively diversified by current residents of the community. A community should consistently ask: Whose voices are missing? What are the barriers to their participation? What can I do to make sure that missing

BOX 15.3   THE AFTERMATH OF THE KOBE EARTHQUAKE

We are old. Even though we may die soon, we want to
go back to Kobe. We hope to die in Kobe.

Izumisano City temporary shelter—woman in her 80s

The Great Hanshin Awaji earthquake of Japan (the Kobe earthquake) occurred on January 17, 1995. The earthquake had a magnitude of 6.8 on the mms scale. More than 6,400 people died; 200,000 people were left temporarily homeless; and 70,000 buildings collapsed, with 55,000 buildings seriously damaged.

The consequence of the earthquake in 1995 was the growth of voluntary and nongovernment activities and the enhancement of cooperation between local government and the residents' association. The Kobe Action Plan was formulated by the people of Kobe six years after the earthquake. The goal of the Kobe Action Plan is to achieve a more complete civil society.

Ten principles formed the basis of the Kobe Action Plan:

1. Dissemination of Kobe experience
2. Unification of livelihood and community
3. Respect for each other
4. People's initiative
5. Decision of "public" field by people
6. New working style
7. Utilization of local knowledge
8. Creation of necessary system
9. New value of life style
10. Realization of decentralized system

Out of these principles, three themes leading to action were developed:

- Theme 1: Community building and planning
- Theme 2: Alternative livelihood
- Theme 3: Living safely in the community

Out of the devastation of the earthquake, the community began to see its relation to the government differently, trying to build a sustainable therapeutic community.

Adapted from Shaw and Goda (2004).

voices are heard? Including multiple voices, and having a wide cross-section of the population in the decision-making process, means that unique and valuable ideas will be included that may protect the interests of the entire community.

15.8.5   MOVE INEQUALITY TO THE CENTER OF THE DISCOURSE

Poverty, racism, and gender inequality create disaster vulnerability. One sure way for disaster professionals to increase the odds that a community will recover quickly would be to address unemployment, underemployment, health care, housing, schools, lending policies, public transportation, and crime. If you can identify and target people who are most vulnerable and build lasting safety nets and capacity for self-advocacy and self-sufficiency, you will create a disaster-resilient community.

15.8.6   Participate in Land-Use and Environmental Decisions

Disaster professionals do not often participate in civic conversations about the hydrocarbon economy. No particular storm is caused by climate change, but increased climate change increases the frequency and intensity of storms, floods, and droughts. Changes in behavior that lead to reductions in carbon emissions (building bike paths, taxing emissions, supporting national renewable energy policy, and ratifying international treaties)—in the long term—contribute to less vulnerable communities. Likewise, the work of arguing in favor of protecting hazardous areas and natural ecosystem should not be the proprietary role of environmentalists: Disaster professionals should be involved, too.

15.8.7   Build Trust in Institutions

When communities have a shared understanding and perception that institutions (like law enforcement, emergency management, etc.) are fair and effective, then trust is built in a community. Participation of institutions in community activities and decisions helps build community trust in institutions (Miller 2007). Thus, when we do community work, we increase disaster resiliency. Because of those ties and trust, community members will cooperate and volunteer with law enforcement (or shelters, etc.) during the disaster. That helping behavior, in itself, increases trust and social ties even more, making the community even stronger for the next disaster. All disaster work should have a double function—one that serves the community during a disaster, and one that serves the community every day in the absence of a disaster.

15.9   SUMMARY

The work of disaster professionals has traditionally focused on building and protecting structures, designing warning systems, and developing response and recovery plans—a necessary but somewhat limited set of roles. Today, we understand that communities will continue to be vulnerable if the community structure itself is weak. Disaster professionals can play a central role in building resiliency that improves a community's ability to respond to stress every day, as well as during extreme natural events. Disasters can have therapeutic or corrosive effects on a community, and the best way to ensure positive effects is to build the capacity for community resiliency. Disaster professionals must be involved in this work of community building if they are to be successful at fostering long-term, sustainable disaster resiliency. Understanding the different forms of community and social networks and the ways in which disaster can strengthen or weaken community ties can help identify the underlying barriers and incentives to building sustainable, resilient communities. If investing in strong communities is the primary goal of disaster professionals, the development of resilient communities is possible.

DISCUSSION QUESTIONS

1. Outline the number of communities that you belong to, such as your family, basketball league, or church group. Determine what types of communities they are: geographic, shared interest, or those of attachment. Then, diagram how they overlap. Let the list sit for several hours and then revisit to see if you have missed any group. What do these lists tell you about who you are?
2. Use Google Images and search for "Looting vs. Finding." Compare the two pictures and captions from the 2005 Katrina hurricane. In what ways did community turn corrosive during this disaster? Can you imagine ways in which disaster professionals could have prevented much of the conflict of Katrina, or, once it happened, could have worked constructively with the conflict to build future social capital?

3. Think about how a community becomes more resilient. For example, what is the level of trust in your community? How would you help increase trust?

4. Consider the preparedness, response, and recovery phases of disasters in your area. As a disaster professional, what nontraditional actions could you take to build community?

ACKNOWLEDGMENTS

The authors acknowledge and thank Eve Passerini for her contributions to the chapter that appeared in the first edition of this book. This chapter represents the writing of the present authors and does not necessarily reflect those of previous authors or contributors to the FEMA Higher Education project on social vulnerability to disaster.

REFERENCES

Adams, V., T. Van Hattum, and D. English. 2009. Chronic disaster syndrome: Displacement, disaster capitalism, and the eviction of the poor from New Orleans. *American Ethnologist* 36 (4): 615–36.

Barton, A. 1970. *Communities in disaster: A sociological analysis.* Garden City, NY: Anchor Books.

Brint, S. 2001. Gemeinschaft revisited: A critique and reconstruction of the community concept. *Sociological Theory* 19 (1): 1–23.

Bruhn, J. 2005. *The sociology of community connections.* New York: Springer Publishing.

Brunsma, D., D. Overfelt, and S. Picou. 2007. *The sociology of Katrina: Perspectives on a modern catastrophe.* New York: Rowman and Littlefield.

Brunsma, D., and S. Picou. 2008. Disasters in the twenty-first century: Modern destruction and future instruction. *Social Forces* 87 (2): 983–91.

Daren, Beville. 2010. Stars align for Nashville flood relief telethon. www.theboot.com/2010/05/16/nashville-flood-relief-telethon/.

Dynes, R., and E. L. Quarantelli. 1968. What looting in civil disturbances really means. *Transaction* 5 (6): 9–14.

Eden, R., and P. Boren. 2008. *Timely assistance: Evaluating the speed of Road Home grantmaking.* Santa Monica, CA: Rand Corp.

Erickson, K. 1978. *Everything in its path: Destruction of community in the Buffalo Creek Flood.* New York: Simon and Schuster.

———. 1994. *A new species of trouble: The human experience of modern disasters.* New York: Norton and Co.

Fletcher, M. 2011. HUD to pay $62 million to La. homeowners to settle Road Home lawsuit. *The Washington Post.* http://www.washingtonpost.com/business/economy/hud-to-pay-62-million-to-la-homeowners-to-settle-road-home-lawsuit/2011/07/06/gIQAtsFN1H_story.html.

Fritz, C. 1961. Disaster. In *Contemporary social problems*, ed. R. Merton and R. Nibet, chap. 14. New York: Harper and Row.

Helton, L., and S. Keller. 2010. Appalachian women: A study of resiliency assets and cultural values. *Journal of Social Service Research* 36:151–61.

Klein, N. 2008. *The shock doctrine: The rise of disaster capitalism.* New York: Henry Holt and Co.

Litman, T. 2005. Lessons from Katrina and Rita: What major disasters can teach transportation planners. Victoria Transportation Policy Institute, Victoria, BC, Canada.

Lowe, J., and T. Shaw. 2009. After Katrina: Racial regimes and human development barriers in the Gulf Coast region. *American Quarterly* 61 (3): 803–27.

Marsh, G., and P. Buckle. 2001. Community: The concept of community in the risk and emergency management context. *Australian Journal of Emergency Management* 16 (1): 5–7.

Mileti, D. 1999. *Disasters by design: A reassessment of natural hazards in the United States.* Washington, DC: Joseph Henry Press.

Miller, L. 2007. Collective disaster responses to Katrina and Rita: Exploring therapeutic community, social capital, and social control. *Southern Rural Sociology* 22 (2): 45–65.

Natural Hazards Research and Application Information Center. 2001. Holistic disaster recovery: Ideas for building local sustainability after a natural disaster. University of Colorado, Boulder. www.colorado.edu/hazards.

Norris, F., S. Stevens, B. Pfefferbaum, K. Wyche, and R. Pfefferbaum. 2008. Community resilience as a metaphor, theory, set of capacities, and strategy for disaster readiness. *American Journal of Community Psychology* 41:127–50.

Obama, B. 2005. Interview by George Stephanopoulos, September 11. *Meet the Press.*

Olson, R. S., and A. C. Drury. 1997. Un-therapeutic communities: A cross-national analysis of post-disaster political unrest. *International Journal of Mass Emergencies and Disasters* 15 (2): 221–38.

Olson, S. 2008. Twitter, Facebook called on for higher purpose. CNET News Blog. http://news.cnet.com/8301-10784_3-9852369-7.html.

Passerini, E. 2000. Disasters as agents of social change in recovery and reconstruction. *Natural Hazards Review* 1 (2): 67–72.

Quarantelli, E. L., and R. R. Dynes. 1976. Community conflict: Its absence and its presence in natural disasters. *Mass Emergencies* 1:139–52.

Rodriguez, H., J. Trainor, and E. Quarentelli. 2006. Rising to the challenge of catastrophe: The emergent and pro-social behavior following Hurricane Katrina. *Annals of the American Academy of Political and Social Science* 604 (1): 82–101.

Shaw, R., and K. Goda. 2004. From disaster to sustainable civil society: The Kobe experience. *Disasters* 18 (1): 16–40.

Smith, Gavin. 2011. *Planning for post-disaster recovery: A review of the United States Disaster Assistance Framework.* Fairfax, VA: Public Entity Risk Institute.

Tierney, K. 2007. From the margins to the mainstream? Disaster research at the crossroads. *Annual Review of Sociology* 33:503–25.

Tierney, K., C. Bevc, and E. Kuligowski. 2006. Metaphors matter: Disaster myths, media frames, and their consequences in Hurricane Katrina. *Annals of the American Academy of Political and Social Science* 604 (1): 57–81.

Tobin, G., and L. Whiteford. 2002. Community resilience and volcano hazard: The eruption of Tungurahua and evacuation of the Faldas in Ecuador. *Disasters* 26 (1): 28–48.

Tonnies, F. 1887/1963. *Gemeinschaft und gesellschaft* [Community and society]. New York: Harper and Row.

Warren, R. 1963. Introd. to *The community in America.* 3rd ed., 1–20. Chicago: Rand McNally College Publishing.

Williams, S. 2008. Rethinking the nature of disaster: From failed instruments of learning to a post-social understanding. *Social Forces* 87 (2): 115–18.

Ya Salaam, K. 2006. Friday, September 2. In *Voices from the storm: The people of New Orleans on Hurricane Katrina and its aftermath,* ed. L. Vollen and C. Ying, 138–39. San Francisco: McSweeney's Books.

16 Measuring and Conveying Social Vulnerability

Deborah S. K. Thomas, Iain Hyde, and Michelle A. Meyer

CONTENTS

16.1 CHAPTER PURPOSE

Having a mechanism for understanding a community's vulnerabilities and capacities in a systematic fashion is necessary for fully translating the concepts of social vulnerability into research and practice. Community vulnerability assessments (CVAs) can put valuable information into the hands of all decision makers, including the public, policy makers, emergency managers, and numerous other members of a community. Most importantly, CVA can incorporate community voices along with traditional data sources, providing a mechanism for participation and a basis for action for all potentially affected groups. This chapter focuses on CVA approaches, including data needs and outcomes.

16.2 OBJECTIVES

As a result of this chapter, readers should be able to:

1. Understand the value of community vulnerability assessment (CVA)
2. Define and explain the basic elements of CVA
3. Describe community-based participatory capacity and vulnerability assessment (CBP-CVA) and what it can offer vulnerability assessments

4. Describe levels of sophistication in conducting various approaches to CVA/CBP-CVA
5. Recognize the link of CVA to the sustainable livelihoods approach
6. Understand the relevance of carefully identifying indicators and the importance of establishing criteria for assessing vulnerability
7. Identify various data sources and mechanisms for collection
8. Understand how GIS (geographic information system) mapping technologies and related tools are utilized in CVA
9. Discuss the steps needed for communities/governments to move beyond the information-gathering stage of identifying social vulnerability issues to incorporating this information into preparedness and mitigation plans

16.3   INTRODUCTION

Previous chapters explored a range of social vulnerability topics in detail, examining how individual and social conditions interplay with hazard events throughout the emergency management cycle. Having an appreciation of how and why these factors come to bear on social vulnerability and capacity is vital to reducing death and destruction from natural and human-induced events. But, we must move beyond just acknowledging these issues to incorporating these concepts directly into emergency management decision-making processes. The social vulnerability paradigm guides comprehensive vulnerability assessments, moving them beyond an evaluation of total populations at risk to a more comprehensive understanding of differential experiences with hazards.

Vulnerability assessments are a means for systematically identifying, analyzing, monitoring, and explicitly integrating social vulnerability into all aspects of preparedness, response, recovery, and mitigation. The information derived from these tools informs every aspect of emergency management, for example, revealing who may need additional assistance in the face of an event, who might struggle with recovery, or how to prioritize mitigation activities. Importantly, vulnerability assessments, when done comprehensively and inclusively, are not just about documenting exposure and susceptibilities; they also highlight strengths and resources that exist in and across communities. Importantly, communities can identify gaps and develop strategies for prioritization of emergency management activities and, ultimately, foster resiliency.

This chapter will explore vulnerability assessments and examine mechanisms for conducting them. The first section of the chapter presents a broad overview of the relevance and general elements of vulnerability assessments and examines various models and approaches. A discussion of indicators, data needs, and collection mechanisms follows, including an emphasis on community-based, participatory processes. Next, the relevance of mapping and geographic information systems (GIS) technologies is reviewed. The last section provides a discussion of specific details necessary for implementation of CVA, as well as strategies for inclusion of CVA outcomes in planning processes.

16.4   IMPORTANCE OF COMMUNITY VULNERABILITY ASSESSMENTS

Although there is no established single approach, CVAs are fundamental mechanisms for measuring and conveying how social conditions, the built environment, community development practices, and political/economic systems contribute to disaster risk in a community. They play an important role in establishing a knowledge base about the hazard and social context of a particular place, revealing the interplay in human–environment interactions at a given location (Turner et al. 2003). Importantly, assessments can be conducted at a variety of scales, either at the community level, regionally, or even nationally, to evaluate and compare the levels of susceptibilities to natural and human-induced events. Much of the following discussion applies at broader scales/levels (state or regional), but the primary emphasis is the community-level assessment, since most mitigation, preparedness planning, response, and recovery efforts are local.

By bringing together information on hazard risk, social vulnerability, and capacities/resources, the basic function of CVA is to reveal social conditions as a fundamental component of the risk equation and directly enmesh them into formal emergency management processes. A CVA ensures that an appraisal of assets and needs is already in position should an event occur to inform response and recovery efforts, and also provides a mechanism for identifying and prioritizing mitigation options. Indeed, CVA can provide a foundation for incorporating emergency/disaster management priorities into ongoing community processes, such as comprehensive plans and land-use regulation, integration increasingly common and promoted as an avenue for effective risk reduction (American Planning Association 2010).

At the local level, building codes, zoning ordinances, and capital improvement plans sometimes address issues of hazard risk. In the United States, comprehensive plans that articulate the long-term vision for development in communities increasingly take hazards into account, though perhaps not as commonly as would be ideal (American Planning Association 2010). Many studies have established that poor populations often live in the most vulnerable areas of their community, for example the regulatory floodplain (Adger 2006; Fothergill and Peek 2004; Thomalla et al. 2006). Integrating hazard analysis and mitigation into the comprehensive plan enables the community to make risk-informed development decisions, such as where to build safely located affordable housing. In addition, it provides the opportunity for the community to achieve multiple objectives and capitalize on cobenefits. One example would be to institute an ordinance to prevent development in the regulatory floodplain while simultaneously developing recreational greenways and preserving wetlands that are essential for water storage and water quality.

In the United States, Presidential Policy Directive 8 (PPD-8) aims to strengthen the security and resilience of the country through the establishment of a system that prepares the nation as a whole to be able to prevent, protect against, mitigate, respond to, and recover from all hazards (PPD-8 2011). Central to the effectiveness of PPD-8 is the notion that the preparedness system enables the nation to make decisions that ultimately reduce risk and shorten the time and minimize the resources required to recover from hazard events. Incorporating CVA into comprehensive development and community planning represents a method for achieving this directive.

The incorporation of social vulnerability into assessment processes starts with the careful development of meaningful databases related to subpopulations described throughout this book. These databases allow first responders and emergency managers to identify areas where people might need evacuation assistance, to estimate sheltering need and supplies, to target the distribution of appropriate educational materials where many do not speak the primary language, or even to be prepared to request state or federal aid to address the needs of these persons. These databases establish a baseline for comparison across space and time, supplying guidance for evaluating mitigation strategies and preparedness activities and the changing requirements of emergency management. CVA also highlights existing shortfalls and gaps in information needed by the community, informing future data collection efforts.

Because places are not static and communities' compositions (built environment as well as social, political, and economic structures) change over time, regularly conducted and updated CVA inventories are useful for identifying successes and the need for adjustment. A CVA is also useful for setting priorities as the voices in a community change. People who move into a community may not be familiar with local hazards or risks, and elected officials with varying knowledge of vulnerability may change office. CVA, then, is a tool to communicate the social-environmental context of hazard risk, thereby increasing awareness within the community as a whole. Ideally, an assessment process unfolds over time, is iterative, and creates community dialogue, establishing communication among all stakeholders.

Vulnerability assessments can influence policy changes that address the root causes of social vulnerability, as well as just evaluating hazards, by linking disaster loss reduction to other community priorities in social services, public and environmental health, and urban/regional/rural planning. These assessments can offer a way of identifying gaps in data, information, and resources;

prioritizing mitigation strategies; developing aid interventions; increasing protection and enhance-ment of economic structures; assisting in the creation of self-protective measures; and supporting institutions in their role of disaster prevention (Cannon, Twigg, and Rowell 2003).

In order to achieve any of these goals, CVA should be conducted with integrity. Results need to avoid common pitfalls that can limit the usefulness of the results for directing policy and affecting pos-itive changes in resilience. The following sections discuss the types of CVAs that communities apply, ideas on generating the best results, and methods for incorporating this information into planning.

16.5   MODELS FOR COMMUNITY VULNERABILITY ASSESSMENT

Capturing community vulnerability and capacity within an assessment process is no easy task, requiring careful consideration to *what* community characteristics will be represented and *how* they will be incorporated into a broad picture of vulnerability. There is not a single, accepted approach, and so initial discussion with stakeholders is essential for setting assessment methods and goals. Fundamentally, the following criteria should be established at the onset of any CVA:

1. Clearly defining purpose, goals, and objectives
2. Selecting data elements that align with these goals
3. Defining a process (rules, guidance, scoping, definitions, evaluation) that realistically acknowledges data, time, and resource considerations
4. Understanding of community-specific cultural and social norms
5. Determining mechanisms for the dissemination of findings and incorporating gathered information into planning and decision-making processes

This section presents a general overview of different assessment models, along with basic steps highlighting community-based, participatory processes and the link to sustainable livelihoods.

Many models exist for conducting CVA, both theoretically based and applied, at all scales/levels, from local to national. Regional, statewide, or even national assessments often focus on macro-level issues that help to identify problems and priorities at a strategic level. The smaller the scale of the study, the more specific the information collected and the more tactical the outcomes of the CVA may be. Further, because vulnerability and capacity are particularly local in nature, commu-nity-based approaches are most relevant for capturing the many forces that contribute to risk. For example, some localized CVAs are conducted on a parcel-by-parcel basis, taking into account how specific property characteristics might influence hazard risks. Birkmann (2006) offers a review of frameworks that inform vulnerability assessments. Some focus exclusively on hazard risk (FEMA 1997; Coburn, Spence, and Pomonis 1994), while others emphasize social, political, and/or eco-nomic vulnerability (Cutter, Boruff, and Shirley 2003). Still others extend into capturing capacity and assets in order to discern resilience (Cutter et al. 2008; Cutter and Finch 2008; Sherrieb, Norris, and Galea 2010). More sophisticated approaches endeavor to systematically merge physical, social sciences, and engineering approaches. Effectively taking structural and agency considerations (see Chapters 1 and 2) into account are particularly challenging.

Approaches to vulnerability assessment can be broadly compared through a review of out-comes, data requirements, and special considerations. Table 16.1 compares five approaches on these axes. The first approach, a single-hazard assessment, represents the most basic approach for a comprehensive understanding of risk, requiring the least resources (in terms of time, money, and human resources) and data inputs. Although a single-hazard modeling technique can be quite sophisticated in and of itself and reveal critical hazard risk, the output is quite linear because it only provides information about a single hazard and commonly neglects the social dimension. Physical models that adequately capture and convey hazard risk are by no means easy, requiring highly researched and developed detection and modeling techniques. Earthquake modeling, for example, is highly technical, as are the monitoring and detection of floods or severe weather, but

TABLE 16.1

Broad Vulnerability Assessment Approaches

Approach	Outcomes	Data Requirements	Considerations
Single-hazard assessment	Documentation and/or models of risk for one hazard	Hazard risk information for the hazard Historical event and impact data Monitoring data to generate models or already-generated model output	In localities with extreme risk from a particular hazard A limited view of hazard risk Socioeconomic conditions, secondary hazards, and environmental impacts are commonly excluded or included in a simplistic fashion
Multihazard assessment	Documentation and/or models of risk for one hazard or all hazards in a given location Mapping and analysis of multiple hazards risks	Hazard risk information for each hazard Historical event and impact data for each hazard Monitoring data to generate models or already-generated model output	More comprehensive picture of hazard risk Challenges of combining and weighting the risk from different hazards Socioeconomic conditions, secondary hazards, and environmental impacts are commonly excluded or included in a simplistic fashion
Basic CVA	Includes multihazard risk assessment Explicit attention to socioeconomic conditions in relation to hazard risk	All the above hazard data Existing secondary data sources for social analysis, such as readily available government census data Additional locally derived socioeconomic data	A start to understanding human-environment interactions when limited resources are available for conducting the analysis Often focus on potential structural impacts without a refined approach to understanding social vulnerability Reliance on secondary governmental data may create incomplete picture of social vulnerability Challenges of how to weight and/or express various indicators of vulnerability
Intermediate CVA/VCA	A more advanced treatment of vulnerability, beyond available census data Includes information on capacity	All the above hazard and socioeconomic data Local-level sources of data, such as property tax/parcel records, school records (free/reduced-cost lunch programs, enrollment, graduation rates), access and functional-needs registries, health registries (birth/death records), low-income housing occupancy, etc. Indicators of capacity, including neighborhood and community resources in nongovernmental organizations, faith-based organizations, and community groups Some primary data collected from surveys or focus groups	Additional locally derived secondary databases are housed in numerous agencies and so require being inquisitive and creative Challenges of integrating data collected for a variety of purposes Challenges of how to weight and/or express various indicators of vulnerability

(continued)

TABLE 16.1 (CONTINUED)
Broad Vulnerability Assessment Approaches

Approach	Outcomes	Data Requirements	Considerations
Community-based, participatory VA (CBP-CVA)	A process that involves capturing local knowledge and perceptions and incorporating into the assessment Expand societal analysis substantially to include both top-down and bottom-up information	All the above hazard and socioeconomic data Primary data through various participatory techniques, such as personal interviews, community information sessions, focus groups, surveys, etc. Inclusion of stakeholders of all types Inclusion of institutions and networks within the community relevant to disaster resilience as well as vulnerability	Provides extremely rich information about socioeconomic conditions and resources/capacity in a community A single model for conducting CBP-CVA does not exist, as numerous approaches exist Intensive process, requiring time, money, and human resources

the output can only provide a partial picture of the total risk for a community without combining with other relevant hazards and social information. These single-hazard assessments do not provide information on what populations are at risk of flooding, what the economic impacts may be, or susceptible infrastructure. As such, CVA should advance beyond detailing a single physical hazard risk to addressing the social condition and more thoroughly capture human–environment interactions. But at the same time, the reality is that as the approach becomes more extensive and inclusive, data needs, the time commitment, human resources required, and financial costs increase. Thus communities will need to balance their needs and their ability to complete the assessment when choosing an approach.

The major challenge of moving beyond single-hazard assessments is the expertise required in each of these topical areas, from natural hazards to human-caused hazards. Fortunately, for many areas of the United States, and even in many parts of the world for some hazard types, much data and information exists on hazard risk, or at least historical hazard data (Thomas et al. 2006; Mileti 1999; Cova 1999). However, this is not equally true for all parts of the globe. As a U.S. example, FEMA's Multi-Hazard Identification and Risk Assessment (1997) guides communities through a hazard assessment approach, and has even been applied internationally in settings with more limited data. While it does not speak to issues of social vulnerability in any significant way, it does provide direction for initial steps in a more robust process. For the purposes of this book, the emphasis is on measuring and understanding social vulnerability beyond the physical hazard risk assessments undertaken in the above approaches; the next section begins to highlight broad steps in this process that can provide useful social vulnerability assessments.

16.5.1 ELEMENTS OF A BASIC COMMUNITY VULNERABILITY ASSESSMENT (CVA)

There are three broad information categories in a basic CVA approach that set the groundwork for presenting a more robust approach to vulnerability assessment. These categories are similar among most place-based studies:

1. Identifying and analyzing hazard risk
2. Identifying and analyzing social vulnerability and capacity of society
3. Identifying high-risk areas, i.e., those areas that have both high hazard potential and high social vulnerability

Cutter et al. (2004) established a process of vulnerability assessment at the local scale in Georgetown County, South Carolina, and Dao and Peduzzi (2003) performed a similar analysis at the global level, using different indicators and weighting schemes (see Section 16.6) but nonetheless attempting to capture these broad categories of information. Of course, assessments conducted at these very disparate scales/levels inform decision making differently (see Section 16.5).

From these broad categories, the following builds on NOAA's Roadmap for Adapting to Coastal Risk (NOAA 2012), which offers a tangible approach to guide communities in the basic steps of CVA. Once a place is clearly defined (location, geographic boundaries) and end-user needs established, the general steps include:

1. Hazard identification
2. Hazard analysis
3. Critical facilities analysis
4. Societal analysis
5. Economic analysis
6. Environmental analysis
7. Mitigation opportunity analysis
8. Capability/capacity analysis
9. Mitigation opportunities analysis

All of these incorporate mapping in order to visually locate high-risk areas: those places that have both a high hazard potential and high social vulnerability.

16.5.1.1   Hazard Identification (1) and Hazard Assessment (2)

In these two steps, a community identifies all of the hazards that exist in their geographic area. These may range from natural hazards (such as earthquakes, hurricanes, flooding, or even disease), human-induced hazards (such as toxic-chemical or hazardous-materials accidents, or oil spills), or a variety that fall somewhere in the middle (such as wildfires or global climate change). Once a complete list of all potential hazards is created, these are prioritized based on likelihood of occurrence combined with the level of impact. A community may decide from the onset that a particular subset of hazards is central, but hazard assessments also assist in setting priorities by highlighting areas of high potential impact (both structural and nonstructural) through probability, magnitude, historical event and/ or loss information, and hazard risk modeling. As an extension, hazard risk should be delineated by the potential consequences of hazard events for specific groups and sectors, including the public, first responders, continuity of operations (including delivery of services), property, facilities and infrastructure, the environment, the economy, and public confidence in jurisdictional governance (EMAP 2010).

16.5.1.2   Critical Facilities Analysis (3)

Incorporation of critical facilities in the CVA is one step for increasing a focus on social vulnerability. Critical facilities and infrastructure are those resources in a community that are essential and vital to its well-being and operation. For example, the U.S. government, through the National Infrastructure Protection Plan, defines critical facilities as those assets that, if damaged or destroyed, would have a debilitating impact on national security, national economic security, national public health or safety, or any combination of those matters (DHS 2009). Critical facilities vary by community, but commonly include entities like fire stations, police, hospitals, emergency shelters, utilities (clean water, sewer, electric/gas, waste disposal), communication networks (phone, mobile), as well as the transportation system (roads, bridges, and tunnels). In some states, a definition of critical facilities and infrastructure may also include nursing homes and congregate-care facilities that have high concentrations of people and energy-extraction or -storage sites as well as other facilities that may contain hazardous materials (CWCB 2010). An inventory of these facilities should be generated at the local level, including location and information about each facility or piece of infrastructure. Once identified, the facilities are examined in combination with the physical hazard risk (1 and 2 above).

16.5.1.3 Societal Analysis (4)

The ultimate goal of CVA is to incorporate knowledge from the social vulnerability paradigm to move beyond an assessment of total population risk to a more comprehensive understanding of differential experiences with hazards. While it is important to estimate total numbers affected—for example, the number of people in the path of a potential dam failure—appreciating that subgroups and neighborhoods have varied abilities to prepare, respond, mitigate, or recover—helps ensure that all people have an equal opportunity for safety and security. Many of the previous chapters identified indicators or variables that reveal aspects of social vulnerability, such as minority populations, poverty status, age distribution, gender, educational attainment, public assistance, rental housing, disability, or a lack of transportation resources. Ultimately, the goal is to identify high-need/high-vulnerability areas/neighborhoods and then account for these in relation to high-hazard risk zones. A basic analysis can rely on readily available secondary data (i.e., already existing data) from local, national, or international government data sources to compile and analyze the information. This is a good first step, but the product is limited by the quality of the data, including the geographic specificity and sampling techniques (Skerry 2000). Importantly, many local governments collect and maintain useful types of secondary data that are often more current than the national or international data, contain different types of information, and are also potentially more accurate. Examples include property tax/parcel records, school records (free/reduced-cost lunch programs, enrollment, graduation rates from secondary school and university), access and functional needs registries, health registries (birth/death records), and low-income housing occupancy, among many others (see Section 16.7 for a discussion on data considerations).

Beyond secondary sources of data, collecting information directly (i.e., primary data collection) through surveys, focus groups, social and/or organizational network analysis, or interviews captures local knowledge and people's perceptions and priorities, and can improve the quality of the social analysis step. Primary data collection could be targeted at issues unavailable through secondary data sources, such as community resources available in faith-based or nongovernmental organizations or often-hidden vulnerable populations, such as the homeless or an HIV/AIDS community.

Once data are compiled and integrated into a common format, they are combined into a social vulnerability index (see Section 16.6 for a further description). Primary data collection (focus groups or surveys, for example) can be used to inform which constellation of social factors identifies the most vulnerable areas in a community. For example, geographic concentrations of high poverty, high crime, and elderly may represent the most vulnerable areas for one community, while another may focus on concentrations of single mothers, low-income children, and those without available health care. The results of this step are combined with output from the other steps to determine high social vulnerability and high-hazard risk areas.

16.5.1.4 Economic Analysis (5)

This phase of the CVA explicitly focuses on the economic sector. As described in Chapter 1, income disparity interfaces with every other vulnerability characteristic; economic strength is related directly to a community's vulnerabilities and capacities. A diverse and healthy economic sector contributes to employment, the tax base, and the overall vitality of a community. Available employment and business opportunities are necessary for community disaster recovery. Thus, understanding the relationship of businesses, industry, and government facilities to hazard risk is also foundational for creating community emergency and disaster plans, as well as business continuity plans, thereby preventing and minimizing disruptions in economic activities.

First, the major sectors of the economy are identified and inventoried (agricultural, mining, construction, manufacturing, transportation, wholesale and retail, services, finance, insurance, real estate, small businesses, or even home-based businesses), including the largest employers and small businesses. This inventory is analyzed to determine what sectors are more susceptible to significant hazard event impacts, including physical and social. For example, a manufacturing facility may be physically at risk of flooding due to location. If it was inoperable during a flood, low-income hourly employees may be the first to lose employment. Or, employees may not be available for work if their neighborhoods and homes are flooded, even if the business is untouched. This impact could ripple from the economic sector into the population if these employees lack the financial resources to withstand temporary or permanent unemployment caused by the disaster.

16.5.1.5   Environmental Analysis (6)

This step aligns with the hazard assessment of steps 1 and 2 by including ecologically sensitive areas and natural resources to the risk assessment. Like in other steps, an inventory and evaluation is conducted, but in this case focused on environmental considerations, which include secondary hazards where the initial event (primary hazard) could cause additional emergency incidents (secondary hazards). For example, an earthquake could cause a gas line to rupture, with an ensuing explosion, or it could cause damage to a dam and result in flooding. Thus, this step includes accounting for facilities and infrastructure that store, transport, or dispose of hazardous and toxic materials, as these could become secondary hazards. Also, ecologically sensitive areas and natural resources that are at risk from either primary or secondary hazards are identified and mapped. Another component of environmental analysis can include inventory of ecosystems that reduce hazard risk and should be protected to reduce future impacts. For example, barrier islands and marshes along coastlines absorb hurricane energy. The environmental analysis is important to encourage mitigation of environmental preservation areas or prepare the community to efficiently repair damage to these resources.

16.5.1.6   Capability/Capacity Analysis (7)

Unfortunately, capability/capacity analyses are often overlooked or minimized in the CVA process, but these should be elevated to a more prominent role. Capabilities or capacities consist of people, organizations, plans, policies, or programs within a community that enable it to effectively assess and reduce vulnerability and increase resilience. Understanding these provides a more comprehensive understanding of what vulnerability-reduction work already takes place and what potential shortfalls may need to be addressed moving forward. Capabilities/capacities encompass public agencies, private businesses, nongovernmental organizations, and even individuals. Examples include:

1. Building codes and zoning ordinances that deal specifically with hazard risk or potential hazard areas
2. Hazard plans (mitigation plans, emergency operations plans, evacuation plans, disaster recovery plans)
3. Education and outreach programs (both from the public and nongovernmental organizations)
4. Community-based mitigation programs (e.g., slash collection and disposal programs in high wildfire risk areas)
5. Access and functional needs registries
6. Nongovernmental and community-based organizations

16.5.1.7   Mitigation Opportunities Analysis (8)

Without a doubt, going through all of the previous steps is extremely informative for understanding loss and informing preparedness and response activities. As important, however, is formulating strategic mitigation opportunities. Mitigation reduces or prevents loss if an event occurs. Thus, this step combines output from all the previous steps to identify where mitigation measures (either structural or nonstructural) would have the greatest potential for loss reduction while considering costs and benefits. For example, a community that identified high risk for their student populations may choose to retrofit schools for earthquakes or ensure that new schools are not built in flood zones.

Still, unlimited funds are not available, and so priorities must be set; CVA provides a mechanism for understanding where and what activities would be most beneficial. Once completed, CVA provides a comprehensive picture of disaster risk that helps a community improve their overall resilience.

16.5.2 COMMUNITY-BASED PARTICIPATORY RESEARCH FOR DISASTER RISK REDUCTION

> We will not succeed in advancing the agenda of the Hyogo Framework for Action if we do not engage local communities in all aspects of strategies for disaster risk reduction. (Gupta 2007)

The Hyogo Framework for Action, adopted by 168 countries, calls attention to the role of the community in disaster loss reduction activities (UNISDR 2005), and the International Strategy for Disaster Reduction (ISDR)'s *Words Into Action: A Guide for Implementing the Hyogo Framework* (UNISDR 2007) emphasizes the importance of community participation. The most sophisticated approach to assessing vulnerability is gathering data beyond that available from government or scientific entities; it is also bottom-up, incorporating information derived from the community in a multimethods approach. Locally derived knowledge can add significant value to understanding local risk. Ethically, if decisions are being made about a community, members of that community should have a voice in setting priorities. This section describes the basics of participatory assessments that represent information-rich and context-specific understandings of vulnerability beyond that of those discussed in the previous section.

While experts may have vast content knowledge about hazards and disaster risk reduction, they frequently do not have the same understanding as those who live, work, and play in local communities. For example, residents may have a better sense of where most vulnerable populations are located, including homebound, elderly, sick, tourists, and those without transportation, among others, than is reflected in formal databases. Further, residents likely have a better sense of local resources and assets, such as religious institutions, community-based organizations, businesses, and governmental structures and how these do, or do not, serve the community. For instance, in creating an inventory of first responders, police stations would likely be identified as an asset in a top-down assessment. However, many local community members may not utilize or even view this as a positive resource, depending on experiences with, and perceptions of, the police. In short, including community-derived information ensures that cultural customs, local wisdom, and prior knowledge about disasters bolster and strengthen other conventional information sources. Incorporating participatory approaches enriches both information and process and likely improves chances for sustainable mitigation (Pearce 2003).

Although there is no gold-standard model for conducting or implementing community-based participatory vulnerability assessments, variations of these processes are being applied in numerous locations globally (Pelling 2007). Known as "community vulnerability assessment," "community-based vulnerability assessment," "community capacity and vulnerability assessment," "participatory vulnerability and risk assessment," or "community-based participatory capacity and vulnerability assessment," these all attempt to give voice to the communities most directly affected by hazards and disasters and reveal the power that communities themselves have to address risk. For the purposes of this section, the term *community-based participatory capacity and vulnerability assessment* (CBP-CVA) is used to capture the idea of stakeholder involvement at the community scale for identifying both capacity and vulnerability. (See Box 16.1.)

The value of CBP-CVA lies in the notion that public participation is critical to any community planning process. The participatory process will be most successful when it is tailored specifically to community needs and characteristics. Berke and Campanella (2006, 199) point out that the prospect of successful implementation of plans increases as participation by those who are most affected by a plan increases. However, in many cases, planning processes do not adequately capture public participation, especially from those who may be more socially vulnerable. Blair (2004, 106) notes that "a lack of guidance on creative or innovative participatory mechanisms raises questions

BOX 16.1   PARTICIPATORY PLANNING FOR DISASTER RESPONSE

A participatory process for emergency planning in one region of the United States illuminates: (1) a method for incorporating the unique challenges vulnerable groups face in emergencies into plans, and (2) a mechanism for gathering information on local capacity so emergency management can quickly draw on these resources. This region used the Voluntary Organizations Active in Disaster (NVOAD n.d.) concept to guide their process and now have an active Community Organizations Active in Disaster Network of social-service, nongovernmental, and faith-based organizations. The leader of the network is a volunteer coordinator for one county in the region and worked for years to develop relationships with organizational representatives from different populations in the region (such as access and functional needs advocacy groups, HIV/AIDS service organizations, homeless shelters, food banks, churches, and neighborhood associations). This group of over 20 organizational representatives meets quarterly with the local government emergency managers to discuss emergency plans, disseminate public education materials, and address needs of specific communities. The group meets more frequently during the development of plans to discuss issues of concern and evaluate these plans before they are codified into practice. For example, a low-income housing organization brought attention to a geographic concentration of low-income households that they knew because of their service provision. This area of the community was small and overlooked in vulnerability assessments that solely used secondary data sources at a larger geographic scale.

Beyond the regular meetings, this network of organizations has conducted one-time participatory programs that target different sectors of the community, including a program for churches and a program for small businesses. The outcomes of the church participatory program included the drafting of emergency plans for each church involved and the identification of vulnerable populations connected to each church. For example, a local Catholic church drew attention to undocumented farm laborers in their community and included outreach and response mechanisms for those people in their internal church emergency planning.

Beyond identifying vulnerable populations and geographies, the connection of these organizations to emergency management has allowed emergency managers to track the capacities that different organizations and their representative populations have. Redeveloped emergency response plans now include volunteer organizations who know the capacity of all other community organizations established in the emergency operation center. Thus, the community now has knowledge of where physical assets (such as chainsaws for tree removal) or human assets (such as volunteers prepared to house displacees) are located in the community sectors and can access those assets in a timely and efficient manner.

The core participants in the network have found that staying connected is time-consuming work, especially during periods of little disaster activity in the area. But they feel that even with sometimes-sporadic involvement, having formed a network and communication lines has improved their ability to respond to the needs of all individuals in their community.

---

regarding the quality of public participation in the planning and implementation of public programs, especially in low-income and rural areas." As such, with good planning, CBP-CVA presents an opportunity to capture citizen needs, insights, and aspirations and incorporate them into analysis in a meaningful and productive manner.

Pelling (2007) divides CBP-CVA into three broad categories:

1. *Procedural approaches*: Generally focus on where the ownership of the process resides, either with local stakeholders themselves or with officials seeking to gain input from those stakeholders.

2. *Methodological approaches*: Emphasize data transfer to and from stakeholders, deriving data from the community (quantitative and qualitative) and then also providing information to the community.

3. *Ideological approaches*: Range from extractive to emancipatory. Extractive processes emphasize information flow, deriving data from the community, whereas emancipatory processes accentuate community self-empowerment to generate change. Emancipatory processes are embedded in theoretical origins promoting *conscientizacão* (awareness or consciousness) as a means of community participation in learning and adaptation of technology (Freire 1973; see also Chapter 2).

These broad categories are not necessarily mutually exclusive, but do at least reveal the necessity of carefully and consciously choosing a participatory approach. Ultimately, the process should be tailored to fit the community and the goals of the assessment. (See also Chapter 15 on the nature of communities and Chapter 17 on community empowerment for a more in-depth treatment of these ideas.)

Several well-developed and documented processes for participatory disaster-loss-reduction activities exist, including Oxfam's Participatory Capacity and Vulnerability Assessment (de Dios 2002), the IFRC's Vulnerability and Capacity Assessment (IFRC 2006), or ADPC's Community-based Disaster Risk Management (Abarquez and Murshed 2004). The community is emphasized in all of these approaches as active agent in the assessment process. Other common characteristics include deriving community-based data for informing risk-reduction activities, community involvement and engagement throughout the process, and open knowledge transfer and communication. Although details vary, some generalized steps convey overarching and guiding themes for participatory disaster loss reduction (see Table 16.2).

As one can imagine, conducting a participatory assessment requires significant background work and relies on in-depth qualitative data collection. Careful planning and preparation are absolutely necessary for producing successful and meaningful outcomes. In fact, the preparation phase requires a significant time commitment; neglecting any aspect will most likely result in less meaningful results and potentially even negative experiences. Once a community is selected, the preparation phase concentrates on clearly defining and preparing for the participatory activities. Significant effort and attention is required to build relationships and rapport in the community, thereby giving the participatory process the greatest chance of success through stakeholder support and ensuring representation from relevant and potentially marginalized, vulnerable groups (see Berke et al. 2011 for an example). For example, incorporating a gendered approach could translate to having separate working groups for men and women, or it could mean focusing on women's groups entirely (Enarson 2003). Another example is the inclusion of children and youth in participatory processes (see Box 16.2). Depending on the stakeholders identified, the types of participation activities, times, and locations of participatory sessions must vary strategically. Through education, inclusion, and self-empowerment, they hold the key for disaster loss reduction from the present into the future. Representation at the table, as it were, will directly affect any findings and so must be vigilantly considered (Beierle and Cayford 2002).

The implementation phase of CBP-CVA includes working session(s) by which community-derived data are collected through a variety of qualitative mechanisms in a comfortable and open setting, again varying based on stakeholder needs. This is followed by a compilation of the findings, analyzing where information converges in common themes or ideas. Ideally, results should be presented to the participants for comment and evaluation to ensure validity of the findings. Lastly, those involved build consensus around findings and set priorities for mitigation and preparedness activities, developing an action plan for implementation, including evaluation.

In theory, the process would be continuous, with adjustments made to the data, priorities, and action plans and refined over time in response to evaluation activities. However, any community-based, participatory process is intensive, often facing limited financial and human resources, as well as competing for people's time and attention; thus, they are difficult to maintain and sustain.

TABLE 16.2

Generalized CBP-CVA Process

Phase	Sample Activities
Planning and preparation	1. Identify the community based on some criteria (hazard risk, local interest, political stability, etc.)
	2. Identify key stakeholders, groups, and leaders to ensure representation from a variety of populations, including children, women, etc.
	3. Choose a conceptual framework to guide designing the process
	4. Meet with relevant stakeholders to define the processes, goals, and objectives
	5. Build rapport with, and understanding of, the community
	6. Determine a time line
	7. Identify what information will be collected and select appropriate data-collection methods
	8. Determine the number and type of participation events
	9. Gain approvals
	10. Organize the events
	11. Conduct analysis of secondary sources of risk information
	12. Conduct a pretest (a test run) of the events and selected methods
Implementation	1. Share the secondary data analysis conducted with existing sources, reviewing with the community
	2. Facilitate dialogue, creating a comfortable, open, and flexible atmosphere
	3. Collect data through a variety of methods (preselected), including visual, oral, written, and/or facilitation
	4. Learn and share knowledge
	5. Create a comfortable, open, and flexible atmosphere
Analysis	1. Systematically organize and compile the data
	2. Bring together all of the various pieces of information, documenting where they converge and diverge
	3. Return to the community with the analysis for input and evaluation
Priority setting and action planning	1. Build consensus around priorities of the findings from the analysis
	2. Identify and design an action plan for mitigation and/or preparedness activities, including opportunities for vulnerability reduction and drawing on and building capacities
	3. Evaluate the implementation of action-plan items

Source: Compiled and derived from de Dios 2002; IFRC 2006; and Abarquez and Murshed 2004.

BOX 16.2 MINOT, ND, PARTICIPATORY PROJECT— PARTICIPATION WITH YOUTH

Following a flood in Minot, ND, the impacted rural communities worked with FEMA recovery planners to develop disaster recovery, redevelopment, and mitigation goals. The recovery planners specifically targeted the youth through several participatory sessions at each school. During these participatory sessions, the students wrote their ideas on small note cards and attached them to topic boards related to different redevelopment sectors for the communities (e.g., parks, tourism, agriculture, safety, housing, education, etc.). The students then went through several days of prioritizing their ideas, which included moving development farther away from the river to avoid future flooding, increasing public safety, and reducing crowding in the schools. Along with feedback from participatory processes with the adults in the communities, local officials and recovery planners developed a plan for implementing each prioritized recovery goal. While not an example of a vulnerability assessment, this participatory process shows that one often-excluded group (youth) can be targeted for involvement of emergency planning and prioritization of mitigation and disaster-recovery items (FEMA 2011).

As such, the importance of identifying clear goals with associated costs, potential funding sources, and feedback loops is paramount. Further, social media and networking technologies offer numerous opportunities for creating sustainable activities around participatory assessment processes (see Chapter 18), although the effort to organize and maintain these is still not free and serves particular purposes with potential pitfalls. Still, even if a participatory assessment occurs singularly, the information generated and the benefits of the process are enormous.

16.5.3 LINK TO SUSTAINABLE LIVELIHOODS

Sustainable livelihood analysis (SLA), commonly applied in many areas of the world and used by organizations internationally, is not entirely distinct from CBP-CVA (see Chapter 3 for a discussion of sustainable livelihoods). In fact, each phase of CBP-CVA can incorporate primary SLA considerations, and conversely SLA could incorporate issues of disaster risk. However, the focus of the analyses is slightly different. SLA stresses the complex set of characteristics (individual, household, and community) that affect people's livelihoods, focusing entirely on the human condition, whereas CBP-CVA considers hazard risk along with social conditions. Along with the varied emphasis, the scale/level of analysis also differs with SLA, which centers on the interrelationships at an individual and household level that give rise to vulnerability. In general, CBP-CVA emphasizes the community.

Furthermore, in SLA, social vulnerability encompasses more than the potential for loss related to hazard risk. According to Cannon, Twigg, and Rowell (2003, 61), social vulnerability in SLA includes:

1. A person's initial well-being (nutritional status, for example)
2. Livelihood and resilience related to economic resources
3. Self-protection (ability and willingness to protect one's self or household)
4. Social protection (structures in the community or region in place to protect from hazards)
5. Social and political networks and institutions

Thus, in this framework vulnerability reduction activities should attempt to expand income and resources, self-empower households and communities, expand access to basic services, and directly address root causes of poverty (CARE 2002; Twigg 2001).

Although useful as a way to observe an overall picture of vulnerability, utilizing descriptive data from conventional sources to offer a baseline for vulnerability assessment does not capture the complexity of individual and social characteristics required by SLA. Thus, social network analysis and household-level surveys and interviews are absolutely necessary. In fact, SLA very explicitly captures data on the full range of individual and community capital, including financial (monetary economic means), physical (basic infrastructure), human (individual characteristics, including health and education), natural (environmental resources), social (social networks and links to institutions), and political (ability to access and use power) (CARE 2002). As an extension, vulnerability reduction is linked explicitly to development, food security, poverty reduction, safe housing, improvements in infrastructure, and effective governance. Although applied at different scales/levels (household versus community), and with a slightly different emphasis on the hazard (peripheral versus central), CBP-CVA and SLA both establish mechanisms for reducing disaster risk.

16.6 ESTABLISHING CRITERIA AND MEASUREMENT APPROACHES

Throughout this chapter, the significance of consciously and carefully designing every element of a vulnerability assessment is emphasized in order to achieve the most meaningful outcomes. This is particularly true for determining measurement criteria for social conditions in an attempt to quantify vulnerability. In some ways, this may seem contrary to the CBP-CVA, but in fact, it can be used in conjunction with it. A quantitatively driven vulnerability assessment does not replace CBP-CVA. Instead, they serve different purposes with slightly unique outcomes, and can inform one another. CBP-CVA emphasizes the process, the learning and understanding that emerge along with producing extremely rich and informative data at a local level, drawing extensively on qualitative methods (Auerbach and Silverstein 2003; Reason 1994). Neither the process nor the information is generalizeable to a broader population, but rather is specific to that locale, revealing complex interactions and in-depth associations that give rise to vulnerability. In fact, because of the nature of the participatory process, even comparisons from place to place are limited. Quantitative CVAs provide a means for measuring, comparing, and monitoring over time. CBP-CVA can be used to inform what quantitative data should be used to track vulnerability over time. Or communities may not be ready or well-suited for a CBP-CVA, so conducting even a simple quantitative CVA is a start to understanding social vulnerability. In the following sections, practical details of vulnerability assessments are discussed, including indicator selection and data quality concerns.

A fundamental component of any data-driven vulnerability assessment requiring careful consideration is identifying and choosing the indicators that represent broader concepts of social vulnerability (e.g., income inequality). Indicators are measures that characterize key elements of a complex system to reflect the current situation and establish rate and direction of change over time or across space. In order to adequately quantify and communicate, indicators should be clearly defined, reproducible, understandable, and practical, reflecting the interests of all relevant stakeholders (e.g., Valentin and Spangenberg 2000).

Over the last decade or more, numerous groups have undertaken work on the development of sustainability and vulnerability indicators (SOPAC 2005; UN 2007). Even so, a single defined set of indicators for social vulnerability does not exist, and the types of data included vary by scale of analysis. For example, global and even regional assessments tend to focus on population numbers and impact with limited information on more detailed population characteristics (Peduzzi, Dao, and Herold 2005; Dao and Peduzzi 2003). These present a broad-brushed depiction of disaster risk. At the regional or local level, more refined indicators are desirable. Thus, it is incumbent for the person or group conducting such an assessment to carefully evaluate which set of indicators best apply to a particular locality through a review of literature and preferably some type of consensus-building activity. Community leaders or government officials may decide, but choosing indicators is an ideal task for the use of community-based, participatory approaches.

Establishing indicators begins with choosing a conceptual framework as applied to a particular scale/level with clearly defined outcomes that tie to the goals and objectives. This in turn guides a selection of categories for which individual indicators can be identified and selected. For example, accounting for health status, the choices for indicators may include infant mortality, life expectancy, number of doctors per 1,000 people, or even number of hospitals per 1,000 people. In considering education, literacy rates, percentage of adults with a high school diploma, or percentage of females completing high school are options. Each of these indicators is a reflection of a slightly different aspect of the vulnerability concern. Additionally, some indicators measuring the same observation have opposite interpretations for a vulnerability assessment. Median house value could signify poverty, but it can also reflect the amount of potential property loss. A corner convenience shop could be considered an asset by residents because of the easy access to some food products, while in other situations it might be a blight property because of loitering or lack of other food resources. Likewise, a high percentage of rental property could be deemed negative in terms of real estate values, but may mean affordable housing in a cohesive neighborhood. Ultimately, relevance, accuracy, and availability of data end up being primary drivers for the selection of indicators.

Once indicators are collected, they can be examined independently across a community or be combined in some fashion into a vulnerability index, a process that is complex and must be carefully planned (Birkmann 2006). As a cursory review, data can be viewed and combined through a normalization process, by categorical scales, or even statistical methods. Normalizing involves translating data into a common unit. For example, median house value and percent female-headed households have different units and so would be placed on the same data scale often based on the average of that particular data set. Categorical scaling involves grouping data together. For example, low-, average-, and high-income groups merge into median house income. The challenge is that cut points must be determined for categories, determining what is low, average, or high. Indicators and outcomes can also be combined statistically to condense the data (e.g., Cutter, Boruff, and Shirley 2003) into a vulnerability index or input into multivariate modeling to establish which independent variables (income, education, age, among others) contribute to an outcome (disaster deaths or property loss, for instance) (e.g., Dao and Peduzzi 2003). Ideally, vulnerability assessments should take a mixed-methods approach that combines measured indicators along with participatory approaches.

16.7 DATA CONSIDERATIONS

Vulnerability assessments are data driven, whether these are derived from existing sources or primary data collection and rely on quality data sources (NRC 1999). The selected conceptual model and corresponding goals and objectives along with the scale of analysis will guide the type of data desired, and at the same time the quality and type of data will directly affect the output. Much information already exists or can be collected, revealing various aspects of vulnerability and capacity (see Table 16.3).

In terms of secondary data, the organization or entity that compiled the data did so for a purpose. Consequently, they may or may not appropriately capture elements of vulnerability and capacity of interest. For example, even when considering postdisaster fatality information, which at first glance seems like it would be a reliable source, several serious issues exist. Accounting for fatalities and death estimates can actually be quite challenging, especially when large numbers of people are involved. How precise is saying 220,000 people perished after the 2004 Indian Ocean tsunami? If someone dies from a heart attack immediately following an earthquake, is this attributable to the event? What if the overall rates for an area are significantly higher than usual? Beyond the accounting issue, even the numbers are frequently aggregated in a way that conceals vulnerability. In other words, deaths by gender, age, race/ethnicity, or even income level are often unavailable, if in existence at all. In sum, data may simply not be collected, have different standards (what is collected and how), be incomplete (missing data), contain some level of error, or lack precision (either geographically or in terms of disaggregated details). Further, data from other organizations or governments may not be readily available or accessible.

Most countries in the world have some type of a national census, but there are concerns when using this data related to variation in the level of analysis, the method of collection, and the types of socioeconomic data included. Many developing countries do not have a detailed resource at the local level, while many developed countries have country-specific versions that are quite detailed, and many countries fall somewhere in the middle of those extremes. In the United States, the census data (collected every 10 years; U.S. Census 2012a) and the American Community Survey (updated every 2 years; U.S. Census 2012b) are common sources of secondary data for conducting a basic CVA, or even as a component of more advanced assessments, because of the vast amount of information on population and housing included. Importantly, even with the large number of indicators easily accessible at a local scale/level, these sources have significant and extensive nuances and limitations, and so should be used with caution. While it is beyond the scope of this volume to detail the data issues specific to these particular sources, users should be aware that the information may misrepresent the current configuration of the locality, sometimes quite considerably. As only one example, certain subpopulations are undercounted, such as minorities or the homeless, among others (Skerry 2000). As a consequence, supplementing census data with other secondary sources is advantageous, as previously mentioned. These could include immigration data, public school records, property tax records, special needs registries, land use and zoning, service agencies, Medicaid and Medicare recipients, subsidized housing, community directories, religious organizations, special interest groups, among numerous others. For example, in the United States, the local or regional planning office is often a good place to start. The point is that local agencies and organizations maintain a variety of useful information; it is a matter of

TABLE 16.3
Sample Information for Vulnerability Assessment Focusing on Social Conditions in U.S. Context

Broad Categories	Sample Information	Potential Source[a]
Demographic	Minority populations	1, 3, 4
	Population over age 65	1, 3, 4
	Population under age 5	1, 3, 4
	Female-headed households	1, 3, 4
	English spoken at home	1
Education	Adults with no high school diploma	1
	Educational programs and initiatives	2, 3, 4
	Preschool programs and enrollment	2
Health	Birth and death records	2
	Health services (hospitals, clinics)	2
	Disease registries	2
	Special-needs registries	2
	Nursing homes	2
	Accessibility of public buildings	2, 3, 4
Economic	Households below poverty	1
	Households with public-assistance income	2
	Rental housing	1
	Children on reduced/free lunch programs	2
	Population covered by insurance	2, 3
Social services	Private and public social-service agencies	2
	Support services to individuals and families that are relevant to disaster response and recovery	2, 3, 4
Political	Sector political representation (or lack thereof)	2, 3, 4
	Efficacy of municipality or local government	2, 3, 4
	Voting levels	2
	Political participation in civic affairs, including building and zoning matters	2, 3, 4
	Governmental organization and coordination around disaster-related issues	2
Infrastructure	Housing units with no vehicle available	1
	Hospitals	2
	Schools	2
	Public transportation	2
Social groups	Neighborhood organizations, such as homeowners' associations, civic clubs	2, 3, 4
	Religious organizations and groups	2, 3, 4
	Special-interest groups	2
Social networks	Family and friend networks	3, 4
	Networks and coordinating groups	3, 4
	Communication networks (newspapers, newsletters, radio stations)	2, 3, 4

[a] Secondary sources: 1 = U.S. Census; 2 = other state or local government agency or organization. Primary sources: 3 = surveys, focus groups, key informant interviews; 4 = participatory process.

spending time seeking it out and evaluating the relevance and quality. However, all data sources, with all they can add to a vulnerability assessment, have errors and biases that should be considered during indicator selection.

Primary data collection methods involve those where information is acquired firsthand. These include surveys, interviews, focus groups, and numerous other tools utilized in the participatory process (Stallings 2002). Each of these approaches has advantages and disadvantages to the types of information obtained. Additionally, each requires vigilant planning, implementation, and analysis in order to appropriately and adequately obtain desired results. For example, if implemented correctly, data from surveys can be generalized to an entire population. However, a survey instrument must be carefully designed, pilot tested, and then administered in order to derive a representative sample of the population. The sampling process ensures that the appropriate number of people are included and from relevant geographic areas and subpopulations. The findings can then reflect characteristics, views, and perceptions of the entire group from which the sample was drawn. Interviews, on the other hand, are not generalizable, but provide a greater detail of information. Focus groups, small groups of people (approximately 6–15 individuals) brought together to discuss a defined set of topics, give people the opportunity to interact, express views, possibly form consensus, and increase awareness. Like interviews, the data are quite detailed, cannot be generalized, and can be quite challenging to analyze.

Surveys, interviews, and focus groups can all be used as part of an advanced CVA, but may or may not be incorporated into a participatory process. Surveys, for instance, could be utilized to derive community-generated data, while not being used within a participatory framework. In this case, experts design and administer the instrument. On the other hand, community members themselves may conduct the surveys or interviews within a participatory framework. An additional set of tools, including participatory mapping, timelines, seasonal calendars, ranking, and transects (walking through a community making observations) and social network analysis, to name a few, are all mechanisms for capturing information in a participatory process (Stoecker 2005). In CVA, for example, low-income households, the elderly, and female-headed households, are commonly identified as highly vulnerable populations. However, in order to obtain an accurate assessment, factors related to social networks should also be considered. For instance, a family with a low income level might have difficulty evacuating unless family or friends live nearby to assist; the social network reduces vulnerability. Social capital (as defined and described in Chapters 2 and 15) has the potential to increase capacity for emergency response, although the relationship is complex (Murphy 2007).

The upshot is that the most sophisticated and advanced vulnerability assessment approaches will incorporate both primary and secondary data and will utilize quantitative and qualitative mixed-methods approaches. (See Tashakkori and Teddle [2003] for more detail on mixed methods in research.) In reality, data collection is a function of availability, time, and money, as compiling data sets requires significant resources and attention. All data are simplifications and generalizations of reality, and as such have both benefits and limitations. Thus, consideration of the limitations or constraints of different data is important when undertaking CVA.

16.8   SOCIAL AND ORGANIZATIONAL NETWORK ANALYSIS AND TECHNOLOGIES

Throughout this book, social networks have been mentioned and discussed numerous times in relation to individual and community vulnerability and capacity. (See Chapters 2 and 3 on social capital or Chapters 15 and 17 on communities and empowerment.) We all have both personal and professional social networks, people with whom we interact, share information and resources, rely upon, and communicate; we are part of a social fabric and do not exist in isolation. As an extension, organizations and agencies also interconnect through networks. Thus, attempting to evaluate and assess social and organizational networks in a formal manner as part of a CBP-CVA provides a basis for understanding strengths and weaknesses in a community, specifically opportunities for building relationships, avenues for disseminating risk information and education, and identifying interconnections through which preparedness, mitigation, response, and recovery can occur.

The principles of social network analysis (SNA) include a methodology that helps to explain how people connect to one another, revealing the structural makeup of interactions and relationships

(Freeman 2004; Scott 2000; Wasserman and Faust 1994). Social networking analysis attempts to systematically understand quantity, quality, group membership, and relationships between people and/or organizations. The emphasis is not on individual characteristics, but rather relationships that reveal the larger social (or organizational) structural pattern (Wasserman and Faust 1994; Scott 2000). Recent studies highlight how the quantity and quality of interactions can affect the community's capacity to handle public health and disaster challenges (Varda et al. 2008; Isett and Provan 2005).

An analysis is conducted using a survey tool that captures information about connectivity of people (or organizations), including inventorying and documenting the type of connections and interactions. Utilizing specialized software (akin to the specialized software used for statistical analysis or GIS), the analysis reports a series of outputs that convey information about the network. For example, "degree centrality" documents the number of connections that one member of the group has to every other member, identifying key players. "Effective network size" establishes the number of unique ties or connections (how big or small the network is). And "closeness centrality" measures how many connections exist between each member in the group and every other member. These are but a few examples of the extensive information gleaned via social or organizational network analysis so that the reader can begin to form an appreciation of how using social and organizational network analyses identifies the underlying barriers and incentives to building sustainable, resilient communities.

New emerging technologies that extend social networks and interactions into a virtual realm allow for a whole new level of near-real-time interactions and information flows (Boyd and Ellison 2008), both among emergency management organizations and professionals and also between emergency management and the public (Hughes and Palen 2012; see also Chapter 18). Social networking sites—such as Facebook, LinkedIn, or Twitter, cell phones (and now smart phones), and information technology platforms for information searching and sharing, like Google—have transformed information flows, with extensive implications for emergency management.

Importantly, the flows are not just about emergency management disseminating information, but also about self-empowerment and self-generated information, as well as sharing of resources. Crowdsourcing uses input from the public, or even professional groups, to gather information through these technologies. As one of numerous and expanding examples, Random Hacks of Kindness (http://www.rhok.org/solutions) is a clearinghouse of open-technology innovations bringing together people's interests and expertise to improve the human condition, including but not limited to reducing disaster impacts, many of which use a crowd-sourced approach. One project described on this site is using text-to-web technology for all water users in Kenya to register complaints about water quality and access issues.

While it is incumbent for emergency management to engage with these new communication technologies, and they provide exciting prospects, we must also be cognizant of several pitfalls. Many mechanisms exist for connecting with people through traditional and expanded social networks, but no single approach for information dissemination and risk communication exists, either with traditional or newer methods. Further, we do not fully understand or appreciate how the newer technologies function within an emergency management context, so evaluation is vital. How, for instance, does one evaluate the quality of the information from such varied sources? And further, how does emergency management compete with now numerous flows of information? What happens to communication if the technology fails? Importantly, adoption of technology varies dramatically across socioeconomic groups and also by organizations: Some people will adopt quickly and utilize extensively, while on the other end of the spectrum, others will never access technology for a variety of reasons (unavailability, expense, etc.). Not insignificantly, privacy and security issues abound in this realm. Who is using the information and how? The bottom line is that these technologies provide emergency managers another important and relevant tool for disseminating and obtaining information, but it must be applied with caution and care.

16.9 MAPPING APPROACHES

Nearly all vulnerability assessments now rely on geographic information systems (GIS) for understanding how hazard risk and vulnerability/capacity interact at a location and vary across space. GIS technologies are essentially computer mapping systems with analytical capabilities that are widely utilized in support of all phases of the emergency management cycle in a variety of ways (Thomas et al. 2006). Spatial technologies actually include a wide range of activities, from remote sensing to GIS to global positioning systems (GPS). As examples, GIS tools are used for risk assessment and communication, damage assessment, coordination and monitoring of cleanup efforts, response planning and coordination, and even evaluation of mitigation alternatives (Tobin and Montz 2004; Radke et al. 2000). (See Photo 16.1.)

GIS is applied extensively as part of the hazard risk assessment process in modeling physical events. Figure 16.1 illustrates a hazard modeling application integrating built-environment data. The Colorado Springs Fire Department (CSFD) is on the cutting edge of developing wildfire protection plans and utilized the Wildlfire Hazard Information Extraction (WHINFOE) model to determine five potential risk levels for wildfire ranging from low to extreme on a parcel level. CSFD assessed risk for more than 35,000 parcels (Colorado Springs Fire Department 2011). The WHINFOE model utilizes 25 weighted factors, including structural characteristics, fuel types and conditions, and topography to determine risk. CSFD collected data through multiple means, including the analysis of parcel data and extensive ground-truthing (confirming data in the field). While this model does not specifically include social vulnerability factors, such as demographics or income levels, it provides a strong model for analyzing specific hazard characteristics against development characteristics to determine an accurate and site-specific level of vulnerability.

The application of geotechnologies to social vulnerability is no less relevant for preparedness, response, recovery, and mitigation, ensuring that vulnerability/capacity is represented and included along with hazard risk. Morrow (1999) emphasizes that knowing where vulnerable neighborhoods exist and understanding their circumstances is a critical step in effective emergency management.

PHOTO 16.1   Bay St. Louis, Mississippi, December 11, 2007. Residents look at new preliminary flood maps at an open house in Hancock County. (Source: Jennifer Smits/FEMA.)

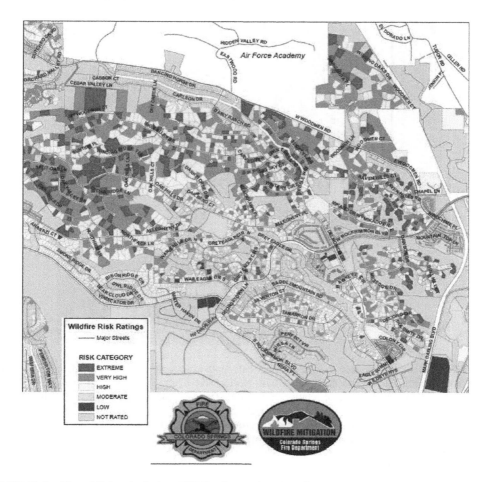

FIGURE 16.1 City of Colorado Springs Wildfire Protection Plan. (Source: Colorado Springs Fire Department. With permission.)

Additionally, Cutter, Mitchell, and Scott (2000) take a multihazard place-based approach to vulnerability assessment that includes both physical risk and social vulnerability. Although focusing on impact assessment and only for earthquakes, floods, and wind, FEMA's HAZUS toolbox does incorporate some elements of vulnerability and was explicitly designed for informing mitigation activities (FEMA 2012). The data and methods are not nearly as developed for depicting the complexities of a community's social vulnerability and capacities as for the modeling of physical events or damage assessment. Still, representing population characteristics and some aspects of vulnerability on a map along with hazard risk reveals the intersection in a powerful way. Additionally, the methodologies have been extended internationally.

Without going into the complexity of the GIS processes or modeling, Figure 16.2 illustrates how informative data displayed on a map can be, easily showing where high-risk locations exist. At the same time, it also demonstrates challenges with conducting a comprehensive hazard and vulnerability assessment. For instance, questions should arise around what is actually displayed. What is the time period for the map? What were the data sources? How was the risk area for each hazard derived? Importantly, social vulnerability, in this instance, is not incorporated in the map in a sophisticated fashion beyond showing flood depths and buildings, though for a vulnerable housing type (mobile homes). Still, maps can form the basis for further discussion and future directions,

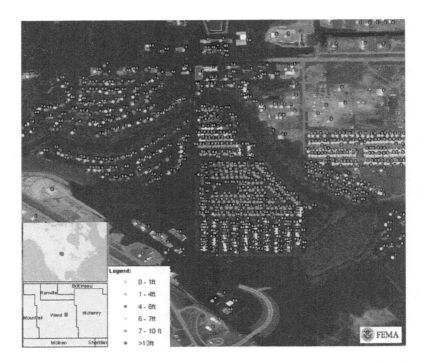

FIGURE 16.2   Minot, ND: Souris (Mouse) River extent, depth of water at structure. HAZUS analysis output examines water depths and mobile homes in Minot, North Dakota, after late June 2011 flooding. Flooding depths are estimated for each structure relative to the ground surface and the June 26th crest using surveyed high-water-mark elevations from the USGS and modeling from U.S. Army Corps of Engineers and Houston Engineering. Protected areas were confirmed on the ground by FEMA/USGS field survey. Satellite imagery acquired Saturday June 25th. (Copyright 2011 GeoEye Enhanced. View License. Oblique imagery acquired by Pictometry. Courtesy of Douglas Bausch, Jesse Rozelle, Sean McNabb, Herbert "Gene" Longenecker, Nicol Robles-Kyle, and Austen Cutrell/FEMA. With permission.)

conveying information in a useful format and informing decision-making processes, including the evaluation of mitigation options and opportunities in the recovery process.

The U.S. Disaster Mitigation Act of 2000 promotes participatory processes and technical vulnerability assessments (mapping hazards and risk) for the preparation of state and local hazard mitigation plans (FEMA 2004). However, in a systematic quality evaluation, the quality of state hazard mitigation plans was found to vary substantially, with most scoring moderately or below in terms of quality (Berke, Smith, and Lyles 2012). A number of states, including California, Arizona, Nevada, Florida, North Carolina, and South Carolina, all have legislation requiring some level of planning in association with natural hazards (APA 2010). The American Planning Association (APA) points out that California's laws include mandates for safety elements in comprehensive plans, as well as mandates for the identification (mapping) of regulatory floodplains, liquefaction zones, and unreinforced masonry buildings in the highest earthquake risk areas and in areas at risk to earthquake-induced landslides. (See Box 16.3 and Figure 16.3.)

Along with its alluring possibilities, geographic modeling of social vulnerability poses many unique challenges, not the least of which is attempting to capture the multifaceted and complex aspects of social systems and human behavior. People utilize communities in different ways. For instance, the distributions of daytime and nighttime populations throughout an urban area are quite different. Further, social, economic, and political systems are not necessarily easy or even possible to record, calculate, and predict in a quantitative manner for inclusion into mathematically based models. Thus, the future of GIS for social vulnerability assessment will undoubtedly involve exploring

> **BOX 16.3 HAITI: ADJUSTING POPULATION DISTRIBUTION IN THE POST-EARTHQUAKE ENVIRONMENT FOR USE WITH THE HAZUS-MH INTERNATIONAL METHODOLOGY**
>
> A study region was created in HAZUS-MH to estimate the social and economic impacts of the January12th, 2010, M7.0 Earthquake in Haiti. The HAZUS International Methodology, "An Updated GIS-Based Methodology for Exporting the HAZUS Earthquake Model for Global Applications" (Bausch, Hansen, Rozelle, McNabb), outlines the procedure of taking U.S. proxy data for any state and applying a multiplier to assign new population values for any country in the world.
>
> This approach provides a baseline population data set that can be customized and altered to more accurately represent the demographic distribution of the country of interest through advanced data collection specific to a location, acquisition of population data specific to a location, ground-truthing, and contribution of local knowledge. Once a population value is established for a particular country, the population can then be used to distribute demographic and building-stock data throughout the country.
>
> Post earthquake, as data and information were gathered and disseminated related to fatalities and displaced populations, these data and information were used to redistribute populations throughout the area for the study region to better reflect the population distribution after the earthquake for use in future analysis. (See Figure 16.3.)
>
> *Source*: International Study Region, analysis and poster created by Douglas Bausch, Jesse Rozelle, Sean McNabb, Herbert "Gene" Longenecker, and Eduardo Escalona/FEMA.

mechanisms for incorporating qualitative along with quantitative information, and then integrating these with social and organizational network analyses that provide a more expansive picture of community vulnerability and capacity. Once on a map, information on social vulnerability and capacity has a strong potential for gaining legitimacy alongside the scientifically measured hazard data.

Participatory GIS (GIS used within the context of CBP-CVA), in particular, has huge potential for social vulnerability assessments. As described previously, mapping is already utilized as a data-capturing tool in CBP-CVA. This approach acknowledges that the vulnerability assessment (and, by extension, emergency management) is not just top-down, but also bottom-up, and can be used to capture indigenous knowledge (Phong et al. 2011). Input from residents is absolutely vital, and the maps become a basis for dialogue, enhancing two-way communication between experts and communities. Additionally, maps can increase education about risk through the process, and people's knowledge and perceptions can be recorded, adding or refining data. In other words, verifying secondary social data becomes possible through local involvement, and priorities can be set by those most affected. (See Photo 16.2.)

In parallel with the expanding social-networking and information-sharing technologies briefly discussed in the previous section, many of these now have a geographic location associated with them and are increasingly being applied across emergency management. In other words, information can be tied directly to maps, which is termed *crowd-sourced* or *volunteered* geographic and georeferenced information. Examples include: everything from photographs posted to all sorts of sites that are geotagged (or referenced to a map); to OpenStreetMap, which uses volunteers to create GIS data available openly and freely (http://www.openstreetmap.org); to Wiki sites that embed mapping activities (http://wiki.openstreetmap.org/wiki/WikiProject_Haiti). Ushahidi has emerged as a leading open-source GIS package that supports the input of crowd-source information, and has frequently been used in disaster applications (http://www.ushahidi.com). Crisis Mappers (http://crisismappers.net) brings together networks of experts, crowd-sourced information, human resources, and expertise (over 4,000 people belong to the Crisis Mapper Network) and innovative geographic

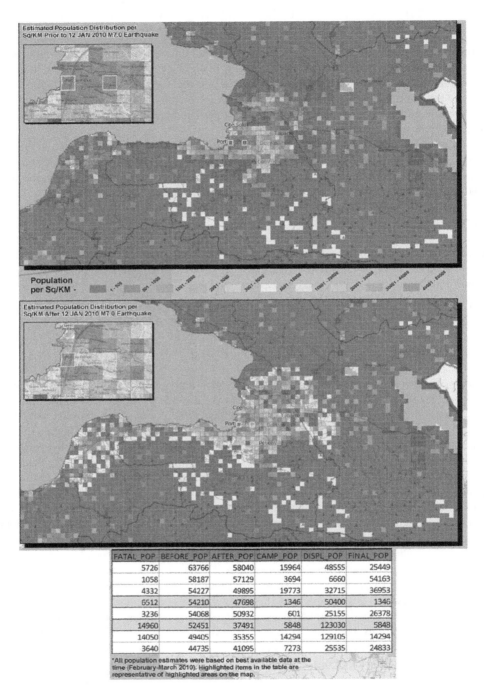

FIGURE 16.3 Haiti: adjusting population distribution in the post earthquake environment for use with the HAZUS-MH international methodology. (With permission.)

PHOTO 16.2   Hoh Indian Reservation, Washington, January 18, 2007. FEMA, state, and Hoh tribal members look at mitigation issues on Hoh Indian Reservation maps in the tribal center. (Source: Marvin Nauman/FEMA photo.)

technologies for innovative solutions for disaster response and risk reduction. Taken together, the opportunities abound.

Nearly all vulnerability assessments incorporate GIS into the process because of the extensive information they integrate and convey. Mapping technologies capture, analyze, and convey data in an extremely accessible manner, one that appeals to the numerous stakeholders in a vulnerability assessment process. Volunteered mapping has rapidly expanded in recent years and introduces many possibilities for conducting more comprehensive and sophisticated vulnerability assessments that have immense promise for disaster relief (Biewald and Janah 2010), response, and risk reduction. Still, much research and investigation is necessary to develop the technology as well as to understand its limitations and possibilities for emergency management (Goodchild and Glennon 2010).

16.10   FINAL CONSIDERATIONS

Just attempting to assess any one aspect of vulnerability can be a daunting process, considering the data, modeling, and analytical complexities, much less adequately combining and integrating the disciplines that inform the process. Terminology, data needs, and methods vary dramatically for every aspect of a vulnerability assessment, and expansive expertise is needed to bridge all of these subtopics. The physical modeling, even by hazard type, is a specialty unto itself. Then there are the specialists in social networking, survey methods, GIS technologies, participatory processes, and the list continues. Clearly, vulnerability assessment requires interdisciplinary approaches, or at a minimum a willingness to draw on information from multiple subject areas. Assembling a team of experts would be beneficial, but this is an involved and intricate process and thus may not be possible, and so partnering with universities, consultants, or individuals in other agencies can be a viable alternative.

Once an assessment is completed, it is equally important to publicize the results and then to ensure their translation through a final report, presentations, new releases, community meetings, a website, and other outlets customized to that location. Ideally, a mechanism for feedback or submitting questions would also be desirable. For example, by working with teachers and school districts, some aspects of the vulnerability assessment can even be incorporated into the school curriculum. The dissemination and feedback processes are essential and should be explicit components of any CVA.

Because a vulnerability assessment is fundamentally about people and the places they live, a heavy responsibility resides with those undertaking the analysis. Mitigation and preparedness are laudable goals, but model outputs could also have negative impacts on communities as well. For instance, if constraints are not clearly explained, results from any loss-estimation model could become the basis for geographical insurance ratings. Another illustration involves portraying vulnerable places. The indices rank neighborhoods and communities based on rather negative criteria. So, while the ultimate goal is to identify pockets of vulnerability to target resources and ultimately reduce loss, this is also a reflection of people's communities, places the residents consider home, not necessarily vulnerable. Data ownership is also relevant. Do residents have a say in what is revealed about their community, especially from a CBP-CVA process where the data are derived from them? Do they continue to have access to the data? The answer to both of these questions should be yes. Ethical considerations point to a need for particular sensitivity when collecting, maintaining, and analyzing data about people, not objects.

16.11 SUMMARY

Vulnerability assessments inform all phases of the emergency management cycle and offer a way to prioritize mitigation activities and increase the efficiency of response. Recognizing from the onset that conducting a vulnerability assessment is not a simple process and requires sufficient resources to achieve goals increases the potential for a successful outcome. The process should be informative, open, carefully designed, flexible, and proactive, not just after a disaster, but also as a preventative measure. Most importantly, results should be translated into decision making. CVA/CBP-CVA, while extremely valuable and necessary, is really only part of the solution, not an entire answer unto itself. The translation of assessments into planning, policy, and decision making that reduces risk for all people is the ultimate goal.

DISCUSSION QUESTIONS

1. Why is a vulnerability assessment useful, and what are its functions?
2. How does a basic CVA reveal community vulnerability?
3. What would the challenges be for implementing a PVCA in your community? What benefits might result?
4. Why do individual and household-level livelihoods matter when considering social vulnerability and capacity?
5. How does a quantitatively driven social vulnerability assessment complement a CBP-CVA? How are the outcomes similar? Different?
6. What are some characteristics of a disaster-resistant community? What indicators would be used to capture this?
7. What types of additional data would be useful for understanding social vulnerability beyond some of the types and sources listed in the chapter?
8. Why is mapping such a powerful tool for vulnerability assessment?
9. What are some challenges to the translation of CVA or CBP-CVA to policy? How might these be overcome?
10. Why are ethical considerations so important both through the CVA/CBP-CVA process and in any final results?
11. What is the relevance of emerging social networking, communication, and geographic technologies for CVA?

ACKNOWLEDGMENTS

The authors acknowledge and thank Pamela Stephens and Jennifer Goldsmith for their contributions to the chapter that appeared in the first edition of this book. This chapter represents the writing of the present authors and does not necessarily reflect that of previous authors.

REFERENCES

Abarquez, Imelda, and Zubair Murshed. 2004. *Community-based disaster risk management: Field practitioners' handbook.* Bangkok, Thailand: Asian Disaster Preparedness Center (ADPC).

Adger, W. N. 2006. Vulnerability. *Global Environmental Change* 16 (3): 268–81.

APA (American Planning Association). 2010. *Hazard mitigation: Integrating best practices into planning.* Planning Advisory Service Report 560. Chicago: American Planning Association.

Auerbach, C. F., and L. B. Silverstein. 2003. *Qualitative data: An introduction to coding and analysis.* New York: New York University Press.

Bausch, D., R. Hansen, J. Rozelle, and S. McNabb. n.d. An updated version: A GIS-based methodology for exporting the Hazards U.S. (HAZUS) Earthquake Model for Global Applications. http://www.usehazus.com/docs/gis_global_hazus_paper.pdf

Beierle, Thomas C., and Jerry Cayford. 2002. *Democracy in practice: Public participation in environmental decisions.* Washington, DC: Resources for the Future.

Berke, P., J. Cooper, D. Salvesen, D. Spurlock, and C. Rausch. 2011. Building capacity for disaster resiliency in six disadvantaged communities. *Sustainability* 3 (1): 1–20.

Berke, P., G. Smith, and W. Lyles. 2012. Planning for resiliency: Evaluation of state hazard mitigation plans under the Disaster Mitigation Act. *Nat. Hazards Rev.* 13 (2): 139–49.

Berke, P. R. and T. J. Campanella. 2006. Planning for postdisaster resiliency. *The Annals of the American Academy of Political and Social Science.* 604 (1): 192–207.

Biewald, L., and L. Janah. 2010. Crowdsourcing disaster relief. *TechCrunch,* August 21. http://techcrunch.com/2010/08/21/crowdsourcing-disaster-relief/.

Birkmann, Jorn, ed. 2006. *Measuring vulnerability to natural hazards: Towards disaster resilient societies.* New York: United Nations University Press.

Boyd, D., and N. Ellison. 2008. Social network sites: Definition, history and scholarship. *Journal of Computer-Mediated Communication.* 13:210–30.

Cannon, Terry, John Twigg, and Jennifer Rowell. 2003. *Social vulnerability, sustainable livelihoods and disasters.* Report to DFID, Conflict and Humanitarian Assistance Department (CHAD) and Sustainable Livelihoods Support Office. Livelihoods and Institutions Group, Natural Resources Institute, Department of International Development, University of Greenwich, U.K., 1–63. http://www.preventionweb.net/english/; www.livelihoods.org/info/docs/vulnerability.doc.

CARE. 2002. *Household livelihood security assessments: A toolkit for practitioners.* Prepared for the PHLS Unit by TANGO International Inc., Tucson, AZ.

Coburn, A. W., R. J. S. Spence, and A. Pomonis. 1994. *Vulnerability and risk assessment.* 2nd ed. UNDP Disaster Management Training Program. Cambridge, U.K.: Cambridge Architectural Research Limited.

Colorado Springs Fire Department. 2011. City of Colorado Springs Community Wildfire Protection Plan, 10–15. http://www.springsgov.com/Page.aspx?navid=101.

Cova, T. J. 1999. GIS in emergency management. In *Geographical information systems,* Vol. 2: *Management issues and applications,* ed. P. A. Longley et al., 845–58. New York: John Wiley and Sons.

Cutter, S., L. Barnes, M. Berry, C. Burton, E. Evans, E. Tate, and J. Webb. 2008. A place-based model for understanding community resilience to natural disasters. *Global Environmental Change* 18 (4): 598–606.

Cutter, S. L., B. J. Boruff, and W. L. Shirley. 2003. Social vulnerability to environmental hazards. *Social Sciences Quarterly* 84:2.

Cutter, Susan L., and Christina Finch. 2008. Temporal and spatial changes in social vulnerability to natural hazards. *PNAS* 105 (7): 2301–6. http://www.pnas.org/content/105/7/2301.short.

Cutter, S. L., J. T. Mitchell, and M. S. Scott. 2000. Revealing the vulnerability of people and places: A case study of Georgetown County, South Carolina. *Annals of the Association of American Geographers* 90:713–37.

CWCB (Colorado Water Conservation Board). 2010. Rules and regulations for regulatory floodplains. http://cwcb.state.co.us/legal/Pages/Rules.aspx.

Dao, Hy, and Pascal Peduzzi. 2003. Global risk and vulnerability index trends per year (GRAVITY). Geneva, Switzerland: UNDP/BCPR. http://www-fourier.ujf-grenoble.fr/~mouton/Publis_HDR_applis/ew_gravity2.pdf.

de Dios, Honorio B. 2002. *Participatory capacities and vulnerabilities assessment: Finding the link between disasters and development*. Oxford, U.K.: Oxfam.

DHS (U.S. Department of Homeland Security). 2009. National Infrastructure Protection Plan partnering to enhance protection and resiliency. http://purl.access.gpo.gov/GPO/LPS113950.

EMAP (Emergency Management Accreditation Program). 2010. *Emergency management standard*. Lexington, KY: EMAP. http://www.emaponline.org/index.php?option=com_content&view=article&id=118&Itemid=110.

Enarson, Elaine. 2003. *Working with women at risk: Practical guidelines for assessing local disaster risk*. Miami: International Hurricane Center, Florida International University.

FEMA (Federal Emergency Management Agency). 1997. *Multi-hazard identification and risk assessment: A cornerstone of the National Mitigation Strategy*. Washington, DC: FEMA.

———. 2004. Multi-hazard mitigation planning guidance under the Disaster Mitigation Act of 2000. Original release March 2004, with revisions November 2006, June 2007, and January 2008. http://www.fema.gov/library/viewRecord.do?id=3115.

———. 2011. *Souris Basin Regional Recovery Strategy*. Washington, DC: FEMA.

———. 2012. HAZUS: FEMA's software program for estimating potential losses from disasters. http://www.fema.gov/protecting-our-communities/hazus.

Fothergill, A., and L. Peek. 2004. Poverty and disasters in the United States: A review of recent sociological findings. *Natural Hazards* 32 (1): 89–110.

Freeman, L. C. 2004. *The development of social network analysis: A study in the sociology of science*. North Charleston, SC: BookSurge, LLC.

Freire, P. 1973. *Education for critical consciousness*. New York: Seabury.

Goodchild, M. F., and J. A. Glennon. 2010. Crowdsourcing geographic information for disaster response: A research frontier. *International Journal of Digital Earth* 3 (3): 231–41.

Gupta, Surajana. 2007. Opening plenary. First global platform on disaster risk reduction (GROOTS). http://www.groots.org/events/june_07_ISDR.html.

Hughes, Amanda L., and Leysia Palen. 2012. The evolving role of the public information officer: An examination of social media in emergency management. *Journal of Homeland Security and Emergency Management* 9 (1): (online).

IFRC (International Federation of Red Cross) and Red Crescent Societies. 2006. *What is VCA? An introduction to vulnerability and capacity assessment*. Geneva, Switzerland: IFRC. http://www.ifrc.org/Docs/pubs/disasters/resources/preparing-disasters/vca/whats-vca-en.pdf.

Isett, K., and K. G. Provan. 2005. The evolution of dyadic interorganizational relationships in a network of publicly funded nonprofit agencies. *Journal of Public Administration and Theory* 15 (1): 149–65.

Mileti, Dennis S. 1999. *Disasters by design: A reassessment of natural hazards in the United States*. Washington, DC: Joseph Henry Press.

Morrow, B. H. 1999. Identifying and mapping community vulnerability. *Disasters* 23:1.

Murphy, B. 2007. Locating social capital in resilient community-level emergency management. *Natural Hazards* 41:297–315.

National Voluntary Organizations Active in Disaster (NVOAD). n.d. http://www.nvoad.org/.

NOAA (National Oceanic and Atmospheric Association) Coastal Services Center. 2012. Roadmap for adapting to coastal risk. http://www.csc.noaa.gov/digitalcoast/training/roadmap.

NRC (National Research Council), Board on Natural Disasters, Commission on Geosciences, Environment, and Resources. 1999. *Reducing natural disasters through better information*. Washington, DC: National Academy Press.

Pearce, L. 2003. Disaster management and community planning, and public participation: How to achieve sustainable hazard mitigation. *Natural Hazards* 28:211–28.

Peduzzi, P., H. Dao, and C. Herold. 2005. Mapping disastrous natural hazards using global datasets. *Natural Hazards* 35:265–89.

Pelling, M. 2007. Learning from others: The scope and challenges for participatory disaster risk assessment. *Disasters* 31 (4): 373–85.

Phong, Tran, Rajib Shaw, Guillaume Chantry, and John Norton. 2011. GIS and local knowledge in disaster management: A case study of flood risk mapping in Viet Nam. *Disasters* 33 (1): 152–69.

PPD-8: National Preparedness, Barack Obama Presidential Policy Directive. 2011. The White House. March 30. http://www.dhs.gov/xabout/laws/gc_1215444247124.shtm.

Radke, J., T. Cova, M. F. Sheridan, A. Troy, M. Lan, and R. Johnson. 2000. Application challenges for GIScience: Implications for research, education, and policy for risk assessment, emergency preparedness and response. *Journal of the Urban and Regional Information Systems Association* 12:15–30.

Reason, Peter. 1994. Three approaches to participative inquiry. In *Denzin and Lincoln, Handbook of qualitative research.* Newbury Park, CA: Sage.

Scott, J. 2000. *Social network analysis: A handbook.* 2nd ed. London: Sage.

Sherrieb, K., F. Norris, and S. Galea. 2010. Measuring capacities for community resilience. *Social Indicators Research* 99 (2): 227–47.

Skerry, Peter. 2000. *Counting on the Census? Race, group identity, and the evasion of politics.* Washington, DC: Brookings Institution Press.

SOPAC (South Pacific Applied Geoscience Commission). 2005. Measuring vulnerability in Small Island Developing States (SIDS): The environmental vulnerability index (EVI). http://www.un.org/esa/sustdev/sids/sidsvind.htm.

Stallings, Robert A., ed. 2002. *Methods of disaster research.* Bloomington, IN: Xlibris Corp.; International Research Committee on Disasters.

Stoecker, Randy. 2005. *Research methods for community change.* Newbury Park, CA: Sage.

Tashakkori, C., and C. Teddle, eds. 2003. *Handbook of mixed methods in social and behavioral research.* Thousand Oaks, CA: Sage.

Thomalla, F., T. Downing, E. Spanger-Siegfried, G. Y. Han, and J. Rockstrom. 2006. Reducing hazard vulnerability: Towards a common approach between disaster risk reduction and climate adaptation. *Disasters* 30 (1): 39–48.

Thomas, D. S. K., K. Ertugay, and S. Kemec. 2006. The role of geographic information systems/remote sensing in disaster management. In *Handbook of disaster research,* ed. H. Rodriguez, E. L. Quarantelli, and R. Dynes. New York: Springer.

Tobin, G. A., and B. E. Montz. 2004. Natural hazards and technology: Vulnerability, risk, and community response in hazardous environments. In *Geography and technology,* ed. S. D. Brunn, S. L. Cutter, and J. W. Harrington Jr. Boston: Kluwer Academic.

Turner II, B. L., Pamela A. Mastson, James J. McCarthy, Robert W. Corell, Lindsey Christensen, Noelle Eckley, Grete K. Hovelsrud-Broda, et al. 2003. Illustrating the coupled human-environment system for vulnerability analysis: Three case studies. *Proceedings of the National Academy of Sciences of the United States of America* 100:14.

Twigg, J. 2001. *Sustainable livelihoods and vulnerability to disasters.* London: Benfield Greig Hazard Research Centre working paper 2. http://www.eird.org/cd/on-better-terms/docs/Twigg-Sustainable-livelihoods-and-vulnerability-to-disasters.pdf.

UNISDR (U.N. Office for Disaster Risk Reduction). 2005. Hyogo Framework for Action 2005–2015: Building the resilience of nations and communities to disasters. http://www.unisdr.org.

———. 2007. Words into action: A guide for implementing the Hyogo Framework. http://www.unisdr.org.

United Nations (UN). 2007. Indicators of Sustainable Development: Guidelines and Methodologies. 3rd Edition. United Nations: New York.

U.S. Census Bureau. 2012a. Census 2010 data. http://2010.census.gov/2010census/data/.

———. 2012b. American Community Survey. http://www.census.gov/acs/www/.

Valentin, A., and J. Spangenberg. 2000. A guide to community sustainability indicators. *Environmental Impact Assessment Review* 20 (3): 381–92.

Varda, D., R. Forgette, D. Banks, and N. Contractor. 2008. Social network methodology in the study of disasters: Issues and insights prompted by post-Katrina research. *Population Research Policy Review* 28 (1): 11–29.

Wasserman, S., and K. Faust. 1994. *Social network analysis.* New York: Cambridge University Press.

RESOURCES

Adams County, Colorado. 2012. Imagine Adams County. http://imagineadamscounty.com/.

Burby, R. 2001. Involving citizens in hazard mitigation planning. *Australian Journal of Emergency Management* 16:3. http://www.em.gov.au/Documents/Involving_citizens_in_hazard_mitigation_planning_making_the_right_choices.pdf.

Caribbean Hazard Mitigation Capacity Building Programme (CHAMP). http://www.cdera.org/projects/champ/mitiplcy/vulnerb.shtml.

Center for Research on the Epidemiology of Disasters (CRED). http://www.cred.be/.

Charlotte-Mecklenburg Emergency Management. 2010. 2010 Hazard Mitigation Plan. http://charmeckem.net/HMP/.

City of Roseville, CA. 2011. *Multi-hazard mitigation plan.* http://www.roseville.ca.us/fire/emergency_pre-paredness/multi_hazard_mitigation_plan.asp.

Crisis Mappers. Crowd-sourcing, Participation, and Distributed GIS for Disaster Management. http://crisis-mappers.net/.

Duda, Kenneth, and Brenda K. Jones. USGS remote sensing for the 2010 Haiti earthquake. ftp://ftp.ecn.purdue.edu/jshan/000000_special_issue/09Duda/text/Duda_USGS%20Haiti%20Coordination_v10Mar2011-1808-forPDF.pdf.

EPA ReVa. http://www.epa.gov/reva/.

Greenwood, Davydd, and Morten Levin. 1998. *Introduction to action research: Social research for social change.* Thousand Oaks, CA: Sage.

Haghebaert, B. Working with vulnerable communities to assess and reduce disaster risk. Humanitarian Practice Network. http://www.odihpn.org/report.asp?id=2888.

Hazard Mitigation Planning Committee (HMPC), Yuba City-Sutter County, California Multi-Hazard Mitigation Plan. 2007. http://www.yubacity.net/documents/News-Events/Multi-Hazard-Mitigation/MultiHazardSection42Vulnerability.pdf.

ISDR. 2006. Let our Children Teach Us! A Review of the Role of Education and Knowledge in Disaster Risk Reduction. United Nations International Strategy for Disaster Risk Reduction. (ISDR) July 2006.

———. Global Network of NGOs for Community Resilience to Disasters. International Strategy for Disaster Reduction (ISDR), October 2006.

Lee County, Florida. 2007. Lee County master mitigation plan. http://www.swfrpc.org/content/Resources/LMMP.pdf.

Los Angeles Times. 2011. Google deploys person finder after Japan earthquake, tsunami leave hundreds dead. March 11. http://latimesblogs.latimes.com/technology/2011/03/google-deploys-person-finder-after-japan-earthquake-tsunami-leaves-hundreds-dead.html.

Michigan Department of State Police. Local Hazard Mitigation Planning Workbook. 2003. EMD-Pub 207. http://www.michigan.gov/documents/7pub207_60741_7.pdf.

Munich Re Foundation. http://www.munichre-foundation.org/StiftungsWebsite/.

Oregon Partnership for Disaster Resilience: Showcase State Program. http://csc.uoregon.edu/opdr/.

Pacific Disaster Center (PDC). 2012. http://www.pdc.org/.

Program to Analyze, Record, and Track Networks to Enhance Relationships (PARTNER). http://www.partner-tool.net/.

ProVention Consortium. http://www.preventionweb.net/english/.

U.S. Census Bureau. 2012. On the Map for Emergency Management. http://onthemap.ces.census.gov/em.html.

U.S. Centers for Disease Control, Committee on Community Engagement. Principles of Community Engagement. http://www.cdc.gov/phppo/pce/part1.htm.

Understanding Risk Network. Understanding Risk: Innovation in Disaster Risk Assessment. 2012. http://www.understandrisk.org/ur/.

Ushahidi. Open Source Mapping. http://www.ushahidi.com/.

Von Kotze, Astrid, and Ailsa Holloway. 1996. Reducing Risk: Participatory Learning Activities for Disaster Mitigation in Southern Africa. Oxfam/IFRC.

INTERACTIVE ONLINE MAPPING EXAMPLES

- California Seismic Hazards Mapping Program. http://www.conservation.ca.gov/cgs/shzp/Pages/Index.aspx.
- FEMA Map Service Center. https://msc.fema.gov/webapp/wcs/stores/servlet/FemaWelcomeView?storeId=10001&catalogId=10001&langId=-1.
- GEOMAC Wildland Fire Support. http://www.geomac.gov/index.shtml.
- Humanitarian Early Warning Service. http://www.hewsweb.org/floods/.
- National Weather Service Weather Mapping. http://www.nws.noaa.gov/outlook_tab.php.
- New Orleans Recovery. http://www.gnocdc.org.
- New York Times. Where to live to avoid a natural disaster. http://www.nytimes.com/interactive/2011/05/01/weekinreview/01safe.html.
- Open Streetmap. http://www.openstreetmap.org, or an example with Haiti: http://wiki.openstreetmap.org/wiki/WikiProject_Haiti.

- SEDAC Global Mapping at Columbia University. http://sedac.ciesin.columbia.edu/maps/client.
- SERVIR Real-time Weather Mapping for Meso America. http://www.servir.net/.
- USAID Famine Early Warning System (FEWS-NET). http://www.fews.net/Pages/default.aspx.
- USGS Earthquake Mapping. http://earthquake.usgs.gov/earthquakes/map/.

17 Social Change and Empowerment

William E. Lovekamp and Sudha Arlikatti

CONTENTS

17.1 CHAPTER PURPOSE

This chapter defines and examines sources of social change and empowerment, and addresses how disasters can influence social change. The chapter also discusses the impacts of several disaster events—the September 11th, 2001, bombings in the United States, the 2004 Indian Ocean tsunami in India, the 2005 Hurricane Katrina in the United States, and the 2010 earthquake in Haiti—to highlight the challenges and impediments to empowerment and social change faced by disadvantaged communities. Each case study emphasizes the unique roles played by nongovernmental and community-based organizations in helping such communities overcome these challenges while bringing about social change at the grassroots level.

17.2 OBJECTIVES

As a result of reading this chapter, the reader should be able to

1. Recognize and develop a critical understanding of the processes of social change and empowerment
2. Understand the importance of nongovernmental and community-based organizations for promoting empowerment and creating social change
3. Acquire knowledge about the history of disaster research and theory to assess how disasters can influence social change
4. Identify change in disaster-stricken communities after the September 11, 2001, bombings in the United States, the 2004 Indian Ocean tsunami in India, the 2005 Hurricane Katrina in the United States, and the 2010 earthquake in Haiti

17.3   INTRODUCTION TO SOCIAL CHANGE

The history of virtually all societies is marked by social change. Social change is defined as "the significant alteration of social structure and cultural patterns through time" (Harper and Leicht 2011, 5). Social structure refers to the "persistent network of social relationships where interaction between persons or groups has become routine and repetitive" (Harper and Leicht 2011, 5). These routine and repetitive patterns of interaction create social institutions or systems. The structure of any society is somewhat specific to that society, depending on the patterns of interaction of social institutions. Culture is "the shared way of living and thinking" (Harper and Leicht 2011, 5) that includes symbols and language, knowledge, beliefs, values, norms, and techniques ranging from common folk recipes to sophisticated technologies and material objects. It is often called the "roadmap of life" within a society. The key to understanding social change is to examine and identify structural issues (e.g., economy, demographic distribution and/or change, complexity of political systems, caste-based differentials) and their relationship to cultural issues (values, how people in society think, what they hope for, how they live). Social change can occur when one or both of these elements are altered.

There are also several important sources of social change such as technology, ideologies, competition, conflict, polity, economic forces, and globalization. Changes in technology, such as the agricultural and industrial revolutions, account for some of the most dramatic and historical social change ever witnessed. Some scholars suggest that humans have recently seen a third technological revolution with the introduction of the microchip, which has resulted in computers and, subsequently, the "information age." Technology not only changes how humans work, but also changes how people interact with one another. Hence, the information age and the use of the Internet, cell phones, iPods, text messaging, Facebook, etc., have altered the way we communicate with others and live.

Additionally, ideologies can promote the status quo or promote social change. Ideologies are cultural beliefs such as democracy, communism, multiculturalism, etc., that justify social arrangements. An ideological change in our society, such as the emphasis on multiculturalism, has transformed education. For example, in the United States there is a great emphasis on English–Spanish bilingualism, English–Spanish public signs in areas with large Hispanic populations, and some states, such as California, allow drivers to take exams in a number of languages.

Competition can also cause social change by "forcing individuals to adopt new forms of behavior to attain desired goals" or be an effect of social change because "a changing society has more goals open to competition than a static society" (Vago 2004, 19). Conflict between different groups has also been identified as a source of social change. While competitors usually have the same goal and are subject to rules of competing, parties in conflict often have different and incompatible goals and may threaten or coerce each other, leading to social change.

Polity, or the political process, can be an additional source of change. People in positions of political power often control and influence access to resources through the political process. Differential access to resources then influences life chances. Furthermore, "Power always implies non-power and therefore resistance" (Vago 2004, 29). Polity characterized by power differentials is thus a dynamic source of change, which further influences economic policies, which in turn change and shape individuals' lives. For example, Karl Marx argued that organization of the economic system determines how other social institutions (religion, politics, family, education, etc.) would be structured. Large corporations increasingly create and control markets and determine what members of society "shall eat, drink, wear, and smoke, and how their homes shall look, and what price they shall pay for what they buy" (Vago 2004, 33). With corporations controlling markets, economic power is often centralized, sparking resistance or conflict among the haves and the have-nots. This has led to social change and sometimes social empowerment.

Finally, globalization has more recently been identified as a source of social change. In fact, it could even be argued that globalization is a form of social change, with expanding economic markets, divisions of labor, and the dissemination of culture within and across societies. Each of these sources can contribute to changes that take place within societies and across cultures.

17.4   DISASTERS AND SOCIAL CHANGE

Researchers have long debated whether disasters can produce large-scale social change. On one hand, researchers argue that major change rarely results from disasters (Wright et al. 1979; Friesema et al. 1979; Rossi, Wright, and Wright 1981). Disasters do not cause growing and prosperous communities to decline, nor do they cause communities on the decline to rise up and become prosperous. Others support the notion that disasters simply accelerate or decelerate preexisting trends present in society (Bates et al. 1963; Oliver-Smith 1986). Finally, some posit that a disaster can create opportunities for major social changes (Dacy and Kunreuther 1969; Cochrane 1975; Abril-Ojeda 1982; Bates 1982; Killian, Peacock, and Bates 1984; Hoover and Bates 1985). Nigg and Tierney (1993)[*] state that research equally supports one of two positions: (1) that disasters contribute to change only by accelerating trends that were already under way prior to impact, and (2) that disasters rarely have noticeable impacts on communities beyond the change caused during and immediately after the disaster occurrence, what would be considered the short-term recovery period.

There are several possible explanations that account for such variation in perspectives or views. One is that there are several different kinds of change. Social change is a complex process (Harper and Leicht 2011) and may include change in personnel, the way parts of structures relate to one another, the function of structures, relationships between structures, and emergence of new structures. There are also several different levels of change (Harper and Leicht 2011), ranging from small group change, changes to organizations, institutions, and society, to global changes. These can all lead to different conclusions about the presence and significance of social change. For instance, "Disaster researchers have studied everything from small, relatively isolated communities or a small number of households or organizations, to large metropolitan communities, clusters of communities and, in a few cases, entire societies" (Morrow and Peacock 1997, 227–28). Therefore, results from one study may not be generalizable to another study.

Even though perspectives on social change and disasters can vary greatly, social change has been an important area of interest from the beginning of disaster research as a field of study. The following four examples demonstrate the long-standing interest in social change. Samuel Prince's investigation of the town of Halifax, Nova Scotia, after the explosion of a munitions ship in 1917 is credited as the first study of the social characteristics of a disaster and social change. He noted that "catastrophes" were not isolated events, but part of the fabric of the community. Because catastrophes interfered with the equilibrium of the social institutions within a given society, they were critical to social change.

In his study of Halifax, Prince (1920) found that the community grew more rapidly after the explosion than it ordinarily might have. More specifically, the explosion prompted increases in building permits, bank clearings, postal and tramway revenues, and generated a renewed interest in voting, city planning and civic improvement, health, education, and recreation. He stated that "Halifax has been galvanized into life through the testing experience of a great catastrophe. She has undergone a civic transformation, such as could hardly otherwise have happened in fifty years" (Prince 1920, 139). In this instance, the disaster created positive social change in Halifax in a way that otherwise would have been impossible or, at the very least, improbable.

Pitrim Sorokin (1942, 9) wrote the first theoretical book on "calamities" where he focused on the effects of the calamities on "behavior, social organization and cultural life of the populations involved." He argued that formal organizational activities and control (especially by government) increases in the postdisaster period as attempts to reestablish equilibrium. Such calamities increase the competition for resources between social groupings of individuals in society where there is an imbalance, which can lead to social change. He also noted that "when [a disaster] overtakes a given

---

[*] For an excellent summary of disasters and social change literature up to 1993, see Joanne M. Nigg and Kathleen J. Tierney (1993), "Disasters and Social Change: Consequences for Community Construct and Affect." Unpublished paper presented at the American Sociological Association Annual Meeting, Miami, Florida. http://dspace.udel.edu:8080/dspace/handle/19716/580.

society, it becomes the focal point of attention in science and art, religion and morals, and other fields" (Sorokin 1942, 156), leading to change in the entire sociocultural landscape.

Gideon Sjoberg (1962, 356) suggested that disasters are a "key variable in altering social structures of industrial–urban societies." Disasters create channels for mobility and create demographic shifts within a society that in "normal" times might not exist or may bring to light structural changes that were already in motion prior to the catastrophe. Sjoberg contended that many of the dramatic social changes in the twentieth century within industrial societies were brought about by social structures responding to catastrophes. Whenever hope is perceived and people are permitted access to mechanisms of social and political power, efforts to bring about social change will be made. Marginalized groups who are already dissatisfied with the social order may seek change through reform or revolution. Similar to Sorokin, he contends that

> actors will struggle to re-establish equilibrium in the system if they see hope for its attainment in a reasonable period. But when they hold little confidence in the utility of their efforts, people will passively accept the disaster's consequences, distasteful though this may be. (Sjoberg 1962, 374)

Russell Dynes (1975) examined opportunities for social change in three types of societies, their vulnerability to disasters, and the likelihood that disasters will produce change. Type I societies are characterized by small populations—organized in terms of family, kin, and clan or tribal relationships—and have a fragile economic base. Disasters can produce considerable disruption and social change in these societies. Type II societies have larger populations and more stable economies where disasters typically produce moderate disruption and social change. Type III societies have large populations and a complex and integrated social structure, such as nation-states, and are most resistant to social change and disruption. They have considerable resources and established institutional structures, such as the Federal Emergency Management Agency (FEMA), the Department of Homeland Security (DHS), and the American Red Cross, in the United States, to cope. Overall, he found that more developed societies are more likely to experience very little social change and disruption than less developed societies.

Additionally, Quarantelli and Dynes (1976) suggested that community conflicts tend to disappear in postdisaster emergency periods, while only to reappear later. The emergency period is characterized by an atmosphere of empathy, resulting in an abundance of aid. The expression of social solidarity and helpfulness among members of affected communities has been described as "utopia" (Wolfenstein 1957), "altruistic" (Barton 1969), or "therapeutic" (Fritz 1961). However, during the disaster recovery period, inequalities often arise in distribution of resources, leading to disagreements in affected communities (Drury and Olson 1998). Additionally, the convergence of new actors may cause conflictual modifications to existing social structures. Altruistic behavior and temporary cessation of predisaster conflicts reemerge, potentially resulting in heightened community conflict or "acrimonious" behavior (Morrow and Peacock 1997; Tierney, Lindell, and Perry 2001). In some cases, the acrimony following disasters has resulted in major issues of political unrest and conflict (Drury and Olson 1998; Bates and Peacock 1987; Blaikie et al. 1994).

Hence, disasters can influence social change, but this is often dependent on the stability of the social structure, the characteristics of the culture, and the ability of groups to mobilize resources and power to fight for change.

17.5 HOW DO MEMBERS OF A SOCIETY BRING ABOUT SOCIAL CHANGE?

While disasters can create opportunities for social change, it is also important to understand the mechanisms that facilitate that change. We begin by discussing empowerment, which is a critically important component of social change and is essential if social change is to be equitable. Empowerment is providing power to people who have been historically marginalized or who are most vulnerable, and providing them with the ability to make choices that are beneficial to them in the future. According to Naila Kabeer (1999, 437), empowerment refers to "the expansion in people's ability to make strategic life choices in a context where this ability was previously denied to them." In examining empowerment, we need to examine "how the matrix of domination is structured along certain axes—race, gender, class, sexuality, and nation—as well as how it operates through interconnected domains of power—structural, interpersonal, disciplinary, and hegemonic" (Collins 2000, 288–89).

In disasters, these systems of oppression and domination, which are usually based on race, ethnicity, social class, caste, gender, age, disability, health, or language, as discussed in previous chapters, limit people's voices, their access to vital preparedness information, and their ability to recover. Simply stated, people who are marginalized and the most vulnerable are often the last to recover. In disaster situations, it is critically important that everyone be considered an equal stakeholder in recovery and that everyone have a voice. Disaster preparedness, response, and recovery must be equitable, and any changes should be empowering for the communities and people who are most directly impacted. (See Photo 17.1.)

A discussion of how members of a society can bring about change in disaster times (define something as a problem, mobilize and take action) and the importance of nongovernmental organizations (NGOs) and community-based, grassroots groups in disaster situations is thus merited. First, the application of the social constructionist perspective to disasters has been very useful for examining social change. This theoretical perspective was originally developed to explain the existence of social problems and how groups define conditions as problems and how they eventually address them. Spector and Kitsuse (1973, 415) define social problems as "the activities of groups making assertions of grievances and claims with respect to some putative conditions." When people make claims that a condition is a problem, which is inherently socially constructed and defined, and respond to the claims, the condition is then regarded as a social problem. Hence, most social constructionist research focuses on claims-making activities and examines how these claims come to be accepted as legitimate and worthy of action (Best 1990).

This perspective has also been applied to the field of disaster research and arguably has made the largest theoretical contribution to disaster research in the United States (Mileti 1999, 211). This perspective "views disasters as socially produced through the formation of a common and shared definition . . . and that disasters do not exist in and of themselves but are the products of how people agree to define them" (Mileti 1999, 210–11). Hence, social constructionism has been used to "examine the meanings of disasters for community residents, reflected in the claims-making activities

PHOTO 17.1 Evidence of empowerment efforts as well as resilience and recovery after Hurricane Katrina. (Photo by Pam Jenkins and Barbara Davidson. With permission.)

through which they define the disaster and translate their understandings into claims for action" (Aronoff and Gunter 1992, 346).

Some scholars have also argued that disasters are best conceptualized as nonroutine social problems (Kreps and Drabek 1996; Kreps 1998). In one of the best examples to date, Stallings (1997) used the social constructionist perspective to examine an earthquake threat as a social problem for involving "people a) reacting to past earthquakes [condition is problematic], b) to press for change in the present, c) in order to avoid an otherwise more negative future [actions will influence social change]" (Stallings 1997, 3). This perspective clearly enables researchers to examine the mechanisms that create change within disaster-affected communities.

Researchers have also examined connections of disasters and involvement in social movements, which clearly have the ability to influence social change. Most social movement literature investigates the relationship between technological or human-induced disasters and the movement's activity. In one example of social movement participation after the Three Mile Island disaster, researchers examined how the construction of shared grievances, established social networks, previous activism, and existing friendship networks all served as catalysts for social movement involvement (Cable, Walsh, and Warland 1988; Walsh and Warland 1983). Following an examination of the two different paths of activism present in the Three Mile Island disaster, the researchers concluded that "recruitment and commitment patterns appear to depend on complex interactions between and among grievances, existing networks, and prevailing ideologies" (Cable, Walsh, and Warland 1988, 966). In technological disasters, blame is often assigned, and communities are much more likely to mobilize and fight for social change that will protect them in the future. (See Photo 17.2.)

Conversely, relatively little research explores the relationship between natural disasters and movements because natural disasters are often incorrectly viewed as "acts of God" or natural, where blame is not assigned. However, Blocker, Rochford, and Sherkat (1991) examined elements of protest movements during a large metropolitan flash flood on Memorial Day weekend in 1984 in Tulsa, Oklahoma. Many people believed the flood resulted from inadequacies of their city to maintain their flood control system. As a result, hundreds of citizens targeted their city government through protests. While not all community members participated, many with similar background characteristics, a strong sense of solidarity, and shared grievances were much more likely

PHOTO 17.2   Community resistance and organizing in New Orleans after Hurricane Katrina. (Photo by Pam Jenkins and Barbara Davidson. With permission.)

to participate (Blocker, Rochford, and Sherkat 1991). Therefore, if people are able to recognize the social structural and political causes of disasters and not dismiss them as "acts of God" or natural, mobilization, movement participation, and change are much more likely to occur.

The role of nongovernmental and community-based organizations in catalyzing social change is critical to our understanding. These organizations are "independent, flexible, democratic, secular, non-profit people's organizations working for and/or assisting in the empowerment of economically and socially marginalized people" (Cousins 1991). Cousins states that they can be

1. Charitable organizations, which typically take a top-down approach to helping others
2. Service organizations, which provide health, family planning, and/or educational services and in which people are expected to participate
3. Participatory organizations, which comprise self-help activities in which local people are involved in the implementation of a project
4. Empowering organizations, which help people help themselves by teaching them an understanding of the social, political, and economic forces that shape their lives

Community-based organizations are a type of nongovernmental organization arising from efforts by local citizens that usually adopt a grassroots approach to helping others or helping others to help themselves and may include religious organizations, women's organizations, social clubs, etc. Community-based organizations are often important in disasters because they provide services that traditional emergency service providers do not, or cannot, provide (Arlikatti, Bezboruah, and Long 2012). Some nongovernmental organizations and many government-based emergency service providers are bound by formalized criteria or regulations in the type of services they can provide or the populations they can serve. Community-based organizations may have less stringent criteria or can be flexible enough that they can meet unique needs of specialized populations.

Community-based organizations are often influential in establishing "unmet needs committees" after disasters to provide services to people who otherwise would "fall between the cracks." They can also provide day-to-day services for specialized populations, such as the disabled, elderly, poor, immigrant, homeless, or special-health-needs communities. They can also help reduce vulnerability to disasters because they know the specialized needs of their clients or community and can bring those needs to the attention of emergency managers and disaster planners. They also engage in coalition building, where they are developing partnerships with each other in collaborative efforts to reduce vulnerabilities of specialized populations or promote social change. (See Photo 17.3.)

In recent years, nongovernmental and community-based organizations have become integral to disaster response and recovery efforts across the globe as they increasingly encourage a bottom-up, approach with public participation. In their edited volume *Beyond the Magic Bullet: NGO Performance and Accountability in the Post–Cold War World*, Edwards and Hulme (1995) specifically describe the roles of nongovernmental and grassroots organizations in international development assistance. This in-depth compilation of works by field experts and researchers discusses the complexities of social change and development, provides frameworks for assessing performance and accountability of NGOs, and offers guidelines for improvements, primarily emphasizing the need for government institutions and NGOs to work synergistically toward building social change and community empowerment.

What follows are four case studies of recent disasters, the September 11, 2001, terrorist attacks and Hurricane Katrina in 2005, both of which have significantly impacted America and its cultural landscape, the impacts of the Indian Ocean tsunami in 2004 on South India, and the 2010 Haiti earthquake. These help illustrate the concepts of community mobilization, empowerment, and social and policy changes in postdisaster contexts.

PHOTO 17.3 Building back better? Improvements to structure and amenities after the tsunami in India. (Photo by Sudha Arlikatti. With permission.)

17.5.1 September 11, 2001, Terrorist Attacks in the United States

We all remember the tragic events that occurred on September 11, 2001. The terrorist attacks and the collapse of the World Trade Center towers will forever be etched into the collective memory of the United States; 2,729 people died, and more than 7,000 were injured or hospitalized (Foner 2005). These events were defining moments that are intrinsically connected in complex ways to both policy and social changes in the aftermath.

The September 11, 2001, terrorist attacks served as what Birkland (2004) calls a "focusing event" and provided policy makers with a window of opportunity for creating change. Some of the most visible policy changes since September 11, 2001, are the creation of the Department of Homeland Security (DHS), the Transportation Security Administration (TSA), the Homeland Security Advisory System, and the National Incident Management System (NIMS). Also, since the terrorist attacks, there has been a resurgence in support for the dominant view of military involvement in disaster response and a de-emphasis on community-based preparedness and mitigation, as evidenced by the elimination of Project Impact (Tierney and Bevc 2007). Birkland (2004) also argues that the Federal Emergency Management Agency (FEMA) has disinvested in and de-emphasized its role in natural disasters and now primarily focuses on homeland security issues since the terrorist attacks, even though disasters pose much greater and more consistent risks than terrorism (Birkland 2004). Today, the Department of Homeland Security contains the following agencies: Citizenship and Immigration Services, Customs and Border Protection, Immigration and Customs Enforcement, Transportation Security Administration (TSA), Coast Guard, Secret Service, and the Federal Emergency Management Agency. The creation of the Department of Homeland Security, the focus on airline security and terrorism via the TSA, the absorption of the U.S. Immigration and Naturalization Service into the DHS, and the absorption of FEMA into DHS to fight the "war" on terrorism are all consistent with this dominant, militaristic view. (For additional thoughts on disasters and conflict, see Box 17.1.)

Not only did the terrorist attacks usher in numerous policy changes, they also prompted many social changes within communities across the United States. One such community, Manhattan, has

BOX 17.1   DISASTERS AS "WAR" AND MILITARISTIC RESPONSE

The view of disasters as similar to war and a military style of response was promoted in the 1950s from anxiety over the Cold War and incorporated into classic definitions of disaster. In the 1960s, Charles Fritz emphasized the following two reasons for the study of disasters: "first, to secure more adequate protection of the nation from the destructive consequences and potential atomic, biological, and chemical attack; and second, to produce the maximal amount of disruption to the enemy in the event of a war" (Fritz 1961, 653). Much of the early disaster research evolved as a response to the institutional demand for understanding how people would react in the face of danger—specifically, how communities would react to dangerous events to gain insight into potential reactions to other destructive external agents, such as war.

This conflict-oriented approach views disaster as a duplication of war, an expression of social vulnerabilities, an entrance into a state of uncertainty, and an attack on groups or communities. Furthermore, this approach focuses on the destructive external agents of disasters and promotes a militaristic response. This militaristic command style of administration was further emphasized when, prior to the creation of the Federal Emergency Management Agency (FEMA) in 1979, most disaster programs were under the Office of Civil Defense and later the Defense Civil Preparedness Agency. After the Cold War era, disaster preparedness and mitigation became more grassroots and community based and continued through the President Clinton era with the creation of Project Impact, a community-based effort at disaster preparedness and mitigation.

the largest Chinese ethnic community in the United States. Chinatown is home to some 56,000 Asian residents, 33,000 workers, and 4,000 businesses that are Chinese owned and operated (Akbar and Sims 2008). Garment work is the largest industry in Chinatown. Before September 11th, there were approximately 246 garment factories in Chinatown employing nearly 14,000 garment workers (Akbar and Sims 2008). In the year following the terrorist attacks, Chinatown's garment industry lost an estimated $490 million with the shutdown of approximately 65 garment factories (Akbar and Sims 2008). It is now estimated that approximately 100 garment factories closed, eliminating about 8,000 Chinese garment worker jobs (Sim 2002).

Also, Chinatown is located less than 10 blocks from "ground zero"—the name that came to be associated with the site where the World Trade Center towers fell. Ground zero was declared a "frozen zone," part of the disaster area that was cordoned off by police and National Guard troops, barring people from entry for several weeks. When the work was still available, many had trouble getting to their homes and to work. Moreover, Chinese who work in Chinatown but live in Brooklyn and Queens had even more difficulties getting into the frozen zone. "Those lucky enough to have kept an old pay stub with the factory address were allowed in; others had to walk around the perimeter until they found a breach in security" (Chin 2005, 195).

Furthermore, the only work remaining for the garment industry was work that was left over from before the terrorist attacks. No new work came into the majority of factories until January 2002 (Chin 2005). Also, while living in the enclave community, many women working in the garment factories were unable to find other work, which was only available outside the community. The networks women had established were often with other women garment workers who knew very little about other jobs available for women outside of Chinatown (Chin 2005). Also, women did not work outside of the community; all of the family members who worked outside of the community were men. As a result, many Chinese women have started to leave Chinatown to look for work; many who traveled to Chinatown from other areas have since found other work in their communities; and many more are learning to speak English as a way of broadening their social networks to ensure that they are more marketable when looking for work. Chin (2005) concludes that garment workers are in the midst of "producing their own sea change" in both the garment industry and their community by changing the way they look for work. The old way of finding jobs through family networks is no longer effective. Garment workers no longer have the right connections, and the old connections they once had no longer point them to secure jobs. The effects of September 11th on the local Chinatown economy have transformed the community in numerous ways. Time will continue to tell the story of social change in Chinatown.

In a second example of social change after September 11, 2001, Muslims experienced many forms of overt and covert prejudice and discrimination after the terrorist attacks. Public perception was that anyone who looked Muslim must have been tied to the terrorists or been part of the attack. This story was solidified with heightened media publicity in Jersey City after the attacks. Jersey City is within a few miles of Manhattan, is racially and ethnically diverse, and is home to a very large Muslim population. The media and the nation focused on Jersey City with hostility partially because of the link the community had with Sheik Omar Abdel-Rahman, who spoke in the community years ago and was convicted of planning the 1993 World Trade Center attack (Bryan 2005). This was also an area of intense FBI (U.S. Federal Bureau of Investigation) infiltration. The FBI, under the order of General John Ashcroft, was ordered to interview some 5,000 male Muslims between the ages of 18 and 33 in their homes or at their workplaces for information relating to terrorism (Bryan 2005; Nabeer 2006). Also, approximately 800 of a total of 1,200 INS (U.S. Immigration and Naturalization Service) detainees were housed in two New Jersey jails located just outside of Jersey City (Bryan 2005).

Muslims across America became the target of hate crimes and discrimination as a result of these events. Many women were harassed or beaten for wearing the *hijab*, a head scarf that has great religious significance, in public. If they chose not to wear the *hijab* in public, they risked not being true to their faith. Muslims were assaulted and scorned on the streets and in banks, coffee shops, grocery stores, etc., by random passers-by, neighbors, and police. The attacks ranged from "children throwing rocks at Muslim women to teenagers throwing beer cans at adult men and women punching Muslim women in the face while attempting to rip off their clothes and tear their veils" (Bryan 2005, 143). In her study of Muslim students, Peek (2003) demonstrates how students did not feel like a part of the larger community because they were portrayed as "the enemy" or "the other"; were excluded from the process of mourning, social bonding, and helping behaviors; and were very concerned about their safety and discrimination.

Despite the severity of the scorn, prejudice, and discrimination following the terrorist attacks, the events led to positive social change for many in the Muslim community in Jersey City and in Muslim communities across the United States. In response to the hostility experienced, many Muslims chose not to blend in or downplay their Arab or Muslim identity (Bryan 2005; Peek 2003). Many believed this to be a critical time to change the way Islam was represented and to educate the media, political leaders, and the larger society about their religion. Muslims began spending more time together reading and discussing the Qur'an; learning Arabic and attending religious services, some for the first time; and paid much closer attention to Islamic rules. The result was that community ties were heightened and Muslim identity and culture were reaffirmed for many after September 11th. Muslim women and men stated that after September 11th, "they gained a renewed sense of purpose in their roles as strong sisters and brothers of Islam" (Bryan 2005, 155). Muslim students in the New York City area believed that "people were genuinely interested in learning about Islam and understanding them and their faith" (Peek 2003, 345). And since September 11th, many American Muslim organizations, both secular and religious, have spoken out publicly and contributed to the national conversation on conflict prevention and terrorism (Huda 2006).

As we can see from the aforementioned examples, while many social processes or changes were already taking place prior to September 11th, such as the move of garment factories out of Chinatown and hostility toward Muslim Americans, the terrorist attacks had a direct and significant impact on each of these communities and facilitated policy and social change in a variety of ways.

17.5.2   The 2004 Indian Ocean Tsunami

On 26 December 2004, an underwater earthquake of magnitude 9.1 on the Richter scale hit north-ern Sumatra in Indonesia, triggering a series of devastating tsunamis along the coasts of most land masses bordering the Indian Ocean and claiming over 300,000 lives in 11 countries. The coastal communities were inundated with waves as high as 30 m (100 ft), destroying hundreds and thou-sands of homes and public buildings around the Indian Ocean, especially in Indonesia, Thailand, Sri Lanka, India, Malaysia, and the Maldives (Arlikatti and Andrew 2012). In India, the damage caused by the tsunami was estimated at USD 2.56, billion directly affecting the livelihoods of 2.8 million people in 1,089 villages (Census of India 2001). The Nagapattinam District along the south-east coast of the Indian peninsula was one of the hardest-hit areas in the state of Tamil Nadu, where 6,000 lives were lost, 196,000 people displaced, and over 28,000 sheltered in temporary relief camps (Prater et al. 2006). Most seriously affected were households from the lower social groups and households whose livelihoods depended directly or indirectly on fishing activities. In addition to public infrastructure, about 84,000 boats were destroyed, more than 32,000 livestock were lost, and about 39,000 hectares of agricultural lands were damaged. Compared to 10 years prior to the tsunami, household incomes from fishing activities fell from 8,000 to 10,000 rupees/week to a mere 1,000 rupees/week after the tsunami. The district of Nagapattinam had a population of 1.5 million (Census of India 2001), with most of the rural households living below the poverty line. Given the high population density along the Tamil Nadu coastline, the bulk of the damage was within half a kilometer from the high-tide line (Kumaran and Negi 2006).

The response to the tsunami-affected populace in South India is a great case in point to demon-strate the importance of cross-sector collaborations in short-term and long-term postdisaster recov-ery projects. With their diverse range of skills and detachment from bureaucracy, traditional NGOs have proven their worth in numerous disasters, as they are able to fill in the gaps left unattended by national and multilateral organizations (Coppola 2006). Whether filling in the gaps left by govern-ments involve providing basic needs, addressing special-interest groups, or raising and allocating funds, NGOs have the capacity to provide services and do so "regardless of race, creed, or nation-ality … and on the basis of need alone" (Coppola 2006, 404). In Nagapattinam, the central, state, and local government agencies worked closely with local NGOs, including Sneha, Seva Bharati, Sevalaya, Revathi, Suyam, Land for Tiller's Freedom Foundation; faith-based groups, including Mata Amritanandamayi Math, Art of Living Foundation, Church's Auxiliary for Social Action; the private sector, including the TATA group, BSNL, Wipro; and international NGOs, including INGOs like Oxfam, Terre Des Hommes, United Nations International Children's Emergency Fund (Arlikatti, Bezboruah, and Long 2012). (See Photo 17.4.)

These collaborations were vital in providing immediate relief and long-term rehabilitation services such as aid distribution, counseling services, shelter management, education, and even rebuilding of new homes, based upon their capacity and expertise. Government officials, led by the district collector of Nagapattinam, met with NGOs and INGOs every evening for two months to be apprised of the situation in various impacted villages. These collaborations proved vital in stem-ming any potential outbreak of epidemics and community conflicts.

Two large-sample quantitative studies were conducted by the Fritz Institute (Thomas 2005, 3) in Indonesia, Sri Lanka, and India (2,300 people surveyed, including 1,000 people from 93 villages in India, 800 people from 98 villages in Sri Lanka, and 500 people from the five most-affected areas in northern Sumatra). These two studies—conducted 60 days and again nine months after the tsunami—focused on survivors' recollections of rescue and relief operations by the local agen-cies and NGOs. Interestingly, they found that, particularly in India, the local government agencies spearheaded the relief operations and were successful in bringing immediate relief to disaster sur-vivors. The government was particularly visible in the burial of the dead (40%) and the provision of water (40%), shelter (32%), and medical care (57%). The local communities were the second most visible relief providers, reaching 20% (average across all services) of those surveyed, and religious

PHOTO 17.4 Missing the livelihoods link? Limited open spaces for fishing activities after the tsunami in India. (Photo by Sudha Arlikatti. With permission.)

organizations (9.9% across all services) and local NGOs (9.5% across all services) had a relatively minor role. In their recall of the services that they received 48 hours after the tsunami, the beneficiaries in India were most satisfied in every category of aid, in contrast to their counterparts in Indonesia, who were the least satisfied in every category.

A number of NGOs and INGOs were also actively involved in the long-term recovery processes and helped with livelihoods restoration and housing recovery as well (Prater et al. 2006). Financial assistance was provided for the purchase of catamarans (derived from the Tamil language, it is a multihulled boat used by local fishermen), motorboats, nets, hooks, and iceboxes as a means of delivering rapid rehabilitation of microeconomic activities existing locally before the disaster (Régnier et al. 2008). NGOs initiated numerous "cash for work" and "food for work" programs involving beneficiaries in saltpan cleaning, desalination of ponds, planting samplings, and creating bioshields as a means of creating alternative employment opportunities.

After the 2004 tsunami, the Tamil Nadu state government undertook construction of permanent houses as part of a rehabilitation program. In the past, the Indian government with the assistance of NGOs has had success in adopting two solutions to providing rural public housing: the "site and services" and the "core housing" approaches. In the site-and-services approach, each family is provided with a small plot and varying levels of services such as: a water tap, stormwater drainage, a sewer connection, paved access, street lighting, etc. Sometimes this is supplemented with the core-housing approach, consisting of a toilet, kitchen, and one room at a minimum and maybe an additional plinth area or a staircase access to the terrace to allow for future expansions. This second approach was the one adopted by the state government of Tamil Nadu, India, in providing housing for disaster victims. The intent was to monitor the rebuilding that followed to verify that it would be tsunami and earthquake resistant as stipulated by the national building code of India 2005 (NBC 2005).

In the summer of 2005, six months after the tsunami, Arlikatti et al. (2010) surveyed 1,000 randomly selected households from 15 coastal villages and one urban settlement in the Nagapattinam district. They found that reconstruction of houses was undertaken by numerous NGOs under the approval and supervision of the NGO Coordination Cell set up by the local district collector's office. This was to ensure that all 81 of the severely impacted coastal villages in the district received equitable aid. All new housing designs adhered to better earthquake and tsunami building codes, and special relocation schemes for people living too close to the high-tide line were also undertaken (ADRC 2005; Arlikatti and Andrew 2012).

A popular premise is that improvements to postdisaster housing structures contribute favorably to the overall perception of household recovery if government agencies and NGOs are responsive to the needs of the populace regarding housing design and the selection of relocation sites for reconstruction and rehabilitation (Arlikatti and Andrew 2012). As Wamsler (2006, 167) notes, "To improve present structures and technologies before importing new ones it is important that urban planners become more aware of local knowledge, assets and the coping strategies of people at risk." By December 2008, there were 71 new housing construction sites in the Nagapattinam district. Lands were provided by the state government in areas zoned as Coastal Regulation Zone III (CRZ-III), and the houses were rebuilt for not more than Rs 150,000,* i.e., approximately \$3,300 including infrastructure costs (Arlikatti and Andrew 2012).†

In a follow-up study conducted in 2008, Arlikatti and Andrew (2012) gauged the perceptions of satisfaction about post-tsunami housing reconstruction among households from 7 of the 16 communities previously surveyed. They found that perceptions of recovery varied among the 558 panel respondents, depending on social class and livelihood type (fishing or agriculture related). The house plans in rehabilitated and newly constructed neighborhoods have changed considerably since the tsunami, with newer homes typically smaller in size, but with a greater number of rooms, a floor-plan design that was approved by the government of Tamil Nadu to ensure parity and equitability across communities. The structural quality of repaired homes has also seen tremendous improvements with the use of earthquake-resistant building codes and better building materials for floors, walls, and roofs of houses. In addition, all new homes adhere to the Coastal Regulation Zone (CRZ) standards that stipulate no new construction up to 500 meters from the high-tide line (HTL). Improvements in household utilities and amenities is also evident, with all new homes being wired for electricity, a water tap inside the home for potable drinking water, and an attached toilet connected to a sewage system.

Despite these and other physical improvements to the built environment, households from the most-backward castes and scheduled castes, lower-income households, and families involved in nonfishing activities had lower perceptions of recovery when compared to those from the backward castes, higher incomes, and those involved in fishing activities (Arlikatti and Andrew 2012). Previous studies have shown similar trends when houses built by NGOs or public agencies failed to take into account local housing culture and Indian *Vastu* principles (similar to *feng shui* principles adopted by the Chinese) and were built away from original settlements for various reasons, including questions of land tenure and ownership and safety concerns, leading to their abandonment by beneficiaries (Barenstein 2010). Further, Andrew et al. (2012) found that beneficiaries of donor-assisted resettlement housing programs perceived a lower sense of recovery than those households that received assistance to repair their homes but remained at their original housing locations, suggesting a need for future studies to look at how and why recipients of different housing programs experience differing recovery trajectories.

Arlikatti and Andrew (2012) note that for many that did not lose family members the tsunami served as a window of opportunity. Many of the survivors are proud owners of property for the first time in their lives. Even women's rights to own property are protected as never before, with the government requiring that a new home be registered jointly by the husband and wife, unlike before the tsunami when only the male head of household owned property. Their villages have better housing stock, tarred roads, and new public buildings like elementary and high schools, trade schools, marriage halls, and day-care centers for infants.

---

* Rs. 150,000 = \$3300 (using the exchange Rate in 2008, of \$1=Rs.45.45).

† CRZ-I pertains to places that are ecologically sensitive areas between 0 to 100 meters from the coastline, CRZ-II covers areas that have already been developed up to or close to the shoreline, CRZ-III covers areas that are relatively undisturbed and those which do not belong to either Category-I or II (as per the 2011 Coastal Regulation Zone (CRZ) Notification released by the Ministry of Environment and Forests Government of India (MoEF n.d.).

However, lessons can be learned and applied to ensure community satisfaction, accelerate the rate of long-term recovery processes, and empower communities to adopt sustainable mitigation practices wholeheartedly. Community involvement is known to restore the self-respect of disaster victims (Babister and Kelman 2002); hence the direct beneficiaries of reconstruction and recovery programs need to be involved right from the outset. It would be worthwhile to involve local community leaders in site selection and plan making to ensure that culturally and climatically sensitive materials are used, to the satisfaction of recipients. Second, the partnership, coordination, and transparency within and between the public, private, and nongovernmental sectors need to be nurtured and strengthened to deliver assistance equitably. The efforts spearheaded by the NGO Coordination Cell under the auspices of the Nagapattinam district collector in Tamil Nadu, India, made these synergistic interactions possible, and these need to be nurtured during peacetime or normal times. Such efforts will sustain transparency and maintain lateral and vertical communication between villagers, NGOs, INGOs, private-sector partners, and local- and state-level agencies, all of which were noteworthy during the response in India (Prater et al. 2006).

17.5.3   2005 HURRICANE KATRINA IN THE UNITED STATES

Hurricane Katrina struck the Mississippi/Louisiana coast, covering approximately 90,000 square miles, as a category 3 storm on August 29, 2005. Hurricane Rita, yet another category 3 storm, followed closely, making landfall along the Texas–Louisiana border in September 2005 adding to the damage and disruption. The uncertainties in the storm's track and intensity, compounded by the fact that Hurricane Rita made landfall less than a month after Hurricane Katrina, led to large-scale evacuations and traffic congestion problems for thousands of Americans (Zhang et al. 2007). Total damages from Hurricanes Katrina and Rita were $150 billion—$135 billion from Katrina and $15 billion from Rita (Schigoda 2011)—with more than 1,800 deaths, several hundred people missing, and almost 1 million area residents forced to evacuate (Gill 2007). Approximately 600,000 households were still displaced one month later: Hurricane shelters housed 273,000 people, and FEMA trailers later housed at least 114,000 people (Schigoda 2011). Also, the storms damaged more than a million housing units in the Gulf Coast region, 134,000 of which were in New Orleans, which comprised 70% of all occupied units (Schigoda 2011). This was one of the largest shifts in a single population in this country since the Dust Bowl of the 1930s and one of the worst disasters to ever impact the United States (see Box 17.2). The general consensus is that while Katrina caused sudden and widespread changes to the physical and social fabric of the area, many changes were already taking place; Katrina simply sped up the process.

Many of the social and policy changes are still emerging after Hurricane Katrina. Therefore, in what follows, we focus primarily on some of the largest recovery and repopulation issues that are taking place as indicators of change. To begin, Green, Bates, and Smyth (2007) state that the most important issues impeding recovery and repopulation of greater New Orleans are levee construction, flood insurance, labor shortages, and an overwhelmed service sector. All of this is central to the repopulation of New Orleans. Generally, people in the New Orleans area do not believe that current levees will protect them from another Katrina, particularly those living below sea level, and Gulf Coast reports are consistent in claiming that the city of New Orleans remains at significant risk of reflooding, even after more than $7 billion was spent to repair and improve the levees (Green, Bates, and Smyth 2007; Katz 2008).

While confidence in levees to protect people and their homes is lacking, there are other factors contributing to slow recovery. For instance, home insurance premiums have skyrocketed. The State Insurance Rating Commission approved increases in premiums of 16%–35% for 2007, some of which had already increased by 40% in 2006 (Warner 2007). Labor shortages have also hampered recovery efforts. Help-wanted signs are still posted all over the Gulf Coast region for tourist and hospitality jobs traditionally filled by residents of the lower income neighborhoods. Also, since there are so few residents to fill many of the day-labor positions, the debris removal and the repair and rebuilding of flood-damaged buildings is being carried out by migrant workers (Green, Bates,

BOX 17.2   REPOPULATION OF NEW ORLEANS

With a pre-Katrina population of 484,674 in 2000 (Schigoda 2011), New Orleans experienced a dramatic population loss after the disaster, but the population had been declining since its peak of 600,000 in 1960 (Jervis 2008). Recent population estimates show that the population is growing, and by December 2008, the number of households actively receiving mail (a crude indicator of repopulation) had reached 73.7% of prestorm levels in New Orleans, compared to 50% one year after Katrina and 69% in August 2007 (GNOCDC 2009). The larger metro area of New Orleans had reached 88.1% repopulation by December 2008 (GNOCDC 2009). The 2010 census shows the New Orleans population at 343,829, 71% of its 2000 pre-Katrina population (Ortiz 2011). Furthermore, the 2010 census shows that the metro area had 1,167,764 people, or 89% of its pre-Katrina population back.

Parish Population Estimates

	Jefferson	Orleans	Plaquemines	St. Bernard	St. Charles	St. John	St. Tammany	MSA
Census 2000	455,466	484,674	26,757	67,229	48,072	43,044	191,268	1,316,510
July 2005	449,640	453,726	28,588	64,683	50,164	45,602	217,551	1,309,954
July 2006	420,891	210,198	21,625	13,875	51,969	47,693	224,227	990,478
July 2007	423,520[a]	239,124[a]	21,540[a]	19,826[a]	52,044	47,684	226,625	1,030,363

Source: U.S. Census Bureau.

Note: 2005 and 2006 estimates were revised with the release of the 2007 census estimates.

[a] Orleans Parish, Jefferson Parish, St. Bernard Parish, and Plaquemines Parish officially challenged their July 2007 census estimates.

While the population is beginning to reach pre-Katrina totals, reoccupation is much slower in areas that were impoverished before the storm, particularly in areas such as the Lower Ninth Ward of New Orleans. For example, by September 2008, the Lower Ninth Ward had only recovered 19% of its July 2005 resident population, while the Central Business District/French Quarter and English Turn, areas least affected by flooding and less impoverished, contain 103% and 107% of their pre-Katrina resident populations, respectively (GNOCDC 2009).

and Smyth 2007). This was partially due to the suspension of the Davis-Bacon Act immediately after the hurricane. The act requires federal contractors to pay the prevailing wage in the area. Once this was suspended, it encouraged many Mexican and Latino immigrants to move to the Gulf Coast area as day laborers, helping with debris removal and disaster-restoration industries. This has resulted in an immigrant labor market that is becoming institutionalized in New Orleans, where many are settling and becoming long-term residents, often living in extremely difficult conditions and subject to exploitation (Donato et al. 2007). Evidence of this institutional shift is apparent in current census data, as New Orleans has gained 3,225 Hispanics, while the metro area has gained 33,500 Hispanics (Plyer 2011).

The overwhelmed service sector is another impediment to recovery. Hospitals, supermarkets, cafes, convenience stores, and schools have been slow to reopen and often operate short staffed and for shorter hours. Charity Hospital, which opened in 1939 with nearly 2,700 beds and had a long-standing tradition of serving poor people in New Orleans despite federal and state disinvestments in health-care provision and subsidization, will not reopen (Katz 2008). Also, the Louisiana State

University Health Sciences Center University Hospital reopened in November 2006 but in a significantly limited capacity, only having 200 beds available (Katz 2008).

Many educational institutions in the Gulf Coast have also struggled to rebuild, redefine themselves, and change their focus. Two years after Katrina, there are widespread teacher shortages, with very few primary and secondary schools reopened, long waiting lists, and long commutes to out-of-neighborhood schools (Green, Bates, and Smyth 2007). As Katz (2008, 18) notes, schools anchor communities and are at the heart of social reproduction—"social practices and forces associated with sustaining production and social life." By December 2008 in Orleans Parish, 65 (70%) private schools had reopened and 89 (70%) public school facilities had reopened—48 as charter schools, 4 as noncharter selective admission schools, 3 as alternative schools, and 34 as noncharter schools run by the Recovery School District—while 8 additional public and 2 private schools opened in the fall of 2008 (GNOCDC 2009). By spring 2011, the city of New Orleans had 63% of its pre-Katrina (2004–2005) public and private enrollment, up from 47% in spring 2007 and 61% in spring 2010 (Ortiz 2011). Additionally, the metro area has reached 80% of its pre-Katrina school enrollment, up from 73% in 2007 and 79% in 2010 (Ortiz 2011). Most of the schools that remained closed were in the most devastated and impoverished areas.

This does not seem to be empowering the poor and minority communities that bore the brunt of the storm. Without schools, how can communities be socially reproduced? Conversely, a new report conducted at the Scott S. Cowen Institute for Public Education Initiatives at Tulane University indicates that while there are still many obstacles, most parents, teachers, and citizens believe that public schools have improved over the last year. They are better than they were before Katrina, and the large number of charter schools that have opened since the storm have boosted community involvement in education (Maxwell 2008). New Orleans is experiencing a new model of education that is decentralized and multidistrict, traditional, and chartered instead of one of financial mismanagement and corruption, academic failure, administrative dysfunction, and an urban school district cited as one of the worst in the country before Hurricane Katrina (Akbar and Sims 2008; Johnson 2008).

Institutions of higher education have also had to overcome their own obstacles and have had to redefine themselves. For example, Esmail, Eargle, and Das (2007) analyzed *Chronicle of Higher Education* articles and coverage of Katrina's impact on colleges and universities and documented changes in location of instruction, programs, teaching methods, learning outcomes, funding, and policy. Tulane and Southern University, among others, did not retain faculty and staff and reduced their degree program offerings. Tulane instituted a community service component, and Delgado Community College has moved more toward vocational learning and expanded offerings for high-demand fields such as construction and nursing. Hurricane Katrina accelerated the growth of the "virtual university," where more courses are now offered online in lieu of the traditional classroom setting. Also, with fewer resources, universities and colleges have been required to use fewer faculty members to teach more students, a trend that was already in progress.

FEMA instituted changes in funding so that private colleges and universities were able to more adequately receive funding in the event of disasters. Previously, private institutions could not receive funding if they had been awarded a small-business loan or sustained operating losses. There are a few relevant examples of the New Orleans area's historically black colleges and universities (HBCUs) using these funds to change in positive ways and move forward. For example, Xavier University will be receiving a $165-million low-interest federal loan to retire a significant amount of its debt incurred from Katrina, and Southern University, which previously never had residence halls, received a $44-million federal loan at 1% interest to be used to build a dormitory complex for 700 students (Mangan 2008). However, Louisiana's higher education commissioner, E. Joseph Savoie has said that despite the promise of funding, FEMA still owes the state's colleges and universities $350 million for damages from Katrina and an additional $37 million from Hurricane Rita's destruction, while private colleges have dipped into endowments and taken out loans (Mangan 2008). On a positive note, by fall 2007, New Orleans's colleges and universities had recovered 74% of their pre-Katrina enrollment, which will significantly help their financial situations and in their more general recovery efforts (GNOCDC 2009). As of fall 2010, they have 88% of their pre-Katrina total enrollment (Ortiz 2011). While there are still many obstacles for education in the coming years, there are signs of hope and change.

An example of social change after Katrina, spearheaded by a faith-based group, has been well documented in the New Orleans Jewish community. In the years following Hurricane Katrina, they have been able to develop a solid plan for changing their community in very positive ways. It is estimated that the pre-Katrina Jewish population was approximately 10,000, down from a Jewish population of nearly 13,000 25 years ago, and about 6,000 in the summer of 2006, a year after Katrina (Chalew 2007; Nolan 2008). As of 2009, the Jewish population in New Orleans (Orleans and Jefferson Parishes) was recorded to be 7,800 (Sheskin and Dashefsky 2010). After Katrina, the community established an online database that was updated daily on the Jewish Federation's website with current contact information for members of the community. This made it possible for people to contact one another from within the community that had been displaced by the storm. The federation publicized meetings to be held in communities where Jewish New Orleanians had resettled and shared information about insurance issues and other resources to assist them in recovery (Chalew 2007). Approximately $20 million was received as donations from the United Jewish Communities and hundreds of synagogues, federations, and private donors from around the country. These funds were allocated directly to every Jewish agency, organization, and synagogue in New Orleans (Chalew 2007).

As a way to rebuild their community, the Jewish Federation of Greater New Orleans developed a "newcomers" plan to attract new, young Jewish people to the community. Newcomers are offered incentives such as a moving grant of up to $3,000, interest-free housing or business loans of up to $15,000 each, rental assistance of up to $2,500, job search and business networking, reduced tuition in the New Orleans Jewish Day School, and free synagogue membership for a year (Chalew 2007). It is currently estimated that the program has attracted approximately 850 newcomers to New Orleans (Nolan 2008). As Michael Weil, executive director of the Jewish Federation of Greater New Orleans, stated, "There is no sense in going back to where we were before the storm. We have the opportunity now to make past dreams and new dreams of a vibrant Jewish New Orleans come true" (Chalew 2007, 86). This is a clear example of social change that is community based and community defined.

Shared migration experiences and a strong commitment to, and leadership in, the Catholic Church demonstrate yet another community's mobilization and reemergence after Katrina. The historically marginalized Vietnamese-American community in New Orleans East has experienced a high rate of return, rapid rebuilding, and high levels of community involvement, despite receiving little city government support and being absent from the national post-Katrina discussions about race, class, and social justice. They have also established themselves very quickly as active stakeholders in their community and the city and organized successfully with African-American community members, environmentalists, and other justice advocates in the Coalition for a Strong New Orleans East to oppose a landfill for hurricane debris to be located two miles from their community (Leong et al. 2007). The social change in these communities is demonstrated through their capacities to not only connect well with their own community members, but to also get connected with other local minority groups. This has enabled the creation of a more extended form of community that has been mobilized to oppose larger structural barriers to recovery, giving them a stronger collective voice. This supports a community-based approach to recovery that can serve as a model for other communities.

Inspirational models of local, community-based leadership and community-based advocacy and activism have also emerged after Katrina by strong women activists who themselves were victims. While men have dominated the cleanup and construction efforts, the work of rebuilding communities and the social service sector and reopening schools will rely heavily on women and their skills and draw extensively from their indigenous knowledge of the local community. One example of these emergent, women-led groups, Women of the Storm, was created predominantly by a privileged group of white women in New Orleans who have actively mobilized a socially and economically diverse group of white, Vietnamese, Latina, and African-American women to educate American governmental leaders about the needs of the people affected by Hurricanes Katrina and Rita for developing safe and secure neighborhoods and communities. They have been successful through advocacy and lobbying in Washington, DC, challenging congressional leaders to visit New Orleans, and offering educational tours, data, and personal narratives of survivors (Pyles and Lewis 2007).

A second example is the New Orleans Regional Alliance Against Abuse (NORAA), another local, women-led, community-based group. This group comprises women social workers who are advocates from various programs and parishes that formed in the weeks following Katrina in Baton Rouge to serve survivors of sexual and domestic abuse in Katrina-affected areas. The group was able to establish new networks across these diverse programs and parishes and effectively create an umbrella group of domestic-violence services to meet the needs of women survivors of domestic violence and sexual assault in the service area impacted by the hurricanes (Pyles and Lewis 2007).

A third example is a group of women advocating for the rights of citizens who were public housing residents, mostly poor and people of color, to return to their homes. They have developed key indicators to recovery such as "a) fair treatment of residents by the U.S. Department of Housing and Urban Development (HUD) and the Housing Authority of New Orleans (HANO) in accordance with federal regulations, b) responding to the needs of residents who have returned, and c) keeping in touch with residents who want to return but are still living away from New Orleans" (Pyles and Lewis 2007). They have organized many activities, including public demonstrations at HUD and HANO offices, leadership-training workshops, job fairs, summer youth programs, and bringing health and mental health services to affected neighborhoods. These are all excellent examples of community-based activism and mobilization by strong women leaders that can serve as models for other disaster-stricken communities across the United States.*

17.5.4 2010 HAITI EARTHQUAKE

At 4:53 a.m. on January 12, 2010, a 7.0-magnitude earthquake struck Haiti, a Caribbean island lying between the Caribbean Sea and the North Atlantic Ocean. With the epicenter occurring in the capital city of Port-au-Prince, the earthquake caused widespread damage to infrastructure, killing an estimated 316,000 people, injuring more than 500,000, and rendering over 1.5 million homeless and living in spontaneous settlements, including over 300,000 children and youth (Ager et al. 2011). The scale of the devastation was in large part due to Haiti's preexisting poverty, morbidity, homelessness, and unemployment (Weisenfeld 2011). The situation in Haiti was abysmal for children even prior to the quakes, with one in four children being malnourished as a result of about 80% of the population living on less than $2 a day. Subsequent to the quake, Haiti ranked 158th of 187 countries in the United Nations Development Programme's human development index (IHDI 2011; HDI 2011), the lowest in the western hemisphere.

However, it must be noted that the outcomes of the collaborative international response to the plight of the Haitians, although disjointed and sometimes even ad hoc, helped to reduce the mortality rate by huge numbers. In the weeks and months following the earthquake, many international voluntary organizations, such as the Toronto Rehabilitation Institute from Canada, worked tirelessly with Healing Hands for Haiti to specifically address the rehabilitation needs of individuals who had sustained spinal cord injuries or needed amputations. These initial lifesaving efforts have created a special-needs population requiring significant long-term care and support (Landry et al. 2010). It remains to be seen if the world medical community, including international and national humanitarian organizations and the health department in the Government of Haiti (GOH), can provide sustained support for this group.

---

* For a comprehensive report of women leaders in the Gulf Coast, see Sarah Vaill (2006), "The Calm in the Storm: Women Leaders in Gulf Coast Recovery." A report by the Women's Funding Network and the Ms. Foundation for Women. http://ms.foundation.org/resources/publications/thecalminthestorm

The challenges faced by aid organizations and the GOH in starting long-term development and rebuilding projects are intrinsically woven around numerous on-ground challenges. One major hurdle in starting the rebuilding of permanent homes is the rather tenuous land tenure system, which even before the earthquake was informal and fraught with disputes (Weisenfeld 2011). In a bid to settle the 680,000 Haitians still living in spontaneous settlements, the UN Human Settlements Programme (UN-HABITAT 2010) is promoting a community-based enumeration program in Haiti similar to the one adopted in Aceh, Indonesia, after the 2004 tsunami. This program has met with great success where formal systems favoring written evidence of land ownership records are impossible to get a hold of after a disaster or a conflict. In these situations, an establishment of land records by bringing key community stakeholders together and having them enumerate who owns which piece of land and who is a tenant of which home works better (Weisenfeld 2011). If such records are sought and legally mandated by the Government of Haiti, it will increase the trust between the populace and the government, and a sense of empowerment to disaster survivors, knowing that their voices are sought. Furthermore, such a well-defined baseline record of land tenure can help in initiating sustainable land-use practices and planning to reduce the impacts from future disasters.

In order to address concerns of child trafficking and slavery, sexual violence, and overall widespread relinquishment of Haitian children living in makeshift tent cities and shelters, numerous local and international humanitarian organizations are working tirelessly. Two of these are Save the Children (n.d.) and Concern Worldwide (n.d.). Within weeks of the earthquake, these organizations partnered with local NGOs to set up transitional schools on the fringes of makeshift tent cities and shelter camps to provide children and youth with child-friendly spaces to jumpstart their recovery. These spaces have changed the lives of over 12,000 children, offering them a sense of safety and stability amidst the chaos of their daily lives. The formalized routine—team-building activities, art, singing, acting, and education—adopted at these schools has helped bring a sense of normalcy back into their lives, made them feel safer and happier despite their deplorable living conditions in the camps, and allowed them to tap into their inner resiliencies. Although there is no hard evidence from Haiti since the 2010 earthquake outlining the short-term and long-term success of providing safe spaces for Haitian children, there are numerous YouTube videos and blogs on the Internet enumerating their benefits (e.g., Save the Children n.d.; Concern Worldwide n.d.). (See Box 17.3.)

Another example of social change in Haiti is through the concerted and collaborative efforts of the international community and the Government of Haiti to reduce gender-based violence (GBV), which is reported to have increased. The U.S. Agency for International Development (USAID), the UN Stabilization Mission in Haiti (MINUSTAH), and local partners are working with residents in temporary shelters and camps, and have installed solar lights in internally displaced persons (IDPs) camps, and also provided headlamps and solar lights to the Haitian National Police to improve night patrols and public safety (Weisenfeld 2011). Mass education campaigning for both men and women about the dangers of GBV and how to protect oneself and one's family members are also under way. USAID and the GOH are also working on strengthening grassroots women's groups and supporting public service announcements (PSAs) on radio and television channels about the issues surrounding GBV, security, and health. The Raising Public Awareness program of USAID, in coordination with the Haitian government, aired "Stop the Rape" (*kwape kadejak*) PSAs on large screens in many of Haiti's spontaneous settlements during the World Cup and on other popular TV programs (Gohmann 2010). These PSAs, which were produced with USAID funding by the Pan-American Development Foundation and Population Services International, raised awareness among the populace about how to report a rape, what resources were available to seek justice, and how to ensure that the perpetrators were prosecuted for this and other violence. The PSAs also provided pertinent information regarding HIV and malaria prevention and hygiene and family planning (USAID n.d.).

Social change has also been mediated by long-distance transnationalism, as demonstrated by the Haitian diaspora. Lundy (2011) interviewed Haitians living outside their country of origin and found them to be even more proud and resilient of their Haitian identity after the earthquake. They were also actively involved in sending medical professionals to Haiti. For example, the Association of

BOX 17.3   SAFE SPACES FOR CHILDREN

The Save the Children Alliance created the Safe Spaces initiative for children and youth liv-ing in internally displaced persons (IDPs) camps and shelters. The Save the Children USA implemented this initiative in Aceh, Indonesia, following the 2004 Indian Ocean tsunami, and the International Rescue Committee (IRC n.d.) adopted this model to open 59 child-friendly spaces in Darfur after the conflict. Madfis, Martyris, and Triplehorn (2010, 847) describe the successful implementation and effectiveness of the USA B-SAFE model adopted in Haiti and the Solomon Islands after the 2007 tropical storm and floods.

B-SAFE is an acronym reflecting the program objectives as listed below:

Build relationships, cooperation, and respect among peers
Screen for high-risk children and youth
Active, structured learning and life-saving information
Facilitate children's natural resilience and return to normalcy
Eestablish a sense of security and self-esteem

In 2007, the Haitian capital of Port-au-Prince suffered destruction when Tropical Storm Noel made landfall and brought heavy rains and flooding in its wake. This disaster left more than 10,000 IDPs seeking schools, hospitals, and churches as temporary shelters. Save the Children USA specifically supported children by creating six "safe spaces" to help them recover from their trauma and provide their parents with time and resources for economic recovery. These spaces functioned for eight hours daily for six weeks and provided a struc-tured schedule that included time for psychosocial games, activities, and study.

Children participated in team- and trust-building activities, role playing, and arts and crafts to encourage reticent disturbed children to become more open and share their experi-ences through painting, singing, and skits. B-SAFE monitoring and performance measure-ment tools, conceptualized using Arntson and Duncan's (2004) evaluation typology on the characteristics of a resilient child, were used by the program managers to measure improve-ments in child and youth behavior. They found that 80% of the children who were shy, lonely, anxious, or demonstrating antisocial behavior at the start of the program showed improved capacity to form relationships, showed trust and respect, and were also able to concentrate. Children indicated that they felt safe, less guilty at having survived the crisis, and were able to resolve conflicts and reconcile differences with other children.

Haitian Physicians Abroad, known by its French acronym AMHE, sent more than 500 volunteers to Haiti. Similarly, the Boston-based group Partners in Health, which operates nine hospitals in Haiti, sent more than 1,000 Creole-speaking volunteers within weeks of the quake. Further, scholars are finding that the Haitian diaspora communities are using political, economic, and communication ties to not only assist loved ones back home, but to concentrate their efforts in having their voices heard in the future of Haiti (Bernard 2010; Esnard and Sapat 2011; Sapat and Esnard 2012).

Finally, the role of the private sector in facilitating empowerment through remittances and maintenance of communication channels needs to be underscored. Western Union quickly intro-duced their "no transfer fee" pricing for any amount sent to Haiti from the United States, Canada, Dominican Republic, Jamaica, and some locations in France, thus enabling every penny of the remittances sent to families back in Haiti being available toward the recovery process. Airlines serving Haiti responded by allowing their Haitian diaspora customers to send relief supplies free of charge, as well as to convert their frequent-flier miles toward donations (Lundy 2011).

Digicel, the largest private mobile telecommunications operator in Haiti, quickly established communication links to Haiti to create a monetary relief fund so that the international community could send remittances online. It also initiated a free SIM card replacement program for those who lost an existing SIM card during the earthquake. They also set up supplemental free-of-charge battery-charging stations throughout Port-au-Prince. Within just a week of the earthquake, most Digicel sites were repaired and functioning across Haiti (Digicel Group 2010), allowing the Haitians and the international aid community a much valued means of communicating when most other infrastructure systems were out. In recognition of their initiatives and innovation, USAID partnered with the Bill and Melinda Gates Foundation to award its first-to-market prize to Digicel in January 2011. They were awarded $2.5 million in prize money for transforming the banking sector in Haiti (USAID 2012).

Now that more than two and one-half years have passed since the January 2010 earthquake in Haiti, governments, NGOs, INGOs, and researchers are engaging in efforts to understand the effectiveness of the international response to Haitians needs. The aftermath of the earthquake prompted the United Nations and other agencies to coordinate their aid to Haiti by creating an Interim Reconstruction Commission run jointly by the president of Haiti and the special UN envoy, Bill Clinton.

Since its creation In March 2010, over $5 billion has been pledged by the world community, and yet only $150 million has been received. The International Rescue Committee (IRC) is having a hard time getting NGOs to work together on identified projects (Pierre-Louis 2011).

And yet, the examples discussed can serve as inspirations to motivate further transnational collaborations that will lead Haiti to a better future. Although it is anticipated that the destruction wrought by the earthquake will serve as a window of opportunity for social change and empowerment in Haiti, it remains to be seen if the international community will continue to partner and demonstrate their sustained support and willingness to work with the Haitian government and health professionals to address the specialized needs of Haitians, especially the disabled, children and youth, and women, as they adapt to their new realities.

17.6 SUMMARY

This chapter examined the relationship between disasters and social change; how members of a community can create change; and the importance of empowerment, mobilization, and community-based organizations. It also presented examples of September 11, 2001, the 2004 Indian Ocean tsunami, Hurricane Katrina in 2005 (Figure 16.2), and the 2010 Haiti earthquake. As demonstrated, disasters often contribute to change by accelerating trends that were already in progress, such as a focus on militarism after the September 11, 2001, terrorist attacks, declines in population, and the presence of racial and ethnic tensions in southern communities impacted by Hurricane Katrina in the United States.

Also, disasters can facilitate or provide opportunities for empowerment of traditionally marginalized groups. For instance, Muslim community members after September 11 have been able to use the attacks to redefine themselves as Muslims, build stronger social connections in their communities, and educate the larger public about Islam in an effort to bring about more tolerance for their religion. Further, the New Orleans Jewish community was able to recreate their identity and recruit newcomers to their faith and community. The New Orleans Vietnamese community was able to reclaim, redefine, and rebuild their community using community-based models of recovery, and strong women activists were able to mobilize and promote empowerment of marginalized women after Hurricane Katrina. It is clear that disasters have the ability to foster community-based social change that empowers traditionally disadvantaged groups, and recovery and reconstruction can be arranged so that the people within those communities have the ability to rebuild their communities so that they best serve their needs.

In India, the post-tsunami housing recovery and rebuilding programs funded through collaborative efforts between the government of India and the nonprofit and private sectors have allowed socially and economically disadvantaged populations from the lower castes to finally own property and a new home. These houses are built to stronger earthquake building codes and are located inland, away from the high-tide line. The government's role in empowering women by implementing the joint owner-ship of home/property requirements for married couples has been critical in helping women reach equal social status. However, it is clear from the Indian context that housing recovery programs are likely to lead to overall dissatisfaction among the recipients if they are not integrated into sustainable-livelihood alternatives and do not allow for minimal input from community members.

As easy as it is to find numerous challenges and areas for improvements, the Haiti case study identified some of the inroads made by humanitarian organizations, including Save the Children and Concern Worldwide in providing "safe spaces" to help build resiliency among Haitian children and youth; UN-HABITAT's initiatives in facilitating community-based enumerations to create a land-tenure baseline record to facilitate the relocation and rebuilding of homes; USAID and the government of Haiti's concerted efforts to reduce gender-based violence; the expansive role of those in the Haitian-diaspora community to help their friends and relatives in Haiti through remittances; and the initiatives of the for-profit sector in enabling channels for remittances, relief aid, and com-munications to assist in recovery.

To this end, we must recognize that disasters are opportunities for policy and social change. We have a responsibility as researchers, policy advocates, emergency managers, and civically engaged human beings to ensure that disasters do not further marginalize groups that have historically been disadvantaged. We need to promote policy and social changes that empower these communities, particularly those historically disadvantaged and disempowered, that have been affected by disas-ters. We cannot allow people in positions of power who have little or no vested interest in or indig-enous knowledge of affected communities to define policy and social changes that will take place within these communities. We must also ensure that disaster preparedness, mitigation, response, and recovery are community based and that people in disaster-impacted communities have the abil-ity to define what is important to them and to determine what changes are in their own best interests. Nongovernmental, community-based organizations and groups are critical to incorporating indig-enous knowledge. We must listen to and incorporate the voices of these groups to promote holistic and equitable disaster recovery.

DISCUSSION QUESTIONS

1. What are the primary sources of social change in a community or society?
2. Explain the relationships between vulnerability, sustainability, community, and social change.
3. Recall the four disaster examples discussed in this chapter. Compare and contrast to iden-tify the most significant barriers to facilitating positive social change in a community impacted by a disaster.
4. What are the most effective means of empowering members of a community after a disaster?
5. If you were an emergency manager of a community, what organizations would you con-sider most important in helping ensure effective community recovery from a disaster?
6. If you were an emergency manager of a community, what organizations would you con-sider most important for promoting social change after a disaster? Who would you contact, what would you tell them, and how would you like them to respond?

REFERENCES

Abril-Ojeda, G. 1982. The role of disaster relief for a long-term development in LDCs. University of Stockholm, Institute of Latin American Studies.

ADRC (Asian Disaster Reduction Center). 2005. Multi-national mission to the tsunami affected areas in India. Final report, 8–13 April 2005. http://www.adrc.asia/publications/india_mission/ENG_Final_Report.pdf.

Ager A., B. Courtney, L. Stark, and T. Daniel. 2011. Child protection assessment in humanitarian emergencies: Case studies from Georgia, Gaza, Haiti and Yemen. *Child Abuse & Neglect* 35:1045–52.

Akbar, R., and M. J. Sims. 2008. Surviving Katrina and keeping our eyes on the prize. *Urban Education* 43 (4): 445–62.

Andrew, S., S. Arlikatti, L. Long, and J. Kendra. 2012. The effect of housing assistance arrangements on household recovery: An empirical test of donor-assisted and owner-driven approaches. *Journal of Housing and the Built Environment*, 1–18. Early view at doi:10.1007/s10901-012-9266-9.

Arlikatti, S., K. Bezboruah, and L. Long. 2012. Role of the voluntary sector in tsunami disaster relief in Southern India: Compensating or complementing? *Social Development Issues* 34 (3): 64–80.

Arlikatti, S., and S. Andrew. 2012. Housing design and long-term recovery processes in the aftermath of the 2004 Indian Ocean tsunami. *Natural Hazards Review* 13 (1) 34–44.

Arlikatti, S., W. G. Peacock, C. S. Prater, H. Grover, and A. S. G. Sekar. 2010. Assessing the impact of the Indian Ocean tsunami on households: The Modified Domestic Assets approach. *Disasters* 34 (3): 705–31.

Arntson, L., and J. Duncan. 2004. *Children in crisis: Good practices in evaluating psychosocial programming.* Westport, CT: Save the Children Federation.

Aronoff, M., and V. Gunter. 1992. Defining disaster: Local constructions for recovery in the aftermath of contamination. *Social Problems* 39 (4): 345–65.

Babister, E., and I. Kelman. 2002. The emergency shelter process with application to case studies in Macedonia and Afghanistan. *Journal of Humanitarian Assistance.* http://sites.tufts.edu/jha/files/2011/04/a092.pdf.

Barenstein, J. D. 2010. Who governs reconstruction? Changes and continuity in policies, practices, and outcomes. In *Rebuilding after disasters: From emergency to sustainability*, ed. G. Lizarralde, C. Johnson, and C. Davidson, 149–76. New York: Spon Press.

Barton, A. 1969. *Communities in disaster: A sociological analysis of collective stress situations.* Garden City, NY: Doubleday and Co.

Bates, F. L., ed. 1982. Recovery, change and development: A longitudinal study of the Guatemalan earthquake. Department of Sociology, University of Georgia, Athens.

Bates, F. L., C. Fogleman, V. Parenton, R. Pittman, and G. Tracy. 1963. *The social and psychological consequences of a natural disaster: A longitudinal study of Hurricane Audrey.* Washington, DC: National Research Council.

Bates, F. L., and W. G. Peacock. 1987. Disasters and social change. In *The sociology of disasters*, ed. R. R. Dynes, B. Demarchi, and C. Pelanda, 291–330. Milan, Italy: Franco Angeli Press.

Bernard, A. 2010. Haitian New Yorkers hold on to their hope. *New York Times*, January 17.

Best, J. 1990. *Threatened children.* Chicago: University of Chicago Press.

Birkland, T. A. 2004. The world changed today: Agenda-setting and policy change in the wake of the September 11 terrorist attacks. *Review of Policy Research* 21 (2): 179–200.

Blaikie, P., T. Cannon, I. Davis, and B. Wisner. 1994. *At risk: Natural hazards, people's vulnerability, and disasters.* New York: Routledge.

Blocker, T. J, E. B. Rochford Jr., and D. E. Sherkat. 1991. Political responses to natural hazards: Social movement participation following a flood disaster. *International Journal of Mass Emergencies and Disasters* 9 (3): 367–82.

Bryan, J. L. 2005. Constructing the true Islam in hostile times: The impact of 9/11 on Arab Muslims in Jersey City. In *Wounded city: The social impact of 9/11*, ed. N. Foner, 133–59. New York: Russell Sage Foundation.

Cable, S., E. J. Walsh, and R. H. Warland. 1988. Differential paths to political activism: Comparisons of four mobilization processes after the Three Mile Island accident. *Social Forces* 66 (4): 951–69.

Census of India. 2001. http://www.censusindia.net/.

Chalew, G. N. 2007. A community revitalized, a city rediscovered: The New Orleans Jewish community two years post-Katrina. *Journal of Jewish Communal Service* 83 (1): 84–87.

Chin, M. M. 2005. Moving on: Chinese garment workers after 9/11. In *Wounded city: The social impact of 9/11*, ed. N. Foner, 184–207. New York: Russell Sage Foundation.

Cochrane, H. C. 1975. *Natural hazards and their distributive effect.* Boulder: University of Colorado.

Collins, P. H. 2000. *Black feminist thought.* New York: Routledge.

Concern Worldwide. n.d. http://www.concernusa.org/Default.aspx.

Coppola, D. 2006. *Introduction to international disaster management.* Oxford, UK: Butterworth-Heinemann.

Cousins, W. 1991. Non-governmental initiatives. In *The urban poor and basic infrastructure services in Asia and the Pacific.* Manila: Asian Development Bank.

Dacy, D. C., and H. Kunreuther. 1969. *The economics of natural disasters.* New York: Free Press.

Digicel Group. 2010. Majority of Digicel cell sites up across Haiti. http://www.digicelgroup.com/en/media-center/press-releases/digicel-in-the-community.

Donato, K. M., N. Trujillo-Pagan, C. L. Bankston III, and A. Singer. 2007. Reconstructing New Orleans after Katrina: The emergence of an immigrant labor market. In *The sociology of Katrina*, ed. D. L. Brunsma, D. Overfelt, and J. S. Picou, 217–34. Lanham, MD: Rowman & Littlefield Publishers.

Drury, A. C., and R. S. Olson. 1998. Disasters and political unrest: An empirical investigation. *The Journal of Contingencies and Crisis Management* 6 (3): 153–61.

Dynes, R. R. 1975. The comparative study of disaster: A social organizational approach. *Mass Emergencies* 1:21–31.

Edwards, M., and D. Hulme, eds. 1995. *Beyond the magic bullet: NGO performance and accountability in the post–Cold War world*. New York: Kumarian Press.

Esmail, A. M., L. A. Eargle, and S. K. Das. 2007. Hurricane Katrina and its impact on education. In *The sociology of Katrina*, ed. D. L. Brunsma, D. Overfelt, and J. S. Picou, 191–202. Lanham, MD: Rowman & Littlefield Publishers.

Esnard, A. M., and A. Sapat. 2011. Disasters, diasporas and host communities: Insights in the aftermath of the Haiti Earthquake. *Journal of Disaster Research* 6 (3): 331–42.

Foner, N. 2005. The social effects of 9/11 on New York City. In *Wounded city: The social impact of 9/11*, ed. N. Foner, 3–27. New York: Russell Sage Foundation.

Friesema, H. P., J. Caporaso, G. Goldstein, R. Lineberry, and R. McCleary. 1979. *Aftermath: Communities after natural disasters*. Thousand Oaks, CA: Sage.

Fritz, C. 1961. Disaster. In *Contemporary social problems*, ed. R. K. Merton and R. A. Nisbet, 651–94. New York: Harcourt Press.

Gill, D. A. 2007. Disaster research and Hurricane Katrina: Guest editor's introduction. *Sociological Spectrum* 27 (6): 609–12.

GNOCDC (Greater New Orleans Community Data Center). 2009. The New Orleans index: Tracking the recovery of New Orleans and the metro area. http://www.gnocdc.org.

Gohmann, A. 2010. Three things you should know about the U.S. government's work in Haiti. Impact blog on USAID from the American People. http://blog.usaid.gov/2010/06/three-things-you-should-know-about-the-u-s-government%E2%80%99s-work-in-haiti/.

Green, R., L. K. Bates, and A. Smyth. 2007. Impediments to recovery in New Orleans Upper and Lower Ninth Ward: One year after Hurricane Katrina. *Disasters* 31 (4): 311–35.

Harper, C. L., and K. T. Leicht. 2011. *Exploring social change: America and the world*. 6th ed. Upper Saddle River, NJ: Prentice Hall.

Hoover, G. A., and F. L. Bates. 1985. The impact of a natural disaster on the division of labor in twelve Guatemalan communities: A study of social change in a developing country. *International Journal of Mass Emergencies and Disasters* 3 (3): 9–26.

Huda, Q. 2006. Conflict prevention and peace-building efforts by American Muslim organizations following September 11. *Journal of Muslim Minority Affairs* 26 (2): 187–203.

HDI (Human Development Index). 2011. Haiti. http://hdrstats.undp.org/en/countries/profiles/HTI.html.

IHDI (International Human Development Indicators). 2011. The 2011 Human Development Index and its components. http://hdr.undp.org/en/media/HDR_2011_EN_Table1.pdf.

IRC (International Rescue Committee). n.d. Safe spaces for children in Darfur. http://www.rescue.org/photo-essays/safe-spaces-children-darfur.

Jervis, R. 2008. New Orleans may have hit plateau. *USA Today*, August 4, 1A.

Johnson, K. A. 2008. Hope for an uncertain future: Recovery and rebuilding efforts in New Orleans's schools. *Urban Education* 43 (4): 421–44.

Kabeer, N. 1999. Resources, agency, achievement: Reflections on the measurement of women's empowerment. *Development and Change* 30 (3): 435–64.

Katz, C. 2008. Bad elements: Katrina and the scoured landscape of social reproduction. *Gender, Place and Culture* 15 (1): 15–29.

Killian, C. D., W. G. Peacock, and F. L. Bates. 1984. The inequality of disasters: An assessment of the interaction between a social system and its geophysical environment. Paper presented at the annual meeting of the Southern Sociological Society.

Kreps, G. A. 1998. Disaster as systemic event and social catalyst: A clarification of subject matter. In *What is a disaster? Perspectives on the question*, ed. E. L. Quarantelli, 31–55. New York: Routledge.

Kreps, G. A., and T. E. Drabek. 1996. Disasters as nonroutine social problems. *International Journal of Mass Emergencies and Disasters* 14 (2): 129–53.

Kumaran, T. V., and E. Negi. 2006. Experiences of rural and urban communities in Tamil Nadu in the aftermath of the 2004 tsunami: Learning from urban disasters, planning for resilient cities. *Built Environment* 32 (4): 375—86.

Landry, M. D., C. O'Connell, G. Tardif, and A. Burns. 2010. Post-earthquake Haiti: The critical role for reha-bilitation services following a humanitarian crisis. *Disability and Rehabilitation* 32 (19): 1616–18.

Leong, K. J., C. A. Airriess, W. Li, A. Chia-Chen Chen, and V. M. Keith. 2007. Resilient history and the rebuilding of a community: The Vietnamese American community in New Orleans East. *The Journal of American History* 94 (3): 770–79.

Lundy, G. 2011. Transnationalism in the aftermath of the Haiti earthquake: Reinforcing ties and second-gener-ation identity. *Journal of Black Studies* 42 (2): 203–24.

Madfis, J., D. Martyris, and C. Triplehorn. 2010. Emergency safe spaces in Haiti and the Solomon Islands. *Disasters* 34 (3): 845–64.

Mangan, K. 2008. New Orleans colleges slog toward recovery from Katrina. *Chronicle of Higher Education* 54 (18): A1–22.

Maxwell, L. A. 2008. New Orleans schools. *Education Week*, April 30: 5.

Mileti, D. S. 1999. *Disasters by design*. Washington, DC: Joseph Henry Press.

MoEF (Ministry of Environment and Forests) Government of India .n.d. Coastal Regulation Zone Notification Ministry of Environment and Forests. (Department of Environment, Forests and Wildlife). http://moef.nic.in/downloads/public-information/CRZ-Notification-2011.pdf.

Morrow, B. H., and W. G. Peacock. 1997. Disasters and social change: Hurricane Andrew and the reshaping of Miami? In *Hurricane Andrew: Ethnicity, gender and the sociology of disasters*, ed. W. G. Peacock, B. H. Morrow, and H. Gladwin, 226–42. New York: Routledge.

Nabeer, N. 2006. The rules of forced engagement: Race, gender, and the culture of fear among Arab immigrants in San Francisco post-9/11. *Cultural Dynamics* 18 (3): 235–67.

NBC (National Building Code of India). 2005. http://www.bis.org.in/sf/nbc.htm.

Nigg, J. M., and K. J. Tierney. 1993. Disasters and social change: Consequences for community construct and affect. Paper presented at the Annual Meeting of the American Sociological Association, 1–50.

Nolan, B. 2008. Revitalizing the Jewish community. *The Times-Picayune*, May 25, 1A.

Oliver-Smith, A. 1986. *The martyred city: Death and rebirth in the Andes*. Albuquerque: University of New Mexico Press.

Ortiz, E. 2011. Facts for Features: Hurricane Katrina recovery. News release. Greater New Orleans Community Data Center. http://www.gnocdc.org/Factsforfeatures/HurricaneKatrinaRecovery/index.html.

Peek, L. 2003. Community isolation and group solidarity: Examining the Muslim student experience after September 11th. In *Beyond September 11th: An account of post-disaster research*, ed. J. Monday, 333–54. Boulder: Institute of Behavioral Science, University of Colorado.

Pierre-Louis, F. 2011. Earthquakes, nongovernmental organizations, and governance in Haiti. *Journal of Black Studies* 42 (2): 186–202.

Plyer, A. 2011. What Census 2010 reveals about population and housing in New Orleans and the metro area. Census fact brief. Greater New Orleans Community Data Center. http://www.gnocdc.org/Census2010/index.html.

Prater, C., W. G. Peacock, S. Arlikatti, and H. Grover. 2006. Social capacity in Nagapattinam, Tamil Nadu, after the December 2004 Great Sumatra earthquake and tsunami. *Earthquake Spectra SE III* 22:715–29.

Prince, S. H. 1920. *Catastrophe and social change*. New York: Longmans, Green & Co.

Pyles, L., and J. S. Lewis. 2007. Women of the storm: Advocacy and organizing in post-Katrina New Orleans. *Affilia* 22 (4): 385–89.

Quarantelli, E. L., and R. R. Dynes. 1976. Community conflict: Its absence and its presence in natural disasters. *International Journal of Mass Emergencies and Disasters* 1:139–52.

Régnier,P., B. Neri, S. Scuteri, and S. Miniati. 2008. From emergency relief to livelihood recovery: Lessons learned from post-tsunami experiences in Indonesia and India. *Disaster Prevention and Management* 17 (3): 410–30.

Rossi, P. H., J. D. Wright, and S. R. Wright. 1981. Assessment of research on natural hazards reassessed in light of the SADRI Disaster Research Program. In *Social science and natural hazards*, ed. J. D. Wright and P. H. Rossi, 143–59. Cambridge, MA: ABT.

Sapat, A., and A. M. Esnard. 2012. Displacement and disaster recovery: Transnational governance and socio-legal issues following the 2010 Haiti earthquake. *Risk, Hazards & Crisis in Public Policy* 3 (1): Article 2.

Save the Children. n.d. http://www.savethechildren.org/.

Schigoda, M. 2011. Facts for features: Hurricane Katrina impact. News release. Greater New Orleans Community Data Center. http://www.gnocdc.org/Factsforfeatures/HurricaneKatrinaImpact/index.html.

Sheskin, I., and A. Dashefsky. 2010. Jewish population in the United States, 2010. Mandell L. Berman Institute, North American Jewish Data Bank. http://www.jewishdatabank.org/Reports/Jewish_Population_in_the_United_States_2010.pdf.

Sim, S. 2002. Chinatown one year after September 11th: An economic impact study. Asian American Federation of New York. http://www.commonwealthfund.org/Bios/S/Sim-Shao-Chee.aspx.

Sjoberg, G. 1962. Disasters and social change. In *Man and society in disaster*, ed. G. W. Baker and D. W. Chapman, 356–84. New York: Basic Books.

Sorokin, P. A. 1942. *Man and society in calamity*. New York: Greenwood Press.

Spector, M., and J. I. Kitsuse. 1973. Toward a sociology of social problems. *Social Problems* 20:407–49.

Stallings, R. A. 1997. Sociological theories and disaster studies. Paper presented at Disaster and Risk Conference. Disaster Research Center, University of Delaware.

Thomas, A. 2005. Improving Aid Effectiveness: Two Studies Suggest Solutions. UN Chronicle. http://www.fritzinstitute.org/PDFs/InTheNews/2006/UNChron_0206.pdf (accessed July 30, 2012).

Tierney, K., and C. Bevc. 2007. Disaster as war: Militarism and the social construction of disaster in New Orleans. In *The sociology of Katrina*, ed. D. L. Brunsma, D. Overfelt, and J. S. Picou, 35–49. Lanham, MD: Rowman & Littlefield.

Tierney, K. J., M. K. Lindell, and R. W. Perry. 2001. *Facing the unexpected: Disaster preparedness and response in the United States*. Washington, DC: Joseph Henry Press.

UN-HABITAT. (United Nations Human Settlements Programme). 2010. Count me in: Surveying for tenure security and urban land management. http://www.unhabitat.org/pmss/listItemDetails.aspx?publicationID=2975.

USAID (United States Agency for International Development). n.d. Addressing gender-based violence through USAID's health programs: A guide for health sector program officers. http://pdf.usaid.gov/pdf_docs/pnadh194.pdf.

USAID (United States Agency for International Development). 2012. Haiti Mobile Money Initiative. http://www.usaid.gov/news-information/fact-sheets/haiti-mobile-money-initiative.

Vago, S. 2004. *Social change*. 5th ed. Upper Saddle River, NJ: Prentice Hall.

Walsh, E. J., and R. H. Warland. 1983. Social movement involvement in the wake of nuclear accident: Activists and free riders in the TMI area. *American Sociological Review* 48 (6): 764–80.

Wamsler, C. 2006. Mainstreaming risk reduction in urban planning and housing: A challenge for international aid organisations. *Disasters* 30(2): 151–77.

Warner, C. 2007. Insurance rate increases OK'd: Coastal parishes to bear bulk of higher charges. *Times-Picayune*, May 25, 1.

Weisenfeld, P. E. 2011. Successes and challenges of the Haiti earthquake response: The experience of USAID. *Emory International Law Review* 25: 1097–1120.

Wolfenstein, M. 1957. *Disaster: A psychological essay*. Glencoe, IL: Free Press.

Wright, J. D., P. H. Rossi, S. R. Wright, and E. Weber-Burdin. 1979. *After the clean-up: Long-range effects of natural disasters*. Beverly Hills, CA: Sage.

Zhang, F., R. E. Morss, J. A. Sippel, T. K. Beckman, N. C. Clements, N. L. Hampshire, J. N. Harvey, et al. 2007. An in-person survey investigating public perceptions of and responses to Hurricane Rita forecasts along the Texas Coast. *Weather and Forecasting* 22 (6): 1177–90.

18 New Ideas for Practitioners

DeeDee Bennett, Brenda D. Phillips, Deborah S. K. Thomas, Eve Gruntfest, and Jeanette Sutton

CONTENTS

18.1 CHAPTER PURPOSE

The purpose of this chapter is to review concepts, approaches, ideas, and tools presented throughout the book and highlight new ideas for incorporating social vulnerability into research and practice, updating the last edition of this book. Much progress has been made toward reducing social vulnerability and building social resilience, but much remains to be done. We invite you to be part of that effort, to remain alert to new materials that become available after the publication of the current edition, and to work collectively to make this world a safer place. This chapter provides a review of the concept of resilience that has permeated throughout this text, along with examples of applications from the United States and the United Kingdom. This chapter also includes a series of checklists designed to be starting points for initial thinking about vulnerability reduction and building resilience in our communities.

18.2 OBJECTIVES

At the conclusion of this chapter, readers should be able to:

1. Understand why emergency management practice must remain dynamic in order to effect transformative change and promote resilience across affected areas and among affected populations
2. Define and illustrate the concept of resilience and ways to use this idea within one's community of practice
3. Explain why the community is actually a composite of communities with varying capacities and vulnerabilities
4. Grasp the significance of the term the "whole community" coupled with implications for community-wide engagement
5. Identify multiple reasons for interdisciplinary coordination across and among physical and social scientists and emergency managers
6. Locate opportunities for remaining current in the field of emergency management practice, particularly with a strong connection to the social and physical sciences
7. Consider new and emerging hazards, such as space weather, and their implications for vulnerable populations
8. Become conversant in the range of technologies, including social media and relevant applications, that connect to the whole community
9. Employ strategies that transform the emergency management workplace into a more diverse, dynamic, and robustly resilient workplace that mirrors the whole community

18.3 INTRODUCTION

To reduce social vulnerability and promote resiliency, we must engage *all* of those impacted by disasters across affected communities. We must work toward creating more resilient communities with populations able to resist the consequences of disaster impacts and to rebound when adversity strikes. To make progress requires an end-to-end-to-end approach engaging all partners from individuals, households, local officials, first responders, researchers, and others, in place of a purely top-down approach (Downton et al. 2005; Morss et al. 2005). The potential impact of leveraging such social capital can be profound. We must, however, move out of our individual silos, disciplines, or locales to work across differences. Indeed, we must use our differences as sources of insight that generate a more robust understanding and set of approaches to risk reduction.

Social science has contributed significantly by providing concepts, theories, and tools that assess and inform practice to help achieve the goal of life safety. Such ideas can be transformative, but also inherently challenge traditional ways of practicing emergency management. American disaster researcher E. L. Quarantelli (1998, 272) was optimistic about changing dominant ways of thinking about and researching disasters:

> [T]he more revolutionary we are in our thinking, the more likely we are to generate a new paradigm for disaster research. At least some of us ought to be revolutionaries rather than reformers. As a long time student of collective behavior and social movements, I am very well aware that the overwhelming majority of revolutions end in failure. But now and then one succeeds and transforms the behavior in the societies in which they occur, often in unexpected ways. So the more venturesome and imaginative among us should be encouraged to see if they can develop different paradigms for disaster research.

As found throughout this volume, it is clear that disasters are not equal opportunity events; they are not social "levelers." Yet despite the prevalent view that those at risk are solely vulnerable, this volume demonstrates the significant capacities that exist even in highly marginalized populations and communities. Empowerment and community-based approaches harness this potential. Indeed,

Jegillos (1999, 8) notes that in the Philippines, experts concur that community-based initiatives are needed rather than a long and failed "history of often uneven, inequitable and unsustainable results from 'top-down' interventions." To reduce risk, we must engage those at risk, respect their social capital and points of view, and provide resources to strengthen those who face the harshest of consequences when disaster strikes.

The transformative value of this volume is also reflected in the words of Ben Wisner (personal communication), an original contributor to the *FEMA Social Vulnerability to Disaster* course materials (on which this book is based) and a noted scholar-practitioner:

> How I learned to think differently. . . . I began with a fairly conventional approach to famine and rural development. But the conventional approach just didn't work in Eastern Kenya. I heard that from dozens of farmers, women and men. And the numbers didn't add up. The more in need of famine relief (measured as a percentage of children under three who were at 80% or below their standard weight for age), the less relief people got! Puzzled, I sought alternative explanations. . . . Then a year or so later, I discovered that people about my age had been finding similar things in West Africa (e.g., cotton exports from Mali going up during the drought and famine there, 1968–1973). . . . Pieces of the puzzle began to fall into place. My own acceptance of an alternative paradigm was born.

Indeed, transformative practice begins with new ideas and approaches, as demonstrated in Box 18.1, where Damai Pakpahan speaks of transforming disaster risk for women and girls after the 2004 Indian Ocean tsunami. Inspired by scholar-practitioners like Pakpahan, this chapter promotes ideas and actionable items grounded in social science.

BOX 18.1   EMPOWERING THE "WHOLE COMMUNITY" IN INDONESIA

Damai Pakpahan received the 2012 Mary Fran Myers award for her courageous leadership after the 2004 Indonesian tsunami (see Box 12.4). Here, she tells us about the efforts put forth by gendered organizations, the challenges they faced, and how the work links to other populations.

> Disasters are so close to us in Indonesia. We have experienced different kinds of disasters from natural to human-made disasters to social-political and armed conflicts. Natural disasters vary from floods to volcanic eruptions to tsunamis. Earthquakes also happen in Indonesia, as the geographical location of Indonesia is a disaster-prone area. We, as Indonesians, have at least faced one, two, or as many as three disasters during our life span. Poor people in Jakarta who live along the banks of the Ciliwung River experience floods annually in the rainy season. My parents' home is located near the Ciliwung River, and I saw my neighbors and relatives who experienced the flooding in their houses. Again, when I was in senior high school, I was involved in a fundraising activity for the victims of flooding of the Code River. As a student activist who opposed the authoritarian regime, I saw these issues through the lens of politics.
>
> The tsunami in Aceh and the earthquake on Nias Island was really an eye opener for linking gender to disaster for me. Before that, although I had learned about gender issues, women's empowerment, and feminism as a student activist in mid 1980s, I thought that disasters impacted everybody the same because all become victims. But the tsunami sharpened my understanding about gender. Because of a gendered division of labor, because of different roles, tasks, and functions—women experience a huge difference with the impact of disasters. I still remember the unfriendly religious interpretation toward women that put the blame on women. They said it was because more women became victims of the tsunami. One religious leader said it was because more women committed sin than men. His argument continued that women victims of the tsunami were found naked (due to the gigantic waves of tsunami), which means that they were sinners. Here we see the bias and stigma placed on women. Even in the distribution of food and nonfood items, women's needs are neglected.

From the women's movement perspective, these kinds of issues have to be resolved. We need to use gendered lenses and women's perspectives too. The Indonesia Coalition for Justice and Democracy (KPI) has been active in disaster since the tsunami in Aceh. The KPI has been actively involved in contributing meaningful and useful support post disaster with women's leadership. In the context of the tsunami in Aceh and Nias, I was stationed in both areas by Oxfam GB as an interim gender advisor. I gave a concise gender introduction to the Oxfam staff all over Aceh and Nias, made the gender assessment for Nias, assessed the partner proposals to ensure that gender issues were there and would address women's empowerment. I have to deal with the issue of sexual harassment too. Other work included network building. Since I am also a feminist and already know many friends and network in Aceh, I can easily meet and learn from friends what happened with the situation of women and children—girls and boys. We started with a Gender Working Group (GWG) with the government, academia, and NGOs together in Aceh. Through GWG, we shared the stories and what would be the planning, action, and monitoring efforts for what is going on in the camps and communities. It was the women's movement who found the case of child trafficking in the postdisaster time.

The model of GWG in Aceh was also brought to Yogyakarta when an earthquake struck in 2006. A cluster approach was introduced in Aceh and Nias by UN agencies (OCHA and UNDP), and this cluster approach was implemented again in Yogyakarta. However, there was no Gender Working Group in place, and we had to lobby and influence the UN and other parties (NGOs) to bring this to their attention and make the arguments over how important is the Gender Working Group (GWG) to the leadership of OCHA/UNDP. Finally we now have a Gender Working Group in Yogyakarta, which was easily reactivated again in the context of the Merapi eruption in 2010, when we made a gender assessment for Merapi survivors.

This model of GWG was brought (thanks to UNFPA) from Yogyakarta to West Sumatra in October 2009 together with the Women's Empowerment Ministry. There were four batches of GWG from Yogyakarta and the Women's Empowerment Ministry's staff from Jakarta to do gender assessment and assist the West Sumatra Province to ensure that women's and children's needs were fulfilled in the postdisaster time. It was not easy to ensure that the government would address seriously women's needs and accept women's leadership. I can still see that military commander—the leader of the postdisaster response—and we had to deal with them and talk seriously without threatening them that they had to address the gender issues, including women's empowerment, such as women participating in the community or camp meeting. (In this context, women were a minority in this elite meeting, and only the KPI attended this kind of meeting.) While with local government, we have to ask and remind them that segregated data based on sex and age is very important and make sure they have that information so that we can know the needs too. One thing, even in the circle of the Women's Empowerment Ministry, is that there is a fear of using the *gender* word. Some of them do not like to talk about gender. One time, when I was just about to discuss gender and disaster in front of the local district staff meeting, one of the staff approached me and asked me not to talk about gender in disaster time. I refused him and calmly said that I will talk about gender in time of disaster, *because gender is everywhere and anytime.*

The situation is still challenging, but we need to continue this struggle to ensure that women, men, girls and boys, transgender people, lesbians, gays, poor people (men and women), and minority groups will get their special needs met in times of disaster and be able to have meaningful participation so that their voices will be heard.

Damai Pakpahan
Bloemfontein, South Africa, 15 July 2012

18.4   RESILIENCE

In Australia, experienced practitioner and scholar Philip Buckle (2000) notes that sociopolitical and even cultural contexts enabled a more rapid adoption of social vulnerability analysis. In Australia, a stronger public sector with more state support of social services led the way. A more collective orientation to political culture, coupled with a formal commitment to egalitarianism and racial justice, supported the change to a "new idea." Australia's national identity as a leader and its resistance to outside ideas and practices also compelled Australians to adopt vulnerability approaches and to work with communities to organize at the grassroots level to build capacity and promote resilience.

As discussed in Chapter 1 and throughout this volume, resilience has emerged as a powerful idea and—when put into action—one that activates social capital in a promising manner (Buckle 2000). Definitions vary, but the core idea of resilience is the ability to rebound when disruptions occur to infrastructure, utilities, neighborhoods, businesses and livelihoods, education, and other critical social structures and relationships that sustain human communities (Liu et al. 2011). What does an emergency manager or practitioner need to know in order to understand vulnerability and promote resilience? Some guiding principles lead us in promising directions (see Box 18.2) and suggest a dedication to active collaboration between emergency managers and the communities they serve. Furthermore, resilience must be developed across the life cycle of disasters, from preparedness through recovery. Coles and Buckle (2004, 14) observed this after multiple disasters in the United Kingdom and Australia. They advise disaster managers to "learn from the practice and experience of the humanitarian and development sectors . . . [including] Agenda 21, the Universal Declaration of Human Rights and the United Nations Millennium Development Goals. All these provide a standard against which we can assess resilience and disaster management."

BOX 18.2   CONNECTING WITH HIGH-RISK POPULATIONS

In order to move toward and adopt a vulnerability approach, practitioners must develop and practice sensitivity to gender, class, ethnicity, and power relations. To illustrate, a gender-sensitive practice might be guided by (Enarson and Morrow 1998; Morrow and Phillips 2008; Enarson and Phillips 2008):

- Using gender analysis in designing and evaluating projects
- Identifying gender bias in organizational culture and practice
- Advocating for gender equity in the planning, implementation, and evaluation of all initiatives to assess and reduce risk
- Working collaboratively and as equals with women
- Working with leading women's groups and organizations at the local level
- Relating relief and reconstruction to the reduction of gender vulnerabilities

Race-conscious practices can also be identified to reduce sources of bias and promote reduction of risk (see Aguirre 1988; Perry and Mushkatel 1986; Bolin and Stanford 1998; Fothergill, Maestas, and Darlington 1999). Strategies for doing so might include:

- Communicating across language barriers to reach diverse groups
- Using culturally appropriate and diverse media to reach racial and ethnic groups, including alternative language stations
- Communicating with community leaders, advocacy groups, and faith-based organizations in all ethnic groups, particularly with locally respected leaders and those organizations that connect to recent immigrants
- Following culturally sensitive guidelines to tailor work to different communities, respecting and following cultural norms within various communities and groups
- Working collaboratively with and empowering ethnic community-based organizations that represent marginalized social groups
- Identifying with marginalized racial and ethnic communities through well-trained professionals, particularly those from within the communities at risk

Practitioners should also work at recognizing and being able to transcend class bias that tends to separate and divide people. Significant social capital exists within all socioeconomic classes, including low-income levels. Based on previous chapters, it is advisable to (Peacock, Gladwin, and Morrow 1997; Bolin and Stanford 1999):

- Advocate for the interests of low-income groups.
- Learn about the living conditions of poor people in their areas of responsibility.
- Identify economic differences between neighborhoods within communities.
- Be sensitive to class-biased assumptions about household structure, employment, and resources.
- Be sensitive to potential class-based barriers to government and nongovernmental relief and recovery services.

In short, Lindell and Prater (2000, 326) urge that:

emergency managers [should] get to know the residents of their communities to identify the ways in which potential implementation barriers affect different segments of the population. Frequent, personally delivered communications about inexpensive hazard adjustments that are targeted to specific segments of the risk area population may be the most effective means of reducing community vulnerability to earthquake hazards.

A research project funded by the United Kingdom's Government Defence Science and Technology Laboratory looked at evidence and case studies surrounding the idea of community resilience (Twigger-Ross et al. 2011). The research uncovered several ways to view resilience. First, resilience can be seen as resistance or a means of "holding the line" (p. 5). Such an element can work during preparedness phases, but it is not considered appropriate when disasters surpass preparedness and mitigation measures—like when the levees failed in New Orleans in the United States from hurricane Katrina. Another way to think about resilience is a *bounce-back*, where the affected area is "getting back to normal" (p. 6). A recent report by the National Academies of Science in the United States (NAS 2012, prepublication edition) defined the concept of resilience as "the ability to prepare and plan for, absorb, recover from and more successfully adapt to adverse events."

Disasters promote opportunities and, when approached through community-based collaboration, can yield significant improvements (Liu et al. 2011). The U.K. researchers also examined resilience as a form of adaptation where people adjust to a "new normal" and refuse to return to the conditions that caused impact (p. 8). Finally, resilience can also be transformative when a "tipping point is reached and it is realized that previously desired community functions are no longer sustainable" (p. 9). Catastrophic events may generate such a scenario (e.g., Hurricane Katrina), although resources and opportunities may not exist sufficiently to reduce future threats (e.g., the earthquake in Haiti).

Any community may follow any of these aspects of resilience. Effective emergency managers see future threats or recent impacts as an opportunity to build community resilience that promotes effective, transformative change. Practitioners will need to realistically assess community willingness, coupled with political will and economic resources to determine priorities and the most viable way forward. Still, emergency managers should not underestimate what can be accomplished, even if progress seems slow. Building effective partnerships takes considerable time in which new coalitions must face and overcome both internal and external obstacles. Indeed, sincere commitment through sustained dialogue serves as a driving force that can become a protracted time of evolution and potential action. Community-based collaboration "can be a way of shaping the economic, social and ecological changes that have been accelerated by human behaviors...[and] ... provide a vehicle not just for change, which can be forced, but for transitions that have legitimacy and support to occur" (Dukes 2011, 212). Social science research confirms that community-based collaboration is, ultimately, worth the effort. Resilience should be viewed as an "ongoing dynamic process" that continues and evolves through time (Twigger-Ross et al. 2011, 9). The starting point is to truly know and engage within one's community and its resources.

18.4.1 Knowing Your Community and Its Resources

Throughout this volume, it is clear that authors and practitioners recommend knowing your community as the one key guiding principle that governs effective practice. A good starting point is to identify social service organizations, nonprofits, faith-based organizations, and advocates within the community (National Council on Disability 2009). These organizations will typically fall into a number of categories relevant to socially vulnerable populations, including those that work with senior citizens, homebound and medically fragile populations, women and children, racial and ethnic minorities, those at risk for violence, the homeless, residents with varying languages and literacy levels, and people with disabilities. A savvy emergency manager will get to know each of these agencies, their personnel, and their capabilities in order to build a cadre of potential partners. Many of them can be brought into the emergency management arena by inviting them to participate through collaborative efforts. In the United States, the National Voluntary Organization Active in Disaster (NVOAD) promotes collaboration. If such an entity does not yet exist, creating a similar interorganizational coalition can serve to organize and facilitate the creation of a useful network and provide disaster-relevant training to member organizations. (For an example, see NVOAD or www.nvoad.org.)

Collaboration within and across communities (either geographically or through cyber-communities) can serve vulnerable populations and help them to aid themselves. Within India, the Self-Employed Women's Association (SEWA) provided tools for women and girls to craft traditional handcrafts. By providing a forum for interaction, women became more confident within their postearthquake environment and ultimately increased their power in their households and through civic governance (Lund and Vaux 2009). A more global effort, Grassroots Organizations Operating Together in Sisterhood (GROOTS), has been assisting women since 1989. They assisted an exchange between India and Turkey, which fostered collaboration between SEWA and women affected when an earthquake struck Turkey (Yonder et al. 2009).

By recognizing the nondisaster roles of local, regional, and even globally operating organizations concerned with community-level impacts, disaster managers reduce vulnerability and foster resilience to disaster. Emergency managers may be surprised to realize that they can increase disaster preparedness through encouraging and supporting local organizing. Fordham (2009) conducted a case study in El Salvador. Though women participated initially out of concern over food and nutrition, they also became involved in creating a community development plan. A health committee formed around water and sanitation, which ultimately led to other committees on waste management and emergencies. As Fordham notes, "It makes sense to organize on the basis of what people recognize as everyday, pressing risks, rather than on the basis of the risk of a disaster which, by comparison, may be a distant threat. It is the process of organizing that is important; the focus of the organization is secondary" (Fordham 2009, 181).

Local community and networked organizations can provide insight into the numbers and kinds of populations that may be at risk locally and offer a valuable connection to them. Though census data can give a general overview (as described in previous chapters), those data remain limited to snapshots and annual estimates. Further, censuses may appear sporadically in some nations that lack the resources for such efforts. Such data often miss emerging populations, including recent immigrants, veterans disabled by recent wars, travelers, people who are homeless, people displaced by conflict, or individuals living in newly created facilities (e.g., prisons, nursing homes, state schools, workshops for the developmentally disabled). But, local community groups and organizations have a sense of these populations. (See Box 18.3.)

BOX 18.3   COLLABORATIVE EFFORTS IN COMMUNITY RESILIENCE: MAHILA PARTNERSHIP

This box presents an effort that connects evidence-based best practices to issues of social vulnerability and resilience. By understanding that livelihoods connect to and foster resilience after disasters, Mahila Partnership promotes local capacity building. As shown here, the critical element emanates from empowering those at risk to identify unmet needs and find collaborative solutions with both short- and long-term impact.

It has become increasingly clear that postdisaster relief and recovery programs must promote long-term risk reduction and address root cause issues that exacerbate impacts of disasters, particularly on women and girls. During disasters and humanitarian crisis, women and girls face daily obstacles related to hygiene, specifically the absence of effective and affordable menstruation management materials and education, forcing changes in their activities that support their role in a postdisaster recovery. Furthermore, the lack of these basic necessities places women and girls at a disadvantage, as it can result in poor hygiene practices that increase the risk of disease and reproductive health issues, and prevent the participation and representation of women at all levels of decision making. When girls and women cannot equally and effectively participate in their community, particularly during recovery from crisis, preexisting gender disparities are magnified.

Building Resilience with Women Post-Disaster

1. Meet with local women
2. Understand health and hygiene needs from their perspectives
3. Provide short-term hygiene kits
4. Collaborate with local sewing cooperative and health clinics on materials for hygiene education and local production of sanitary pads
5. Invest in local cottage industry to establish capacity to manufacture products for hygiene materials
6. Employ and train local women
7. Source Mahila Hygiene Kits from the women we work with and other sustainable enterprises

Following an examination of research in disaster risk reduction as well as firsthand experiences over the past five years, Mahila Partnership has developed programs helping women and girls impacted by disasters reclaim their esteem, health, and economic future by providing access to critical health and hygiene education and materials. Women who have access to health and hygiene materials are healthier and more confident, and are more likely to participate in the community and thrive personally and financially, especially in postdisaster scenarios.

To be successful, two overarching considerations need to exist: partnership and investments. Successful programs illustrate partnerships driven by local participation and ownership. Partnerships involve local-community actors who have a long-time active presence in a community and serve as a repository for knowledge of the needs of the women and girls in the community. Following disasters, Mahila Partnership starts first with an aid-based intervention. As part of its intervention, Mahila searches for possible partners who are rooted in the community and can help focus and guide possible long-term solutions. Once its aid-based solutions are realized, Mahila uses its on-the-ground contacts to search for long-term partners in order to transform its work by investing in a long-term sustainability model. Using principles of social entrepreneurship and accountability, and aligning funding support to outcomes, local partners actively generate economic recovery, reducing future vulnerability to disasters. Furthermore, investing in women and girls before, during, and after disasters has a multiplier effect, given that they are typically responsible for taking care of others, particularly children and the elderly.

One Mahila project in Haiti empowers a women's sewing cooperative (haitiprojects.org) to design and produce reusable sanitary pads for Haiti Project's local women's clinic and, eventually, to be sold in the local market. Women work together to craft sanitary pads to be used in the clinic for educating women and girls about menstruation and reproductive health. Still in its testing phase, this single project promises to address a root-cause health issue: the need for sanitary solutions and education. This need not only affects women in rural Haiti, but affects 200 million women in low-income countries every day—the *struggle to find adequate sanitary products, clean water for washing, or private places for changing sanitary pads.*

In Haiti and other countries where Mahila works to provide postdisaster hygiene kits and support local cottage industry production of sanitary pads, 1 million women in need of sanitary supplies will receive sanitary pads over the next five years.

Source: Mahila Partnerships. For more information please visit www.mahilapartnership.org.

Organizations, including the faith-based sector, provide critical services to many at risk. For example, though the poverty rate remains fairly constant in many nations, a dynamic population moves into and out of poverty all the time. Similarly, homelessness seems constantly present but, again, a changing body of people move into and out of homelessness daily. Organizations that provide transitional facilities serve as a means to contact and inform those who are homeless about disaster preparedness, evacuation, and recovery. The transitional nature of such populations means that although the social problems of poverty and homelessness will always influence the practice of emergency management, the people we will try to reach will change. Local organizations provide useful ties to such dynamic populations.

18.4.2   THE "WHOLE COMMUNITY"

Knowing your community means the *whole community*, with no exceptions. In the United States, the Federal Emergency Management Agency (FEMA) recently adopted an approach consistent with evidence-based best practices contained within this volume and with ideas expressed in this chapter. FEMA (2011) generated the idea of the *whole community* through a national dialogue that took place over several years. FEMA began by recognizing that people live in a diverse mosaic of communities within communities, an observation consistent with social science writing on communities affected by disaster (Marsh and Buckle 2001; Buckle 2000). Engaging the diversity within and across communities is critical to risk reduction. As FEMA administrator Craig Fugate observed, "We fully recognize that a government-centric approach to disaster management will not be enough to meet the challenges posted by a catastrophic incident. That is why we must fully engage our entire societal capacity" (FEMA 2011, 2).

The *whole community* approach is more than an idea; it is a method of engaging the community—together. FEMA recognized the challenge of tasking emergency managers with involving a diverse array of groups and organizations. The FEMA approach supports perspectives that define emergency management as a people profession requiring effective communication, abilities to inspire trust, and a willingness to take the long road through collaboration. Indeed, FEMA finds that "a community's needs should be defined on the basis of what the community requires without being limited to what traditional emergency management capabilities can address" (FEMA 2011, 8). Quick fixes do not work; rather, building trusted, credible relationships over time does.

The *whole community* approach rests on several key principles. A first principle directs emergency managers to "understand and meet the actual needs of the whole community." Doing so requires practitioners to understand a community's demographic makeup, cultural contexts, and social structures—all of which emanate from and resonate within a strong social science framework. Second, as documented in multiple chapters in this volume, we must "engage and empower all parts of the community" (see Box 18.2), including local stakeholders from individuals through the key organizations and agencies mentioned earlier. A third principle directs us to "strengthen what works well in communities on a daily basis." This means focusing on "building community resilience" to "strengthen the institutions, assets, and networks that already work well in communities" (FEMA 2011, 5). (For a tabletop exercise engaging the whole community, see the Resources section of this chapter.)

Whole-community principles move emergency managers into six strategic themes (FEMA 2011, 5, verbatim):

- Understand community complexity.
- Recognize community capability and needs.
- Foster relationships with community leaders.
- Build and maintain partnerships.
- Empower local action.
- Leverage and strengthen social infrastructure, networks and assets.

As an idea, the *whole community* builds upon solid social science findings that recommend engaging and empowering people and organizations within and across areas likely to be affected by disaster. In a disaster event, especially one that surpasses available resources to respond, we will need each other. Emergency managers who recognize this and participate in community-based efforts will reduce impacts on the public and on their own organizations. Behind the scenes of such public collaboration, scientists and emergency managers must forge stronger connections in order to reduce threats to public safety.

18.5   COLLABORATION AMONG SOCIAL AND PHYSICAL SCIENTISTS AND EMERGENCY MANAGERS

Collaboration between social scientists, physical scientists, and practitioners is vital for reducing vulnerability and increasing resilience, though this has remained a serious challenge for decades. (See Box 18.4.) Several main obstacles to successful collaboration include the following:

- Most physical and social scientists operate within narrow disciplinary stovepipes that do not incorporate or involve practitioners.
- Most social and physical scientists, even if they want to collaborate with each other, have very limited knowledge of each other's concepts and tools related to natural hazards. The same has been historically true between scientists and practitioners. We simply do not talk across our disciplines and workspaces very well.
- Physical scientists and practitioners tend to underestimate the value of the social sciences and how best to incorporate a fair understanding of human behavior in the face of risk and natural hazards. Reducing losses from tornadoes, for example, has at least as much to do with human response to warnings as it does to increasing lead time, a practical problem that requires collaboration among all those involved in research and practice on public safety.
- Limited funding, particularly for the social sciences, and minimal budgets for many practitioners keep them isolated and unable to collaborate effectively.

The process of predicting human behavior is at least as complicated as predicting the weather that results from changing atmospheric conditions. Yet, billions of dollars in research funding have advanced the state of physical science in predicting volcanic eruptions, tsunamis, hurricanes, tornadoes, and many other hazards. Achieving parallel progress on the human behavior side will also require years of research and, as is accepted in science, it will not be a direct route to success. A

BOX 18.4   LINKING ACADEMICS, PRACTITIONERS, AND EMERGENCY MANAGERS: A DISABILITY FOCUS

The Emergency Preparedness Initiative Global (EPI Global) is a small not-for-profit that evolved from 10 years of active programming under the National Organization on Disability. Freestanding and independent now, EPI Global's vision is to promote inclusive emergency management practices that benefit all people across the globe. This is based on the belief that people from all backgrounds and circumstances should be an integral part of planning for, responding to, recovering from, and mitigating the impact of natural and human-made disasters.

Thus, EPI Global's mission is to serve as a bridge that informs and empowers emergency management practitioners and stakeholder communities to collaborate effectively and to identify issues and find solutions across the life cycle of emergency management, resulting in a better-prepared public and a more capable response community.

EPI Global recognizes the need to cross-share information among subject-matter experts from all areas and covers traditionally underserved-population issues that are independent stratifications but overlap in many combinations including, among others, age, disability, gender, economic status, race, and culture.

An example of new and broad-reaching programming is a five-part webinar series begun in July 2012 on the topic of gender and disaster and cosponsored with the U.S. Gender and Disaster Resilience Alliance. The inaugural session—a cross-cutting overview—had attendees joining from New Zealand, Australia, Aceh (Indonesia), the United Kingdom, Canada, and across the United States and maxed out available slots allocated for attendance.

considerable shift in funding social science disaster research is a necessary means to accomplishing this parallel but joint research agenda.

Social science integration with engineering, especially in the area of computer and information sciences, is becoming vital when designing communication tools for at-risk populations. The same silos that currently exist between the physical and social sciences pervade the information and communication technology design process as technologies continue to develop without the end user in mind. Software and hardware products must take into consideration the various populations that may employ information and communication technologies (ICTs), as well as make use of social science knowledge on aspects of disaster mitigation, preparedness, response, and recovery. While populations at risk have tremendous ability and capability to adapt existing technologies for novel rescue and response activities, it will benefit individuals and organizations across the disaster time continuum to utilize social science knowledge for design of applications and communications technologies prior to a disaster event.

For instance, in the United States, the National Weather Service (NWS) is starting to incorporate societal impacts in its forecasts. Previously, in severe summer weather conditions, the forecasters were concerned mostly with predictions of the size of hail. Hailstones measuring three-quarters of an inch and wind speeds of 58 miles per hour were required to meet the criteria for a severe thunderstorm. Now forecasts also take into account whether the storm will affect rush-hour traffic or have other impacts that will affect large numbers of people.

The National Weather Service also has a new "roadmap" that highlights how forecasters are directly addressing decision support for households, emergency managers, coaches, transportation departments, managers of large venues, and others. The roadmap is part of the weather-ready national initiative that is bringing forecast offices and regional offices in closer touch with expressed stakeholder needs (Figure 18.1). This roadmap shows how the agency should pay closer attention to local and regional emergency managers' particular weather concerns.

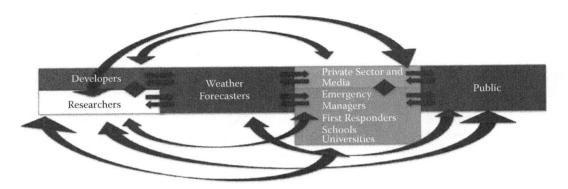

FIGURE 18.1   Model of relationship between stakeholders and forecast software developers in an integrated hazards information service. Social scientists have established a process that brings stakeholders' perspectives (emergency managers, forecasters, and others) in direct dialog with forecasting software developers. This work has started to build professional relationships between these traditionally disconnected groups. The software designers realize that the new tools they design will likely be utilized by the stakeholders. The stakeholders are trusted partners in the development of the new software, and so they invest time working with the developers. (*Source*: J. Spinney and E. Gruntfest, "What makes our partners tick? Using ethnography to inform the Global System Division's development of the Integrated Hazards Information Service [IHIS]," 2012.)

Key to increasing understanding between social and physical scientists is the extension of social vulnerability research into relevant areas of expertise, coupled with integration of emergency management professionals. Meteorologists who warn the public must understand the significance and required content of the messages they deliver so that they are meaningful to people with disabilities, seniors, children home alone, or administrators of congregate-care facilities. Engineers who design structural features to mitigate risk must couple that effort with accessibility standards. Safe rooms (meeting the FEMA 361 standard), for example, must be redesigned to permit wheelchair access both above and below ground.

18.6   PROFESSIONAL DEVELOPMENT

The road to a complete acceptance and use of social science concepts and tools has not been a smooth one, and has not been entirely achieved. Two currently divergent roads must meet: collaboration of social scientists with physical scientists and integration of social science research with emergency management. Social scientists should become familiar with field techniques, data, tools, and concepts used for understanding the physical aspects of hazards, and physical scientists must conversely understand the relevance and basics of social science. This interdisciplinary cross-fertilization is required to accelerate the changes that will allow the research and stakeholder communities to learn from experience and reduce losses overall. This new community of scientists and practitioners could aid in cross-hazard work extending to issues related to climate change, floods, hurricanes, and every other hazard type. Emergency management professionals should be connected with academics and scientists—and vice versa. Without working collaboratively, we cannot hope to achieve effective risk reduction for vulnerable populations.

Research suggests that knowledge transfer from researchers to practitioners occurs in a slow and unwieldy fashion (Mileti 1999; Fothergill 2000). Academic research tends to move into the public domain faster than that governed by proprietary or private interests (though it can be bought through consulting contracts). However, academic researchers must work within a framework that demands certain standards, including publication in top-notch scientific journals and presentations at professional conferences, which slows knowledge transfer. Annual reviews, salary increments, and tenure all ride on these accomplishments. These venues, however, are not the place where most emergency managers glean information. Further, academics often write in jargon and in order to communicate within and across scientific communities—rather than with emergency managers. Thus a disconnect exists between these unfortunately separated communities.

Emergency managers tend to prefer information sources that include emergency management conferences, Listservs, courses available through FEMA or state agencies, and professional networks (Mileti 1999; Fothergill 2000). Direct experience is also valued, often above and beyond that acquired through research sources or academic degree programs. Though the field is changing continually, the research-based discipline of emergency management remains in its emerging decades, but with an increasing number of degree programs developing worldwide, an even greater array of certificates, minors, and related opportunities exist. At present only a handful of doctoral programs deliver research-based content to the next generation of researchers or scholar-practitioners.

During the last three decades, the field of emergency management has increasingly professionalized through the adoption of credentials, professional organizations, and both training and degree work. The FEMA Higher Education Project in the United States has led many efforts to encourage the growth of emergency management and related degree programs. Well over 200 colleges and universities now offer degrees, certificates, or other programs (both traditional and online) that are helping to build the next generation of emergency managers. A number of those degree programs include course content or even stand-alone courses on vulnerability. Courses can also be found in a number of social science programs, such as a department of sociology, on populations at risk (many of them offered by authors in this volume). Unfortunately, social vulnerability is not necessarily at the core of many of these programs, but at least it has become increasingly recognized. Ultimately, all programs should integrate some social vulnerability core education and training, even if it is not the entire emphasis of a program. For example, Hesston College in Kansas developed a curriculum focused primarily on vulnerability reduction. Their efforts represent a stellar step toward transforming practice by using a vulnerability program. Worldwide, additional programs in a variety of discipline-based and interdisciplinary efforts have developed in Australia, New Zealand, Nepal, Canada, Turkey, and the United Kingdom. (For a current list, see http://www.training.fema.gov/EMIWeb/edu/collegelist/OtherCountries/.)

These trends reflect a larger pattern of increasing specialization and the demand for formal credentials (Wilson 2000; Neal 2000; Darlington 2000), which should have vulnerability grounded in cutting-edge social science as a fundamental component. Employers also are increasingly expecting that those they hire will possess abilities to think across disciplines and fields of work, engage in effective community relations, interact with a diverse public, and collaborate with local citizens. Some suggest that emergency managers today represent "a new generation of emergency planners" rather than the old-school approach of top-down management styles (Dynes 1994, 156). In emergency management, disasters drive change.

In the United States, Hurricane Katrina spurred on new approaches as well, with progress occurring at the federal level. FEMA, for example, has revised the National Response Framework to incorporate disability concerns. The National Housing Strategy (2009) recognizes the complexity of postdisaster housing given income and other issues. In addition to planning and tools specific to disabilities, FEMA has moved to embrace a "functional needs" approach. By emphasizing the functions that people need to meet (e.g., communications, transportation, medical needs, nutrition, etc.), the person becomes recognized, supported, and empowered to be more independent and active during disaster (see Resources section). The European Union has moved to formalize and professionalize its outreach when disaster occurs as a consequence of learning from the 2010 Haiti earthquake (Brattburg and Sundelius 2011).

Remaining current in the field is critical, both in terms of current research and practice. Additionally, trends outside the field may also have great influence. To illustrate, we move now to considerations of new and emerging hazards and the rapidly evolving area of social media and related technologies.

18.7   NEW AND EMERGING HAZARDS

As this book was going to press, a coronal mass ejection (CME) left the sun and moved quickly toward the Earth. Commonly referred to as "space weather," the phenomenon represents a new hazard among both social scientist researchers and practitioners. What is familiar, though, is the need to alert the public to impending consequences of this new hazard. Accordingly, the U.S.-based National Weather Service Space Weather Prediction Center (http://www.swpc.noaa.gov/) now issues alerts from a multilevel warning framework. The various levels describe the power of the space weather (including CMEs, solar flares, solar radiation storms, and geomagnetic storms) to influence the Earth. Potential disruptions may include problems with cell phones, radios, GPS navigation (automobiles, watercraft, and both commercial and military aircraft), and electrical power grids. These disruptions can cause considerable chaos in very rare but very high-impact events—powerful enough to interrupt the electrical grid along the U.S. eastern seaboard, possibly for months. Imagine the consequences for socially vulnerable populations such as those dependent on oxygen, users of mobility devices, people and professionals that rely on cell phones for communications (including first responders), and on the transportation industry—with significant consequences for the economy. Could such an event occur? History tells us that we need to be ready. An extremely powerful solar flare that occurred in 1859 produced a very intense geomagnetic storm with impressive results. While many people enjoyed the aurora lights seen in northern skies, telegraph operators faced disrupted communications, sparks that flew from their equipment, and related fires. The only thing that limited the damage was the primitive technology and lack of networked systems.

Experts concur that the power grid, along areas like the U.S. east coast, requires significant upgrades to stabilize the system against such effects. In 2012, physical scientists gathered at the annual Space Weather Enterprise Forum in Washington, DC, to discuss "solar maximum" and extreme space weather events. The report issued from this event reads:

> The next peak of solar activity expected in 2013 has already begun, and the effects of these powerful space weather events are negatively impacting the technical infrastructure that underpins our economy and society. The Nation faces many uncertainties from increasing reliance on space weather–affected technologies for communications, navigation, security, electrical power generation and distribution, and other activities. We also face increasing exposure to space weather-driven human health risks as trans-polar flights and space activities, including space tourism and space commercialization, increase. (OFCM 2012, 2)

At present, information transfer about space weather from experts to the public appears to occur through several means: social media and websites, on-air meteorologists who mention the effects (e.g., aurora and cell-phone disruptions), and weather-related services—a process in which emergency managers are only beginning to develop public education procedures. The extent to which the public understands the need to prepare for and develop resilience in a space weather event remains unknown. What is clear is that emergency managers will need to translate effectively information like this, sent out by the Federal Emergency Management Agency in response to a March 7, 2012, event:

> Space weather for the past 24 hours has been strong. G2 geomagnetic storms, S1 solar radiation storms and radio blackouts reaching the R3 level occurred. Space weather for the next 24 hours is predicted to be moderate, with G2 geomagnetic storms, S1 solar radiation storms and R1 radio blackouts expected.

Understanding levels of the storms, their physical properties, and the human impacts requires strong collaboration between our respective communities.

To foster a better dialogue between these communities—both of which are dedicated to life safety and motivated to make their work relevant to today's society—we offer these recommendations:

- Participate in each other's Listservs and engage in dialogue with each other over issues relevant to socially vulnerable populations.
- Attend and present at emergency management conferences.
- Contact academic researchers to acquire copies of their research and invite them to give local presentations at emergency management agencies.
- Involve academic researchers and social and physical scientists in consulting contracts designed to develop, for example, special-needs emergency operations plans, evacuation protocol, shelter arrangements, and recovery programs.
- Attend workshops that involve both social scientists and emergency managers working on common problems, for example, those found at the National Hurricane Conference.

Clearly, the key to such a transformative move toward scholar-practitioners or "pracademics" requires interdisciplinary conferences, publications, and programs that train and educate both emergency managers and researchers in relevant disciplines. In short, emergency managers must actively continue to learn as new ideas, findings, and hazards become known.

18.8 TOOLS AND TECHNOLOGIES

In the last several decades, technology has progressed at an increasingly rapid pace. New tools have been introduced that expand our information gathering and communication ability. Some tools are not exactly new, but have been repurposed in vastly different ways than initially conceived. An example would be the cell phone. In the United States, 83% of adults own a cell phone (Smith 2011), and global cell phone ownership is also extremely high, even in developing nations, where cell phone technology leapfrogged the installation of landlines (UNITU 2012). Initially designed for voice calls, the modern cell phone allows users to send text messages, send and receive e-mails, view the Internet, take pictures, post on social media, and even deposit checks into their banking institution!

18.8.1 CELL PHONES

New technology, including cell phones, is increasingly being used during emergencies and disasters. How, where, when, and by whom these devices are used become important questions for researchers and practitioners. Their use may also have serious implications for socially vulnerable populations during emergencies, especially new technologies that connect with or are used primarily through cell phones because of the differences in use among different demographics. For instance, some ethnic minorities are more intense and frequent users of the cell phone than whites in the United States. Additionally, parents use their cell phones more than those without children, and low- and high-income individuals use their cell phones more than those in the middle class (Lenhart 2010).

Due to the differences in use, some newer technologies may actually help practitioners disseminate information to certain socially vulnerable populations. In this section, we present several examples of new technology used in practice, developed, or researched for use during disasters. Additionally, devices and concepts that have not been researched but may potentially impact socially vulnerable populations are presented.

18.8.2 ENGAGING THE COMMUNITY WITH NEW TECHNOLOGIES: A FOCUS ON WARNINGS

Consider the efforts of Jim Davis, the emergency coordinator for Pittsylvania County in Virginia. Davis first contacted a local community college regarding his concern for local residents who are deaf. He worked with the college to write a grant proposal to a local Lions Club, which provided some funding to purchase weather radios. Davis worked to adapt those radios so that they would vibrate pillows when he issued a warning, and the devices were then given out to local residents who are deaf. One individual responded exactly as Davis had hoped, by becoming increasingly concerned about the risks faced by residents who are deaf. Davis then offered local Community Emergency Response Training (CERT) through local trainers and a certified sign-language interpreter. Now, rather than being dependent on others for assistance during a disaster, local residents who are deaf can assist and support using their newly acquired skills. Davis transformed a formerly vulnerable population into one with capacities helpful to their families, neighborhoods, and community. For his efforts, Davis received the 2007 Clive Award at the National Hurricane Conference. Davis's efforts worked because he (1) built a partnership among local organizations; (2) provided accessible equipment at no cost to recipients, who tend to experience low incomes; (3) empowered local residents to work at their own preparedness; and (4) transformed vulnerability into resilience.

It is clear from Chapter 8 on disability that people who are deaf or hard of hearing do not get warning messages as easily as those who can, literally, hear warning sirens. In Oklahoma, a program called *OK-Warn* was developed out of the State Office of Emergency Management. Participants, accumulated on a database through the state agency, receive pager or e-mail warnings. What is important about *OK-Warn* is that it allows individuals to select the type of warning they wish to receive. By understanding that people acquire information in different ways and by designing a warning system to meet that preference, it is possible to enhance warning receipt and interpretation and to motivate compliance with protective action instructions. *OK-Warn* received the 2008 Clive Award. *OK-Warn*'s efforts worked because they (1) respected the ways in which a local population preferred to receive information; (2) provided an affordable means to receive warnings; (3) offered accessible devices; and (4) networked among state agencies to connect information to affected populations.

Research efforts at the Wireless Rehabilitation Engineering Research Center for Wireless Technologies (Wireless RERC), funded by the National Institute on Disability and Rehabilitation Research and the U.S. Department of Education, has shown that wireless technologies are increasingly important for people with disabilities and the elderly. As a result of their latest survey of user needs, text messaging is an invaluable method of communication for the deaf and hard-of-hearing. Additionally, most of the people with disabilities who were surveyed think it would be beneficial to use wireless technologies for communication during an emergency. During field trials for people who are blind/low-vision and people who are deaf/hard-of-hearing, the Wireless RERC used Commercial Mobile Alert System (CMAS) and short-message service (SMS) messaging for a tornado warning. On average, 90% of trial participants (both CMAS and SMS) were interested in having a mobile wireless alerting system (Mitchell, Bennett, and Laforce 2011).

CMAS, also called Wireless Emergency Alert (WEA), is a new means to issue warnings to the public. It will be limited to a 90-character message. The types of alerts sent will include presidential notifications, amber alerts, and warnings for tsunamis, tornadoes, flash floods, hurricanes, typhoons, dust storms, extreme winds, blizzards, and ice storms (NRC 2011). These alerts are tied to the location of your cell phone, and so messages are relevant to your current location. The CMAS service is offered free and does not count toward data or text-messaging charges. The messages come from authorized government agencies, including local and state emergency management agencies, FEMA, the Federal Communications Commission (FCC), the Department of Homeland Security (DHS), and the National Weather Service (NWS). Currently, several phones are CMAS capable, but not all, and so these are not capable of receiving the wireless emergency alert. Individuals wishing to opt out of the service can refrain from receiving all alerts except presidential notifications. A list of CMAS-capable phones is available through the commercial mobile wireless carriers. CMAS- and WEA-compatible phones are currently available. (For more information, see the Federal Communications Commission website at http://transition.fcc.gov/pshs/services/cmas.html.)

18.8.3 SOCIAL MEDIA

Social media are platforms that allow its users to set up a profile, interact with other users voluntarily, as well as connect and view other users' profiles (Boyd and Ellison 2008). There are several different social media platforms. The most common in the United States are *Facebook*, *Twitter*, *YouTube*, *LinkedIn*, and *Flickr*. Social media are often accessed via the Internet on desktop computers, laptops, smart mobile phones, and tablets (Wotham 2010). However, recent developments have allowed for individuals to participate in Twitter via any phone using their "speak-to-Tweet" service. The public uses these dynamic methods of communications for both personal and public events, most often without external incentives.

Social media are rapidly being used in emergency warning, response, and recovery for all types of disasters. During emergencies and disasters, researchers have documented this new media used by victims, emergency management officials (at all levels), volunteer groups, and news reporters (Sutton, Hansard, and Hewett 2011; Starbird and Palen 2011). Social media have already been used during a number of events, including the 2007 Virginia Tech shooting (Palen 2008), the 2007 California wildfires (Sutton, Palen, and Shklovski 2008), the 2010 Haiti earthquake (Crowe 2012), the 2010 Hawaii tsunami warning (Sutton, Hansard, and Hewett 2011), the 2011 Australian floods (IANS 2011), and the Egyptian Civil Unrest/Revolution of 2011 (Crowe 2012). They have been used specifically to warn constituents, locate victims, disseminate important information, organize fundraisers, seek volunteers and donations, gather resources, and gain national support and attention (Shklovski, Palen, and Sutton 2008; Palen and Hughes 2009; Mills et al. 2009; Heveren and Zach 2010). Further, social media can be used to monitor and track disaster communication in order to gauge perceptions, interactions, and needs (Edmonds et al. 2010; Schmidt 2012).

Crowd sourcing is often done in conjunction with social media sites, often via mobile phone and wireless technologies, and involves the input of data from the public (Gao, Barbier, and Goolsby 2011; Hesse 2010). Sometimes, though not always, the information can be displayed in map form. As one example, Ushahidi is a crowd-sourcing platform started in 2008, initially to develop reports of violence after a political election in Haiti (Ushahidi 2011), and was extensively used during the 2010 Haiti earthquake. People employed Ushahidi to mobilize relief efforts by creating a tool for citizens and relief workers to communicate about search and rescue operations and location of supplies (Heinzelman and Waters 2010). Additionally, reports concerning individual safety, shelter, and resource needs were plotted geographically by frequency onto a map, which was updated in real time dynamically (Heinzelman and Waters 2010).

18.8.4 Mapping Technologies

GIS applications can be useful during response and recovery—by getting search and rescue to specific locations quickly and efficiently. Social media efforts can also be used to determine the status of store inventories in affected areas. (Fugate 2011)

Geographical Information Systems (GIS) gather, analyze, manage, and display geographic information in support of all phases of the emergency management cycle (see Chapter 16). People are most familiar with maps as an output, and expanding online and mobile products have increased the availability of spatial information. Geographic technologies are used in support of response efforts, and though improving, many challenges still exist for the real-time data and information that are needed (Zerger and Smith 2002). Mobile geographic information technologies are now being used to allow individuals to upload GIS information on mobile wireless devices (Erharuyi and Fairbairn 2003). Additionally, GIS is used for a wide variety of applications in emergency management, including locating shelters, damage assessment, event modeling, impact assessment, vulnerability assessments, coordination and monitoring of cleanup efforts, response planning and coordination, recovery planning/monitoring/evaluation, and evaluation of mitigation alternatives (Thomas, Ertugay, and Kemec 2006; Tobin and Montz 2004; Radke et al. 2000). While much potential exists for the application of geographic technologies for disaster risk reduction, much research and investigation is still necessary to develop the technology science, as well as understand limitations and possibilities for emergency management (Goodchild and Glennon 2010).

18.8.5 Mobile Applications

Mobile applications or "apps" are small programs, primarily uploaded to smart phones and tablets. Apps enable the user to keep static information on their phone and/or dynamically link to other data, such as from the Web, GPS, GIS, or social media. There are a number of apps that have been developed for disaster-related information. For instance, FEMA has an app that contains information on household disaster preparedness and is primarily static information. Additionally, the Oklahoma Mesonet app contains mainly dynamic content that gives the users real-time emergency alert information on storms, tornadoes, and flooding within the state. The American Red Cross has also developed an app that provides the public with information about shelters in the area, blood drives, and ways to help during a disaster. Mobile apps for disasters have become increasingly popular after the Japanese Tohoku earthquake (Saltzman 2011). Since then, the disaster alert app, earthquake watch apps, emergency radio apps, and disaster readiness apps have been developed to help individuals prepare (Saltzman 2011; Chansanchai 2011).

18.8.6 Challenges to Using the New Technologies

The use of Web-based and online technologies should always generate a discussion about privacy and security (Mills et al. 2009). While this has not deterred the public from using social media platforms (Mills et al. 2009), it may be a deterrent to many emergency management agencies, in addition to the technological challenges and hurdles, and keep them from adopting. Spam, hacking, and false information also occur frequently.

Misinformation and rumors may spread quickly via online networks and are serious concerns (Fisher 2008). During the Japan earthquake and tsunami in 2011, inaccurate information and unreliable tweets were repeated (Acar and Muraki 2011). Misinformation and rumor can spread extremely rapidly and with more impact than more traditional communications conduits. During Hurricane Katrina, widespread claims of violence and chaos from print, online news, and broadcasters were often unsubstantiated and subsequently corrected. This could have led to the slow response and tarnished the images of the victims, often from socially vulnerable populations (Pierre and Gerhart 2005). However, there is a self-correcting culture on some social media networks (Sutton 2010; Surowieki 2004). For example, Twitter users have been noted to correct or address information that is not entirely accurate (Sutton 2010). How the self-correcting nature of social media sites works should be the subject of increased studies. Importantly, social media will work best when used in conjunction with other means of dissemination.

While there is the seemingly lack of adoption by those directly impacted, and by emergency management professionals, increasing examples are occurring of successful integration into response efforts (Sutton 2010). For example, FEMA has taken many steps to increase participation in social media, noting that it can be a very valuable resource (Fugate 2011). And, more frequently, local emergency management has embraced social media during disaster (Associated Press 2010; IANS 2011), which could lead to a wider audience receiving messaging. We also have seen increased adoption by those directly affected by the emergency since 2007 (Sutton, Palen, and Shklovski 2008; Palen and Hughes 2009; Mills et al. 2009; Sutton, Hansard, and Hewett 2011).

There are also challenges when using open- and crowd-sourced materials. For example, verifying, monitoring, and sorting through the large amount of data can be overwhelming (Heinzelman and Waters 2010). Further, while the information provided may be accurate, it may not always correspond to disaster relief activities. When mapping, incorrect locations may be displayed and placed on a map (Gao, Barbier, and Goolsby 2011). Importantly, reliance on technology requires that the technology is working before, during and after a crisis, which is not always the case. Finally, while several of these new technologies are being implemented and adopted for use during emergencies, there is very little research on how socially vulnerable subsets of the population utilize these platforms and devices. We still are unable to quantify how many more people may be reached by using these new technologies or how this would bring forth effective warnings and quality response and relief efforts.

18.9 IMPLICATIONS FOR ACTION

In this section, we consider strategies that transform practice, particularly in the emergency management workplace. Following this section, we address key activities of emergency management that tend to be organized around a series of phases. Though the names of the phases vary from nation to nation, they tend to fall into predisaster, impact, and postdisaster phases. To launch the reader into action, we summarize evidence-based best practices in checklist form across key areas.

18.9.1 INTEGRATING AT-RISK POPULATIONS INTO EMERGENCY MANAGEMENT WORKPLACES

Although some movement toward a vulnerability perspective can be identified, the process will reveal its greatest integration when the occupations of emergency management and related fields truly reflect the populations they seek to support. Unfortunately, there are clear indicators that only limited progress has been made. For example, male students still dominate most emergency management and related degree programs (Neal 2000). One explanation is that students tend to be drawn from first-responder-type or military-related occupations, which have historically been male. In a study of Florida's county-level emergency management offices, Wilson (2000) found that only 15% of the directors and 13.5% of the assistant directors were female. As of mid-2012, a woman had not yet led the U.S. FEMA, although Secretary Janet Napolitano currently oversees the Department of Homeland Security. In New Zealand, women have risen through the ranks of the Ministry of Civil Defence and Emergency Management, as has been observed in Australia and the United Kingdom. Still, a woman in command of emergency management functions remains rare worldwide.

A number of barriers exist to limit the increased participation of women, racial and ethnic minorities, and people with disabilities in emergency management practice (see also Chapter 6). Underrepresentation tends to stem from historic patterns of gender roles or from able-ism or racism. With regard to gender, for example, it could be possible to hire from, or recruit students from, fields that women tend to dominate such as social work, women's studies, psychology, health care, or public health, rather than an overreliance on the male-dominated first-responder and military professions. Job descriptions can advertise more widely than traditional fields in order to recruit a diverse set of candidates with skills commensurate with those identified here, particularly sensitivity to a wide range of circumstances (poverty, age-related situations, disabilities) and well-versed with interpersonal skills. Alternative arrangements can be made as well, such as hiring female- or minority-owned consultants and businesses that support the practice of emergency management.

Racial barriers compound overt and covert resistance to women and men of color in professions related to emergency management and in employment, retention, and promotion practices in emergency management agencies. Cultural-diversity programs and mentoring efforts can make a difference. It is clear that we have a long way to go even to sensitize workplaces to the needs of diverse populations. The Emergency Management Ontario (Canada) office has undertaken efforts to sensitize staff to disability concerns, such as offering lunchtime sign-language classes. Their other efforts include raising prospective service animals from puppies to adults. Staff members indicate that they have raised their awareness to disability issues and express commitment to rescuing service animals in a disaster.

18.9.2 PRACTICAL CHECKLISTS FROM EVIDENCE-BASED BEST PRACTICE

This section consists of a series of features that suggest evidence-based best practices specific to an area of concern for emergency managers. Readers are advised to refer to specific chapters on related topics for additional information, resources, and useful references.

18.9.2.1 Warnings

The warning phase of disaster, for both rapid-onset and advance-notice disasters, can be challenging. The one-size-fits-all approach does not work—just as sirens are simply one tool in a robust warning system. Emergency managers find themselves working diligently to disseminate warnings in ways that reach all populations at all levels of education, income, trust levels, and access points. This checklist identifies useful ways to do so, particularly as a starting point in trying to reach the "whole community."

- Identify the whole community, beginning with community demographics from census data and moving out to organizations that represent and/or advocate for a range of people living in the area.
- Research past events to identify who was injured or killed, and see if patterns can be discerned (e.g., seniors, children, people with disabilities).
- Convene public forums in convenient locations (senior centers, retirement communities, schools for the deaf or blind, veterans organizations, faith centers, etc.) to talk (or sign) about how emergency managers try to disseminate warnings and what they mean. Invite open discussion about past disasters and how people gathered information.
- Conduct outreach to populations in need of warning receipt and identify the impediments they experience with the ways that currently exist, and then determine their preferred ways to receive communications.
- Form a public support team to look for funding to offer weather radios, technology for people who are blind or deaf, and more. Involve local community-based, faith-based, and civic organizations in the effort—as well as those at risk.
- Involve stakeholders in designing and testing warning messages to identify possible problems, holes, and issues in wording and dissemination.
- Determine who is a trusted, credible authority within the populations at risk and integrate them into public education and information dissemination efforts.
- Become a more trusted, credible authority by becoming known within the populations at risk. Attend festivals, events, and locations where people gather, and become a familiar face.
- Create public service announcements (PSAs) for local media with and by the populations at risk—in their jargon, language, signs, and other ways they commonly communicate.
- Identify points of information dissemination on warnings such as senior centers, maternity hospitals, doctor's offices, advocacy organizations, and community-based efforts that reach the homebound.
- Maintain and update efforts on at least an annual basis as populations change constantly—they age, develop new disabilities, move into the area, or have children.

18.9.2.2 Evacuation

The efforts described in the preceding section can aid with evacuation planning and procedures. By knowing and involving the whole community, emergency managers can more easily identify transportation concerns. Whether we need to move people to cooling centers in a heat wave or across the state when hurricanes make landfall, certain procedures stand out:

- Evacuation planning *with* affected populations is key. The needs of women avoiding abusive situations will differ from those of medically dependent and home-based elderly.
- A variety of agencies and organizations can be tapped to assist and are likely to be needed in the event that a widespread, long-term event occurs. In many communities, Citizen Corps teams can be involved as well.
- Transportation assets need to be inventoried and mapped vis-à-vis locations of at-risk populations, preferably on a GIS system.

- Human evacuation planning must be accompanied by similar efforts for pets, service animals, large animals, livestock, and exotic animals. Humane societies, animal response teams, veterinarians, and shelter providers all need to be part of this effort.
- Training of agencies, organizations, workers, and leaders involved in activating transportation will be needed on a regular basis. Turnover of both paid and volunteer personnel make it necessary to update people routinely.
- Training specific to people's mobility needs and cognitive conditions needs to be included for first responders and others likely to be involved in transportation.
- Trusted, credible authorities and leaders must be involved in explaining to people that a real threat exists, that people like them must leave, and that appropriate transportation and shelters will be available.
- Authorities and leaders need to reach out to social networks of neighbors, families, coworkers, health officials, advocates, and others to convince those at risk that they must leave.
- PSAs of people like the affected population participating in evacuation procedures should be widely disseminated—in multiple languages, at varying literacy levels, and with both pictorial images and with the use of sign language. Native speakers are critical in this effort.
- A range of media, including social media, must be activated to spur communication within social networks.
- As with recent hurricanes in the United States, resources for evacuation (e.g., entitlement funds) need to be released when an event occurs close to the end of the month, when people are waiting for their funds. Local agencies and host communities need to be informed that arriving evacuees may need additional assistance to return home or with other critical needs such as medications that they left behind or could not replace prior to departure.
- Arriving locations need to be ready for the whole community to arrive, which means advance training for shelter providers in particular.
- Evacuation exercises need to be conducted with the populations and agencies likely to be involved.

18.9.2.3 Shelters

The U.S. Department of Justice has issued recommendations regarding accessibility standards for local shelters. Based on the Americans with Disabilities Act, the standards provide guidance on a number of issues from aisles and doorway widths to cot heights for various kinds of disabilities to kitchen access for people with diabetes. A helpful checklist and guidebook can be downloaded to assess local shelters for accessibility and can be found at http://www.ada.gov/pcatoolkit/chap-7shelterchk.pdf. In addition, FEMA recently issued a new set of guidance materials for functional needs in general populations. It can be found at this website: http://www.fema.gov/pdf/about/odic/fnss_guidance.pdf.

More broadly, international guidelines for relief camps and similar temporary shelters can be found in multiple languages at the Sphere Project (http://www.sphereproject.org/handbook/). Perhaps as important as international humanitarian relief standards is the understanding that shelter providers should:

- Recognize that local religious and cultural practices may influence the placement of facilities.
- The type of refuge that is used may need to be considered. In the rush to temporarily provide respite from the conditions, inappropriate materials may be used that exacerbate local climate conditions. Hastily introduced materials may also prove to stay in place as long-term solutions. Preplacement and preplanning with people subject to repetitive risks can reduce such consequences.
- Gender issues are essential elements of international relief camp planning. Safety, security, privacy, and modesty requirements must be recognized.

- Camps must be accessible, particularly when disasters increase the prevalence of those with disabilities.
- Relief facilities must be located free of additional hazards, but sufficiently close to allow for residents to reclaim livelihoods and rebuild homes.

18.9.2.4 Recovery

After most disasters, social service and civic organizations step in to assist with recovery needs, particularly rebuilding the homes of low-income families and households. However, there is considerably more to recovery than just homes. Temporary housing units, which are funded or provided by FEMA to qualified survivors, have historically lacked accessible standards. In a post-Katrina lawsuit (*Brou v. FEMA*, also named DHS), a settlement provided for a process to identify applicants of accessible FEMA trailers. A local advocacy organization assisted with identifying those in need and FEMA worked to provide such units. As another example, Louisiana domestic violence organizations discovered that FEMA lacked any policy regarding trailer occupancy or resident protection should a resident be subject to domestic violence.

In the aftermath of a disaster, recovery planners often look to the general needs of the community rather than considering the particular needs of socially vulnerable populations and how the community could be transformed to create a safer, more affordable, and increasingly accessible location. Consider, for example, if a community might:

- Convene recovery meetings in the laundry rooms of public housing units and other convenient locations so that low-income families could attend and participate.
- Redesign damaged public transportation to be accessible for seniors, children, and people with disabilities.
- Refuse to take lands of historically disenfranchised groups in order to rebuild.
- Collect and distribute donations that people really need and want as compared to what an outside community thinks the affected might be able to use. Items must be consistent with local cultures, faiths, physical environments, and livelihoods.
- Listen to the displaced to hear what they need to get home again, in a safer, more resilient community.
- Cast a wider net with economic redevelopment by offering microloans for home-based work, creating a citywide free Internet to encourage telecommunicating and greener recovery, and encouraging loans to small businesses. Such efforts help small businesses to retain racial and ethnic diversity and promote gendered recovery.
- Incorporate local concerns with environmental damage, such as those espoused by Native American tribes along Louisiana's Gulf Coast, into restoration efforts that would stem storm surge in future events.
- Maintain the quality of indigent health care and specialized health care for seniors, children, and people with disabilities.
- Link housing, work, transportation, and health-care facilities so that movement among these different critical locations is easier, accessible, and more affordable.
- Incorporate local cultural heritage into the rebuilt architecture.
- Mitigate future risks without undue impact on those who might be displaced by some measures such as elevations that affect seniors and people with disabilities.
- Incorporates features like elevators to allow people with mobility disabilities to avoid displacement from familiar locations.
- Maintain communication with displaced populations during the recovery process. While communications may become fewer in number, emergency management agencies need to remain a visible and vocal part of the recovery information dissemination process.

18.9.2.5 Resilience through Sustainable Development and Integrated Approaches

As was explored in Chapter 3, decreasing vulnerability and reducing the impacts of disasters for all necessitates pursuing sustainable development practices. Doing so increases the likelihood that disaster and emergency management becomes integrated with environmental, social, and economic practices for creating resilient communities. Further, pursuing an integrated approach ensures that emergency management does not occur in a silo and independently of other community processes, and can yield significant cobenefits. For example, practitioners can:

- Integrate disaster risk reduction principles into local and regional development plans, including comprehensive and land use efforts.
- Attend community planning and safety meetings, even when not specifically about emergency preparedness. Additionally, attempt to get on the agenda for these meetings.
- Minimize and prevent disaster impacts through strategic mitigation actions that are equitably applied.
- Develop relationships with community-based organizations that interface with and understand the needs of vulnerable populations.
- Invoke participatory processes as mainstream approaches, including all stakeholders from diverse backgrounds and experiences.
- Ensure that development initiatives instituted in the United States and internationally address disaster risk reduction.
- Design international development and disaster aid to build capacity in the recipient countries and communities, empowering local endeavors rather than imposing outside views and approaches.

18.10 SUMMARY

The chapters of this new volume are a must-read for the hazards community, including all brands of scientists (social and physical) and practitioners. Ultimately, it is our hope that every academic program will have at least one class that concentrates entirely on social vulnerability and the potential for reducing disaster loss by increasing capacity and by building resilience from a social science perspective. Ideally, social vulnerability and social science approaches would be embedded throughout education, training, practice, and research, including an emphasis on the active role of community and the necessity of integrating social and physical sciences along with engineering.

DISCUSSION QUESTIONS

1. How and where are emergency managers integrating the new concept of resilience? With what kinds of results?
2. Why is there a disconnect between researchers and practitioners? How can you be part of building a bridge between these two communities?
3. What is the value of connecting the physical and social sciences to emergency management practice? How should we go about doing that? As a case in point, think about the possibility of a major geomagnetic storm striking the Earth. What would the consequences be if the power grid went down in your area for 3–6 months? What are the implications for planning, preparedness, mitigation, response, and recovery? Who within the whole community needs to be engaged?
4. How do you plan to remain current in the field? What kinds of opportunities can you identify for continuing educational opportunities where you live?
5. What are the apps that you and your colleagues use? Why are they useful? Do the people that you want to reach (in socially marginalized populations) use those apps? What are the barriers to such adoption?

6. How would you recruit a woman of color into an emergency management workplace and ensure that you retain her as a valued employee of the organization?

7. Your aunt has been active in organizing others to resist the tribe's plan to license a nearby waste-treatment plant. She is a single parent who has been saving money to return to college and complete her education, but isn't sure what profession she wants to enter. What would she bring to emergency management? How could her success be nurtured?

8. Describe the knowledge, skills, and abilities needed for an emergency manager developing a community education plan for your community. What would a professional trained to use a social vulnerability perspective bring to the job that others might not? How would that professional promote resilience?

REFERENCES

ABC News. 2010. Social media helped with Hawaii tsunami evacuation. ABC News. http://abcnews.go.com/US/wireStory?id=9981620.

Acar, A., and Y. Muraki. 2011. Twitter for crisis communication: Lessons learnt from Japan's tsunami disaster. *International Journal of Web Based Communities* 7 (3): 392–402.

Adamski, S. 2011. Using your cell phone before, during and after a disaster. FEMA blog. http://blog.fema.gov/2011/03/using-your-cell-phone-before-during-and.html.

Aguirre, B. 1988. The lack of warnings before the Saragosa tornado. *International Journal of Mass Emergencies and Disasters* 6 (1): 65–74.

Bolin, R. C. and L. Stanford. 1998. *The Northridge earthquake: Vunerability and disaster.* London: Routledge.

Boyd, D., and N. Ellison. 2008. Social network sites: Definition, history and scholarship. *Journal of Computer-Mediated Communication* 13:210–30.

Brattburg, E., and B. Sundelius. 2011. Mobilizing for international disaster relief: Comparing U.S. and E.U. approaches to the 2010 Haiti earthquake. *Journal of Homeland Security and Emergency Management* 8 (1): 1–22.

Buckle, P. 2000. *Assessing resilience and vulnerability in the context of emergencies: Guidelines.* Melbourne, Australia: Victorian Department of Human Services.

Chansanchai, A. 2011. Mobile apps help in a hurricane. MSNBC. http://usnews.nbcnews.com/_nv/more/section/archive?author=athimachansanchai&nvo=6000&16707124%7Cao/o7Cnu%7C30%7Cl%7Ct%7Ca%7C6000=.

Coles, E., and P. Buckle. 2004. Developing community resilience as a foundation for effective disaster recovery. *Australian Journal of Emergency Management* 19 (4): 6–15.

Crowe, A. 2012. *Disasters 2.0.* Boca Raton, FL: CRC Press.

Darlington, J. 2000. The profession of emergency management: Educational opportunities and gaps. Presentation to the Natural Hazards Workshop, Boulder, CO. http://training.fema.gov/EMIWeb/edu/highpapers.asp.

Downton, M., R. Morss, E. Gruntfest, O. Wilhelmi, and M. Higgins 2005. Interactions between scientific uncertainty and flood management decisions: Two case studies in Colorado. *Environmental Hazards* 7:134–46.

Dukes, et al. 2011. Community-Based Collaboration: Bridging socio-ecological research and practice. University of Virginia Press.

Dynes, R. 1994. Community emergency planning: False assumptions and inappropriate analogies. *International Journal of Mass Emergencies and Disasters* 12 (2): 141–58.

Edmonds, J., L. Raschid, H. Sayyadi, and S. Wu. 2010. Exploiting Social Media to Provide Humanitarian Users with Event Search and Recommendations. Proceedings of the 7th International ISCRAM Conference (May). Seattle, Washington (page 489).

Enarson, E. and B. Morrow. 1998. *The gendered terrain of disasters: through women's eyes.* Westport, CT: Greenwood Publishing.

Enarson, E. and B. Phillips. 2008. Introduction to a New Feminist Disaster Sociology. Pp. 41-74 in Phillips, Brenda and Betty Hearn Morrow, editors. 2008. Women and Disasters: from theory to practice. Philadelphia, PA: International Research Committee on Disaster Book Series, Research Committee #39 ofthe International Sociological Association (Xlibris).

Erharuyi, N., and D. Fairbairn. 2003. Mobile geographic information handling technologies to support disaster management. *Geography* 88 (4): 312–18.

FEMA. 2009. National Housing Strategy Available at http://www.fema.gov/nationaldisaster-housing-strategy-resource-center, last accessed December 18, 2012. Washington, D.C.: FEMA.

FEMA (Federal Emergency Management Agency). 2011. Whole community. http://www.fema.gov/whole-community.

Fisher, H. W. 2008. *Response to disaster: Fact versus fiction and its perpetuation.* Lanham, MD: University Press of America.

Fordham, M. 1998. Participatory planning for flood mitigation: Models and approaches. *Australian Journal of Emergency Management* Summer:27–33.

———. 2009. We can make things better for each other: Women and girls organise to reduce disasters in Central America. In *Women, gender and disaster: Global issues and initiatives*, ed. E. Enarson and P. Chakrabarti, 175–88. New Delhi: Sage.

Fothergill, A. 2000. Knowledge transfer between researchers and practitioners. *Natural Hazards Review* 1 (2): 92–98.

Fothergill, A., E. Maestas, and J. Darlington. 1999. Race, ethnicity and disasters in the United States: A review of the literature. *Disasters* 23 (2): 156–73.

Fugate, C. 2011. Keynote address presented at 2011 ESRI Federal User Conference, Washington, DC.

Gao, H., G. Barbier, and R. Goolsby. 2011. Harnessing the crowdsourcing power of social media for disaster relief. *IEEE Intelligent Systems* 26 (3): 10–14. http://wordpress.vrac.iastate.edu/REU2011/wp-content/uploads/2011/05/Harnessing-the-Crowdsourcins-Power-of-Social-Media-for-Disaster-Relief.pdf.

Goodchild, M. F., and J. A. Glennon. 2010. Crowdsourcing geographic information for disaster response: A research frontier. *International Journal of Digital Earth* 3 (3): 231–41.

Heinzelman, J., and C. Waters. 2010. Crowdsourcing crisis information in disaster-affected Haiti: Special report for the United States Institute of Peace, Washington, DC.

Hesse, M. 2010. Crisis mapping brings online tool to Haitian disaster relief efforts. *Washington Post.* http://www.washingtonpost.com/wp-dyn/content/article/2010/01/15/AR2010011502650.html.

Heverin, Thomas and Zach, Lisl. 2010. Microbloggingfor Crisis Communication: Examination ofTwitter Use in Response to a 2009 Crisis in the Seattle-Tacoma, Washington Area. Proceedings of the 7th International ISCRAM Conference, Seattle, USA May 2010. [page 489].

Jegillos, S. 1999. Fundamentals of disaster risk management: How are Southeast Asian countries addressing this? In *Risk, sustainable development and disasters: Southern perspectives*, ed. A. Holloway, 7–16. Cape Town, South Africa: Periperi Publications.

Lenhart, A. 2010. *Adults, cell phones and texting.* Washington, DC: Pew Research Center Publications.

Liu, A., R. Anglin, R. Mizelle Jr., and A. Plyer, eds. 2011. *Resilience and opportunity: Lessons from the U.S. Gulf Coast after Katrina and Rita.* Washington, DC: Brookings Institution.

Lund, F., and T. Vaux. 2009. Work-focused responses to disasters: India's Self Employed Women's Association. In *Women, gender and disaster: Global issues and initiatives*, ed. E. Enarson and P. Chakrabarti, 212–23. New Delhi: Sage.

Marsh, G., and P. Buckle. 2001. Community: The concept of community in the risk and emergency management context. *Australian Journal of Emergency Management* 16 (4): 5–7.

Mileti, D. 1999. *Disasters by design.* Washington, DC: Joseph Henry Press.

Mills, A., R. Chen, J. Kee, and H. R. Rao. 2009. Web 2.0 emergency applications: How useful can Twitter be for emergency response? *Journal of Information Privacy & Security* 5 (3): 3–26.

Mitchell H., D. Bennett, and S. Laforce. 2011. Planning for accessible emergency communications: Mobile technology and social media. Paper presented at the 2nd AEGIS Accessibility Research Everywhere Conference and Final Workshop, Brussels, Belgium.

Morss, R., O. Wilhelmi, E. Gruntfest, and M. Downton. 2005. Flood risk uncertainty and scientific information for decision making: Lessons from an interdisciplinary project. *Bulletin of the American Meteorological Society* 86 (11): 1594–1601.

NAS (National Academy of Sciences). 2012. *Disaster resilience: A national imperative.* Committee on Increasing National Resilience to Hazards and Disasters, Committee on Science, Engineering, and Public Policy. Washington, DC: The National Academies Press (prepublication version, subject to further editorial revisions).

National Council on Disability. 2009. Effective emergency management: Making improvements for communities and people with disabilities. Washington D.C.: National Council on Disability.

Neal, D. 2000. Developing degree programs in disaster management: Some reflections and observations. *International Journal of Mass Emergencies and Disasters* 18 (3): 417–37.

NRC (National Research Council). 2011. Public response to alerts and warnings on mobile devices: Summary of a workshop on current knowledge and research gaps. Washington, DC: National Academies Press.

OFCM (Office of the Federal Coordinator of Meteorology). 2012. Space Weather Enterprise Forum, summary report. http://www.ofcm.gov/swef/2012/SWEF%20SumReport%20v%20final.pdf.

Palen, L. 2008. Online social media in crisis events. *Educase Quarterly*, no. 3: 76–78. http://net.educause.edu/ir/library/pdf/eqm08313.pdf.

Palen, L., and A. Hughes. 2009. Twitter adoption and use in mass convergence and emergency events. Paper presented at the 6th International ISCRAM Conference, Gothenburg, Sweden.

Perry, R. W. and A.H. Mushkatel. 1986. Minority citizens in disasters. Athens, GA: University of Georgia Press.

Phillips, Brenda and Betty Hearn Morrow, editors. 2008. Women and Disasters: from theory to practice. Philadelphia, P A: International Research Committee on Disaster Book Series, Research Committee #39 of the International Sociological Association (Xlibris).

Pierre, R. E., and A. Gerhart 2005. News of pandemonium may have slowed aid. *Washington Post*, October 5, 2005. http://www.washingtonpost.com/wp-dyn/content/article/2005/10/04/AR2005100401525.html.

Quarantelli, E. L. 1998. Epilogue: Where have we been and where might we go? In *What is a disaster?* ed. E. L. Quarantelli, 234–73. New York: Routledge.

Radke, J., T. Cova, M. F. Sheridan, A. Troy, M. Lan, and R. Johnson. 2000. Application challenges for GIScience: Implications for research, education, and policy for risk assessment, emergency preparedness and response. *Journal of the Urban and Regional Information Systems Association* 12:15–30.

Saltzman, M. 2011. Japan quake popularizes disaster apps. *USA Today*. http://www.usatoday.com/tech/news/2011-03-17-disaster-apps.htm.

Schmidt, C. W. 2012. Using social media to predict and track disease outbreaks. *Environmental Health Perspectives* 120 (1): A30–A33.

Shklovski, I., L. Palen, and J. Sutton. 2008. Finding community through information and communication technology during disaster events. Paper presented at CSCW Conference Proceedings, San Diego, CA.

Smith, A. 2011. *Americans and their cell phones*. Washington, DC: Pew Research Center Publications.

Starbird, K., and L. Palen. 2011. *Voluntweeters: Self-organizing by digital volunteers in times of crisis*. ACM: Vancouver, BC, Canada.

Surowieki, J. 2004. *The wisdom of crowds*. New York: Doubleday.

Sutton, J. 2010. Twittering Tennessee: Distributed networks and collaboration following a technological disaster. Paper presented at the 7th International ISCRAM Conference, Seattle, WA.

Sutton, J., B. Hansard, and Paul Hewett. 2011. Changing channels: Communicating tsunami warning information in Hawaii. Paper presented at the 3rd International Joint Topical Meeting on Emergency Preparedness and Response, Robotics, and Remote Systems, Knoxville, TN.

Sutton J., L. Palen, and I. Shklovski. 2008. Backchannels on the front lines: Emergent uses of social media in the 2007 Southern California Wildfires. Paper presented at the 5th International ISCRAM Conference, Washington, DC.

Thomas, D. S. K., K. Ertugay, and S. Kemec. 2006. The role of geographic information systems/remote sensing in disaster management. In *Handbook of disaster research*, ed. H. Rodriguez, E. L. Quarantelli, and R. Dynes. New York: Springer.

Tobin, G. A., and B. E. Montz. 2004. Natural hazards and technology: Vulnerability, risk, and community response in hazardous environments. In *Geography and technology*, ed. S. D. Brunn, S. L. Cutter, and J. W. Harrington Jr. Boston: Kluwer Academic Publishers.

Twigger-Ross, C., T. Coates, H. Deeming, P. Orr, M. Ramsden, and J. Stafford. 2011. Community resilience research: Evidence review report to the Cabinet Office and Defence Science and Technology Laboratory. Collingwood Environmental Planning Ltd., London.

UNITU (United Nations Telecommunication Union). 2012. http://www.un-ngls.org/spip.php?page=article_s&id_article=848.

Ushahidi. 2011. About us. http://www.ushahidi.com/about-us.

Wilson, J. 2000. The state of emergency management 2000: The process of emergency management professionalization in the United States and Florida. Unpublished doctoral dissertation. Department of Sociology and Anthropology, Florida International University, Miami.

Wortham, Jenna. 2010. Cell Phones Now Used More for Data Than for Calls. *New York Times. B1*. Retrieved on July 7, 2012 from http://www.nytimes.com/2010/05/14/technology/personaltech/14talk.html [page 489]

Yonder, A., Akcar, S. and P. Gopalan. 2009. Women's participation in disaster relief and recovery. In Women, gender and disaster: Global issues and initiatives, ed. Enarson, E. and Chakrabarti, P. pp. 189–211. New Delhi, India: Sage Publications India Pvt Ltd.

RESOURCES

- Australia led the way on establishing resilience resources. A set of materials for assessing resiliency can be found at http://www.radixonline.org/resources/buckle-guidelines.pdf.
- A Community Resilience Index, developed by the Gulf of Mexico Alliance's Coastal Community Resilience Priority Issue Team, the Mississippi-Alabama Sea Grant Consortium, and the Louisiana Sea Grant College (and others) provides a self-assessment tool usable at the community level. A handbook and toolbox can be found at http://www.gulfofmexicoalliance.org/issues/resilience.php.
- FEMA's downloadable Whole Community Tabletop Exercise can be found at http://www.fema.gov/library/viewRecord.do?id=5932.
- The FEMA Higher Education Project with links to college and university programs can be found at http://www.training.fema.gov/EMIweb/edu/collegelist/.
- Global Risk Forum (GRF Davos) (http://www.idrc.info/pages_new.php/-About-IDRC/236/1/) provides a platform for "attempt[ing] to find answers and solutions to today's challenges in managing risk, reducing disasters and adapting to climate change."
- Integrated Research on Disaster Risk (http://www.irdrinternational.org/) promotes integrated research for the reduction of disaster risk.
- The NOAA Coastal Services Center offers a Digital Center with a variety of tools incorporating social science data. Information can be found at http://www.csc.noaa.gov/digitalcoast/socialcoast. The site maintains the view that "Social science data offers users the opportunity to better understand people, their institutions, and their decision-making processes. The social science disciplines provide insight into why people make the choices they do, given the information they have available."
- International Federation of Red Cross and Red Crescent Societies' mission includes "providing [humanitarian] assistance without discrimination" and "with a view to preventing and alleviating human suffering" (http://www.ifrc.org/).
- PreventionWeb (http://www.preventionweb.net/english/) acts as an information clearinghouse for all types of disaster risk reduction activities.
- Understanding Risk Network (http://www.understandrisk.org/ur/) brings together a community to "share knowledge and experience, collaborate and discuss innovation and best practice in risk assessment."
- The United Kingdom Cabinet Office has developed a Web page with extensive resources on community resilience. You can find case studies, best practices, and more at http://www.cabinetoffice.gov.uk/content/community-resilience.
- The United Nations Development Programme provides resources for areas troubled with disasters (e.g., tsunamis, earthquakes, explosions) and violence at http://www.undp.org/content/undp/en/home/ourwork/crisispreventionandrecovery/overview.html.
- The United Nations Office for Disaster Risk Reduction (http://www.unisdr.org/) highlights international efforts and coordination for disaster risk reduction around the world.
- USAID's site has information on current disasters as well as preparedness and mitigation initiatives at http://transition.usaid.gov/our_work/humanitarian_assistance/disaster_assistance/. Many countries have international aid organizations beyond the U.S. example.
- The U.S. Census has created a new tool for mapping and reporting. Called ONTheMap for Emergency Management, the tool can be found at http://onthemap.ces.census.gov/em.html.

Index

#0301 - 051017 - C0 - 254/178/29 [31] - CB - 9781466516373